FAMILY THERAPY AND RESEARCH

FAMILY THERAPY AND RESEARCH

An Annotated Bibliography of Articles, Books, Videotapes, and Films Published 1950-1979

Second Edition

Ira D. Glick, M.D.
Professor of Psychiatry
Cornell University Medical College
and
Associate Medical Director
For Inpatient Services
Payne Whitney Clinic
The New York Hospital-Cornell Medical Center
New York

David H. Weber, M.D.
Instructor of Psychiatry
Cornell University Medical College
and
Associate Coordinator
for Family Therapy
The New York Hospital-Cornell Medical Center
Westchester Division
New York

David Rubinstein, M.D.
Clinical Professor of Psychiatry
Department of Psychiatry
Temple University School of Medicine
Philadelphia

John T. Patten, M.D.
Clinical Instructor of Psychiatry
Cornell University Medical College
New York

GRUNE & STRATTON
New York   London
Paris   San Diego   San Francisco   São Paulo
Sydney   Tokyo   Toronto

Library of Congress Cataloging in Publication Data
Main entry under title:

Family therapy and research.

   Rev. ed. of: Family therapy and / Ira D.
Glick, Jay Haley, 1971
   Includes index.
1. Family psychotherapy—Bibliography. I. Glick,
Ira D., 1935-   II. Glick, Ira D., 1935-
Family therapy and research.
Z6664.N5F34 1981 [RC488.5] 016.61689'156 81-7230
ISBN 0-8089-1431-6   AACR2

Grune & Stratton, Inc.
111 Fifth Avenue
New York, New York   10003

Distributed in the United Kingdom by
Academic Press Inc. (London) Ltd.
24/28 Oval Road, London NW 1

Library of Congress Catalog Number 81-7230
International Standard Book Number 0-8089-1431-6

Printed in the United States of America

CONTENTS

1. FAMILY THERAPY

Included in this section are papers on the theory of family therapy as well as on special techniques. The emphasis is on the conjoint treatment of the whole family, but the section includes a few references to studies of members treated simultaneously in individual treatment. If the treatment involved several families in a session, the reference is not included here but under section 1.2, "Multiple Family Therapy." If the focus is on treating married couples only and not the whole family, the reference is not listed here but under section 1.3, "Marital and Couple Therapy."

This section deals with articles on the treatment of several whole families together as well as groups of marital couples. (See also section 1.1, "Family Therapy—Theory and Technique," and section 1.3, "Marital and Couple Therapy.")

This section includes papers on the treatment of couples, primarily married couples, but also other heterosexual and homosexual couples. The emphasis is on conjoint therapy, but a few papers describe members of couples treated in separate interviews.

Listed here are papers describing family therapy occurring in conjunction with some other procedure, such as placing a child in a foster home, using a day hospital, seeing members in individual or group therapy, or hospitalizing all family members.

This section emphasizes training in the practice of family therapy, but it also includes articles on the general teaching of a family orientation.

4.   FAMILY DESCRIPTION

4.1   MARITAL DESCRIPTION   169

Included here are papers describing couples, married and unmarried, but not the whole family. Some papers on couple therapy are cross-referenced, but generally papers describing couples are listed here and those emphasizing the treatment of couples are listed under section 1.3, "Marital and Couple Therapy."

4.2   SIBLING STUDIES   180

Papers listed here deal with the siblings in families in which a member is an "identified patient."

4.3   FAMILY — MULTIPLE GENERATION   182

Included here are papers dealing with extended kin and other multigenerational involvements. The emphasis is on the network of relatives that is wider than the nuclear family.

4.4   FAMILY CRISIS STUDIES   185

The emphasis here is on times of crisis in families and on the treatment of crises.

4.5   THE FAMILY IN THE COMMUNITY   190

Included here are discussions of family involvement with schools, gangs, and a network of helpers; articles on effects of hospitalization of a family member, and studies on cross-cultural comparisons. (See also section 3.6 "Family Theory.")

5.   TYPES OF FAMILIES

5.1   CONTRASTING FAMILY TYPES   201

Listed here are papers dealing with the problem of classifying families into types, as well as papers contrasting one type of family with a control type; for example, a comparison of families of good and bad premorbid schizophrenics would be listed here, as would studies contrasting schizophrenic and normal families.

5.2   FAMILY MEMBER WITH PSYCHOTIC DISORDER   214

Includes mostly papers on families with a member diagnosed schizophrenic, but also other psychotic disorders, for example, acute psychotic episode by DSM III classification.

5.3   FAMILY MEMBER WITH DISORDER USUALLY FIRST EVIDENT IN CHILDHOOD   238

This section includes papers on school problems, mental retardation, and other studies where the identified patient is a child.

5.4   FAMILY MEMBER WITH DISORDER USUALLY FIRST EVIDENT IN ADOLESCENCE   242

Listed here are papers that focus on adolescent problem children and their families. It includes discussions of families with a child defined as delinquent. Suicide is also included in papers listed here. Also included are articles about disorders usually first evident in adolescence, e.g., anorexia nervosa.

Included here are studies of families in which a member is nonpsychotic, "neurotic," or has characterological problems or in which no specific type of pathology is indicated.

Papers listed here deal with family health and medical problems as well as with specific types of physical abnormalities as they relate to the family. Psychosomatic studies and papers on liaison psychiatry with families are included here.

Listed here are papers dealing with descriptions of family dynamics and methods of intervention with low socioeconomic class families.

Listed here are papers that survey the literature of a particular aspect of the family as well as papers that present a large amount of bibliographical material.

7. BOOKS

Included here are articles on specific topics brought together and edited in one volume.

Included here are monographs, texts, literature surveys, and research reports written by single or multiple authors.

A number of audiovisual works have been made by individuals or groups. Those listed here are ones that are easily available for general distribution.

INTRODUCTION

This bibliography is divided into two sections: articles and books, and videotapes and films.

The section on articles and books published from 1950 through 1979 attempts, like its predecessor, to include all that has been written on family therapy and family research studies relevant to psychiatry, psychology, and social work. The many papers and books on the family in the area of sociology and anthropology have been excluded. Also excluded are popular books and magazine articles for the nonprofessional. Frequently the decision of what to include has been difficult; for example, the therapy of family members treated outside the family is not completely covered, even though the family is sometimes mentioned.

Studies of individuals in families or research based on individual records or reports are included only if they deal with differences between types of families within a family orientation; for example, statistical studies of the frequency of divorce in America would not be included, but an article comparing such statistics in families with a schizophrenic member to the general population would be included.

Users of the previous edition of this book will recognize a few changes in organization. The references are still arranged by subject and by author in alphabetical order within a subject category (referred to as *sections*).

Several changes have been made in the section titles, for example, outcome studies have been given a category separate from those on therapy to reflect the importance of and growing interest in these papers. The titles in section 5 have been reworded to better correspond to the DSM-III classification of psychiatric disorders.

As before, placement of a particular article is sometimes arbitrary. When an article deals with more than one subject, the entire annotated reference is placed in the section it primarily fits. The reference only is repeated in other appropriate sections, with a notation referring the reader to the section containing the entire text. This change from the previous edition, which repeated the entire text in two or more sections, was made in order to keep the book of manageable size, since the number of new abstracts in the last decade approximates the total of the first two decades (1950-1970).

The annotations for each reference vary in length and completeness; they are intended to give the gist of an article so the reader can determine whether it is relevent to his or her interests. The length of the abstract does not reflect the quality of the article.

The section on videotapes and films attempts to cover the work of many of the well-known therapists and theoretical models. Clinical presentations have been chosen, rather than didactic presentations, since they are more illustrative.

There are many more videotapes than films selected. Many commercial and documentary films have been made about families and marriage. These were felt often to be too general, of less use to a clinician, and listed elsewhere in film bibliographies. Many excellent audiotapes exist that are not listed.

The use of videotape for teaching and for communication of ideas is in its infancy. Although the technology, use, and ownership of videotape and videotape equipment are still expanding, there is no administrative structure for distribution. The expensive and time-consuming production is largely in the hands of a few enthusiastic individuals. Issues of confidentiality and loss of quality with use and reproduction are also of concern.

Many important videotapes exist that are not in this bibliography. Often they are in the hands of institutions or individuals, but for many of the reasons mentioned they are not available for rental or purchase. Descriptions of some of the tapes are as complete as we could make them, given the information available to us.

PREFACE

There is a growing consensus that the field of family theory and therapy has grown to be a powerful force in that area of the scientific marketplace that is concerned with understanding and changing behavior.

The best evidence of a field's maturity is not claims by its advocates, but the quality and quantity (as an indication of the interest in a field) of its data base. The second edition of *Family Therapy and Research* has grown from a paperbound monograph of 164 pages published by Family Process in 1965 and entitled *Psychiatry and the Family*, in which articles from the years 1960 to 1964 were abstracted by Jay Haley and Ira D. Glick, to a new edition covering the years 1950 to 1970 which was edited by Glick and Haley* and published by Grune & Stratton in 1971 to the gratifying acceptance of residents, clinicians, and theoreticians in the family field.

Now in 1981, with the spread of the family model across international boundaries, it seemed appropriate to revise the bibliography and to expand it to include the last decade, thus covering the period from 1950 to 1980. We thank Jay Haley for entrusting this task to us, and I have enlisted the help of my colleague at the Payne Whitney Clinic, David Weber (now at the New York Hospital-Cornell Medical Center, Westchester Division), for much of the abstracting, editing, and reorganization. David Rubinstein, who has been one of the leaders in the field, has taken on the task of abstracting the articles in *Family Process* from 1970 to 1979. He has completely rewritten most of these abstracts. John Patten, another member of our family therapy group at Payne Whitney Clinic, who has had a special interest in the use of videotapes and movies, has enthusiastically written short reviews in order to acquaint students, teachers, and clinicians with this available material.

Betty Scott and Margaret Weber have our thanks for superbly handling the difficult task of organizing and revising our abstracts.

We apologize to those persons whose article, book, videotape, or film we missed in our search. We request that you write to us with the appropriate citation, and we will include it in the next edition of this bibliography.

We are grateful to Donald Block, editor of *Family Process*, who has allowed us to reprint the abstracts published in *Family Process*. As the challenge of evaluating the effectiveness of psychotherapy looms in the 1980s, we hope that this bibliography will be useful not only in meeting that need but also in stimulating a creative use of the literature of the past in order to understand and alleviate the problems of the family for the future.

---

*Norman W. Bell also assisted with a number of articles in the social science field.

1. FAMILY THERAPY

1.1 FAMILY THERAPY—THEORY AND TECHNIQUE

ACKERMAN N. W. The Art of Family Therapy. In N. W. Ackerman (Ed.), *Family therapy in Transition.* Boston: Little, Brown, 1970.
A brief, personal comment on family interviewing with the emphasis upon humor and first names. "The art of family therapy is, in fact, a unique, spontaneous expression of self in the therapeutic role."

ACKERMAN, N. W. Child participation in family therapy. *Family Process, 1970, 9:*403–410.
An essay on the need for full involvement of children in family therapy. The therapist may be more involved with one generation than with all three. Suggestions for including younger children in therapy are made.

ACKERMAN, N. W. Emergency of family Psychotherapy on the present scene. In H. Stein (Ed.), *Contemporary psychotherapies.* New York: Free Press, 1961
A clinical essay reviewing the development of family therapy: it's rationale, diagnostic techniques, and methods of treatment. It gives an overview of the field of family therapy, highlighting the "more important concepts pertinent to the family approach to diagnosis and therapy."

ACKERMAN N. W. Eulogy for Don D. Jackson. *Family Process*, 1970, *9:*117–122.
A tribute to one of the major figures in the field of family therapy and research, highlighting his ideas and contributions.

ACKERMAN, N. W. The family approach to marital disorders. In B. Greene (Ed.), *The psychotherapies of marital disharmony.* New York: Free Press, 1955.
A diagnostic scheme for understanding the problem, treatment goals, rationale, and techniques of family therapy.

ACKERMAN, N. W. Family Focused therapy of schizophrenia. In A. Scher & H. Davis (Eds.), *The outpatient treatment of schizophrenia.* New York: Grune & Stratton, 1960.
Given at a conference on the outpatient treatment of schizophrenia, this clinical essay is on schizophrenia and the family. The family is relevant not only to the course and outcome of therapy but to the origin of schizophrenia; therefore, treatment should include the whole family together rather than only the identified patient. Techniques of treating the family are described.

ACKERMAN, N. W. Family interviewing: The study process. In N. W. Ackerman (Ed.), *Family therapy in transition.* Boston: Little, Brown, 1970.
A discussion of family interviewing, indications for family therapy, the process of family therapy with case examples, and methods for stimulating deeper motivation on the part of the family members.

ACKERMAN, N. W. Family psychotherapy and psychoanalysis: Implications of difference. *Family Process*, 1962, *1,* 30–43.
An essay on the techniques of family psychotherapy, followed by a comparison with psychoanalytic concepts and therapy. The two treatment methods are viewed as complementary—"psychoanalytic treatment focuses on the internal manifestations of disorder of the individual personality. Family treatment focuses on the behavior disorders of a system of interacting personalities, the family group."

ACKERMAN, N. W. Family psychotherapy—Theory and practice. *American Journal of Psychotherapy, 1966, 20,* 405–414.
A discussion of the theory, history, methods, goals, and future of family therapy. Functions of the therapist are stressed.

ACKERMAN, N. W. Family psychotherapy today. *Family Process*, 1970, *9,* 123–126.
Major trends and crucial issues in family therapy are identified

ACKERMAN, N. W. Family psychotherapy today: Some areas of controversy. *Comprehensive Psychiatry*, 1966, *7,* 375–388.
A detailed discussion of thirteen controversial areas relating to family therapy, i.e., rationale, goals, role of transference, definition, indications and contraindications, "depth" material, acting out, "intimate or secret" matters, relation to other forms of treatment, strength, and weaknesses, and who is qualified to do family treatment.

ACKERMAN, N. W. Family therapy. In S. Arieti (Ed.), *American Handbook of psychiatry* (Vol. III). New York: Basic Books, 1966.
A chapter in a textbook, of psychiatry covering the following aspects of family therapy: theoretical background, homeodynamics, diagnosis and interventions rationale, indications and contraindications.

ACKERMAN. N. W. A family therapy session. In N. W. Ackerman (Ed.), *Expanding theory and practice in family therapy*. New York: Family Service Association of America, 1967.
A transcript of an interview with a family as recorded on audiotape, plus the therapist's interpretive comments.

ACKERMAN, N. W. Further comments on family psychotherapy. In M. Stein (Ed.), *Contemporary psychotherapies*. New York: Free Press, 1961.
A clinical essay specifically focusing on techniques of family therapy from first contact with the family. A case example is presented in support of some of the theoretical notions. Several contraindications of family therapy are described.

ACKERMAN, N. W. The future of famiy psychotherapy. In N. W. Ackerman (Ed.), *Expanding theory and practice in family therapy*. New York: Family Service Association of America, 1967.
A clinical essay tracing the development of family therapy, defining it, and pointing out what it is used for. Shortcomings of psychoanalysis are described, as are weaknesses in group therapy and child theory. Family therapy is therapy "in vivo, not in vitro." It could become the "very core of the newly emerging community psychiatry."

ACKERMAN, N. W. *To catch a thief. In N. W. Ackerman (Ed.), Family therapy in transition*. Boston: Little, Brown, 1970.
A family interview presented verbatim with comments by the therapist on what was going on.

ACKERMAN, N. W. & BEHRENS, M. The family approach in levels of intervention. *American Journal of Psychotherapy, 1968, 22*, 5–14.
Family therapy is seen as complementary to individual therapy. Rationale and applicability are discussed in order to make clear the central thesis of the paper that treatment must be problem oriented, *not* technique oriented; that is, different levels of intervention are used depending on the family and the stage of treatment.

ACKERMAN, N. W. & FRANKLIN, P. F. Family dynamics and the reversibility of delusional formation: A case study in family therapy. In I. Boszomenyl-Nagy & J. L. Framo (Eds.), *Intensive family therapy*. New York: Harper & Row, 1965.
A report on a case of a 16-year-old schizophrenic and her family in which treatment "of the whole family seemed to move toward reversal of the patient's psychotic experience." Interview data and comment are provided.

ALEXANDER, I. E. Family therapy. *Marriage and Family Living*. 1963, *25*, 146–154.
A review of the history of family therapy followed by a description of the author's experience with family therapy combined with other methods of treatment. Typical processes during family therapy are described, as well as indications for this form of treatment.

ANDERSON, C. M. & MALLOY, E. S. Family photographs: In treatment and training. *Family Process*, 1976, *15*, 259–264.
Photographs may be used in family therapy to illustrate specific themes of male and female stereotypes based on power, dependency, or intimacy.

ANDERSON, D. Nursing therapy with families. *Perspectives in Psychiatric Care*, 1969, *1*, 21–27.
An essay on the use of family therapy by nurses in both inpatient and outpatient settings. Appropriate theory, rationale, and techniques are described with liberal use of case examples.

APONTE, H. J. Organizing treatment around the family's problems and their structural bases. *Psychiatric Quarterly*, 1974, *48*, 209–227.
This is a theoretical article based on the author's clinical work in a child guidance clinic (which has a "family orientation" rather than a "psychoanalytic" orientation). The symptoms of the child are reactions to pathology in the family constellation. Techniques of treatment include getting the family to agree on the problem, identifying the participants to which the problem is related, and making pledges to work on changing the structural base of the problem. Several case examples are presented in support of the usefulness of the model.

ARLEN, M. S. Conjoint therapy and the corrective emotional expreience. *Family Process*, 1966, *5*, 91–104.
The use of family therapy with families containing a person with severe character disorder described within a framework of providing a corrective emotional experience.

ATTNEAVE, C. L. Therapy in tribal settings and urban network intervention. *Family Process*, 1969, *8*, 192–210.
A comparison of network therapy and interventions in a network clan of a tribal minority culture. An example of treatment with an Indian tribe is contrasted with urban network treatment where the clanlike social structure must be reconstituted.

AUGENBRAUN, B., REID, H., & FRIEDMAN, D. Brief Intervention as a preventive force in disorders of early childhood. *American Journal of Orthopsychiatry*, 1967, *37*, 697–702.

Three family interviews with follow-ups 6 to 9 months later was the technique used in this pediatrics practice when the identified patient had symptoms (such as bed wetting, nightmares, etc.) with no apparent organic etiology. The technique is based on the idea that these symptoms may indicate underlying family problems. Families are seen together rather than separately. No results are offered (except for case examples), but the technique is thought to be effective.

BARCAI, A. & RABKIN, L. Y. Excommunication as a family therapy technique. *Archives of General Psychiatry*, 1972, *27*, 804–808.
A clinical paper based on experience with 11 families in which "schismatic relations" between the parents prevent effective discipline of children. During the course of therapy, the family excommunicates the identified patient (i.e., refuses to associate with the member, usually an adolescent) until certain conditions are met. The theory, indications, and possible effects of this technique are discussed.

BARDILL, D. Family therapy in an army mental hospital hygiene clinic. *Social Casework*, 1963, *44*, 452–457.
From an outpatient Army mental hygiene clinic, the author presents his experience in using family therapy with adolescents. Manifest problems represent a breakdown in the family system. Aims and techniques are discussed and illustrated by clinical examples.

BARTOLETTI, M. Conjoint family therapy with clinic team in a shopping plaza. *International Journal of Social Psychiatry*, 1969, *15*, 250–257.
A mental health clinic in a shopping center provided brief conjoint family therapy to the community. Staff consisted of a psychiatrist, psychologist, and social worker. Treatment plan was divided into a diagnostic treatment segment of two months and then a second two month treatment period. A variety of interventions utilizing various combinations of family members were utilized.

BEAL E. W. Use of the extended family in the treatment of multiple personality. *American Journal of Psychiatry*, 1978, *135*, 539–542.
A case report of a 27-year-old woman with multiple personalities who was treated with a family system approach after somatic treatment and individual psychotherapy had failed. The family therapy emphasized unresolved triangular relationships in her family of origin, which were reflected in her "alternate" selves. Advantages and disadvantages of the different models are contrasted.

BEALL, L. The corrupt contract: Problems in conjoint therapy with parents and children. *American Journal of Orthopsychiatry*, 1972, *42*, 77–81.
Three case examples from an outpatient clinic illustrate that the initial therapeutic contract can make the problems of the family worse rather than better.

BEATMAN, F. L. Intergenerational aspects of family therapy. In N. W. Ackerman (Ed.), *Expanding theory and practice in family therapy*. New York: Family Service Association of America, 1967. See reference in Section 4.3.

BEATMAN, F. L. The training and preparation of workers for family–group treatment. *Social Casework*, 1964, *45*, 202–208.
An essay describing the method of training for social workers learning family therapy (called "family-group treatment"). Group processes as a method for supervision are used in preference to individual supervision because of "the requirements of treating the family rather than the individual." Specific methods used and discussed are group supervision, sitting in on a family session, viewing through a one way screen, films, and tape recordings.

BEATMAN, F. L. Trends toward preventive practice in family service. In. N. W. Ackerman, F. L. Beatman, & S. Sherman (Eds.), *Exploring the base for family therapy*. New York: Family Service Association of America, 1961.
A clinical essay with stress on prevention of serious emotional disorder in the family. The family agency seems the logical agency to do this. Schema includes taking an inventory, fortifying the healthy components in the family, and directing the family for further help where needed.

BEATMAN, S. SHERMAN, S., & LEADER, A. Current issues in family treatment. *Social Casework*, 1966, *47*, 75–81.
This is a clinical essay on "controversial" issues in family treatment. There is a discussion on privacy and confidentiality, of family therapy on children (which is felt to be overstressed in view of the fact that children usually know the problems prior to therapy), whom to include in sessions, how to formulate a treatment plan, and a discussion of transference reactions.

BECK, M. The management of hostility in family treatment. *Journal of Psychiatric Treatment and Evaluation*. 1979, *1*, 13–14.
Using 5 case examples, 4 interventions are suggested for openly treating hostile families. The "object-related question" temporarily distracts the family, "taking the attack upon oneself" provides better examples for dealing with

attacks, "joining the attack" will support a usually passive member when he or she first tried self-assertion and "attacking the attacker" is a confrontation for narcissistic members. Indications and contraindications for these techniques are discussed.

BECKER, J. Good premorbid schizophrenic wives and their husbands. *Family Process*, 1963, *2*, 34–51.
A report of conjoint family therapy with seven female schizophrenics and their husbands. The women's backgrounds, premorbid marital life, and course of illnes are described. Results of treatment were that "five families appeared to benefit substantially, one somewhat, and one not at all."

BEELS, C. C. & FERBER, A. S. Family therapy: A view. *Family Process*, 1969, *8*, 280–318.
A "personal view of the literature of family therapy" with an evaluation of the teaching and practice of different therapists.

BEHRENS, M. & ACKERMAN, N. The home visit as an aid in family diagnosis and therapy. *Social Casework*, 1956, *37*, 11–19.
A paper based on the authors' clinical work in which the home visit is used as an aid in family diagnosis and therapy when the identified patient is a child. Observations are based on family interaction patterns, physical environment, and atmosphere of the home. A case example is given to illustrate the authors' technique.

BELL, J. E. The family group therapist: An agent of change. *International Journal of Group Psychotherapy*, 1964, *14*, 72–83.
An essay on the therapist's role in family therapy. Topics discussed are indications for whom to include in therapy, the theoretical basis for seeing the family *as a group*, and the task of the therapist with particular emphasis (rather than insight).

BELL, J. E. *Family group therapy*. Public Health Monograph No. 64, Department of Health, Education, and Welfare, 1961.
A manual of family therapy that discusses rationale for and the techniques of family therapy phase by phase from the first conference through the terminal phase.

BELL, J. E. The future of family therapy. *Family Process*, 1970, *9*, 127–141.
The concept of family therapy as a technology is presented. The notion of family treatment through a transcultural framework is suggested. The development of preventive and educational programs by family therapists is discussed.

BELL, J. E. Recent advances in family group therapy. *Journal of Child Psychology and Psychiatry*, 1962, *3*, 1–15.
A review of family group with various definitions of the family and an emphasis upon the social psychological approach to the unit. Includes a discussion of the development of the family group, its stability, its problems, and the process of bringing about change.

BELL, J. E. A theoretical position for family group therapy. *Family Process*, 1963, *2*, 1–14.
An essay delineating some of the author's thoughts on family therapy over the past 11 years. The author emphasizes that from the onset of therapy the focus should be on the group rather than the individual. Contrast with group therapy is made, some questions of technique discussed, and a process of family change is set.

BENTOVIN, A, & KINSTON, W. Brief focal family therapy when the child is the referred patient. *Journal of Psychology and Psychiatry*, 1978, *19*, 1–12.
This is a study in two parts on the application of brief "focal" techniques to family therapy. The Tavistock clinic's "workshop" procedure was used for 29 cases over 1 year. The first part of the study outlines the procedure and describes 2 case examples. The second part describes the assessment methodology and a review of the results. Successful outcome criteria were set by the workshop prior to treatment, which included 6 to 20 family sessions for work on a focal problem (e.g., scapegoating of identified child patient). Results were scored on an 8-point scale by the treatment team at the end of treatment and at a 3- and 6-month follow-up. Results showed 66 percent improvement in the identified patient and 38 percent in the family as a whole. Parental psychiatric disturbance was found to correlate significantly with failure.

BERKOWITZ, D. A. On the reclaiming of denied affects in family therapy. *Family Process*, 1977, *16*, 495–501.
This paper emphasizes the continued relevance of a psychodynamic, interpretative approach for families with unresolved grief. In order to work through these feelings of grief, each family member must acknowledge the affect as present and internalized in the self. The disclaimed emotions remain powerful unconscious motivations of behavior, exerting their influence despite their denial.

BLOCH, D. A. Family therapy, group therapy. *International Journal of Group Psychotherapy*, 1976, *26*, 289–299.
Part of a symposium of family and group therapy, this paper discusses the family as a "natural group." Issues that arise in family therapy are always relevant to each individual, unlike group therapy in which "happenstance"

determines the relevance to an individual and in which "the group never becomes the patient." Disadvantages of the family as a treatment system (e.g., its greater resistance to change) are also discussed.

BLOCH, D. A. Symposium: Family therapy and group therapy—similarities and differences. Family therapy, group therapy. *International Journal of Group Psychotherapy*, 1976, *26*, 289–299.
The second paper in this series is from the perspective of a family therapist. Family therapy has the advantage of working with the real family rather than the "substitute family" (the group). Its core assumption is change in the system, *not* in the individual. Advantages and disadvantages of the family as a therapy system are discussed, and the future of the family is pondered.

BODIN, A. Conjoint family therapy. In W. Vinacke (Ed.), *Readings in general psychology*. New York: American Book Company, 1968, pp. 213–219.
An overview of conjoint family therapy as it evolved and the theories behind it, focusing on general systems theory, communication theory, social learning, and interactional concepts—its technique and comparisons of individual and family therapy. Finally, an attempt is made to give an overview of its place in the fields of psychiatry and psychology. Interpersonal actions are increasingly viewed as the context in which intrapersonal phenomena emerge.

BODIN, A. M. & BODIN, L. J. The topsy-turviness of Mrs. Piggle Wiggle: Its symbolic significance. *Family Process*, 1977, *16*: 117–118.
This is a brief note on the importance of the use of paradoxical intention as applied to young children and to the treatment of families.

BOSZORMENYI-NAGY, I. Intensive family therapy as a process. In I. Boszormenyi-Nagy & J. L. Framo (Eds.), *Intensive family therapy*. New York: Harper & Row, 1965.
"Intensive family therapy differs from all other mental health approaches in its application of principles and techniques derived from dynamic individual psychotherapy and, to a lesser extent, from group therapy, in helping all family members through direct observation and modification of their interactions." A report on the treatment of 50 families is included with case illustrations.
Intensive family therapy derives its application of principles and techniques from dynamic individual psychotherapy and, to a lesser extent, group therapy. Its objective is to help all family members through direct observation and modification of their interactions. Case illustrations and a report on the treatment of 50 families are included.

BOSZORMENYI-NAGY, I. Loyalty implications of transference model in psychotherapy. *Archives of General Psychiatry*, 1972, 27, 374–379.
This is a clinical paper exploring the relation of the transference in individual psychotherapy to transference in family therapy. Transference in family therapy relies on the hierarchy of obligations and loyalties within the family. Such loyalties and unconscious obligations to other family members create resistances to progress. Changing in therapy by individual family members implies forsaking old family loyalties.

BOSZORMENYI-NAGY, I., & FRAMO, J. L. Family concept of hospital treatment of schizophrenia. In J. Masserman (Ed.), *Current psychiatric therapy* (Vol. II). New York: Grune & Stratton, 1962.
A research project investigating schizophrenia in an inpatient psychiatric unit. Psychopathology of the family of the schizophrenic has been neglected. To this end, hospital treatment is oriented around a number of techniques involving the family. One of these techniques is conjoint family therapy, which had been conducted with 12 selected families over a 3-year period. Responses to these changing forms of treatment are described.

BOVERMAN, M., & ADAMS, J. R. Collaboration of psychiatrist and clergyman: A case report. *Family Process*, 1964, *3*, 251–272.
A description of a psychotic patient and family treated in collaboration. The different functions of psychiatrist and clergyman are discussed, with each presenting his view of the case.

BOWEN, M. Family psychotherapy. *American Journal of Orthopsychiatry*, 1961, *31*, 40–60.
A discussion of the research program in which parents and their schizophrenic offspring lived together on a psychiatric ward. The paper includes a description of the history of the project, the sample of families, and the theoretical approach. The emphasis is on the family as a unit of illness rather than on individuals in the family group. Principles and techniques of family therapy emphasize utilizing a family leader and avoiding both individual relationships with family members and the position of omnipotence, which the family attempts to place the therapist. Results are discussed and examples given with case material.

BOWEN, M. Family psychotherapy with schizophrenia in the hospital and in private practice. In I. Boszormenyi-Nagy & J. L. Framo (Eds.), *Intensive family therapy*. New York: Harper & Row, 1965.
A theory of the family and family therapy with sections on differences between family and individual theory, a summary of the family theory of emotional illness with the emphasis upon schizophrenia, the parental transmission of problems to the child, the clinical approach to modify the family transmission process, and principles and techniques of this family therapy approach.

BOWEN, M. The use of family theory in clinical practice. *Comprehensive Psychiatry,* 1966, *7,* 345–373.
An essay based on the author's clinical experience describing the history, current states, and future of the "family movement." The family is discussed as representing different types of systems. The "medical model" is not used. Clinical uses and techniques of family therapy are discussed on the basis of the author's theoretical orientation.

BOYD, E., CLARK, J., KEMPLER, H., et al. Teaching interpersonal communication to troubled familes. *Family Process,* 1974, *13,* 317–336.
This study uses several social and family theorists' assumptions on the development of generalizations by family members. Change by one family member means that he or she must be seen differently by the other family members. The experimenters set up an operational model in which family members pursue the following steps: (1) observe each other; (2) compare notes with a co-observer; (3) share observations with those observed; and (4) receive feedback from the observed member. This process, coupled with an analytic approach geared toward insight, created change in familial communication patterns, attitudes, and behavior.

BRANDZEL, E. Working through the Oedipal struggle in family unit sessions. *Social Casework,* 1965, *46,* 414–422.
A discussion of the use of family-unit sessions to help a family work through its problems with a young adolescent. Case examples are given.

BRESLOW, D. B., HRON, B. G. Time-extended family interviewing. *Family Process,* 1977, *16,* 97–103.
This paper presents a time-extended family interviewing technique in which the therapist prolongs the traditional 1-hour interview to 3 to 7 hours. Extended sessions promote movement because: (1) they contribute to heightened investment and hopefulness; (2) they produce greater willingness to risk dealing with a painful issue because of increased likelihood of closure; and (3) they provide time to experience on an emotional level an issue that previously has been intellectualized. This technique facilitates the understanding of families' defenses and resistances.

BREUNLIN, D. C., & SOUTHGATE, P. An interactional approach to dysfunctional silencing in family therapy. *Family Process,* 1978, *17,* 207–216.
Silencing is viewed as dysfunctional if it occurs repeatedly and independently of content or if it functions as a negative feedback to limit changes. Dysfunctional silencing is manifested by efforts of one or more family members, in tacit collusion with another member, to limit change by blocking communication. The interactional approach utilizes conflict–resolution techniques and videotape feedback.

BRODEY, W. M. A cybernetic approach to family therapy. In G. H. Zuk & I. Boszormenyi-Nagy (Eds.), *Family therapy and disturbed families.* Palo Alto: Science & Behavior Books. 1967.
See Reference in Section 3.6.

BRODEY, W. M., & HAYDEN, M. Intrateam reactions: Their relation to the conflicts of the family in treatment. *American Journal of Orthopsychiatry,* 1957, *27,* 349–356.
A clinical report emphasizing the notion that reactions of treating personnel to each other are in part a reenactment of conflicts of the family. Data were obtained from an outpatient child guidance clinic team of psychotherapist and caseworker. Five case examples were given to support this hypothesis. By focusing on the reaction of the workers, signiicant dynamic trends can be identified and therapy can be accelerated. The building of family conflicts that influence the intrateam reactions depends upon the power of the family conflict and the sensitivity of the team's equilibrium to this particular stress.

BROWN, S. Family therapy viewed in terms of resistance to change. In I. M. Cohen (Ed), *Psychiatric research report 20.* Washington, D.C.: American Psychiatric Association, 1966.
Family therapy from a psychoanalytic and "child guidance" point of view with the emphasis on resistance to change. Case examples are given.

BURKS, H., & SERRANO, A. The use of family therapy and brief hospitalization. *Diseases of the Nervous System,* 1965, *26,* 804–806.
Experience with setting up an inpatient service in conjunction with an outpatient child guidance clinic (which had a strong bias to family therapy) is described. Patients were between 12 and 16 years old and diagnosis varied from neurosis to psychosis. Hospitalization was short (usually under two months) and was family oriented, using techniques adapted from the multiple impact therapy technique. Results, including a 1-year follow-up, with 25 patients are described.

BYNG-HALL, J. Family myths used as defence in conjoint family therapy. *British Journal of Medical Psychology,* 1973, *46,* 239–250.
This clinical paper examines the family myth as a defense against family therapy. Data came from clinical experience with 50 families in an outpatient clinic. Most of the identified patients were adolescents. The family myth derives from life events and experience in the family and provides a bridge between life events and unconscious fantasies. In treatment, efforts should focus on working toward a more reality-based consensus of the family rather than on attempting to destroy the old myth.

CAMP H. Structural family therapy: An outsider's perspective. *Family Process*, 1973, *12*, 269–277.
This paper outlines some of the useful models and orientations included in structural family therapy, drawn from literature, discussions, talks, and videotapes with the purpose of facilitating the model's adoption by agencies desiring to utilize this orientation.

CARROLL, E. J. Family therapy: Some observations and comparisons. *Family Process*, 1964, *3*, 178–185.
A discussion of family therapy with comparisons with individual therapy. Differences between the two methods are listed. Four kinds of operations in the field of family therapy are noted: emphasis upon the family as individuals, focus upon shifting dyads such as between mother-child and therapist-child, focus upon the family unit with only the patient as a messenger for the family, and emphasis upon the family and a segment of the community as an open system.

CARROLL, E. J. Treatment of the family as a unit. *Pennsylvania Medicine*, 1960, *63*, 57–62.
A lecture comparing psychotherapy and pscyhoanalysis to family therapy. Rationale for this form of treatment and techniques for working with a couple as well as with an entire family are described. One case example is given in illustration.

CARROLL, E. J., CAMBOR, C. G., LEOPOLD, J. V., et al. Psychotherapy of marital couples. *Family Process*, 1963, *2*, 25–33.
A general discussion of indications for and advantages and disadvantages of family therapy. Two case reports are given. Of 6 cases seen by the group, 4 made significant gains, while the other 2 were unimproved.

CHARNY, I. Family interviews in redefining a 'sick' child's role in the family problem. *Psychological Reports*, 1962, *10*, 577–578.
A child guidance clinic suggests that, at the beginning of treatment, family therapy offers significant advantages over individual treatment of parent and child. The problem in the family can be defined, the child can be released from the scapegoat role, and the parents can be involved in treatment.

CLARKIN, J. F., FRANCES, A. J., & MOODIE, J. L. Selection criteria for family therapy. *Family Process*, 1979, *18*, 391–403.
This paper presents a decision tree model outlining the factors that incline a clinician to perform a family evaluation and to determine the duration and intensity of family treatment. It also includes a systematic compilation of the indications and contraindications for family and marital therapy. The model is based on a utilization review format.

CLOWER, C., & BRODY, L. Conjoint family therapy in outpatient practice. *American Journal of Psychotherapy*, 1964, *18*, 670–677.
This essay describes techniques, selection criteria, indications, and treatment goals for conjoint family therapy in an outpatient setting. Conjoint family therapy is compared to both individual and group therapy.

COE, W. A behavioral Approach to Disrupted Family Interactions. *Psychotherapy: theory, research, and practice*, 1972, *9*, 80–85.
One case example is presented in support of the notion that family therapy based on behavioral modification is useful as a short-term therapy for children with "emotional problems."

COHEN, C. I., & CORWIN, J. An application of balance theory to family treatment. *Family Process*, 1975, *14*, 469–479.
See reference in Section 3.6.

COHEN, I. M. (Ed.), *Family structure, dynamics and therapy* (Psychiatric Research Report 20). Washington, D.C.: American Psychiatric Association, 1966.
A collection of material that includes discussions of research methods, family functioning, communication styles, dynamics, family myths, family relations in which there is a retarded member, family relations in which the patient has 14+6 cps EEG positive spike patterns, family resistances, methods for family work-ups, techniques for dealing with the low-socioeconomic family, effects of videotape playback on family members, family therapy as an alternative for psychiatric hospitalization, use of heterosexual cotherapists, and multiple impact therapy as a teaching device.

CORNWELL, G. Scapegoating: A Study in family dynamics. *American Journal of Nursing*, 1967, *67*, 1862–1867.
In a study of two low-socioeconomic families, which included mother and son, the mechanics of scapegoating were described. Each member of the families took mutually reinforcing roles in the process. A discussion followed on the means of intervention in the process.

COUNTS, R. M. Futher thoughts on family therapy. *Contemporary Psychoanalysis*, 1974, *10*, 496–501.
The paper describes indications and contraindications for individual and family therapy, further examining the similarities and differences between the individual psychoanalytic approach and the family-systems approach. Patient's, family's, and therapists's conceptualizations of the problem determine indications and contraindications for family therapy and individual therapy.

COYLE, G. L. Concepts relevant to helping the family as a group. *Social Casework*, 1962, *43*, 347–354.
An essay on the concepts of the family group as the unit of treatment. It is suggested that 3 trends are being classed together in the family movement: an increased emphasis on the relationships of the individual with his or her immediate family members, the attempt to use concepts about the family drawn from the social sciences, and an examination into the research of small group behavior. A framework of the social process within the family group is offered with 6 aspects or dimensions.

CURRY, A. E., The family therapy situation as a system. *Family Process*, 1966, *5*, 131–141.
A discussion of the processes that occur between a family unit and the family therapist, which involve neutralizing the therapist, re-establishing the family's pretherapy equilibrium, and disrupting the overall family therapy situation. Processes of coalition, coalescence, and coagulation are presented with examples.

CURRY, A. Toward the phenomenological study of the family. *Existential Psychiatry*, 1967, *6*, 35–44.
A paper exploring the theoretical basis for conjoint family therapy from the "phenomenological" point of view (defined as observing the phenomenon as it manifests itself). Modes of interrelating, affective responses, and methods of communication of both normal and pathological families are analyzed from this point of view.

CUTTER, A. V. & HALLOWITZ, D. Diagnosis and treatment of the family unit with respect to the character-disordered youngster. *Journal of American Academy of Child Psychiatry*, 1962, *1*, 605–618.
A description of a treatment program involving 56 cases of families with children with character disorders. Case examples are provided with results indicating that 60 percent of the families made "consistently good progress."

CUTTER, A. V., & HALLOWITZ, D. Different approaches to treatment of the child and the parents. *American Journal of Orthopsychiatry*, 1962, *32*, 152–158.
The authors contrast the concept of the "child as the patient and the parents as collaborators" with the recognition of the importance of familial relationships and their impact on the developing child." They offer 7 treatment approaches that include different combinations of family members and therapists with the criterai for their application. Diagnosis and treatment are directed toward the child, mother, and father, and the pathogenic weaknesses and breakdowns in their relationships with each other.

DAVID, A. Using audio tape as an adjunct to family therapy: Three case reports. *Psychotherapy*, 1970, 7, 28–32.
A tape was made during a session in the therapist's office, and after the session the family took the tape home and listened to it. Later in the course of treatment the procedure was reversed. Three case reports, all treated over 6 months with successful outcome, are presented in support of the usefulness of the technique. The model of the therapeutic session is "extended via tape into the home without the direct control of the therapist."

DE SHAZER, S. Brief therapy: Two's company. *Family Process*, 1975, *14*,79–93.
The triad is described as a key element in family therapy and can provide a valuable concept when designing interventions. Some interventions are described that have proved effective in dealing with the "stuck" triangle. The "odd-man out" principle is explored. By intervening to create new alliances the therapist can broaden the family's behavioral repertoire.

DEMING, B., & KIMBLE, J. J. Adapting the individual problem-oriented record for use with families. *Hospital and Community Psychiatry*, 1975, *26*, 334–335.
The problem-oriented record was adapted for use in conjunction with family therapy and is thought to offer considerable advantage over other types of records developed for individual psychiatry. Techniques for use are described.

DEUTSCHER, M. Brief family therapy in the course of first pregnancy: A clinical note. *Contemporary Psychoanalysis*, 1970, 7, 21–35.
A contribution to the psychology of pregnancy from a family point of view. Psychodynamics and treatment techniques during the first trimester, second trimester, third trimester, delivery, and postpartum are discussed. The sample taped interviews with 10 young middle-class couples seen in the second trimester and in the third month postpartum. All pregnancies were without complications. Data was "impressionistic, subjective, and phenomenoligically descriptive," so as to "give the feel" of the experience.

DWYER, J. H., MENK, M. C., & VAN HOUTEN, C. The caseworker's role in family therapy. *Family Process*, 1965, *4*, 21–31.
An approach to family therapy developed in a residential treatment center for children. The whole family is seen by a psychiatrist and then a caseworker sees the parents while the psychiatrist sees the child. The caseworker deals with the parents' responses to the family sessions.

EISLER, R. M.& HERSEN. M. Behavioral techniques in family-oriented crisis intervention. *Archives of General Psychiatry*, 1973, *28*, 111–116.

Three case reports are presented to illustrate the usefulness of behavioral techniques to rapidly alter family structure during "crisis" treatment at a university clinic. Instruction is provided in rapid behavior assessment of interactive patterns and in use of such techniques as feedback, modeling, and reciprocal reinforcement.

EIST, H. I., & MANDEL, A. U. Family treatment of ongoing incest behavior. *Family Process*, 1968, 7, 216–232.
A description of a case in which there was ongoing incest behavior. Family treatment was used and the techniques are discussed.

ELLES, G. Family treatment from a therapeutic community. *Confinia Psychiatrica*, 1965, 8, 9–14.
From an inpatient ward where the identified patient had a personality disorder, some families were treated with some or all members of the family receiving individual therapy, while other families were treated by family therapy in the home. Discussion of experiences, but no data, is presented comparing the two forms of treatment.

ENGLISH, O. S., SCHEFLEN, A. E., HAMPE, W. W. & AUERBACH, A. H. Strategy and structure in psychotherapy. *Behavioral Studies Monograph* (No. 2) Eastern Pennsylvania Psychiatric Institute, 1965.
A companion volume to *Stream and Structure of Communication Behavior* (A. E. Scheflen) which includes 3 research studies of the family therapy interview by Whitaker and Malone.

EPSTEIN, N. B. Family Therapy. *Canadian Mental Health*, 1962, 10, 5–9.
A sound conceptual framework for family therapy based on rigorous research is urged in this review of transactional versus interactional dynamics and different techniques of family therapy.

EPSTEIN, N. B. & CLEGHORN, J. The family transactional approach to general hospital psychiatry: Experiences, problems, and principles. *Comprehensive Psychiatry*, 1966, 7, 389–396.
This paper deals with the experiences and problems arising, and principles derived from, the introduction of concepts of family dynamics and family therapy in the psychiatry departments of two general hospitals. These concepts were used in the outpatient department, community department, inpatient service, and the day hospital. Ongoing supervision for family as well as for individual therapy is stressed.

EPSTEIN, N. B. Treatment of the emotionally disturbed pre-school child: A family approach. *Canadian Medical Association Journal*, 1961, 85, 937–940.
A clinical essay focusing on the assumption that when the identified patient is a child, the family must be included in the treatment. First a family diagnostic interview is held, followed by a staff discussion of the dynamics and recommended further work-up. Possible therapeutic programs prescribed include (1) treatment of the family as a unit, (2) treatment of two or more members of the family as a group, dependency upon "exigencies" arising as the treatment progresses, (3) treatment by individual psychotherapy for the identified patient, (4) treatment of the "significant dyad," e.g., mother–child, and (5) the child may be placed in group, or in individual and group therapy. A case example is presented to illustrate the approach.

ERICKSON, M. The identification of a secure reality. *Family Process*, 1962, 1, 294–303.
Case report of treatment of an 8-year-old boy who was progressively defiant to his mother. The author's formulation of the case and treatment with boy and mother are described.

ERLICH-AMITAI, H. S., & BLOCH, D. A. Two families: The origins of a therapeutic crisis. *Family Process*, 1971, 10, 37–52.
This paper examines the treatment by individual and family therapy of a hospitalized young woman as it reflects the historical and current family dynamics of the patient and of her individual psychotherapist. The proposition is made that the therapist–patient dyad serves as the interface of two larger social systems, the respective family units of the two participants.

FELDMAN, L. B. Strategies and techniques of family therapy. *American Journal of Psychotherapy*, 1976, 30, 14028.
This theoretical paper describes a conceptual model for strategies and techniques of family therapy. The family therapist's manner of relating, the strategies or techniques he or she employs, the presenting problem or problems particularly characteristic of the family, and the developmental phase of the family therapy process are described. Manner of relating, empathy, respect, genuineness, strategy, and technique focus, as well as specific and global strategies are also discussed.

FELDMAN, M. J. Privacy and conjoint family therapy. *Family Process*, 1967, 6, 1–9.
A discussion of whether a greater or lesser degree of privacy effects the nature of therapeutic disclosures by contrasting individual and conjoint family therapy. There is no simple relationship between degree of privacy and scope of disclosure, and the private nature of individual therapy can lead to an ethical position that can detrimentally elevate an individual's welfare above others.

FELLER, C. The use of teaching stories in conjoint family therapy. *Family Process*, 1976, 15, 427–431.

The author suggests that change, the goal of all therapy, can be facilitated through use of a teaching story. He describes a teaching story as a therapeutic communication that offers the benefits of both an educational factor and a therapeutic paradox. Several examples of teaching stories are offered, and the implications of this personal sharing by the therapist are explored.

FERBERT, A. S., & BEELS, C. C., Changing family behavior programs. In N. W. Ackerman (Ed.) *Family therapy in transition.* Boston: Little, Brown, 1970.
A description of an approach to family therapy in which "the family comes to the therapist with a script which they have repeatedly rehearsed, but which they cannot get into production . . . His job is to make them aware of the staging, gestures, blocking, and business, and then help them restage it or rewrite it if need be. Case illustrations are provided.

FERREIRA, A. J. Family myths. In I. M. Cohen (Ed.), *Psychiatric research reports 20.* Washington, D.C.: American Psychiatric Association, 1966.
A discussion of the myths families develop with an illustration of the contrast of a family's report and its behavior in a test setting. The relevance of family myths in family therapy is discussed.

FERREIRA, A. J. Family therapy: A new era in psychiatry. *Western Medicine,* 1967, *8,* 83–87.
A clinical essay focusing on development, rationale, goals, and techniques of family therapy. The difference in orientation from individual therapy is described. Family therapy is seen as more than "a new technique in psychotherapy"; it constitutes, in fact, the beginning of an entirely new chapter on understanding behavior.

FERREIRA, A. & WINTER, W. Stability of interactional variables in family decision-making. *Archives of General Psychiatry,* 1966, *14,* 352–355.
In order to test the stability over time and after family therapy of 3 variables in family decision-making, 23 randomly selected families (10 abnormal and 13 normal) were retested 6 months after the original research project. The abnormal families had received therapy. Research indicated that there was no significant difference between the means observed in test and retests of the 3 variables for either normal or abnormal families. It is concluded that these 3 variables (spontaneous agreement, decision-time, and choice-fulfillment) were consistent over time and were not changed by family therapy.

FINE, S. Troubled families: Parameters for dianosis and strategies for change. *Comprehensive Psychiatry,* 1974, *15,* 73–78.
This clinical essay stresses the importance of using the family model to understand and treat mental illness. There are sections on diagnosis, response of families to stress, strategies for change, and defensive reactions of families in response to the therapist's strategies.

FLECK, S. Some general and specific indications for family therapy. *Confinial Psychiatrica,* 1965, *8,* 27–36.
From his clinical work with inpatient schizophrenic families, the author presents indications for family therapy based on the stage of hospitalization. Three phases described are the admission, the period of hospital adjustment, and the reintegration with the community. Family therapy complements, but does not replace, other treatment modalities.

FLOYD, G. J. Managing member silence in family therapy. *Journal of Psychiatric Nursing and Mental Health Services,* 1973, *11,* 20–24.
This is an essay based on data from the author's clinical practice describing various interpretations of silence in family therapy. Extensive silences increased the likelihood that the identified patient would drop out of family therapy. The more silent family members were, the less likely the active member of the family would gain therapeutic benefit. Methods for managing silence in individuals and the whole family are described and a case example presented.

FORREST, T. Treatment of the father in family therapy. *Family Process,* 1969, *8,* 106–118.
A discussion of family therapy with special emphasis upon dealing with the father. The goals are to provide him with emotional support, strengthen his sexual identity, and develop his skills as head of the family group.

FOSTER, R. M. & LOMAS, D. F. Anger, disability and demands in the family. *American Journal of Orthopsychiatry,* 1978, *48,* 228–236.
This is a theoretical discussion of "how parents of children brought to mental health treatment facilities can tell their children not to get angry." Unconsciously held views of a child as "disabled" and unable to express anger without increased disability are expressed through ineffective demands on the child's behavior. This can prevent the best use of coping mechanisms. Implications for therapy are briefly discussed.

FRAMO, J. L. Family of origin as a therapeutic resource for adults in marital and family therapy: You can and should go home again. *Family Process,* 1976, *15,* 193–210.
The author presents a method of involving the family of origin in marital and family therapy. This method is demonstrated through case studies and expresses the author's thesis that marital problems are extensions of

relationship problems that exist in the families of origin and are best addressed through therapeutic interaction with the original families. Theory is elaborated and compared with Bowen's approach. Methods for overcoming resistance are described, and a preliminary evaluation of clinical outcomes is discussed.

FRAMO, J. My families, my family, *Voices*, 1968, *4*, 18–27.
In support of the idea that treating families revives feelings of the therapist toward his or her *own* past and present family, the author has presented material from family sessions followed by his own thoughts and feelings. Material relating to childhood, marriage, parenthood, and adulthood are reviewed.

FRAMO, J. L. Personal reflections of a family therapist. *Journal of Marriage and Family Counseling*, 1975, *1*, 15–28.
This essay describes a wide variety of issues in the family therapy field. Aspects of theory, technique, therapist reactions, and results are discussed. The "subjective side of doing family therapy" (that is, therapist reactions) are discussed extensively.

FRAMO, J. L. Rationale and techniques of intensive family therapy. In I. Boszormenyi-Nagy and J. L. Framo (Eds.), *Intensive family therapy*. New York: Harper & Row, 1965.
A description of the principles derived from the family therapy approach at the Eastern Pennsylvania Psychiatric Institute and the techniques found to be useful, promising, limited or antitherapeutic.

FRAMO, J. Symptoms from a family transactional viewpoint. In Nathan W. Ackerman, (Ed.), *Family therapy in transition*. New York: Little, Brown, and Company, 1970, pp. 125–171.
This is a clinical essay using numerous case examples to make the point that psychiatric symptoms are a manifestation of a change in family homeostasis, as well as an intrapsychic and interactional conflict. Symptom choice, maintenance and reduction of symptoms, as well as sharing and exchange of symptoms, are discussed.

FRAMO, J. L. The theory of the technique of family treatment of schizophrenia. *Family Process*, 1962, *1*, 119–131.
See Reference in Section 1.4.

FRANKLIN, P. Family therapy of psychotics. *American Journal of Psychoanalysis*, 1969, *29*, 50–56.
This is a case report of a schizophrenic child and his parents and grandmother who were treated individually and with family therapy over 7 years. The author's thesis is that schizophrenic symptoms are a manifestation of a process that "involves the entire family." The identified patient and the family improved after treatment.

FREEMAN, V. J. Differentiation of 'unity' family therapy approaches prominent in the United States. *International Journal of Social Psychiatry*, special edition, 1964, *2*, 35–46.
A review and classification of family therapy describing 6 and 8 "unit" or "conjoint" methods closely related approaches. Similarities between methods are discussed in terms of frame of reference, family composition, and activity of the therapist. A bibliography of 53 references on family therapy is included.

FREEMAN, V. S., KLEIN, A. F., RIEHMAN, L. M., et al. "Family group counseling" as differentiated from other "family therapies." *International Journal of Group Psychotherapy*, 1963, *13*, 167–175.
An essay proposing treatment of the family using a "modification of social group work methods" which the authors call "family group counseling." The method focuses on group interactive processes rather than individual intrapsychic processes. A schema is presented to differentiate this method from other types of family therapy and from other therapies.

FRIEDMAN, A. S. The incomplete family in family therapy. *Family Process*, 1963, *2*, 288–301.
A discussion of the incomplete family in treatment with emphasis on obstacles that prevent progress in therapy. A case example is given with verbatim excerpts.

FRIEDMAN, A. S. The "well" sibling in the "sick" family: A contradiction. *International Journal of Social Psychiatry*, special edition 1964, *2*, 47–53.
See Reference in Section 4.2.

FRIEDMAN, E. H. The birthday party: An experiment in obtaining change in one's own extended family. *Family Process*, 1971, *10*, 345–359.
The author describes a technique in providing "disequilibrating" information and experience to his own extended family with the purpose of inducing change in stable patterns of interaction. A follow-up and some personal observations and commentaries evaluate the usefulness of the technique.

FRIEDMAN, P. H. Outline (alphabet) of 26 techniques of family and marital therapy: A through Z. *Psychotherapy: Theory, Research, and Practice*, 1974, *11*, 259–264.
Based on the literature and the author's clinical work, an outline guide of marital and family therapy techniques is presented. There is a long list of references.

FRIEDMAN, P. H. Personalistic family and marital therapy. In A. A. Lazarus (Ed.), *Clinical behavior therapy*. New York; Brunner/Mazel, 1972.
This chapter describes the theory and techniques of family and "personalistic family" therapy, a kind of therapy based on family therapy and behavioral therapy models with the additional technique that "the therapist shares the role in his own family with the patients." Nonsystematic follow-up revealed that 70 percent to 80 percent of the families were "successfully treated."

GEHRKE, S., & KIRSCHENBAUM, M. Survival patterns in family conjoint therapy. *Family Process*, 1967, *6*, 67–80.
A discussion of 20 families studied in family therapy with the emphasis upon different patterns of emotional survival myths in the family. Three types of family are contrasted: the repressive family, the delinquent family, and the suicidal family. The survival myth is the illusion of family members that they must continue their existing family ways of relating in order to survive psychologically.

GEDDES, M. & MEDWAY, J. The symbolic drawing of the family life space. *Family Process*, 1977, *16*, 219–228.
This article describes the technique of the symbolic drawing of the family life space. It compares the technique with other techniques for facilitating communication and interaction, and it illustrates the clinical use this technique serves as: (1) a diagnostic source providing information regarding the structural configuration of a family; (2) a therapeutic tool measuring the degree of intrafamilial congruence; and (3) a research device providing measurements of changes of familial structure.

GERRISH, M. The family therapist is a nurse, *American Journal of Nursing*, 1968, *68*, 320–323.
One case example is presented in support of the family approach in treatment of a 52–year–old depressed housewife, her husband, and young daughter. It was reported that the family was functioning well 2 years following treatment.

GOLDENBERG, I. & GOLDENBERG, H. A family approach to psychological services. *American Journal of Psychoanalysis*, 1975, *35*, 317–328.
This theoretical essay offers a critique of individual psychotherapy versus the advantages of family therapy. Theories of family pathology, models, techniques, and indications are reviewed, and the relationship of family therapy to behavior therapy, multiple-impact therapy, home visits, crisis therapy, network therapy, and multiple-family group therapy are discussed.

GOLDMAN, J. & COANE, J. Family therapy after divorce: Developing a strategy. *Family Process*, 1977, *16*, 357–362.
This paper presents a 4-part model for intervention with families after divorce. It consists of: (1) the redefinition of the family as including all members; (2) the reaffirmation of generational boundaries in order to reduce the parentification process, often intensified by the parent's physical absence; (3) the replay of the history of the marriage to correct developmental distortions and to offer an opportunity to mourn the loss of the intact family; and (4) the facilitation of an emotional divorce. A case study illustrates the procedure.

GOOLISHIAN, H. A. A brief psychotherapy program for disturbed adolescents. *American Journal of Orthopsychiatry*, 1962, *32*, 142–148.
A report on the multiple-impact psychotherapy of the youth development project of the University of Texas Medical Branch. The program is based on the assumptions that to attempt psychotherapy with adolescents was to deal with chronic pathological family interaction, and that behavioral changes in adolescents take place rapidly. With intensive brief psychotherapy a family can work toward self rehabilitation. The interdisciplinary team meets with the family group for 2 or 3 full days, with follow-up sessions 6 months and a year later. The procedural pattern is flexible and includes full family sessions, individual and overlapping interviews, and psychological testing. Variations in procedure and treatment goals are discussed.

GRANLICK A. Family psychotherapy: General and specific considerations. *American Journal of Orthopsychiatry*, 1962, *32*, 515–526.
A general discussion of family therapy with a partial review of the history. The procedure for family therapy is described as "any psychotherapeutic approach to the primary patient which consciously includes members of his family, seen either separately or jointly with the primary patient." The emphasis is upon family treatment of patients in an inpatient setting, with a focus upon the aims and the value of this approach.

GRANLICK, A., & SCHWEEN, P. H. Family therapy. In I. M. Cohen (Ed.), *Psychiatric research report 20*, Washington, D. C.: American Psychiatric Association, 1966.
The traditional general practitioner "may be looked upon as the forerunner of the present day psychiatric family therapist." The value of treating the family unit is discussed. Indications for family therapy, its purposes, and the importance of dealing with the family of the discharged patient are emphasized.

GRANLICK, A, & YELIN, G. Family therapy in a private hospital setting. *Current Psychiatric Therapy*, 1969, *9*, 179–180.

This is a clinical report of family therapy as used in an inpatient hospital setting. Problems, technique, and rationale are discussed.

GREENBERG, I. M., GLICK, I. D., MATCH, S., & RIBACK, S. S. Family therapy: Indications and rationale. *Archives of General Psychiatry*, 1964, *10*, 7–25.
Indications for and results of family therapy with a series of 20 patients, mostly schizophrenic, in an open hospital, inpatient setting are discussed. Indications list diagnostic as well as therapeutic goals. 6-month follow-up results of 13 cases are presented, and a rationale using ego, psychological, and group process terms is included. A review of the family therapy literature is presented.

GROSSER, G., & PAUL, N. Ethical issues in family group therapy. *American Journal of Orthopsychiatry*, 1964, *34*, 875–885.
An essay focusing on two aspects of family therapy: (1) effects of family therapy on family solidarity and intrafamily relationships and (2) special features in the "doctor–patient" relationship. The therapist should be nonaligned when resolving conflicts. Attempting to understand the conflicts and then letting the family solve them in a more constructive manner than they had previously. Some of the ethical issues raised about family therapy have come from psychiatrists rather than from "the public." This may be due to "countertransference" problems of the therapist.

GROUP FOR THE ADVANCEMENT OF PSYCHIATRY, Committee on the Family. *The field of family therapy*. New York, 1970.
A report on the field of family therapy that is meant to be a "snapshot" taken during the winter of 1966–1967. Data based upon a questionnaire answered by 312 persons who considered themselves family therapists, as well as on the opinions of the members of the family committee. The work deals with the practitioners of family therapy, families typically entering treatment, goals and conceptual approaches, techniques used, and possible ethical problems.

GROUP FOR THE ADVANCEMENT OF PSYCHIATRY, Committee on the Family. *Integration and conflict in family behavior. Report No. 27.* Topeka, Kansas, 1954.
A report by the committee on the Family of GAP dealing with organizing data on the study of the family. It discusses the relation of the family to the social system, the system of values to which the family is oriented, and Spanish–American family patterns as well as American middle-class family patterns. 67 pp.

GUERNEY, B., & GUERNEY, L. F. Choices in initiating family therapy. *Psychotherapy*, 1964, *1*, 119–123.
A discussion of the decisions involved in family therapy, such as which members to include, whether to have individual sessions as well as group sessions, and how many therapists to include.

GUTHEIL, T. G., AVERY, N. C. Multiple overt incest as family defense against loss. *Family Process*, 1977, *16*, 105–116.
This paper presents a case report of father–daughter incest that illustrates the way in which overt incest can function as a multi-determined familial defense against separation and loss. The authors maintain the psychodynamic view that incest expresses the collective psychopathology of all the family members, as well as their common adaptational capacities.

GUTTMAN, H. A. The child's participation in conjoint family therapy. *Journal of American Academy of Children*, 1975 *14*, 490–499.
Using numerous case examples, the author suggests that children, although included, are often neglected during the actual family therapy process. The usual mistake is to ask the child "how and why" questions, rather than to interpret their nonverbal behavior and play. Techniques to understand and to use this material in family therapy, as well as techniques for encouraging the child's interaction with the family (for example, family sculpture), are discussed.

GUTTMAN, H. A. A contraindication for family therapy . *Archives of General Psychiatry*, 1973, *29*, 352–355.
Four case reports are presented in support of the notion that conjoint family therapy is contarindicated when the identified patient is on the verge of decompensating or has decompensated or has recently recompensated from acute psychosis. It is hypothesized that the reason the identified patient gets worse in family therapy is because his anxiety increases and he is unable to express his discomfort when be becomes aware of his "ambivalent dependency" on his parents. If family therapy is used in such cases, it should be directive at first and then more insight oriented when the patient's defensives are "more solidly reconstituted."

HALEY, J. Approaches to family therapy. *International Journal of Psychiatry*, 1970, *9*, 233–242.
A description of the differences in premises and approach of the beginning and the experienced family therapist.

HALEY, J. Communication and therapy: Blocking metaphors. *American Journal of Psychotherapy*, 1971, *25*, 214–227.
This is an essay on differential effectiveness of various treatment strategies. Symptoms are seen as not only a bit of information relating to interpersonal interactions, but also to the therapist. For the symptom to change, the situation

should change, and evaluation measures should include the presence or absence of a "better behavior," and the realization whether the system in which the behavior took place has also changed.

HALEY, J. Family therapy: A radical change. In J. Haley (Ed.), *Changing families*. New York: Grune & Stratton, 1971. A review of the development of the family therapy field with emphasis upon the shift in unit from 1 person to 2 or 3 or more persons. Consequences to theory and the effect on the professions is described.

HALEY, J. Strategic therapy when a child is presented as the problem. *Journal of American Academy of Child Psychiatry*, 1973, *12*, 641–659.
This is a clinical paper describing strategic therapy, that is, therapy based on determining "which conceptual unit will make it easy to bring about change" in the family. The course of treatment and treatment approaches are focused on involving the peripheral adult with the child and disengaging the over-involved parent and child. Several case examples are presented to illustrate the technique. A comparison is made with the traditional approach, which focuses on the child.

HALEY, J. Whither family therapy. *Family Process*, 1962, *1*, 69–100.
A review of various family therapy with a comparision of family and individual therapy. Family and individual therapy have in common a series of paradoxes, which patients face as long as they present disturbed behavior.

HALEY, J. Why a mental health clinic should avoid family therapy. *Journal of Marriage and Family Counseling*, 1975, *1*, 3–13.
This essay describes the changes that take place in an institution when the family therapy approach is adopted. Inconsistencies between the individual and family approaches, including differences in diagnostic models, training methods, and problems in the professional hierarchy, are discussed. A variety of ways to prevent adoption of a family approach are listed.

HALLOWITZ, D. Family unit treatment of character-disordered youngsters. *Social Work Practice*. New York: Columbia University Press, 1963.
A report on the family treatment of 38 children with a diagnosis of character disorder. Procedures and descriptions of the family are offered along with tabular reports of outcome. 61 percent had a favorable outcome with the treatment averaging 17 hours per case.

HALLOWITZ, D., & CUTTER, A. V. The family unit approach in therapy: Uses, process, and dynamics. *Casework Papers*. New York: Family Service Association of America, 1961.
Conjoint family interviewing in a clinic is described in terms of its use as an intake procedure during individual treatment of child and parents and as a continuous form of treatment. When used as a continuous method of treatment contraindications exist when the emotional disturbances in the child or the parents "have become intrapsychically ingrained in the form of a neurosis or psychosis" and when there are "basic disturbances in the marital relationship." Yet the treatment is effective with children with character disorders. A case is discussed.

HAMMER, L. I. Family therapy with multiple therapists. In Masserman, J. H. (Ed.), *Current psychiatric therapies*. New York: Grune & Stratton, 1967, pp. 103–111.
A clinical essay on the use of a technique called "multiple therapy" (defined as more than one person engaged in the solution of family problems). This technique defines the family therapist as almost anyone who has contact with the case and who uses a theoretical framework based on understanding problems from a family viewpoint. Methods of diagnosis, technique, advantages, and disadvantages are discussed.

HANDLON, J. H., & PARLOFF, M. B. The treatment of patient and family as a group: Is it group psychotherapy? *International Journal of Group Psychotherapy*, 1962, *12*, 132–141.
Family group therapy differs from conventional group therapy in many important aspects. The permissive atmosphere of group therapy is difficult in family therapy because the patient feels unique and lacks equal power status and protection and because the family comes to therapy with shared mythology and reality distortions.

HANSEN, C. An extended home visit with conjoint family therapy. *Family Process*, 1968, 7, 67–87.
An approach to family therapy that involved staying in the home with the family for a week to intervene therapeutically in a family's life. Benefits and problems of this approach are discussed.

HARBIN, H. T. Cure by ordeal: Treatment of an obsessive-compulsive neurotic. International Journal of Family Therapy, 1979, *1*, 324–332.
A case report of family therapy with a 16-year-old female identified patient with a severe compulsive disorder. Individual treatment for 2½ years had been unsuccessful: family treatment lasted 8 months and is described in 3 stages. The last stage involved a prescription of an "ordeal" for the patient. At the end of each day that she had displayed ritualistic behavior, she had to exercise for ½ hour at midnight. A review of the literature is included.

HARE-MUSTIN, R. T. Treatment of temper tantrums by a paradoxical intervention. *Family Process*, 1975, *14*, 481–485.
Paradoxical intention enables patients to develop detachment and gain distance from their behavior leading to behavior change. Tantrums occurring daily disappeared entirely after the second session. A 9-month follow-up revealed no further tantrums.

HARMS, E. A socio-genetic concept of family therapy. *Acta Psychotherapy*, 1964, *12*, 53–60.
An essay which criticizes Ackerman's rationale and technique of family therapy. The author proposes that family therapy be called "socio-genetic family group therapy," because to understand a family one has to understand sociologic as well as genetic points of view. The author also takes into account the concepts of normality. Six points-of-insight in order to proceed are presented.

HAWKINS, R. P., PETERSON, R. F., SCHWEID, E., & BIJOU, D. Behavior therapy in the home: Amelioration of problem parent-child relations with the parent in a therapeutic role. *Journal of Experimental Child Psychology*, 1966, *4*, 99–107.
A conditioning approach to changing parent-child relations by programming the parents to deal differently with the child.

HENRION, R.P. Family nurse therapist: A model of communication. *Journal of Psychiatric Nursing.* 1974, *12*: (6), 10–13.
Case examples are used to support the hyposthesis that "success of family therapy depends upon how effectively the therapist utilized communication skills with family members."

HIRSCHE, R. & IMHOF, J. E. A family therapy approach to the treatment of drug abuse and addiction. *Journal of Psychedelic Drugs*, 1975, *7*, 181–185.
This is a clinical report of application of the family model when drug abuse is the presenting problem. The sample was 47 families seen during the intake phase, using family evaluation techniques. Treatment was family therapy in combination with psychopharmacotherapy. No results are reported, but the approach was thought "to be very encouraging."

HIRSCHOWITZ, R. G. Family coping patterns in times of change. *Social Psychiatry*, 1974/1975, *21*, 37–43.
Based on principles of preventitive as well as clinical psychiatry, this essay reviews causes, natural history, and techniques in helping families cope with change. A model based on individual, family, and social psychiatric models is presented. The change process is described, and it is stressed that the family will have to learn to change as rapidly as "modern life." Unhealthy, as well as healthy, patterns of coping are described, and techniques for family therapeutic interventions are delineated.

HOFFMAN, L. Deviation amplifying processes in natural groups. In J. Haley (Ed.), *Changing families*. New York: Grune & Stratton, 1971.
A theoretical paper on the limitations of a homeostatic theory to deal with change. The family view, systems theory, and sociological ideas about deviants are brought together in a discussion of the process of change in systems in which a deviation is amplified.

HOFFMAN. L., & LONG, L. A systems dilemma. *Family Process*, 1969, *8*, 211–234.
A description of a man's breakdown in terms of the social systems within which he moved, and the attempts to intervene with treatment to bring about change. The ecological field of a person is the area considered.

HOLLANDER, L. Rethinking child and family treatment. In Sankar, D. V. (Ed.), *Mental health in children*. Westbury, New York: PJD Publications Ltd., 1975.
See reference in section 1.7.

IRWIN, E. D., MALLOY, E. S. Family puppet interview. *Family Process*, 1975, *14*, 179–191.
This paper reviews family assessment and focuses on the family puppet interview. It is a symbolic and interactive procedure involving the whole family for the purpose of diagnosis and therapy. The procedure is described and several illustrative cases are presented.

JACKSON, D. D. Action for mental illness—What Kind? *Stanford Medical Bulletin*, 1962, *20*, 77–80.
An essay discussing the treatment of schizophrenia. It is pointed out that in addition to somatic methods, the family should be involved in family therapy throughout hospitalization and in the posthospital phase to decrease morbidity. The patient should be encouraged to leave the hospital from the moment he or she enters it, and family therapy should be held in the home.

JACKSON, D. D. Aspects of conjoint family therapy. In G. H. Zuk & I. Boszormenyi-Nagy (Eds.), *Family therapy and disturbed families*. Palo Alto: Science & Behavior Books, 1967.

A discussion of the difference between the family therapy approach and psychoanalysis with an example of a "Lolita-type" case. The individual and the family are like the wave and particle theories of light, and that merging the two is not quite possible.

JACKSON, D. D. Conjoint family therapy. *Modern Medicine*, 1965, *33*, 172–198.
A clinical article discussing the history of, rationale for, and techniques of family therapy. Schizophrenia is seen as a reaction to a disturbance in family communication. Families operate in a homeostatic system and the disturbances of one member affect other members.

JACKSON, D. D. Family interaction, family homeostasis, and some implications for conjoint family psychotherapy. In J. Masserman (Ed.), *Individual and familial dynamics*. New York: Grune & Stratton, 1959.
A clinical paper focusing on family homeostasis and its importance to the development of pathology. When homeostasis in the family breaks down, it can be expected that one member of the family will develop symptoms. To treat the system, the entire family must be involved, therefore offering a distinct advantage over "collaborative" therapy.

JACKSON, D. D. Family therapy in the family of the schizophrenic. In H. Stein (Ed.), *Contemporary psychotherapies*. New York: Free Press, 1961.
A clinical essay dealing with the rationale for the development of family therapy. Data based on interviews with 15 schizophrenic families and several delinquent families. Goals and techniques of family therapy are described by use of an extensive transcript from a case. Mother, father, siblings, and identified patients are all caught in a reverberating circuit of pathology. Further research with controls is needed.

JACKSON, D. D. The monad, the dyad, and family therapy. In A. Burton (Ed.), *Psychotherapy and Psychosis*. New York: Basic Books, 1961.
A clinical paper on the treatment of schizophrenics using family therapy. One case example is used to support a theoretical framework of family therapy, and advantages and disadvantages of conjoint therapy are discussed. Transference and countertransference problems and the therapist's ability to grasp the data are central issues.

JACKSON, D. D. & SATIR, V. A review of psyciatric developments in family diagnosis and family therapy. In N. W. Ackerman, F. L. Beatman, & S. Sherman (Eds.), *Exploring the base for family therapy*. New York: Family Service Association of America, 1961.
A discussion of the family point of view in psychiatry with a classification of the various approaches to treating the family. A review of the historical development and present attempts to investigate family process.

JACKSON, D. D., & WEAKLAND, J. H. Conjoint family therapy: Some considerations on theory, technique, and results.*Psychiatry*, 1961, *24*, 30–45.
See Reference in Section 5.2

JACKSON, D. D., & YALOM, I. Family research on the problem of ulcerative colitis. *Archives of General Psychiatry*, 1966, *15*, 410–418.
See Reference in Section 5.6

JACKSON, D. D., & YALOM, I. Conjoint family therapy as an Aid in psychotherapy. In A. Burton (Ed.), *Family therapy of schizophrenia in modern psychotherapeutic practice*. Palo Alto: Science & Behavior Books, 1965.
A clinical report presenting one case in support of the notion that family therapy is useful for breaking an impasse in individual therapy. A case example is presented in detail and it is shown how the pathology of the family prevented progress in individual therapy.

JACKSON, D. D., & YALOM, I. Family homeostasis and patient change. In J. Masserman (Ed.), *Current Psychiatric Therapies* (Vol. IV). New York: Grune & Stratton, 1964.
By use of a case report of conjoint family therapy, the hypothesis is tested that "the schizophrenic family is a specific system, which, when altered, results in a change in the identified patient's symptoms and this change correlates with a noticeable alteration in the behavior of other family members." Specific techniques are described in detain—particularly "the therapeutic double bind and prescriptions of behavior."

JEFFERSON, C. Some notes on the use of family sculpture in therapy. *Family Process*, 1978, *17*, 69–76.
This article describes the use of family sculpting in 3 cases in different ways. In each case, the author explains how the therapists made the choices involved in directing the therapeutic process. At best, clients become aware of their responsibility in maintaining patterns of behavior and may elect other options for their behavior within the system.

JENSEN, D., & WALLACE, J. G. Family Mourning process. *Family Process*, 1967, *6*, 56–66.
A discussion of mourning as a family crisis involving all members. Two case examples are given. Therapy is seen as intervening in maladaptive family interaction patterns resulting from the loss of a member.

KADUSHIN, P., CUTLER, C., WAXENBERG, S., & SAGER, C. The family story technique and intrafamily analysis. *Journal of Projective Techniques of Personality Assessment*, 1969, *33*, 438–450.
This is a report of a new technique, the family story technique (FST), to assess affect, interactional patterns, and future outlook in the family. It is said to be useful as a diagnositc and research tool and to compare families with one another once normative data have been accumulated on a wide variety of families.

KADUSHIN, P., WAXENBERG, S., & SAGER, C. Family story technique changes in interactions and affects during family therapy. *Journal of Personality Assessment*, 1971, *35*, 62–71.
This is one of a series of reports on the family story technique (FST) to explore changes over the course of brief family therapy. The study was done at an outpatient community mental health center with a sample of 38 women, 33 men, and 13 children in 39 families. About half were white and one half black and Puerto Rican. The FST was submitted to each family individually early in therapy and again near the end (about the twelfth to the fifteenth session). Results revealed a reduction in hostility between mothers and children and a more realistic view of family relationships. There was a decrease in family anxiety and an increase in anger on the part of adult females, as well as reduction in children's projected guilt.

KAFFMAN, M. Family diagnosis and therapy in child emotinal pathology. *Family Process*, 1965, *4*, 241–258.
A description of families treated in Israel based upon 194 kibbutz families and 126 families living in Haifa. Family treatment is said to be effective and case examples are given.

KAFFMAN, M. Short term family therapy. *Family Process*, 1963, *2*, 216–234.
A report on the use of family therapy in a child guidance clinic in Israel with the emphasis upon short-term family treatment. The rationale, mehtodology, limitations, and initial evaluations of results are presented for 70 consecutive cases referred to the clinic.

KANTOR, R. E., & HOFFMAN, L. Brechtian theater as a model for conjoint family therapy. *Family Process*, 1966, *5*, 218–229.
A model for family therapy is offered in terms of the theater with particular emphasis upon Brecht's approach. Various procedures by Brecht are described as they apply to the family therapy process.

KAPLAN, M. L., KAPLAN, N. R. Individual and family growth: A Gestalt approach. *Family Process*, 1978, *17*, 195–205.
This paper is about the application of gestalt therapy to family therapy. The emphasis is on current experience, on affective experience, and on the totality of the family unit as an interactive, self-maintaining system. The aim is to produce an awareness of the family's current emergent experiences so that its members collaborate with the therapist in reducing the restrictions on themselves, in expanding their awareness, and in discovering their resources.

KAPLAN, S. L. Structural family therapy for children of divorce: Case reports. *Family Process*, 1977, *16*, 75–83.
This paper illustrasted strategies utilized in the resolution of clinical problems associated with the divorce process by changing the structural configuration in situations such as: mother, child, maternal grandparents; overprotective mother and child; helpless and mildly neglectful mother; father and child; new family formations; and remarriage.

KARDENER, S. The family: Structure, pattern, and therapy. *Mental Hygiene*, 1968, *52*, 524–531.
Following a review of the concept of the family as an etiologic agent in the development of psychopathology, 7 types of problem constellations, 4 types of family interrelationships, and 7 danger signals alerting the family to potential trouble are described. Role of therapist is outlined to deal with these problems.

KATKIN, S. Charting as a multipurpose treatment intervention for family therapy. *Family Process*, 1978, *17*, 465–468.
Using a review of literature and brief case reports, this paper discusses "charting" as a behavioral modification technique. This technique produced quick and sometimes dramatic changes. Its efficacy can be explained by integrating the viewpoints of behaviorist and of family therapy approaches.

KAZAMIAS, N. Intervening briefly in the family system. *International Journal of Social Psychiatry*, 1979, *25*, 104–109.
One case is presented to support the notion that brief, intense interventions can lead to more functional transactions within the family. The identified patient was an adolescent son who repeatedly ran away from home.

KEITH, D. V. Use of self: A brief report. *Family Process*, 1974, *13*, 201–206.
The portrayal of a therapist's use of self during a 3-year-old child's temper tantrum in which an impasse had been reached during therapy with the child's mother. The therapist was able to free the flow of feelings and produce behavoir change in both mother and child. The therapist also gained insight into this child's feelings of pain, anger, and omnipotence.

KEMPLER, W. Experimental family therapy. *International Journal of Group Psychotherapy*, 1965, *15*, 57–72.
A review of the author's experience in the use of a family approach to both diagnosis and treatment in the management of psychiatric problems. "Experimental family therapy" is a psychotherapeutic approach to the treatment of emotionally disturbed individuals within the framework of the family. Its core is the exploration of the "what and how" of the "I and thou" in the "here and now."

KEMPLER, W. Experimental psychotherapy with families. *Family Process*, 1968, 7, 88–89.
A description of a particular approach to family therapy with illustrative examples. The emphasis is upon the here and now and upon personal growth for family and therapist.

KEMPLER, W. Family therapy of the future. *International Psychiatry Clinics*, 1969, *6*, 135–158.
This is an essay on what family therapy will be like "in the future." Psychotherapy will be experiential. The orientation will shift from "objective–individual" to "subjective–interpersonal," and the focus will be on the present, on what is happening at this particular moment. There will be no such thing as diagnosis.

KEMPSTER, S. W., & SAVITSKY, E. Training family therapists through "Live" supervision. In N. W. Ackerman, F.L. Beatman, & S. Sherman (Eds.), *Expanding theory and practice in family therapy*. New York: Family Service Association of America, 1967.
A clnical essay focusing on techniques of supervision of family therapy. Family therapy and the process of live supervision should be introduced early in the course of training therapists. Staff and family reaction was "generally favorable, with adverse reactions rare."

KING, C. Family therapy with the deprived family. *Social Casework*, 1967, *48*, 203–208.
From the author's clinical work with delinquent boys at the Wiltwyck School, techniques of working with low socioeconomic-class patients and their families are described. Selection, rationale, and scope of family therapy are discussed. Basic techniques consist of educational and therapeutic maneuvers focusing on clarity of communication and the teaching of parent–child and sibling roles.

KLUGMAN, J. Owning and disowning: The structural dimension. *Family Process*, 1977, *16*, 353–356.
See reference in Section 3.6.

KNOBLOCHOVA, J., & KNOBLOCH, F. Family psychotherapy. In *Aspects of family mental health in europe*. Public Health Papers, No. 28, World Health Organization, 1965.
A report of the author's experience in a university hospital in Czechoslovakia using family therapy. Theoretical background and techniques are discussed.

KOEHNE-KAPLAN, N. S. The use of self as a family therapist. *Perspectives in Psychiatric Care*, 1976, *XIV*, 29–33.
A clinical paper addressing the notion that the use of the self is *the* primary tool for family therapy. In contrast to the literature, which speaks mostly about therapeutic process, the author offers an "exercise" designed to "illustrate the therapist's use of self."

KOVACS, L. A therapeutic relationship with a patient and family. *Perspectives in Psychiatric Nursing*, 1966, *4*, 11–21.
A case report in which family therapy was employed in treatment of a patient from the first admission to a private hsopital, to transfer to a state hospital, and finally to reunion with the family after discharge.

KWIATKOWSKE, H. Family art therapy. *Family Process*, 1967, *6*, 37–55.
A discussion of using art therapy as a therapeutic technique with families. In the previous 5 years 47 families have participated in family art therapy. The approach is described with a case example.

L'ABATE, L., & WEEKS, G. A bibliography of paradoxical methods in psychotherapy of family systems. *Family Process*, 1978, *17*, 95–98.
See reference in Section 6.0.

LANDES, J., & WINTER, W. A new strategy for treating disintegrating families. *Family Process*, 1966, *5*, 1–20.
A communal therapy procedure in which patient families and the families of therapists participated in a 48-hour weekend. The experience, problems, and results of such a weekend are described.

LANGSDORF, R. Understanding the role of extrafamilial social forces in family treatment: A critique of family therapy. *Family Theraply*, 1978, *5*, 73–80.
See reference in Section 4.5.

LANGSLEY, D. G. Three models of family therapy. *Journal of Clinical Psychiatry*, 1978, *11*, 792–795.
An overview of 3 models of family therapy: (1) the prevention model suggests the identification of high-risk groups for disorganization under stress leading to individual symptoms; (2) the crisis model follows the development of acute

symptomatology and sees the family as the patient while still focusing on relieving that symptomatology; and (3) the rehabilitation model aims at altering long-term patterns (e.g., persistent marital conflict). Examples of each model and suggestions for research designs are given. Thirty-four references are included.

LANGSLEY, D., PITTMAN, F. S., MACHOTKA, P., & FLOMENHAFF, K. Family crisis therapy: Results and implications. *Family Process*, 1968, 7, 145–159.
A report on the crisis treatment unit established at Colorado Psychiatric Hospital in Denver. A total of 186 cases selected randomly were treated by brief family treatment and compared with control cases hospitalized in the usual way. Preliminary results are reported.

LEADER, A. L. Current and future issues in family therapy. *Social Service Review*, 1969, 43, 1–11.
A clinical essay focussing on current "hot" issues in family therapy. Family therapy (a way of thinkilng about emotional problems) is differentiated from family group treatment techniques (defined as the different techniques of family therapy). At times the focus should be on the whole family and at other times on individual members. Different ways of using the family interview are discussed.

LEADER, A. L. Denied dependency in family therapy. *Social Casework*, 1976, 57, 637–643.
A clinical essay focusing on the problem of "dependency needs" that are appropriate but not acknowledged in the course of family processes. Family therapy techniques deal with these denied dependencies and their manifestations are discussed so that some balance can be achieved between realistic dependency needs and pathological dependency.

LEADER, A. L. The role of Intervention in family-group treatment. *Social Casework*, 1964, 45, 327–332.
A clinical essay on techniques of active intervention in family therapy. Active intervention is indicated because the family interactional patterns are deeply intrenched and difficult to break, there is a great deal of denial, and usually there is tremendous diffuseness. By using this technique, the problem can be shifted from the presenting problem to the underlyilng problem. Difficulties of active intervention and reasons for these difficulties are discussed.

LEFER, J. Counter-resistance in family therapy. *Journal of Hillside Hospital*, 1966, 15, 205–210.
This essay stresses the role of countertransferential feelings of the therapist to the family being treated. Material was taken from supervision of 6 residents, who reported from notes taken during the session or written immediately afterwards. Countertransference is manifested in distrubed feelings toward the family, stereotypy, love and hate responses, and carrying over affects after the session. The need for supervision of the therapist and self-knowledge in order to avoid difficulties is underlined.

LEIK, R. K., & NORTHWOOD, L. K. Improving family guidance through the small group experimental laboratory. *Social Work*, 1965, 9, 18–25.
A research article on using the experimental laboratory for: (1) contributing to general principles to guide counseling and guidance personnel, (2) providing a diagnostic vehicle for a given case, and (3) treatment evaluation. Interaction research studies are reviewed, and it is pointed out that the laboratory can be useful for training.

LENTHALL, G. A. Tribute to two masters. *Family Process*, 1975, 14, 379–388.
Two of Betty MacDonald's children's stories provide a focus for viewing change. The viewpoint used is that of a clinical hypnotist with a family-systems orientation.

LEVETON, A. Family therapy as the treatment of choice. *Medical Bulletin of the U.S. Army in Europe*, 1964, 21, 76–79.
The author discusses his experience with family therapy with 70 families in a military setting in which family therapy was the initial treatment method employed regardless of the presenting complaint. Of the 70 families, half involved hsuband and wife, and half involved a child and parents. Rationale for family therapy, as well as family dynamics, roles and ideologies are discussed and a case history presented. In general, family therapy, in contrast to individual psychotherapy, deals more with the present and future, rather than exploration of the individual or collective past.

LEVINE, R. Treatment in the home. *Social Work*, 1964, 9, 19–28.
A clinical report of treatment of 7 low-income, multiproblem families who came to a mental hygiene clinic for help with the identified patient, usually a child. Treatment of the family rather than the individual was begun because it seemed more economical, more family members could be helped, and the therapist could be more accurate in understanding problems. Treatment was done in the home. Techniques included "talking," "demonstration," and family activity. The 7 families were rated in terms of improvement, from most improved to least improved.

LEWIS, J., & GLASSER, N. Evolution of a treatment approach to families: Group family therapy. *International Journal of Group Therapy*, 1965, 15, 505–515.
A report of the involvement of families of mentally-ill patients in a therapy program treatment center. Three groups were set up: family members *excluding* patients, patients alone, and patients and families together. Impressions of this type of family involvement are described.

LIBERMAN, R. Behavioral approaches to family and couple therapy. *American Journal of Orthopsychiatry*, 1970, *40*, 106–119.
This is an essay attempting to apply some of the basic principles of "imitative learning and operant conditioning" to family therapy. Four case examples are given in support of some of the techniques. Advantages of this approach "remain to be proven by systematic research." Comparisons with techniques based on psychoanalytic principles are described.

LIBERMAN, R. P. Behavioral methods in group and family therapy. *Seminars of Psychiatry*, 1972, *4*, 145–156.
A critical article describing the use of behaivor therapy in combination with family therapy. Method is to make base-line observations of family interactions for at least the first 2 weeks. Problem behaviors that need modifying are specified. A program manual describing methods of reinforcement, extinction, and of specifying behaviors to be recorded is presented. Results with 11 families indicated that significant changes occurred in deviant behaviors. One case example is given to illustrate this approach.

LONG, R. The path toward psychodrama family process. *Group Psychotherapy*, 1966, *19*, 43–46.
In an inpatient setting, where psychodrama is one of the treatment techniques used, the author describes his realization that families seem to be involved in the pathogenesis of mental illness. He suggests that bringing in the *real* family to the psychodrama sessions might be useful and describes some problems that arose as a result.

LUM, K. Towards multicentered marital therapy. *Psychotherapy*, 1973, *10*, 208–211.
Multicentered marital therapy is defined as a type of therapy "using self-disclosure and it dyadic effect in juxtaposition with empathy." The therapy is described in detail along with the role of the therapist and its use with other techniques.

MACGREGOR, R. Communicating values in family therapy. In G. H. Zik & I. Boszormenyi-Nagy (Eds.), *Family therapy and disturbed families*. Palo Alto: Science & Behavior Books, 1967.
A discussion of family therapy form the point of view of the therapist attempting to change a family's system of values. A case illustration defends the advocation of conventional middle-class values. Includes an attempt to differentiate deliberate influence from unwitting culture conflict between therapist and patient.

MACGREGOR, R. Group and family therapy: Moving into the present and letting go of the past. *International Journal of Psychotherapy*, 1970, *20*, 495–515.
As part of a symposium on the relationship of group psychotherapy to other treatment modalities involving groups, this paper compares similarities and differences among the theories and techniques of various family therapists. Strategies of family therapy are discussed. A primary family therapy goal is the optimal resumption of productive functioning, while group therapy focuses on "repair of personality malfunction."

MACGREGOR, R. Multiple impact psychotherapy with families. *Family Process*, 1962, *1*, 15–29.
A description of the treatment approach used by the outpatient psychiatric clinic staff for adolescents at the University of Texas Medical Branch Hospitals at Galveston. Fifty-five families are described in which an adolescent was the primary patient and the families were in some sort of crisis. Multiple-impact therapy is a form of diagnositc and therapeutic intervention that uses the entire time and facilities of an orthopsychiatric team in different combinations for half a week. The method and some preliminary results based on 6 and 18 month follow-up studies are reported.

MACGREGOR, R. Progress in multiple impact therapy. In N. W. Ackerman, F. L. Beatman, & S. Sherman (Eds.), *Expanding theory and practice in family therapy*. New York: Family Service Association of America, 1967.
A report on the youth development project in Galveston where multiple impact therapy developed. The approach is described with emphasis upon the bringing together of "a relatively open system, the team," with "a relatively closed system, the family functioning in a defensive way." Procedures and concepts are described.

MACHOTKA, R., PITTMAN, F. S., & FLOMENHAFT, K. Incest as a family affair. *Family Process*, 1967, *6*, 98–116.
A discussion of incest from the point of view of the whole family. Two cases of father–daughter and one of sibling incest are discussed with the emphasis upon the crucial role of the nonparticipating member, the concerted denial of the incest, and on where the focus of therapy should be.

MACKIE, R. Family problems in medical and nursing families. *British Journal of Medical Psychology*, 1967, *40*, 333–340.
From 9 cases treated over 4 years and a review of the literature, the author presents parts of 3 cases in which the presenting patient was a doctor or nurse. Of the 9 cases, 7 improved with family therapy and 2 did not. The doctor or nurse will "defend himself or herself against the direct expression of sick or dependent parts of himself or herself and will instead project these onto the spouse or onto other relatives."

MADANES, C., HALEY, J. Dimensions of family therapy. *Journal of Nervous Mental Diseases*, 1977, *165*, 88–98.
A descriptive paper focusing on different types of family therapy: (1) psychodynamic, (2) experiential, (3) behavioral, (4) systems and (5) communication. These types of family therapy are compared in approach (e.g., emphasis on past versus present; the number of people present), goals, and techniques (e.g., interpretive versus directive work).

MANDELBAUM, A. Diagnosis in family treatment. *Bulletin of the Menninger Clinic*, 1976, *40*, 497–504.
The importance of diagnosis in family treatment is emphasized. Diagnostic techniques include not only gathering historical information but also employing action-oriented measures such as family sculpting.

MANDELBAUM, A. A family centered approach to residential treatment. *Bulletin of the Menninger Clinic*, 1977, *41*, 27–39.
In this theoretical paper by a director of a family therapy training program, 2 case examples are used to illustrate the arguments for a family-systems approach to the treatment of hospitalized adolescents and young adults. Both identified patients were severely disturbed, nonpsychotic, young adults who improved with family treatment.

MARKOWITZ, I., TAYLOR, G., & BOKERT, E. Dream discussion as a means of reopening blocked familial communication. *Psychotherapy and Psychosomatic*, 1968, *16*, 348–356.
Based on the clinical notion that parents exclude the child in family dialogue, these family therapists use the dreams of the children "as a focus for familial discussion." It is thought to be an "indicator of the degree of honesty of communication present in the family." Numerous case examples are given in support of this view.

MARX, A., & LUDWIG, A. Resurection of the family of the chronic schizophrenic, *American Journal of Psychotherapy*,1969, *23*, 37–52.
A careful review of the author's experience treating psychiatric inpatients by systematically involving the family of the patient. Sample was 44 chronic schizophrenic patients and families over a 2-year-period. Family resistances and methods to deal with these resistances are discussed. The treatment program included family–therapist meetings, patient–family–therapist sessions, multiple family group meetings, and multiple family conjoint therapy sessions. Some of the effects of this treatment program, both positive (patient and family improvement) and negative (member of the family decompensating), as well as the methods of dealing with these implications and ethics of this approach are discussed.

MAZUR, V. Family therapy: An approach to the culturally different. *International Journal Social Psychiatry*, 1973, *19*:114–120.
See reference in Section 4.5.

MCDANALD, E. C. Out-patient therapy of neurotic families. In I. M. Cohen (Ed.), *Psychiatric research report 20*. Washington, D. C: American Psychiatric Association, 1966.
"Impressions about the psychotherapy of predominantly neurotic families on an out-patient basis." The emphasis is on considerations for excluding family members, factors that impede change, and indications for family therapy.

MCPEAK, W. R. Family interactions as etiological factors in mental disorders: An analysis of the american journal of insanity, 1844–1848. *American Journal of Psychiatry*, 1975, *132*, 1327–1329.
See reference in Section 3.6.

MENDELL, D. & FISCHER, S. A multigeneration approach to the treatment of psychopathology. *Journal of Nervous Mental Diseases*, 1958, *126*, 523–529.
This essay describes techniques of treating the family, rather than the identified patient, for various problems seen in *a private psychiatric population. TAT and Rorschach material were important parts of the diagnostic evaluation.*

MERENESS, D. Family therapy: An evolving role. *Perspectives in Psychiatric Care*, 1968, *6*, 256–259.
This essay discusses the role of the psychiatric nurse in family therapy. Rationale and indications for family therapy are discussed. Nurses are seen as "uniquely well equipped to accept the role of family therapist." Training for nurses should include functioning as a cotherapist, being taught the body of knowledge concerning family dynamics, and learning treatment techniques. Moving outside the "traditional role of the psychiatric nurse" is suggested.

MESSER, A. Family treatment of a school Phobic child. *Archives of General Psychiatry*, 1964, *11*, 548–555.
Case report of family treatment of a phobic child and his family. Hypothesis was that the phobia expressed publicly a disruption in the family equilibrium.

MESSER, A. The "phaedra complex." *Archives of General Psychiatry*, 1969, *21*, 213–218.
A case report centering around the dynamics of a stepparent–stepchild attraction. There is dilution of the "incest barrier." The mother–son incest taboo is far stonger than that involving father and daughter. Inability to cope with

this potential conflict, particularly when the parents are in a disturbed or mutually frustrating relationship, can lead to problems with the children who are often the identified patients.

MIDELFORT, C. F. Use of members of the family in treatment of schizophrenia. *Family Process*, 1962, *1*, 114–118.
See Reference in Section 1.4

MILLER, S. A study in family dynamics. *Perspectives of Psychiatric Care*, 1963, *1*, 9–15.
One case example that describes individual, interpersonal, and sociocultural dynamics. Treatment included helping the family to deal with problems of everyday living, to set goals for the future, and to accomplish developmental tasks.

MINUCHIN, S. Conflict-resolution family therapy. *Psychiatry*, 1965, *28*, 278–286.
A description of a method of family therapy developed at Wiltwyck School for Boys in which the therapist brings members of the family behind a one-way mirror to observe the conversation of the remaining family members. This procedure is effective with multiproblem families. The family member is usually asked in family therapy to be a participant-observer and in this method these two functions are separated. "The one-way mirror maintains the emotional impact of interpersonal experiences, while it does not provide an opportunity for impulsory discharge." The family members impulse to react with action, which is generally characteristic of the families treated, is delayed and channeled into verbal forms.

MINUCHIN, S. Family structure, family language and the puzzled therapist. In O. Pollak (Ed.), *Family theory and family therapy of female sexual delinquency*. Palo Alto: Science & Behavior Books, 1967.
An approach to family therapy derived from treating low socioeconomic families at the Wiltwyck School for Boys. "We began to look anew at the meaning and effectiveness of therapist interventions and to focus on two aspects of the family—family language and family structure." Ways of challenging the family structure and other procedures are described with illustrations.

MINUCHIN, S. Family therapy: Technique or theory? In J. Masserman (Ed.), *Science and Psychoanalysis (Vol. XIV): Childhood and adolescence*. New York: Grune & Stratton, 1969.
A discussion of family therapy with the emphasis upon the need to take into account the total ecology of the family.

MINUCHIN, S. Psychoanalytic therapies and the low socioeconomic population. In J. Marmor (Ed.), *Modern psychoanalysis*. New York: Basic Books, 1968.
The failure of psychoanalytic therapies and psychotherapy to reach the low socioeconomic population is discussed in terms of the implicit requirements of those approaches and the characteristics of the population. Alternate approaches such as living group therapy, remedial learning therapy, and family therapy are discussed.

MINUCHIN, S. The use of an ecological framework in the treatment of a child. In E. J. Anthony & C. Koupernik (Eds.), *The child in his family*. New York: Wiley, 1970.
A discussion of the 3 elements in the study of the child: the child as an individual, his environment, and the linkage between. The ecological point of view is discussed and a case of an adolescent with *anorexia nervosa* is discussed in terms of his family and the family therapy approach to the problem.

MINUCHIN, S., AUERSWALD, E., KING, C., & RABINOWITZ, C. The study and treatment of families that produce multiple acting-out boys. *American Journal of Orthopsychiatry*, 1964, *34*, 125–134.
An early report of experience with families of delinquent boys, social class V, at the Wiltwyck School for Boys in New York. The report focuses on some aspects of familial functioning, in particular "the socializing function of parental control, guidance and nurturance." The group's technique of family diagnosis and therapy with delinquent families is also presented.

MINUCHIN, S., & BARCAI, A. therapeutically induced family crisis. In J. Masserman (Ed.), *Science and psychoanalysis (Vol. XIV):Childhood and Adolescence*. New York: Grune & Stratton, 1969.
A report on a family treatment approach in which a crisis is induced and resolved. A family with a child regularly hospitalized for diabetic acidosis was treated by being assigned tasks that induced a crisis situation to which the family members had to respond by changing.

MINUCHIN, S., & MONTALVO, B. Techniques for working with disorganized low socioeconomic families. *American Journal of Orthopsychiatry*, 1967, *37*, 880–887.
A paper describing some modifications of family therapy techniques useful for dealing with some families of low socioeconomic class. The techniques include changing the family composition so that some members observe the family sessions through a one-way mirror, separately treating various subgroups within the natural family (e.g., all adolescents), actively manipulating subgroups in relation to the whole family group, and finally helping the family members to *discuss* what they want to *act* on.

MITCHELL, C. A casework approach to disturbed families. In N. W. Ackerman, F. L. Beatman, & S. Sherman (Eds.), *Exploring the base for family therapy*. New York: Family Service Association of America, 1961.
The family from the point of view of the caseworker, with emphasis upon family diagnosis and treatment.

MITCHELL, C. Integrative therapy of the family unit. *Social Casework*, 1965, *46*, 63–69.
A discussion of the family unit therapy approach as practiced at the Jewish Family Service in New York. Concepts are presented with a case example.

MITCHELL, C. The uses and abuses of co-therapy as a technique in family unit therapy. *Bulletin of the Family Mental Health Clinics J. F. S.*, 1969, *1*, 8–10.
A clinical essay on the advantages and problems of using cotherapists in family therapy.

MITCHELL, C. The use of family sessions in the diagnosis and treatment of disturbances in children. *Social Casework*, 1960, *41*, 283–290.
A discussion of family casework in which the family as a whole is interviewed. The family session is supplemented by interviews of family pairs, triads, or individuals. Sessions with the whole family provide unique insights on many levels, help a child accept treatment more readily, lay bare the involvement of all family members in the problem, and further the growth of all family members.

MIYOSHI, N. & LIEBMAN, R., "Training Psychiatric Residents in Family Therapy." *Family Process*, 1969, *8*, 97–105.
A report on training psychiatric residents in family therapy at Mercy-Douglass Hospital in Philadelphia. Problems and benefits are discussed.

MONEA, H. A family in trouble (A case study of a family in conjoint family therapy). *Perspectives of Psychiatric Care*, 1974, *12*, 165–170.
One family with a drug-abusing member was treated by conjoint family therapy (including the use of sculpting). The family improved.

MOSHER, L. R. Schizophrenogenic communication and family therapy. *Family Process*, 1969, *8*, 43–63.
A description of a technique of family therapy with a family of a schizophrenic. The emphasis is on the structural and process aspects of the family's communication, and case material is used for illustration.

MOSHER, L., & KWIATKOWSKA, H. Family art evaluation: Use in families with schizophrenic twins. *Journal of Nervous Mental Diseases*, 1971, *153*, 165–179.
Family art as a useful method or diagnosis of relationships in families with no, 1 or 2 schizophrenic twins is discussed. The procedures are outlined, and the results (based on the scores from 2 "blind" raters) of 3 families (1 normal, 1 discordant for schizophrenia, and 1 concordant for schizophrenia) were rated on 12 variables and analyzed. The parents of the concordant twins did the most poorly and the parents of the control twins did the best. A large statistical study is essential for confirmation of the results.

MOTTOLA, W. Family therapy: A review. *Psychotherapy: Theory, Research & Practice*, 1967, *4*, 116–124.
See reference in Section 6.0.

MUELLER, P. S., & ORFANIDIS, M. M. A method of co-therapy for schizophrenic families. *Family Process*, 1976, *15*, 179–191.
The authors describe a method of family therapy for families with a diagnosed schizophrenic child in which male and female cotherapists adopt structured roles. Therapy focuses on individuating and differentiating the relationships between nuclear and extended family members that interfere with autonomic development. Case studies are presented that illustrate the stages of therapy, i.e., initiation, breaking of fusion, repair of alienation, and solidifying the marital alliance and generational boundaries. The authors suggest that ongoing family therapy is important to maintain therapeutic gains in behavior patterns.

MURNEY, R., & SCHNEIDER, R., Family Therapy: Understanding and changing behavior. In F. McKinney (Ed.), *Psychology in action*. New York: Macmillan, 1957.
A review of articles describing rationale, indications, methods, and theory of family therapy for the beginning psychologist.

MURRAY, M. E. Family character analysis. *American Journal of Psychoanalysis*, 1979, *39*, 41–53.
The application of psychodynamic theories of character analysis to family therapy is discussed. The family, like an individual, has an "ego" based on object relations and manifesting unconscious conflicts (interpersonal rather than intrapsychic). Characteristic patterns of resistance to change are also discussed. A framework for family therapy, which utilizes these theories on family dyadic and individual levels, and a clinical example is presented.

NATIONAL CLEARINGHOUSE FOR MENTAL HEALTH INFORMATION.*Family therapy: A selected Annotated Bibliography.* Bethesda: Public Health Service, 1965.
An annotated bibliography of the literature on family therapy up to 1964, which includes general theoretical articles, therapy with adolescents, child-oriented family therapy, therapy in the home, therapy with families of psychiatric inpatients, marital counseling, therapy with schizophrenics, and training family therapists.

ORGUN, I. N. Playroom setting for diagnostic family interviews. *American Journal of Psychiatry*, 1973, *130*, 540–542.
Case examples are used to illustrate the advantages of a playroom setting (to an office) for family diagnostic interviews with children under 10 years of age. Therapists and family members meet in a playroom 1 week after the identified patient is seen alone. Two years of experiences with this technique suggest that: it offers the advantage of a less stressful atmosphere than in an office; the child is less anxious; diagnostic clues can be obtained by observing parents' use of toys; and there is decreased parental anxiety about future play therapy for the child.

ORVIN, G. H. Intensive treatment of an adolescent and his family. *Archives of General Psychiatry*, 1974, *31*, 801–806.
Family dynamaics are an important part of the evaluation in a "new" program for treatment of adolescents. Therapy includes marital therapy, family therapy, and mulitple family group therapy. No results are reported.

OSBERG, J. W. Initial impressions of the use of short-term family group conferences. *Family Process*, 1962, *1*, 236–244.
A discussion of early experiences with 38 families seen in group treatment over a 4-year period in a psychiatric outpatient clinic. The evaluation, initial session, and succeeding sessions are described with a case example.

OSMAN, S. My stepfather is a she. *Family Process*, 1972, *11*:209–218.
A clinical report of the treatment of a lesbian couple and their two sons. Family therapists are frequently called upon to intervene professionally with new family forms, although they must be aware of their own value system and how cultural biases shape the treatment process. Therapy may benefit children by introducing them to a different value orientation.

OSTENDORF, M. The public health nurse role in helping a family to cope with mental health problems. *Perspectives in Psychiatric Nursing*, 1967, *5*: 208–213.
This article develops a *modus operandi* for a public health nurse to deal with families with mental health problems. She can help the family to deal with daily problems of living, to increase the stability of one family member ("which will subsequently benefit the entire family"), and to strengthen the family's ability to cope with future mental problems.

PAIDOUSSI, E. Some comparisons between family therapy and individual therapy. *Bulletin of the Family Mental Health Clinic, J.F.S.,* 1969, *1*, 11–12.
This is a clinicial essay dealing with differences between these two kinds of therapy. Family therapy involves working with interactions, more here and now material, requires more involvement and more leadership on the part of the therapist.

PAPP, P., SLIVERSTEIN, O. & CARTER, E. Family sculpting and preventive work with "well families." *Family Process*, 1973, *12*, 197–212.
A description of an experimental community prevention project. Family sculpting was applied to 3 groups of families in the community who were not in an immediate crisis. Significant modifications in the family structure were obtained. The conclusions derived from observations were that: (1) structuring tends to enhance rather than hamper the spontaneous release of affect; (2) presenting teaching concepts can lead away from intellectualization, not toward it; (3) limiting group interaction intensifies rather than diminishes the effect of the group; and (4) deliberately changing one's behavior can lead to insightful changes.

PARLOFF, M. B. The family in psychotherapy. *Archives of General Psychiatry,* 1961, *4*, 445–451.
A discussion of the research trends in family therapy with emphasis upon some of the theoretical modifications that accompany present forms of family therapy. In treatment, a shift has been made from family members seen individually by different therapists to a single therapist treating several family members. The influence of group therapy provided "the greatest single advance in the interpersonal relationship treatment technique," and from there it was a short step to working with a patient's actual family rather than his transference family. The patient (a child) began to be seen less as a victim and more as a part of the organic unit of the family.

PARLOFF, M. B. Symposium: Family therapy and group therapy—Similarities and differences. Discussion: The narcissism of small differences—and some big ones. *International Journal of Group Psychotherapy,* 1976, *26*: 311–319.
The final paper in this series of four discusses the previous two. In lieu of the fact that neither treatment has been advanced to the point where it can answer the questions—what kinds of changes are produced in what kinds of problems, by what kinds of therapists, using what kinds of techniques, under what kinds of conditions—it is difficult to make comparisons that are meaningful but easy to spend a great deal of time debating the "intermediate goals and

techniques" of the therapies. That is, the outcome for the "ultimate goals" in terms of reducing symptom distress either in individuals or families is not addressed by either therapy.

PATTERSON, B., MCNEAL, S. HAWKINS, N., & PHELPS, R. Reprogramming the social environment. *Journal of Child Psychology and Psychiatry,* 1967, *8:* 181–185.
A case report of conditioning techniques used to reprogram parent and child, and not just the child alone, so that they become mutually reinforcing. The patient was a 5-year-old autistic child. Observation of the new conditioning was done in the home. There were 12 conditioning sessions lasting from 10 to 20 minutes over a 4-week period. Changes in behavior were noted.

PATTERSON, G. R., SHAW, D. A., & EBNER, M .J. Teachers, peers, and parents as agents of change in the classroom. In S. A. N. Benson (Ed.), *Modifying deviant social behaviors in various classroom settings.* Eugene: University of Oregon, 1969.
An approach to correcting deviant behavior in the classroom by using a combined systems and reinforcement theory approach.

PATTISON, E. M. et al. A psychosocial kinship model for family therapy. *American Journal of Psychiatry,* 1975, *132:* 1246–1251.
See reference in Section 3.6.

PATTISON, W. M. Treatment of alcoholic families with nurse home visits. *Family Process,* 1965, *4,* 75–94.
The use of public health nurses to make home visits is described in terms of preventive crisis intervention and family therapy. The results of a study of 7 families are offered with case examples showing that the public health nurse can play a decisive role, particularly with lower class, multiproblem families.

PAUL, N. L. Effects of playback on family members of their own previously recorded conjoint therapy material. In I. M. Cohen (Ed.), *Psychiatric Research Report 20.* Washington, D.C.: American Psychiatric Association, 1966.
A discussion of the use of playback of tape-recorded conjoint family therapy material to help families "recognize or assess the respective contributions each makes to the maintenance of maladaptive functioning . . . " Case examples are given with discussion of the responses of the families.

PAUL, N. L. The role of a secret in schizophrenia. In N. W. Ackerman (Ed.), *Family therapy in transition.* Boston: Little, Brown, 1970.
A case of a family of a schizophrenic with a secret. Excerpts from family interviews are included to illustrate decoding the transactions among the family members.

PAUL, N. The use of empathy in the resolution of grief. *Perspectives/Biology and Medicine,* 1967, *11,* 153–169.
This is an essay on a technique in family therapy in which it is felt that there is a direct relationship between the maladaptive response to the death of a loved person and the fixity of symbiotic relationships within the family. The patient's symptom is a defense against the grief. Use of empathy by the therapist in resolving the grief helps to change the symptomatology.

PAUL, N. L. & GROSSER, G. H. Family resistance to change in schizophrenic patients. *Family Process,* 1964, *3,* 377– 401.
A description, with case excerpts, of the patterns of family response to schizophrenic patients that develop during the early phase of conjoint family therapy. Families express desire for the patients to change while attempting to maintain the status quo in family relationships in ways that reinforce the patient's symptomatology.

PAUL, N. L., & GROSSER, G. Operational mourning and its role in conjoint family therapy. *Community Mental Health Journal,* 1965, *1,* 339–345.
Studies of records of 50 families with a schizophrenic member and 25 families with at least one psychoneurotic member revealed "patterns of inflexible interaction and maladaptive response to object loss." The way the sample was obtained is not stated. It is hypothesized from this data that incomplete mourning after object loss leads to an inability to deal with future object loss and this defect is transmitted to other family members. This is thought to lead to a "fixation of symbiotic relationships in the family." Therefore, "one possible way to dislodge this fixation would be to mobilize those affects which might aid in disrupting this particular kind of equilibrium." "Operational mourning" is the technique evolved to do this and is believed to "involve the family in a belated mourning experience with extensive grief reactions." A case report is included.

PERLMUTTER, M., LOEB, D., GUMPERT, G., O'HARA, F., & HIGBIE, I. Family diagnosis and therapy using videotape playback. *American Journal of orthopsychiatry,* 1967, *37,* 900–905.
A paper describing the uses of videotape for teaching, research, and treatment. Videotape was useful in diagnosis, in getting family consensus on "what happened" and in therapist supervision.

PITTIMAN, F., DEYOUNG, C., FLOMENHAFT, K., KAPLAN, D., & LANGSLEY, D. Crisis family therapy. In J. Masserman (Ed.), *Current Psyciatric Therapies* Vol VI. New York: Grune & Statton, 1966.
A report of the authors' experiences in using a family approach rather than hospitalization or individual psychotherapy to deal with acute crisis situations. Setting was an acute treatment facility that hospitalizes about 75 percent of patients referred. Of these, 25 percent were referred to the family treatment unit, which consisted of a psychiatrist, social worker and nurse. Fifty cases were referred to this unit, and, in 42, hospitalization was "avoided completely." Techniques of treatment are discussed.

PITTMAN, F., LANGSLEY, D., & DEYOUNG, C. Work and school phobias: A family approach to treatment. *American Journal of Psychiatry*, 1968, *124*, 1535–1541.
Eleven cases of work phobia (the patient experienced over anxiety associated with having to go to work or staying at work) are thought as being "the adult form of school phobia." Treatment goal is to allow the wife or mother to allow the man to separate. One year follow-up shows that 5 cases treated with conjoint family therapy were able to return to work; the 6 in long term individual therapy had not.

PITTMAN, F. S., LANGSLEY, D. G., FLOMEHAFT, K. DEYOUNG, C. D., & MACHOTKA, I. Therapy techniques of the family treatment unit. In J. Haley (Ed.), *Changing families.* New York: Grune & Stratton. 1971.
A report on the therapy techniques of a crisis treatment unit in Denver that did brief family therapy to prevent hospitalization. Different approaches are described.

PITTMAN, F. S., LANGSLEY, D. G., KAPLAN, D. M. FLOMENHAFT, K. & DEYOUNG, C. Family therapy as an alternative to psychiatric hospitalization, In I. M. Cohen (Ed.), *Psychiatric Research Report 20.* Washington, D.C. American Psychiatric Association, 1966.
A report on the crisis treatment team at the Colorado Psychopathic Hospital, which treated a random selection of patients and their families as an alternative to hospitalization. Case examples are given.

POLLACK, O., & BRIELAND, D. The midwest seminar on family diagnosis and treatment. *Social Casework*, 1961, *42*, 319–324.
A project to develop a model for family diagnosis and treatment that would be useful for the teaching and practice of social work. A discussion of various aspects of family dynamics, treatment, and treatment problems that are important to case work is presented.

POTASH, H. & BRUNELL, L. Multiple-conjoint psychotherapy with folie à deux. *Psychotherapy: Theory, Research, and Practice, 11*, 270–276.
One case example of a *folie à deux* is presented in support of the concept that family therapy is useful in the treatment of this syndrome.

RABINER, E. L., MOLINSKI, H., & GRALNICK, A. Conjoint family therapy in the inpatient setting. *American Journal of Psychotherapy.* 1962, *16*, 618–631.
A general discussion of the adaptation of family therapy to the inpatient setting, with its advantages and difficulties illustrated by cases.

RABINOWITZ, C. Therapy for underprivileged "delinquent" families. In O. Pollack & A. S. Friedman (Eds.), *Family dynamics and female sexual delinquency.* Palo Alto: Science & Behavior Books, 1969.
See Reference in Section 5.7.

RAKOFF, V., SIGAL, J., & EPSTEIN, N. Working-through in conjoint family therapy. *American Journal of Psychotherapy*, 1967, *21*, 782–790.
Several clinical examples are given in support of this notion that the psychoanalytic concept of "working-through" is useful in conjoint family therapy. In family therapy the material is not a specific conflict, but rather problems that the family is currently discussing. In family therapy the therapist must be more persistent than in individual therapy. In addition "characteristic patterns in the family" are also to be "worked through."

RASHKIS, H., "Depression as a Manifestation of the Family as an Open System," *Archives of General Psychiatry*, 1968, *19*, 57–63.
See Reference in Section 5.4.

REBNER, I. Conjoint family therapy. *Psychotherapy: Theory, Research and Practice*, 1972, *9*, 62–66.
A clinical essay reviewing the historical development of family therapy. Several case examples are given illustrating its usefulness. It is not a panacea for all psychiatric conditions.

RICE, D. G., FEY, W.F., & KEPECS, J. G. Therapist experience and "style" as factors in co-therapy. *Family Process*, 1972, *11*, 1–15.
A self-description questionnaire of general in-therapy behavior, attitudes toward co-therapy, and ratings of co-

therapy effectiveness was given to 25 experienced (E) and 25 inexperienced (IE) therapists who treated a total of 48 couples in co-therapy. Major findings indicated that (1) 6 different "styles" emerged via a factor analysis of therapists' self-descriptions of in-therapy behavior; (2) E and IE therapists as a group had different personal therapeutic styles and preferences as to the style preferred in a co-therapist; (3) subjectively rate effectiveness of co-therapy correlated with the degree of comfort felt by the therapist in the relationship and the acceptance by the co-therapist; and (4) there was evidence of a point of "diminishing returns" in satisfaction for therapists in general, which came with increasing experience in doing co-therapy. The article concludes with a commentary by Carl A. Whitaker, M.D., who describes his own "evolution" through the "styles" of in-therapy behavior.

RICHMAN, J. The family therapy of attempted suicide. *Family Process*, 1979, *18*, 131–142.
Suicide is a multi-determined act based upon a variety of factors among which family tensions and patterns of interaction predominate. The basic goals of therapy are to help initiate and to catalyze a healing process that will enable the participants to accept changes in both individual and family existence; to decrease the amount of destructive family interaction; to deal with the anxiety accompanying growth and development; to make contact with and among family members; and to provide hope.

RICHTER, H. Familientherapie. *Psychotherapy and Psychomatics*, 1968, *16*, 303–318.
An essay on the development of family therapy as an important new application of "psychoanalysis." An indication for family therapy is whenever a family is exposed to a common psychological problem and is capable of making this problem accessible to a therapeutic approach. This article is in German.

RIESS, B. F. Family therapy as seen by a group therapist. *International Journal of Group Psychotherapy*, 1976, *26*, 301–309.
Group and family therapies are compared from the point of view of a theorist in group therapy research. The two therapies are found to be widely varying approaches to different problems. In family therapy, the family gradually becomes a patient itself; this does not happen in group therapy in which members use the treatment to correct individual problems.

RIESS, B. F. Symposium: Family therapy and group therapy—Similarities and differences. Family therapy as seen by a group therapist. *International Journal of Group Psychotherapy*, 1976, *26*, 301–309.
Differences between family therapy and group therapy are described. Of the two therapies, only the "curative factors" of group therapy have been subject to some research. The two approaches are different in intent and deal with different problems.

RITCHIE, A. Multiple impact therapy: An experiment. *Social Work*, 1960, *5*, 16–21.
A description of the multiple impact therapy used in the youth development project at the University of Texas Medical Branch in Galveston. The method consists of a brief, usually 2-day, intensive study and treatment of a family in crises by a guidance team composed of psychiatrist, psychiatric social worker, and clinical psychologists. the team deals with a family 6 or 7 hours a day for 2 days. These families come from 50 to 450 miles away, and the method was developed for families who could not regularly visit. There are 2 basic assumptions to the method: a family facing a crisis is more receptive to change than at other times, and dramatic change occurs in early stages of treatment.

ROBINSON, L. R. Basic concepts in family therapy: A differential comparison with individual treatment. *American Journal of Psychiatry*, 1975, *132*, 1045–1048.
A clinical essay comparing the differences between family psychotherapy and individual psychotherapy models. Three dimensions are explored: personality development, symptom formation, and techniques to produce therapeutic change. Family therapy is based mostly on interactional system concepts, while individual psychotherapy is based mostly on "intrapsychic," noninteractional concepts.

ROHDE, I. The nurse as a family therapist. *Nursing Outlook*, 1968, *16*, 49–52.
One case example is presented in support of the idea that the nurse can be a valuable team member in family therapy.

ROMAN, M. Symposium: Family therapy and group therapy—Similarities and differences: Introduction. *International Journal of Group Psychotherapy*, 1976, *26*, 281–287.
The first in a series of four papers gives an overview and a review of the literature.

ROSENTHAL, M. J. The syndrome of the inconsistent mother. *American Journal of Orthopsychiatry*, 1962, *32*, 637–643.
A report on a method of treatment of mothers who are inconsistent with matters of discipline of their acting-out problem children. These mothers regard their disciplinary efforts as proof of their hostility toward their children and exploration of motivations tends to increase guilts. The treatment recommended focuses sharply upon the disciplinary problem and is oriented toward alleviation of the mother's guilt by helping her become more consistent and effective in her disciplining of the child. The procedure is often dramatically effective.

ROSMAN, B. L., MINUCHIN, S. & LIEBMAN, R. Family lunch sessions: An introduction to family therapy in Anorexia Nervosa. *American Journal of Orthopsychiatry*, 1975, *45*, 846–853.
A clinical paper advocating the use of the "family lunch" (i.e., observation of the entire family in the treatment setting) as a diagnostic and therapeutic technique in the treatment of anorexia nervosa. Method was chart review of 17 hospitalized patients of whom 8 had sufficient pre- and post-session weight data. Results, using the McNemar test, indicated that the indentified patients gained a significant amount of weight after the family-lunch intervention. Rationale and implications are discussed.

RUBENSTEIN, D. Family Therapy. *International Psychiatric Clinics*, 1964, *1*, 431–442.
This essay is oriented toward the teaching of family therapy. Rationale and techniques are discussed, and it is stressed that this form of family therapy can be taught to trainees in the same way that other techniques of psychotherapy are taught. Usually trainees sit in with an experienced staff member as a cotherapist.

RUBINSTEIN, D. Family therapy. In E. A. Spiegel (Ed.), *Progress in neurology and psychiatry (Vol. XVIII)*. New York: Grune & Stratton, 1963.
A review article of the literature on family dynamics and therapy for 1961 and 1962. The literature grouped in the following categories: (1) theory and research, (2) dynamics, (3) technique, and (4) miscellaneous.

RUBINSTEIN, D. Family therapy. In E. A. Spiegel (Ed.), *Progress in neurology and psychiatry (Vols. XX, XXI)*. New York: Grune & Stratton, 1965, 1966.
The 1965 review emphasizes a shift to the creation of a conceptual framework to understand the dynamics of the family system. There are 52 references. In the 1966 annual review, there is a similar emphasis with articles summarized under the following headings: theory and research, dynamics, technique, and miscellaneous. Included are 54 references.

RUBINSTEIN, D. Family therapy of schizophrenia—Where to?—What next? *Psychotherapy and Psychosomatics*, 1975, *25*, 154–162.
See reference in Section 6.0.

RUBINSTEIN, D., & WEINER, O. R. Co-Therapy teamwork relationships in family therapy. In G. H. Zuk and I. Boszormenyi-Nagy (Eds.), *Family therapy and disturbed families*. Palo Alto: Science & Behavior Books, 1967.
A description of co-therapy experiences at the Eastern Pennsylavnia Psychiatric Institute. "We feel that if one therapist were to deal alone with the intense negative transference of a family system, the result might be overwhelming for the therapist." Dynamics of team relationships are discussed.

RYAN, F. Clarifying some issues in family group casework. *Social Casework*, 1967, *48*, 222–226.
An essay attempting to answer some difficult issues in family group casework (defined as casework with the entire family present rather than just an individual). Family casework should be done with all family members present, although it does not preclude treatment of individual members by other therapists. Both historical and here-and-now issues are important.

SAFER, D. J. Family therapy for children with behavior disorders. *Family Process*, 1966, *5*, 243–255.
A report on short-term therapy of 29 children with behavior disorders and their families. All cases were selected because they were either unmotivated or unacceptable for individual psychotherapy. Treatment approach is described, and 40 percent showed improvement.

SAGER, C. An overview of family therapy. *International Journal of Group Psychotherapy*, 1968, *18*, 302–312.
Several issues concerning family therapy are raised including: a commentary on its develpoment; its interdisciplinary approach; its effectiveness as a form of treatment; the implications of research when the identified patient is schizophrenic; the openness of the therapists in the field; and the advantages and disadvantages of cotherapists.

SAKAMOTO, H. Family focused therapy of schizophrenia. *Japanese Journal of Psychotherapy*, (Tokyo) 1975, *1*, 124–132.
An essay suggesting tht family therapy may be useful as a treatment for schizophrenia. There is a review of the literature and summaries of some of the work of well-known therapists.

SANDER, F. M. Family therapy or religion: A re-reading of T. S. Eliot's *The Cocktail Party. Family Process*, 1970, *9*, 279–296.
An analysis of the play, *The Cocktail Party*, from the view of analytic sociology with the emphasis upon family therapy as a response to changes in the structure of contemporary families.

SATIR, V. M. Communication as a tool for understanding and changing behavior. *Proceedings, Human Growth and Diversity*. California Association of School Psychologists and Psychometrists, 16th Annual Conference, 1965.
A clinical essay on the notion that communication and its analysis can lead to understanding interactional processes

between family members and within the family system. The basic goal in all therapy is "to change the self concept from which more appropriate ways of dealing with others and the objective world can be developed."

SATIR, V. M. The family as a treatment unit. *Confinla Psychiatrica*, 1965, *8*, 37–42.
With the emphasis on concepts of interaction, the family is discussed as a closed and open system, and "appropriate outcomes" for the family are "decisions and behavior which fit the age, ability, and the role of the individuals, which fit the role contracts and the context involved, and which further the common goals of the family."

SATIR, V. M. Family systems and approaches to family therapy. *Journal of Fort Logan Mental Health Center*, 1967, *4*, 81–93.
An essay focusing on development of the concept of the family as a system, how it functions, and what happens when it breaks down.

SATIR, V. M. The quest for survival: A training program for family diagnosis and treatment. *Acta Psychotherapy*, 1963, *11*, 33–38.
A review of the training program for family therapists at the Mental Research Institute given to psychiatrists, psychologists, and social workers who work in a variety of settings: state hospitals, outpatient clinics, probation departments, and family service agencies. Setting, goals, and procedures of the training are described.

SCHAFFER, L., WYNNE, L. C., DAY, J., RYCKOFF, I. M. & HALPERIN, A. On the nature and sources of the psychiatrist's experience with the family of the schizophrenic. *Psychiatry*, 1962, *25*, 32–45.
A detailed discussion of the experience of the therapist as he performs family therapy with the family of the schizophrenic, where "nothing has a meaningful relation to anything else." This therapy is said to be different from work with other families. Case illustrations are given.

SCHEFLEN, A. E., *Stream and structure of communicational behavior*. Behavioral Series Mongraph No. 1, Eastern Pennsylvania Psychiatric Institute, Philadelphia, 1965. A context analysis of a family therapy session of Whitaker and Malone. The examination of the interview is in detail and includes kinesic, linguistic, and contextual description.

SCHEFLEN, A. E. Susan smiled: On explanation in family therapy. *Family Process*, 1978, *17*, 59–68.
A review of the concept of "message" and "metamessage" in the context of family therapy. The interpretation of behavior is biased by a variety of conceptual models and paradigms, resulting in different explanations which the psychotherapist uses. The therapist's use of explanations may reflect a political power maneuver in therapy, i.e., to maintain control over one or more of the family members for the duration of the course of therapy. Explanations can be utilized as temporary tactics in a long-term strategy.

SCHOMER, J. Changing the matriarchal family's perception of the father. *Bullentin of Family Mental health Clinic. J.F.S.*, 1969, *1*, 13–14.
In working class families, in which the family dynamics are often set up around matriarchal control of the family, the family will often tend to exclude the father from family therapy. In one case in which the therapist insisted that the father attend, the identified patient showed improvement; in another case, the father's presence gave the family a chance to "ventilate rage"; and in a third case the family terminated therapy without improvement.

SCHREIBER, L. E. Evaluation of family group treatment in a family agency. *Family Process*, 1966, *5*, 21–29.
A report on the experience of a family service agency in the treatment of 72 families. Within 3 months, 61 percent showed improvement in communication processes and 56 percent in the presenting behavior problem of the child. Of those who continued beyond 3 months, 96 percent showed improvement in communication processes and 92 percent in the behavior of the child.

SCHUSTER, F. Summary description of multiple impact psychotherapy. *Texas Reports on Biology and Medicine*, 1962, *17*, 120–125.
A report of the multiple impact psychotherapy project used at a child guidance clinic in Texas. Families come from great distances and are seen intensively for two days, both individually and in various family situations. The preliminary 1-year or 1-month follow-ups attest that this method is "at least as effective as individual treatment in many adolescent referrals."

SEDERER, L. I. & SEDERER, N. A family myth: Sex therapy gone awry. *Family Process*, 1979, *18*, 315–321.
A case study in which sexual dysfunction served as a myth to hide more functional problems. The authors comment that sex therapy may exaggerate the importance that sexuality plays in family dynamics.

SEEGER, P. A. A framework for family therapy. *Japanese Journal of Mental Health Services*, 1976, *14*, 23–28.
One notion of a theme of family therapy based on the work of Glasser and Howell. The family therapist should identify needs, communicate needs, and work out strategies to achieve the needs. Four case examples are presented to illustrate the thesis.

SELINGER, D. & BARCAI, A. Brief family therapy may lead to deep personality change. *American Journal of Psychotherapy,* 1977, *296,* 302–309.
One case example is presented in support of the hypothesis that brief family therapy has the potential to lead to long lasting individual personality changes. The identified patient was a 15½-year-old boy with the symptom of a falsetto voice. Father, mother, and child were seen in 12 family therapy sessions with changes in the boy's self-image documented in "man-figure" drawings. Nine-month-follow-up revealed no recurrence of the presenting symptom and an improvement in social and familial relationships of the identified patient.

SELVINI PALAZZOLI, M. BOSCOLO, L. CECCHIN, G. F., et al. Family rituals: A powerful tool in family therapy. *Family Process,* 1977, *16,* 445–453.
This article describes the prescription of a family ritual aimed at the destruction of a three generation myth. Using a case illustration the authors analyze in detail the meaning of family rituals from a system's viewpoint.

SHACHOR, S. & TELPAZ, N. Mental health care by a family oriented general practice team. *International Journal of Social Psychiatry,* 1976, *22,* 96–100.
Advantages of a family)orientation approach in terms of prevention and treatment versus the traditional individually oriented approach are discussed within context of a community mental health center.

SHELLOW, R. S., BROWN, B. S. & OSBERG, J. W. "Family group therapy in retrospect: Four years and sixty families. *Family Process,* 1963, *2,* 52–67.
A review of experience with family group therapy (author's term for conjoint family therapy) with 60 families in a child guidance clinic over a 4-year period. Referal sources were mainly from physicians and school. Several "hidden" factors influenced choice of this form of therapy by staff members: (1) the identified patient was often the oldest child and (2) there was a large proportion of school-achievement problems represented.

SHERMAN, M. H., BLAIR, A., PANKEN, S., PLATT, R., & SCHOMER, J. Some dimensions of style in family therapy. *Psychotherapy: Theory, Research and Practice,* 1972, *9,* 67–75.
Five cases are given in support of the hypothesis that there is a "critical event" during family therapy (defined as an intervention) that produces movement in the therapy process. Method was to use protocols from 5 different families of 5 different therapists, asking both the family and therapist to write down their perceptions of the critical event. Results were equivocal.

SHERMAN, S. N. The concept of the family in casework therapy. In N. W. Ackerman, F. L. Beatman, & S. Sherman (Eds.), *Exploring the base for family therapy.* New York: Family Service Association of America, 1961.
A clinical essay stressing the family when focusing on the individual in casework, individual behavior is a function of the family group, and the family is in homeostasis. The differences between family therapy and casework are discussed.

SHERMAN, S. N. Family therapy as a unifying force in social work. In N. W. Ackerman (Ed.), *Expanding theory and practice in family therapy.* New York: Family Service Association of America, 1967.
Family therapy has changed the way caseworkers practice, not only in terms of seeing families together, but in thinking about the individual from a family point of view. Family therapy may bridge the gap between casework and group work and between social theory and psychological theory.

SHERMAN, S. N. Family treatment: An approach to children's problems. *Social Casework,* 1966, *47,* 368–372.
The use of family therapy in cases where the identified patient is at latency age is discussed. Previously, family agencies have not used family treatment for disorders in this age group, preferring individual therapy. Family treatment is seen as helpful in ameliorating the children's problems and is the treatment of choice over individual therapy, especially applicable as a "first phase of treatment and to many children's problems in a working-through phase."

SHERMAN, S. Inter-generational discontinuity and therapy in the family. *Social Casework,* 1967, *48,* 216–221.
The best medium for affecting the rapid social changes that are occurring in our society may be the family. Family casework as a technique to accomplish this is discussed. Several case illustrations are offered in support of this idea.

SHERMAN, S. N. Joint interviews in casework practice. *Social Work,* 1959, *4,* 20–28.
An attempt "to place joint interviews within the methodology of casework." The purpose and concept of family interviewing is discussed with case examples.

SHERMAN, S. N. Sociopsychological character of the family-group treatment. *Social Casework,* 1964, *45,* 195–201.
A family service agency reports that both interpersonal and intrafamilial conflicts are being discussed in family therapy. Several case examples are given.

SHERR, C., & HICKS, H. Family drawings as a diagnostic and therapeutic technique. *Family Process,* 1973, *12*:439–460.

This article describes and summarizes the technique of family art therapy, through the presentation of a case in which this technique was utilized in association with family therapy. Family art therapy provided highly significant diagnostic data not previously observed and served as a dramatic agent for change, which was evidenced in the family sessions.

SIGAL, J. J., RAKOFF, V., & EPSTEIN, N. B. Indications of therapeutic outcome in conjoint family therapy. *Family Process*, 1967, *6*, 215–226.
A report on a study that attempted to predict the eventual success of family therapy by examining the degree of family interaction and emotional involvement as described by therapists in the initial stages of treatment. "The clinical observations in this study cause some doubts about the value of the interactional frame of reference in conjoint family therapy."

SIMON, R. Sculpting the family. *Family Process*. 1972, *11*:49–57.
An essay on clinical aspects of family sculpting (members of a family create a physical representation of their relationships at a given point in time by arranging themselves and/or objects in space). Indications and techniques are described.

SKINNER, A. Indications and contraindications for conjoint family therapy. *International Journal of Social Psychiatry*, 1969, *15*, 245–249.
Advantages, disadvantages, indications and contraindications of family therapy show that it is economical, and useful for diagnostic purposes and for keeping within the family responsibility for solving the presenting problem. Its primary limitation is that "changes is restricted to what is accepted by the family as a whole, *rather than* adapted to the needs of any one individual." Families with paranoid and schizoid mechanisms are most responsive to family therapy; those with depressive symptoms are least so.

SKYNNER, A. A group-analytic approach to conjoint family therapy. *Journal of Child Psychology and Psychiatry*, 1969, *10*, 81–106.
This essay describes the Author's use of group principles and psychoanalytic principles in conjoint family therapy in the setting of a children's psychiatric clinic. These principles are contrasted with family approaches, and advantages and disadvantages in dealing with problems in which the identified patient is a child are discussed. A case history is presented in support of several of the author's ideas, There is an extensive review of the literature.

SKYNNER, A. School phobia: A reappraisal. *British Journal of Medical Psychology*, 1974, *47*:1–16.
A clinical paper focusing on the management of school phobia using techniques of family therapy rather than individual therapy. The therapist needs to be "in charge." Medication may be prescribed for both children and parents to help them cope with changing family patterns. Case examples are presented in support of the techniques.

SLUZKI, C. E. The coalitionary process in initiating family therapy. *Family Process*, 1975, *14*:66–77.
The use of "coalitionary structure" by a single therapist is described based on the notion that the process of negotiation and establishment of coalitions in a family can be closely related to the vicissitudes of the power relationships within that family system. Through monitoring this variable the therapist can establish basic ground rules to effect a course of treatment. Analysis of the coalitions allows calibration and refinement of therapeutic techniques.

SLUZKI, C. Family interaction and symptoms. *Revista Interamericana de Psicologia*, 1968, *2*, 283–288.
Symptoms are seen as having an interactional effect on other family members. The identified patient is not a "victim," but is as much a part of this system as anyone else. The therapist must maintain equidistance from all members of the group in order to avoid coalitions.

SLUZKI, C. E. E Grupo Familiar del Paciente Internado (The family group of the in-ward patient). *Acta Psiquiatrica Y Psicologica De America Latina*, 1963, *9*, 304.
Based on Don D. Jackson's family typology, a description of the family group circumstances and behavior that may favor mental illness in one member and the attitude of the different types of families in regard to the admission of one member to a mental hospital and to release from it. Prognosis can be predicted in each case if one takes into account the type of family and its behavior during the onset of the mental illness. Recommendations are made for family group therapy simultaneously to the admission of the single patient.

SMITH, I. W., & LOEB, D. The stable extended family as a model in treatment of atypical children. *Social Work*, 1965, *10*, 75–81.
See Reference in Section 5.3

SMITH, L., & MILLS, B. Intervention techniques and unhealthy family patterns. *Perspectives of Psychiatric Nursing*, 1969, 7:112–119.
A clinical paper describing characteristic family patterns and intervention techniques that a nurse may use in family therapy. One of the main goals is to improve, clarify, and facilitate communication in the family.

SOCIAL WORK PRACTICE, *Selected Papers, 90th Annual Forum, National Conference on Social Welfare, Cleveland, Ohio, May 19–24, 1963.* New York: Columbia University Press, 1963.
Papers on family diagnosis and treatment, family unit treatment of character-disordered youngsters, and on schizophrenia and family therapy are included in this collection from a social work conference. 255 pp.

SONNE, J. C. Insurance and family therapy. *Family Process*, 1973, *12*, 399–414.
See reference in Section 4.5.

SONNE, J. C. Entropy and family therapy: Speculations on psychic energy, thermodynamics, and family interpsychic communication. In F. H. Zuk & I. Boszomenyi-Nagy (Eds.), *Family therapy and disturbed families*. Palo Alto: Science & Behavior Books, 1967.
An attempt to link concepts from the physical sciences with observations of schizophrenogenic families in treatment, with special emphasis upon the concept of entropy.

SONNE, J. C., & LINCOLN, G. Heterosexual co-therapy team experiences during family therapy. *Family Process*, 1965, *4*, 177–197.
A description of co-therapy experiences with the family of the schizophrenic. The emphasis is upon clarifying and unifying the male–female co-therapy team during the treatment.

SONNE, J. C., & LINCOLN, G. The importance of a heterosexual co-therapy relationship in the construction of a family image. In I. M. Cohen (Ed.), *Psychiatric research report 20*. Washington, D. C: American Psychiatric Association, 1966.
A discussion of the use of co-therapy to provide a heterosexual image in the treatment of the family of the schizophrenic.

SONNE, J. C., SPECK, R. V., & JUNGREIS, J. E. The absent-member maneuver as a resistance in family therapy of schizophreniz. *Family Process*, 1962, *1*, 44–62.
A report of a specific type of resistance encountered while using family treatment in 10 families containing a schizophrenic offspring. The absent-member maneuver, defined as the absence of a family member from the family sessions, was seen in one form or another in all 10 families. Some of the dynamics of this maneuver are discussed. The authors believe that the absent member (often seen as "healthy" by the rest of the family) tends to pathologically maintain unresolved Oedipal problems in the family.

SORRELLS, J., & FORD, E. Toward an integrated theory of families and family therapy. *Psychotherapy*, 1969, *6*, 150–160.
A theory of family functioning and family treatment in which all family members have self-needs, self-wants, and a self-concept is presented. The family operates in a system using certain communication devices that maintain a homeostasis. Concepts of status quo, decision-making, autonomy, and distortion of feedback are discussed. Treatment techniques of the contract, diagnosis, interventions, and goals, are described.

SPARK, G. Parental involvement in family therapy. *Journal of Marriage and Family*, 1968, *30*, 111–18.
An essay from a child guidance clinic in which family therapy is presented as offering significant advantages over traditional individual therapy with family members, since there is less tendency for the parents to project onto the children and dependency needs and separation fears can be discussed. Relationships between over- and under-involved parents become more malleable to change and new homeostatic equilibria can be reached.

SPARK, G. M., & BRODY, E. M. The aged are family members. *Family Process*, 1970, *9*, 195–210.
A discussion of the involvement of older family members and the important roles they play in family dynamics. Including them in treatment can prevent cyclical repetition of pathological relationship patterns.

SPECK, R. V. Family therapy in the home. *Journal of Marriage and Family*, 1964, *26*, 72–76.
An essay based on the author's clinical experience in family therapy in the home. Advantages of this technique are discussed and several aspects are described: the absent member, the most distrubed family member, the youngest member, the role of pets, the extended family, and family secrets.

SPECK, R. V. Family therapy in the home. In N. W. Ackerman (Ed.), *Expanding theory and practice in family therapy*. New York: Family Service Association of America, 1967.
A research project in which family therapy was conducted at home. Advantages and disadvantages in techniques are discussed. Family therapy in the home is thought to be advantageous over therapy in the office, but no definitive experiment has yet been done. At least one home visit should be made to every family.

SPECK, R. V. Psychotherapy of the social network of a schizophrenic family. *Family Process*, 1967, *6*, 208–214.
A description of the social network approach to treatment. Procedure, goals, and future directions are described.

SPECK, R. V., & ATTNEAVE, C. Network therapy. In J. Haley (Ed.), *Changing families*. New York: Grune & Stratton, 1971.
A report on network therapy in which all of the significant people of a natural group are brought together in relation to a problem. The theory, practice, techniques, and effects of assembling the "tribe" are described.

SPECK, R. V., & RUEVENI, U. Network therapy: A developing concept. *Family Process*, 1969, *8*, 182–191.
A description of network therapy in which all members of the kinship system, all friends of the family, and other significant people are brought together. A description of the method and a case illustration is offered.

SPEER, D. C. Family systems: Morphostasis and morphogenesis, or "Is homeostasis enough?" *Family Process*, 1970, *9*, 259–278.
The role of family homeostasis in conjoint family therapy is reviewed from the standpoint of a sociocultural systems framework as presented by Buckley. Homeostasis, by itself, is demonstrated to be insufficient as a basic explanatory principle for family systems and may limit the therapeutic family process. An attempt is made to relate the concepts of inability, positive feedbacks, morphogenesis, and "variety" to some of the clinical literature.

SPIEGEL, J. P. The family: The channel of primary care. *Hospital and Community Psychiatry*, 1974, *25*, 785–788.
Family therapy is seen as a modality useful for primary prevention. Three serious problems that exist in the field are described: (1) theoretical inconsistency; (2) lack of attention to ethnic and subcultural differences in families; and (3) economic issues. Current and future roles, as well as the history of the movement are described.

SPIEGEL, J., & BELL, N. The family of the psychiatric patient. In S. Ariti (Ed.), *American handbook of psychiatry (Vol. I)*. New York: Basic Books, 1959.
See Reference in Section 3.6

STACHOWIAK, J. Psychological distrubances in children as related to disturbances in family interaction. *Journal of Marriage and Family*, 1968, *30*, 123–127.
Family therapy is compared to individual psychotherapy. Data is from a child guidance clinic. The therapist is portrayed as an active teacher, "whose main concern is that of inducing change in the family's rigid and stereotyped pattern of interactions."

STEWART, R. H., PETERS, T. C., MARSH, S., & PETERS, M. J. An object-relations approach to psychotherapy with marital couples, families and children. *Family Process*, 1975, *14*, 161–178.
Based on object relations theory, ideas about the dynamics of interpersonal relationships are presented. Included are the following concepts: (1) there is a necessity for partners to disown and project, which serves as a defense mechanism against "fluid and/or joint ego boundaries;" (2) the therapist's countertransference reactions are seen as a valid reflection of the patient's struggle; (3) the adult or child who is the identified patient is often a carrier of the split-off unacceptable impulses of the other(s); and (4) the individual is perceived as part of a unit with an inherent healthy reparative function. Therapeutic implications are listed.

STIERLIN, H. Group fantasies and family myths—Some theoretical and practical aspects. *Family Process*, 1973, *12*, 111–125.
This paper examines shared fantasies and myths that evolve in small groups, such as Bion and Balint groups, and in families. They fulfilled defensive and protective functions for the family group. Defensively, they are utilized against painful confrontations with aspects of their real, past and present, living experiences. They also may protect the family group from intrusions and unsettling judgments from the outside world. The therapist must realize that myths safeguard the family members' involvement with each other, and that they are maintained as long as they are needed.

STREAN, H. S. A family therapist looks at "Little Hans." *Family Process*, 1967, *6*, 227–234.
A re-examination of the case of "little Hans" from the point of view of the family as the unit of diagnosis and treatment. The case is said to be "an excellent illustration of how a symptom or one member binds and protects a whole family constellation."

STREAN, H. S. Treating parents of emotionally distrubed children through role playing. *Psychoanalytic Review*, 1960, *47*, 67–75.
A procedure for treating mothers of distrubed children by exposing them to a contact "where the therapist consciously attempted to set an example for the parent-patient." Case examples are presented. Offers of educational guidance are defeated but accepting and encouraging the mother's point of view while being firm provides the parent a new symbolic parent and a corrective emotional experience which she may eventually repeat with the child.

THORMAN, G. *Family therapy: Help for troubled families*. New York: Public Affairs Pamphlet No. 356, 1964.
Rationale, indications, family dynamics, techniques, and future trends are described.

TITCHENER, L., & GOLDEN, M. Predictions of therapeutic themes from observation of family interaction evoked by the "revealed differences" technique. *Journal of Nervous Mental Disorders*, 1963, *136*, 464–474.
See Reference in Section 3.3

TESCHER, B. A nurse, a family, and the velveteen rabbit. *Family Process*, 1971, *10*, 303–310.
This paper describes a series of family sessions with a lower class Spanish-speaking family in which communication was chaotic. Structuring techniques helped to achieve a better communicational pattern and immediate goals were set up in a short period. The author compared the family's process with a popular parable.

THARP, R., & OTIS, G. Toward a theory for therapeutic intervention in families. *Journal of Consulting and Clinical Psychology*, 1966, *30*, 426–434.
Using data from the author's clinical work, family roles are categorized into 5 functional entities: solidarity, sexuality, internal instrumentality, external relations, and division of responsibility. Wthin these, a discrepancy between the expectations and the actual performance can lead to symptoms. Interventions to make the roles more consonant are described. Three case studies are presented in support of these concepts.

TROEMEL-PLOETZ, S. She is just not an open person: A linguistic analysis of a restructuring intervention in family therapy. *Family Process*, 1977, *16*, 339–352.
This paper is based on a linguistic analysis of a dialogue between a couple and a therapist during the sixth session of the couple's therapy. The linguistic properties of the therapist's utterances show that the restructuring is achieved by particular syntactic, semantic, and pragmatic features of the utterances. It is shown that coherences with respect to the sequence of linguistic acts and moves between the speakers in a given situation forces an interpretation of the various utterances as a connected text. The therapeutic effect is attributed to the restructuring character of the intervention which sufficiently shifts the balance first between the therapist and one spouse, and then between both spouses.

VAGLUM, P. Contrasting multi-generational attitudes toward psychosis in two Norwegian families. *Family Process*, 1972, *11*, 311–320.
This is a study of 2 families, each with a young adult schizophrenic female member. Family A was seen for 25 sessions over a period of 12 months; family B for 15 sessions over 9 months, with also 4 home visits. Results show 2 phases in the families' reaction. In the first phase, when the patients' symptoms were relatively moderate, both families' reaction patterns were dominated by mutual traditions of isolating themselves from the outside world. The daughters were kept at home and no therapist was contacted. When the deviant behavior became marked, however, they responded in accord with other aspects of family culture and the patterns of reaction became totally dissimilar: "Keep and Hide" (family A) and "Push out and Forget" (family B). The authors believe that close studies of families might give a better understanding of individual psychology, social psychology, sociology, and socioeconomic conditions involved in each pattern, as well as of the forces to be faced in attempting to change these patterns.

VAN BLAADEREN-STOCK, C. An approach to family therapy along analytic lines. *International Journal of Group Psychotherapy.*, 1970, *20*, 241–244.
This clinical paper describes a case in which the presenting symptoms of the identified patient, a child, had their origin in a pathogenic relationship between the parents. Once this was diagnosed, marital therapy replaced conjoint family therapy. Therapists should be flexible in switching back and forth from family to marital therapy, depending upon the circumstances of the case.

VASSILIOU, G. Milieu specificity in family therapy. In N. W. Ackerman (Ed.), *Family therapy in transition*. Boston: Little, Brown, 1970.
A description of the Greek family, its historical development, and its problems as seen from a family therapy point of view.

VIORST, J. Therapy for the whole family. *Science News*, 1963.
A clinical essay defining family therapy and describing indications, advantages, problems, and dangers inherent in the use of "new techniques."

WAIRI, M. Nurse participation in family therapy. *Perspectives of Psychiatric Care*, 1965, 3:8–13.
Based on the idea that the illness of one family member is related to the disturbance of the total family, this is a clinical essay dscribing the role of the nurse in family treatment. The nurse is encouraged to take a role in family treatment along with other team members.

WALLERSTEIN, J. S., & KELLY, J. B. Brief interventions with children in divorcing families. *American Journal of Orthopsychiatriy*, 1977,l 47:23–39.
This is another in a series of papers from a divorce-counseling project. The focus in this paper is on preventive clinical interventions developed for children of various ages in divorcing families. Developmental assessment was achieved with a "brief" history from the parents, detailed information from school, and "direct observation" of the child.

WALLERSTEIN, J. S., & KELLY, J. B. Divorce counseling: A community service for families in the midst of divorce. *American Journal of Orthopsychiatry*, 1977, *47*:4–22.
This paper covers treatment strategies, interventions, failures, therapist's role, and professional dilemmas in divorce counseling of 60 families with 131 children between the ages of 3 and 18 at the time of divorce. The technique of counseling was to see one parent and child separately by the same therapist three to six times over a month-period.

WARKENTIN, J. Psychotherapy with couples and families. *Journal of the Medical Association of Georgia*, 1969, *49*, 569–570.
An essay based on the author's clinical work on family psychotherapy as an additional treatment which can be used in the treatment of emotional disorders. Discussion of dynamics and problems with a case example.

WEAKLAND, J. Family therapy as a research arena. *Family Process*, 1962, *1*, 63–68.
A paper emphasizing the appropriateness and importance of using conjoint family therapy not only for therapeutic purposes, but also for reserach. Several questions pertinent to family treatment are raised (such as "what immediate or longer-term results in family behavior are produced by any given moves on the part of the therapist"), and finding the answers to these questions in the family treatment situation is discussed.

WEAKLAND, J. H., FISCH, R., WATZLAWICK, P., et al. Brief therapy: Focused problem resolution. *Family Process*, 1974, *13*, 141–168.
Using briefer versions of more conventional forms of individual and family therapy as well as 6 years of research on rapid problem resolution, these authors have developed a "brief therapy." The major techniques employed in this therapy are paradoxical instruction and therapeutic double-binding. With treatment limited to a maximum of 10 sessions and to very specific goals of behavioral change, these authors and coworker engaged 97 client/families in therapy. These client/families had various diagnoses and/or complaints. Success or continued changes in behavior were noted in three-fourths of this sample.

WEINER, M. F. "Individual" versus conjoint therapy. *Diseases of the Nervous System*, 1975, *36*, 546–549.
Indications and contraindications for individual psychotherapy, group psychotherapy, and family therapy are prescribed, using a schema based on the clinical psychopathology with subcategories of locus and duration of symptoms and commitment of family members to work on certain marital problems. Data are from the author's private practice.

WELLINGTON, J. A case for short-term family therapy. *Psychotherapy*, 1957, *4*, 130–132.
Based on a case of a 14-year-old female who was treated with family theraply over 12 sessions with good results (she had had 5 pervious years of individual psychotherapy at age 12), it is argued that short-term family therapy is often as effective as long-term therapy.

WERKMAN, S. L., MALLORY, L., & HARRIS, J. The common psychiatric problems in family practice. *Psychosomatics*, 1976, *17*, 3,
This is a clinical report of the extent and type of psychiatric problems existing in family practice. Method was to send a structured questionnaire to 202 family practitioners who attended a postgraduate seminar. Results indicated that marital conflicts are one of the most frequent problems encountered in family practice. Such physicians wanted to learn more about marital and family diagnosis and treatment than about any other new technique.

WERTHEIM, E. S. Positive mental health, western society, and the family. *International Journal of Social Psychiatry*, 1975, *21*, 235–246.
This essay describes the author's brand of family therapy, called "Family unit therapy." The focus is the family rather than the identified patient, and primary treatment concepts include: family emotional autonomy, self-regulation, and competence.

WHITAKER, C. Family treatment of a psychopathic personality. *Comprehensive Psychiatry*, 1966, *7*, 397–402.
From part of a summary of treatment of a woman, identified as having "8 years of treatment, 3 psychotherapists, 2 near successes of suicide, and 2 successful divorces," and her family, the author has evolved a theory of the development of the psychopathic personality. The child divides a weak parental relationship and then adopts this approach to all situations in later life. A team approach is suggested.

WHITAKER, C. A. Psychotherapy of the absurd: With a special emphasis on the psychotherapy of aggression. *Family Process*, 1975, *14*, 1–16.
In his discussion of hostility in the family system, Whitaker suggests that the "here and now" facilitates the ability of the therapist to shift roles. The process of family therapy is defined as occurring in two phases: (1) transference, and (2) the existential, adult-to-adult phase. Six modes of therapeutic intervention are discussed. The focus is on augmenting the unreasonable quality of symptoms to the point of absurdity in an effort to break the old patterns of thought and behavior.

WHITAKER, C., & BURDY, J. Family psychotherapy of a psychopathic personality: Must every member change? *Comprehensive Psychiatry*, 1969, *10*, 361–364.
This is the second of 2 reports of family treatment in which the identified patient was diagnosed as a psychopathic personality. The patient was seen with the family for 1½ years, and, for 6 months more, she was seen individually. In this case the identified patient changed while the other family members did not.

WHITAKER, C., FELDER, R. E., & WARKENTIN, J. Countertransference in the family treatment of schizophrenia. In I. Boszomenyi-Nagy & J. L. Framo (Eds.), *Intensive family therapy*. New York: Harper Row, 1965.
A discussion of family treatment with the emphasis upon the problems that emerge in the therapist. In the treatment of the schizophrenic family the therapist must be involved but avoid being absorbed "into its quicksand kind of meshing." Adequate therapy of the therapist, being part of a professional group, having a satisfying family life of his own, and supervision help resolve the countertransference problem.

WHITAKER, C., & MILLER, M. H. A reevaluation of "psychiatric help" when divorce impends. *American Jornal of Psyciatry*, 1969, *126*, 57–64.
See Reference in Section 1.3

WHITE, S. L. Family dinner time: A focus for life-space diagrams. *Clinical Social Work Journal*, 1976, *4*, 93–101.
Deriving from the author's clinical practice, a technique for family evaluation is described. It involves having the family do a diagram of the seating arrangement of the nuclear family and having the family associate to that diagram. The rationale is that the "family mealtime may be thought of as a micorcosm of the family in sociological and dynamic terms." It is thought to be especially useful with nonverbal families. Using a sample of 10 men in group therapy, 1 investigator used the data from this technique and compared it to another investigator's description of the families attained from information in the intake files. More relevant material on the family was found from the family diagram than from the intake files.

WHITIS, P. R. The legacy of a child's suicide. *Family Process*, 1968, 7, 159–169.
A discussion of the effect on a family of a child's suicide illustrated with a case report. Prompt therapeutic intervention is recommended for the bereaved family.

WILKINSON, C., & REED, C. An approach to the family therapy process. *Diseases of the Nervous System*, 1965, *26*, 705–714.
An essay describing experience using family therapy as a new technique in an outpatient clinic. The rationale, dynamics, and treatment process noted by the author is described.

WILLIAMS, F. Family therapy: A critical assessment. *American Journal of Orthopsychiatry*, 1967, *37*, 912–919.
An essay exploring some of the uses and misuses of family therapy. It is useful for diagnosis, to help parents to deal with children less than 5 years old to enlist the parents as allies in treatment of severely psychotic children, and in making order out of a chaotic family situation. Inadequate training and supervision, potential for the therapist's acting out, and discarding psychoanalytic principles in a premature separation of intrapsychic and interpersonal approaches are dangers discussed.

WINER, L. R. The qualified pronoun count as a measure of change in family psychotherapy. *Family Process*, 1971, *10*, 243–247.
This experiment was based on the observation and recorded materials of 4 couples, seen 40 times during a 16- to 43-month period in multiple family therapy at the Georgetown University department of psychiatry. Using Bowen's concept of health as the differentiation of self from the "undifferentiated family ego-mass" and based on the premise that behavior can be inferred by what people say about themselves and significant others, two hypotheses were formulated. As a person changes and becomes more "differentiated," (1) the amount of "I" statements would increase, and (2) the amount of "we," "our," and "us" statements would decrease. Preliminary findings indicate that the "change ratio" is useful in determining differentiation and that these families did change.

WOLD, P. Family structure in three cases of anorexia nervosa: The role of the father. *American Journal of Psychiatry*, 1973, *130*, 1394–1397.
A clinical essay based on 3 cases of anorexia nervosa. The weight loss in the identified patient represented hostile attitues toward the father, based in part on each parent placing the identified patient in the positon of his or her mother toward whom neither parent could express hostility. Family therapy led to improvement in 2 cases of the 3 cases.

WORLD HEALTH ORGANIZATION. *Aspects of family mental health in europe*, Public Health Papers 28. New York, 1965.
Eight papers which were "working papers presented at a Seminar on Mental Health and the Family held by the WHO regional office for Europe at Athens in 1962" and specially commissioned chapters. These include, "The Mother and the Family." "The Child in the Family." "Working Women and the Family." "Marriage Problems and their

Implications for the Family." "Family Psychotherapy." "Mental Health and the Older Generation." "School for Parents," and "The Hampstead Child-Therapy Clinic."

WYATT, G. L., & HERZAN, H. M. Therapy with stuttering children and their mothers. *American Journal of Orthopsychiatry*, 1962, *32*, 645–659.
A study of the therapy of stuttering children which indicates that therapy should start from a sound theory of the interpersonal aspects of language learning in children, the techniques should be adpated to the age of the child, and the mother should be included in the treatment program. Twenty-six childran were included in the sample with some children seen in the presence of their mothers and some seen separately. Stuttering was considered to be the result of a disruption of the complementary patterns of verbal interaction between mother and child.

WYNNE, L. C. Some indications and contraindications for exploratory family therapy. In I. Boszomenyi-Nagy & J. L. Framo (Eds.), *Intensive family therapy*. New York: Harper & Row, 1965.
A discussion of the indications and contraindications "for one form of family therapy: long-term, exploratory, conjoint family therapy used as a main mode of therapy." This discussion attempts "to summarize my current views, subject to revision, of some of the issues pertinent to an appraisal of the place of family therapy in the psychiatric repertory."

WYNNE, L. C. The study of intrafamilial alignments and splits in exploratory family therapy. In N. W. Ackerman, F. L. Beatman, & S. Sherman (Eds.), *Exploring the base for family therapy*. New York: Family Service Association of America, 1961.
See Reference in Section 5.2

WYNNE, L., RYCKOFF, I., DAY, J., & HIRSCH, S. Pseudo-mutuality in the family relations of schizophrenics. *Psychiatry*, 1958, *21*, 205–220.
See Reference in Section 5.2

WYNNE, L. C., RYCKOFF, I., DAY, J., & HIRSCH, S. I. Psuedo-mutuality in the family relations of schizophrenics. In N. W. Bell, & E. F. Vogel (Eds.), *A modern introduction to the family*. Glencoe: Free Press, 1960.
See Reference in Section 5.2

ZIERER, E., STERNBERG, D., FINN, R., & FARMER, M. Family Creative Analysis: Its role in treatment. Part I. *Bulletin of Art Therapy*, 1966, *5*, 47–65.
A report on the use of creative analysis (which is a technique by which paintings are used to understand the functioning of the ego) and its application to family treatment. The family agrees on a project to be done and then the sketch is made by one or many members of the family. It is then divided into as many sections as there are participants. From an understanding of the painting, the therapist then interprets the family and their conflicts. Observations are shared with the treatment team of the inpatient unit it which the identified patients are staying and also with the members of the family. Short- and long-range goals of family treatment are formulated and worked out in at least 15 projects.

ZIERER, E., STERNBERG, D., FINN, R., & FARMER, M. Family creative analysis: Its role in treatment. *Bulletin of Art Therapy*, 1966, *5*, 87–104.
This is the second in a series of papers describing the use of "creative analysis" in the treatment of families. Method has been previously described. In this paper, a case example is presented demonstrating the method. Changes in the family were compared with evaluation before treatment, using the Interpersonal Checklist. Creative analysis is seen as an adjunct of an approach stimulating a healthy "reintigration of the family as a network of mutually need-gratifying members."

ZUK, G. Family therapy. *Archives of General Psychiatry*, 1967, *16*, 71–79.
A theoretical paper on family therapy in which the author puts forth a model that contrasts with the "insight-centered" psychoanalytic model. The therapist is a "go-between" for family members, and attempts to get them to change. Techniques of doing this, as well as the family's defensive reactions, are described.

ZILBACH, J. J. The family therapy: Discussion. *Journal of the American Academy of Child Psychiatry*, 1974, *13*, 459–467.
A discussion of two previous papers in this journal exploring polarization between family therapists and child psychiatrists. It is pointed out that family therapists often exclude young and old members of families in treatment and thus, ironically, fragment families.

ZUK, G. Family therapy: Formulation of a technique and its theory. *International Journal of Group Psychotherapy*, 1968, *18*, 42–57.
As an alternative to the "insight model" of family therapy, to *go-between* process is described. The therapist defines issues, acts as a go-between for family members, and sides for or against family members. Tactics of the family to forestall this are listed. The family is thought to change "in order to forestall the therapist's expected demands for much greater change or in order to foil other attempts of his to control the relationship."

ZUK, G. The Go-between process in family therapy. *Family Process*, 1966, *5*, 162–178.
A discussion of family therapy from the point of view of the "go-between process." Four variations are described with case examples.

ZUK, G. A further study of laughter in family therapy. *Family Process*, 1964, *3*, 77–89.
A discussion of the function of laughter in the family illustrated with excerpts from family therapy sessions. It is proposed that laughter is an important means of qualifying meaning for the purpose of disguise.

ZUK, G. On the pathology of silencing strategies. *Family Process*, 1965, *4*, 32–49.
A description and categorization of the ways people impose or enforce silence on one another. "There is a causal relation between silencing strategies and pathological silence and babbling which may themselves be used as powerful silencing strategies."

ZUK, G. On silence and babbling in family psychotherapy with schizophrenics. *Confinia Psychiatrica*, 1965, *8*, 49–56.
From the author's clinical work, 2 cases are presented in support of this idea that both silence and babbling can be understood as attempts to interrupt communication and silence others' interactions. They are often seen in schizophrenia, but patients learn these strategies from their parents. Techniques for dealing with this in treatment are discussed.

ZUK, G. On the theory and pathology of laughter in psychotherapy. *Psychotherapy*, 1966, *3*, 97–101.
An essay based on the author's previous research, some clinical work and other notions on the meaning of laughter. Bizarre laughter in schizophrenics, which often seems unexplainable, became clear when it was systematically studied in the family setting. It was found to be due to a "wish to communicate information *differentially* to members of the family group." Clinical uses of laughter are discussed.

ZUK, G. Prompting change in family therapy. *Archives of General Psychiatry*, 1968, *19*, 727–736.
An essay describing the author's ideas of why families change and the techniques to foster it. Families will tend to follow a therapist's direction but will resist it at the same time. They will also resist the idea that the identified patient's improvment is related to their involvement. A case is report in support of these observations.

ZUK, G. The side-taking functioning in family therapy. *American Journal of Orthopsychiatry*, 1968, *38*, 553–559.
One of a series of theoretical papers describing family therapy in terms of the therapist acting as a "go-between" and as a "side-taker." Pros, cons, rationale, and hoped-for results are discussed.

ZUK, G. Triadic-based family therapy. *International Journal of Psychiatry*, 1969, *8*, 539–569.
This is a theoretical paper putting forth the theory that family therapy is more than just a dyadic affair and can be best understood in triadic terms (that is, at least 3 people involved, some of whom can be fantasized or introjects). The therapist acts as a "go-between" between 2 individuals or groups at odds with one another. Techniques of family therapy based on these theoretical constructs are presented.

ZUK, G. H. Values and family therapy. *Psychotherapy: Theory, Research & Practice*, 1978, *15*, 48–55.
This theoretical paper proposes a method for brief family therapy based on the idea that many families are in conflict over two value systems. These are defined as "continuity" and "discontinuity" values. They are compared in affective, ethical, cognitive, and task-oriented terms. The therapist is supporting one value or the other when acting as a "go-between," "side-taker," or "educator."

ZUK, G. When the family therapist takes sides: A case report. *Psychotherapy*, 1968, *5*, 24–28.
This is one of a series of papers on the "go-between process" (therapist as a facilitator of communications among family members), as used in family therapy. Previous papers illustrate what happens when the family therapist does not take sides; this paper describes the timing and method when the therapist does take sides. Its purpose is to understand pathogenic relating of families and to "replace it if possible with a more productive pattern."

ZUK, G., & RUBINSTEIN, D. A review of concepts in the study and treatment of families of schizophrenics. In I. Boszormenyi-Nagy & J. L. Framo (Eds.), *Intensive family therapy*. New York: Harper & Row, 1965.
A review of conceptual trends in family treatment of schizophrenics, which discusses the shift from parent pathology to nuclear family to three generational involvement.

1.2 MULTIPLE FAMILY THERAPY

BARCAI, A. An adventure in multiple family therapy. *Family Process*, 1967, *6*, 185–192.
A discussion of scapegoating as it was dealt with in multiple family therapy with 3 families with schizophrenic sons. When the therapist found himself unable to counteract the dehumanization and disrespect shown to the schizophrenic sons by their parents, he restructured the group, making the son the group leader.

BEARMAN, K. Multiple family therapy. *Mental Hygiene*, 1966, *50*, 367–370.
Multiple conjoint family therapy (treating 2 or more families simultaneously) was used in a large VA hospital for 1 year. Sample included alcoholics and some "nonsevere" psychotics with sociopaths and "severe" psychotics excluded. Techniques are described. Preliminary results indicated that no patient has been rehospitalized (30–40% rehospitalization was expected).

BLINDER, M., COLMAN, A., CURRY, A., & KESSLER, D. "MCFT": Simultaneous treatment of several families. *American Journal of Psychotherapy*, 1965, *19*, 559–569.
A critique of multiple-conjoint family therapy (a type of group meeting composed of 6 to 8 family units) done on inpatient service. Stages that the group goes through are described in achieving the goal of a more healthy equilibrium. This technique is a "potent method" for working through family problems and making the posthospital adjustment more successful.

BURTON, G., & YOUNG, D. Family crisis in Group therapy. *Family Process*, 1962, *1*, 214–223.
A report of the experiences of two therapists doing group counseling of 12 couples, each of which includes an alcoholic husband. The paper is specifically concerned with the reporting of family crises in the group. It is the author's impression that group members "use the crisis reports of each other in furthering an understanding of their own situations and in gaining courage to experiment in modifying their own behavior."

COUGHLIN, F., & WIMBERGER, H. C. Group family therapy. *Family Process*, 1968, *7*, 37–50.
A treatment program using multiple family therapy with 10 families seen in a group. All families were seen together for the first 3 sessions, and then parts of families were seen in different combinations. It is said to be a useful, short-term treatment technique, and 8 of the 10 families improved.

CURRY, C. Therapeutic management of multiple family group. *International Journal of Group Psychotherapy*, 1965, *15*, 90–96.
A report on the use of the treatment techniques of having multiple family groups meeting together. What was discussed and how it was discussed are described. These techniques appear to be less threatening than conjoint family therapy, but also less intensive.

DAVENPORT, Y. B., EBERT, M. H., ADLAND, M. L., & GOODWIN, F. K. Couples group therapy as an adjunct to lithium maintenance of the manic patient. *American Journal of Orthopsychiatry*, 1977, *47*, 495–502.
See reference in Section 1.4.

DAVIES, Q., ELLENSON, G., & YOUNG, R. Therapy with a group of families in a psychiatric day center. *American Journal of Orthopsychiatry*, 1966, *36*, 134–147.
Clinical impressions of treatment of "several" patients with their families all in one group, meeting weekly and using current concepts of family diagnosis and treatment are described. Work was done in a day treatment center of a general hospital. Theoretical principles, objectives, and group process are described. This treatment was found to be "a useful form of therapy."

DURELL, V. Adolescents in multiple family group therapy in a school setting. *International Journal of Group Psychotherapy*, 1969, *19*, 44–52.
This is a clinical report of 4 families in multifamily therapy over 11 sessions in a junior high school setting where the identified patients are having difficulty in school. The course of a group is discussed, and therapy was helpful in terms of the patient's school performance. Problems with school administration were discussed.

GOTTLIEB, A., & PATTISON, E. M. Married couples group psychotherapy. *Archives of General Psychiatry*, 1966, *14*, 143–152.
A general discussion or a group therapy with marital couples with emphasis upon how the marriage influences group dynamics, how the spouse influences the other spouse's psychotherapy, and the particular positions of cotherapists in a group of couples. Arguments for and against the procedure are presented, and a clinical illustration is offered.

GURMAN, A. S. Group marital therapy: Clinical and empirical implications for outcome research. *International Journal of Group Psychotherapy*, 1972, *21*, 174–189.
A clinical paper reviewing group therapy with marital couples and including goals, indications, contraindications, and assessment of outcome.

HENDRIX, W. Use of multifamily counseling groups in treatment of male narcotic addicts. *International Journal of Group Psychotherapy*, 1971, *21*, 84–90.
From a group of male inpatients at a narcotics addiction treatment agency who were participating in multifamily therapy, a random sample of one third were studied. Results after a 1-year-follow-up indicated that their outcome was better than outpatients not treated with multifamily therapy. Limitations of the study are discussed.

HUBERTY, D. J. Adapting to illness through family groups. *International Journal of Psychiatric Medicine*, 1974, *5*, 231–242.
See reference in Section 5.6.

JARVIS, P., ESTY, J., & STUTZMAN, L. Evaluation and treatment of families at fort logan mental health center. *Community Mental Health*, 1969, *5*, 14–19.
A survey paper of trends in evaluation of treatment of patients from an inpatient facility of a psychiatric hospital. More evaluations are being carried out in the patient's home or in the community rather than in the hospital itself. There is greater involvement of "extended families" and of children (and in the case of children, involvement at an earlier age) in evaluation and treatment. There is great use of multiple family group therapy rather than conjoint family therapy.

JONES, W. The villain and the victim: Group therapy for married couples. *American Journal of Psychiatry*, 1967, *124*, 351–354.
The author's experience with group therapy where the group is made up of married couples. One indication for such therapy is when "conjoint marriage therapy" is deadlocked.

JULIAN, B., VENTOLA, L., & CHRIST, J. Multiple family therapy: The interaction of young hospitalized patients with their mothers. *International Journal of Group Psychotherapy*, 1969, *19*, 501–509.
A clinical report of multiple family therapy of adolescents, diagnosed as schizophrenic, all of whom are hospitalized. The family group is here made up of only the identified patient and the mother. There were 4 females and 2 males. The group met once weekly. Progress and problems of the group are discussed.

KIMBRO, E., TASCHMAN, H., WYLIE, H., & MACLENNAN, B. Multiple family group approach to some problems of adolescence. *International Journal of Group Psychotherapy*, 1967, *17*, 18–24.
A report of the author's experience with multiple family groups (3 families in each group). Theoretical considerations, process, problems, goals, and role of the therapist are discussed. This form of therapy is thought to incorporate the advantages of traditional, group, and family therapy, in addition to adding a dimension of its own.

KLIMENKO, A. Multifamily therapy in the rehabilitation of drug addicts. *Perspectives of Psychiatric Care*, 1968, *6*, 220–223.
A report of experiences at a halfway house for treatment of narcotics addicts, using multifamily therapy conducted by two cotherapists. Rationale is that "successful efforts to break the habit are directly related to family cohesiveness." A family member is loosely defined to include any person with whom an addict is closely involved. Sessions are once a week, lasting 1½ hours. No data are presented, but it is the author's impression that "family disturbances are a major influencing factor in the life of a drug addict."

LAQUEUR, H. P. General systems theory and multiple family therapy. In W. Gray, F. Duhll, & N. Rizzo (Eds.), *General systems theory and psychiatry*. Boston: Little, Brown, 1969.
A discussion of multiple family therapy from the point of view of systems theory. The general theoretical base for multiple family therapy is offered within this framework.

LAQUEUR, H. P. Multiple family therapy and general systems theory. In N. W. Ackerman (Ed.), *Family therapy in transition*. Boston: Little, Brown, 1970.
The family from the point of view of general systems theory with the emphasis upon treating groups of families. Theory and technique are described with examples.

LAQUEUR, H. P. Multiple family therapy and general systems theory. *International Psychiatric Clinic*, 1970, *7*, 99–124.
A discussion of multiple family therapy using the concepts of general systems theory. The family and its components are viewed as subsystems of a larger field of interrelations whose interface problems can be studied and dealt with.

LAQUEUR, H. P., LABURT, H. A. Family organization on a modern state hospital ward. *Mental Hygiene*, 1964, *48*, 544–551.
A description of the participation of an auxiliary composed of families of hospitalized patients. The families raise funds, participate in the ward activities, and are involved in group therapy as family groups. The goal is "to integrate the family into the patient's treatment plan."

LAQUEUR, H. P., LABURT, H. A., & MORONG, E. Multiple family therapy. In J. H. Masserman (Ed.), *Current psychiatric therapies* (Vol. IV):*Psychoanalysis and social process*. New York: Grune & Stratton, 1964.
A description of the treatment of families in group sessions in which a therapist sees several families at once. The context of the treatment is a therapeutic community ward in a state hospital. The procedure, its rationale, and impressions of results are given for a sample of 80 families treated with this method.

LAQUEUR, H. P., LABURT, H. A., & MORONG, E. Multiple family therapy: Further developments. *International Journal of Social Psychiatry*, 1964, *2*, 70–80.
An expanded discussion of the treatment of families in groups at Creedmoor State Hospital. Setting, objectives, problems, and techniques of the method are discussed.

LAQUEUR, H. P., WELLS, D., & AGRESTI, M. Multiple family therapy in a state hospital. *Hospital and Community Psychiatry*, 1969, *20*, 13–20.
This is a report of multiple family therapy in a state hospital setting. Sessions were held for 75 minute once a week, with one therapist throughout hospitalization and sometimes during aftercare. The sample consisted primarily of young schizophrenics. Rationale, dynamics, techniques, practical matters, and advantages and disadvantages as compared to conjoint family therapy are discussed.

LEICHTER, E., & SCHULMAN, G. Emerging phenomena in multi-family group treatment. *International Journal of Group Psychotherapy*, 1968, *18*, 59–69.
A case report of 3 families who met together as a group over 9 months. Some of the dynamics and uses of this technique are discussed.

LEICHTER, E., & SCHULMAN,L G. L. Multifamily group therapy: A multidimensional approach. *Family Process*, 1974, *13*, 95–110.
This article outlines the philosophical orientation of this approach for the nonhospitalized client and family. Some guidelines for group selection and other process and procedural issues and strategies are summarized. The dynamics of this approach are cited through case presentation.

LIBO, S., PALMER, C. & ARCHIBALD, D. Family group therapy for children with self-induced seizures. *American Journal of Orthopsychiatry*, 1971, *41*, 506–509.
A clinical paper reporting 2 cases of children with self-induced seizures. One child was 12, the other 10; both were neurologically unremarkable, had low intelligence, and failed to respond to various anti-convulsant medications. Treatment was family therapy by cotherapists with *both* families seen together. Sixteen biweekly sessions were held over a year's time. Results indicated a decreased number of seizures in both patients, with family relations improving in both cases, although fathers participated in a very limited fashion.

LUBER, R. F., & WELLS, R. A. Structured, short-term multiple family therapy: An educational approach. *International Journal of Group Psychotherapy*, 1977, *27*, 43–58.
This paper describes an approach to multifamily groups that is based on the direct teaching of communication skills and problem-solving techniques developed in the day hospital of an urban community mental health center. Outcome was evaluated by administering to all members (of 2 groups) 3 rating scales of interpersonal and family relationships before and after treatment. Results showed more gains for the group that was "healthier" before treatment.

MARKOWITZ, M., & KADIS, A. L. Parental interaction as a determining factor in social growth of the individual in the family. *International Journal of Social Psychiatry*, 1964, *2*, 81–89.
A general discussion of marriage and the family based upon treatment of married couples in group therapy. The emphasis is on unresolved problems and conflicts in the parents leading to unconscious alliances fostered in the child, with a breakdown of the potential for corrective experience. Examples from analytic group therapy are given.

MARX, A., & LUDWIG, A. Resurrection of the family of the chronic schizophrenic. *American Journal of Psychotherapy*, 1969, *23*, 37–52.
A careful review of the author's experience treating psychiatric inpatients by systematically involving the family of the patient. Sample was 44 chronic schizophrenic patients and families over a 2-year period. Family resistances and methods of dealing with these resistances are discussed. The treatment program included family–therapist meetings, patient–family–therapist sessions, multiple family group meetings, and multiple family–conjoint therapy sessions. Some of the effects of this treatment program, both positive (patient and family improvement) and negative (member of the family decompensating), as well as the methods of dealing with these probelms and practical theoretical implications and ehtics of this approach, are discussed.

MESSINGER, L., WALKER, K. N., & FREEMAN, S. J. J. Preparation for remarriage following divorce: The use of group techniques. *American Journal of Orthopsychiatry*, 1978, *48*, 263–272.
As a clinical pilot study, 22 couples were seen in 4 small groups by one of the authors for 4 sessions. The couples were self-selected, were all either in or contemplating a remarriage. The discussion focused on defining their problems in common. Results showed that, although the groups were different in individual make-up, the issues that emerged were similar: transition from marriage to separation and redefinition of ties, roles, and identities.

OSTBY, C. H. Conjoint group therapy with prisoners and their families. *Family Process*, 1968, 7, 184–201.
A report on a family treatment program at a correctional institution. The approach used was multiple family therapy. The special effect of the prison setting and case examples are described.

PAPANEK, H. Group psychotherapy with married couples. In J. H. Masserman (Ed.), *Current Psychiatric Therapies* (Vol. V): *Psychoanalytic education*. New York: Grune & Stratton, 1965.
An essay on the use of group therapy with married couples. The couple is seen together (not in group therapy) only as an introductory phase to gather historical data.

POWELL, M., & MONOGHAN, J. Reaching the rejects through multifamily group therapy. *International Journal of Group Psychotherapy*, 1969, *19*, 35–43.
A clinical report based on use of multifamily therapy (2 or more families meeting together). The setting was a child guidance clinic. Data was obtained from 5 groups, each consisting of 3 families. Each family included mother, father, and the identified patient, with siblings introduced when it was considered "appropriate." They were mostly of low socioeconomic class. One group was reported on, and the results indicaated that communication improved with all family members. Premature termination was not a problem.

RAASOCK, J., & LAQUER, H. P. Learnilng multiple family therapy through simulated workshops. *Family Process*, 1979, *18*, 95–98.
This paper describes how multiple family therapy (MFT) can be learned more rapidly through simulated workshops. The most difficult step in real and simulated MFT is "taking off" and "landing." Specific exercises facilitate these early phases of treatment. Group input for assessment of the sessions is essential to facilitate the termination phase.

REISS, D., & COSTELL, R. The multiple family group as a small society: Family regulation of interaction with nonmembers. *American Journal of Psychiatry*, 1977, *134*, 21–24.
A research study of the mechanism of family interaction with nonmembers. Method was to study a multiple family group over 59 weeks involving 18 families. Data was collected about seating patterns and patterns of verbal communication. Results indicated that changes in either the parents of adolescents in the group were quickly matched by comparable changes in the other generation. Results suggest "a continuously operating family control mechanism governing participation of members in interaction with nonmembers."

SIMON, L. Marital counseling: A dynamic-holistic approach. *American Journal of Psychoanalysis*, 1978, *38*, 243–254.
A clinilcal study of "group marital treatment" in an urban mental health clinic. Twenty-seven couples in 6 groups were given 8 weekly sessions; 21 who finished self-rated their outcome at the end of treatment. Results showed 50 percent at least moderately improved. The theoretical basis and techniques of the treatment are also discussed to support the conclusion that this form of treatment can make significant changes in a brief time.

STRELNICK, A. H. Multiple family group therapy: A review of the literature. *Family Process*, 1977, *16*, 307–325.
This review focuses upon multiple family group therapy—its origin, settings, techniques, group development, goals, and dominant themes and parallels in family and group work. Outcome and the dynamics contributing to family change are discussed.

1.3 MARITAL AND COUPLE THERAPY

ADDARIO, D., & RODGERS, T. A. Some techniques for the initial interview in couples therapy. *Hospital and Community Psychiatry*, 1974, *25*, 799–800.
This is a working guide of a technique for the initial interview in marital therapy. There is a discussion of the seating arrangement. The therapist lays out ground rules and suggests a theoretical framework for the couple. Each partner is

asked to do a self-assessment scale aimed at assessing his or her desire to stay in the marriage. This is followed by a discussion of family behavior. The session is terminated with homework for each of the partners, and a therapeutic contract is made. Nonsystematic feedback suggests the technique is useful.

ALGER, I. Joint plsychotherapy of marital problems. In Masserman, J. H. (Ed.), *Current Psychaitric Therapies*. New York: Grune & Stratton, 1967, pp. 112–117,
A clinical essay on the use of marital psychotherapy for problems that seem to have a marital rather than an intrapsychic basis. The author prefers seeing the couple with a cotherapist. Videotaped playbacks have been used with "good results."

ALGER, I., & HOGAN, P. Enduring effects of videotape playback experience on family and marital relationships. *American Journal of Orthopsychiatry*, 1969, *39*, 86–96.
The third in a series of papers describing the use of videotape playbacks in family and marital therapy. Sample included 75 families from the author's private practice. Equipment and techniques are described. Playback is said to be valuable as an adjunct to therapy in encouraging more "intense emotional involvement" on the part of the patients, in making available more objective data on the therapeutic process, and in clarifying complex behavior patterns and sequences as well as relating verbal and nonverbal levels. It is thought to be effective on repeated trials over a period of time and to have a residual effect lasting over a period of months and "even years."

ALGER, I., & HOGAN, P. The use of videotape recordings in conjoint marital therapy. *American Journal of Psychiatry*, 1967, *123*, 1425–1430.
A description of some findings obtained using videotape playback of parts of conjoint marital therapy sessions (i.e., treatment of husband and wife by one or two therapists). The setting was private practice with over 100 sessions with ten different couples. The videotape technique is thought to be useful in helping patients to see themselves in new ways, to understand the concept of multiple levels of messages and to help the marital partners take a more objective position to understand their interaction and therefore decrease "blaming."

APPEL, K. E., GOODWIN, H. M., WOOD, H. P., & ASKREN, E. L. Training in psychotherapy: The use of marriage counseling in a university teaching clinic. *American Journal of Psychiatry*, 1961, *117*, 709–711.
In the department of psychiatry at the University of Pennsylvania School of Medicine, residents may participate in a teaching program that includes treatment of married couples. Marriage counseling is discussed, and there is a case example of a case presentation given to psychiatric residents.

BECKER, B. J. Holistic analytic approaches to marital therapy. *American Journal of Psychoanalysis*, 1978, *38*, 129–142.
See reference in Section 4.1.

BECKER, J. Good premorbid schizophrenic wives and their husbands. *Family Process*, 1963, *2*, 34–51.
A report of conjoint family therapy with 7 married female schizophrenics and their husbands. Their backgrounds, premorbid marital life, and course of illness are described. Results of treatment were that "5 families appeared to benefit substantially, 1 somewhat, and 1 not at all."

BELL, J. E. Contrasting approaches in marital counseling. *Family Process*, 1967, *76*, 16–26.
A discussion of marital treatment with the emphasis upon the therapist–marital couple relationship as a social system. Treatment of the marital partners individually and together is contrasted.

BELLVILLE, T. P., RATHS, Q. N., & BELLVILLE, C. J. Conjoint marriage therapy with a husband-and-wife team. *American Journal of Orthopsychiatry*, 1969, *39*, 473–483.
A clinical report of marital therapy in which the cotherapists were husband and wife. Advantages, differentness of transference, identification when the therapists are also a couple, problems of tension between the therapists, selection of therapist couples, and the personality patterns of the patients treated are discussed. The sample was 44 couples with the primary complaint of "sexual incompatability." They were treated in 16 weekly sessions. The results indicated that 26 were rated as successfully treated and 18 as unsuccessful.

BERENSTEIN, I. On the psychotherapy of the marital couple. *Acta Psyquiat. Psycol. Amer. Lat*, 1968, *14*, 301–308.
Family therapy of a couple from the author's private practice is described. Emphasis is placed on understanding projective identification (undefined in the translation), analysis of conflicts, and acting out.

BERGER, M. M., & BERGER, L. F. Couple therapy by a married couple. *Journal of the American Academy of Psychoanalysis*, 1979, 7, 219–240.

Based on 13 years of clinical experience, this is an overview of marital therapy by a team of married cotherapists. Subjects discussed include evaluation, goals of marital treatment, and treatment difficulties. The special contribution of married cotherapists is communicating that they are also working continuously on their relationship.

BERMAN, E. M., & LIEF, H. I. Marital treatment from a psychiatric perspective: An overview. *American Journal of Psychiatry*, 1975, *132*, 583–592.
See reference in Section 6.

BOLTE, G. L. A communications approach to marital counseling. *Family Coordinator, 19*, 32–40, 1970
A clinical essay based on the thesis that communications difficulties provide an important avenue for understanding marital conflict. Therefore an interactional approach is advised for treating problems. Communication difficulties are outlined and interventions are suggested. Interactional techniques are seen as only one part of the marriage counselor's repertoire.

BRODY, S. Simultaneous psychotherapy of married couples. In J. Masserman (Ed.), *Current Psychiatric Therapies* (Vol. I). New York: Grune & Stratton, 1961.
Current advances in the field of family interaction and communication indicate many advantages to simultaneous therapy of couples by one psychiatrist rather than by two which tends to "atomize" family interaction. The author discusses the problems in treating a married individual and a couple, and points out the great assistance provided to a "deadlocked" therapy by the introduction of the marital partner into concurrent therapy.

CARROLL, E. J., CAMBOR, C. G., LEOPOLD, L. J. V., MILLER, M. D., & REIS, W. J. Psychotherapy of marital couples. *Family Process*, 1963, *2*, 25–33.
A general discussion of indications for advantages and disadvantages of family therapy. Two case reports are given. Of 6 cases seen by the group, 4 made significant gains, while the other 2 were unimproved.

CHARNY, I. W. Marital love and hate. *Family Process*, 1969, *8*, 1–24.
A discussion of marriage with the emphasis upon how marital fighting is "inevitable, necessary, and desirable—not simply an unhappy by-product of emotional immaturity or disturbance."

COCHRANE, N. Some reflections on the unsuccessful treatment of a group of married couples. *British Journal of Psychiatry*, 1973, *123*, 395–402.
A married couples' therapy group was ineffective in changing either marital patterns or individual psychodynamics. The intent was to run 75 weekly sessions of 1½ hours duration. Three of the 5 couples terminated prematurely, and the last 2 terminated at the 67th session. The approach was based primarily on interpretation of the interaction with emphasis on both present and past dynamics and difficulties in communication. Reasons for the failure in outcome effectiveness are discussed and were felt to be caused, in part, by the therapist's "single handed, detached and nondirective approach." Cotherapists are suggested for such groups.

DINABURG, D., GLICK, I. D., & FEIGENBAUM, D. Marital therapy of women alcoholics. *Journal of Studies on Alcohol*, 1977, *38*, 1247–1258.
A case report and follow-up over 9 years of an alcoholic woman. The patient and husband were treated for 35 sessions by cotherapists in conjoint marital therapy. Although there was improvement in the family patterns and in drinking behavior during the treatment, the improvement did not last after termination. The case suggests that marital therapy in the *absence of other treatment interventions* is ineffective in changing the long-run course of women alcoholics.

ELKIN, M. Short-contact counseling in a conciliation court. *Social Casework*, 1962, *43*, 184–190.
A description of the purpose and procedures of the marital counseling program of the Conciliation Court of Los Angeles County. The court offers short-contact marital counseling service for couples on the verge of separation or divorce. The background, purpose, procedures and effectiveness of the service are presented.

FITZGERALD, R. V. Conjoint marital psychotherapy: An outcome and follow-up study. *Family Process*, 1969, *8*, 261–271.
A report on an outcome study of couples seen in conjoint marriage therapy. A sample of 57 couples were followed up after 2½ years with an interview by telephone. Of the couples who were seen because an individual sought therapy, 76 percent were improved. Of those who presented an ongoing marital conflict as the presenting problem, 75 percent improved.

FOX, R. E. The effect of psychotherapy on the spouse. *Family Process*, 1968, *7*, 7–16.
A discussion and review of the literature of the effect on a spouse when the partner is in individual psychotherapy. Problems of gathering data are presented and the ethical problem of adverse effects upon the spouse are discussed.

FRY, W. F. The marital context of an anxiety syndrome. *Family Process*, 1962, *1*, 245–252.
A report from a project studying schizophrenic communication, whose hypothesis is that "the relationship with the

marriage partner is intimately related to the psychopathology of the patient." The patients in the report had the syndrome of anxiety, phobias, and stereotyped avoidance behavior. Spouses are described, and it was found that the onset of symptoms correlated with an important change in the life of the spouse and the symptoms seemed to keep the couple united.

GEHRKE, S., & MOXOM, J. Diagnostic classifications and treatment techniques in marriage counseling. *Family Process*, 1962, *1*, 253–264.
A report by two case workers describing a marital counseling method with the diagnostic classifications and treatment techniques used. Indications for joint interviews with husband and wife are given.

GEIST, J., & GERBER, N. Joint interviewing: Treatment technique with marital partners. *Social Casework*, 1963, *41*, 76–83.
Conjoint family interviewing is indicated: (1) when there is a breakdown in communication; (2) when there is distrust of the other partner's actions; (3) when individual work does not progress; (4) when there is lack of focus in individual interviews; (5) when the joint interviews seem to be more constructive than individual. Techniques for joint interviews are discussed, as are methods of termination and contraindications.

GETTY, C., & SHANNON, A. Nurses: Co-therapists in a family setting. *Perspectives of Psychiatric Nursing*, 1967, *5*, 36–46.
A clinical paper describing one case in which an outpatient married couple was seen in family therapy by two nurses who were co-therapists. Co-therapists are seen as "models of communication."

GILL, H., & TEMPERLEY, L. J. Time-limited marital treatment in a foursome, *British Journal of Medical Psychology*, 1974, *47*, 153–162.
The second in a series of papers describing a case report of marital therapy done by cotherapists of each sex over a *time-limited basis*. In this report, problems of the case and techniques are described, e.g., marital fusion as a defense against past conflicts, impotence, mutual denigrating of the role of women, and mutual working through of conflicts dating from adolescence.

GOLDBERG, M. Conjoint therapy of male physicians and their wives. *Psychiatric Opinion*, 1975, *12*, 19–23.
The author describes his work in marital therapy with over 200 couples of which the identified patient was a male physician. Usual duration of treatment was 6 months to 1 year involving 20 to 40 sessions. Dynamics, techniques, problems, and process are described. No results are reported, except that "such couples have done rather better than other couples I work with."

GOODWIN, H. M., & MUDD, E. H. Marriage counseling: Methods and goals. *Comprehensive Psychiatry*, 1966, *7*, 450–461.
This clinical essay on marriage counseling covers values and basic concepts, indications, goals, structure and process. Marital counseling is most effective in an unpressured, unaccusing atmosphere in which can take place give and take, catharsis, new perspectives, and the supportive efforts of new and mutually acceptable interaction patterns.

GOTTLIEB, A., & PATTISON, E. M. Married couples group psychotherapy. *Archives of General Psychiatry*, 1966, *14*, 143–152.
A general discussion of group therapy with marital couples with emphasis upon how the marriage influences group dynamics, how the spouse influences the other spouse's psychotherapy, and the particular positions of cotherapists in a group of couples. Arguments for and against the procedure are presented as well as a clinical illustration.

GREENE, B. L. Introdution: A multioperational approach to marital problems. In B. L. Greene (Ed.), *The psychotherapies of marital disharmony*. New York: Free Press, 1965.
This essay describes the author's personal experience, as well as the advantages and disadvantages, in prescribing counseling, psychoanalysis, collaborative therapy, current therapy, conjoint therapy, or some combination of all.

GREENE, B. L. Management of marital problems. *Diseases of the Nervous System*, 1966, 27, 204–209.
An essay describing some theoretical principles, classifications, and treatment techniques for marital problems. Described are indications and contraindications of (1) counseling, (2) classic one-to-one psychotherapy, (3) collaborative treatment (marital partners treated by different therapists), (4) concurrent treatment (both partners treated by same therapists), (5) conjoint family therapy, (6) conjoint marital therapy, and (7) combinations of all six.

GREENE, B. L. Marital disharmony: Concurrent analysis of husband and wife. *Diseases of the Nervous System*, 1960, *21*, 73–78.
A preliminary report of the concurrent analysis of 14 couples which the author began following 3 successive failures in collaborative psychoanalysis (each partner treated by a different analyst). Theoretical considerations, philosophy of treatment, and some results are reported.

GREENE, B. L., BROADHURST, B. P., & LUSTIG, N. Treatment of marital disharmony: The use of individual, concurrent and conjoint sessions as a combined approach. In B. L. Greene (Ed.), *The psychotherapies of marital disharmony*. New York: Free Press, 1965
This clinical essay describes the use of an approach involving individual, concurrent, and conjoint sessions for marital problems. The indication is when "both triadic and dyadic transactions are necessary either for successful treatment of the marital transaction or of one of the partners." Advantrages and disadvantages of this technique compared to other techniques are discussed. No results are offered.

GREENE, B. L., LUSTIG, N., & LEE, R. R. Marital therapy when one spouse has a primary affective disorder. *American Journal of Psychiatry*, 1976, *133*, 827–830.
A clinical essay focusing on the marital dynamics when one spouse has a primary affective disorder. Sample was 100 upper-middle or upper-class couples from the author's private practice. Family psychotherapy in combination wilth somatic therapy is recommended as the treatment of choice.

GREENSPAN, STANLEY, I., & MANNINO, FORTUNE, V. A model for brief intervention with couples based on projective identification. *American Journal of Psychiatry*, 1974, *131*, 1103–1106.
Two case examples are presented in support of the concept that projective identification (defined as a mechanism by which "internal conflicts are translated into more concrete modes of perceiving and behaving in family relationships") interferes with "growth" of the marital unit and causes marital problems. Therapeutic intervention is organized around time-limited, problem-oriented marital therapy with a goal of putting each partner in touch with those aspects of the other's character that are omitted from awareness.

GULLERUD, E. N., & HARLAN, V. L. Four-way joint interviewing in marital counseling. *Social Casework*, 1962, *43*, 532–537.
A clinical report of marital therapy using cotherapists of different sexes. Indications include (1) the inability of the marital partners to agree on common goals, (2) excessive dependence, (3) need for support by the caseworker of the same sex, (4) diagnostic purposes, and (5) when an impasse is reached in individual sessions. Interview procedures, dynamic considerations, advantages, and evaluations are discussed.

GURMAN, A. S. The effects and effectiveness of marital therapy: A review of outcome research. *Family Process*, 1973, *12*, 145–170.
See reference in Section 2.0.

GURMAN, A. S. Marital therapy: Emerging trends in research and practice. *Family Process*, 1973, *12*, 45–54.
Marital therapy literature was reviewed to examine trends in research and clinical practice. From a few (N=5) articles in the period prior to 1940, the number of publications grew to 415 during the period 1970–1972. Despite this rapid growth, the field lacked a comprehensive, theoretical foundation. What had emerged was both an eclecticism of disciplines and an eclecticism of therapeutic techniques, pointing to the need of a consistent theoretical formulation as well as a structured set of therapeutic interventions.

GURMAN, A. S., & KNISKERN, D. P. Behavioral marriage therapy: II. Empirical perspective. *Family Process*, 1978, *17*, 139–148.
See reference in Section 6.0.

GURMAN, A. S., & KNUDSON, R. M. Behavioral marriage therapy: I. A psychodynamic-systems analysis and critique. *Family Process*, 1978, *17*, 121–138.
See reference in Section 6.0.

GURMAN, A. S., KNUDSON, R. M., & KNISKERN, D. P. Behavioral marriage therapy: IV. Take two aspirins and call us in the morning. *Family Process*, 1978, *17*, 165–180.
See reference in Section 6.0.

HALEY, J. Marriage therapy. *Archives of General Psychiatry*, 1963, *8*, 213–234.
A discussion of the treatment of conflicts in marriage. Certain types of marital relationships, the kinds of conflicts which arise, and the ways a therapist intervenes to induce change are discussed. It is suggested that conflicts occur when husband and wife define their relationship in conflicting ways thereby imposing paradoxical situations. The resolution of the conflict can occur when the couple faces paradoxical situations provided by marriage therapists.

HALLOWITZ, D., CLEMENT, R., & CUTTER, A. The treatment process with both parents together. *American Journal of Orthopsychiatry*, 1957, *27*, 587–608.
Based on clinical experience at a child guidance center, the authors stress the need to see both parents of the identified patient together rather than separately. No sessions with all members of the family together were used.

HANSEN, C. An extended home visit with conjoint family therapy. *Family Process*, 1968, 7, 67–87.

An approach to family therapy that involved staying in the home with the family for a week to intervene therapeutically in a family's life. Benefits and problems of this approach are discussed.

HARE-MUSTIN, R. T. A feminist approach to family therapy. *Family Process*, 1978, *17*, 181–194.
This paper makes the point that family therapists need to examine the consequences of traditional socialization practices that primarily are biased against women. The consistent reinforcement of stereotyped sex roles takes place in family therapy practice. There is a need to re-evaluate these stereotyped roles and statuses for females and males in our society by applying feminist principles to such areas as the marriage contract, tasks, communication, generational boundaries, labeling deviance, therapeutic alliances, and modeling.

HARPER, R. Marriage counseling as rational process-oriented therapy. *Journal of Individual Psychology*, 1970, *16*, 197–207.
An essay based on the point of view that marriage counseling is "synonymous with" psychotherapy. Both lead to "revision of interpersonal dynamics." Major processes and techniques in marriage counseling are discussed and compared to similar processes in psychotherapy.

HEARD, D. B. & KEITH A case study of structural family therapy. *Family Process*, 1978, *17*, 338–356.
An edited case presentation of marital therapy of a couple whose child was the presenting problem. Two themes are presented: The structuring of therapy along critical stages that need appropriate timing; and the use of a task to induce structural realignment in the family. Excerpts and commentaries illustrate these themes.

HICKOK, J. E. & KOMECHAK, M. G. Behavior modification in marital conflict: A case report. *Family Process*, 1974, *13*, 111–119.
This paper reports on the combination of confrontation of relevant behavioral awareness and a token economy to treat one marital dyad on the brink of divorce. The theoretical basis of this treatment approach is that each individual's conscious awareness of the topography, frequency, and parameters of his or her own behavior and the consequences of these behaviors on the spouse can create change. The token system was operative for a 6-week period, discontinued for 2 weeks and reinstituted. It was found that during the third week the rewarded behaviors increased and continued during the cessation of the token economy as indicated by a 2-month-follow-up home visit. It is believed that as the couple became more aware of their behaviors and reactions to their behaviors, the reinforcers became more intrinsic and the behavior began maintaining itself.

HOEK, A. & WOLLSTEIN, S. Conjoint psychotherapy of married couples: A clinical report. *International Journal of Social Psychiatry*, 1966, *12*, 209–216.
This is a clinical report of 30 cases in which the identified patient and spouse were treated conjointly by cotherapists. Indications, objectives, treatment focus, type of cases, clinical findings, and a case illustration are presented in support of this method of treatment. No results are reported.

HOLLENDER, M. Selection of therapy for marital problems. *Current Psychiatric Therapies*, 1971, *11*, 119–128.
This clinical essay attempts to lay guidelines for selection of therapy for marital problems. Questions to be answered in approaching the problem are should therapy be recommended, and if so, what kind?, and if therapy is recommended, should it be marital-oriented or person-oriented? Examples are presented in support of the points made.

HURVITZ, N. Marital problems following psychotherapy with one spouse based upon spouses referred later for marriage counseling. The problem is not only that individual treatment might break up a marriage but that "the relationship between the spouses, which should be used to benefit them both, is further disturbed." Marital treatment approach using the individual therapy as a problem area in the marriage is described.

JACOBSON, N. & WEISS, R. L. Behavioral marriage therapy. III: The contents of Gurman, et al. may be hazardous to our health. *Family Process*, 1978, *17*, 149–163.
See reference in Section 6.0.

JONES, W. The villain and the victim: Group therapy for married couples. *American Journal of Psychiatry*, 1967, *124*, 351–354.
The author's experience with group-therapy in which the group is made up of married couples. One indication for such therapy is when "conjoint marriage therapy" is deadlocked.

KADIS, A. A new approach to marital therapy. *International Journal of Social Psychiatry*, 1964, *10*, 261–265.
An essay on a new technique for marital therapy in which the therapist "rechannels communication so that the therapist becomes primarily the listener and tries to maximize interpartner communication." Steps to achieve this end are described.

KALINA, E. Psychoanalytic psychotherapy with a couple considered as brief therapy. *Acta Psiquiatrica Y Psicologica De America Latina*, 1968, *14*, 311–316.
From the author's private practice, several case examples are presented in support of the idea of family therapy as a primary treatment tool. Diagnosis prior to starting therapy is stressed. The main technical tool is seen as "the interpretation of the unconscious transference fantasy."

KARDENER, S. H. Convergent internal security systems—A rationale for marital therapy. *Family Process*, 1970, *9*, 83–91.
A theoretical frame of reference within therapeutic interventions may be made in the treatment of couples. The notion of the need to restage the parental relationship is demonstrated with two clinical examples.

KERN J. Conjoint marital psychotherapy: An interim measure in the treatment of psychosis. *Psychiatry*, 1967, *30*, 283–293.
See Reference in Section 1.4.

KRELL, R. & MILES, J. Marital therapy of couples in which the husband is a physician. *American Journal of Psychotherapy*, 1976, *30*, 267–275.
This clinical paper focuses on problems and treatment of 10 couples in which the identified patient is a physician. Individual psychotherapy appeared contraindicated; prognosis "improved dramatically" with inclusion of wife in therapy.

KRESSEL, K. & DEUTSCH, M. Divorce therapy: An in-depth survey of therapists' views. *Family Process*, 1977, *16*, 413–443.
A semi-structured interview with 21 therapists on the criteria for a constructive divorce, the obstacles for achieving such a divorce, and the strategies and tactics of "divorce therapy." The primary criterion of a constructuve divorce is the successful completion of the process of "psychic separation" and the protection of the welfare of minor children. Therapy may focus on the decision to get divorced and/or the negotiation of the terms of a settlement.

LASKIN, E. Breaking down the walls. *Family Process*, 1968, *7*, 118–125.
A report on the treatment of a couple by a variety of approaches with a recommendation that a therapist maintain maximum flexibility and innovativeness in treatment.

LEHRMAN, N. S. The joint interview: An aid to psychotherapy and family stability. *American Journal of Psychotherapy*, 1963, *17*, 83–94.
Using parts of transcripts of 3 cases, the author discusses some of the principles and techniques of the joint interview of husband and wife that he uses as an aid to psychotherapy in "defining and resolving intrafamilial friction, and at times of impasse."

LESLIE, G. R. Conjoint therapy in marriage counseling. *Journal of Marriage and Family*, 1964, *26*, 65–71.
A clinical essay by a sociologist focusing on development of conjoint interviewing in family therapy and in marital counseling. Marital counselors have not tended to take full advantage of joint interviewing. Conjoint therapy aids in the identification and working through distortions, helps hold transference and counter-transference in check, quickly brings marital conflicts into the open and into the counseling sessions, and emphasizes current relationship problems. Contraindications include lack of training by the therapist, inability of the marital partners to use conjoint sessions, and a strong paranoid system in one partner.

LLOYD, R. A. & PAULSON, I. Projective indentification in the marital relationship as a resistance to psychotherapy. *Archives of General Psychiatry*, 1972, *27*, 410–413.
One case is presented in support of the notion that marital treatment is useful to overcome resistance to individual psychotherapy in a couple presenting with mutual projective identification. Results showed the couple to be more "accessible" to individual treatment afterward.

MARTIN, P. A. Treatment of marital disharmony by collaborative therapy. In B. L. Greene (Ed.), *The psychotherapies of marital disharmony*. New York: Free Press, 1965.
A clinical paper describing collaborative therapy of marital partners, based on treatment of 50 couples. "It is not the reality of the situation which is important, it is the distortion of reality that provides the clinical material." Advantages and disadvantages of the collaborating psychiatrists meeting regularly are discussed.

MARTIN, P. A. & BIRD, H. W. An approach to the psychotherapy of marriage partners—The stereoscopic technique. *Psychiatry*, 1953, *16*, 123–127.
In response to therapeutic impasse in individual treatment of 4 patients, the spouses of these patients were referred to another therapist for simultaneous individual treatment. The 2 therapists then met "during which each psychiatrist presented his reconstructed version of important events in the life of the partner he was treating." Advantages and disadvantages of this technique are discussed.

MAURIN, J. Conflict within the marital dyad. *Journal of Psychiatric Nursing and Mental Health Services*, 1974 *12*, 27–31.
A description of marital therapy with a particular focus on "how to perform or who should perform household tasks." Based on family therapy, role therapy, and communication therapy, several case examples are presented in support of the author's strategy. Work with the marital dyad alleviates problems of the identified patient.

MUDD, E. H. & GOODWIN, H. M. Counseling couples in conflicted marriages. In B. L. Greene (Ed.), *The psychotherapies of marital disharmony*. New York: The Free Press, 1965.
A clinical essay describing the definition, goals, and techniques of marital counseling developed over 25 years of work. The aim is to bring an adequate adaptation to external reality.

NADELSON, C., BASSUK, E. L., HOPPS, C. R., et al. Conjoint marital pyschotherapy: Treatment techniques. *Diseases of the Nervous System*, 1977, *38*, 898–903.
A study of evaluation and treatment procedures for couple therapy in a clinic of a major teaching hospital. The program described includes three evaluation sessions; the setting of specific goals; an initial phase of treatment (focused on communication patterns and tools for effective problem solving); a middle phase (working through transference resistance); and a termination phase (working through loss of therapist but not complete resolution of transference). A review of the literature of the theoretical basis for conjoint therapy is included.

NADELSON, C., BASSUK, E., HOPPS, C.R., et al., Evaluation procedures for conjoint marital psychotherapy. *Social Casework,* 1975, *56*, 91–96.
A clinical report of evaluation procedures used for treatment of marital therapy. Data was obtained from 25 married couples over a 2-year period in an outpatient setting. Not only should the marital interaction be evaluated but each partner should be evaluated "individually." Case examples are presented to illustrate the evaluation procedures and reasons for choice of treatment.

NADELSON, C. C., BASSUK, E. L., HOPPS, C. R., & BOUTELLE, W. E. The use of videotapes in couples therapy. *International Journal of Group Psychotherapy*, 1977, *27*, 241–253.
Videotaping playback in treatment can be useful to deal with resistance and denial and to refocus on main themes. In supervision, it facilitates communication and allows students to respond with different perceptions and experience.

OLSEN, E. The marriage—A basic unit for psychotherapy. *American Journal of Psychiatry*, 1971, *127*, 945–947.
The "psychotherapist can be more effective working within an existing system than establishing a competing dyadic relationship with one of the spouses." Rationale is that both partners are in an interlocking system, and therefore the marital system can be better helped to "grow" in family therapy than in individual psychotherapy.

PADBERG, J. "Bargaining" to improve communications in conjoint family therapy. *Perspectives of Psychiatric Care*, 1975, *13*, 69–72.
One case example illustrates the notion that bargaining in marital therapy can improve family communication and change family patterns.

PAPANEK, H. Group psychotherapy with married couples. In J. Masserman (Ed.), *Current psychiatric therapies* (Vol. V). New York: Grune & Stratton, 1965.
An essay on the use of group therapy with married couples. The couple is seen together (not in group therapy) only as an *introductory phase* to gather historical data.

PATTON, J., BRADLEY, J. & HRONOWSKI, M. Collaborative treatment of marital partners. *North Carolina Medical Journal*, 1958, *19*, 523–528.
A clinical report of three psychiatrists who met regularly over 18 months to discuss their cases being treated by individual psychotherapy. As the discussions progressed, conceptualizing the psychiatrists' patients in terms of the patients' thinking shifted from individual dynamics to the realization that the individual symptomatology was representative of family problems. Treatment of the family was suggested.

PAUL, N. L. The role of mourning and empathy in conjoint marital therapy. In G. H. Zuk & I. Boszormenyi-Nagy (Eds.), *Family therapy and disturbed families*. Palo Alto: Science & Behavior Books, 1967.
An experimental technique consisting of the induction of a belated mourning reaction as a way of treating couples. Intense grief, unrecognized and unresolved, has a latent strength.

PASMORE, J. What is marital therapy? *Psychotherapy and Psychosomatics*, 1975, *25*, 149–153.
Based on material from the author's clinical practice, definition, conditions, aims, and techniques of marital therapy are discussed.

PECK, B. B. The extruded third: An interpersonal approach to couples treatment. *Psychotherapy*, 1973, *10*, 62–65.
A clinical paper describing a process in marital therapy in which one person is constantly pushed out of a dyad.

Initially, one member of the couple and the therapist have "a thing" (defined as finding a point of contact between the therapist and one partner). This causes a change of equilibrium, and the therapist is brought closer to the other partner. In the final phase, the therapist is extruded and presumably the couple has established new patterns of relating, resolving the impasse that brought them into therapy.Advantages and disadvantages of this technique are discussed.

PERLMAN, C., & GIVELBER, F. Women's issues in couples treatment—The view of the female therapist. *Psychiatric Opinion*, 1976, *13*, 6–12.
See reference in section 4.1

PITTMAN, F. S., & FLOMENHAFT, K. Treating the doll's house marriage. *Family Process*, 1970, *9*, 143–156.
Intervention procedures in the type of marriage in which one spouse's incompetance is required or encouraged by the other. Therapy works best when the emphasis is upon respect for unique individual needs within the framework of the marriage.

POLLAK, O. Sociological and psychoanalytic concepts in family diagnosis. In B. L. Greene (Ed.), *The psychotherapies of marital disharmony*. New York: Free Press, 1965.
A clinical essay describing a sociologic and psychoanalytic model of marriage problems. In the marital conflict the therapist must identify the problem, identify the obstacle to improvement, and then offer himself as an ally.

RAVICH, R. Game-testing in conjoint marital psychotherapy. *American Journal of Psychotherapy*, 1969, *23*, 217–229.
A report on the "game-test" for both family diagnosis and family therapy. Methodology is described and four typical patterns of interaction are identified: (1) competitive, (2) alternating, (3) dominant-submissive, and (4) Mixed, that is, elements of all the above three. Based on these patterns, techniques for therapy are described.

RAVICH, R. Short-term intensive treatment of marital discord. *Voices*, 1966, *2*, 42–48.
A case in support of the notion that short-term intensive treatment can give a "reasonably quick resolution of discord." The couples are given the Deutsch-Krause game as a diagnostic tool. (This game is oriented around the idea that the couple must work together to solve a task). In this technique, the couple is seen together 3 or 4 times a week for 2 or 3 weeks, and occasionally separately.

REDING G. R., CHARLES, L., & HOFFMAN, M. Treatment of the couple by a couple. II: Conceptual framework, case presentation, and follow-up study. *British Journal of Medical Psychology,* 1967, *40*, 243–252.
A report of the author's experience using a male and female co-therapist for marital therapy. Previously the "four-way" treatment was seen a combination of two individual treatments. This has been given up and extensive use of transference and counter-transference interpretation has been made. Discussions of theory, process, and a case are presented. Telephone follow-up 3 to 30 months after termination of 10 of 15 couples treated by this method are reported.

REDING, G. R., & ENNIS, B. Treatment of the couple by a couple. *British Journal of Medical Psychology*, 1964, *37*, 325–330.
A description of a treatment of married couples by two psychotherapists. The dynamics of the "four-way" interview are described, with emphasis upon the relationship between the therapists.

RICKARBY, G. A. The wider uses of conjoint psychotherapy. *British Journal of Medical Psychology*, 1976, *49*, 183–187.
Using 3 case histories of compulsive gambling, alcoholism, and pathological grief, the possible usefulness of conjoint therapy for these "individual" problems is discussed.

ROBERTS, F. Conjoint marital therapy and the prisoners' dilemma. *British Journal of Medical Psychology*, 1971, *44*, 67–74.
One case example is presented in support of the notion that in marital therapy the partners are each "a cell" and cannot communicate with each other in a manner that allows them to trust the other and "escape from the dilemma." The purpose of marital therapy is to reopen useful communication. Aspects of the change in communication and symptom patterns for each partner is discussed.

ROMAN, M., BAUMAN, G., BORELLO, J., et al. An effect of change in patient status of marital interaction. *Family Process*, 1976, *15*, 251–258.
See reference in Section 4.1.

RUBINSTEIN, D. Distortion and dilemma in marital choice. *Voices*, 1966, *2*, (3) 60–64.
From an extensive case example, this essay hypothesizes that in a disturbed marital relationship there are distortions and dilemmas that can be summarized as follows: (1) the marital pair does not relate as real persons; (2) they relate through each other to the internal introjects, (3) they try to change each other into an internal introject to solve longstanding conflicts; (4) they become "bad objects"; and (5) as long as there is an externalized "bad object," the

idealized "good" introject can be kept alive and sought. Family therapy attempts to uncover these distortions and help the marital pair to see each other realistically.

SAGER,C. The conjoint session in marriage therapy. *American Journal of Psychoanalysis*, 1967, *27*, 139–146.
Diagnostic interviews, therapeutic techniques, indications and contraindications in marital therapy are discussed.

SAGER, C. The development of marriage therapy: An historical review. *American Journal of Orthopsychiatry*, 1966, *36*, 458–468.
An historical review of the literature of marital therapy, and an attempt to integrate current theoretical and therapeutic techniques. Transference from both a transactional and psychoanalytic frame of reference are discussed and is felt to be a valuable tool in marital therapy.

SAGER, C. J. Marital psychotherapy. In Masserman, J. H. (Ed.), *Current psychiatric therapies*. New York: Grune and Stratton, 1967, pp. 92–102.
An essay on marital psychotherapy from a clinical viewpoint. Indications, contraindications, diagnostic, and treatment techniques (with specific emphasis on the "nature and use of transference"), problems, and advantages are presented. Behavioral changes are more likely to occur if the therapist concentrates on the interaction between spouses rather than on "insight."

SAGER, C. J. The role of sex therapy in marital therapy. *American Journal of Psychiatry*, 1976, *133*, 555–558.
Case material from a sex therapy clinic is used to discuss therapeutic focus and the relationship between marital and sex therapy. Both techniques are seen as useful parts of a clinician's armamentarium in dealing with complex problems when the identified patient has either a problem in sexual function or a problem in marital function.

SAGER, C. Transference in conjoint treatment of married couples. *Archives of General Psychiatry*, 1967, *16*, 185–193
A theoretical paper on transference, which is defined as the transfer of relations exhibited toward infantile objects to contemporary objects. Various types are mentioned, and methods to utilize the transference in therapy are put forth. Conjoint family therapy offers a significant advantage over individual therapy because the triangular nature of the situation yields greater possibilities for transference reactions.

SATIR, V. Conjoint marital therapy. In B. L. Greene (Ed.), *The psychotherapies of marital disharmony*. New York: Free Press, 1965.
A clinical article describing rationale and techniques of family therapy. Interpersonal relationships involve two levels of communication, both of which have to be interpreted and worked on to effect change. In this technique the therapist has to be more active than in other therapies and must act as a "model of communication."

SEEMAN, M. V. & EDWARDES-EVANS, B. Marital therapy with borderline patients: Is it beneficial? *Journal of Clinical Psychiatry*, 1979, *40*, 308–312.
A case report of a 3-month trial of unsuccessful marital treatment for patients with borderline personality disorders complaining of marital incompatibility.

SEGRAVES, R. T. Conjoint marital therapy: A cognitive behavioral model. *Archives of General Psychiatry*, 1978, *35*, 450–455.
This theoretical article recommends a framework for brief conjoint marital treatment to make it both clinically relevant and empiricaly testable. There is a need to integrate contributions from psychoanalytic, systems, communications, and behavioral theories. People have cognitive schemas for the perception of their spouses which are often negative or limited; the model is presented in a series of hypotheses focused on the tactics of changing these schemas. Suggestions are offered for testing the hypotheses. Sixty-five references are included.

SILK, S. The use of videotape in brief joint marital therapy. *American Journal of Psychotherapy*, 1972, *26*, 417–424.
Two case examples are used to support the notion that use of videotapes is more helpful than more traditional family therapy approaches. The technique "must be individualized," but here a combination of videotaping individual as well as conjoint sessions was used, letting one or both partners view it. After the first session, the couple has "something tangible to work on"; after the second, "an objective portrayal of the situation"; and after the third, the couple was given a problem-solving situation that clearly brought out problems in the relationship.

SILVERMAN, J. The women's liberation movement: Its impact on marriage. *Hospital and Community Psychiatry*, 1975, *26*, 39–40.
See reference in Section 4.1.

SKIDMORE, R. A., & GARRETT, H. V. The joint interview in marriage counseling. *Marraige and Family Living*, 1955, *17*, 349–354.
A clinical essay suggesting that joint interviews rather than individual interviews are helpful in marriage counseling. Three cases are presented, and advantages as well as safeguards of such interviews are discussed.

SLUZKI, C. & BLEICHMAR, H. The interactional approach to marital therapy. *Acta Psiquiatrica Y Psicologica De America Latina*, 1968, *14*, 325–328.
The interactional model of couples in family therapy is stressed using techniques for both understanding and treating.

SMITH, V., & ANDERSON, F., Conjoint interviews with marriage partners. *Marriage and Family Living*, 1963, *25*, 184–188.
Joint interviews in marriage counseling are seen as an additional technique, with assumptions, advantages, and disadvantages discussed. Objectives based on clearcut clinical needs should be spelled out in advance, rather than having them come about due to resistance of the client or to administrative decision.

SPARK, G. M. Marriage is a family affair. *Family Coordinator*, 1977, *26*, 167–174.
An essay that advocates an intergenerational approach to marital therapy. The importance and value of working on spouses' families of origin is discussed from the theoretical aspects of marital mythology and intergenerational loyalties and obligations. Specific techniques are outlined and examined in a clinical illustration.

STRAYHORN, J. Social-exchange theory: Cognitive restructuring in marital therapy. *Family Process*, 1978, *17*, 437–448.
This paper examines problem areas in marital relationships that are amenable to cognitive structuring therapy. They include different rules for communicating "value messages."; they depend primarily upon painful channels for sending and receiving value messages; and they acknowledge that each partner's quota of value messages from the other partner is either exaggerated or inflated by fear of abandonment of devaluation. The therapeutic task and the marital alliance have to elucidate each of these three difficulties.

STUART, R. B. Token reinforcement in marital treatment. In P. H. Glasser & L. N. Glasser (Eds.), *Families in crisis*. New York, Harper & Row, 1970.
The tasks of the marriage therapist are . . . to identify the desired ("loving") behaviors sought by each spouse from the other; to identify the contingencies that can be used to accelerate and maintain these behaviors; and to increase the probability that each of these behaviors will occur." Procedures and results with 5 couples are presented.

STURGES, S. Folie á deux in a husband and wife. *Bulletin of the Menninger Clinic*, 1967, *31*, 343–351.
A case report of a mutually shared well-systemized delusion in a husband and wife. Individual and family dynamics underlying this delusion are discussed.

SUMMERS, F. Severe hypertension treated successfully by marital psychotherapy. *American Journal of Psychiatry*, 1978, *135*, 989–990.
See reference in Section 5.6.

TEISMANN, M. W. Jealousy: Systematic, problem-solving therapy with couples. *Family Process*, 1979, *18*, 151–160.
The concept of the "therapeutic triangle" and the use of paradox and symptom transfer, as well as the introduction of serious playfulness, are discussed as methods for treating marital jealousy.

TERUEL, G. Considerations for a diagnosis in marital psychotherapy. *British Journal of Medical Psychology*, 1966, *39*, 231–237.
An essay describing a method to "understand certain patterns of interrelationships between a man and a wife." When a spouse is referred for treatment, the other spouse is invited for a joint interview, and the therapist tries to get the marriage partners to present the data in their own words. Five cases and the theory used to understand what is being seen in the joint interview are presented.

THOMPSON, P. & CHEN, R. Experiences with older psychiatric patients and spouses together in a residential treatment setting. *Bulletin of the Menninger Clinic*, 1966, *30*, 23–31.
A report of an experimental program of geriatric treatment in an inpatient psychiatric hospital setting. Husbands and wives were often hospitalized together. Family dynamics and treatment approaches are discussed.

TITCHENER, J. The problem of interpretation in marital therapy. *Comprehensive Psychiatry*, 1966, 7, 321–337.
Based on the dynamics of a couple, the rationale and methods of a theory of interpretation in marital therapy is discussed.

TONGE, W. L. Marital therapy: How to choose the wrong treatment. *Psychotherapy and Psychosomatics*, 1975, *25*, 163–167.
Three cases are offered to support the thesis that there are different indications and contraindications for conjoint therapy, individual psychotherapy for one or both partners, and behavior therapy. Individual psychotherapy is thought to be indicated when the complaint is about "the self," and conjoint therapy when the complaint is about "the other."

TOOMIM, M. K. Structured separation with counseling: A therapeutic approach for couples in conflict. *Family Process*, 1972, *11*, 299–310.
Besides immediate divorce, indefinite separation, and discontented clinging, couples in conflict can be presented with a fourth alternative: a moderatley structured, time-limited period of separation with counseling. The recommendations of this article rest on a 1-year follow-up conducted with 18 couples who completed a 3-month structured trial separation with counseling. The article describes the parameters of the separation structure and the main areas to be attended to in separation counseling.

VOSBURG, R. Conjoint therapy of migraine: A case report. *Psychosomatics*, 1972, *13*, 61–63.
Family therapy with weekly sessions lasting 3 months was prescribed for a 44-year-old male with migraines associated with anger toward his wife. After 8 sessions the patient was free of headaches and was not on any medication; however, at the point where the marriage had to be renegotiated, the couple terminated treatment. Based on the observed family dynamics, it was thought the migraine was related to "suppressed feelings of resentment."

WADESON, H. Conjoint marital art therapy. *Psychiatry*, 1972, *37*, 39–98.
An essay describing the use of marital art therapy for both the study and treatment of marital disorders. Advantages include immediacy, graphic representation of the couple's life, permanence, and "sheer pleasure." A number of exercises are described including making a picture together, abstracting the marital relationship simultaneously but separately in a picture, and self-portrait exercises. Case examples illustrate the techniques.

WARKENTIN, J. Psychotherapy with couples and families. *Journal of the Medical Association of Georgia*, 1960, *49*, 569–570.
See Reference in Section 1.1.

WARKENTIN, J., & WHITAKER, C. "Marriage—The cornerstone of the family system. In O. Pollak & A. S. Friedman (Eds.), *Family dynamics and female sexual delinquency.* Palo Alto: Science & Behavior Books, 1969.
A description of the inner assumptions and postulates about human nature and marriage of two experienced therapists.The emphasis is upon the importance of the therapist's views about life when dealing with a family.

WARKENTIN, J. & WHITAKER, C. The secret agenda of the therapist doing couples therapy. In G. H. Zuk & I. Boszormenyi-Nagy (Eds.) *Family therapy and disturbed families.* Palo Alto: Science & Behavior Books, 1967.
A discussion of the treatment of married couples with the emphasis upon the profound influence of the therapist's own pattern of personal living. Includes the author's premises about marriage.

WARKENTIN, J. & WHITAKER, C. Serial impasses in marriage. In I. M. Cohen (Ed.), *Psychiatric research report No. 20.* American Psychiatric Association, 1966.
A discussion of marriage as both a legal and an emotional commitment with special emphasis upon the times "when we may expect difficulty and even impasse in the development of the emotional marriage." These times include the wedding night, pregnancy, the second baby, and the "ten year syndrome."

WATSON, A. S. The conjoint psychotherapy of marriage partners. *American Journal of Orthopsychiatry*, 1963, *33*, 912–923.
A discussion of the premises, technique, technical problems, and technical advantages of conjoint psychotherapy of marital partners. Several indications for this method are stated: (1) family relationships in which the distortions are gross and reality disrupted, and (2) cases in which problems are largely of an acting-out, characterological nature.

WHITAKER, C. Psychotherapy with couples. *American Journal of Psychotherapy*, 1958, *12*, 18–23.
A clinical report on the use of marital therapy as an alternative to the use of individual psychotherapy. Sample was 30 couples all of whom were in outpatient treatment. There were no individual meetings during the course of treatment. Results indicated that of the 30 couples, 6 dropped out. In 2 caes the marital therapy was preliminary to individual therapy. Ten couples showed no progress in at least 1 member, and it is unclear what happened to the other couples.

WHITAKER, C., & MILLER, M.H. A reevaluation of "psychiatric help" when divorce impends. *American Journal of Psychiatry*, 1969, *126*, 57–64.
An examination of the effect of therapeutic intervention on one or another side in a marriage in which divorce is being considered. Being neutral is improbable, and the authors suggest involving the whole family.

WOLMAN, R. Women's issues in couples treatment—The view of the male therapist. *Psychiatric Opinion*, 1976, *13*, 13–19.
See reference in Section 4.1.

1.4 FAMILY THERAPY COMBINED WITH OTHER METHODS

ARBOGAST, R. The effect of famiy involvement on the day care center treatment of schizophrenia. *Journal of Nervous and Mental Diseases*, 1969, *149*, 277–280.
A pilot study to assess the relationship between the presence of a seriously disturbed parent or spouse in the home environment and the effectiveness of treatment in a day hospital setting of a consecutive series of schizophrenic patients. Eight of 17 patients were considered to be living with a psychotic or borderline family member. The group *without* seriously disturbed relatives in their environment improved significantly more in their treatment.

BARTON, W. E., & DAVIDSON, E. M. Psychotherapy and family care. In J. Masserman (Ed.), *Current psychiatric therapies* (Vol. I). New York: Grune & Stratton, 1961.
Family care is an alternative to the dilemma of returning patients to their families, where they are caught up in a pathological role or remaining in the artificial environment of a hospital with pressures toward regression. Group therapy with aftercare patients and similar techniques are said to be appropriate for family care patients with the new environment, providing a testing ground for patterns in living and an emotional climate for growth.

BASAMANIA, B. W. The emotional life of the family. Inferences for social casework. *American Journal of Orthopsychiatry*, 1961, *31*, 74–86.
A casework view of the Bowen research project in which families with a schizophrenic member were hospitalized. Observations of 11 families are categorized into (1) interrelated personality problems among family members, and (2) interaction problems among family members. Case examples are given. A discussion of family therapy procedures is presented with the emphasis upon relating to more than one individual at a time. Inferences for social casework emphasize the dimension of the emotional life of the family rather than the integration of sociological concepts with casework practice.

BEIT-HALLAHMI, B., & COLON, F. Involving family members in student counseling. *Psychotherapy: Theory, Research & Practice,* 1974, *11*, 265–269.
Two case examples are presented in support of the hypothesis that family therapy is useful in situations in which the identified patients are students at a university counseling center. The core dynamic issues focus around separation from parents. It is felt that the family therapy is a useful *adjunct* to the individual psychotherapy.

BELMONT, L. P., & JASNOW, A. The utilization of cotherapists and of group therapy techniques in a family oriented approach to a disturbed child. *International Journal of Group Psychotherapy*, 1961, *11*, 319–328.
A case history of the treatment of a 9-year-old disturbed boy and his parents. The boy was first placed in a boy's group and the parents were seen in several joint sessions and then placed in a man's group and a woman's group. Later they were seen together with the child and with the two therapists in joint sessions. The authors suggest that they offered the family a series of controlled therapeutic settings which approximated more and more closely the actual family setting.

BING, E. The conjoint family drawing. *Family Process*, 1970, *9*, 173–194.
Clinical material is presented to demonstrate the value of the conjoint family drawing technique as a diagnostic tool and therapeutic device. Fourteen randomly chosen families whose children were referred to a child psychiatry clinic were studied. They collaborated in an observed structured performance-task-oriented session. Six relevant dimensions were identified from the data.

BOWEN, M. A family concept of schizophrenia. In D. D. Jackson (Ed.), *The etiology of schizophrenia*. New York: Basic Books, 1960.
Clinical observations based upon a research study of the families of schizophrenics is presented, including a report on the project in which whole families of schizophrenics were hospitalized.

BOWEN, M. Family Psychotherapy. *American Journal of Orthopsychiatry*, 1961, *31*, 40–60.
See Reference in Section 1.1.

BOYD, J. H. The interaction of family therapy and psychodynamic individual therapy in an inpatient setting. *Psychiatry*, 1979, *42*, 99–111.
This paper reviews the literature on inpatient psychiatry with respect to the inclusion of family therapy. The literature seems to be divided into proponents for either individual psychodynamic therapy or family therapy as a *sole* modality of treatment. Based on his experience as a resident on a university teaching unit at a Veteran's hospital, the author believes the two can be used successfully together. Disagreements between the two approaches on a theoretical level are discussed and one case example is described.

BRODY, E. Modification of family interaction patterns by a group interview technique. *Journal of Group Psychotherapy,* 1956, *6*, 38–47.
As part of a study of prefrontal lobotomy, family members of 11 patients, who were to undergo this procedure, were seen for 5 months before the operation until at least 1 week after the operation. Frequency was from once weekly during the first few months to as infrequently as once a month during the last few months. Individual interviews with

family members were also used. The family interviews seemed to result in "an increased capacity for action by the family previously immobilized."

BRODY, E., & SPARK, G. Institutionalization of the aged: A family crisis. *Family Process*, 1966, 5, 76–90.
A discussion of the importance of involving the family in the decision about institutionalizing an aged person. Case examples are given.

BROWN, G., BIRLEY, J., & WING, J. Influence of family life on the course of schizophrenic disorders: A replication. *British Journal of Psychiatry*, 1972, 121, 241–258.
A clinical study investigating the hypothesis that "a high degree of expressed negative emotion" will cause relapses in schizophrenia independent of other factors. Results indicated that there was a significant association between critical comments, presence of hostility, and emotional overinvolvement and relapse. Treatment can consist of regular phenothiazine medication and avoidance of tooclose contact with a highly emotional relative.

BULBULYAN, A. Psychiatric nurse as family therapist. *Perspectives of Psychiatric Care*, 1969, 7, 58–68.
From a community mental health center, a psychiatric nurse, under the supervision of a psychiatrist, presents a case in which she used family therapy. Dynamics and treatment techniques, which are important for psychiatric nurses in such a setting are presented.

BURKS, H., & SERRANO, A. The use of family therapy and brief hospitalization. *Diseases of the Nervous System*, 1965, 26, 804–806.
Experience with setting up an in-patient service in conjunction with an out-patient child guidance clinic (which had a strong bias to family therapy) is described. Patients were between 12 and 16 years old and diagnosis varied from neurosis to psychosis. Hospitalization was short (usually under 2 months) and was family oriented, using techniques adapted from the multiple impact therapy technique. Results, including a 1-year follow-up of 25 patients are described.

BURNS, K., & FRIEDMAN, S. In support of families under stress: A community based approach. *Family Coordinator*, 1976, 26, 41–46.
Community support persons (CSP) (teachers, mental health workers, etc.) can change outcome for families in which the identified patient is a child with an emotional illness who is enrolled in a residential reeducation center. The CSP was matched with a family for a 4- to 5-hour period with the aim of "building trust and gaining insights into the strengths and stresses which face the family." No results are reported.

BURTON, G., & YOUNG, D. Family crisis in group therapy. *Family Process*, 1962, 1, 214–223.
A report of the experiences of two therapists doing "group counseling" of 12 couples, each of whom had an alcoholic husband. The paper is specifically concerned with the reporting of family crisis in the group. It is to the authors' impression that group members "use the crisis reports of each other in furthering an understanding of their own situations and in gaining courage to experiment in modifying their own behavior."

CHARNY, I. W. Integrated individual and family psychotherapy. *Family Process*, 1966, 5, 179–198.
An essay on using individual and family interviews concurrently and flexibly, since the strengths of both approaches can be utilized as the case requires. Case examples are given.

CHAZAN, R. A group family therapy approach to schizophrenia. *Israel Annals of Psychiatry and Related Disciplines*, 1974, 12, 177–193.
A clinical report of multiple family therapy on an inpatient unit. Sample was made up of acutely ill psychiatric patients with most diagnosed as schizophrenic, but some are manic-depressive, neurotic, and personality disordered. Method was multiple family therapy with 4 or 5 families. Techniques and problems are discussed; the group can "bring about a significant change of family dynamics and the long-term well-being of the identified patient."

COHEN, M., FREEDMAN, N., ENGELHARDT, D., & MARGOLIS, R. Family interaction patterns, drug treatment, and change in social aggression. *Archives of General Psychiatry*, 1968, 19, 50–56.
This study hypothesizes that family interaction patterns can be changed by the use of phenothiazine medication. The sample was 126 schizophrenic patients, 18 to 48 years of age, who were attending an outpatient clinic for at least 3 months. A randomized, double blind assignment to chlorpromazine, promazine, or a placebo was made and a social behavior interview was given at the end of 3 months, focusing on the measure of conflict and tension in the home. Results indicated that the most significant decrease in aggression occurred among the chlorpromazine-treated patients from low conflict and low tension homes. Regardless of treatment, there was no change in social aggression in patients from high conflict and tension homes. These results were interpreted as meaning that phenothiazines will significantly reduce patient's aggressive behavior when the behavior is *dissonant* with family interactional patterns.

COLEMAN, S. B., & DAVIS, D. I. Family therapy and drug abuse: A national survey. *Family Process*, 1978, 17, 21–29.
See reference in Section 3.1.

ÇOLON, F. Family ties and child placement. *Family Process*, 1978, *17*, 289–312.
One of a series from a symposium on "The family and child placement practices." It examines the effects of current child placement practices on the child's ties to his or her biological, foster, and adoptive families and explores alternative practices. These include joint custody of children, short-term foster care, long-term foster care, adoptive care with familial connection, etc.

COUNTS, R. M. Family therapy as a parameter of individual psychotherapy. *Contemporary Psychoanalyis*, 1973, *9*, 502–513.
This essay compares family therapy to individual therapy from the point of view that "family therapy can be used as a method of preparing some patients for individual therapy or psychoanalysis. Family therapy seems particularly indicated for "poorly individuated persons" defined as those (1) whose egos are poorly defined; (2) who are unduly dependent; (3) who can't cope with intimacy; (4) who are usually psychotic or have a character disorder; (5) who act out intensively in psychoanalysis or psychotherapy; and (6) who have the tendency for intrapsychic disruptive impact on the intrapsychic integration of another. A case is presented to illustrate some of the points made. Two short, critical discussions of the article are also presented.

DAILEY, W., & WELLISCH, D. Managing family convicts of halfway house residents. *Hospital and Community Psychiatry*, 1974, *25*, 583–584.
One case is presented to support the hypothesis that family therapy is a crucial part of the treatment for successful management and rehabilitation of chronic psychiatric patients living in halfway houses.

DAVENPORT, Y. B., EBERT, M. H., ADLAND, M. L., & GOODWIN, F. K. Couples group therapy as an adjunct to lithium maintenance of the manic patient. *American Journal of Orthopsychiatry*, 1977, *47*, 495–502.
In a follow-up study from an outpatient clinic, 12 patients previously hospitalized for mania and treated postdischarge with couples group therapy as well as lithium maintenance were compared to 11 on lithium alone on the measure of marital success at follow-up (2-10 years). The index group did significantly better on social functioning and family interaction. The authors conclude that differential effectiveness is not established because the groups differed significantly pretreatment in age, age of onset, and length of marriage, but they believe that couples group treatment is particularly useful for bipolar patients and may enhance the prophylactic effects of lithium.

DESPOTOVIC, A. Alkohalizam, narkomanije i porodica. (alcoholism, drug addictions and family.) *An. Zac. Ment. Zdr., Beograd*, 1974, *6*, (No. 2–3): 191–202. *Journal of the Studies of Alcoholism*, 1976, *37*, 1456–1457.
A clinical report from the Institute of Alcoholism in Belgrade. Treatment of alcoholism is based on a combination of individual psychotherapy and family psychotherapy plus group psychotherapy within a therapeutic community. The treatment objective is to change behavioral patterns; it is explicitly stated that personality change is not essential.

DREIKURS, R. Family group therapy in the Chicago community child guidance center. *Mental Hygiene*, 1951, *35*, 291–301.
From a child guidance center, 5 different types of group therapy are described. Included in this classification is family therapy. Family dynamics are discussed.

DWYER, J. H., MENK, M. C., & VAN HOUTEN, C. The caseworker's role in family therapy. *Family Process*, 1965, *4*, 21–31.
An approach to family therapy developed in a residential treatment center for children. The whole family is seen by a psychiatrist and then a caseworker sees the parents while the psychiatrist sees the child. The caseworker deals with the parents' responses to the family sessions.

EMDE, R., BOYD, C., & MAYO, G. The family treatment of folie à deux. *Psychiatric Quarterly*, 1968, *42*, 698–711.
A case report of a mother and daughter who shared delusions. Family dynamics that explain this phenomenon are presented. Treatment consisted of family therapy, milieu therapy, and phenothiazines.

EPSTEIN, N., & CLEGHORN, J. The family transactional approach in general hospital psychiatry: Experiences, problems, and principles. *Comprehensive Psychiatry*, 1966, 7, 389–396.
Concepts of family dynamics and family therapy are used in the psychiatry departments of the out-patient department, community department, in-patient service, and the day hospitals of two general hospital. Ongoing supervision in family and in individual therapy is stressed.

EWING, J. A., LONG, V., & WENZEL, G. G. Concurrent group psychotherapy of alcoholic patients and their wives. *International Journal of Group Psychotherapy*, 1961, *11*, 329–338.
A description of concurrent but separate group psychotherapy meetings of alcoholic outpatients and their wives. The authors find that more husbands continue to attend group meetings if the wife is involved, and there is greater improvement in alcoholic patients whose wives also attend group meetings. The participation of the wife in the husband's drinking is examined. An example is the wife who accidentally put a shot of whiskey into her husband's iced tea after he had stopped drinking. The authors highly recommend involving the wives of alcoholics in group therapy.

FINE, S. Family therapy and behavioral approach to childhood obsessive-compulsive neurosis. *Archives of General Psychiatry*, 1973, *28*, 695–697.
Two cases are presented in support of the notion that family therapy and behavioral therapy are helpful in the treatment of obsessive-compulsive neurosis.

FLECK, S. Psychotherapy of families of hospitalized patients. In J. Masserman (Ed.), *Current psychiatric therapies* (Vol. III). New York: Grune & Stratton, 1963.
An essay describing therapeutic principles and approaches to the families of hospitalized patients. A crisis somewhere in the family usually precipitates hospitalization, and attention to both patient and family as well as some relatively long-range decisions about service rendered to the family should be made early in the course of the patient's hospitalization. Flexibility in approach is stressed.

FLECK, S. Some general and specific indications for family therapy. *Confinia Psychiatrica*, 1965, *8*, 27–36.
See reference in Section 1.1.

FRAMO, J. L. The theory of the technique of family treatment of schizophrenia. *Family Process*, 1962, *1*, 119–131.
A rationale for and experiences with family therapy of schizophrenia is described based on work with hospitalized young adult female schizophrenics, all of whom were also receiving intensive individual and group psychotherapy. Techniques used by this group are described.

GOLDSTEIN, M. J., RODNICK, E. H., EVANS, J. R., et al. Drug and family therapy in the aftercare of acute schizophrenics. *Archives of General Psychiatry*, 1978, *35*, 1169–1177.
See reference in Section 2.0.

GRALNICK, A. Conjoint family therapy: Its role in rehabilitation of the inpatient and family. *Journal of Nervous and Mental Disease*, 1963, *136*, 500–506.
Family therapy for inpatients is recommended when a patient is not improving and the conflict appears related to the family, when the patient cannot communicate his thoughts and feelings to his family without help, when an unusually pathological relationship appears and feelings to family without help, when an unusually pathological relationship appears to exist with family members, and when rupture of a marital relationship seems imminent.

GREEN, R. Collaborative and conjoint therapy combined. *Family Process*, 1964, *3*, 80–89.
A discussion of conjoint and collaborative therapy with families with a recommendation for a combined approach where the family members are seen both individually and conjointly. A case illustration of a married couple is given.

GRUNEBAUM, H. U., & WEISS, J. L. Psychotic mothers and their children: Joint admission to an adult psychiatric hospital. *American Journal of Psychiatry*, 1963, *119*, 927–933.
A description of 12 infants and young children cared for by their mothers on the adult ward of the Massachusetts Mental Health Center. The mothers were hospitalized for severe emotional disorders, but were still able to care for their children. Such joint admissions are said to be practical in selected cases and can make a substantial contribution to the mother's recovery.

HANSEN, C. An extended home visit with conjoint family therapy. *Family Process*, 1968, *7*, 67–87.
An approach to family therapy which involved staying in the home with the family for a week to intervene therapeutically in a family's life. Benefits and problems of this approach are discussed.

HARBIN, H. Conjoint family therapy by the same therapist. *Diseases of the Nervous Systems*, 1975, *36*, 20–25.
Based on the author's clinical practice, 'his essay explores the techniques and problems that can arise when there is simultaneous individual psychotherapy id family therapy given by the same therapist. Confidentiality, transference, countertransference, and techniques of therapy are discussed.

HARBIN, H. T. Families and hospitals: Collusion or cooperation? *American Journal of Psychiatry*, 1978, *135*, 1496–1499.
A description of common problems in family treatment on a psychiatric inpatient unit of a large university teaching hospital. Families use a variety of mechanisms to attempt changing the ward staff's approach in order to avoid changing their family structure, which they resist as a necessary part of their sick member's treatment. Attempts to "split" or hamper the staff are usually made by "going to a higher authority," and, if successful, will undermine the patient's and family's treatment.

HARBIN, H. T. A family-oriented psychiatric inpatient unit. *Family Process*, 1979, *18*, 281–291.
This article describes the structure and operations of a psychiatric inpatient unit that was developed with the goal of integrating family-oriented treatment approaches into its therapeutic program. One initial effort is made by all the staff members to engage the family in the treatment program, including the negotiation of some agreement by the

family as to the problems necessitating hospitalization. If the family is resistant to engage themselves in the program, they are informed that their patient will have to leave the hospital.

JARVIS, P., ESTY, J., & STUTZMAN, L. Evaluation and treatment of families at the Fort Logan mental health center. *Community Menal Health Journal*, 1969, 5, 14–19.
A survey paper of trends in evaluation of treatment of patients from an in-patient facility of a psychiatric hospital. More evaluations are being carried out in the patient's home or in the community rather than in the hospital itself. There is greater involvement of "extended families" and of children (and involving them at an earlier age) in both evaluation and treatment. There is great use of multiple-family group therapy rather than conjoint family therapy. There is less formal training of family therapists than other forms of therap. There were no evaluative procedures of the variuos forms of family therapy being used.

KAFKA, J., & MCDONALD, J. The latent family in the intensive treatment of the hospitalized schizophrenic patient. In J. Masserman (Ed.), *Current psychiatric therapies* (Vol. V). New York: Grune & Stratton, 1965.
Describes the author's use of the family in an in-patient setting where the primary treatment method was individual psychotherapy. Differences of this approach compared to both family therapy alone or individual therapy alone are discussed.

KERN, J. Conjoint marital psychotherapy: An interim measure in the treatment of psychosis. *Psychiatry*, 1967, 30, 283–293.
A case report of use of family therapy in an in-patient setting where there was a stalement in individual treatment. In this case, a basically pathological relationship was re-established for use of family therapy as an alternative to no relationship which was leading to permanent hospitalization of the identified patient.

KLAPMAN, H., & RICE, D. An experience with combined milieu and family group therapy. *International Journal of Group Psychotherapy*, 1965, 15, 198–206.
A case report of a family in which the primary patient was a 13-year-old boy. The family was thought to be more difficult than usual. Treatment was milieu therapy plus a once-a-week meeting of the family and members of the treament team, including psychiatrist, social worker, teacher, occupational therapist, and two ward staff members.

KLEIN, H., & ERLICH, H. S. Some dynamic and transactional aspects of family therapy with psychotic patients. *Psychotherapy and Psychosomatics*, 1975, 26, 148–155.
A clinical essay stressing the importance of using the family model in treating psychotic patients. The authors suggest that cotherapists are more useful in families in which the identified patient is schizophrenic. (as contrasted with "more authoritarian, 'director' model of intervention")

KNOBLOCHOVA, J., & KNOBLOCH, F. Family therapy in Czechoslovakia: An aspect of group-centered psychotherapy. In N. W. Ackerman (Ed.), *Family therapy in transition*. Boston: Little, Brown, 1970.
Family therapy in the stricter sense is said to be relatively rare in Prague, but some form of family psychotherapy in a broad sense is an indispensible part of every case. A case illustrates the approach.

KOHLMEYER, W. A., & FERNANDES, X. Psychiatry in India: Family approach in the treatment of mental disorders. *American Journal of Psychiatry*, 1963, 119, 1033–1037.
This discussion of the family unit in India precedes a report of the new policy of the mental health centre of the Christian Medical College in which one or two members of the family must stay with the patient throughout his treatment as an inpatient. Thus a relatively small psychiatrically trained staff can handle a large number of patients, even if acutely disturbed.

KOSSORIS, P. Family therapy: An adjunct to hemodialysis and transplantation. *American Journal Nursing*, 1970, 70, 1730–1733.
A clinical paper pointing out that the stresses associated with renal dialysis and transplantation create symptoms in *not only* the patient, but the family. Family therapy has been useful in the treatment of such symptoms.

KUGEL, L. Combining individual and conjoint sessions in marital therapy. *Hospital and Community Psychiatry*, 1974, 25l, 795–798.
One case is presented in support of the hypothesis that marital problems are best treated with a combination of both individual and family therapy, 3 sessions a week, over a limited period of time. Advantages over a traditional one-to-one approach in a rural setting are described.

LANDES, J., & WINTER, W. A new strategy for treating disintegrating families. *Family Process*, 1966, 5, 1–20.
A communal therapy procedure in which patient families and the families of therapists participated in a 48-hour weekend together. The experience, problems, and results of such a weekend are described.

LANGDELL, J. Family treatment of childhood schizophrenia. *Mental Hygiene*, 1967, *51*, 387–392.
Case report of treatment of a child with childhood schizophrenia using both individual and family therapy. Improvement in the child followed improvement in parental intrapersonal and interpersonal conflicts.

LAQUEUR, H. P., & LABURT, H. A. Family organization on a modern state hospital ward. *Mental Hygiene*, 1964, *48*, 544–551.
A description of the participation of an auxilliary composed of families of hsopitalized patients. The families raise funds, participate in the ward activities, and are involved in group therapy as family groups. The goal is "to integrate the family into the patient's treatment plan."

LAQUER, H. P., LABURT, H. A., & MORONG, E. Multiple family therapy. In J. Masserman (Ed.), *Current psychiatric therapies* (Vol. IV). New York: Grune & Stratton, 1964.
A description of the treatment of families in group sessions in which a therapist sees several families at once. The context of the treatment is a therapeutic community ward in a state hospital. The procedure, its rationale, and impressions of results are given for a sample of 80 families treated with this method.

LAQUER, H. P., WELLS, C., & AGRESTI, M. Multiple family therapy in a state hospital. *Hospital and Community Psychiatry*, 1969, *20*, 13–20.
A report of "multiple-family therapy" in a state hospital setting. Sessions were held for 75 minutes once a week, with one therapist, throughout hospitalization and sometimes during aftercare. Sample consisted primarily of young schizophrenics. Rationale, dynamics, techniques, practical matters, and advantages and disadvantages over conjoint family therapy are discussed.

LEICHTER, E., & SHULMAN, G. The family interview as an integrative device in group therapy with families. *International Journal of Group Psychotherapy*, 1963, *13*, 335–345.
A report of the author's experiences in using the family interview (i.e., a meeting with the identified patient's family) as an adjunctive treatment process to group therapy. The family interviews are used in a variety of ways, e.g., diagnosis at the onset of group treatment, integrating changes achieved in total family functioning, and at the conclusion of the group therapy.

LIDZ, T. The influence of family studies on the treatment of schizophrenia. *Psychiatry*, 1969, *32*, 237–251.
See Reference in Section 5.2

LINDBERG, D. R., & WOSMEK, A. W. The use of family sessions in foster home care. *Social Casework*, 1963, *44*, 137–141.
A discussion of the use of family sessions with a foster child and his new foster family. The therapeutic purpose is to help the family accept the child's needs, to help the child deal with the problem of attachment to his or her own family and the foster family, and to clarify misunderstandings which might arise with the caseworker.

LLOYD, R. A., & PAULSON, E. Projective identification in the marital relationship as a resistance to psychotherapy. *Archives of General Psychiatry*, 1972, *27*, 410–413.
See reference in Section 1.3.

MIDELFORT, C. F. Use of members of the family in treatment of schizophrenia. *Family Process*, 1962, *1*, 114–118.
A report of the author's experiences using family members as companions and attendants for schizophrenic patients hospitalized in a general hospital and treated with family therapy as well as with other somatic and pharmacologic agents.

MINARD, S. Family systems model on organizational consultation: Vignettes of consultation to a day care center. *Family Process*, 1976, *15*, 313–320.
The author describes the effects of a "dysfunctional system" on the behavior of staff and children in a day care center and suggests that an organizational approach to behavioral problems based on Bowen's family systems theory allows for more effective and efficient intervention than does an individual approach.

MOSS, S. Z., & MOSS, M. S. Mental illness, partial hospitalization, and the family. *Clinical Social Work*, 1973, *1*, 168–176.
This clinical paper describes the role of the family in the treatment of chronic emotional illness when the setting is a day hospital, part of a community mental health center in a "low socioeconomic neighborhood." Weekly sessions with the entire family were rarely held because only a small number of families were able to attend, but a variety of other ways in which the family was directly and indirectly involved are described—for example, a weekly discussion group in which patients individually discuss their own families. Role of the family in terms of long-term prevention of chronic illness patterns is discussed.

NAKHLA, F., FOLKART, L., & WEBSTER, J. Treatment of families as in-patients. *Family Process*, 1969, *8*, 79–96.

A report on work at the Cassel Hospital in England where 35 families were hospitalized for an average period of 8 months on the average. The treatment was intensive, analytically oriented psychotherapy against the background of a therapeutic community. Rationale, problems, advantages, and case illustrations are given.

NOONE, R. S., & REDDIG, R. L. Case studies in the family treatment of drug abuse. *Family Process*, 1976, *15*, 325–332.
Using case studies to illustrate, the problem of drug abuse is explained as an indication of developmental difficulties in the family rather than as social deviance. Treatment focus should be on facilitating movement through unresolved family crises so that individual and family energy can be redirected toward growth and personal development rather than on maintenance of rigid interactional patterns, which may interfere with the possibility of change.

RABINER, E. L., MOLINSKI, H., & GRALNICK, A. Conjoint family therapy in the inpatient setting. *American Journal of Psychotherapy*, 1962, *16*, 618–631.
A general discussion of the adaptation of family therapy to the in-patient setting with its advantages and difficulties illustrated with cases.

SCHWEEN, P., & GRALNICK, A. Factors affecting family therapy in the hospital setting. *Comprehensive Psychiatry*, 1966, 7, 424–431.
Dicusses the modifications necessary when doing family therapy in a hospital setting. Transference and counter-transference problems, administrative problems, and the role of the other patients in treatment are mentioned.

SEARLES, H. F. The contributions of family treatment to the psychotherapy of schizophrenia. In I. Boszormenyi-Nagy & J. L. Framo (Eds.), *Intensive family therapy*. New York: Harper & Row, 1965.
A discussion of the importance of the family in the treatment of schizophrenia with the emphasis upon processes which are predominantly intrapsychic differentiated from processes which are predominantly interpersonal.

SHAPIRO, E. R., SHAPIRO, R. L., ZINNER, J., & BERKOWITZ, D. A. The borderline ego and the working alliance: Indications for family and individual treatment in adolescence. *International Journal of Psychoanalysis*, 1977, *58*, 77–87.
An explanation of the author's observation that in the treatment of the borderline adolescent the working alliance is often facilitated by concurrent family therapy (with the same therapist). The developmental model of the borderline character (i.e., a failure of separation–individuation leading to pathological use of splitting and projection) suggests a poor prognosis with classical psychoanalytic psychotherapy, because the necessary working alliance is not formed and uncontrolled regressions or transference psychoses can occur. The use of family therapy to facilitate alliance formation is advocated instead of other methods (e.g., "manipulations" or "limit-setting"). Clinical observations from 1 case are used to support these conclusions and 36 references are included.

SMITH, I. W., & LOEB, D. The stable extended family as a model in treatment of atypical children. *Social Work*, 1965, *10*, 75–81.
A report of a multiple-impact therapeutic program in the treatment of 6 severely disturbed children and their families. Three boys and 3 girls, aged 4 through 7 were referred as mentally retarded, were intolerable in school, and appeared psychotic in the first interview. Two female therapists, assuming grandmotherly roles, treated the families conjointly in 3 overlapping phases: (1) individual treatment for the patient and parents, (2) family group therpay, and (3) peer experiences for all family members. Patients showed rapid symptomatic recovery, enabling them to return to school and participate in social situations. Parents and siblings, relieved of anxiety, functioned more efficiently and experienced improved interpersonal relationships.

SZALITA, A. The combined use of family interviews and individual therapy in schizophrenia. *American Journal of Psychotherapy*, 1968, *22*, 419–430.
A discussion of the use of the family interviews when doing individual therapy with schizophrenics. Information is provided for both therapists and patient.

TAUBER, G. Prevention of posthospital relapse through treatment of relatives. *Journal of Hillside Hospital*, 1964, *13*, 158–169.
Observations of a caseworker working with families of psychiatric patients discharged from a voluntary psychiatric hospital. The hypothesis presented is that intensive casework service with the family as well as the patient is necessary to prevent posthospital relapse. Problems of working with these families as well as technigues of treatment are described.

VAUGHN, C. E., & LEFF, J. P. The influence of family and social factors on the course of psychiatric illness. *British Journal of Psychiatry*, 1976, *129*, 125–137.
An extension of the Brown, et al., 1972 project concerning the influence of family life on the course of schizophrenia. That study suggested that the index, "emotion expressed" by key relatives about the patient at the time of admission, proved to be the best single predictor of symptomatic relapse in the 9 months after discharge from the hospital. The

present study attempted to replicate this study using a sample of patients with schizophrenia and with depressive neurosis. Methodology was the same as the earlier study. Results confirmed those of earlier study in that the expressed emotion of the relative again seemed to be associated with relapse independent of all other social and clinical facts investigated. Treatment implications suggested that patients from "high expressed emotion" homes, identified a being high risk, should be maintained on drugs, and should see the relatives as little as possible.

VIKERSUND, G. Family treatment in psychiatric hospitals. *Psychotherapy and Psychosomatics*, 1968, *25*, 333–338.
A report of the author's experience in setting up a family treatment center in which an entire family is admitted into a hospital for family therapy. Inpatient treatment of the entire family is indicated only where outpatient treatment is not feasible. The report focuses on *indications* for this form of treatment: (1) in hysterical young married women who develop severe anxiety neurosis after the first or second child; (2) on depressive reactions due to unsuccessful marriages where the partner is mentally ill; (3) in young patients in conflict with their parents; (4) in alcoholic patients; (5) in sexual deviates; (6) and in neurotic marriages. No results are reported.

WEISFELD, D., & LASER, M. S. Divorced parents in family therapy in a residential treatment setting. *Family Process*, 1977, *16*, 229–236.
This paper describes the experience of involving divorced parents in the family therapy of their child in a residential treatment center. Case material illustrates sources of resistance and various techniques. This approach decreased recidivism and contributed to improvement in the children's functioning in school, home, and community activities.

ZIEBER, E., STERNBERG, D., FINN, R., & FARMER, M. Family creative analysis I: Its role in treatment. *Bulletin of Art Therapy*, 1966, 5, 47–65.
A report on the use of creative analysis (which is a technique by which paintings are used to understand the functioning of the ego) and its application to family treatment. The family agrees on a project and then a sketch is made by one or more members of the family. It is then divided into as many sections as there are participants. From an understanding of the drawing, the therapist then interprets the family and their conflicts. Observations are shared with the treatment team of the inpatient unit in which the identified patients are staying and also with the members of the family. Short- and long-range goals of family treatment are formulated and worked out in at least 15 projects.

ZWERLING, I., & MENDELSOHN, M. Initial family reactions to day hospitalization. *Family Process*, 1965, *4*, 50–63.
A report of a study on the relationship between the course of hospital treatment and certain family responses at the time ofadmission of a psychotic member. The sample consists of 100 patients consecutively admitted to a day hospital. It includes responses to admission, to family treatment, and to improvement.

1.5 FAMILY THERAPY TRAINING

APPEL, K. E., GOODWIN, H. M., WOOD, H. P., & ASKREN, E. Training in psychotherapy: The use of marriage counseling in a university teaching clinic. *American Journal of Psychiatry*, 1961,*117*, 709–711.
In the department of psychiatry at the University of Pennsylvania School of Medicine, residents may participate in a teaching program which includes treatment of married couples. Marriage counseling is discussed and a case example of the type given to psychiatric residents.

BARD, M., & BERKOWITZ, B. A community psychology consultation program in police family crisis intervention: Preliminary impressions. *International Journal of Psychiatry*, 1969, *15*, 209–215.
See Reference in Section 4.4

BEAL, E. W. Current trends in the training of family therapists. *American Journal of Psychiatry*, 1976, *133*, 137–141.
Fifteen training programs for family therapists are described and compared based upon a scale published by the Group for the Advancement of Psychiatry, which identifies the theoretical spectrum of each of the centers. Results indicate that the centers vary from experiential to structural (with a few in the middle that combine both orientations). It was concluded that training programs suffer from the absence of an adequate diagnostic nomenclature for family therapy and from an insufficiently designed conceptual framework.

BEATMAN, F. The training and preparation of workers for family–group treatment. *Social Casework*, 1964, *45*, 202–208.
An essay describing the method of training for social workers learning family therapy. Group processes as a method for supervision are used in preference to individual supervision because of "the requirements of treating the family rather than the individual." Specific methods used and discussed here are group supervision, sitting in on a family session, viewing through a one way screen, films and tape recordings.

BEELS, C. C., & FERBER, F. Family therapy: A view. *Family Process*, 1969, *8*, 280–318.
See Reference in Section 1.1

BERG, B. Learning family therapy through simulation. *Psychotherapy: Theory, Research & Practice*, 1978, *15*, 56–60.
A method using simulated families in training family therapists is described. Four students role play a dysfunctional family and other students role play co-therapists and consultants. The method appears to hold promise for training students *before* working with actual families.

BODIN, A. Family therapy training literature: A brief guide. *Family Process*, 1969, *8*, 727–729.
The literature on training in family therapy is described and a bibliography of 32 articles listed.

BODIN, A. M. A review of family therapy, training, and study in the San Francisco Bay area. *Family Process*, 1971, *10*, 111–121.
See reference in Section 6.0.

BODIN, A. Videotape applications in training family therapists. *Journal of Nervous and Mental Disease*, 1969, *148*, 251–262.
Uses a videotape in both training and treatment are described. Training applications include: (1) taping prior to particular courses, (2) tape libraries, (3) splitting audio and visual channels, (4) "on line" feedback, (5) self-presentation exercises, and (6) comparative analyis of a trainee's performance. Several different applications in regard to therapy are also presented. Trainees themselves may be exposed to a wide variety of ways of using videotapes.

BRYANT, C. M., & GRUNEBAUM, H. U. The theory and practice of the family diagnostic . I: Practical aspects and patient evaluation. II: Theoretical aspects and resident education. In I. M. Cohen (Ed.), *Psychiatric research report No. 20*. Washington, D.C. American Psychiatric Association, 1966.
A presentation of a family diagnostic procedure at the Massachusetts Mental Health Center, which includes a description of methodology and theoretical considerations as well as resident teaching. Family members are interveiwed individually and together on the subject of what brings the patient to the hospital. The training of the psychiatric resident is said to be broadened by participation.

BULBULYAN, A. Psychiatric nurse as family therapist. *Perspectives in Psychiatric Care*, 1969, 7, 58–68.
From a community mental health center, a psychiatric nurse presents a case in which she used family therapy. Dynamics and treatment techniques are presented. It is felt that this is an improtant technique for psychiatric nurses to use in such a setting.

BURDILL, D. R. The simulated family as an aid to learning family group treatment. *Child Welfare*, 1976, *55*, 703–709.
In this technique for teaching family therapy, the students take the roles of the family members. Procedures, selection of players, formulating the problem, the value of the experience, and ground rules are described.

CLEGHORN, J. M., & LEVIN, S. Training family therapists by setting learning obejctives. *American Journal of Orthopsychiatry*, 1973, *43*, 439–446.
Specific learning objectives at several stages of family training are discussed. A detailed list of perceptual, conceptual, and executive skills to be set as objectives is given for both basic and advanced levels of learning.

COLMAN, A. The effect of group and family emphasis on the role of the pyschiatric resident of an acute treatment ward. *International Journal of Group Psychotherapy*, 1965, *15*, 516–525.
A report of a psychiatric resident on his experiences and impressions on a ward, which stressed group and family dynamics rather than individual approaches. The ward is described, and the resident's self-image is discussed and compared with the staff and patient expectations of the resident.

CONSTANTINE, L. L. Designed experience: A multiple, goal-directed training program in family therapy. *Family Process*, 1976, *15*, 373–387.
This paper describes the experiential and theoretical features of a goal-directed family therapy training program that focuses on nonpathological family processes. Utilizing an integrated learning model, it is structured in terms of definite training goals and provides a unifying theroetical framework. The basic elements and structure of the program are discussed in detail as well as the problems and potential of the course.

EHRLICH, F. M. Family therapy and training in child psychiatry, *Archives of General Psychiatry*, 1973, *12*, 461–472.
An essay describing the integration of a family therapy training program with a traditional training program for child psychiatrists that stressed psychoanalytic psychotherapy. Family therapy training was introduced because of failures in individual treatment, presence of multiple family problems, and families that were unable to "tolerate" prolonged evaluation and then individual treatment. The training programs is described. It is suggested that family therapy is useful "especially with the disorganized, impoverished segment of our clinic population . . . . Teaching of the family therapy model does not interfere with learning of a psychoanalytic model."

ERICKSON, G. Teaching family therapy. *Journal of Education and Social Work*, 1973, *9*, 9–15.
This is an essay on teaching family therapy to social workers. Comparisons between individual therapy and family therapy are made, as well as the problems of teaching family therapy to students who have been trained using an individual orientation. Core concepts of family dynamics and treatment are stressed, and problems in implementing these concept are discussed.

FERBER, A., & MENDELSOHN, M. Training for family therapy. *Family Process, 1969, 8*, 25–34.
A description of the program of training in family therapy at the Albert Einstein College of Medicine in New York. The different levels of the program, the assumptions on which it is based, and the content is discussed.

FLINT, A. A., & RIOCH, M. J. An experiment in teaching family dynamics. *American Journal of Psychiatry*, 1963, *119*, 940–944.
A discussion of a course in family dynamics for a group of women with no prior formal experience or training in the mental health field. The course included tape recordings of family therapy, literature review, observation of family screening interviews, observation of collateral group therapy, and structural interviews of parents. The students were able to benefit without having too heavy a therapeutic responsibility in this difficult field. The program is recommended for training other psychotherapists.

FLOMENHAFT, K., & CARTER, R. E. Family therapy Training: Program and outcome. *Family Process,* 1977, *16*, 211–218.
A report on the content and results of a 4-year-old family therapy training program organized by the Pennsylvania Commonwealth Office of Mental Health for staff of mental health agencies. Three hundred practitioners have been trained in family therapy, and 64 local family therapy trainers have been developed. Local trainers offered programs to an additional 200 mental health professionals and human services workers.

FLOMENHAFT, K., & CARTER, R. E. Family therapy training: A statewide program for mental health centers. *Hospital and Community Psychiatry*, 1974, *25*, 789–791.
This essay describes a training program stressing the "family approach" for staff members of community mental health centers. Orientation consists of lectures, readings, videotapes, and demonstrations. Each participant is supervised with at least two families, using two kinds of supervision—on-the-spot supervision with a one-way mirror and video recordings of the session. Evaluation of the training program with a sample of 53 of 67 participants indicated that he trainees liked the program, liked the teachers, did more family therapy, and got a new way of looking at psychiatric problems.

GARRIGAN, J. J., & BAMBRICK,, A. F. Introducing novice therapists to "go-between" techniques of family therapy. *Family Process*, 1977, *16*, 237–246.
This paper describes the competencies, objectives, and criteria for evaluation used during a time-limilted (150 hours) training program with the "go-between" model for novice therapists. Novice therapists solely trained in "go-between" did significantly well with families having a child attending classes at Centennial School of Lehigh University. The childrens' behavior improved both in the classroom and at home. The parents were able to establish communication in more meaningful ways.

GERSHENSON, J., & COHEN, M. S. Through the looking glass: The experiences of two family therapy trainees with live supervision. *Family Process*, 1978, *17*, 225–230.
This paper examines live supervision of family therapy from the viewpoint of the trainee. Live supervision is an importnat technique with intense emotinoal responsiveness in the trainees, especially at times when the trainee is experiencing confusion during the family session.

HALL, R. L. A paraprofessional's view of supervision. *Family Process*, 1972, *11*, 163–169.
The experience of a black paraprofessional community worker is presented with special emphasis on the problems of shifting to a family-oriented view in her work. Problems associated with the supervisory reationship are discussed.

KEMPSTER, S. W., & SAVITSKY, E. Training family therapists through live supervision. In N. W. Ackerman (Ed.), *Expanding theory and practice in family therapy*. New York, Family Service Association of America, 1967.
Family therapy and the process of and techniques of live supervision should be introduced early in the course of training therapists. Staff and family reaction was "generally favorable, with adverse reactions rare."

KRAFT, I. A. Multiple impact therapy as a teaching device. In I. M. Cohen (Ed.), *Psychiatric research report No. 20*. Washington, D.C: American Psychiatric Association, 1966.
A discussion of the value of multiple impact therapy in the training of psychiatric residents with the emphasis upon work experience with other professionals as well as family understanding.

MALONE, C. A. Observations of the role of family therapy in child psychiatry training. *Journal of the American Academy of Child Psychiatry*, 1974, *13*, 437–458.

A clinical essay discussing the polarization between individually oriented therapists in diagnosis and treatment of children. A description is given of the way in which family therapy is believed to be useful in its generated clinical orientation, in treating particular problems, in diagnosis, and in consultation. Problems in family therapy training are discussed.

McDERMOTT, J. F., JR., & CHAR, W. F. The undeclared war between child and family therapy. *Journal of the American Academy of Child Psychiatry*, 1974, *13*, 422–436.
A clinical essay describing the different viewpoints, history, and myths of family therapy versus individual psychoanalytic orientation in regard to diagnosis and treatment of childhood disorders. The authors believe that there is an overemphasis on the family as the cause of all symptoms in the child, that there is more to treatment of the child than improved communication in the family, and that therapists in a community mental health center need to have more, rather than less, training to be competent. It is concluded that child psychiatry needs therapists with training in both theories.

MERENESS, D. Family therapy: An evolving role. *Perspectives of Psychiatric Care*, 1968, *6*, 256–259.
This essay discusses the role of the psychiatric nurse in family therapy. Rationale and indications for family therapy are discussed. Nurses are seen as "uniquely well equipped to accept the role of family therapist." Training for nurses should include functioning as a co-therapist, being taught the body of knowledge concerning family dynamics, and learning treatment techniques. Moving outside the "traditional role of the psychiatric nurse" is suggested.

MEYERSTEIN, I, Family therapy training for paraprofessinoals in a community mental health center. *Family Process*, 1977, *16*, 477–493.
This article describes an "ecologically oriented" training program for paraprofessionals who work with high-risk clients in a community mental health center. Formats, such as group supervision, peer supervision, and live supervision are described. Recommendations are made for teaching paraprofessionals working in these centers.

MIYOSHI, N., & LIEBMAN, R. Training psychiatric residents in family therapy. *Family Process*, 1969, *3*, 97–105.
A report on training psychiatric residents in family therapy at Mercy-Douglas Hospital in Philadelphia. Problems and benefits are discussed.

MONTALVO, B. Aspects of live supervision. *Family Process*, 1973, *12*, 343–359.
This article describes the process of "live" supervision. The supervisor watches the session usually behind a one-way mirror and interrupts to supervise directly. An agreement and discussion before and after the session provides the ground rules to assure that the therapist will not be inhibited in the spontaneity of therapy. Some of the advantages include the avoidance of gaps in the therapist's self-reports to the supervisor.

NADELSON, C. C., BASSUK, E. L., HOPPS, C. R., & BOUTELLE, W. E. The use of videotapes in couples therapy. *International Journal of Group Psychotherapy*, 1977, *27*, 241–253.
See reference in Section 1.3.

NAPIER, A. The consultation-demonstration interview. *Family Process*, 1976, *15*, 419–426.
The author explores the difficulties encountered by a consultant involved in family therapy demonstrations and workshops. Organization and planning are key issues if the endeavor is to be meaningful to both family and professionals. Using examples from his personal experience, the author makes specific recommendations for maximizing the benefits of the process. The key factor in a successful interview is the determination of the therapist to provide the family with a therapeutically meaningful experience.

OLSON, U., & PEGG, P. F. Direct open supervision: A team approach. *Family Process*, 1979, *18*, 463–469.
This article reviews the procedure, advantages, and disadvantages for training of direct open supervision in which the supervisor is present in the room with the trainee and the family and makes immediate and direct interventions, which are communicated explicitly during the course of the session. This method combines elements of live supervision with team participation.

PERLMUTTER, M., LOEB, D., GUMPERT, G., O'HARA, F., & HIGBIE, I. Family diagnosis and therapy using videotape playback. *American Journal of Orthopsychiatry*, 1967, *37*, 900–905.
A paper describing the uses of videotapes in teaching, research on family dynamics, and treatment. Videotape was found useful in diagnosis, in getting family consensus on "what hapened," and in therapist supervision.

PINSOF, W. M. The family therapist behavior scale (FTBS): Development and evaluation of a coding system. *Family Process*, 1979, *18*, 451–461.
The family therapist behavior scale (FTBS) was designed to identify and study clinically relevant, verbal behaviors of short-term, problem-oriented family therapists. Validity was assessed by testing the scale's ability to discriminate significant, predicted differences between the in therapy behaviors of 8 novice family therapists conducting observed interviews and 8 advanced family therapists conducting supervisory interviews. Two coders rated 3 5-minute samples

from each of the 16 videotapes with the FTBS. The validity results supported over 50 percent of the 16 research hypotheses. The implications of these findings are examined.

RAASOCH, J., & LAQUER, H. P. Learning multiple family therapy through simulated workshops. *Family Process*, 1979, *18*, 95–98.
See reference in Section 1.2.

ROESKE, N. The junior medical student as diagnostician of the family of an emotionally disturbed child. *Journal of Medical Education*, 1972, *47*, 51–56.
As part of a course on clinical psychiatry given to junior medical students, each student was given the responsibility of working up the family of a child with "emotional pathology." Part of the goals of the course included "appreciation of the family ability to integrate its emotional and social units with individual patterns of behavior." The evaluation began with a 15-minute review of the referral information followed by a meeting of the student and family while the supervisor observed through a one-way mirror. Audiovisual tapes were sometimes made and reviewed later. A team conference followed in which students "formulated hypotheses regarding each family." Students then worked with the family for a number of weeks and discussed recommendations for treatment. Evaluation of the program revealed there was no difference between medical student teams and nonmedical student teams regarding the family's accpetance or rejection of treatment recommendations.

RUBINSTEIN, D. Family therapy. *International Psychiatric Clinics*, 1964, *1*, 431–442.
Ratinoale and techniques of teaching family therapy are discussed, and it is stressed that this form of family therapy can be taught to trainees in the same way that other techniques of psychotherapy are taught. Trainees usually sit in with an experienced staff member as a cotherapist to start.

SANDER, F. M., & BEELS, C. C. A didactic course for family therapy trainees. *Family Process*, 1970, *9*, 411–423.
A description of a family therapy training progrm given at a medical college to experienced practitioners. The thrust was to conduct a *didactic* course on theory and practice that was less clinically oriented than most. The course bibliography is included.

SATIR, V. M. The quest for survival: A training program for family diagnosis and treatment. *Acta Psychotherapy*, *1963, 11*, 33–38.
A review of the training program for family therapists at the mental research institute given to "psychiatrists, psychologists, and social workers who work in a variety of settings: state hospitals, outpatient clinics, probation departments, and family service agencies." Setting, goals, and procedures of the training are described.

SCHOPLER, E., FOX, R., & COCHRANE, C. Teaching family dynamics to medical students. *American Journal of Orthopsychiatry*, 1967, *37*, 906–911.
In an attempt to orient fourth-year medical students to child psychiatry, each group of 6 to 8 students was assigned to one family for study during their psychiatry rotation. One student was assigned to each family member in addition, and observations of family interaction were made a routine part of the diagnostic procedure. A family interaction situation was set up using the method of Drechsler and Shapiro. Ten families were rated by the students watching through a one-way mirror. This seemed to be a useful way of observing family interaction and of teaching family dynamics to students.

SCHULMAN, G. L. Teaching family therapy to social work students. *Social Casework*, 1976, *57*, 448–457.
A report from a family therapy training program for social work students describing an approach in which cognitive and experiential processes are interwoven. Students see videotapes and live interviews. Experiential processes include role playing, sculpting the past or present, and other nonverbal techniques. Phases that the class moves through in learning are described.

SHAPIRO, R. J. Problems in teaching family therapy. *Professional Psychology*, 1975, *6*, 41–44.
A report of a 5-year family therapy teaching program involving graduate students, postdoctoral fellows in clinical psychology, and psychiatric residents. Greatest difficulty was the shift in orientation from individual to family. Methods of teaching included case material, reading, and videotape.

SHAPIRO, R. J. Some implications of training psychiatric nurses in family therapy. *Journal of Marriage and Family Counseling*, 1975, *1*, 323–330.
The problems of implementing utilization of psychiatric nurses as family therapists in a clinical psychiatric setting are discussed. In order for the nurses to actually do the therapy, the larger institutional system had to be modified. Ways to bring about change are discussed.

SHERMAN, S. Aspects of family interviewing critical for staff training and education. *Social Service Review*, 1966, *40*, 302–308.
An essay focusing on training of social workers stressing that conjoint family therapy interviews, rather than

individual interviews, are helpful in understanding family dynamics, as well as in treating the case. The caseworker can be prepared for the group supervision, use of film or videotapes, direct observation, and participation as cotherapists.

SLUZKI, C. E. On training to "think interactionally." *Social Science and Medicine*, 1974, *8*, 483–485.
An essay defining characteristics and strategies useful for teching trainees in a family medicine training program how to think interactionally. Strategies used include: 1) stating the program's ideology clearly; 2) keeping the terminology clear and avoiding labels, e.g., "psychiatric," "behavioral," etc.; and 3) teaching and keeping the institution's focus on "family process, community process, systems theory, group dynamics, and human ecology." Problems of learning such an approach are analyzed and solutions suggested.

STAMBLER, M., & PEARLMAN, C. Supervision as revelation of the pattern: I Ching comments on "The Open Door." *Family Process*, 1974, *13*, 371–384.
This short paper and attached commentaries by Ravich and Levenson raise some interesting theoretical and practical issues in the use of I Ching (or the Book of Changes) for the purpose of supervision. The major focus of the article is the discussion of the parallels between the structural family paradigm and results from consulting I Ching. A clinical example is included.

STANTON, M. D. Family therapy training: Academic and internship opportunities for psychologists. *Family Process*, 1975, *14*, 433–439.
Institutions that train psychologists in psychotherapy skills have generally neglected the family approach. Information is provided on university departments of psychology internship facilities that include family therapy training in their programs.

STANTON, M. D. Psychology and family therapy. *Professional Psychology*, 1975, *6*, 45–49.
A review of the relationship of clinical psychologists to the field of family therapy. There is a relative lack of interest by psychologists. A family approach is particularly well suited to behavioral techniques and the psychologist's reserach skills. Therefore, an increase in training and interest in family therapy is recommended to psychologists.

TOMM, K. M., & WRIGHT, L. M. Training in family therapy: Perceptual, conceptual and executive skills. *Family Process*, 1979, *18*, 227–250.
An outline of skills required for trainees in family therapy based on an integrated treatment model within a systems framework. Four major functions performed by a family therapist are categorized (engagement, problem identification, change facilitation, and termination) and further differentiated into general therapeutic competencies. Specific perceptual, conceptual, and executive skills are included in the form of instructional objectives and are listed under each competency.

UMBARGER, C. The paraprofessional and family therapy. *Family Process*, 1972, *111*, 147–162.
This paper defines the functions and identify of the paraprofessional family therapist, a new career development for the undereducated adult and an outgrowth of the community mental health field. Some of the problems involved in this role are outlined. The need for a concept of service that can combine management of reality with beneficial restructuring of psychological systems is pointed out.   nother issue is that the clinical functions taught in training need to be related to the problems of the urban poor to enable the paraprofessional with a role fitted to their new career.

VANDERVOORT, H. E., & RANSOM, D. C. Undergraduate education in family medicine. *Journal of Medical Education*, 1973, *48*, 158–165.
A clinical essay emphasizing the point that training in family medicine has been based almost exclusively on utilizing the model of "individual distress theories." An approach based on "the family approach" would seem more logical for family medicine. Problems in implementing such an approach and a model training program are described.

WEINGARTEN, K. Family awareness for nonclinicians: Participation in a simulated family as a teaching technique. *Family Process*, 1979, *18*, 143–150.
A course in family theory adapted to "well" families that combines didactic and experiential teaching techniques. Students participate in a simulated family for 12 weeks. This ourse allows family therapists to teach family dynamic processes to the lay public and the "well" person.

1.6   FAMILY CONSIDERATION IN INDIVIDUAL DIAGNOSIS

ACKERMAN, N. W. A dynamic frame for the clinical approach to family conflict. In N. W. Ackerman, F. L. Beatman, & S. Sherman (Eds.), *Exploring the base for family therapy*. New York: Family Service Association of America, 1961.
A diagnostic scheme, as well as therapeutic principles, in dealing with a disturbed family is described. The diagnostic task is to establish the specific dynamic relationship between the family members. Strengths as well as weaknesses should be carefully delineated.

ACKERMAN, N. W. Prejudice and scapegoating in the family. In G. H. Zuk & I. Boszormenyi-Nagy (Eds.), *Family therapy and disturbed families.* Palo Alto: Science & Behavior Books, 1967.
A description of families in terms of the victim who is scapegoated, the destroyer or persecutor who is specially prejudiced against the victim, and the family healer who neutralizes the destructive powers of the attack.

ACKERMAN, N., & BEHRENS, M. The family group and family therapy: The practical application of family diagnosis. In J. Masserman & J. Mareno (Eds.), *Progress in psychotherapy (Vol. III). Techniques of psychotherapy.* New York: Grune & Stratton, 1958.
A clinical essay pointing out limitations of individual psychotherapy in dealing with emotional illness. Family diagnosis and evaluating family functioning is emphasized. Several case examples are given to illustrate clinical procedures.

BEHRENS, M. & ACKERMAN, N. W. The home visit as an aid in family diagnosis and therapy. *Social Casework*, 1956, *37*, 11–19.
See Reference in Section 1.1.

BEHRENS, M. & SHERMAN, A. Observations of family interaction in the home. *American Journal of Ortho-psychiatry*, 1959, 29, 243–248.
See Reference in Section 3.3.

BERNAL Y DEL RIO, V. Family interviews: A technique for the selection of psychiatric residency candidates. *Psychiatric Quarterly*, 1972, *46*, 504–512.
A clinical paper that describes a process of selection of psychiatric residents when both husband and wife are applicants. The selection procedure included a joint interview. Sample was 6 couples who applied.

BRYANT, C. M., & GRUNEBAUM, H. U. The theory and practice of the family diagnostic. I: Practical aspects and patient evaluation. II: Theoretical aspects and resident education. In I. M. Cohen (Ed.), *Psychiatric research report No. 20.* Washington, D.C.: American Psychiatric Association, 1966.
A presentation of a family diagnostic procedure at the Massachusetts Mental Health Center which includes a description of methodology and of theoretical considerations as well as resident teaching. Family members are interviewed individually and together about the subject of what brings the patient to the hospital. The training of the psychiatric resident is said to be broadened by participation.

COHEN, R. L., CHARNY, I. W., & LEMBKE, P. Parental expectations as a force in treatment. *Archives of General Psychiatry*, 1961, *4*, 471–478.
A discussion of parental involvement with severely disturbed children based upon 175 cases referred to the inpatient unit at Oakbourne Hospital. It is suggested that intake diagnostic procedures include exploration of parental motivation to anticipate later parental resistance to the child's treatment.

DAVANZO, H. The family group and dynamic psychiatric diagnosis. *International Journal of Group Psychotherapy*, 1962, *12*, 496–502.
Three cases are reported in support of the idea of using the family interview as a diagnostic device. Advantages and disadvantages are discussed.

DRECHSLER, R. J., & SHAPIRO, M. I. A procedure for direct observation of family interaction in a child guidance clinic. *Psychiatry*, 1961, *24*, 163–170.
A procedure for making direct observations of a family as part of the intake procedures of a child guidance clinic. A psychiatrist interviews the family, the family is observed alone, and the family answers a 20-item questionnaire while being observed. The procedural aim was to sample family interactions in a way that would fit economically into ongoing clinic policy. The interview clarifies the presenting problem. A task for the family provides a stage upon which the family acts out the interactive patterns in their relationships.Case illustrations are provided.

EHRENWALD, J. Family diagnosis and mechanisms of psychosocial defense. *Family Process*, 1963, 2, 121–131.
Second of a series of papers attempting to delineate patterns of family interaction for the purposes of arriving at a diagnostic schema for the family as a whole. Method used is an inventory of 30 traits and attitudes "descriptive of interpersonal habitual relationships in family members." Four major patterns have emerged from the author's work with families and are described.

EPSTEIN, N. B. Treatment of the emotionally disturbed preschool child: A family approach. *Canadian Medical Association Journal*, 1961, *85*, 937–940.
A clinical essay focusing on the assumption that when the identified patient is a child, the family must be included in the treatment. First a family diagnostic interview is held, followed by a staff discussion of the dynamics, and then further work-up is recommended. Possible therapeutic programs prescribed include (1) treatment of the family as a unit; (2) seeing two or more members of the family as a group, dependent upon "exigencies" arising as the treatment progresses; (3) treatment as individual psychotherapy for the identified patient; (4) treatment including the

"significant dyad, e. g., mother–child; (5) placing the child in group therapy; or (6) placing the child in individual plus group therapy. A case example is presented to illustrate the approach.

GORAD, S., MCCOURT, W., & COBB, J. The communications approach to alcoholism, *Quarterly Journal on the Study of Alcoholism*, 1971, *32*, 651–668.
This essay postulates that alcoholism can be best understood using three models: (1) the "family model," (2) the transactional model, and (3) the communication model. Drunkenness is viewed as a way of sending a relationship-defining message while denying responsibility for the message. Drinking is viewed as one element in a disturbed interpersonal system. The primary conflict is around control, and drinking is the alcoholic's best weapon in the fight. A case history illustrates some of the points.

GREENBAUM, M. Joint sibling interview as a diagnostic procedure. *Journal of Child Psychology and Psychiatry*, 1965, *6*, 227–232.
A report of a diagnostic procedure in which two siblings are interviewed jointly or observed playing together as part of a family workup. Techniques are described. Setting is a children's out-patient clinic which offers the advantages of actually seeing how the patient interacts with others, lessens the artificial nature of the patient-therapist contact, and gives the therapist a chance to observe the health of at least one other sibling in the family.

GROTJAHN, M Analytic family therapy: A study of trends in research and practice. In J. Masserman (Ed.), *Individual and familial dynamics*. New York: Grune & Stratton, 1959.
An essay focusing on the "psychoanalytic approach to the dynamics of the family." Freudian theory dwells heavily on inborn patterning of personality in the first years of life but not on the importance of the later levels of social participation. Freudian observations have been based on reconstruction from individual psychoanalysis. A schema for family diagnosis is outlined and compared to psychoanalytic diagnostic schemes.

JACOB, C. The value of the family interview in the diagnosis and treatment of schizophrenia. *Psychiatry*, 1967, *30*, 162–172.
Using several case examples, the author's hypothesis is that a single family interview can be an important additional factor in the evaluatino of certain schizophrenic patients by providing information that would otherwise be unavailable or relatively inaccessible. This interview can also be therapeutic, and by studying the protocol in the interview, it also can provide clues to countertransference and other errors in technique.

JARVIS, P., ESTY, J., & STUTZMAN, L. Evaluation and treatment of families at Fort Logan Mental Health Center. *Community of Mental Health*, 1969, *5*, 14–19.
A survey paper of trends in evaluation of treatment of patients from an inpatient facility of a psychiatric hospital. More evaluations are being carried out in the patient's home or in the community rather than in the hospital itself. There is greater involvement of "extended families" and of children (and of involving them at an earlier age) in evaluation and treatment. There is great use of multiple-family group therapy rather than conjoint family therapy.

KAFFMAN, M. Family diagnosis and therapy in child emotional pathology. *Family Process*, 1965, *4*, 241–258.
A description of families treated in Israel based upon 194 kibbutz families and 126 families living in Haifa. Family treatment is said to be effective and case examples are given.

KEENEY, B. P. Ecosystemic epistemology: An alterantive paradigm for diagnosis. *Family Process*, 1979, *18*, 117–129.
This paper proposes an alternative paradigm for diagnosis based on cybernetics, ecology, and systems theory. Theoretical statements concerning this approach are delineated with specific references to major family therapists. this discussion provides a foundation for diagnosis that takes ecological relationship systems into account.

MAHON, E. & EGAN, J. The use of family interviews in child psychotherapy. *International Journal of Child Psychotherapy*, 1973, *2*, 365–378.
Five cases are presented to emphasize the point that family diagnostic interviews are an important part of treatment of children with emotional disorders. The information gained cannot be obtained by seeing each member of the family separately.

MARTIN, F., & KNIGHT, J. Joint interviews as part of intake procedure in a child psychiatric clinic. *Journal of Child Psychology and Psychiatry*, 1962, *3*, 17–26.
An intake procedure for pre-adolescent children in use at the Tavistock Clinic, London, is described and illustrated with case material. Based upon current concepts of family dynamics, the procedure entails the use of one or more initial joint interviews between both parents and members of the psychiatric team (psychiatrist, caseworker, and psychologist). The advantages over the traditional procedure include better contact with fathers, an increased opportunity for direct observation of family interaction, and an increased assessment of differing motivations for approaching the clinic.

MENDELBAUM, A. Family process in diagnosis and treatment of children and adolescents. *Bulletin of the Menninger Clinic*, 1971, *35*, 153–166.
An essay based on the notion that using the "family model" in understanding the dynamics and in treatment of children who are hospitalized inpatients can be useful. A number of case examples are presented in support of this idea.

MENDELL, D., & FISCHER, S. A multi-generation approach to the treatment of psychopathology. *Journal of Nervous and Mental Disease*, 1958, *126*, 523–529.
Techniques of treating the family rather than the identified patient for various problems seen at a private psychiatric population. TAT and Rorschach material were important.

MENZIES, M., BEDLAK, S., & MCRAE, L. An intensive approach to brief family diagnosis at a child guidance clinic. *Canadian Psychiatric Journal*, 1961, *6*, 295–298.
Two case examples are given in support of a treatment method of families who come to a child guidance clinic and are not from the immediate community. It is suggested that parents and patient come for a 2- to 3-day period to participate in both individual as well as joint interviews.

RICHMAN, J., & WHITE, H. A family view of hysterical psychosis, *American Journal of Psychiatry*, 1970, *127*, 280–285.
Four case reports are presented of hysterical psychosis with the emphasis of familial rather than individual psychodynamics as being etiologic. Psychotic symptoms could be understood in terms of dominant family problems, themes, myths, and fantasies.

SERRANO, A. C., McDANALD, E. C., GOOLISHIAN, H. A., MacGREGOR, R., & RITCHIE, A. M. Adolescent maladjustment and family dynamics. *American Journal of Psychiatry*, 1962, *118*, 897–901.
A summary of the dynamics of 63 disturbed adolescents and their families. The patients are said to fall into four diagnostic categories each associated with a type of family interaction. These categories of maladjustment reaction in adolescence are the infantile, the childish, the juvenile, and the preadolescent. The adolescent functions as a stabilizing factor in the family and when his behavior becomes unendurable to himself, the family, or society, this precipitates a crisis which mobilizes the family to seek help.

SERRANO, A. C., & WILSON, N. S. Family therapy in the treatment of the brain damaged child. *Diseases of the Nervous System*, 1963, *24*, 732–735.
In treating children diagnosed as having organic brain syndromes, the authors emphasize using evaluation of the total family constellation (here using multiple impact therapy), as well as using the more traditional physical and psychological studies.

SHERMAN, S. N. Practice implications of psychodynamic and group therapy in family interviewing. *The family is the patient*. (Monograph VII). New York: National Association of Social Workers, 1965, pp. 40–47.
An essay stressing the importance of relating an individual symptom to the structure and interactional processes within the family. It is useful for both diagnostic and therapeutic purposes. The therapist must take into account both individual psychodynamics, as well as interactional processes.

TOOLEY, K. M. Irreconcilable differences between parent and child: A case report of interactional pathology. *American Journal of Orthopsychiatry*, 1978, *48*, 703–716.
This is a clinical case report of two families in which the interaction between parents and child was based on the parents' view of the child as "bad." The authors find that the parents use the child to displace their unacceptable impulses and went to evaluations for confirmation of their beliefs, not treatment. Five-year follow-up on one child (direct contact and projective testing) is the basis for the conclusion that separation from such parents is the treatment of choice and may require legal action.

TYLER, E. A., TRUUMAA, A., & HENSHAW, P. Family group intake by a child guidance clinic team. *Archives of General Psychiatry*, 1962, *6*, 214–218.
A report on an intake method devised by the Riley Child Guidance Clinic at the Indiana University Medical Center. The procedure substitutes the family group for the usual signle informant and uses 3-man team in place of a single interviewer. Experience with the procedure with 100 cases is described in terms of the main problems, the teaching aspects, nature of diagnosis, team work, and family responses.

VAN AMEROGEN, S. Initial psychiatric family studies. *American Journal of Orthopsychiatry*, 1954, *24* 73–84.
Based on treatment failures for a child guidance clinic over the previous 3-year period, it was concluded that the failures were possibly the result of the fact that the total family dynamics were not taken into consideration. For this reason, the author presented a revised scheme for initial psychiatric work-up. One or two interviews were held with both parents conjointly, and two or three interviews were held with the child alone. The child also had psychological testing. The family study was terminated by a final planning conference usually with both parents.

WEISS, V. Multiple client interviewing: An aid in diagnosis. *Social Casework*, 1962, *43*, 111–113.
This essay from a family service agency points out that often seeing others in addition to the identified patient is helpful in establishing a diagnosis. Indications for whom should be included are discussed.

Social Work Practice, 1963, Selected Papers. (90th Annual Forum National Conference on Social Welfare, Cleveland, Ohio, May 19–24, 1963.) New York: Columbia University Press, 1963.
A collection of papers given at a social work conference which includes a paper on family diagnosis and treatment, family unit treatment of character-disordered youngsters, and a paper on schizophrenia and family therapy. 255 pp.

1.7   FAMILY CONSIDERATION IN INDIVIDUAL TREATMENT

ACKERMAN, N. W. Disturbances of mothering and criteria for treatment. *American Journal of Orthopsychiatry*, 1956, *26*, 252–263.
A clinical paper discussing theory and practice of mothering and its disturbances. Critique of traditional techniques used in the child guidance clinic are presented and suggestions for therapy are made. Disturbances of mothering can be seen as by-products of intrafamilial difficulties of the mother with other family members as well as a disturbance in individual psychodynamics.

ACKERMAN, N. The emergence of family diagnosis and treatment: A personal view. *Psychotherapy*, 1967, *4*, 125–129.
An essay on the history of family diagnosis and therapy. The role of the family in the etiology of psychopathology was a longstanding "blind spot." Family psychotherapy is gradually developing as a form of psychotherapy with indications and contraindications of its own. Comparison studies with other forms of psychotherapy should be done.

ACKERMAN, N. W. Interpersonal disturbances in the family. *Psychiatry*, 1954, *17*, 359–368.
Involves in part an historical review of the handling of family problems by psychotherapeutic means. Previously, family problems have been handled in terms of individual psychotherapy, couple psychotherapy, and by various members of the family being seen separately but simultaneously by different or the same therapists. Even if every member of a family were given individual psychotherapy, it still would not constitute a psychotherapy of the family. Some suggestions for working with family problems are made.

ACKERMAN, N. W. The psychoanalytic approach to the family. In J. Masserman (Ed.), *Individual and familial dynamics*. New York: Grune & Stratton, 1959.
A clinical essay defending the use of some psychoanalytic concepts as a basis for family therapy: unconscious communication; use of diagnostic family interviews; and an illustration of techniques of family therapy. Conjoint interviews can be an aid to individual psychoanalysis.

ACKERMAN, N. W. Toward an integrative therapy of the family. *American Journal of Psychiatry*, 1958, *114*, 727–733.
See References in Section 3.6

ACKERMAN, N. W., & SOBEL, R. Family diagnosis. *American Journal of Orthopsychiatry*, 1950, *20*, 744–753.
To understand the preschool child who is a patient, it is necessary to consider the psychosocial effects of the family members upon each other. Treatment of the young child should begin with treatment of the family group.

ARLEN, M. S. Conjoint therapy and the corrective emotional experience. *Family Process*, 1966, *5*, 91–104.
The use of family therapy with families containing a person with severe character disorder described within a framework of providing a corrective emotional experience.

ANDERSON, C. M. Family intervention with severely disturbed inpatients. *Archives of General Psychiatry*, 1977, *34*, 697–702.
This paper focuses on the use of the family model and techniques for short-term work with the families of severely distrubed inpatients. Issues discussed range from initial information gathering (should not be accusatory and guilt provoking) to including the family in aftercare planning. Techniques for involving resistant families are emphasized and difficulties encountered by staff in coping with families are also discussed.

APPLETON, W. S. Mistreatment of patient's families by psychiatrists. *American Journal of Psychiatry*, 1974, *131*, 655–657.
A clinical essay with case examples stressing the point that pathological families have not been proven to be a cause of schizophrenia and therefore indiscriminate blame and mistrust of the family, overtly or covertly, by the treating therapist is not helpful to the identified patient or his family. Suggestions to help therapists treat families are made.

BARCAI, A. The reaction of the family system to rapid therapeutic change in one of its members. *American Journal of Psychotherapy*, 1977, *31*, 105–115.
In this clinical paper from Israel, 3 case reports are presented to illustrate the effect of rapid and dramatic change in patients in individual therapy on other family members. The family is seen as a system with interlocking parts. Factors in predicting the possible responses of family members include the speed, direction, and meaning of the change to the family member. It is the responsibility of the therapist to anticipate such meaning and impact of change and plan for it in therapeutic interventions.

BEAL, E. W. Use of the extended family in the treatment of multiple personality. *American Journal of Psychiatry*, 1978, *135*, 539–542.
See reference in Section 1.1.

BEATMAN, F. L. Family interaction: Its significance for diagnosis and treatment. *Social Casework*, 1957, *38*, 111–118.
A discussion of the importance of considering the dynamics of the family illustrated with a case example.

BENNEY, C., & PECK H. The family as a factor in the rehabilitation of the mentally ill. *Mental Hygiene*, 1963, *47*, 372–379.
A report of the author's experiences in a rehabilitation workshop treating psychiatric patients. The value of using family dynamics in the individual approach to the patient, as well as bringing in the whole family, is stressed.

BERENSTEIN, I. On the psychotherapy of the marital couple. *Acta Psyquiatrica Y Psiocologica De America Latina*, 1968, *14*, 301–308.
Family therapy of a couple is described. Emphasis is placed on understanding projective identification, analysis of conflicts, and acting out—all based on a psychoanalytic understanding of the patient techniques.

BOSZORMENYI-NAGY, I. Loyalty implications of the transference model in psychotherapy. *Archives of General Psychiatry*, 1972, *27*, 374–380.
A discussion of limits on therapeutic change that may occur in individual child psychotherapy because of loyalties to other family members. Transference to the therapist may imply disloyalty, and symptom change can mean betrayal. It is necessary to synthesize intrapsychic, psychodynamic knowledge with a family systems orientation. A therapeutic strategy which utilizes this approach is outlined.

BRODY, E. Modification of family interaction patterns by a group interview technique. *International Journal of Group Psychotherapy*, 1956, *6*, 38–47.
As part of a study of perfrontal lobotomy, family members of 11 patients who would undergo this procedure were seen for 5 months before the operation until at least 1 year after the operation. Frequency was from once weekly during the first few months to as infrequently as once a month during the last few months. Individual interviews with family members were also used. The family interviews seemed to result in "an increased capacity for action by the family previously immobilized."

BROOKS, W. B., DEANE, W. N., LAGOV, R. C., & CURTIS, B. B. Varieties of family participation in the rehabilitation of released chronic schizophrenic patients. *Journal of Nervous and Mental Diseases*, 1963, *136*, 432–444.
A study of the posthospital course of 170 chronic schizophrenic patients. The data were abstracted from records. The social, economic, and psychiatric outcomes are correlated with various aspects of the family's participation in the rehabilitation process. A major factor in the success of this group is said to be the breaking of pathological ties with the family and the forming of new, healthier relationships.

BROWN, S. Family therapy viewed in terms of resistance to change. In I. M. Cohen (Ed.), *Psychiatric research report No. 20*. Washington, D.C.: American Psychiatric Association, 1966.
Family therapy from a psychoanalytic and "child guidance" point of view with the emphasis on resistance to change. Case examples are given.

BYNG-HALL, J., BRUGGEN, P. Family admission decisions as a therapeutic tool. *Family Process*, 1974, *13*, 443–459.
This is a description of a new approach in deciding to admit an adolescent to a mental hospital. The family made this decision rather than the psychiatrist in an attemlpt to prevent "ejection" of adolescents from troubled families. Hospital admissions were reduced, and implications of this result are discussed. Five case examples are presented.

CHANDLER, E., HOLDEN, H., & ROBINSON, M. Treatment of a psychotic family in a family psychiatry setting. *Psychotherapy and Psychosomatics*, 1968, *16*, 333–347.
This case report is in support of an experimental approach to a family by a psychologist, social worker, and

psychiatrist working in a psychoanalytically oriented psychiatric outpatient clinic. Whereas, previously, each member of the family had had a separate therapist, in this case, the family was seen together by all 3 therapists. Following the family meeting, each of the 2 sons saw a therapist, and the parents together saw one therapist ("It was not possible to find another worker for the 2 parents.") Accounts of each of the therapists in their work with each of the individuals is described. Goals of the family were to regard themselves as separate individuals.

COOPER, S. New trends in work with patients: Progress or change? *Social Casework*, 1961, *42*, 342–347.
Discusses the notion that treatment of the individual patient often stems from problems in the family as a whole. Individual dynamics and therapy should be kept in mind along with consideration of family dynamics. Indications for each type of treatment should be carefully considered in each case.

DAVIDSON, S. School phobia as a manifestation of family disturbance: Its structure and treatment. *Journal of Child Psychology and Psychiatry*, 1960–1961, *1*, 270–288.
30 Cases of school phobis were studied at a child guidance clinic. Data were gathered from social histories and from individual interviews with patients and their parents. Family dynamics and methods of individual treatment are discussed.

DELL, N., TRIESCHMAN, A., & VOGEL, E. A sociocultural analysis of resistances of working-class fathers treated in a child psychiatric clinic. *American Journal of Orthopsychiatry*, 1961, *31*, 388–405.
The authors' hypotheses is that fathers have been excluded from the treatment process in the child guidance clinic setting. Ten working-class father were seen for periods ranging from 1 to 4 years. It was part of concurrent, simultaneous treatment of the identified patient (the child) and the mother. Familial dynamics are discussed. The child's treatment may be facilitated when the father is seen.

DEMERS, R., & DAVIS, L. Influence of prophylactic lithium treatment on marital adjustment of manic-depressives and their spouses. *Comprehensive Psychiatry*, 1971, *12*, 348–353.
Fourteen married, manicdepressive patients, who were being treated with lithium at an outpatient clinic, were investigated together with their spouses, using the Marital Partner Attitude Test and a global rating scale of the status of the marriage in order to document the notion that lithium treatment will change the perceived psychological state of the identified patient and his or her mate in relation to each other. The results indicated there was a statistically significant decrease in the number of undesirable attributes of the patient following treatment but not of desirable attributes. A prospective study was suggested to replicate these findings.

DIETZ, C., & COSTELLO, M. Reciprocal interaction in parent-child relationship during psychotherapy. *American Journal of Orthopsychiatry*, 1956, 26, 376–394.
A 4-year-old child was the identified patient. The parents were seen together by one therapist and the child by another therapist. It was pointed out the parents and the child had interactional effects on each other's pathology.

DYSINGER, R. A family perspective of the diagnosis of individual members. *American Journal of Orthopsychiatry*, 1961, *31*, 61–68.
Based on the authors' clinical experience and a research project on family groups of schizophrenic children all living in a ward setting, the authors hypothesize that psychiatric illness may be a function of disturbance in the family. Families with schizophrenic members seem to be involved "in an intense emotional process with one another" and have difficulty in being effective in just about any area. They aren't aware that their judgment is undependable. A case example supports these hypotheses.

ELLES, G. Family treatment from a therapeutic community. *Confinia. Psychiatrica*, 1965, *8*, 9–14.
Some families were treated with some or all members of the family receiving individual thearpy, while other families were treated by family therapy in the home. Discussion of experiences, but no data, is presented comparing the 2 forms of treatment.

FAUCETT, E. Multiple-client interviewing: A means of assessing family process. *Social Casework*, 1962, *43*, 114–119
One case example is offered in support of the notion that the identified patient in casework if often acting out some of the family problems. "The focus of the therapy of the patient must be on the family's most burdensome problem."

FELDMAN, L. B. Depression and marital interaction. *Family Process*, 1976, *15*, 389–395.
A clinical illustration is used to describe a comprehensive theory of depression that considers the significance of biological, intrapsychic behavioral, and family systems aspects. Treatment focuses on enhancing the process of "morphogenesis" based on the notion that interrelational homeostasis perpetuates the pathology and must be changed for improvement to occur.

FORREST, T. The family dynamics of maternal violence. *Journal of American Academy of Psychoanalysis*, 1974, *2*, 215–230.
Based on psychiatrtic and nonpsychiatric literature and 3 cases of women in treatment—one who had actually

murdered a child, one who had participated in child assault, and one who had had a dream of murdering a child—the author discusses the "family dynamics" of maternal violence.

FOX, R. E. The effect of psychotherapy on the spouse. *Family Process*, 1968, *7*, 7–16.
A discussion and review of the literature of the effect on a spouse when the partner is in individual psychotherapy. Problems of gathering data are presented, and the ethical problem of adverse effects upon the spouse is discussed.

FRANKEL, S. An indication for conjoint treatment: An application based on an assessment of individual psychopathology. *Psychiatry Quarterly*, 1977, *49*, 97–109.
Two case examples are presented to contrast unseccessful individual treatment to successful conjoint treatment for patients who consistently blame another person, usually a spouse, for their problems and who do not reflect on internal difficulties.

FRIEDMAN, T., ROLFE, P., & PERRY, S. Home treatment of psychotic patients. *American Journal of Psychiatry*, 1960, *116*, 807–809.
A report of the first 15 months of operation of the psychiatric home treatment service of the Boston State Hospital, whose aim was "better management of mental illness at a time of stress and to see it appropriate alternatives to hospitalization might be possible." Each case was seen by psychiatrist and social worker. Sixty percent of the cases were able to return home. Families were included in the planning for the identified patient; no family therapy was done.

GLASSMAN, R., LIPTON, H., & DUNSTAN, P. Group discussions with a hospitalized schizophrenic and his family. *International Journal of Group Psychotherapy*, 1959, *9*, 204–212.
From an inpatient hospital service, this is a case report of treatment of a schizophrenic patient at the time of an acute crisis in his hospitalization. The crisis was the return of the patient to his family. The crisis was handled through treatment of the patient and family together in 10 1-hour sessions over a period of 17 weeks.

GOLL, K. Role structure and subculture in families of elective mutists. *Family Process*, 1979, *18*, 55–68.
A presentation of 10 case records that describe a theory of treatment of elective mutism. The key is to "break down the family's distrust of the outer world" before social training of the identified patient is started.

GRAD, J., & SAINSBURG, P. Mental illness and the family. *Lancet*, 1963, *1*, 544–547.
An analysis of the effects on the family of psychiatric illness of one member of the family before and after treatment. The sample was 410 patients from 2 psychiatric facilities in England. Problems reported by families were analyzed; the sicker or older the patient, the greater the number of problems reported by the family. The number of problems reported by families was reduced significantly after treatment of the patient.

GRANLICK, A. The family in psychotherapy. In J. Masserman (Ed.), *Individual and familial dynamics*. New York: Grune & Stratton, 1959.
From an inpatient unit, diagnostic and treatment techniques involving the family are described. "The therapeutic community" that integrates the family into the treatment program must be developed.

GROTJAHN, M. Letter to the Editor. *Psychoanalysis Forum*, 1966, *1*, 426.
In relation to Freud's insight into family dynamics, there is a hypothetical interview with Freud in which he advises another analyst not to continue treatment with an alcoholic due to the "masochism of the wife, which would be an 'obstacle' to the treatment." It is deduced that Freud realized the wife's "important part in the husband's drinking habits."

HAHN, I. Family therapy: A child-centered approach to disturbed parent–child relationships. *Pennsylvania Psychiatric Quaterly*, 1964, *4*, 58–62.
Family oriented treatment (includilng "therapist, child and usually both parents") seemed to offer advantages over the "typical psychoanalytical approach." Sample was 15 families where the child was the identified patient, referred to either a child guidance clinic or private practice. All cases improved and telephone follow-up in seven cases six months "corroborated the results."

HATFIELD, A. B. The family as partner in the treatment of mental illness. *Hospital & Community Psychiatry*, 1979, *30*, 338–340.
A report of a survey of the experience of families in which the identified patient has a chronic schizophrenic disorder. eight-nine members of a voluntary self-help organization completed standard questionnares on the effects of illness on the family and the services needed in order to cope. Result showed serious disruption of family functioning and gradual learning of coping mechanisms. Families of schizophrenics need information, support, and more reaching out by professionals.

HOLLANDER, L. Rethinking child and family treatment. In Sankar, D. V. (Ed.), *Mental health in children*. Westbury, New York: PJD Publications Ltd., 1975.
This essay uses a number of clinical examples to discuss the transition for child psychiatrists from a "child-focused" model to a family systems model. In the absence of treatment outcome data, treatment options are discussed.

HOLLENDER, M. H., MANN, W. A., & DANEHY, J. H. The psychiatric resident and the family of the hospitalized patient. *Archives of General Psychiatry*, 1960, *2*, 125–130.
Problems of the resident who must deal with the families of patients hospitalized in acute diagnostic and treatment centers. An examination of the difficulties of residents in this area, a discussion of the ambiguities in the situation, such as whether the resident represents the patient or the hospital, and comments on whether or not the resident should be the one who maintains contact with the family.

HALLER, L. L. Family systems theory in psychiatric intervention. *American Journal of Nursing*, 1974, *74*, 462–463.
From the vantage point of a primary therapist at a community mental health center, this clinical essay suggests that to manage the kinds of problems that are present in such a setting the family view point should be encouraged. Concepts such as looking at process rather than content, family interaction patterns, and family intervention tactics are discussed, and a case is presented to illustrate the point. Results of family treatment in the one case presented revealed no change in the family system or identified patient (schizophrenic).

HOWELLS, J. G. Child-parent separation as a therapeutic procedure. *American Journal of Psychiatry*, 1963, *19*, 922–926.
A discussion of the idea that separation of child from mother (defined as "the child is physically apart from its parents") is not always harmful, and in fact can be useful in treatment. A summary of the author's previous investigations is included and a sharp differentiation made between separation and deprivation.

HURVITZ, N. Marital problems following psychotherapy with one spouse. *Journal of Consulting Psychology*, 1967, *31*, 38–47.
A discussion of the ways marital problems are complicated or created by individual treatment of one spouse based upon spouses referred later for marriage counseling. The problem is not only that individual treatment might break up a marriage but that "the relationship between the spouses, which should be used to benefit them both, is further disturbed." Marital treatment approach using the individual therapy as a problem area in the marriage is described.

JACKSON, D. D., & YALOM, I. Conjoint family therapy as an aid in psychotherapy. In A. Burton (Ed.), *Family therapy of schizophrenic in modern psychotherapeutic practice*. Palo Alto: Science & Behavior Books, 1965.
See Reference in Section 1.1

JOSSELYN, I. The family as a psychological unit. *Social Casework*, 1953, *34*, 336–343.
Based on the author's clinical experience, the idea is presented that the family can be viewed as a psychological unit. Not only does the family influence the individual, but the individual has a crucial impact of the family unit. Thus individual psychopathology can be better understood by understanding the family psychopathology.

KLAPMAN, H., & RICE, D. An experience with combined milieu and family group therapy. *International Journal of Group Psychotherapy*, 1965, *15*, 198–206.
A case report of a family in which the primary patient was a 13-year-old boy. The family was thought to be more difficult than usual. Treatment was milieu therapy plus a once-a-week meeting of the family and members of the treatment team, including psychiatrist, social worker, teacher, occupational therapist, and two ward staff members.

LEWIS, J., & GLASSER, N. Evolution of a treatment approach to families: Group family therapy. *International Journal of Group Psychotherapy*, 1965, *15*, 505–515.
A report of the involvement of families of mentally ill patients in a therapy program treatment center. Three groups were set up: family members excluding patients, patients alone, and patients with families together. Impressions of this type of family involvement are described.

LIEBMAN, R., HONIG, P., & BERGER, H. An integrated treatment program for psychogenic pain. *Family Process*, 1976, *15*, 397–405.
This paper describes an integrated treatment program which was developed and applied over a 3-year period to a group of 10 children referred to the Philadelphia Child Guidance Clinic for evaluation of persistent abdominal pain. The roles of the pediatrician and the psychiatrist and the characteristics of the family are examined and the goals and strategies of treatment are identified. An integrated treatment approach was found effective in the treatment of recurrent abdominal pain of psychogenic origin.

LINDON, G. A psychoanalytic view of the family: A study of family member interactions. *Psychoanalytic Forum*, 1968–69, *3*, 13–65.
A transcript of a panel discussion in which 3 papers were read and were discussed by 7 panelists. The data from these

papers dealt with: a case report on a patient and the effects of her analysis on her family; the simultaneous analysis of father and son; and a theory of the family, which is illustrated by several case vignettes and from the literature.

LOMAS, P. Family role and identity formation. *International Journal of Psychoanalysis*, 1961, *42*, 371–380.
A report of a case of a 30-year-old woman with fears of traveling, being poisoned, blindness, and going insane. Her parents were in conflict over a change in their social situation, and the anxiety over family disintegration was dealt with by a myth of mutual love and loyalty. The basic marital disharmony resulted in each parent seeing the patient as a loved object to supplant the marriage partner.

LONG, R. The path toward psychodrama family process. *Group Psychotherapy*, 1966, *19*, 43–46.
In an inpatient setting, where psychodrama is one of the treatment techniques used, the author describes his realization that families seemed to be involved in the pathogenesis of mental illness. He suggests that bringing in the real family to the psychodrama sessions might be useful and describes some problems which arose as a result.

MADDISON, D. C. The integrated therapy of family members—A case report. *International Journal of Group Psychotherapy*, 1961, *11*, 33–48.
A case report of a mother and daughter dealt with by the joint interview technique with a brief survey of some of the family therapy reports. An 18-year-old patient with recurrent nightmares was seen individually, then her mother was seen individually, and finally both were seen conjointly while continuing individual sessions. The emphasis is upon analytical oriented individual psychotherapy from the same psychiatrist with occasional combined interviews where every opportunity was taken to analyze the patient's reactions to the triangular situation.

MARKOWITZ, I. Family therapy in a child guidance clinic. *Psychiatric Quarterly*, 1966, *40*, 308–319.
An essay describing some limitations of family therapy. Cases were from a child guidance clinic in which a child was the primary patient. Limitations are "when individual psychopathology is so severe that the family cannot be harmonious."

MARTIN, F. E. Some implications from the theory and practice of family therapy for individual therapy (and vice versa). *British Journal of Medical Psychology*, 1977, *50*, 53–64.
See reference in Section 3.6.

MENDELBAUM, A. Family process in diagnosis and treatment of children and adolescents. *Bulletin of the Menninger Clinic*. 1971, *35*, 153–166.
See reference in Section 1.6.

MENZIES, M. The angry parent in family-oriented therapy. *Canadian Psychiatric Association Journal*, 1965, *10*, 405–410.
A clinical essay focused on "the hostility of the parent towards the child" with the data obtained from "working with parents during the past 14 years." Dynamics centering on hostility as a "defensive reaction" are discussed as are principles of treatment.

MITCHELL, C. B. Family interviewing in family diagnosis. *Social Casework*, 1959, *40*, 381–384.
A discussion of the importance of family interviews for diagnosis. "In the course of a series of interviews with the entire family, distrubance in any one individual serves to illuminate graphically the family distrubance of which it is symptomatic."

MITCHELL, C.B. Problems and principles in family therapy. In N. W. Ackerman (Ed.), *Expanding theory and practice in family therapy*. New York: Family Service Association of America, 1976.
A clinical essay by a caseworker using family dynamics to understand individual problems. Problems and benefits from the family approach are outlined, and a case example is given in support of several of the points.

MONTALVO, B. Observations on two natural amnesias. *Family Process*, 1976, *15*, 333–342.
This paper explores the role and effecxt of interpersonal "sequences" in determining amnesias, compared to the usual focus of intrapsychic conflict. The process of "vanishing" is examined in light of the ways in which therapists and clients control their contribution to their interpersonal interaction. In this way, they influence whether or not they will be remembered and whether the memory will be positive or negative. An excerpt of a therapy session with an 8-year-old girl is used to illustrate the author's hypothesis.

MONTALVO, B., & HALEY, J. In defense of child therapy. *Family Process*, 1973, 12, 227–244.
This paper present child therapy as dealing with the presenting symptom of a family: the child. Thus by accepting the scapegoat function of the child, the therapist does not arouse resistance in the family. This approach leaves the therapist free to convey effective suggestions in brief contacts with the parents. These suggestions may bring about change in the family and consequent change in the child.

MUNRO, F., & BIDWELL, B. Joint interviews in the treatment of mothers and their young children. *Journal of Child Psychology and Psychiatry*, 1965, *5*, 231–239.
Report of 3 cases in which the child was the primary patient and in which treatment was done using 2 therapists, 1 for mother and 1 for the child, both in intercommunicating rooms. Advantages and disadvantages of the technique are discussed.

PATTISON, E. M. The fatal myth of death in the family. *American Journal of Psychiatry*, 1976, *133*, 674–678.
A patient's psychopathology appeared to be related to death of a parent. It was hypothesized that such a process was due to the inability of the family to integrate death as a "natural part of the process of living."

PATTON, J., BRADLEY, J., & HRONOWSKI, M. Collaborative treatment of marital partners. *North Carolina Medical Journal*, 1958, *19*, 523–528.
A clinical report of 3 psychiatrists who met regularly over 18 months to discuss their cases being treated by individual psychotherpay. As the discussions progressed, conceptualizing the psychiatrist's patients in terms of the patients' thinking shifted from individual dynamics to the realization that the individual symptomatology was representative of family problems. Treatment of the family is suggested.

PING-NIE, PAO. The use of patient–family–doctor interview to facilitate the schizophrenic patient's return to the community. *Psychiatry*, 1960, *23*, 199–207.
A discussion of the use of conjoint interviews with family members to ease a schizophrenic patient's move from the hospital to the outside world. After intensive psychotherapy, a crisis may come when the patient is faced with going home. After preparing both family members and patient, joint interviews are held which allow the family members and patient to deal with each other in preparation for living together with less distress. Four cases are given as examples, including one where the outcome was unfavorable.

RAE, J. The influence of the wives on the treatment outcome of alcoholics: A follow-up study at two years. *The British Journal of Psychiatry*, 1972, *120*, 601–613.
A two-year, follow-up study examining the influence on treatment outcome of wives of 58 alcoholic, male inpatients. Clinical variables were related to MMPI of patients and wives. Relapsing patients significantly more often had wives with a Psychopathic Deviate Profile. Results indicated that outcome is significantly related to marital interaction processes.

RAUTMAN, A. L. Meeting a need in child guidance. *Family Process*, 1965, *4*, 217–227.
A procedure for dealing with families with child problems by interviewing a marital pair in their home in "as personal and relaxed a setting as possible consistent with professional standards."

REIDY, J. J. An approach to family-centered treatment in a state institution. *American Journal of Orthopsychiatry*, 1962, *32*, 133–141.
A report on methods of treatment in a children's psychiatric state hospital, the Esther Loring Richards Children's Center in Maryland. The treatment assumes that the child's problems are due in part to detrimental family relationships ad that the function of the hospital is "to help the child become well enough to return to the community." A community agency maintains continuing interest in the child and provides the necessary help to the family; the child returns home each weekend. Emphasis is placed upon parental adjustment to changes in the child and, in those cases in which a child is discharged to a foster home, weekend visits are also allowed, thus enabling the new family unit to develop.

RINSLEY, D. B., & HALL, D. D. Psychiatric hospital treatment of adolescents. *Archives of General Psychiatry*, 1962, *7*, 286–294.
See Reference in Section 5.4

ROSENSTOCK, H. The summit-annotated contract technique for hospitalized adolescents. *American Journal of Psychiatry*, 1975, *132*, 7457.
A short clinical report of a technique for use with adolescents in the terminal phase of psychiatric hospitalization. The intention of the technique is to maintain in the post-hospital phase the therapeutic gains made in the hospital. The technique is useful for families with a non-psychotic, "acting-out," identified patient. Near the end of the hospitalization, patient, parents, and therapist meet together and write a "contract" that describes the new homeostasis in detail. It specifies the conditions by which the patient returns to family life. One case of the first 20 families is presented to illustrate the technique. No follow-up results are presented, but the technique is thought to be useful.

SAVITSKY, E., & SHARKEY, H. Study of family interaction in the aged. *Journal of Geriatric Psychiatry*, 1972, *5*, 3–19.
Is a clinical study describing interpersonal relations in the aged. In treating such patients with emotional disorders, it

is felt that family interviews are crucial to diagnosis and management. Staff countertransference in institutions can significantly hinder treatment for such a population.

SCHERZ, F. Multiple client-interviewing: Treatment implications. *Social Casework*, 1962, *43*, 120–124.
From a family service agency, indications or contraindications for having more than the identified patient present at interviews is discussed. Individual and group treatment can be used in various combinationa. Techniques for multiple client interviewing are put forth.

SEARLES, H. F. The contributions of family treatment to the psychotherapy of schizophrenia. In I. Boszormenyi-Nagy and J. L. Framo (Eds.), *Intensive family therapy*. New York: Harper & Row, 1965.
See Reference in Section 1.4

SHERESHKY, P. Family unit treatment in child guidance. *Social Casework*, 1963, *8*, 63–70.
An essay reviewing concepts about the family and its effect on individual psychopathology with the specific focus on how that concept could be useful to case workers in a child guidance clinic. Following a brief review of the literature, aims and specific techniques to accomplish this purpose are discussed. Differences from the traditional focus on the "mother–child relationship" and individual psychotherapy casework are pointed out.

SHERMAN, S. N. Joint interviews in casework practice. *Social Casework*, 1959, *4*, 20–28.
An attempt "to place joint interviews within the methodology of casework." The purpose and concept of family interviewing is discussed with case examples.

SILVERMAN, D. C. Sharing the crisis of rape: Counseling the mates and families of victims. *American Journal of Orthopsychiatry*, 1978, *48*, 166–173.
This is a clinical paper which offers suggestions to counselors of rape victims on methods to involve the mates and family members in intervention. The author, from an urban psychiatric liaison–consultation service, believes this is essential because, even when the victim does not wish to talk, other members need to discuss their reactions and misconceptions of the rape experience, which will importantly affect the victim's adjustment.

SIPORIN, M. Family-centered casework in a psychiatric setting. *Social Casework*, 1956, *37*, 167–174.
One case is presented in support of the author's notion that casework can be best done by keeping both individual as well as family dynamilcs in mind. A review of the family approach in casework is presented.

SLAVSON, S. R. Coordinated family therapy. *International Journal of Group Psychotherapy*, 1965, *15*, 177–187.
A report on a new plan of family treatment in which primary patient (here adolescents) were placed in treatment in "para-analytic group psychotherapy," with the group being derived according to sex and a 2-year-age range. Fathers and mothers of the primary patient wre seen in separate groups.

SOLOMON, A. P., & GREENE, B. L. Concurrent psychoanalytic therapy in marital disharmony. In B. L. Greene (Ed.), *The psychotherapies of marital disharmony*. New York: Free Press, 1965.
The authors describe treatment of a marital problem using concurrent psychoanalytic therapy for both partners by the same therapist. Indications, contraindications, and techniques are discusses and supported by case examples. It is useful in understanding family transactions.

STANTON, M. D. A neglected facet of second-order effecs in mental health treatment. *Professional Psychology*, 1975, *6*, 237–238.
This is an essay which asserts that family system change is overlooked as a second-order effect of individual psychotherapy. Second order effects are defined as those outside the planned control of the therapist. A negative second-order effect is when patients drop out due to threats to family loyalties. Seeing families directly or paying more attention to the family system in individual treatment is useful to minimize such negative results.

SZALITA, A. The combined use of family interviews and individual therapy in schizophrenia. *American Journal of Psychotherapy*, 1968, *22*, 419–430.
Seeing the family together as an adjunct to individual, psychoanalytically oriented psychotherapy with schizophrenic patients is thought to be useful. Data comes from the author's out-patient private practice. Schizophrenia is not seen as a "disease of the family."

SZALITA, A. The relevance of the family interview for psychoanalysis. *Contemporary Psychoanalysis*, 1971, *8*, 31–44.
Based on data from the author's private practice, it is suggested that family therapy is useful in conjunction with psychoanalysis. Data was derived from those cases in which one or both spouses were in analysis with the author. Family interviewing can be useful (1) during psychoanalytic training to help the candidate avoid a transference problem; (2) as an adjunct to individual psychoanalysis to shorten the process; (3) to correct distorted impressions; and (4) for diagnostic purposes.

TANGARI, A. Family involvement in the treatment of a psychiatric inpatient. *Hospital and Community Psychiatry*, 1974, *25*, 792–794.
A report of the family approach in an inpatient psychiatric unit with an average of 6 to 8 weeks' stay. Staff thinks "family" from admission to discharge. There are frequent patient–staff meetings of 30 to 50 people divided into 2 to 4 small groups. The focus of these meetings is on current difficulties. Staff impression is that this modality helps.

VAN AMEROGEN, S. Initial psychiatric family studies. *American Journal of Orthospychiatry*, 1954, *24*, 73–84.
Based on treatment failures of a child guidance clinic over a 3-year period, it was concluded that the failures were possibly the result of the fact that the total family dynamics were not taken into consideration. For this reason, the author presented a revised scheme for initial psychiatric work-up. One or 2 interviews were held with both parents conjointly, 2 or 3 interviews with the child alone. The child had psychological testing. the family study was terminated by a final planning conference, usually with both parents. Two cases are presented in support of this treatment approach.

WHITTAKER, C., & BURDY, J. Family psychotherapy of a psychopathic personality: Must every member change? *Comprehensive Psychiatry*, 1969, *10*, 361–364.
The second of two reports of family treatment in which the identified patient was diagnosed a psychopathic personality. The patient was seen with the family for 1½ years and for 6 months more she was seen individually. Her brother left family therapy after about 6 interviews. In this case the identified patient changed while the other family members did not.

2. FAMILY THERAPY OUTCOME

ALEXANDER, J. F., & BRUCE, V. P. Short-term behavioral intervention with delinquent families: Impact on family process and recidivism. *Journal of Abnormal Psychology*, 1973, *81*, 219–225.
A clinical controlled study comparing the effects of "behaviorally" oriented family therapy, "client-centered" family therapy, and no therapy at all for families with a delinquent member. Sample included 99 families randomly assigned to treatments. Results indicated the efficacy of the behavioral family therapy in reducing recidivism.

ARBOGAST, R. The effect of family involvement on the day care center treatment of schizophrenia. *Journal of Nervous and Mental Diseases*, 1969, *149*, 277–280.
A pilot study to assess the relationship between the presence of a seriously distrubed parent or spouse in the home environment and the effect of treatment in a day hospital setting of a consecutive series of schizophrenic patients. The group without seriously distrubed relatives in their environment improved significantly more in their treatment.

BELLVILLE, T. P., RATHS, O. N., & BELLVILLE, C. J. Conjoint marriage therapy with a husband-and-wife team. *American Journal of Orthopsychiatry*, 1969, *39*, 473–483.
A clinical report of marital therapy where the co-therapists were husband and wife. Advantages, differences of transference and identification when the therapists are also a couple, problems of tension between the therapists, selection of therapist couples, and the personality patterns of the patients treated are discussed. Sample was 44 couples with the primary complaint of "sexual incompatibility." They were treated in 16 weekly sessions. The results indicated that 26 were rated as successfully treated and 18 as unsuccessfully treated.

BIRD, H. W., & SCHUHAM, A. I. Meeting families' treatment needs through a family psychotherapy center. *Hospital & Community Psychiatry*, 1978, *29*, 175–178.
An uncontrolled report of the experience of a small, private family therapy center, Five professionals of different disciplines conducted a complicated 5-phase evaluation on 42 families over 2 years. This included an initial telephone assessment, 3 self-administered forms, the Holmes and Rahe Social Readjustment Rating Scale, the Coddington Inventory, clinical interviews, psychological testing (MMPI, Rorschach, TAT) and a team meeting. Based on this, 36 began treatment (mostly marital treatment) averaging 14 weekly sessions. Of the 21 families who completed treatment, 16 were rated improved at end of treatment.

BURKS, H., & SERRANO, A. The use of family therapy and brief hospitalization. *Diseases of the Nervous System*, 1965, *26*, 804–806.
Experience with setting up an inpatient service in conjunction with an outpatient child guidance clinic (which had a strong bias to family therapy) is described.Patients were between 12 and 16, and diagnosis varied from neurosis to psychosis. Hospitalization was short (usually under two months) and was family oriented, using techniques adapted from the multiple impact therapy technique. Results, including a 1-year follow-up, with 25 patients are described.

COUGHLIN, F., & WIMBERGER, H. C. Group family therapy. *Family process*, 1968, *7*, 37–50.
A treatment program using mulitple family therapy with 10 families seen in a group. All families were seen together for the first 3 sessions, and then parts of families were seen in different combinations. It is said to be a useful, short-term treatment technique and 8 of the 10 families improved.

CROW, M. J. Conjoint marital therapy: A controlled outcome study. *Psychol Med*, 1978, *8*: 623–636.
A study comparing the outcome of 2 types of marital treatment. Forty-two couples were treated with 5 to 10 sessions of conjoint marital treatment, with 14 couples each randomly assigned to either "directive," "interpretive," or supportive (used as a control group) therapy. Assessment was by self-report and independent ratings on 5 questionnaires at 7 times before, during, and after (up to 18 months) treatment. Data analysis were by use of multivariate analysis. Results suggested that the directive approach was superior to the control treatment on several measures from the end of treatment through the 18-month follow-up. The interpretive therapy showed significant superiority *only at* the 18-month follow-up. The directive approach is recommended for *most* couples.

CROWE, M. J. Conjoint marital therapy: Advice or interpretation? *Journal of Psychosomatic Research*, 1973, *17*, 309–316.
A report on the methodology for an outcome study of marital therapy, comparing an interpretive approach with a direct, behavioral approach based on operant conditioning principles. A control group will receive common sense, nondirective, and noninterpretive therapy. All 3 types of treatment will be given by the same therapist. Assessment will be done by an independent assessor, blind to treatment, and by questionnaires filled out separately by each partner, covering work, leisure, social, and sexual spheres, as well as symptoms. Sessions will be given every other week, usually up to 10 sessions, but cases could be stopped earlier. An example of each of the 3 approaches is given, and preliminary impressions of treatment are reported.

CUTTER, A. V., & HALLOWITZ, D. Diagnosis and treatment of the family unit with respect to the character-disordered youngster. *Journal of the American Academy of Child Psychiatry*, 1962, *1*, 605–618.
A description of a treatment program of families with children with a diagnosis of character disorder. There are "56 cases currently active" and the results indicate that 60 percent "have been making consistently good progress." Descriptions of the treatment with case examples are provided.

DEWITT, K. N. The effectiveness of family therapy. *Archives of General Psychiatry*, 1978, *35*, 549–561.
A review of the outcome research on family therapy from 1961–1974 with a focus on therapy that involves at least two generations. Results of studies with comparison groups indicate that family therapy is superior to no treatment and to treatment with nonconjoint methods. Review of patient factors, thrapist factors, and treatment factors affecting outcome indicates that such variables *do* affect the outcome. There is an extensive list of references.

ELY, A. L., GUERNEY, B. G., JR., & STOVER, L. Efficacy of the training phase of conjugal therapy. *Psychotherapy*, 1973, *10*, 20–207.
This report evaluates the "training phase" of conjugal therapy, defined as a technique to promote expression, feelings, attitudes, and communications). Subjects were 46 volunteer, married graduate and undergraduate student couples randomized into an experimental treatment group and a control group (put on a waiting list). Measurement instruments included the Ely Feeling Questionnaire, Role-Playing Situations, Primary Communication Inventory, and the Conjugal Life Questionnaire. The conjugal therapy program is described. Results indicate that there was significant improvement in the experimental treatment group over the control group.

ESTERSON, A., COOPER, D., & LAING, R. Results of family-oriented therapy with hospitalized schizophrenics. *British Medical Journal*, 1965, *2*, 1462–1465.
A report of a clinical study of 20 male and 22 female schizophrenics treated by conjoint family milieu therapy plus tranquilizers (given in "reduced" doses). No individual psychotherapy or other somatic treatment was used. Results indicated that all patients were discharged within 1 year of admission, the average length of stay was 3 months, and 17 percent were readmitted within a year of discharge. Of 32 patients discharged to jobs, 26 worked for a whole year after discharge, 2 for from 6 months to a year, and 4 not at all. There was not control group, but the readmission rate was about the same as with other forms of treatment. During the follow-up period, less than half of the patients were on psychotropic medication.

FERREIRA, A., & WINTER, W. Stability of interactional variables in family decision-making. *Archives of General Psychiatry*, 1966, *14*, 352–355.
In order to test the stability over time, and after family therapy, of 3 variables in family decision-making, 23 randomly selected families (10 abnormal and 13 normal) were retested 6 months after the original research project. The abnormal families had received therapy. Results indicated that there was no significant difference between the means observed in test and retests fo the 3 variables for either normal or abnormal families. It is concluded that these 3 variables (spontaneous agreement, decision-time, and choice-fulfillment) were consistent over time and were not changed by family therapy.

FISHER, S., & MENDELL, D. The spread of psychotherapeutic effects from the patient to his family group. *Psychiatry, 1958, 21*, 133–140.
One of a series of papers on the effect of family therapy on an entire family. Some 10 patients in the author's private practice, who were willing to participate in the study, were given the Rorshcach test and the TAT. Data were analyzed based "purely on inspection, impression, and striking individual correlations of events." The authors conclude that significant changes in the patient are accompanied by clearcut changes in the other members of the family. Case examples are given in support of this position.

FITZGERALD, R. V. Conjoint marital psychotherapy: An outcome and follow-up study. *Family Process*, 1969, *8*, 261–271.
A report on an outcome study of couples seen in conjoint marriage therapy. A sample of 57 couples were followed up after 2½ years with an interview by telephone. Of the couples who were seen because an individual sought therapy, 76 percent were improved. Of those who presented an ongoing marital conflict as the presenting problem, 75 percent improved.

FLOMENHAFT. K., KAPLAN, D., & LANGSLEY, D. Avoiding psychiatric hospitalization. *Social Casework*, 1969, *14*, 38–46.
One of a series of articles comparing "outpatient family crisis therapy" with psychiatric hospitalization. The methodology has been previously described. Results achieved by both of these two methods were equivalent. However, the authors stressed out-patient treatment is more economical and less "stigmatizing."

FRIEDMAN, A. S. Interaction of drug therapy with marital therapy in depressive patients. *Archives of General Psychiatry*, 1975, *32*, 619–637.
A controlled study of the comparative effects of marital therapy and an antidepressant drug (amitriptyline) and of the drug-psychotherapy interaction. Patients were randomly assigned to four treatment groups, in a two-by-two factorial design: (1) drug-marital therapy; (2) drug-minimal contact; (3) placebo-marital therapy; and (4) placebo-minimal contact. Course of treatment was 12 weeks, setting was an outpatient clinic, and patients had the primary diagnosis of depression. Results indicated that both the marital therapy and the drug therapy had significant advantage over controls. Drug therapy worked faster and was more efficient in relieving symptoms an giving better global improvement, but marital therapy was significantly better in improving family role task performance. It was concluded that both drug therapy and marital therapy could be additive rather than mutually exclusive.

GOLDSTEIN, M. J., RODNICK, E. H., EVANS, J. R., et al. Drug and family therapy in the aftercare of acute schizophrenics. *Archives of General Psychiatry*, 1978, *35*, 1169–1177.
An outcome study that examines the effect of crisis family therapy (6 sessions) and high- and low-dose therapy. One hundred and four young schizophrenic patients were treated at a community mental health clinic after an average 14 day hospitalization. They were stratified for premorbid adjustment by the UCLA Social Attainment Scale and then randomized to .25 or 1.0 ml fluphenazine enanthate biweekly for 6 weeks, with or without weekly family sessions. Results measuring symptoms and relapse rate at 6 weeks and at 6 months showed a significant advantage for the high dose with family treatment group and worse results for the low dose without. The authors conclude that the effects are specific, vary significantly with premorbid adjustment and support this combined aftercare treatment approach.

GRAD, J., & SAINSBURG, P. Mental illness and the family. *Lancet*, 1963, *1*, 544–547.
An analysis of the effects on the family of psychiatric illness of one member of the family before and after treatment. The sample was 410 patients from psychiatric facilities in England. Problems reported by families were analyzed; the sicker or older the patient the greater the number of problems reported by the family. The number of problems by families was reduced significantly after treatment of the patient.

GREENBERG, I. M., GLICK, I. D., MATCH, S., & RIBACK, S. S. Family therapy: Indications and rationale. *Archives of General Psychiatry*, 1964, *10*, 7–25.
Indications for and results of family therapy with a series of 20 patients, mostly schizophrenic, in an open hospital, inpatient setting. Indications list diagnostic as well as therapeutic goals. Six-month follow-up results of 13 cases are presented, and a rationale using ego psychological and group process terms is included. A review of the family therapy literature is presented.

GURMAN, A. S. The effects and effectiveness of marital therapy: A review of outcome research. *Family Process*, 1973, *12*, 145–170.
This article reviews the liiterature on outcome research in marital therapy. The overall improvement rate across the studies reviewed was 66 percent, compared to 16 percent "spontaneous" improvements. Attention was called to the possibility of deterioration of marital relationships due to therapy; although exact figures are not available this seems to be rare (about 2 percent). The merits of cotherapy versus single therapy in marital treatment have not been proven.

GURMAN, A. S., KNISKERN, D. P. Technolatry, methololatry, and the results of family therapy. *Family Process*, 1978, *17*, 275–281.
A critical commentary of Wells and Desen's article reviewing research outcomes on nonbehavioral family therapies. The authors question whether standard criteria are sufficient to study the outcomes of family therapy. Relationship factors as well as "inferential" measures, rather than "objective" change measures, should be used in judging outcome and results.

HAHN, I. Family therapy: A child-centered approach to distrubed parent–child relationships. *Pennsylvania Psychiatric Quarterly*, 1964, *4*, 58–62.
Family oriented treatment (including "therapist, child and usually both parents") seemed to offer advantages over the "typical psychoanalytical approach." Sample was 15 families, where the child was the identified patient, referred to either a child guidance clinic or private practice. All cases improved and telephone follow-up in 7 cases afer 6 months "corroborated the results."

HALLOWITZ, D. Family unit treatment of character-disordered youngsters. In *Social work practice*. New York: Columbia University Press, 1963.
A report on the family treatment of 38 children with a diagnosis of character disorder. Procedures and descriptions of the family are offered along with tabular reports of outcome. 61 percent had a favorable outcome with the treatment averaging 17 hours per case.

HARDCASTLE, D. R. A Mother–child, multiple-family, counseling program: Procedures and results. *Family Process*, 1977, *16*, 67–74.
The purpose of this study was to determine the effects of a family counseling program on: (1) parents' family satisfaction, perceived integration, and family congruence; (2) the number of positive and negative responses communicated among family members; and (3) an undesirable behavior exhibited by one child in the family. Mother and child taught other family members the principles learned during multiple-family sessions. Results observed in a sample of 14 experimental families and 11 control families indicated: (1) parents receiving family counseling increased significantly their family satisfaction and perceived-integration scores as compared to those parents not receiving counseling; (2) families receiving counseling increased significantly the number of positive responses among them compared with the control families; (3) children receiving counseling decreased significantly the frequency of exhibiting specific undesirable behavior; and (4) no significant differences were found between the two groups in parents' family congruence scores and in the number of negative communicated responses among family members.

HAWKINS, R. P., PETERSON, R. F., SCHWEID, E., & BIJOU, S. W. Behavior therapy in the home: Amelioration

of problem parent-child relations with the parent in a therapeutic role. *Journal of Experienced Child Psychology*, 1966, *4*, 99–107.
A description of the behavior modification approach to bringing about changes in a family. Theory and techniques are described as well as outcome.

KAFFMAN, M. Short term family therapy. *Family Process*, 1963, *2*, 216–234.
A report on the use of family therapy in a child guidance clinic in Israel with the emphasis upon short-term family treatment. The rationale, methodology, limitations, and initial evaluations of results are presented for 70 consecutive cases referred to the clinic.

KRITZER, H., & PITTMAN, F. S. Overnight psychiatric care in a general emergency room. *Journal of Hospital and Commnity Psychiatry*, 1968, *19*, 303–306.
A clinical article reviewing the experience with 36 psychiatric patients who came to the emergency room because of a crisis. As alternatives to in-patient hospitalization, overnight hospitalization, and the emergency room was used. Rationale was that their presenting problem was often a manifestation of underlying family problems, and by temporarily relieving the crisis and working out the future management, in-patient hospitalization could be avoided. Results indicated that of 36 patients, 11 were essentially sent to a psychiatric hospital, 22 were discharged directly from the emergency room, and 3 signed out against medical advice.

LANGSLEY, D., FLOMENHAFT, K., & MACHOTKA, P. Follow-up evaluation of family crisis therapy. *American Journal of Orthopsychiatry*, 1969, *39*, 753–759.
One of a series of papers on a research project in which families were assigned randomly either to traditional hospital treatment of family crisis therapy with a focus on family therapy. Six-month follow-up evaluations of 150 family crisis therapy cases and 150 hospital treatment cases demonstrated that patients are less likely to be rehospitalized in the former group.

LANGSLEY, D., PITTMAN, F., & SWANK, G. Family crisis in schizophrenics and other mental patients. *Journal of Nervous and Mental Diseases*, 1969, *149*, 270–276.
A further report on a study using crisis therapy as an alternative to psychiatric hospitalization. In this study, 50 families which included a schizophrenic patient and 50 which included nonschizophrenic mental patients, were studied with the means of an instrument which quantified the events leading to a crisis in the family and the management of such crises. Nonschizophrenic mental patients were better able to handle crises and interact with their families. Discussion of these findings is presented.

LANSKY, M. R., & DAVENPORT, A. E. Difficulties in brief conjoint treatment of sexual dysfunction. *American Journal of Psychiatry*, 1975, *132*, 177–179.
Ten couples from a military population were treated with both Masters and Johnson's sexual therapy and family therapy for sexual dysfunction. Eight received treatment *only* for symptomatic sexual difficulties, 2 received the family treatment in addition. Results indicate that only 2 couples of the 10 improved. Reasons for this outcome are discussed.

LEVINE, R. Treatment in the home. *Social Work*, 1964, *9*, 19–28.
A clinical report of treatment of 7 low-income multiproblem families who came to a mental hygiene clinic for help with the identified patient, usually a child. Treatment of the family rather than the individual was begun because it seemed more economical, more family members could be helped, and the therapist could be more accurate in understanding problems. Treatment was done in the home. Techniques included talking, demonstration, and family activity. The 7 families were rated in terms of improvement.

MACKIE, R. Family problems in medical and nursing families. *British Journal of Medical Psychology*, 1967, *40*, 333–340.
From 9 cases treated by the author over 4 years and a review of the literature, the author presents parts of 3 of the cases in which the presenting patient was a doctor or nurse. Of the 9 cases, 7 improved with family therapy and 2 did not. The doctor or nurse will "defend himself against the direct expression of sick or dependent parts of himself and will instead project these onto the spouse or onto other relatives.

MASTEN, A . S. Family therapy as a treatment for children: Critical review of outcome research. *Family Process*, 1979, *18*, 323–335.
This article reviews the value of family therpy as a treatment for child psychopathology by examining pertinent outcome research. Fourteen studies that met 3 criteria are included in the review: (1) a child or adolescent was the identified patient; (2) therapy included at least on parent and the child; and (3) outcome was evaluated in terms of the child's symptoms. There were only two well-controlled studies; all others showed major shortcomings. Empirically, there is evidence that family therapy is an effective treatment for these problems. However, there are no sufficient data available to demonstrate the merits of family therapy over individual child therapy.

MILLER, W. H., & GOTTLIEB, F. Predicting behavioral treatment outcome in disturbed children: A preliminary report of the responsivity index of parents (RIP). *Behavior Therapy*, 1974, *5*, 210–214.
This clinical study attempts to predict outcome of family therapy where the identified patient is a nonpsychotic child, using the MMPI scores of the mother. Method was to devise outcome criteria based on family follow-up at six months. Using a step-wise analysis on a new sample based on "responsivity" of the mother's intervention or "balance of internalization/externalization behavioral attributes" could predict outcome in 80 percent of the cases. Father's MMPI predict outcome only at the chance level. This is a pilot study, and results are considered to be suggestive only.

MURRELL, S. Intra-family variables in psychotherapy outcome research. *Psychotherapy*, 1970, *7*, 19–21.
This is a report of a pilot study to investigate the relationship between intra-family variables and individual therapy outcome. The sample was from a child mental health center. Children were in individual therapy; parents were in group therapy. Before starting group therapy, both husband and wife filled out the Leary Interpersonal Checklist. Measures of the discrepancies between husband and wife were used in these descriptions. Results suggested a relationship between inter-spouse discrepancy and therapy outcome, "the tendency being for a high degree of discrepancy to be related to successful outcome."

OSBERG, J. W. Initial impressions of the use of short-term family group conferences. *Family Process*, 1962, *1*, 236–244.
A discussion of early experiences with 38 families seen in group treatment over a 4-year period in a psychiatric outpatient clinic. The evaluation, initial session, and succeeding sessions are described with a case example.

PATTERSON, B., MCNEAL, S., HAWKINS, N., & PHELPS, R. Reprogramming the social environment. *Journal of Child Psychology and Psychiatry*, 1967, *8*, 181–185.
A case report in which the hypothesis was that conditioning techniques could be used to reprogram the parent and the child so that they become mutually reinforcing in contrast to conditioning the child alone. The patient was a 5-year-old autistic child. Observation of the new conditioning was done in the home of the patient and both parents. There were 12 conditioning sessions lasting from 10 to 20 minutes over a 4-week period. Changes in behavior were noted.

PITTMAN, F., DEYOUNG, C., FLOMENHAFT, K., KAPLAN, D., & LANGSLEY, D. Crisis family therapy. In J. Masserman (Ed.), *Current Psychiatric therapies* (Vol. VI). New York: Grune & Stratton, 1966.
A report of the author's experiences in using a family approach in dealing with acute crisis situations, rather than using hospitalization or individual psychotherapy. Setting was an acute treatment facility which hospitalizes about 75 percent of patients referred. Of these, 25 percent were referred to the family treatment unit consisting of a psychiatrist, social worker, and nurse. Fifty cases were referred to this unit and, in 42, hospitalization was "avoided completely." Techniques of treatment are discussed.

PITTMAN, E., LANGSLEY, D, & DEYOUNG, C. Work and school phobias: A family approach to treatment. *American Journal of Psychiatry*, 1968, *124*, 1535–1541.
Eleven cases of work phobia (the patient experienced overt anxiety associated with having to go to work or staying at work) are thought of as being "the adult form of school phobia." Treatment goal is to allow the wife or mother to allow the man to separate. One year follow-up showed that 5 cases treated with conjoint family therapy returned to work; the 6 in long-term individual therapy did not.

POLAK, P. R., EGAN, D., VANDERBERGH, R., & WILLIAMS, W. V. Prevention in mental health: A controlled study. *American Journal of Psychiatry*, 1975, *132*, 146–149.
See reference in Section 4.4.

POSTNER, R. S., GUTTMAN, H. A., SIGAL, J. J., et al. Process and outcome in conjoint family therapy. *Family Process*, 1971, *10*, 451–473.
This experiment was designed to measure change in participation and affective expression by family members during the course of conjoint family therapy as it relates to the outcome of therapy. Forty-nine coded transcript segments of 11 families were examined for affective expressions. Quantity and direction of expression were recorded as well as the therapist's verbal interactions with these families. Using a two-way analysis of variance to indicate statistical differences of the high and low outcome groups indicated an increase of "welfare" feelings, a sharp decrease in "neutral" statements, and an initial rise and leveling off "emergency" statements for both groups during process changes with little or no change between groups. Characteristics of the good outcome group also included a father who could "out talk" the mother in a family and a mother who spoke little in initial sessions. Implications for future experimentation and hypothesis testing are discussed.

RAKOFF, V. M., SIGAL, J. J., & EPSTEIN, N. B. Predictions of therapeutic process and conjoint family therapy. *Archives of General Psychiatry*, 1975, *32*, 1013–1017.
A controlled clinical study attempting to predict process and outcome in family therapy. Sample was drawn from 20 families in family therapy in an outpatient clinic of mostly upper lower-class clientele. Treatment was done by

therapists of different disciplines supervised by senior staff members. Predictions of process and outcome were made by a "team of experienced family therapists." Using the Family Category Scheme, predictions of change versus the changes actually observed were rated on a 4-point scale. Results indicated that the team was (1) unable to predict process; (2) underrated treatment effectiveness; and (3) were most successful predicting changes in behavior.

REDING, G., CHARLES, L., & HOFFMAN, M. Treatment of the couple by a couple. II: Conceptual framework, case presentation, and follow-up study. *British Journal of Medical Psychology*, 1967, *40*, 243–252.
A report of the authors experience using a male and female cotherapist for marital therapy. Previously the "four-way" treatment was seen as a combination of two individual treatments. This has been given up and extensive use of transference and countertransference interpretation have been made. Discussions of theory, process, and a case are presented. Telephone follow-up 3 to 30 months after termination of 10 to 15 couples treated by this method are reported.

ROBINS, L. N. Problems in follow-up studies. *American Journal of Psychiatry*, 1977, *134*, 904–907.
See reference in Section 3.5.

RO-TROCK, G. K., WELLISCH, D. K., & SCHOOLAR, J. C. A family outcome study in an inpatient setting. *American Journal of Orthopsychiatry*, 1977, *47*, 515–522.
A controlled study comparing family therapy with individual therapy for hospitalized adolescents. Two groups of inpatients were each randomly assigned to either individual therapy of family therapy. Objective and subjective measures of family interaction were made pre- and post-treatment. Prehospitalization functioning level was compared at 3-month follow-up. None of the family treatment adolescents were rehospitalized, versus 6 in the individual treatment group, and community readjustment was better, thus supporting the conclusion that family therapy is more effective than individual therapy in this sample of patients.

RUBINSTEIN, D. Rehospitalization versus family crisis intervention. *American Journal of Psychiatry*, 1972, *129*, 715–720.
Three case reports are presented to support the idea that a family-oriented crisis intervention approach to therapy will prevent rehospitalization at times of crisis. Treatment was done by a multidisciplinary team at a regional teaching center, who particularly used home visits. Results in an uncontrolled pilot study showed that only 3 of 27 patients seen in 6 months required rehospitalizaiton.

RUSSELL, A. Limitations of family therapy. *Clinical Social Work Journal*, 1976, *4*, 83–92.
Two case examples are presented in support of the idea that there is an unknown percentage of families who present for treatment for whom family therapy will not be effective. Reasons for this include lack of outcome studies discriminating as to effectiveness, a variety of poor prognosis factors (for example, lack of motivation), and specific difficulties in separating adolescents from their families.

SAFER, D. J. Family therpay for children with behavior disorders. *Family Process*, 1966, *5*, 243–255.
A report on short term therapy of 29 children with behavior disorders and their families. All cases were selected because they were either unmotivated or unacceptable for individual psychotherapy. Treatment approach is described and 40 percent showed improvement.

SANDER, F. M. Freud's "A case of successful treatment by hypnotism (1892–1893)": An uncommon therapy? *Family Process*, 1974, *13*, 461–468.
In Freud's first reported successful treatment by hypnosis he describes an enmeshed family. His treatment approach combined the uses of hypnosis and paradox, which resulted in behavior change. This author draws parallels between Freud's treatment approach and to Haley/Erickson family systems theory described in the book, *"Uncommon Therapy'* (for example, that it is valuable to view a psychiatric symptom as a symptom of family interpersonal relationships occurring particularly during transitional stages of family development). However, Freud indicated in his case only short-lived changes, or "symptom retrieval." The author fears the same for the case of family therapy if the goal of treatment is based solely on symptom removal.

SCHREIBER, L. E. Evaluation of family group treatment in a family agency. *Family Process*, 1966, *5*, 21–29.
A report on the experience of a family service agency in the treatment of 72 families. Within 3 months, 61 percent showed improvement in communication processes and 56 percent in the presenting behavior problem of the child. Of those who continued beyond 3 months, 96 percent showed improvement in communication processes and 92 percent in the behavior of the child.

SCHUSTER, F. Summary description of multiple impact psychotherapy. *Texas Report of Biology Medicine*, 1962, *17*, 120–125.
A report of the multiple impact psychotherapy project used at a child guidance clinic in Texas. Families come from great distances and are seen intensively for two days, both individuallly and in various family situations. The preliminary 1-year and 1-month follow-ups attest that this method is "at least as effective as individual treatment in many adolescent referrals."

SHAPIRO, R. J. Therapist attitudes and premature termination in family and individual therapy. *Journal of Nervous and Mental Diseases*, 1974, *159*, 101–107.
The second report of a study randomizing patients to individual versus family evaluation and therapy in an outpatient clinic. Methodology has been previously described. Each patient and family was rated by the therapist on: (1) "the therapist's affective responses to the patient, (2) degree of psychopathology; and (3) treatment prognosis." Results indicated the most significant difference between "continuers" and "terminaters" was that therapists were consistently much more positive with continuers than with dropouts. However, this difference was less marked for families than for individual patients.

SHAPIRO, R. J., & BUDMAN, S. H. Defection, termination, and continuation in family and individual therapy. *Family Process*, 1973, *12*, 55–67.
This study focuses on comparative rates of defection (failure to appear for the first session), permature termination (1 to 3 sessions), and continuation (more than 3 sessions) of treatment, in a sample of patients who were referred for either individual (N=183) or family therapy (N=66). Structured telephone interviews were used to determine the reasons for termination or continued treatment. Results showed: (1) drop-out rates for family therapy are significantly higher than for individual treatment (29 percent in families versus 16 percent in individual treatment); (2) major reasons for terminating or continuing treatment, in either modality, seem related to patients' and families' perceptions of their therapists (lack of activity for family therapists, and lack of empathy in individual therapists); and (3) fathers of patients played a key role in determining continuation in treatment.

SHELLOW, R. S., BROWN, B. S., & OSBERG, J. W. Family group therapy in retrospect: Four years and sixty families. *Family Process*, 1963, *2*, 52–67.
A review of experience with family group therapy (authors' term for conjoint family therapy) with 60 families in a child guidance clinic over a 4-year period. Referral sources were mainly from physicians and school. Several "hidden" factors influenced choice of this form of therapy by staff members: (1) the identified patient was often the oldest child, and (2) there was a large proportion of school achievement problems represented.

SIGAL, J. J., BARRS, C. B., & DOUBILET, A. L. Problems in measuring the success of family therapy in a common clinical setting: Impasse and solutions. *Family Process*, 1976, *15*, 225–233.
This study compares treatment outcomes after 4½ years for 62 families treated in therapy for approximately one year in a psychiatric outpatient clinic and 31 families who refused treatment after no more than two sessions. New symptoms were reported by more families in the treated group than in the untreated group. No significant difference in reported improvement and family functioning level was found. Flaws in data collection and methodology are identified and suggestions are made for future research using process or correlational studies to improve service.

SIGAL, J. J., RAKOFF, V., & EPSTEIN, N. B. Indications of therapeutic outcome in conjoint family therapy. *Family Process*, 1967, *6*, 215–226.
A report on a study that attempted to predict the eventual success of family therapy by examining the degree of family interaction and emotional involvement as described by therapists in the initial stages of treatment. "The clinical observations in this study raise some doubts about the value of the interactional frame of reference in conjoint family therapy."

SLIPP, S., ELLIS, S., & KRESSEL, K. Factors associated with engagement in family therapy. *Family Process*, 1974, *13*, 413–427.
In order to understand, "why families continue with or terminate conjoint family treatment," these authors compared 38 families who continued with therapy with 13 families who dropped out on a variety of antecedent variables. They found 3 predictors that were importnat to consider: (1) which spouse initiated the search for treatment; (2) the level of authoritarianism in spouses; and (3) the family socioeconomic status. Families that had a severely disturbed member had a poor rate of engagement, except in those families where both spouses did not have high authoritarianism attitudes. When both spouses initiated treatment, engagement was nearly perfect. Difficulties in engaging families from the lowest socioeconomic class may be partly related to the authoritarianism attitudes of the husband.

SLIPP, S., & KRESSEL, K. Difficulties in family therapy evaluation. I: A comparison of insight versus problem-solving approaches. II. Désign critique and recommendations. *Family Process*, 1978, *17*, 409–422.
This paper includes 2 parts. In Part I, an outcome study comparing 2 methods of family treatment is reported. Families were randomly assigned to insight oriented treatment (N=10) or a Problem-Solving intervention (N=10). The results on self-report measures of family functioning indicated that the Problem-Solving intervention yielded more improvement after 3 months. In Part II, the study is critically reviewed. Special attention is given to issues involving the selection of treatment and control conditions, sampling, and the measurement of outcome.

SMITH, I. W., & LOEB, D. The stable extended family as a model in treatment of atypical children. *Social Work*, 1965, *10*, 75–81.
A report of a multiple-impact therapeutic program in the treatment of 6 severely disturbed children and their families. Three boys and 3 girls, aged 4–7 were referred as mentally retarded, were intolerable in school, and appeared psychotic in the first interview. Two female therapists, assuming grandmotherly roles, treated the families conjointly

in 3 overlapping phases: (1) individual treatment for the patient and parents, (2) family group therapy, and (3) peer experiences for all family members. Patients showed rapid symptomatic recovery, enabling them to return to school and participate in social situations. Parents and siblings, relieved of anxiety, functioned more efficiently and experienced improved interpersonal relationships.

SOLOMON, M. Family therapy dropouts: Resistance to change. *Canadian Psychiatric Journal*, 1969, *14*, 21–29.
A clinical paper that retrospectively hypothesizes that resistance to change in the family was responsible for the family's unilateral decision to terminate treatment. Data came from 5 families treated from 4 to 17 sessions on an outpatient basis. Treatment stopped at the point where change had to be made in the husband–wife relationship. (The change was perceived by the family as a threat to stability). The role of therapist is *provoking* termination of therapy was discussed, and a comprehensive review of the literature on family resistance was made.

STUART, R. B. Token reinforcement in marital treatment. In P. H. Glasser & L. N. Glasser (Eds.), *Families in crisis*.
New York: Harper & Row, 1970.
"The tasks of the marriage therapist are . . . to identify the desired ("loving") behaviors sought by each spouse from the other; second, to identify the contingencies which can be used to accelerate and maintain these behaviors; and third, to increase the probability that each of these behaviors will occur." Procedures and results with 5 couples are presented.

WAINWRIGHT, W. H. The reaction of mothers to improvement in their schizophrenic daughters. *Comprehensive Psychiatry*, 1960, *1*, 236–243.
At the Payne Whitney Psychiatric Clinic 8 mother–schizophrenic daughter combinations were interviewed and observed for a period ranging from 4 to 48 months, including up to 30 months after the patient's hospital discharge. Of these 8 mothers, 2 responded favorably to their daughter's improvement, 2 showed fluctuation in resopnse which seemed dependent upon the severity of the daughter's symptoms, and 4 mothers showed signs of illness as their daughters improved. The author sees a common need with these 4 mothers to keep the daughter partially ill. Where hostility emerges during the recovery phase, he suggests evaluation for treatment of the mother.

WELLINGTON, J. A case for short term family therapy. *Psychotherapy*, 1957, *4*, 130–132.
Based on a case of a 14-year-old female who was treated with family therapy over 12 sessions with good results (she had had 5 previous years of individual psychotherapy at age 12), it is argued that short-term family therapy is often as effective as long-term therapy.

WELLS, R. A., DILKES, T. C., & TRIVELLI, N. The results of family therapy. A critical review of the literature.
Family Process, 1972, *11*, 189–207.
See reference in Section 6.0.

WELLS, R. A., & DEZEN, A. F. Ideologies, idols (and graven images?): Rejoinder to Gurman and Kniskern. *Family Process*, 1978, *17*, 283–286.
A response to Gurman and Kniskern's critical commentaries about their own review article, appearing in the same issue. Agreements and disagreements with the commentaries are discussed regarding design criteria for family therapy outcome research; and the role of objective change measures in psychotherapy outcome research is also discussed.

WELLS, R. A., & DEZEN, A. F. The results of family therapy revisited: The nonbehavioral methods. *Family Process*, 1978, *17*, 251–274.
A 5-year critical survey (1971–1976) of literature reporting the outcome of the nonbehavioral family therapies. A noticeable trend is the utilization of family therapy as an alternative to psychiatric hospitalization in psychosomatic problems in children and adolescents and as an alternative to individual psychotherapy. There is a discussion of outcome research design.

WHITAKER, C. A. Psychotherapy with couples. *American Journal of Psychotherapy*, 1958, *12*, 18–23.
A clinical report on the use of marital therapy as an alternative to the use of individual psychotherapy with the identified patient. Sample was 30 couples all of whom were in outpatient treatment, and there were no individual meetings during the course of treatment. Results indicated that of the 30 couples, 6 dropped out, in 2 cases the marital therapy was preliminary to individual therapy. 10 couples showed no progress in at least one member, and it is unclear what happened to the other couples.

WOODWARD, C. A., SANTA-BARBARA, J., LEVIN, S., et al. Aspects of consumer satisfaction with brief family therapy. *Family Process*, 1978, *17*, 399–407.
A study of brief family therapy based on a family satisfaction questionnaire administered to 279 families at 6 months after treatment for problems generated in a child with academic and/or behavioral problems at school. Families were generally satisfied with the overall services received but expressed widely varying degrees of satisfaction with various aspects of treatment. Forty-five percent of the sample did not feel that the services provided were comprehensive and adequate. Despite this criticism, the majority of families were functioning well at the time follow-up was assessed by a

number of independent measures. Global satisfaction is not the only index of treatment effectiveness; many dissatisfied families experienced successful treatment outcomes.

WOODWARD, C. A., SANTA-BARBARA, J., LEVIN, S., et al. The role of goal attainment scaling in evaluating family therapy outcome. *American Journal of Orthopsychiatry*, 1978, *48*, 464–476.
As part of a study of family therapy outcome, the adequacy of Goal Attainment Scaling for evaluating brief family therapy is described. Two-hundred and seventy-nine families were treated by 80 experienced therapists who constructed specific goals for each patient and family early in treatment, and these were later used in follow-up interviews. Interrater reliability was high and content analysis of the goals set and met is discussed. Although external measurements of validity are presented only elsewhere, the authors conclude that this scaling method is useful as an outcome measure.

ZIERER, E., STERNBERG, D., FINN, R., & FARMER, M. Family creative analysis: Its role in treatment. *Bulletin of Art Therapy*, 1966, *5*, 87–104.
The second in a series of papers describing the use of "creative analysis" in the treatment of families. A case example is presented demonstrating the method. Changes in the family were compared with evaluation before treatment, using the interpersonal check-list. Creative analysis is seen as an adjunct of an approach stimulating a health "re-integration of the family as a network of mutually need-gratifying members."

3. FAMILY RESEARCH

3.1 FAMILY DATA FROM RECORDS

AHMED, F. Family and mental disorders in Pakistan. *International Journal of Social Psychiatry*, 1968, *14*, 290–295.
In order to study the effect of the structure of the family on mental illness, 967 cases from a privately owned psychiatric clinic in Pakistan were studied, using retrosepctive case records. Only psychotics and neurotics were used from the larger sample. Results revealed that there were more female psychotics, that psychotic patients were closer in age to their parents, that, the father's age was usually less than 25 for the psychotics and more than 25 for the neurotics, that more psychotics were the oldest in the family and more neutorics were the youngest in the family. There was more psychopathology in the family of psychotics than neurotic patients. No relationship was found between mental disorders and marital status, "family system," (term unexplained), siblings, parental loss in childhood, and mother's age at birth.

AVALLONE, S., ARON, R., STARR, P., & BREETZ, S. How therapissts assign families to treatment modalities: The development of the treatment method choice sort. *American Journal of Orthopsychiatry*, 1973, *43*, 767–773.
A research study in a private outpatient clinic for children attempted to parcel out factors that influence choice of psychotherapy. Instruments used were a 197-item-Q-sort based on statements of preference (not practive) for treatment modality from the clinic therapists (psychiatrists, psychologists, and social workers), 86 demographic variables, and the Douglas Thom Child Guidance List of presenting complaints. Results indicate that 127 of the 197 factors reached significance in terms of consensus. Indications and contraindications for individual therapy, family therapy, marital therapy, group therapy, and combinations thereof are listed.

BECK, S. F. Families of schizophrenic and of well children: Methods, concepts, and some results. *American Journal of Orhtopsychiatry*, 1960, *30*, 247–275.
A report on a research study attempting to differentiate and compare families with schizophrenic children, families with neurotic children, and families with normal children. a list of trait items about individuals in 106 families were Q-sorted by a psychiatrist and three social workers. The clusterings are said to indicate similarities and differences.

BROOKS, W. B., DEANE, W. N., LAGOV, R. C., & CURTIS, B. B. Varieties of family participation in the rehabilitation of released chronic schizophrenic patients. *Journal of Nervous and Mental Diseases*, 1963, *136*, 432–444.
A study of the post-hospital course of 170 chronic schizophrenic patients. The data were abstracted from records. The social, economic and psychiatric outcomes are correlated with various aspects of the family's participation in the rehabilitation process. A major factor in the success of this group is said to be the breaking of pathological ties with the family and the forming of new, healthier relationships.

BROWNING, C. J. Differential impact of family disorganization on male adolescents. *Social Problems*, 1960, *8*, 37–44.
Samples of 60 nondelinquent, 60 delinquent-truancy, and 60 delinquent-auto theft (boys, age 15) were identified. Data were obtained from school, police, and probation records, from interviews with mothers, from family solidarity and marital adjustment scales filled out by parents, and California test of personality scales filled out by the boys. The incidence of broken homes is higher in the delinquent groups, but this variable is not a consistently good indicator of family disorganization and needs refinement.

BROWNING, D. H., & BOATMAN, B. Incest: Children at risk. *American Journal of Psychiatry*, 1977, *134*, 69–72.
A clinical paper reviewing 14 cases of incest seen in a child psychiatry clinic using the material from the charts. The findings revealed that the "typical family constellation" consisted of a "chronically depresseed mother, an alcoholic and violent father or stepfather, and an eldest daughter who was forced to carry many of the mother's responsibilities with ensuing role confusion." Treatment varied as to the case, some of the cases receiving family therapy, and other cases receiving individual therapy for the mother.

BUCK, C. W., & LADD, K. L. Psychoneurosis in marital partners. *British Journal of Psychiatry*, 1965, *3*, 587–590.
A study of records of physicians' diagonses from a health insurance plan in a Canadian city. There was a definite association between the occurence of psychoneurotic illness in husbands and wives who had been married for many years, little association for partners recently married, and no association during the pre-marital period. The authors interpret these findings as evidence that a process of contagion rather than mate selection determines the concordance between marital partners in psychoneurotic illness.

COLEMAN, S. B., & DAVIS, D. I. Family therapy and drug abuse: A national survey. *Family Process*, 1978, *17*, 21–29.
This report describes a national study of the role of family therapy in drug abuse cases. One of the findings was that there are relationships between the degree of heroin abuse and both the extend to which family therapists are trained and the degree to which an agency really uses family therapy as a major treatment. Low-opiate groups get more family

therapy, a more adequately trained family therapist, and an agency that fosters family therapy as a central mode of rehabilitating the addict.

DAVIDSON, S. School phobia as a manifestation of family disturbance: Its structure and treatment. *Journal of Child Psychology and Psychiatry*, 1960–61, *1*, 270–288.
Thirty cases of school phobia were studied at a child guidance clinic. Data was gathered from social histories and from individual interviews with patients and their parents. Family dynamics and methods of individual treatment are discussed.

DUHRESSEN,L A. Preventive massnahmen in der familie. *Psychotherapy and Psychosomatics*, 1968, *16*, 319–322.
This article focuses on the *preventive* aspects of family therapy. Characteristics of family life in other cultures are first described, and then psychopathology of specific family types is presented. A case report is presented in support of this thesis.

EVANS, H. A., CHAGOYA, L., & RAKOFF, V. Decision making as to the choice of family therapy in an adolescent inpatient setting. *Family Process*, 1971, *10*, 97–110.
Reasons for the avoidance and/or termination of conjoint family therapy (CFT) in an adolescent inpatient setting where such treatment is part of the espoused policy were examined. The study includes an examination of the records, covering 2 years, of 100 adolescents, male and female, ages 12–21, hospitalized for schizophrenia, character and psychosomatic disorders, depressive and adolescent adjustment reaction, and borderline and manic-depressive psychosis. Material in the charts indicated that 50 received CFT; 50 did not. Drawing on the responses to questionnaires sent to patients' families, the material on the charts, the authors comment on the reason given for not CFT. They conclude that when CFT was not carried out a combination of realistic barriers and unconscious factors were operative, including therapist's inability to deal with various resistances.

HILGARD, J., & NEWMAN, M. F. Parental loss by death in childhood as an etiological factor among schizophrenic and alcoholic patients compared with a non-patient community sample. *Journal of Nervous and Mental Disease*, 1963, *137*, 14–28.
Hospital records were examined and a sample of 1,561 schizophrenic patients and 929 alcoholic patients were compared with a control sample of 1.096 cases. Schizophrenics had lost one or both parents more often than the control group. Parent loss is said to be one of the factors assiciated with an increase in vulnerability in coping with the stresses of adult life.

HILGARD, J., & NEWMAN, M. F. Early parental deprivation as a function factor in the etiology of schizophrenia and alcoholism. *American Journal of Orthopsychiatry*, 1963, *33*, 409–420.
A study designed to consider the age at which loss by death was sustained during childhood by hospitalized schizophrenic and alcoholic patients. Comparison was made using hospital admission records of 1521 schizophrenic patients, 929 alcoholic patients and a control group of 1,096 cases selected using an area-sampling technique from an urban community. It was concluded that mother loss among women in both diagnostic categories was earlier than in the control group who lost mothers. Schizophrenic women showed loss of both mother and father at a significantly earlier age than the control subjects.

JACKSON, D. D., BLOCK, J., & PATTERSON, V. Psychiatrists conceptions of the schizophrenic parent. *Archives of Neurologic Psychiatry*, 1958, *79*, 448–459.
Twenty psychiatrists were asked for their conceptions of the mothers and fathers of schizophrenics. Three types of mothers are 3 types of fathers were described. This data was then compared with Q-Sorts done on 20 mothers and 20 fathers of 20 schizophrenic patients. Two out of 3 mother types described by psychiatrists correlated highly. None of the father descriptions correlated statistically.

JENKINS, R. The varieties of children's behavioral problems and family dynamics. *American Journal of Psychiatry*, 1968, *124*, 1440–1445.
Fifteen hundred children attending a psychiatric clinic were separated into 3 groups by computer clustering of their symptoms, and correlated with family types. Overanxious children are likely to have an anxious, infantilizing mother. A critical, depreciative, punitive, inconsistent mother or stepmother is typical for the unsocialized, aggressive child. Socialized delinquents are likely to come from large families characterized by parental neglect and delegation of parental responsibilities.

KREITMAN, N. Mental disorder in married couples. *Journal of Mental Science*, 1962, *108*, 438–446.
To determine the incidence and nature of mental illness in the spouses of psychiatric patients, the records of the Chichester psychiatric service in England were examined. The findings indicate that the incidence of mental illness in spouses of psychiatric patients is higher than among the general population. Various hypotheses to account for this finding are discussed.

LAGRONE, D. M. The military family syndrome. *Americn Journal of Psychiatry*, 1978, *135*, 1040–1043.
This is a clinical study of diagnosis and treatment of military families. The method was to review case records of 792 children and adolescents seen in a militay outpatient clinic over a 2-year period. The data suggested that there was a high incidence of "behavioral disorders." The author hypothesizes that such disorders are a result of an "acting out" of the problem between the military and the family through the cildren. Family therapy is the suggested "treatment of choice." It is believed that this may be more effective than the individual psychotherapeutic approach.

LANE, E. A., & ALBEE, G. W. Early childhood differences between schizophrenic adults and their siblings. *Journal of Abnormal Social Psychology*, 1964, *68*, 193–195.
The IQ tests which had been taken when they were in the second grade were obtained for 36 men and women who were later hospitalized for schizophrenia. These IQ results were compared with those of their siblings taken at the same time. The mean IQ of those who later became schizophrenic was lower than those of the siblings. A control group did not show such differences.

LEVINGER, G. Sources of marital dissatisfaction among applicants for divorce. In P. H. Glasser & L. H. Glasser (Eds.),*Families in crisis*. New York: Harper & Row, 1970.
A study of dissatisfaction in marriage based upon 600 couples, with data derived from records of marriage counselors doing mandatory interveiws as part of the application for divorce. Spouse complaints are classified and discussed.

McCORD, W., PORTA, J. & McCORD, J. The familial genesis of psychoses. *Psychiatry*, 1962, *25*, 60–71.
A study of the influence of early environment on the development of psychosis based upon data gathered during the childhood of subjects who later became psychotic. In the middle 1930's in Massachusetts a sample of boys was observed as a part of a study on the prevention of delinquency. These past case histories were examined and 12 prepsychotics were matched with nonpsychotic controls. The familial environments of the prepsychotics differed from those of the nonpsychotics in a number of ways. Typically the prepsychotics were raised in an environment directed by an overprotective mother and an absent or passive father. This "silver cord syndrome" has also been noted by other investigators who used a retrosepctive approach.

McCORD, W., McCORD, J., & VERDEN, P. Familial correlates of psychosomatic symptoms in male children. *Journal of Health and Human Behavior*, 1960, *1*, 192–199.
Further study of data from the Cambridge-Somerville Youth Study (1935–1945). Data were available on the physical condition of youths, their family backgrounds, and delinquent activities. Hypotheses that children with psychosomatic disorders would have been raised in families with a high degree of interpersonal stress and with anxious, hypochondriacal, symptom-ridden parents were not confirmed. But when boys are cross-classified as extropunitive or intropunitive, some regularities are observable. It is concluded that degree of extropunitiveness and nature of parental "sick-role" models are variables which affect childhood deseases.

MORRIS, G., & WYNNE, L. Schizophrenic offspring, parental styles of communication. *Psychiatry*, 1965, *28*, 19–44.
A study of parental styles of communication and schizophrenic children. Data were selected from excerpts of transcripts of conjoint family sessions with 12 families. Predictions about the most disturbed offspring were made by a judge blind to the clinical aspects of the case. Predictive criteria were then reformulated using the data from a parallel study utilizing psychological test material as predictors. These reformulated criteria were then utilized for blind predictions on 8 new families. Results indicated that the style of the family communication can be relaxed to the thought and effect disorder in schizophrenics.

NOVAK. A. L., & VAN DER VEEN, F. Family concepts and emotional disturbance in the families of disturbed adolescents with normal siblings. *Family Process*, 1970, *9*, 157–171.
A sample of 13 families with an adolescent who had applied to an outpatient clinic for treatment was contrasted with a group of similar families selected through a school. A Q-Sort procedure was used with individual family members. "Real family concepts" and "ideal family concepts" were obtained and differences were found between the 2 groups and between disturbed children and their normal siblings.

PAUL, N., & GROSSER, G. Operational mourning and its role in conjoint family therapy. *Community Mental Health Journal*, 1965, *1*, 339–345.
Studies of records of 50 families with a schizophrenic member and 25 families with at least one psychoneurotic member revealed "patterns of inflexible interaction and maladaptive responses to object loss." The way the sample was obtained is not stated. It is hypothesized from this data that incomplete mourning after object loss leads to an inability to deal with future object loss and this defect is transmitted to other family members. This is thought to lead to a "fixation of symbolic relationships in the family."

RABKIN, L. Y. The patient's family: Research methods. *Family Process*, 1965, *4*, 105–132.
A review of family research with special emphasis upon the family of the schizophrenic. Critical examination is done of

case history studies, interviewing studies, psychodiagnostic testing, questionnaire studies, and observational research. A bibliography of 99 references is included.

RYDER, R. G. A topography of early marriage. *Family Process*, 1970, *9*, 385–402.
See reference in Section 4.1.

SAGER, C., GRUNDRACH, R., KRAMER, M., LANZ, R., & ROYCE, J. The married in treatment: Effects of psychoanalysis on the marital state. *Archives of General Psychiatry*, 1968, *19*, 205–217.
In order to ascertain the effects of psychoanalysis on the marital state, a study of 736 married patients (432 womena and 304 men), age 21 to 68 in middle and upper socioeconomic class who were being treated in psychoanalysis, was done. 79 psychoanalysts supplied data on any ten consecutive patients. It was obtained through a closed ended questionnaire. 12 percent of the patients had concurrent group therapy, 2 percent were in conjoint marital therapy and about 20 percent of the patients had one or more conjoint consultations with their spouse and analyst. Results indicated that marriages rated poor initially improved. Marriages rated better also improved. There was no evidence that as one marital partner got better another got worse. Overall individual patient improvement was rated at about 60 percent of the cases. Of the spouses who were in treatment, good effects were more frequently reported in cases in which both husband and wife were treated by the same psychoanalyst.

SPITZER, S. P., SWANSON, R. M., & LEHR, R. K. Audience reactions and careers of psychiatric patients. *Family Process*, 1969, *8*, 159–181.
A study of the reaction of families and the ways these reactions influence the psychiatric patient career. The histories of 79 first admission patients were examined and patient and a family member were interviewed. Two dimensions of family reaction to deviance are described leading to a typology of 8 career patterns which allows for the classification of 95 percent of the cases reviewed.

WARING, M., & RICKS, D. Family patterns of children who become adult schizophrenics. *Journal of Nervous and Mental Disease*, 1965, *140*, 351–364.
See Reference in Section 5.2.

WEAKLAND, J. H., & FRY, W. F. Letters of mothers of schizophrenics. *American Journal of Orthopsychiatry*, 1962, *32*, 604–623.
See Reference in Section 5.2.

WENDER, P. H., ROSENTHAL, D., KETY, S. S., SCHULSINGER, F., & WELNER, J. Crossfostering: A research strategy for clarifying the role of genetic and experiential factors in the etiology of schiozphrenia. *Archives of General Psychiatry*, 1974, *30*, 121–128.
This clinical study attepts to determine whether psychiatric disorder occurs more frequently than chance when the offspring do *not* carry a genetic load for schizophrenia. Sample included all persons residing in Copenhagen who had been adopted between 1924 and 1927 and resulted in 69 index adoptees born of parents who had at some time been diagnosed as schizophrenic or probably schizophrenic and who were adopted by nonbiologically related parents. There were 69 matched controls. Results indicated that deviant child rearing did *not* increase the risk of schizophrenic illness in individuals without schizophrenic genetic endowment. A genetic effect, but *not* an environmental effect, in the transferance of schizophrenia was identified. It was tentatively concluded that familial psychotic illness does *not* play a causal role in the etiology of schizophrenia.

3.2 FAMILY DATA FROM INDIVIDUALS

ANTHONY, E. J. The mutative impact of serious mental and physical illness in a parent on family life. In E. J. Anthony & C. Koupernik (Eds.), *The child in his family*. New York: Wiley, 1970.
See reference in Section 3.6.

BAUMANN, G., & ROMAN, M. Interaction testing in the study of marital dominance. *Family Process*, 1966, *5*, 230–242.
A sample of 50 couples was exposed individually and conjointly to the Wechsler Bellevue. In the conjoint testing, the couple was asked to reach agreement on the response. Comparisons of the individual test and the conjoint test were made, as well as measures of dominance in the couple when tested together.

BAXTER, J. C., ARTHUR, S., FLOOD, C., & HEDGEPETH, B. Conflict patterns in the families of schizophrenics. *Journal of Nervous and Mental Disease*, 1962, *135*, 419–424.
Families of 12 male and 6 female schizophrenics were interviewed individually and as a group to explore conflict patterns in relation to the sex of the child. The amount of conflict is said to be comparable in the 2 groups while

patterns of conflict differ. There is more interparental conflict in the group of families with a male patient and more involvement of the patient in conflict in the group with a female patient.

BAXTER, J. C., & BECKER, J. Anxiety and avoidance behavior in schizophrenics in response to parental figures. *Journal of Abnormal Social Psychology*, 1962, *64*, 432–437.
See Reference in Section 5.2.

BEAVERS, W. T., BLUMBERG, S., TIMKEN, D. R. & WEINER, M. F. Communication patterns of mothers of schizophrenics. *Family Process*, 1965, *4*, 95–104.
A study of the ways the mothers of schizophrenics communicate with an interviewer. Nine mothers of schizophrenics were contrasted with 9 mothers of hospitalized nonschizophrenic patients. The mother of schizophrenics communicated their feelings in a quantitatively more ambiguous fashion.

BECK, S., & NUNNALLY, J. Parental attitudes in families. *Archives of General Psychiatry*, 1965, *13*, 208–213.
Differences in attitudes of parents of schizophrenic children compared with those of parents with well children. Eighteen attitudes were measured using the semantic differential test of Osgood (measures concepts like "My Child, Pregnancy," etc.). Schizophrenic families were obtained from 32 families of children resident in a therapeutic school; well-children families came from the community. Concepts associated with greater mental health by the well families included "my mother, the kind of father I am, the kind of mother I am, myself when I was a father, clinic mothers, and clinic our family." There was no difference between samples in the other nine concepts.

BENTINCK, C. Opinions about mental illness held by patients and relatives. *Family Process*, 1967, *6*, 1932–207.
1967, *6*, 1932–207.
The nature of the attitudes at home about mental illness in families of male schizophrenics was studied. A control group of male medical patients was used. The data was gathered by a questionnaire administered in a home interview. The sample was 50 schizophrenics and 50 relatives, and 50 medical patients and 50 relatives. Opinions of relatives of schrizophrenics had "more in common with blue collar employees than with mental health professionals."

BERGER, A. A test of the double blind hypothesis of schizophrenia. *Family Process*, 1965, *4*, 198–205.
198–205.
A samlple of 20 schizophrenics, 18 maladjusted nonschizophrenics, 20 hospital employees, and 40 students were exposed to a questionnaire of items rated for their double blind nature. Differences were found.

BOSS, P. G., McCUBBIN, H. I., & LESTER, G. The corporate exectutive wife's coping patterns in response to routine husband-father absence. *Family Process*, 1979, *18*, 70–86.
This study examines the effect of the routine absence of corporate husband/fathers in intact families.A coping inventory was adminstered to 66 corporate wives. Results, using factor analysis, showed that the wives coped with the stress of routine father absence by either fitting into the corporate life style; or developing themselves, and establishing their independence. These findings offer support for the idea that individual psychological variables need to be considered along with systems variables in the development of family stress theory.

BOSWELL, J. LEWIS, C., FREEMAN, D., & CLARK, K. Hyperthyroid children: Individual and family dynamics. *Journal of American Academy Child Psychiatry*, 1967, *6*, 64–85.
A retrospective study describing 12 children (10 girs, 2 boys; 6 negro, 6 white; 4 lower, 8 middle-class), who developed hyperthyroidism between the ages of 4 and 14. Data were gathered from individual psychiatric interviews, psychologic tests, parents, and from social agencies—but not from family interviews. Parents were found to have given minimal care and expected maximum self-sufficiency from the child. Children were found to be fixated at a pregenital stage.

BROWN, R. A. Feedback in family interviewing. *Social Work*, 1973, *18*, 52–59.
A research paper describing a type of feedback called "ascription," which is defined as the therapist using a declarative statement to communicate information concerning a family member with whom he is interacting at the moment. Data were obtained from tape-recorded interviews with families by social workers. Five hundred twenty-six ascriptions were identified from 21 1-hour interviews. Each example was analyzed by three judges using questionnaires completed by the social workers. Of the 526 statements, 85 percent stimulated verbal responses from families. The therapist should know his purpose (for example, improving communication) in making the ascription. It is hypothesized that ascriptions produce changes in the family system if they bring the worker and the family together in a way that is "dynamic and meaningful to them both."

CAPLAN, G. Patterns of parental response to the crisis of premature birth: A preliminary approach to modifying the mental health outcome. *Psychiatry*, 1960, *23*, 365–374.
Types of response to the crisis of a premature birth were derived from interview data on 10 cases where the baby weighed less than 4 pounds, and the records were sufficiently detailed so a case could be assigned unambiguously to an extreme category of healthy or unhealthy outcome. Cases were classified as "healthy outcome" if all relationships

in the family were as healthy or more healthy than before the birth and if parent–child relationships were healthy at the end of 12 weeks. "Unhealthy outcomes" were the reverse.

CAPUTO, D. V. The parents of the schizophrenic. *Family Process*, 1963, *2*, 339–356.
A study to assess the role of the parents in the development of schizophrenia, with particular emphasis upon the passive father and dominating mother notion. Parents were given individual tests, and after taking a parent attitude inventory they were asked to discuss the items on which they had disagreed. These discussions were assessed with the Bales method. Reversal of role was not found to be a significant factor, and a hostile atmosphere is indicated in the home of the potential schizophrenic.

CHEEK, F. E. Family socialization techniques and deviant behavior. *Family Process*, 1966, *5*, 199–217.
A study based upon Parsons' theoretical framework in which deviant behavior is related to imbalance of systems inputs and outputs at various stages of development. A sample of 120 male adults, from 4 different groups: schizophrenics, normals, alcoholics, and reformatory inmates were exposed to a questionnaire on family problem situations. Differences were found and it is suggested that Parsons' theoretical scheme could be translated it into reinforcement theory.

CLARK, A. W., & VAN SOMMERS, P. Contradictory demands in family relations and adjustment to school and home. *Human Relations*, 1961, *14*, 97–111.
Intensive case studies of families of 20 maladjusted and 20 adjusted children, all families having 1 or more adults other than the parents living in the family. The concern was with "the process of explaining an unsatisfactory relationship between any two individuals in terms of the influence of a third individual." Data was obtained by detailed, focused interviews, questionnaires to school staffs, group interviews with peers, and tests of ability. School difficulties were associated with unsatisfactory relationships in the home, such as dependence of one parent upon the other adult. Unsatisfactory relationships of adults contribute to withdrawal of father from family activities, difficulties between adults and children, maladjustment of children at home and school, and to recurrence of symptoms in parents.

COE, W. C., CURRY, A. E., & KESSLER, D. R. Family interactions of psychiatric patients. *Family Process*, 1969, *8*, 119–130.
A study using a questionnaire to examine family interaction patterns with emphasis upon everyday activities. Forty males and 40 females and their relatives who were psychiatric inpatients were contrasted with 54 husband and wife volunteers. Results include the finding that more family decision-making is left to the child in the patient families. The members tend not to recognize disagreement in their interactions.

COHAN, M., FREEDMAN, N., ENGELHARDT, D., & MARGOLIS, R. Family interaction patterns, drug treatment, and change in social agression. *Archives of General Psychiatry*, 1968, *19*, 1950–1956.
A study testing the notion that family interactional patterns will significantly modify the effect of phenothiazine treatment. Sample was 54 male and 72 female schizophrenics in an outpatient setting. Using a double bind procedure, patients were given chlorpromazine, promazine, or a placebo. All got supportive individual psychotherapy. A "close relative" was the source of the data to measure conflict and patient's behavior in the home. Results indicated that most patient improvement occurred in patients of chlorpromazine living in "least conflict homes." Medication was less effective where family conflict was high.

COHLER, B., WEISS, J., GRUNEBAUM, H., LIDZ, C. & WYNNE, L. MMPI profiles in hospitalized psychiatric patients and their families. *Archives of General Psychiatry*, 1972, *26*, 71–78.
To test the hypothesis that there would be significant differences in the families of schizophrenics, borderlines, neurotics, and non-neurotic psychiatric controls, a sample of 6 control families who had not had psychiatric treatment and 50 families who had had a child hospitalized for "emotional disturbance" were given the MMPI. Of the 50 patients, 23 were schizophrenic, one manic-depressive, 16 borderline, and 10 neurotic. None was hospitalized at the time of data collection. Using multivariant statistical profile similarities, there were no differences among either the fathers, mothers, or siblings of the offspring in the 4 diagnostic groups. It was concluded that these families could not be differentiated on the basis of self-reports of psychiatric symptoms.

CORNELISON, A. R. Casework interviewing as a research technique in a study of families of schizophrenic patients. *Mental Hygiene*, 1960, *44*, 551–559.
A discussion of casework interviewing in family study as experienced by a caseworker with the Lidz project. The families of 16 cases were studied by individual interviews with family members. Group interviews have been recently initiated. Caseworker–family contact beings upon hospital admission, if not sooner, and family patterns are frequently illuminated by the various and varying attitudes displayed toward the caseworker. A general discussion is offered of the special usefulness of combined casework service and research, practical aspects of the method, and problems involved.

CROMWELL, R. E., KEENEY, B. P. & ADAMS, B. N. Temporal patterning in the family. *Family Process*, 1976, *15*, 343–348.
This is a pilot study in which an open-ended questionnaire concerning orientation to "morningness" and "nightness" was adminstered to 28 married graduate students. Hypotheses concerning matched and mismatched couples were derived from analysis of the questionnaire responses. The authors conclude that "temporality" in families is a studiable question and that family members are aware of their awake-sleep patterns and the effect on their relationships.

DAVIDSON, S. School phobia as a manifestation of family disturbance: Its structure and treatment. *Journal of Child Psychology and Psychiatry*, 1960–61, *1*, 270–288.
Thirty cases of school phobia were studied at a child guidance clinic. Data were gathered from social histories and from individual interviews with patients and their parents. Family dynamics and methods of individual treatment are discussed.

DAVIS, D. Family processes in mental retardation. *American Journal of Psychiatry*, 1967, *124*, 340–350.
A lecture pointing out that in addition to genetic factors, mental retardation may result from failure of the family to give the child protection from stress during critical periods of learning in early childhood. Data were obtained from 50 cases (36 boys and 14 girls) with I.Q. below 75 (median 55)—all cases were seen by the author prior to age seven. Retrospective historical data were obtained from parents—mothers were found to be depressed through much of the child's life including the period prior to recognition of the child's retardation. These mothers were found to have lost their fathers during adolescence and to have gotten "ineffective lifelong support" from the maternal grandmother. Prevention and treatment are discussed.

DENIKER, P., DESAUGY, D., & ROPERT, M. The alcoholic and his wife. *Comprehensive Psychiatry*, 1964, *5*, 374 384.
A study focusing on the relationship between the alcoholic and his wife by studying 3 groups of patients: 50 alcoholics with psychiatric disorders called "psychiatric alcoholics," 50 alcoholics with cirrhosis or gastritis called "digestive alcoholics," and 67 in a control group where the husband was matched for age and socioeconomic status. All couples were interviewed using a questionnaire designed for this study. Compared with the digestive alcoholics and the controls, the psychiatric alcoholics showed a relationship to birth order, had fathers who were also alcoholics, made lower salaries, had dominant wives, and drank relatively little at home. The wife of the psychiatric alcoholic "tends to unconsciously maintain her husband's alcoholism."

DOWNING, R., COMER, N., & EBERT, J. Family dynamics in a case of Gilles de la Tourette's Syndrome. *Journal of Nervous and Mental Disease*, 1964, *138*, 548–557.
A case report of a patient with Gilles de la Tourette's syndrome in which all the members of the family were interviewed and tested with a WAIS, Rorschach, TAT, and word association test. A Leary interpersonal check list was done in the home. From this data a dynamic, genetic, and familial formulation of the case was made.

DUPONT, R., & GRUNEBAUM, H. Willing Victims: The husbands of paranoid women, *American Journal of Psychiatry*, 1968, *125*, 151–159.
In an attempt to understand the dynamics of spouses of paranoid women, cases with paranoid delusions (both inpatient and outpatient) were evaluated over a three-year period. Data were collected on nine women with paranoid state, using clinical interviews with the husband alone, wife alone, and the couple together, plus the MMPI and interpersonal checklist. Results indicated that the wife expressed the anger and dissatisfaction in the marriage, while the husand manifested passivity and apparent reasonableness and thus seemed to be a "willing victim."

DUPONT, R., RYDER, R., & GRUNEBAUM, H. Unexpected results of psychosis in marriage. *American Journal of Psychiatry*, 1971, *128*, 735–739.
As part of an ongoing study of the relationship of psychosis and marriage, the effect of the psychosis on the spouse was explored. The sample included 44 outpatient couples, one member of which had been diagnosed as psychotic. The tests administered included an MMPI, TAT, and a Henmon-Nelson Test of Mental Ability. In addition, a 1-hour joint interview with special attention to the impact of illness on the marriage was conducted. Findings suggested that "a large number of couples have described the psychotic episode and their attempts to cope with it as a strongly *positive* experience."

ELDER, G. H. Structural variations in the child-rearing relationship. *Sociometry*, 1962, *25*, 241–262.
Seven types of parent–adolescent interdependence, ranging from parental autocracy to parental ignoring, were identified by focused interviews. Questionnaires to 7,400 Ohio and North Carolina adolescents reveal that parental dominance is most common in lower-class, large, Catholic families. Parental autocracy is most likely to be associated with negative evaluations of parental policies by adolescents and with mutual rejection of each other.

ELDER, G. H. & BOWERMAN, C. E. Family structure and child-rearing patterns: The effect of family size and sex composition. *American Sociological Review*, 1963, *28*, 891–905.
The effects of family size, sex composition, and social class on the involvement of the father in child rearing, on the type of parental control exerted, and on the disciplinary techniques used were studied. Data were obtained from a 40 percent sample (N=1261) of all seventh grade white Protestant students of unbroken homes in central Ohio and central North Carolina. Family size and sex composition were found to have effects on child-rearing methods, but the effects are highly contingent on the sex of the child and the social class of the family.

EPSTEIN, N. B., & WESTLEY, W. A. Parental interaction as related to the emotional health of children. *Social Problems*, 1960, *8*, 87–92.
The 9 healthiest of 160 university freshmen and their families were evaluated. The child's emotional health is not related to the parents' sexual adjustment, but is related to the dependency needs of the father and the father's executive ego function. It is concluded that the parental sexual relationship is a poor indicator of family health and that the father's family position is important.

FARBER, B. Perceptions of crisis and related variables in the impact of a retarded child on the mother. *Journal of Health and Human Behavior*, 1960, *1*, 108–118.
An extension of earlier findings that a retarded child produces a tragic crisis (shock of diagnosis) or a role organization crisis (inability to develop roles to cope with the child). A sample of 268 mothers and fathers of retarded children were interviewed and adminstered questionnaires. The hypotheses concern the reaction of mothers to the crises, role definitions of mother, and her self-perceived health. The general conclusion is that health–symptom status of mother is related to the type of crisis experienced.

FARINA, A. Patterns of role dominance and conflict in parents of schizophrenic patients. *Journal of Abnormal and Social Psychology*, 1960, *61*, 31–38.
Parents of 12 good premorbid schizophrenics, 12 poor premorbids, and 12 children hospitalized for tuberculosis were interviewed. They were exposed individually and as pairs to hypothetical incidents with children. The joint conversations were analyzed for dominance and conflict. Father dominance was associated with good premorbid adjustment of the son and mother dominance with the poor premorbids. Parents of schizophrenics displayed more conflict than the control parents.

FELDMAN, M. J. Privacy and conjoint family therapy. *Family Process*, 1967, *6*, 1–9.
A discussion of whether greater or lesser degrees of privacy effects the nature of therapeutic disclosures by contrasting individual and conjoint family therapy. There is no simple relationship between degree of privacy and kind and scope of disclosure. The private nature of individual therapy led to an ethical position which elevates an individual's welfare above others, which may even be to their detriment.

FERBER, A., KLIGLER, D., ZWERLING, I., & MENDELSOHN, M. Current family structures. *Archives of General Psychiatry*, 1967, *16*, 659–667.
The hypothesis was that the family, in order to maintain equilibrium, will extrude to the hospital certain members (most usually those members functioning peripherally). Data were obtained from an emergency room psychiatric population of a large municipal hospital. Nine hundred and thirty-seven patients and/or their "closest companion" filled out a family information form. Families of psychiatric patients were compared with families from the general population. Relability on the raw data was 90 percent. Findings were that being married (rather than single, widowed, etc.), coming from a family of procreation, coming from an intact family, and being an emotionally important member of the household are associated with a lower risk of becoming a patient and of having a better outcome from treatment.

FISCHER, A. The importance of sibling position in the choice of a career in pediatric nursing. *Journal of Health and Human Behavior*, 1962, *3*, 283–288.
Questionnaires on sibling status and various other background characteristics and attitudes were administered to 109 student nurses in a children's hospital. The hypothesis that senior siblings are more likely to become pediatric nurses than junior siblings holds only for sibling groups of four or more. Futher analysis shows that sex composition of the sibling group also affects this career choice. A theory to cover all sibling group sizes, based on opportunities for identification with feminine models is advanced. It is suggested that sibling position, handled more complexly, may be as significant as clinical studies suggest.

FISHER, S., & MENDELL, D. The communication of neurotic patterns over two and three generations. In N. W. Bell & E. F. Vogel (Eds.), *A modern introduction to the family*. Glencoe: Free Press, 1960.
A report on a study of similarities in the patterning of fantasy and behavior in 2 or more generations of family groups. The data included projective tests and psychiatric interviews. Six families with 3 generations of kin and 14 families with 2 generations of kin were examined and impressions are given.

FITZGERALD, R. V. Conjoint Marital Psychotherapy: An outcome and follow-up study. *Family Process*, 1969, *8*, 261–271.

A report on an outcome study of couples seen in conjoint marriage therapy. A sample of 57 couples were followed up after 2½ years with an interview by telephone. Of the couples who were seen because an individual sought therapy, 76 percent were improved. Of those who presented an ongoing marital conflict as the presenting problem, 75 percent improved.

FREEMAN, H. E. Attitudes toward mental illness among relatives of former patients. *American Sociological Review*, 1961, *26*, 59–66.
The relatives of 649 newly discharged mental hospital patients (of a total population of 714) were successfully interviewed to investigate their attitudes about a etiology of mental illness, the mental hospital, the normalcy of patients after mental illness, and the responsibility of patients for thier condition. As in other surveys, age and education were associated with attitudes. "Enlightened" attitudes were not associated with social class measured independently of education, but were associated with verbal skill. It is suggested that verbal skill may be more important than style of life. However, attitudes were related to the patients' post-hospital behavior, and appear to be complexly determined and deeply rooted."

FREEMAN, H. E. & SIMMONS, O. G. Feelings of stigma among relatives of former mental patients. *Social Problems*, 1961, *8*, 312–321.
Feelings of stigma were elicited from the families of 649 of a cohort of 714 functional psychotics released from hospitals in eastern Massachusetts. Data were gathered by means of standard items in a structured interview with a relative a month after the patient's release. One-quarter of the sample reported feelings of stigma, while two-thirds acknowledged management problems. These feelings are associated with the patient's posthospital behavior, the education, class status, and personality characteristics of the relatives. Wives are more likely than other kin to feel stigma.

GANGER, R., & SHUGART, G. The heorin addict's pseudoassertive behavior and family dynamics. *Social Casework*, 1966, *57*, 643–649.
A discussion of heroin addiction based upon interviews with addicts and family members. Addiction is said to have a function within the family and the authors conclude, "Our clinical observations and our experience with casework treatment provided to the total family unit, including the addicted person, lead us to the conviction that addiction is specifically a 'familiogenic' disease; consequently, any attempt to cure it must be undertaken within the context of the family unit."

GARMEZY, N., CLARKE, A. R., & STOCKNER, C. Child rearing attitudes of mothers and fathers as reported by schizophrenic and normal patients. *Journal of Abnormal Social Psychology*, 1961, *63*, 176–182.
A group of 15 good premorbid and 15 poor premorbid schizophrenic patients were asked to think back to when they were 13 or 14 years old and try to remember their mothers and fathers at that time. The experimenter then presented them with 75 statements describing various child rearing attitudes and asked the patients if their parents would have agreed or disagreed with each item. A group of 15 patients hospitalized for medical problems was used as a control. The results indicate that the subject's level of social maturity and the extent of attitudinal deviance ascribed to parents are related. Poor premorbids reveal maternal dominance whereas good premorbids ascribe heightened paternal dominance in their responses.

GERBER, G. L. Conflicts in values and attitudes between parents of symptomatic and normal children. *Psychological Reports*, 1976, *38*, 91–98.
A clinical research study comparing conflicts between parents of normal children to conflicts between parents of symptomatic children regarding: (1) values relating to the child's symptoms, and (2) acceptance. Three groups of 10 parents of male children ages 8–13 with either emotional disturbance, primary learning disorder, or no disorder were matched by family size and intactness, and tested with the Allport-Vernon-Lindzey Study of Values Scale and a questionnaire on acceptance–rejection attitudes. Results showed significant increases of conflict ove values only for the learning disorder group (significance tested by analysis of variance) and increase of conflict over acceptance–rejection for both symptomatic groups (significance by Fisher probability). The author concludes that parents of symptomatic children tend to develop greater differences between them in these areas.

GETZELS, J. W. & JACKSON, P. W. Family Environment and cognitive style: A study of the sources of highly intelligent and of highly creative adolescents. *American Sociological Review*, 1961, *26*, 351–359.
A study of adolescent boys and girls, 28 highly intelligent but not creative and 26 creative but not concomitantly intelligent, chosen from a school population on the basis of testing. These students proved equally superior in achievement to the remainder of the student body although they differed both functionally and in their goals. The central issue of this report deals with the role of the family environment in the differentiation of kinds of intellectual ability through interviews with the mothers. Significant group differences were found in parental type education, childhood memories, reading interests, values, degree of satisfaction with child and school, and so on. The authors find less anxiety in the highly creative home and therefore more freedom for "individual divergence."

GILL, H. S. The influence of parental attitudes on child's reaction to sexual stimuli. *Family Process*, 1970, *9*, 41–50.

The general aim of this study was to consider the role of child–parent interaction in determining the child's perceptions. An assessment was made in 25 families of children's adequacy (and/or reporting) of sexual themes depicted in a set of pictures. Results support that the child incorporates the meanings inherent in the communications of his/her mother and father.

GOODRICH, W., RYDER, R., & RAUSH, H. Patterns of newlywed marriage. *Journal of Marriage and the Family*, 1968, *30*, 383–391.
A report of an exploratory study of 50 average, middle-class marriages examined during the fourth month with interview, problem solving situations, and questionnaires. Eight patterns of marriage are suggested.

GRAD, J., & SAINSBURG, P. Mental illness and the family. *Lancet*, 1963, *1*, 544–547.
An analysis of the effects on the family of psychiatric illness of one member of the family before and after treatment. The sample was 410 patients from psychiatric facilities in England. Problems reported by families were analyzed: the sicker or older the patient the greater the number of problems reported by the family. The number of problems reported by families was reduced significantly after treatment of the patient.

GREEN, A., GAINES, R., & SANDGRUND, A., Child abuse: Pathological syndrome of family interaction. *American Journal of Psychiatry*, 1974, *13*, 882–886.
This is a descriptive study of the famiy dynamics in cases of child abuse. Data were obtained from 60 families, mostly black and Hispanic, and of low socioeconomic class; children ranged from 5 to 13. A structured interview was conducted with mother alone and in a fifth of the cases with mother and child together. Results suggested that the behavior is a result of the interaction of the personality of the parent, which makes him "abuse-prone," the vulnerability of the child to scapegoating, and environmental stress for that particular mother.

GRUNEBAUM, H., ABERNATHY, V., ROFMAN, E., & WEISS, J. The family attitudes, common practices, and motivations of mental patients. *American Journal of Psychiatry*, 1971, *128*, 740–744.
This is a clinical investigation of family planning practice of a group of hospitalized psychiatric patients. The sample consisted of 21 randomly selected female inpatients from a wide range of socioeconomic status. They were diagnosed as 7 schizophrenics, 10 neurotic or psychotic depressions, and 4 "borderline." There was a high frequency of divorce, separation, marital disharmony, and unwanted pregnancies. Twenty-six unwanted pregnancies were reported by 13 women; 8 felt the pregnancies contributed to their emotional breakdown. Psychodynamic reasons for the ineffectiveness of contraceptive practice were explored.

GREENBERG, I. M. & ROSENBERG, G. Familial correlates of the 14 and 6 CPS EEG positive spike pattern. In I. M. Cohen (Ed.), *Psychiatric reserch report 20.* Washington, D.C.: American Psychiatric Association, 1966.
A report on the results of a study of the families of young hospitalized psychiatric patients in which central nervous system function, individual psychodynamics, cognitive style, and social and familial factors are considered. A sample of nine patients were contrasted with ten with no EEG abnormality. Differences were found in the families.

HAGNELL, O. & KREITMAN, N. Mental illness in married pairs in a total population. *British Journal of Psychiatry*, 1974, *125*, 293–302.
This is one of a series of papers investigating the concordance of mental illness in spouses. Data were obtained by direct interview from a circumscribing population of a small town in Sweden *over a 10-year span*. Results indicated there was a general tendency for spouses to show a progressive increase in morbidity with increasing duration of marrige. Wives are more susceptable than husbands to illness in the partner. Chronicity of illness in husbands could not be shown to influence the morbidity of wives, but remission of illness did relate to lower illness rates in wives.

HARMS, E. Defective parents, delinquent children. *Corrective Psychiatry*, 1962, *8*, 34–42.
A discussion of the relationship between delinquency and defective parents. In 300 cases of children stealing and lying, it was found that in 264 of them "at least one parent was, in one respect or another, deficient." Where the father is the defective factor, the boys will be found to be lying and the girls stealing. Where the mother is the defective factor, the girls will be found lying and the boys stealing.

HERSHEY, S. & WERNER, E. Dominance in marital decision making in women's liberation and non-women's liberation families. *Family Process*, 1975, *14*, 223–233.
Fourteen couples in which the wives were associated with the Women's Liberation Movement (WLM) and 14 "traditional" couples were interviewed using a modified version of the Revealed Differences Technique. Analysis indicated that the WLM wives were more "self-reliant," while the control wives were more "passive and dependent." The two did not differ significantly on the "Speaks First" and "Decisions Won" indices of dominance and conflict measures.

HIGGINS, J. Sex of child reared by schizophrenic mothers. *Journal of Psychiatric Research*, 1966, *4*, 153–167.
In an attempt to assess the effect of child-rearing by schizophrenic mothers, two groups of 25 children of schizophrenic mothers were studied. One group was reared by the mothers and the other group was reared from an

early age by agents without psychiatric illness. The sample was tested using a psychiatric interview of the child only, several psychological tests, and a report from the school. Results failed to support the hypothesis that the mother-reared children would display greater maladjustment on the various measures than would the reared-apart children.

HIRSCH, S. & LEFF, J. Parental abnormalities of verbal communication in transmission of schizophrenia. *Psychological Medicine*, 1971, *1*, 118–127.
In an attempt to determine parental abnormality in terms of communication of schizophrenia, a replication of Singer and Wynne's study using a Rorschach protocol and employing blind testing conditions and blind scoring transcriptions was undertaken. The sample was 20 schizophrenic and 20 neurotic inpatients. The findings of Singer and Wynne's study were not confirmed. A statistically significant difference between the deviant scores of both groups was found, but the marked overlap of the distribution of scores was not compatible with theories previously advanced. There were no differences between groups in number of words spoken.

ILFELD, F. W. Current social stressors and symptoms of depression. *American Journal of Psychiatry*, 1977, *134*, 161–166.
The relationship between depression and pre-illness "social stressors" was studied. Subjects were 2299 adults, age 18–65, and data were gathered using an open- and closed-ended questionnaire (specially designed for the study) as well as the Psychiatric Symptom Index. Results indicate that over a fourth of the variance in depressive symptoms is accounted for by 5 "social stressors." Depression is most closely related to social stresses of marriage and parenting. Treatment implication are that a focus on intervention and prevention in areas of family and marital life is desirable.

JOHNSTON, R. & PLANASKY, K. Schizophrenia in men: The impact on their wives. *Psychiatric Quarterly*, 1968, *42*, 146–155.
A study on an in-patient unit rating 36 wives of chronic in-patients. Data were obtained from independent interviews with spouses by four raters on the unit. As the patients regressed, about half the spouses rejected (divorced, separated, etc.) their husbands. Reasons for this are discussed.

JONES, J. E. Patterns of transactional style deviance in the TAT's of parents of schizophrenics. *Family Process*, 1977, *16*, 327–337.
This study demonstrates that parents of schizophrenics show more "transactional style deviance" in diverse situations than do other parents. In a sample of 44 intact families of nonschizophrenic outpatient adolescents, a manual for scoring such deviance on stories told for 7 TAT cards was developed. Six factors were developed. High scores on 2 particular factors were found only in the parents of hospitalized schizophrenics. Parents of young adult schizophrenics were more likely to show high scores on at least one of these 6 factors than other parents. It was possible to discriminate parents of schizophrenia spectrum from other parents.

KAGEL, S. A., WHITE, R. M. & COYNE, J. C. Father-absent and father-present families of disturbed and nondisturbed adolescents. *American Journal of Orthopsychiatry*, 1978, *48*, 342–352.
This is a research study on the effect of absent fathers on mental health of teenage sons. The sample was 24 families from Mental Health Clinics and 24 matched controls from local schools; with half of each group "father-absent." Measurements were the Family Environment Scale questionnaire and a semi-structured interview of mothers and sons. The data was analyzed using analysis of variance. Results did not support the hypothesis that there are special conditions in father-absent homes which contribute to adolescent maladjustment.

KELLAM, S. G., ENSMINGER, M. E. & TURNER, R. J. Family structure and the mental health of children: Concurrent and longitudinal community wide studies. *Archives of General Psychiatry*, 1977, *34*, 1012–1022.
A study of different family structures (defined by types of adults present) and the mental health of children, as measured by rating scales of psychological well being and by the Social Adaptation Status. Families were grouped into ten major classes (86 different combinations of adults); ratings were made of children by mothers, clinicians, teachers and themselves in first and then third grade; and data was analyzed using a log-linear analysis of hierarchical models treatment. Results showed that "mother alone" families had the greatest risk of poor mental health, "mother-father" the least risk, while the risk of "mother-2nd other adult" families varied by the second other adult. The often used other category of father-absent families is too ambiguous and should be discarded.

KEMPLER, W., IVERSON, R., & BEISSER, A. The adult schizophrenic and his siblings. *Family Process*, 1962, *1*, 224–235.
Sixty-five siblings in a group of 16 schizophrenic families were interviewed using a structured protocol to explore parent-child relationships as seen by the siblings. Findings included distortions in communications by both patients and siblings, and appeared unrelated to the schizophrenic process. Four subjects, all of whom were "favorite" children in the familiy, showed no such distortions. A transcript from a single family is presented in illustration.

KREITMAN, N. The patient's spouse. *British Journal of Psychiatry*, 1964, *110*, 159–174.
A group of 75 patients and 95 controls, closely matched for sex, social class, father's social class, education, and number of children, were subjects of a mail survey using the Maudsley personality inventory, the Cornell medical

index, and biographical details for the purpose of describing spouses of mental patients and their relationship with the marriage partner. Compared with controls the patient's spouses were more neurotic and had more physical and psychological symptoms which increased as the marriage went on. Wives were more likely than husbands to reflect the illnesses of spouses.

KREITMAN, N., COLLINS, J., NELSON, B., & TROUP, J. Neurosis and marital interaction: I. Personality and symptoms. *British Journal of Psychiatry*, 1970, *117*, 33–46.
This is one of a series of studies of the effects of neurosis on the patient's marriage and the marital partner. A sample of 60 male patients from an outpatient clinic, together with their wives, was compared with a control group from the community, matched for socioeconomic class. Both husbands and wives were interviewed jointly, using a semi-structured interview, the Cornell Medical Index and the Maudsley Personality Inventory; a reliability and validity study was done. The results indicated that compared with controls, the patient's wives were (1) higher on symptoms of previous psychiatric illness, (2) the wives' disability tended to increase as the marriage increased, and (3) the wives were no different from the control wives at the onset of marriage, thus failing to support the hypothesis that a "neurotic" husband will pick a "neurotic" wife.

KREITMAN, N., COLLINS, J., NELSON, B., & TROUP, J. Neurosis and marital interaction: IV. Manifest psychological interaction. *British Journal of Psychiatry*, 1971, *119*, 243–252.
This study looked at manifest psychological interactions using the Lorr and Terrill Scales. Reliability and validity studies were done. Results indicated that compared to controls, the patient-husbands manifested less positive affection, but there was no difference for wives. More assertive husbands displayed less affection toward and received less affection from their wives. Duration of marriage did not appear to be related to patterns of husband–wife correlation as assertiveness or affection. Problems of sampling marital behavior, as well as other design details, are discussed.

KUDASHIN, P., WAXENBERG, S., & SAGER, C. Family story technique changes in interactions and affects during family therapy. *Journal of Personality Assessment*, 1971, *35*, 62–71.
One of a series of reports on the Family Story Technique (FST) to explore changes over the course of brief family therapy. The study was done at an outpatient community mental health center with a sample of 38 women, 33 men, and 13 children, in 39 families. About one half were white and one half were black and Puerto Rican. The FST was submitted to each family individually early in therapy and near the end (around the 12th to the 15th session). Results reveal that there was a reduction in hostility between mothers and children and a more realistic view of family relationships. There was a decrease in family anxiety and an increase in anger on the part of adult females, as well as reduction in children's projected guilt.

LESLIE, G. R., & JOHNSON, K. P. Changed perceptions of the maternal role. *American Sociological Review*, 1963, *28*, 919–928.
The generalization that childrearing methods have become more permissive is questioned. Several hypotheses relating changed perceptions to the normative patterns receiving authoritative support in that generation, the amount of exposure to the normative pattern at the time the mother role is being enacted, and the explicitness of the norms associated with various areas of childrearing are set forth. Questionnaire data from 297 of 418 woman graduates of the 1949 class of a midwestern university covered their own and their mothers' practices in several areas: sex and modesty training, agression toward mother, and the encouragement of self-direction. Predictions are confirmed, thus raising questions about the true nature of change and validity of generalizing from one aspect of the maternal role to another.

LEVITT, H., & BAKER, R. Relative psychopathology of marital partners. *Family Process*, 1969, *8*, 33–42.
A study examining whether the member of a marriage who seeks treatment is the more disturbed of the spouses. A sample of 25 patients and their spouses were examined with questionnaire and psychological tests. Eleven psychologists served as judges to examine the test results and identify the "sicker" member. In 13 of the 25 cases the identified patient was judged to be sicker.

LEWIS, V. S., & ZEICHNER, A. N. Impact of admission to a mental hospital on the patient's family. *Mental Hygiene*, 1960, *44*, 503–509.
A report on a study of the effect on families when a member is hospitalized for mental illness. The study is based upon interviews with members of the family of 109 patients admitted to Connecticut's three state mental hospitals. Reported with tables are such categories as the recognition and acceptance of mental illness, the ways of coping with the patient's illness, assessment of help of resources tried, and treatment given prior to hospitalization.

LIDZ, T., CORNELISON, A., FLECK, S., & TERRY, D. The intrafamilial environment of a schizophrenic patient: I. The Father. *Psychiatry*, 1957, *20*, 329–342.
To understand the role of the family in the etiology and pathogenesis of schizophrenia. 14 families with a hospitalized schizophrenic were studied for periods varying from 6 months to over 2 years. Data collection included interviewing all members of the family (individually), observations, and records of interactions of family members with each other and with the hospital personnel, home visits, and projective testing of all family members. Focus was on the fathers, in

view of the fact that so much previous work had focused on mothers alone. Fathers were found to be "very important, albeit often extremely disturbing, members of the families, whose presence and influence cannot be neglected." Five different types of fathers are described.

LIDA, T., FLECK, S., ALANEN, Y. O., & CORNELISON, A. Schizophrenic patients and their siblings. *Psychiatry*, 1963, *26*, 1–18.
A study of the siblings of schizophrenics based upon individual interviews of family members, observation of family members with each other and hospital staff, and projective tests. Sixteen families were studied for periods ranging from 6 months to 6 years. As many siblings were psychotic as were reasonably well adjusted, and all except 5 or 6 of the 24 siblings suffered from severe personality disorders. Siblings of the same sex as the patient were more disturbed than those of the opposite sex.

LIDZ, T., PARKER, B., & CORNELISON, A. The role of the father in the family environment of the schizophrenic patient. *American Journal of Psychiatry*, 1956, *113*, 126–132.
One of a series of papers on a study of the families of schizophrenic patients. Families in which there was both a mother and father present were interviewed separately, in pairs, and in groups. The identified patient was an inpatient and came from upper class or upper middle-class families. Sixteen families (of which 5 identified patients were female and 11 were male) were studied. The fathers are seen as "noxious" in the development of schizophrenia. Three types are described: (1) fathers of schizophrenic daughters who are constantly battling their wives and seeking to enlist the support of their daughters, (2) fathers who feel their sons are rivals for their wives, and (3) passive, withdrawn, and absent fathers.

LU, Y. C. Contradictory parental expectations in schizophrenia. *Archives of General Psychiatry*, 1962, *6*, 219–234.
A report of some preliminary findings of an investigation of the families of schizophrenias. The emphasis is upon a comparison of the parents' relationship with the patient and with nonschizophrenic siblings in an attempt to explain why one child in a family develops schizophrenia and not another. The parents expect a hilgher degree of dependence from the preschizophrenic than from the nonschizophrenic child, and they also expect a higher degree of achievement and responsibility. The author suggests that the relational pattern of contradictory parental expectations and the child's persistent effort to fulfill them could be called a "quadruple bind."

LINTON, H., BERLE, B. B., GROSS, M., & JACKSON, E. Reaction of children within family group as measured by the bene-anthony tests. *Journal of Mental Science*, 1962, *107*, 308–325.
A study of 69 children in 28 families who were given the Bene-Anthony family relations test where they were asked to match statements with representations of family members. The test scores were rated high or low on 6 qualitative variables in family life. The child rated as sick by pediatrician and nurse was more involved with parent of the opposite sex, and in families with episodes of illness the children express a marked preference for the mother. Significant patterns were found in boys and girls of different age groups and in the group as a whole.

LU, Y. C. Mother–Child role relations in schizophrenia: A comparison of schizophrenic patients with non-schizophrenic siblings. *Psychiatry*, 1961, *24*, 133–142.
An investigation into why one child in a family develops schizophrenia and another does not, based upon interviews with 50 chronic schizophrenic patients, their siblings, and their parents. The patient is largely confined to his parents and especially his mother while the siblings have several significant other relationships.

LUCKEY, E. B. Marital satisfaction and congruent self-spouse concepts. *Social Forces*, 1960, *39*, 153–157.
Satisfactory (S) and less satisfactory (LS) married couples were identified by Locke's marital adjustment scale from a population of 594 married students. Couples in the two groups independently completed the Leary interpersonal check list regarding the self and spouse. The congruence of the husband's perception of himself and his wife's perception of him was related to satisfaction, but the congruence of the wife's self concept and her husband's perception of her was not. Some implications and explanations of these results are offered.

LUCKEY, E. B. Perceptional congruence of self and family concepts as related to marital interaction. *Sociometry*, 1961, *24*, 234–250.
Forty-one satisfactorily married (S) and 40 less satisfactorily married (LS) couples completed Leary interpersonal check lists on self, spouse, mother, father, and ideal self. S and LS subjects were compared on agreement of self concept and spouse's concept of subject, of self and ideal self, of self and parents, of spouse and parent, of idea self and spouses. The many differences between S and LS subjects are used to refine the proposition that marital satisfaction is related to perceptual congruence, and to evaluate a theory of marital interaction.

MANN, J., & STARR, S. The self-report questionnaire as a change agent in family therapy. *Family Process*, 1972, *11*, 95–105.
This study reports on a daily self-reporting questionnaire given for 12 weeks to a group of 68 "normal" couples, married at least 10 years, in regrads to their sexual behavior. Questions focused principally on specific sexual activities that subjects had perfomred, wanted to perform, or fantasized about performing. An experimental subgroup

of 51 males and 34 females were exposed to 4 sessions of "stag" films at weekly intervals after having completed the first 4 weeks of daily reporting. The remaining members of the sample attended 4 comparable session at which nonerotic films were shown. The results indicated that sexual activity had reached its peak of frequency and variety for all groups in the 4 weeks preceding the showing of the films. Furthermore, the erotic films did not exercise sufficient influence to restore the activity of the group to the peak frequencies achieved during the first 4 weeks. The assumption is made that self-monitoring may induce behavioral change, and a suggestion is made that daily self-questionnaires may have an application to a variety of clinical problems in family interaction.

McCONAGHY, N., & CLANCY, M. Formal relationships of allusive thinking in university students and parents. *British Journal of Psychiatry*, 1968, *114*, 1079–1087.
The notion was tested that when a person showed allusive thinking (defined as similar to "loosening of associations" but called "allusive" to avoid the implication of pathology), at least one of his parents would also show this type of thinking. Sample was 38 university students and their parents. Measures used were the object sorting test and the F-scale of the MMPI. Results showed that the students with allusive thinking did have parents with similar thoughts, but they did not have schizophrenic pathology.

McCORD, W., McCORD, J., & HOWARD, A. Early familial experiences and bigotry. *American Social Review*, 1960, *25*, 717–772.
The Authoritarian Personality concluded that bigots have experienced stern, moralistic, rejecting childrearing. The conclusion, much challenged, is evaluated in the light of data from the Cambridge-Somerville youth study. Ratable data on prejudices are available for 45 of 200 subjects reinterviewed in 1948 and 1956. No relation between degree of prejudice and family experiences as determined earlier could be established. The interpretation is suggested that prejudice in the lower class is a part of a generally stereotyped culture and does not relate to personality needs or family environment.

McGHIE, A. A comparative study of the mother–child relationship in schizophrenia. I: The interview. II: Psychological testing. *British Journal of Medical Psychology*, 1961, *34*, 195–221.
In Part I of this two-part article there is a description of interviews with 20 mothers of schizophrenics, 20 mothers of neurotics, and 20 mothers of normals. Findings about families of schizophrenics reported in the literature were generally confirmed. There is more marital disharmony in the schizophrenic group and the fathers are said to be weak. However, mothers of schizophrenics do not appear as overprotective as mothers of neurotics. In Part II, the test findings for the three groups are reported. They were given a childrearing questionnaire, a sentence completion test, a word connection test, and the Rorschach test.

MENDALL, D., CLEVELAND, S. E., CLEVELAND, & FISHER, S. A five-generation family theme. *Family Process*, 1968, *7*, 126–132.
A study examining projective test fantasies of family members. Five generations of one family including examination of 27 members, were conducted. It was found that a family selects one or two central themes which are perpetuated in the responses of family members across generations.

MEYEROWITZ, J. H., & FELDMAN, H. Transition to parenthood. In I. M. Cohen (Ed.), *Psychiatric research reports 20*. Washington, D.C.: American Psychiatric Association, 1966.
A report based on a study of 400 couples (individual interviewing). Experiences during the first pregnancy are described as well as experiences when the child is 1 month and 5 months old.

MEYERS, D., & GOLDFARB, W. Studies of perplexity in mothers of schizophrenic children. *American Journal of Orthopsychiatry*, 1961, *31*, 551–564.
In order to document the association of parental complexity (defined as passivity, uncertainty, lack of spontaneity, absence of empathy, with diminished awareness of the child's needs, bewilderment, and blandness in the fact of unacceptable behavior in the child, and an absence of parental control), 23 mothers of schizophrenic children and 23 mothers of normal public school children were studied. Techniques included a participant–observation technique, in which the observer spent 3 hours with the family at home, and a semistructured open-ended interview of the mothers. Results indicated that the mothers of the schizophrenic children, without organic involvement, have a greater difficulty in appropriately structuring their child's environment, while the mothers of the organic group cannot be differentiated from mothers of the normals.

MILLER, D. R., & WESTMAN, J. C. Reading disability as a condition of family stability. *Family Process*, 1964, *3*, 66–76.
A report of a study of the relationship between reading disability in a child and the condition of the family. The subjects were 18 boys in out-patients care. The family members were given individual tests, data were drawn from individual therapy sessions, and there were periodic visits to home and school. A matched control group was compared. It is postulated that parents and children resist change in the reading disability because it contributes to the family's survival.

MITCHELL, H. E. Application of the Kaiser method to marital pairs. *Family Process*, 1963, 22, 265–279.
A discussion of the Leary measurement as used on 20 maritally conflicted alcoholics and their spouses. Questions concerning resemblances and differences are raised. The major emphasis is "not to be substantive findings but to demonstration of the feasibility of the Kaiser method as a technique for measuring interpersonal dimensions of marital and family dynamics."

MORRISON, J. R. Parental divorce as a factor in childhood psychiatric illness. *Comprehensive Psychiatry*, 1974, *15*, 95–102.
Based on the association in the literature of psychiatric disorder with divorce, 126 children with diagnosed mental illness were studied to see the correlation with marital status. Out of the 126 probands, 34 were divorced and 5 were separated. Results indicated that diagnosis of the child did *not* correlate with divorce except in one case: enuresis persisted past age 5. Over half of the divorced parents had a psychiatric disorder (compared with one-quarter of the non-divorced parents), but the differences were due to an excess of alcohol and/or sociopathic divorced fathers. Divorced mothers have more affective disorder. The data did not support the hypothesis that divorce precipitates symptoms in the child that necessitate his being treated children or that react with depression.

MORRISON, J. R., & STEWART, M. A. A family study of the hyperactive child syndrome. *Biological Psychiatry*, 1971, *3*, 189–195.
To explore the hypothesis that behavior of hyperactive children was inherited, 59 children who had been diagnosed as hyperactive in an outpatient child psychiatric clinic, were compared with 41 children admitted to a hospital for non-psychiatric conditions. A partially structured interview was given covering childhood and school experience, medical and psychiatric symptoms and treatment, and mental health of relatives. Interviewers were blind. Results indicated that significantly more of the parents of hyperactive than control children had been hyperactive as children, and as adults had a high prevalence of sociopathy, hysteria, and alcoholism.

MUNTZ, H. Thought disorder in the parents of thought disordered schizophrenics. *British Journal of Psychiatry*, 1970, *117*, 707–708.
In order to terst the hypothesis that there is a thought disorder in the parents of schizophrenic patients, the Banister Repertory Grid Test and the Mill Hill Vocabulary Test were given to parents of 18 schizophrenic patients with a thought disorder and 22 without such a thought disorder (who had other psychiatric illnesses). Results in contrast to other studies indicated that there was a significant relationship between thought disorder in the parents and thought disorder in the children.

NAVRAN, L. Communication and adjustment in marriage. *Family Process*, 1967, *6*, 173–184.
A sample of married couples was exposed to the marital relationship inventory and the primary communication inventory, two questionnaires which were given to the couples individually. The 24 couples having a "happy" relationships were contrasted with 24 having an "unhappy" relationship. Differences were found and "marital adjustment was shown to be positively correlated with capacity to communicate."

NEALON, J. The adolescent's hospitalization as a family crisis. *Archives of General Psychiatry*, 1964, *11*, 302–312.
A study of the reactions of 25 sets of parents to the hospitalization of an adolescent member of the family. Data were collected from parents' initial interviews with case-worker ("Generally one or two, but ranging up to six"). Interviews were held before admission, or as soon as possible afterward. The hospitalization was defined as a family crisis because "of the impact of mental illness in the family, family disruption precipitating and following hospitalization, and the parent's expectation of the hospitalization." Family-oriented approach is stressed, and implications for treatment are discussed.

OLSON, D. H. The measurement of family power by self-report and behavioral methods. *Journal of Marriage and the Family*, 1969, *31*, 545–550.
A study comparing self report and observed behavior on the question in power in marriage. Thirty-five couples were given questionnaires and their responses compared with their behavior in the laboratory dealing with real problems. No relationship was found between what the couples said about the distribution of power in the marriage and what was observed when they dealt with one another. Explanatory factors are offered, and the conclusion is reached that this research reinforces "the idea that methodological research of this type should precede, rather than follow, substantive research in the field."

OTTO, H. A. Criteria for assessing family strength. *Family Process*, 1963, *2*, 329–339.
A discussion of family strengths and resources with the data collected by questionnaire. Twenty-seven families were queried. Married couples met for group discussions on family strengths. A set of criteria for assessing family strengths is offered.

PANNOR, R., BARAN, A., & SOROSKY, A. D. Birth parents who relinquished babies for adoption revisited. *Family Process*, 1978, *17*, 329–337.

As part of a series on "The Family and Child Placement Practices," this paper reports on the attitudes and feelings of birth parents reported years after their babies were adopted. Thirty-eight parents were interviewed (36 female and two male, ages 20 to 62). The age of the child was birth to 6 months. Analysis of the data indicated that the majority of birth parents were married and had children at the time of the study, but continued to have feelings of loss, pain, and mourning, years after relinquishment. A great majority wanted the children to know they still cared about them and had an interest in knowing what kind of persons they had grown up to be. Eight-two percent said they would be amenable to a reunion if the adoptee wished it when he reached adulthood.

PARAD, H. J., & CAPLAN,L G. A framework for studying families in crises. *Social Work*, 1960, *5*, 3–15.
An approach to the observation and study of the family in crisis. Family members are seen individually and as a group in the home while engaged in household activities. The concepts of family lifestyle, problem-solving mechanisms, and need-response patterns are illustrated with a case history. It is suggested that intervention is most effective at the moment the family is in crisis.

PARSONS, A. Family dynamics in south Italian schizophrenics *Archives of General Psychiatry*, 1960, *3*, 507–518.
If family factors play an etiological role in schizophrenia, comparative studies of the family background of schizophrenics in different cultures is important. After observation of south Italian patients in the United States, a sample of 25 patients hospitalized in public hospitals in Naples and vicinity was investigated. Patterns in the families are described in terms of exclusive dyads, imbedded dyads, comptitive and unstable situations, and isolates. Comparing pathological family constellations in different cultures, the taboo areas are important, and the problem of idfferentiating the normal from the pathologicl must be resolved. "We would doubt that these probelms can ever be resolved in a framework in which any particular set of social values or conditions is considered as inherently schizogenetic."

PERKINS, T. F., & KAHAN, J. P. An empirical comparison of natural-father and stepfather family systems. *Family Process*, 1979, *18*, 175–183.
This study exasmined differences between 40 natural-father and stepfather family systems. Family triads consisting of the husband, the wife, and a child (age 12 to 15 years) were studied. Four instruments were used: the Family Concept Q-Sort, a Semantic Differential, a demographic questionnaire, and an interaction–reaction questionnaire. Results indicated that stepfather families differed from natural-father systems on psychological adjustment, satisfaction with family, reciprocal understanding, and perceived goodness and potency. These differences affect the entire step-parent family system and its ability to function adequately.

PETURSSON, E. A study of parental deprivation and illness in 291 psychiatric patients. *International Journal of Social Psychiatry*, 1961, *7*, 97–105.
A group of 291 patients with functional psychiatric illness was observed by the author and information gathered about their parents from them, from spouses or relatives, or by direct observation in some instances. The parents suffered from functional psychiatric illness in 77.5 percent of the cases. The incidence of broken homes was 31.7 percent. There appeared to be a high incidence of patients developing the same type of psychiatric illness as the parents in various categories. Well integrated family units occurred in the background of patients in only 11.7 percent of the cases.

PLIONIS, F. M. Family functioning and childhood accident occurrence. *American Journal of Orthopsychiatry*, 1977, *47*, 250–263.
The hypothesis that the adequacy of family functioning is associated with the rate of children's accidents was tested using a semistructured interview of 15 families with a child hospitalized for treatment of an accidental injury. Family functioning was rated using Geisner's Scale, and the alternative hypothesis (that accident occurrence is related to family stress) was tested with the Holmes-Rahe Social Readjustment Scale. Raters were blind to previous accident history, which was defined as number in child's life/age. The data, when analyzed by Spearman Correlation Coefficient and Mann-Whitney U Test, showed no relation to family stress. Relation to functioning existed only for a subgroup (N=10) of index child's age 3–11. Implications for liability assessment and preventive treatment are discussed and 65 references are included.

PURCELL, K., & METZ, S. R. Distinctions between subgroups of asthmatic children: Some parent attitude variables related to age of onset of asthma. *Journal of Psychosomatic Research*, 1962, *6*, 251–258.
A continuation of the authors' previous work with asthmatic children at the Children's Asthma Research Institute and Hospital in Denver. Previous work had tentatively classified these 86 children as "steroid dependent" and "rapidly remitting" in terms of their clinical course once at the hospital and separated from home. Parents' attitudes were measured using the parent attitude research instrument. Positive findings of this study were than within the group of rapidly remitting children, relatively late age of onset (after 12–18 months) was associated with autocratic and restrictive attitudes on the part of their mothers. These findings were not substantiated by the other group.

QUERY, J. M. N. Pre-morbid adjustment and family structure: A comparison of selected rural and urban schizophrenic men. *Journal of Nervous and Mental Disease*, 1961, *133*, 333–338.

A study which reviews schizophrenia in relating to cultural and familial settings. The hypothesis is that premorbid adjustment of rural schizophrenics will be better than that of urban subjects because the rural setting includes a more patriarchal family structure, more emphasis upon individualism, and better sex-role identification. Case history data were examined in terms of the Phillip's scale and supplemented by family interviews. Fifty-one families were interviewed and the hypothesis was supported by the evidence.

RABKIN, L. Y. The patient's family: Research methods. *Family Process*, 1965, *4*, 105–132.
A review of family research with special emphasis upon the family of the schizophrenic. Critical examination is done of case history studies, interviewing studies, psychodiagnostic testing, questionnaire studies, and observational research. A bibliography of 99 references is included.

REISS, D. Varieties of consensual experience. I: A theory for relating family interaction to individual thinking. *Family Process*, 1971, *10*, 1–28.
The central notion of this theory is that families develop shared constructs of their immediate environment and the family's place in it. Three varieties of such consensual experience are described: consensus-sensitive, environment-sensitive, and interpersonal distance-sensitive. The relation of these types to families of schizophrenics, middle class normal families, and families of delinquents respectively is investigated.

REISS, D. Varieties of consensual experience. II: Dimensions of a family's experience of its environment. *Family Process*, 1971, *10*, 28–35.
A description is given of the experimental effort used to test for the presence, validity, and sufficiency of the three dimension (family problem-solving effectiveness, coordination, and penchant for closure) of family consensual thinking descried in Part I of this two part paper. The procedure utilized a card-sorting problem devised by Shipstone and based on previous work by Miller, Chomsky, and Reiss. Family members worked alone on an initial task, then as a family unit, and thirdly alone again on a final task. A number of indices were constructed to compare a family's performance from one task to another. Results indicated that these dimensions accounted for 82 percent of variance between families and that the productive capacity of the tests are good except for closure. The predicted and unexpected results are discussed.

REISS, D. Varieties of consensual experience: III: Contrasts between families of normals, delinquents, and schizophrenics. *Journal of Nervous and Mental Disease*, 1971, *152*, 73–95.
This is another in a series of studies comparing normals, delinquents, and schizophrenics. A selective review of the literative permitted predictions that normal families would experience the environment as "logical and masterable"; that families of delinquents would experience themselves in a universe where others' opinions and behavior were irrelevant, and families with schizophrenice would experience the environment as confusing and hostile and strive towards shared, stylized, distorted notions of it as a means of mutual projection and support. Most of the predictions were confirmed, using objective measures (previously described in other reports).

REISS, D., & ELSTEIN, A Perceptual and cognitive resources of family members. *Archives of General Psychiatry*, 1971, *24*, 121–134.
Three groups of families, each consisting of a father, mother, and a hospitalized child, were tested with a battery of perceptive and cognitive tests. Children were the identified patient. Eight had paranoid, and eight were controls with other psychiatric diagnoses. Results indicated families of schizophrenics had lower scores for the Shipley-Hartford Abstraction Test and showed more frequent overexclusions on Epstein's Inclusion Test and substantial reduced reversal rates on reversal figures. Schizophrenic families had an inability to discern the underlying patterns, were rigid, and used personal rather than conventional reality in interpreting the results.

REISS, P. J. The extended kinship system: Correlates of and attitudes on frequency of interaction. *Marriage and Family Living*, 1962, *24*, 333–339.
A report of a study of urban middle-class kinship systems with emphasis upon frequency of contact and attitudes about it. A sample was selected from the metropolitan Boston area and interviewed. The conclusions are that frequency of interaction are not explained by the sex, ethnic background, or family cycle phase of these respondents. Degree of kin relationship and distance of residence of kin are the most important variables. Half of the respondents felt the frequency of contact with kin has been insufficient and there is a desire for kin to live close but not too close.

ROSENBAUM, M., & RICHMAN, J. Family dynamics and drug overdoses. *Life-Threatening Behavior*, 1972, 2, 19–25.
This is a clinical study describing the family dynamics of 40 suicidal patients, 18 of whom had relatives. The sample was seen at a large city hospital. An open-ended questionnaire was administered separately to each family member and in a family interview. Results indicated that there was direct participation of other family members in the suicidal act.

ROSENBERG, C. The young addict and his family. *British Journal of Psychiatry*, 1971, *118*, 469–470.
To test the hypothesis that siblings of patients with adolescent drug abuse would also have psychiatric illness, a

sample was obtained of 35 families (26 male, 9 female), each containing an adolescent drug abuser of amphetamines, barbituates, LSD, cocaine, or heroin. Information was obtained mostly from mothers alone, but occasionally from fathers by means of a questionnaire (what type was not specified). The results indicated that over one third of the parents and older siblings of the index patient had had psychiaric treatment. Fathers and brothers had behavior disorders and personality disorders, while mothers and sisters had neurotic or depressive symptoms. It was concluded that the index patients' drug abuse was a symptom of a wider family problem.

ROSENTHAL, D., WENDER, P., KETY, S., et al. Parent–child relationships and psychopathological disorder in the child. *Archives of General Psychiatry*, 1975, *32*, 466–476.
This is one of a series of studies exploring the relative effects of hereditary and rearing on development of psychopathology. Two hundred fifty-eight subjects were placed into one of four groups: (1) index adoptees who had a biological parent with schizophrenic or manic-depressive disorder, but who were given up for adoption early in life; (2) control adoptees who were simlarly adopted, but whose biological parents had no known psychiatric illness; (3) sujbects who did not have a biological parent with a schizophrenic or manic–depressive disorder, but who were adopted and reared by persons who did have such disorder, and (4) non-adoptees who had a schizophrenic or manic-depressive parent and were reared in the parental home at least during their first 15 years of life. Data were obtained from the identified patient only. content focused on aspects of each subject's life with his rearing parents, both in childhood and as adults. Results suggested that both heredity and the quality of rearing affect development of psychopathological disorder, but the amount of variance explained by rearing tends to be low.

ROSENTHAL, M. J., NI, E., FINKELSTEIN, M., & BERKWITZ, G. K. Father–child relationships and children's problems. *Archives of General Psychiatry*, 1962, 7, 360–373.
A group of 405 new patients coming into the Institute for Juvenile Research in Chicago were examined to determine whether the emotional problems of children were related to certain types of father–child relationships. The relationship was examined by interviews with parents and children. Certain of the children's problems were found to be correlated with types of father–child relationships being studied while others were not.

ROSMAN, B., WILD, C., RICCI, J., FLECK, S., & LIDZ, T. Thought disorders in the parents of schizophrenic patients: A further study utilizing the object sorting test. *Journal of Psychiatric Research*, 1964, *2*, 211–221.
This is a second replication of a study by McConughy who found that parents of schizophrenic patients received scores in the object sorting test that were indicative of pathology in conceptual thinking. Sixty-eight parents of schizophrenic patients and 115 control parents were used. The hypothesis of greater frequency of pathological scored in the patient-parent group was supported only with subjects from higher levels of intelligence, education and occupation.

RUBIN, J. A., & MAGNUSSEN, M. G. A family art evaluation. *Family Process*, 1974, *13*, 185–200.
These authors illustrate and discuss a two-hour art evaluation used in a child-guidance center. The evaluation consists of three tasks: (1) individually creating a picture from a scribble; (2) individually creating a family portrait; and (3) jointly deciding upon and creating a mural. Specific rationale for order and contents of tasks are discussed. Sources and amount of data lead to clear cut diagnostic conclusions and treatment recommendations.

RUTTER, M. Sex differences in children's responses to family stress. In E. J. Anthony & C. Koupernik (Eds.), *The child in his family*. New York: Wiley, 1970.
A questionnaire study investigating the impact on the child of marital problems and parental psychiatric disorders. Antisocial behavior in boys is associated with disturbance in family relationships but the marriage rating bore no relation to the rate of disorder in girls. Theoretical discussion is offered.

RYLE, A., & HAMILTON, M. Neurosis in fifty married couples. *Journal of Mental Science*, 1962, *108*, 265–273.
An investigation of 50 working class marital couples to record the prevalence of neurosis as indicated by the Cornell medical index, the records of the general practitioner with whom the families were registered, and the home interviews of a psychiatric social worker, The information from these sources was compared and the presence of neurosis was correlated with some aspects of adverse childhood experience, marital adjustment, consumer status and social integration.

SAFILIOS-ROTHSCHILD, C. Deviance and mental illness in the Greek family. *Family Process*, 1968, 7, 100–117.
A study of spouses of hospitalized mental patients in Greece to determine attitudes about deviance and mental illness. The defining of behavior as deviant will depend upon cultural definitions. Whether the deviance is defined as mental illness depends upon other factors. Here the "degree of marital satisfaction seems to be the determining factor as to whether or not the normal spouse will" label the deviance as mental illness.

SAGER, C., GRUNDRACH, R., KRAMER, M., LANZ, R., & ROYCE, J. The married in treatment: Effects of psychoanalysis on the marital state. *Archives of General Psychiatry*, 1968, *19*, 205–217.
In order to ascertain the effects of psychoanalysis on the marital state, a study of 736 married patients (432 women and 304 men) age 21 to 68 in middle and upper socioeconomic class who were being treated in psychoanalysis, was done. Seventy-nine psychoanalysis supplied data on "any 10 consecutive patients" and it was obtained through a

closed-ended questionnaire. 12 percent of the patients had concurrent group therapy, 2 percent were in conjoint marital therapy and about 20 percent of the patients had one or more conjoint consultations with their spouse and analyst. Results indicated that marriages rated poor initially improved and marriages rated better also improved. There was no evidence that as one marital partner got better another got worse. Overall individual patient improvement was rated at about 60 percent of the cases. Of the spouses who were in treatment, good effects were more frequently reported in cases in which both husband and wife were treated by the same psychoanalyst than when one spouse was treated by another therapist.

SAMPSON, H., MESSINGER, S., & TOWNE, R. D. Family processes and becoming a mental patient. *American Journal of Sociology*, 1962,1 *68*, 88–96.
Accommodation of the familiy to the deviant behavior of the future patient, and the disruption of this accommodation which leads to hospitalization are described for a series of 17 married mothers. Patients were located at time of first admission and extensive data collected by interviews with family members, by professionals involved at any stage, and by direct observation in home and hospital. Types of accommodation found were (1) spouses isolated, emotionally distant from each other, and (2) family not self-contained but revolved about a maternal figure who took over wife's duties. Each type has characteristic ways of disrupting, resulting in different implications to hospitalization.

SAMPSON, H., MESSINGER, S., & TOWNE, R. D. The mental hospital and family adaptations. *Psychiatric Quarterly*, 1962, *36*, 704–719.
The authors' purpose was to examine the effects of hospitalization on the family, not only during the hospitalization but also after discharge. Seventeen families in which the wife–mother was hospitalized for the first time and was diagnosed by the state hospital as schizophrenic, were studied using interviews and records up to 23 years after release. Emphasis is placed on a more deliberate therapeutic intervention based on study of the crisis that precipitated hospitalization and ways in which these crises are coped with by the family.

SCHUERMAN, J. Marital interaction and posthospital adjustment. *Social Casework*, 1972, *53*: 163–172.
It was hypothesized that expectations for emotional gratification in marriage of the identified patient (who was hospitalized) would correlate with outcome. Twenty-two married, ages 20 to 45, living with husbands at the time of admission, and living close enough to follow-up, were sampled. Eleven of the 22 were "depressed," 8 were "schizophrenic," and the remaining 3 were alcoholic or having an anxiety reaction. A semi-structured interview, as well as checklist focusing on emotional gratification in marriage were developed. Interviews were done by 2 people, and interrater reliability was 0.62 to 0.83. Outcome was measured at 6 months. Among 7 scales, only 1, "emotional responsiveness," correlated with outcome; the more emotionally responsive the spouse, the better the outcome.

SINGER, M. T., & WYNNE, L. C. Communication styles in parents of normals, neurotics, and schizophrenics: Some findings using a new Rorschach scoring manual. In I. M. Cohen (Ed.), *Psychiatric Research Report 20*. Washington, D.C.: American Psychiatric Association, 1966.
A report of a study of 250 families in which the Rorschach was used as a stimulus for individual family members. Styles of parental communication are described and findings reported.

SINGER, M. T., & WYNNE, L. C. Differentiating characteristics of parents of childhood schizophrenics, childhood neurotics, and yound adult schizophrenics. *American Journal of Psychiatry*, 1963, *120*, 234–243.
A study where parents of 20 autistic children were blindly differentiated at a statistically significant level of accuracy from parents of 20 neurotic children. The data were TAT and Rorschach tests of the parents. Additionally, the parents of adolescent and young adult schizophrenics were compared with the parents of autistic children and differences were found.

SINGER, M., & WYNNE, L. Principles for scoring communication defects and deviances in parents of schizophrenics: Rorschach and TAT scoring manuals. *Psychiatry*, 1966, *29*, 260–289.
A continuation of previous studies in which the authors have predictively related parental behavior on psychological tests with psychiatric diagnosis of their offspring. Two scoring manuals for use with the Rorschach and with the TAT are presented in an effort to pinpoint certain selective features of parental behavior which can be quickly scored (previous studies used inferences which required a great deal of time in analyzing a battery of tests). A discussion of the tests and their clinical correlates in the family of schizophrenics is also provided.

SINGER, M. T., & WYNNE, L. C. Thought disorder and family relations of schizophrenics. III: Methodology using projective techniques. IV: Results and implications. *Archives of General Psychiatry*, 1965, *12*, 187–212.
A continuation of the study of families through the use of projective tests with the emphasis upon predicitng the form of thinking and degree of disorganization of each patinet from the tests of other members of his family, and the blind matching of patients and their families. The series includes a full discussion of various aspects of schizophrenia and the family.

SPITZER, S. P., SWANSON, R. M., & LEHR, R. K. Audience reactions and careers of psychiatric patients. *Family Process*, 1969, *8*, 159–181.

A study of the reaction of families and the ways these reactions influence the psychiatric patient career. The histories of 79 first admission patients were examined and the patient and a family member were interveiwed. Two dimensions of family reaction to deviance are described leding to a typology of 8 career patterns which allow for the classification of 95 percent of the cases reviewed.

STABENAU, J. R., TUPIN, J., WERNER, M., & POLLIN, W. A comparative study of families of schizophrenics, delinquents, and normals. *Psychiatry*, 1965, *28*, 45–59.
A report of a comparison of five families with a schizophrenic, five families with a delinquent, and five normal families tested with the revealed differences test, the object sorting test, and the thematic apperception test. "Data from the three different tests suggest that in the schizophrenic and delinquent families there were both individual disturbances in thought process and impaired communication at the family level." "There was relatively little evidence of communication impairment at the individual or family level in the normal families."

STENNETT, R. Family diagnosis: MMPI and CIP results. *Journal of Clinical Psychology*, 1966, *22*, 165–167.
MMPI and CIP (California test of personality) tests were done on 230 families over a 5-year period in an out-patient clinic to answer several questions about family dynamics. Families were urban, Protestant, and white, with wide socioeconomic status. The CIP was given to children from age 4 up to 13. Findings were that a significant number of family members other than the identified patient had personality problems of their own, that there was a significant correlation in the level of psychopathology between the parents of troubled families, but no evidence was found of conflicting or complementary personality characteristics in the parents.

VAN der VEEN, F., HUEBNER, B., JORGENS, B., & NEJA, P. Relationships between the parents' concept of the family and family adjustment. *American Journal of Orthopsychiatry*, 1964, *34*, 45–55.
To study the "significance of the family unit for the well-being of the individual" and "the perceptions of the family unit by each individual," two groups of ten families each were selected. One group was composed of families from the community which functioned well (called the higher adjustment group). The other group was composed of families which had applied to a guidance center for help with one of their children. They were matched a to sex and position of the child and size of family. Tests used were the family concept Q-Sort, family semantic test, and a martial questionnaire. Results indicated that the adjustment of the families was a function of: (1) the amount of agreement between the "real" family concept of the parent and "ideal" family concept as determined by professionals; (2) the agreement between the "real" and "ideal" family concepts of the parent; and (3) the agreement between the "real" family concepts of the mother and father.

VAN der VEEN, F., & NOVAK, A. L. The family concept of the disturbed child: A replication study. *American Journal of Orthopsychiatry*, 1974, *44*, 763–772.
A replication of a previous study that revealed that family satisfaction and effectiveness were perceived to be significantly lower by distrubed adolescents than by their siblings or by normal controls. Methodology was previously described, but, in summary, the study used a sample of nonrandomly selected adolescents who were applying for help at a mental health clinic compared with one of their siblings and selected junior high school students. the Family Concept Test and the Maudsley Personality Inventory were the instruments used. Data was analyzed using analysis of variance and covariance. Results replicated the previous study. Implications for therapy are discussed.

WALSH, F. W. Breaching of family generation boundaries by schizophrenics, disturbed, and normals. *International Journal of Family Therapy*, 1979, *1*, 254–275.
See reference in Section 5.2.

WARING, M., & RICKS, D. Family patterns of children who become adult schizophrenice. *Journal of Nervous and Mental Disease*, 1965, *140*, 351–364.
A study comparing family variables of three groups of adult patients, who were seen as adolescents at a child guidance center. The three groups were (1) 30 patients, who as adults developed schizophrenia and remitted (defined as leaving the hospital), (2) 20 patients, who as adults developed schizophrenia and did not remit, and (3) a control group of 50 patients, selected from the clinic population, who did not develop schizophrenia and were never hospitalized. Data were obtained retrospectively from work-ups at the time the patients were adolescents, and also from subsequent follow-ups with schools, hospitals, and other agencies, and finally in some cases with interviews with patient and family. There were significant familial differences between the remitting and unremitting groups, and less significant differences between the total schizophrenia group and the controls.

WATZLAWICK, P., BEAVIN, J., SIKORSKI, L., et al. Protection and scapegoating pathological families. *Family Process*, 1970, *9*, 27–39.
An instrument for diagnoses in family therapy was developed that elicited complementary patterns of protection and scapegoating. The report is based on data obtained from 48 white middle-class families and 129 children ranging in age from 8 to 20 years. There were 51 identified patients. No normal families were used. Statistical significance was demonstrated in several areas.

WEIS, D. P. Children's interpretations of marital confict. *Family Process*, 1974, *13*, 385–393.
This experimental study was constructed to investigate the process of developing structures for interpreting and resolving interpersonal conflicts by latency age children. The theoretical base of this study is drawn from Piaget. The experimental sample included 128 children evenly distributed by sex and age, from intact middle and upper middle class homes. The children were asked to respond to 8 story situations depicting 4 major themes involving some type of "discord" or conflict between marital partners. Coding schemes were devised to measure developmental differences in the number of factors the children could consider simultaneously, their levels of abstraction in problem conceptualization and problem resolution. Results indicate the inability of latency age children to take into account large numbers of factors. Implications of this experilment are discussed.

WEISMAN, I. Exploring the effect of the marital relationship on child functioning and parental functioning. *Social Casework*, 1963, *44*, 330–334.
A report on a study investigating the relationship between child functioning and marital patterns. A sample was drawn of clients from the community service society of New York. The data consisted of the judgments of the caseworkers who used a rating scale to indicate severity and persistence of conflict in several areas of child functioning and paternal patterns.

WESTLEY, W. A., & EPSTEIN, N. B. Report on the psychosocial organization of the family and mental health. In D. Willner (Ed.), *Decisions, values and groups*. New York: Pergamon Press, 1960.
A report of a study designed to investigate the relationship between family functioning and development of either mental health or pathology. The sample was 531 students of the first year class at a university who were given a Rorschach, Gordon-Personality test, and interviewed by a psychiatrist. Out of these, 20 were classified as being the most emotionally healthy and of these, 17 were in the study, in view of the fact that they were available and their families agreed to participate. There is a schema for description, analysis, and evaluation of the family which is extensively illustrated using a case example. Common features of these emotionally healthy families are described.

WILLI, J. Joint Rorschach testing of partner relationship. *Family Process*, 1969, *8*, 64–78.
A test of marital partners by the conjoint Rorschach procedure. A sample of 80 pairs was examined with each person administered the Rorschach individually and then again administered it conjointly with the partner. The goal was to measure the relative strength of the partners and how the personality of the subject changes in the discussion with the other.

WINTER, W. D., FERREIRA, A. J., & BOWERS, N. Decision-making in married and unrelated couples. *Family Process*, 1973, *12*, 83–94.
See reference in Section 4.1.

WOLMAN, B. B., The fathers of schizophrenic patients. *Acta Psychotherapy and Psychosomatics*, 1961, *9*, 193–210.
Observations on the fathers of schizophrenic patients based upon 33 patients seen in individual and group therapy, and interviews with their family members. Although some fathers performed adequately outside the family circle, each deomnstrated childlike dependency upon the wife and inability to play the role of father. Fathers are grouped as sick, prodigies, rebellious, and runaways.

YARROW, M. R., CAMPBELL, J. D., & BURTON, R. V. Reliability of maternal retrospection: A preliminary report. *Family Process*, 1964, *3*, 207–218.
An examination of the retrospective method of family research where the data are based on self report of family members about the past. A study is reported where retrospection of mothers is obtained through interview methods and these data are compared with the reports of those mothers at the earlier period. The results "demonstrate a very large error in retrospective interview data on parent–child relations.

3.3   FAMILY DATA FROM OBSERVATION OF GROUP

ABARBANEL, A. Shared parenting after separation and divorce: A study of joint custody. *American Journal of Orthopsychiatry*, 1979, *49*, 320–329.
This is an inquiry into the effectiveness of joint custody. Data from four families was obtained from clinical interviews of parents and children, home visits, interviews of teachers, the BEM Sex-Role inventory, and questionnaires about parental values and influence. Results identified four factors in successful arrangements; commitment, mutual support, flexibility in sharing responsibility, and agreement on implicit rules.

ACKERMAN, N. W. Prejudicial scapegoating and neutralizing forces in the family group, with special reference to the role of family healer. *International Journal of Social Psychiatry*, 1964, *2*, 90–96.
A discussion of conflict in the family based upon films of family diagnostic sessions. The emphasis is upon prejudicial

scapegoating within a pattern of interdependent roles: those of the persecutor, the scapegoat, and the family healer. It is said that disturbed families break up into warring factions with a leader of each faction, a victim of prejudicial attack, and a person who provides the emotional antidote. The health–sickness continuum is influenced by the shifting balance of the struggle.

ALEXANDER, B. K., & DIBB, G. S. Interpersonal perception in addict families. *Family Process*, 1977, *16*, 17–28.
This paper reports on an investigation of interpersonal perception in 8 families in which addicted offspring maintained close parental ties. A technique called the "Interperception Matrix" was used and findings were compared with those observed in 8 matched control families. Results tended to validate clinical opinions that social perception in addict families contribute to perpetuate opiate addiction by undermining the addicts' self-esteem.

ASTON, P., & DODSON, G. Family interaction and emotional adjustment in a sample of normal schoolchildren. *Journal of Child Psychology and Psychiatry*, 1972, *13*, 77–91.
This is a clinical study attempting to discern differences in parental behavior toward children considered "noraml" (that is, having never received special psychological, educational or legal attention). Sample was 25 children (11 boys and 14 girls) ages 10 to 11, from upper middle class families with both parents living at home. Families were rated on a family task, children on adjustment using the Briston Social Adjustment Guide. Children were divided into three categories—adjusted, middle, and disturbed—with nine in the first group, eight each in the second and third. Significant differences were found between the adjusted and the disturbed groups for parental behavior during the family discussion task. Disturbed mothers were found to be "over-prominent and over-attentive"; disturbed fathers were withdrawn.

BASAMANIA, B.W. The emotional life of the family: Inferences for social casework. *American Journal of Orthopsychiatry*, 1961, *31*, 74–86.
A casework view of the Bowen research project where families with a schizophrenic member were hospitalized. Observations of 11 families are categorized into (1) interrelated personality problems among family members, and (2) interaction problems among family members. Case examples are given. A discussion of family therapy procedures is presented with the emphasis upon relating to more than one individual at a time. Inferences for social casework emphasize the dimension of the emotional life of the family rather than the integration of sociological concepts with casework practice.

BAUMANN, G., & ROMAN, M. Interaciton testing in the study of marital dominance. *Family Process*, 1966, *5*, 230–242.
A sample of 50 couples was exposed individually and conjointly to the Wechsler Bellevue. In the conjoint testing, the couple was asked to reach agreement on the response. Comparisons of the individual test and the conjoint test were made, as well as measures of dominance of the couple tested together.

BAXTER, J. C., & ARTHUR, S. C. Conflict in families of schizophrenics as a function of premorbid adjustment and social class. *Family Process*, 1964, *3*, 273–279.
A group of 16 hospitalized male schizophrenics was grouped into four classes on the basis of the patients' premorbid adjustment and social class. Standard interviews with the parents were rated for conflict."Results indicate that the amount of conflict expressed by the parents varies jointly with the premorbid level of the patient and the social class of the family."

BAXTER, J. C., ARTHUR, S., FLOOD, C., & HEDGEPETH, B. Conflict patterns in the families of schizophrenics. *Journal of Nervous and Mental Disease*, 1962, *135*, 419–424.
Families of 12 male and six female schizophrenics were interviewed individually and as a group to explore conflict patterns in relation to the sex of the schizophrenic child. The amount of conflict is said to be comparable in the two groups while patterns of conflict differ. There is more interparental conflict in the group of families with a male patient and more involvement of the patient in conflict in the group with a female patient.

BECKER, J. V., & MILLER, P. M. Verbal and nonverbal marital interaction patterns of alcoholics and nonalcoholics. *Journal of Studies on Alcohol*, 1976, *37*, 1616–1624.
See reference in Section 4.1.

BECKER, J., TATSUOKA, M., & CARLSON, A. The communication value of parental speech in families with distrubed children. *Journal of Nervous and Mental Disease*, 1966, *141*, 359–364.
Hypothesis was the communicativeness of parents with emotionally distrubed children (1) sets of parents who had children coming to a clinic) would be lower than that of parents with normal children (12 parent sets who were paid volunteers). Communicativeness was assessed by Taylor's cloze procedure. The speech of nonclinic mothers was significantly more communicative than that of nonclinic fathers, clinic mother, and clinic fathers. The latter three groups did not differe among themselves.

BEHRENS, M. Brief home visits by the clinic therapist in the treatment of lower-class patients. *American Journal of Psychiatry*, 1967, *124*, 371–375.

A paper reviewing the author's experience with home visits. The sample was 80 patients attending an out-patient clinic. These were chronic schizophrenics, the majority black and female of socioeconomic class IV or V with certain exceptions. Home visits were made on the average of one some visit per year per patient, usually in the late afternoon and lasting 30 to 40 minutes. At first they were done only at time of crisis situations, later routinely. The visits have been found useful in obtianing data about the patient and family, improving the relationship between patient and therapist, and in decreasing rehospitalizations.

BEHRENS,L M., & AKCERMAN, N. The home visit as an aid in family diagnosis and therapy. *Social Casework*, 1956, *37*, 11–19.
See Reference in Section 1.1

BEHRENS, M., & GOLDFARB, W. A study of patterns of interaction of families of schizophrenic children in residential treatment. *American Journal of Orthopsychiatry*, 1958, *28*, 300–312.
An attempt to differentiate families of schizophrenic children from those of nonschizophrenic children with a sample of 20 families who had a child diagnosed as schizophrenic and with five with a behavior disorder, all of whom were in-patients. There were ten normals, all children living at home. Data were collected using family interaction scales, and observations were recorded in the homes for both the normals and the patients when they were home on a visit. One person made all the observations. This observer knew which families had a schizophrenic child and which did not. Results indicate that the schizophrenic families were more pathological than the normal families and the families with behavior disorders.

BEHRENS, M., MEYERS, D. I., GOLDFARB, W., GOLDFARB, N., & FIELDSTEEL, N. D. The Henry Tittleson Center family interaction scales. *Genetic Psychology Monograph*, 1969, *80*, 203–295.
A report of the manual used for the use of the family interaction scales. The scales appraise the functioning of family groups, and derive from a clinical interest in the relationship between the identified patient and the family. Data are obtained through a three-hour home visit at mealtime. Scales have been used to evaluate the functioning of the family with a schizophrenic child, to compare families which include children with variuos diagnoses with normal families and to determine the nature of changes in family functioning over a specified length of time. A description of scales and in instructions, and three-family illustrations are described.

BEHRENS, M., ROSENTHAL, A. J., & CHODOFF, P. Communication in lower class families of schizophrenics. *Archives of General Psychiatry*, 1968, *18*, 689–696.
Part II: observation and findings, of a study of low-socioeconomic families of schizophrenics. The study was done in the home where the family was focussed upon a task, particularly the Rorschach. Raters were asked to predict type of family from written transcripts. Results indicate that communication and interaction patterns of lower class families with a schizophrenic differ from families whose class background is similar.

BEHRENS, M., & SHERMAN, A. Observations of family interaction in the home. *American Journal of Ortho-psychiatry*, 1959, *29*, 243–248.
An essay on the author's previous studies using home visits in evaluating family interactional patterns to differentiate schizophrenic families from nonschizophrenic families. Difficulties in this type of research are discussed and suggestions for further data collection are made. It is felt that this is a useful technique for diagnostic, treatment, and research purposes."

BERMAN, G. Communication of affect in family therapy. *Archives of General Psychiatry*, 1967, *17*, 154–158.
An experiment attempting to determine how affect is communicated in family sessions. The method was to take tape-recorded dialogue between three subjects in family therapy, transcribe it, and give the typewritten dialogue to seven observers (four social workers and three psychiatric residents). They were asked to rate the affective content of each speech. Findings were that verbal affect correlates with written dialogue, the preceding written and verbal dialogue will influence the raters' judgment of the affect of the subsequent speech, and that nonverbal affect will more strongly influence the raters' judgment than verbal affect. Methodology and application of the findings are discussed.

BING, E. The conjoint family drawing. *Family Process*, 1970, *9*, 173–194.
To assess family functioning, the family is asked to do a conjoint drawing. A sample of 14 families with a problem child was given the task and the results are reported.

BOWEN, M. A family concept of schizophrenia. In D. D. Jackson (Ed.), *The etiology of schizophrenia*. New York: Basic Books, 1960.
Clinical observations based upon a research study of the families of schizophrenics. The book includes a report on the project where whole families of schizophrenics were hospitalized.

BRODY, E. Modification of family interaction patterns by a group interview technique. *International Journal of Group Psychotherapy*, 1956, *6*, 38–47.
As part of a study of prefrontal lobotomy, family members of 11 patients who would undergo this procedure were seen

for five months before the operation until at least one year after the operation. Frequency was from once weekly during the first few months to as infrequently as once a month during the last few months. Individual interviews with family members were also used. The family interviews seemed to result in "an increased capacity for action by the family previously immobilized."

BRODEY, W. Some family operations in schizophrenia. *Archives of General Psychiatry*, 1959, *1*, 379–402.
See Reference in Section 5.2

BROWN, B. S. Home visiting psychiatrists. *Archives of General Psychiatry*, 1962, *7*, 98–107.
As part of an exploration of alternatives to psychiatric hospitalization, an investigation was done of home visiting by 34 psychiatrists with varied practice patterns. Data were gathered by interviews on frequency of visit, attitudes, and experiences. Nine of the psychiatrists had never done a home visit, 13 had done one to five a year, seven had made six to 25 visits per year, and five had made from 50 to 400 visits yearly. The type of practice apparently is the greatest determinant. Psychoanalytically oriented psychiatrists do least. The consensus of the group of psychiatrists is that home visits have doubtful utility. The movement to break down rigid boundaries between home and hospital may lead to a renaisance of home visiting.

BUGENTAL, D., LOVE, L., & KASWAN, J. Videotaped family interaction: Differences reflecting presence and type of child disturbance. *Journal of Abnormal Psychology*, 1972, *79*, 285–290.
This is a study comparing communication patterns of families containing "normal" children with those containing children with "emotional disturbance." The method was to use an unstructured situation including all family members and to measure activity, directing behavior, and positive versus negative evaluation. Analysis of covariance revealed significant differences between fathers, but not between mothers or children. Fathers of "disturbed" children showed "controlling" and/or dependent behavior: fathers of distractible children were evaluatively extreme and talkative; fathers of withdrawn children were neutral, nondirecting, and talkative; fathers of agressive children were negatively expreme, directing, and untalkative.

CANTWELL, D. P., BAKER, L., & RUTTER, M. Families of autistic and dysphasic children. I: Family life and interaction patterns. *Archives of General Psychiatry*, 1979, *36*, 682–687.
This is a study comparing the functioning of families of nonretarded autistic children (N=15) versus language disordered children as a control group (N=14). The groups were matched for age, sex, I.Q. and differed primarily in the social and behavioral characteristics of an autistic child. Measures of parent-child interaction and family life were made by semistructured interviews, scaled professional observations and parent questionnaires. There were no significant differences bewteen groups. It is concluded that there is no psychopathogenic family origin to infantile autism.

CAPUTO, D. V. The parents of the schizophrenic. *Family Process*, 1963, *2*, 339–356.
A study to assess the role of the parents in the development of schizophrenia, with particular emphasis upon the passive father and dominating mother notion. Parents were given individual tests and after taking a parent attitude inventory they were asked to discuss the items on which they had disagreed. These discussions were assessed with the Bales method. Reversal of role was not found to be a significant factor, and a hostile atomsphere is indicated in the home of the potential schizophrenic.

CHEEK, F. A serendipitous finding: Sex role in schizophrenia. *Journal of Abnormal Social Psychology*, 1964, *69*, 392–400.
One of a series of reports on an ongoing research project studying the family environment in schizophrenia. Interaction profiles of 67 young adult schizophrenics (40 male and 27 female) were compared with those of 56 normals (31 male and 25 female). Profiles were derived from 48 minutes of recorded interaction between father, mother, and paient with a variation of the Bales interaction categories. Male schizophrenics persented an interaction equivalent of withdrawal, with low total activity rates and low dominance behaviors. In contrast, female schizophrenics proved to be more active than female normals.

CHEEK, F. Family interaction patterns and convalescent adjustment of the schizophrenic. *Archives of General Psychiatry*, 1965, *13*, 138–147.
This is a study attempting to examine the relationship between family interaction patterns and outcome in schizophrenia. Data were obtained from 51 patients who had been hospitalized between the ages of 15 and 26, all of whom had living mothers and fathers. Each family member filled out a questionnaire relating to interaction patterns, all three family members together worked on 2 questionnaire problems, and an interview with the mother on the adjustment of the patient was evaluated by means of a 40-item 4-point rating scale. One week later in the home of the patient, 2 more 15-minute discussions among family members were recorded. Fifty-six normal families were studied with identical procedures used as with the schizophrenics. Results indicated that it was the characteristics of the parents, rather than the degree of sickness of the patient "which was the decisive factor in producing a poor outcome."

CHEEK, F. The father of the schizophrenic: The function of a peripheral role. *Archives of General Psychiatry*, 1965, *13*, 336–345.

In view of the absence of data on the role of the father in the intra-familial environment of the schizophrenic, Bales interaction process analysis technique and the social system theoretical framework of Parsons are used for studying the interaction of 67 families of young adult schizophrenics (40 male and 27 female). This was compared to 56 families with non-psychotic young adults (31 male and 25 female). Cases were evaluated a year and a half following discharge from the inpatient setting. All discussions were tape-recorded and coded, using the Bales interaction categories. Additionally, each ot the three members of the family was asked to fill in a questionnaire examining expectations and perceptions of how the other three might behave in relation to one another in certain typical family problems. Schizophrenic fathers occupy a peripheral position in the family in which the mother and patient are closest by default. Profiles of mothers of schizophrenics, however, differed more widely from those of normals than fathers.

CHEEK, F. Parental role distortions in relation to schizophrenic deviancy. In I. M. Cohen (Ed.), *Psychiatric Research report No. 20*. Washington, D.C.: American Psychiatric Association, 1966.
A study investigating the nature of schizophrenic interaction in the family, and the relation of family interaction to the outcome of the schizophrenic. The study combined questionnaire and observational data. The sample included 67 schizophrenic contrasted with 56 nonpsychotic young adults.

CHEEK, F. The "schizophrenic mother" in word and deed. *Family Process*, 1964, *3*, 155–177.
A study of the mothers of schizophrenics by direct observation of their behavior in a standard conversation with spouse and schizophrenic offspring. The data were analyzed with a revised version of the Bales process analysis. Sixty-seven families of schizophrenics were contrasted with 56 normal families. Differences in the characteristics of the mothers were found.

DAY, J., & KWIATKOWSKA, H. The psychiatric patient and his "Well" sibling: A comparison through their art productions. *Bulletin of Art Therapy*, 1962, *1*, 51–66.
This is a clinical paper comparing the "well" sibling to the "sick" sibling in families with a schizophrenic member. The setting was an inpatient ward, and observations were taken from the art work of the paried siblings during art therapy. The data from 3 families reveal that the "sick" sibling are productions are quite disorganized, while the "well" sibling's productions are more normal, but often "incongruous or unusual" and worse in unstructured situations. From other clinical data on 35 families, it is the authors' impression that the "well" siblings are less "emotionally involved" in the family, have more childhood friends than the patient, but have much less "depth of character and personality" than normals.

DRECHSLER, R. J., & SHAPIRO, M. I. Two methods of analysis of family diagnostic data. *Family Process*, 1963, *2*, 367–379.
A description of the conjoint use of clinical and statistical analysis of the same data. Thirteen families were interviewed and also given a standard family task (discussing a questionnaire) to perform alone. Samples of the tape recordings were extracted and frequency count made of how often one person spoke to another. Clinical impressions were compared and similarities found.

DREYER, C. A., & DREYER, A. S. Family dinner time as a unique behavior habitat. *Family Process*, 1973, *12*, 291–301.
This paper describes the dinner ritual in a sample of 40 white, middle-class families, which reveals a patterning of behavior. In this sample, the family eats together at the dinner table; the parents are constantly teaching the young child, admonishing him about his behavior at the table; and, the ritual is a highly socializing experience. Conversation at the dinner table is predominantly adult; the parents talk significantly more than the children, accounting for almost two-thirds of the total amount of speech at the table.

DUPONT, R., & GRUNEBAUM, H. Willing victims: the husbands of paranoid women. *American Journal of Psychiatry*, 1968, *125*, 151–159.
In an attempt to understand the dynamics of spouses of paranoid women, cases with paranoid delusions (both in-patient and out-patient) were evaluated over a three-year period. Data were collected on nine women with paranoid state, using clinical interviews with the husband alone, wife alone, and the couple together, plus the MMPI and interpersonal checklist. Results indicted that the wife expressed the anger and dissatisfaction in the marriage, while the husband manifested passivity and apparent resonableness and thus seemed to be a "willing victim."

ELBERT, S., ROSMAN, B., MINUCHIN, S., & GUERNEY, F. A method for the clinical study of family interaction. *American Journal of Orthopsychiatry*, 1964, *34*, 885–894.
Two methods are described to obtain the data on family interactions which were developed by the family research unit at the Wiltwick School for Boys. Families were from low socioeconomic status with more than one delinquent child. The family interactions apperception test is a TAT style test consisting of ten pictures showing family members in different activities. The family task is designed to permit observations of the family relations and their interactions. The family is seated in a room and by operating a tape recorder they hear six different tasks, which they must all discuss and answer together. During the time they are discussing the tasks, continuous report on nonverbal behavior is being dictated by an observer (looking through a one way mirror). Verbal behavior is recorded by a tape recorder.

ENGLISH, O. S., SCHEFLEN, A. E., HAMPE, W. W., & AUERBACH, A. H. Strategy and structure in psychotherapy. *Behavioral Studies Monograph No. 2*. Philadelphia: Eastern Pennsylvania Psychiatric Institute, 1965.
A companion volume to *Stream and structure of communicational behavior* (by A. E. Scheflen) which includes three research studies of a family therapy interview by Whitaker and Malone.

FARINA, A. Patterns of role dominance and conflict in parents of schizophrenic patients. *Journal of Abnormal Social Psychology*, 1960, *61*, 31–38.
See Reference in Section 3.2

FARINA, A., & DUNHAM, R. M. Measurement of family relationships and their effects. *Archives of General Psychiatry*, 1963, *9*, 64–73.
A group of families of male hospitalized schizophrenic patients, divided into good premorbind and poor premorbid, were given a structural test. Each family member is exposed to some hypothetical problem situations with children, and the family is then brought together and exposed to the same situation. Indices of dominance, such as length of speeches, and indices of confilct were constructed. Immediately following this, a group of the patients were given a visual-task individually and contrasted with a group given the same taks a week after the situation test. The conclusions are that fathers are more dominant in good premorbid cases and mothers more dominating in bad premorbids. Conflict scores are higher for good premorbids.

FERREIRA, A. J. Decision-making in normal and pathologic families. *Archives of General Psychiatry*, 1963, *8*, 68–73.
See Reference in Section 3.4

FERREIRA, A. J., & WINTER, W. D. Decision-making in normal and abnormal two-child families. *Family Process*, 1968, *7*, 17–36.
See Reference in Section 3.4

FERREIRA, A. J., & WINTER, W. D. Family interaction and decision-making. *Archives of General Psychiatry*, 1965, *13*, 214–223.
See Reference in Section 3.4

FERREIRA, A. J. & WINTER, W. D. Information exchange and silence in normal and abnormal families. *Family Process*, 1968, *7*, 251–278.
A comparison of normal and abnormal families which measured exchange of information and amount of time spent in silence in doing a task. A sample of 30 normal and 45 abnormal families were contrasted by a rater judgment of tape recordings. Differences were found.

FERREIRA, A. J., & WINTER, W. D. Stability of interactional variables in family decision-making. *Archives of General Psychiatry*, 1966, *14*, 352–355.
See Reference in Section 1.1

FERREIRA, A. J., WINTER, W. D., & POINDEXTER, E. J. Some interactional variables in normal and abnormal families. *Family Process*, 1966, *5*, 60–75.
A study contrasting normal and abnormal families, with the abnormals including schizophrenic, delinquent, and maladjusted children. The families were exposed to three TAT cards at a time. and asked to make up a story tying them together. Differences were found between the types of families.

FISCH, R. Home visits in a private psychiatric practice. *Family Process*, 1964, *3*, 114–126.
A discussion of home visiting with the merits described in terms of involving the entire family, decreasing family defensiveness, gaining new information about the patient's setting, and preventing hospitalization. Examples of experiences in home visits are given.

FOSTER, F. G., & KUPFER, D. J. Anorexia nervosa: Telemetric assessment of family interaction and hospital events. *Journal of Psychiatric Research*, 1975, *12*, 19–35.
One anorexic patient on an inpatient service and the family were studied using a telemetry-mobility sensing system and quantitating the amount of motor activity, clinical course, and other psychophysiologic measures. It was concluded that such a technique had great potential for measurements of outcome of hospital treatment.

FRIEDMAN, A. S. Family therapy as conducted in the home. *Family Process*, 1962, *1*, 132–140.
A discussion of the rationale for, experiences with, and problems resulting from home visits of schizophrenic patients and their families.

FRIEDMAN, C. J., & FRIEDMAN, A. S. Characteristics of schizophrenic families during a joint story-telling task. *Family Process*, 1970, *9*, 333–353.

A comparison of families with a schizophrenic, and normal families in the task of telling a story. Observer ratings were used for the interaction and judges ratings for the final joint family story. Differences were found.

GARMEZY, N., FARINA, A., & RODNICK, E. H. The structured situation test: A method for studying family interaction in schizophrenia. *American Journal of Orthopsychiatry*, 1960, *30*, 445–451.
A group of 36 sets of parents composed of parents of good premorbids, or parents of sons with TB ("normals"), were exposed to 12 hypothetical misbehaviors of a son. Individually and then together they were asked to indicate how to handle the situation. From tape recordings of the interviews, measures of dominance behavior and conflict were made, such as who spoke first and last, acceptance of another's solution, amnount of interruption, and so on. Fathers of good premorbids were dominant, as were mothers of poor premorbids. The parents of normals share dominance. Poor premorbids show greater conflict than normals.

GERBER, G. L., & KASWAN, J. Expression of emotion through family grouping schemata, distance, and interpersonal focus. *Journal of Consulting and Clinical Psychology*, 1971, *36*, 370–377.
This is a study of psychological closeness within a family using a sample obtained from 60 children attending a remedial summer school because of learning difficulties. Of those 60, 14 had both a mother and father, and of these 14, 10 participated and used the "family doll placement technique," which measured family grouping, distance, and interpersonal focus. Results indicated that positive emotional themes were represented by closer doll placements than negative themes.

GLASSER, P. H. Changes in family equilibrium during psychotherapy. *Family Process*, 1963, *2*, 245–264.
A report of a study of role changes in three families when a parent undergoes psychotherapy. Family members were interviewed, families were observed and interviewed as a group during home visits, reports of therapists and psychiatric and social work records were examined. Case examples are given and the reaction of the family to the process of treatment is described in terms of the changes in family equilibrium.

GOLDSTEIN, M., JUDD, L., RODNICK, E., ALKIRE, A., & GOULD, E. A method for studying social influence and coping patterns within families of disturbed adolescents. *Journal of Nervous and Mental Disease*, 1968, *127*, 233–252.
The first report of a project dealing with family interaction patterns between parents and adolescents. Twenty families with the identified patient aged 13 to 19 were seen for five sessions at the UCLA psychology clinic. Data collected included psychological testing (TAT and a partial WAIS), psycho-physiological recordings, and videotape recordings of both actual and simulated verbal interaction. The results of simulated interactions indicated that social power usage among family members was related to type of psychopathology manifested by the adolescents.

GOODRICH, W., & BOOMER, D. S. Experimental assessment of modes of conflict resolution. *Family Process*, 1963, *2*, 15–24.
A report of an experimental technique for studying the coping behavior of husband and wife when they attempt to resolve a marital conflict. Fifty paid volunteer couples between 18 and 27 years of age were asked to match colors—some unmatchable—to see how the couple coped with puzzling or ambiguous situations. A general discussion of results is given relating the "ability to achieve perspective on the situation and maintenance of self-esteem" to adequacy of coping.

GOODRICH, W., RYDER, R., & RAUSH, H. Patterns of newlywed marriage. *Journal of Marriage and the Family*, 1968, *30*, 383–391.
A report of an exploratory study of 50 average, middle-class marriages examined during the fourth month with interviews, problem solving situations, and questionnaires. Eight patterns of marriage are suggested.

HALEY, J. Cross-cultural experimentation: An initial attempt. *Human Organism*, 1967, *3*, 110–117.
See Reference in Section 3.4

HALEY, J. Observation of the family of the schizophrenic. *American Journal of Orthopsychiatry*, 1960, *30*, 460–467.
A report on a research project examining families containing a schizophrenic child by observation of conjoint family therapy sessions, filmed structured interviews, and experimental situations. The family is seen as a self-corrective system which is governed by the behavior of each family member. The limited range of a family system can be described in terms or rules and prohibitions which, when infringed, activate family members to behave in such a way as to reinforce the system. The general communicative behavior of the schizophrenic family is described.

HALEY, J. Research on family patterns: An instrument measurement. *Family Process*, 1964, *3*, 41–65.
A report of an investigation of patterns of interchange in families. The questions are whether families follow patterns, whether "normal" and "abnormal" families differ, and whether patterns change over time. A group of 40 normal and 40 abnormal families were given a standard stimulus for conversation and a frequency count was made of the order in which family members speak. Families were found to follow patterns and differences were found between the normal and abnormal groups.

HALEY, J. Speech sequences of normal and abnormal families with two children present. *Family Process*, 1967, *6*, 81–97.
A sample of 50 abnormal and 40 normal families were contrasted in an experimental setting where a measurement was made of the sequence in which family members speak. Differences had been found in a previous study where the families were tested in triads. In this study, where the sibling was included as well as the index child, differences were not found between the two groups.

HENRY, J. The study of families by naturalistic observation. In I. M. Cohen (Ed.), *Psychiatric research report No. 20.* Washington, D.C.: American Psychiatric Association, 1966.
A discussion of the observation of psychotic children in the home with the emphasis upon the methodology and the experience of such observations are undertaken, it quickly becomes apparent that the data are so rich as to compel re-examination of old theories and suggest hypotheses leading to new ones."

JACKSON, D. D., RISKIN, J., & SATIR, V. A method of analysis of a family interview. *Archives of General Psychiatry*, 1961, *5*, 321–339.
The authors examined the first five minutes of a family therapy interview without knowing the diagnosis of the child in the family. This "blind" analysis included a prediction of the psychopathology of the patient and some character traits of his brother. The information available was only the parents' conversation which was examined from the point of view of their communicative behavior, their needs and defenses, and possible early life experiences which would lead them to interact in this way. The purpose of the study was to illustrate a method of analyzing a family system.

JONES, D. M. Binds and unbinds. *Family Process*, 1964, *3*, 323–331.
A description of a family, with excerpts of verbatin conversation, which discusses the processes of the family members binding and unbinding in relation to one another.

JONES, M. W., et al. Parental transactional style deviance as a possible indicator of risk for schizophrenia. *Archives of General Psychiatry*, 1977, *34*, 71–77.
This research and clinical study attempts to delineate the role of intrafamilial transaction in the etiology of schizophrenia. TAT stories of 44 families who had a high risk for developing schizophrenia were recorded on audio tapes. Seventeen were in a high-risk group, 15 in an intermediate-risk group and 12 iln a low-risk group. Results indicate that high-risk male adolescents come from two symptom groups—withdrawn adolescents and adolescents in an active family conflict. High-risk parents tend to show transactional style deviance in direct interaction with their child and in a written statement describing the child's problem. Results suggest that parents with an adolescent who is hypothesized to be at risk for schizophrenia show particular subclinical forms of disturbance in their interactions.

KAUFAMN, I., FRANK, T., HEIMS, L., HERRICK, S., REISER, D., & WILLER, L. Treatment implications of a new classification of parents of schizophrenic children. *American Journal of Psychiatry*, 1960, *116*, 920–924.
A report of a study of the personalities of 80 schizophrenic children's parents. Material was gathered from psychotherapy, psychological testing, and direct observation of parent-child interaction. Parent personalities are classified as "spychoneurotic," "somatic," "pseudodelinquent," and "overly psychotic." The first two types of personalities were found more frequently in an out-patient setting, while the last two were found more frequently in a state hospital setting. Treatment for these parents is discussed.

KLOPPER, E. J., TITTLER, B. I., FRIEDMAN, S., et al: A multi-method investigation of two family constructs. *Family Process*, 1978, *17*, 83–93.
This paper examines "prominence" and 'inter-personal distance," by using data obtained from 15 families with a symptomatic child. Prominence Measures (talking time, family task outcome, prominence in symbolic representation of the whole family) and Inter-personal Distance Measures (amount of talk with dyads, dyadic distance in figure placements, seating arrangements) were obtianed from videotaped sessions and the results of figure placement procedures. It is suggested that current distress in families may increase the clarity of the prominence hierarchies and dyadic distances that emerge.

LEIK, R. K. Instrumentality and emotionality in family interaction. *Sociometry*, 1963, *26*, 131–145.
A comparison of discussion groups where nine families composed of father, mother, and daughter participated in triadic sessions. One third of the discussion groups were made up of all fathers, all mothers, or all daughters. Another third were composed of a father, a mother, and a daughter not of the same family. The final third was of natural families. The three groups were exposed to standard questions and observed. Categories of acts were derived from the Bales system with an emphasis upon instrumentality versus emotionality. It was found that sex role differentiation tends to disappear in family groups and the relevance of instrumentality and emotionality is quite different for family interaction than for interaction among strangers.

LENNARD, H. L., BEAULIEU, M. R., & EMBREY, N. G. Interaction in families with a schizophrenic child. *Archives of Geneal Psychiatry*, 1965, *12*, 166–183.

A study contrasting ten families with a schizophrenic child and seven normal families. The families have a 15-minute discussion of three topics related to a child's life. The conversations are recorded, transcribed, and coded along 12 dimensions. Differences are found between the two groups, and there is a discussion of the theoretical background and methodological problems.

LERNER, P. Resolution of intrafamilial role conflict in families of schizophrenic patients. I: Thought disturbance. *Journal of Nervous and Mental Disease*, 1966, *141*, 342–351.
Hypothesis was that there would be differences in the processes used to solve intrafamilial role conflict in parents with schizophrenic sons with marked thought disorder (12 families), less severe thought disorder (12 families), and control families (12 families). Thought disorder was measured by Rorschach protocol using the genetic level score of Becker. Intrafamilial role conflict solving was measured using a situational test with Strodtbeck's "revealed differences" technique. Results supported the hypothesis. Methodology of such research is discussed.

LERNER, P. Resolution of intrafamilial role conflict in families of schizophrenic patients. II: Social maturity. *Journal of Nervous and Mental Disease*, 1967, *4*, 336–341.
A study attempting to evaluate the relationship between resolution of intrafamilial role conflict and premorbid level of social competence in schizophrenics. Sample and methods were the same as in a previous study except that here social competence was measured by a scale developed by Zigler and Phillips. Findings were that control families compromised and acknowledged disagreement, while schizophrenic families did not but let the mother or father decide.

LEVIN. G. Communicator–communicant approach to family interaction research. *Family Process*, 1966, *5*, 105–116.
A family experiment in which the experimenter asks the subject to make a tape recording which might be played subsequently to some specific other person in his family. The recording includes specific instructions about a simple task. Individuals from families containing a schizophrenic (a sample of 33) were contrasted with normal individuals. the recordings were not actually played to family members, but the instructions were analyzed and classified with differences found bewteen the two groups.

LEVINE, R. Treatment in the home. *Social Work*, 1964, *9*, 19–28.
A clinical report of treatment of seven low-income, multiproblem families who came to a mental hygiene clinic for help with the identified patient, usually a child. Treatment of the family rather than the individual was begun because it seemed more economical, more family members could be helped, and the therapist could be more accurate in understanding problems. Treatment was done in the home. Techniques included "talking," "demonstration," and family activity. The seven families were rated in terms of improvement.

LEVINGER, G. Supplementary methods in family research. *Family Process*, 1963, *2*, 357–366.
See Reference in Section 3.5

LEVINGER, G. Task and social behavior in marriage. *Sociometry*, 1964, *27*, 433–448.
This study hypothesized that in a family, task-behavior (designated as subject-object activity) is specialized while social behavior (designated as subject-subject activity) is mutual. Sample is 60 middle-class couples with children interviewed clinically (separately and together) and performing together on several tasks: a vocabulary test, a color symbol test, and an adaptation of the Wechsler-Bellevue digit-symbol test. Social-behavior performance is the essence of marital relations as seen by both spouses and it is mutual, rather than specialized.

LEVY, J., & EPSTEIN, N. An appliction of the rorschach in family investigation. *Family Process*, 1964, *3*, 344–376.
A description of family testing using the Rorschach as a stimulus for conversation. Includes a detailed presentation of the individual and family responses to a set of cards by one family.

LIDZ, T., CORNELISON, A., FLECK, S., & TERRY, D. The intrafamilial environment of a schizophrenic patient. I: The father. *Psychiatry*, 1957, *20*, 329–342.
To understand the role of the family in the etiology and pathogenesis of schizophrenia, 14 families with a hospitalized schizophrenic were studied for periods varying from six months to over two years. Data collection included interviewing all members of the family (individually), observations and records of interactions of family members with each other and with the hospital personnel, home visits, and projective testing of all family members. Focus was on the fathers, in view of the fact that so much previous work had focussed on mothers alone. Fathers were found to be "very important, albeit often extremely disturbing, members of the families whose presence and influence cannot be neglected."

LIDZ, T., CORNELISON, A., FLECK, S., & TERRY, D. Intrafamilial environment of schizophrenic patients. II: Marital schism and marital skew. *American Journal of Psychiatry*, 1957, *114*, 241–248.
A study of the intrafamilial environment of the schizophrenic patient. In this study of 14 families, eight were split in two factions by "overt schism between the parents." Thus the identified patient cannot use one parent as a model for

identification or as a love object without losing the support of the other parent. The other six families were "skewed" (defined as psychopathology in the dominant parent) which was accepted or shared by the other without trying to change it. Case examples are given.

LIDZ, T., FLECK, S., ALANEN, Y. O., & CORNELISON, A. Schizophrenic patients and their siblings. *Psychiatry* 1963, *26*, 1–18.
A study of the siblings of schizophrenics based upon individual interviews of family members, observation of family members with each other and hospital staff, and projective tests. Sixteen families were studied for periods ranging from six months to six years. As many siblings were psychotic as were reasonably well adjusted, and all except five or six of the 24 siblings suffered from severe personality disorders. Siblings of the same sex as the patient were more disturbed than those of the opposite sex.

LIDZ, T., PARKER, B., & CORNELISON, A. The role of the father in the family environment of the schizophrenic patient. *American Journal of Psychiatry*, 1956, *113*, 126–132.
One of a series of papers on a study of the families of schizophrenic patients. Families in which there was both a mother and father present were interviewed separately, in pairs, and in groups. The identified patient was an in-patient and came from upper-class or upper middle-class families. Sixteen families (of which five identified patients were female and 11 were male) were studied. The fathers are seen as "noxious" in the development of schizophrenia. Three types are described: (1) fathers of schizophrenic daughters who are constantly battling their wives and seeking to enlist the support of their daughters, (2) fathers who feel their sons are rivals for their wives, and (3) passive, withdrawn, and absent fathers.

LIEBER, D. J. Parental focus of attention in a videotape feedback task as a function of hypothesized risk for offspring schizophrenia. *Family process*, 1977, *16*, 467–475.
Twenty-five families of disturbed, nonpsychotic, adolescents were observed in a structured task in which they discussed their reactions to viewing themselves interacting on videotape. Audiotaspes obtained were scored following the Singer-Wynne concept of transactional style deviance and related to prior assessments of parental communication disorder based on individual parental TAT protocols. The results confirmed the Singer-Wynne hypothesis of the cross-situational stability of transactional style deviance. A striking finding was that an index of positive focusing behavior differentiates more strongly parents of adolescents hypothesized to be at varying levels of risk for schizophrenia than does the measure of transactional style deviance.

LOVELAND, N. T. The family Rorschach: A new method for studying family interaction. *Family Process*, 1963, *2*, 187–215.
A report of a study in which the Rorschach was used as a standardized stimulus for family conversations. The procedure is descirbed, the advantages and disadvantages are discussed and excerpts from a family Rorschach are presented.

MANNING, J., & GLASSER, B. The home visit in the treatment of psychiatric patients awaiting hospitalization. *Journal of Health and Human Behavior*, 1962, *3*, 97–104.
As an experimental project, 16 patients on a waiting list for hospitalization were visited in their homes by a social worker and/or nurse, psychologist, or psychiatrist. Case materials are presented to demonstrate the reasons for home visiting, and the benefits that were seen. It is felt that home visits are helpful both diagnostically and in terms of treatment.

MARTIN, B. Family interaction associated with child distrubnces assessment and modification. *Psychotherapy*, 1967, *4*, 30–35.
A report testing the author's notion that disturbances in the interaction between parents and child can lead to disturbed behavior in the child. An experimental procedure was developed in order to limit communication to just one member of the family at a time. Sessions were recorded on audiotape and rated according to degree of blaming. In a pilot study of four families, two received modification procedures designed to decondition blaming, and two did not. The experimental families showed a greater proportion of decrease in blaming scores.

MATTA, S., & MULHARE, M. T. Breaking a cycle of hospitalization through the psychiatric house call. *Hospital and Community Psychiatry*, 1976, *27*, 346–348.
A case report supports the technique of home visits focusing on family dynamics and treatment techniques to break the cycle of repeated hospitalizations for schizophrenics.

McPHERSON, S., GOLDSTEIN, M., & RODNICK, E. Who listens? Who communicates? How? Styles of interaction among parents and their disturbed adolescent children. *Archives of General Psychiatry*, 1973, *28*, 393–403
The hypothesis that differential patterns of intrafamilial communication contribute to the development of a particular form of disturbed adolescent behavior was investigated using a sample of 28 adolescents referred for evaluation of "behavior disturbance" who had two parents willing to cooperate in a research project. The families were divided into four groups: (1) aggressive, asocial adolescents; (2) adolescents in active family turmoil and conflict; (3) passive,

negative adolesctnes; and (4) withdrawn, socially isolated adolescents. There was dyadic and triadic discussions that were taperecorded and transcribed. Statements were coded according to the Mishler and Waxler procedure. Results indicated that each family type had specific types of communication patterns.

MEYERS, D., & GOLDFARB, W. Studies of perplexity in mothers of schizophrenic children. *American Journal of Orthopsychiatry*, 1961, *31*, 551–564.
In order to document the association of parental complexity (defined as passivity, uncertainty, lack of spontaneity, absence of empathy, with diminished awareness of the child's needs, bewilderment, blandness in the face of unacceptable behavior in the child, and an absence of parental control), 23 mothers of schizophrenic children and 23 mothers of normal public school children were studied. Techniques included a participant-observation technique, in which the observer spent three hours with the family at home, and a semistructured open-ended interview of the mothers. Results indicated that the mothers of the schizophrenic children with organic involvement have a greater difficulty in appropriately structuring their child's environment, while the mothers of the organic group cannot be differentiated from mothers of the normals.

MINUCHIN, S., & MONTALVO, B. An approach for diagnosis of the low socioeconomic family. In I. M. Cohen (Ed.), *Psychiatric research report No. 20*, Washington, D.C.: American Psychiatric Association, 1966.
A report on the diagnostic techniques used in appraising the individual and the family at the Wiltwyck School for Boys. The emphasis is upon communication style and affect. Clinical illustrations are provided.

MISHLER, E. Families and schizophrenia: An experimental study. *Mental Hygiene*, 1966, *50*, 552–556.
A discussion of a way of testing families with a schizophrenic member and contrasting them with normal families. Findings are not given, but illustrations are offered of ways the families respond in the test situation.

MISHLER, E., & WAXLER, N. Family interaction in schizophrenia. *Archives of General Psychiatry*, 1966, *15*, 64–75.
A study which describes only methodology used in an experimental study of family interactions in schizophrenia. Subjects were 30 schizophrenic families (in which a schizophrenic child was hospitalized) and 16 normal families recruited from the community. Schizophrenic patients were newly admitted to the hospital, unmarried, white, living in the Boston area, living at home with both parents (who had to be alive and living together), and had one unmarried sibling of the same sex. Experimental procedure was Strodtbeck's revealed differences test. Coding and data anallysis procedures are described.

MORGAN, R. W. The extended home visit in psychiatric research and treatment. *Psychiatry*, 1963, *26*, 168–175.
A report of some data on 14 cases and techniques involved in the extended home visit by the social worker. The material presented is said to give support to the idea that highly relevant data pertinent to psychiatric research and treatment is obtained and is worth the time, cost, and emotional expense involved.

MORRIS, G., & WYNNE, L. Schizophrenic offspring and parental styles of communication. *Psychiatry*, 1965, *28*, 19–44.
One of a series of papers reporting a study of parental styles of communication and schizophrenic children. Data were selected from excerpts of transcripts of conjoint family sesions with 12 families. Predictions about the most disturbed offspring were made by a judge blind to the clinical aspects of the case. Predictive criteria were then reformulated using the data from a parallel study utilizing psychological test material as predictors. These reformulated criteria were then utilized for blind predictions on eight new families. Results indicated that the style of the family communication can be related to the thought and affect disorder in schizophrenics.

MURRELL, S., & STACHOWIAK, J. Consistency, rigidity, and power in the interaction patterns of clinic and non-clinlic families. *Journal of Abnormal Psychology*, 1967, *72*, 265–272.
In order to study interaction patterns in families, 11 families, each having at least two children who were attending a child guidance clinic, were matched with 11 control families whose names were obtained from school, who were thought to be normal. All families included both parents and the two oldest children. They were matched on the basis of age, sex, sibling position, and parental educational attainment. Families were observed by two raters through a one-way mirror and were asked to (1) plan something together as a family, (2) answer a list of 11 questions about the families and agree on the answers, (3) list adjectives regarding their family, and (4) make up stories to 7 TAT pictures. Results indicated that in all 22 families, the pattern of who talks to whom was consistent. Secondly, the control patients had more rigidity in speaking than the "sick" families. Thirdly, in sick families the older child had more power within the family than in the controls, and fourthly, the sick families were not as productive as the well families.

NELSON, B., COLLINS, J., KREITMAN, N., & TROUP, J., Neurosis and marital interaction. II: Time sharing and social activity. *British Journal of Psychiatry*, 1970, *117*, 47–58.
The second in the series of studies on neurosis and marital interactions, this one tests patterns of time-sharing and social activity in marriages of patients and controls. The instrument was a "time budget for a one-week period." Results indicated that patients and wives spent more time in face-to-face contact than controls, had less social activity than controls, and that the wives were less independent than the controls.

NIELSON, J. Home visits by psychiatrists. *Comprehensive Psychiatry*, 1963, *4*, 442–461.
The author reports on another aspect of the Samso Project (Samso is an island off the Danish mainland), that is the home visits of psychiatrists for diagnostic and therapeutic purposes. It is felt that one home visit is of diagnostic importance in nearly all types of mental illness, and of therapeutic importance in all elderly and all psychotic, except paranoid patients. A home visit is advised for neurotic patients when supportive and dynamic family therapy is used.

NIELSEN, N. P., & NAVA, V. Il ranking Rorschach Test Ed il PARI nello studio delle interazoni in un gruppo di famiglie di schizorenici. (The consensus Rorshcach Test and the PARI in a study of interactions in a group of families of schizophrenics.) *Rivisita di Psyichiatria* (Roma), 1975, *10*, 345–364.
This is one of a series of studies (methodology previously described) using the PARI to understand family interaction in schizophrenia. Results indicated that in such families: "(1.) A smaller number of individual choices; (2.) A greater frequency of an official speaker for the family; (3.) Greater difficulty in agreeing on collective responses; (4.) A tendency to agree on collective responses because of task pressure, rather than as an expression of real agreement; (5.) Greater tendency to persuade or impose a collective response; and (6.) Greater frequency for firm alliances between single members of the family."

ODOM, L., SEEMAN, J., & NEWBROUGH, J. A study of family communication patterns and personality integration in children. *Child Psychiatry and Human Development*, 1971, *1*, 275–285.
A clinical pilot study attempting to generate an hypothesis about the role of intrafamilial communication patterns in the psychological adjustment of children. Method was to sort a subsample of a fifth grade class ranked on "personality integration" using the Bill Lewis Reputation Test and the Radke-Yarrow Teacher Rating Scale. On the ratings of high-adjustment and low-adjustment families, four famlies (out of five) who volunteered to participate in the high-adjustment group and three (of three) families in the low-adjustment group were used. An observer, blind to adjustment of the family, observed the family while they did a family task using the Rorschach cards, High-adjustment families, compared to low-adjustment families, had a greater range of communication skills, more role clarity, less psychological distance between family members, and greater decentralization in decision-making.

OLSON, D.H. The measurement of family power by self-report and behavioral methods. *Journal of Marriage and the Family* , 1969, *31*, 545–550.
A study comparing self report and observed behavior on the question of power in marriage. Thirty-five couples were given questionnaires and their responses compared with their behavior in the laboratory dealing with real problems. No relationship was found between what the couples said about the distribution of power in the marriage and what was observed when they dealt with one another. Explanatory factors are offered, and the conclusion is reached that this research reinforces "the idea that methodological research of this type should precede, rather than follow, substantive research in the field."

PARAD, H. J., & CAPLAN, G. A framework for studying families in crises. *Social Work*, 1960, *5*, 3–15.
An approach to the observation and study of the family in crisis. Family members are seen individually and as a group in the home while engaged in household activities. The concepts of family life-style, problem-solving mechanisms, and need-response patterns are illustrated with a case history. It is suggested that intervention is most effective at the moment the family is in crisis.

PLIONIS, E. M. Family functioning and childhood accident occurrence. *American Journal of Orthopsychiatry*, 1977, *47*, 250–263.
The hypothesis that the adequacy of family functioning is associated with the rate of children's accidents is tested using a semistructured interview of 15 families (mother only in 10) with a child hospitalized for accidental injury. Family functioning was rated using Geisner's Scale, and family stress was rated using the Holmes-Rahe Social Readjustment Rating Scale. Data analysis was by Spearman Correleation Coefficients and Mann Whitney U Test. No relation was found to family stress and none to family functioning for the whole group, but when only families with index child's age 3–11 (N=10) were considered, there was a highly significant relationship to adequacy of the marital relationship, child training methods and family social activities, but not to the child-parent relationship or individual members adjustments. A 65 reference review of the literature is included.

RAVICH, R. Game-testing in conjoint marital psychotherapy. *American Journal of Psychotherapy*, 1969, *23*, 217–229.
A report on the "game-test" for both family diagnosis and family therapy. Methodology is described and four typical patterns of interaction are identified: (1) competitive, (2) alternating, (3) dominant-submissive, and (4) mixed. Based on these patterns techniques for therapy are described.

REISS, D. Individual thinking and family interaction. I: Introduction to an experimental study of problem-solving in families of normals, character disorders, and schizophrenics. *Archives of General Psychiatry*, 1967, *16*, 80–93.
This is a report of an experimental study of the relationship between individual thinking and family interaction. Experimental procedures and methods of measuring modes of analysis are discussed. Subjects were families of five normals, five character disorders, and six schizophrenics. The test used was a puzzle that required active use of cognitive and conceptual capacities. The method of analysis was derived from the work of Riley whose systematic approach included computing scores from the raw data and developing rules concerning inferences.

REISS, D. Individual thinking and family interaction. II: A study of pattern recognition and hypothesis testing in families of normals, character disorders, and schizophrenics. *Journal of Psychiatric Research*, 1967, *5*, 193–21.
This is the second in a series of studies of the relationship between family process and individual thinking. Methodology has been discussed in a previous study. Results indicate that following a period of family interaction, members of normal families showed improvement in pattern recognition, members of families of schizophrenics showed deterioration or no change; and members of character disorder families were in between.

REISS, D. Individual thinking and family interaction. III: An experimental study of categorization performance in familes of normals, those with character disorders, and schizophrenics. *Journal of Nervous and Mental Disease*, 1968, *146*, 384–404.
The second of a series of studies to measure the relationship between individual family interaction and individual thinking, and to determine what differences in this relationship exist among families of normals, personality disorders, and schizophrenics. Method was to give the families a puzzle, tape their discussion, and to code verbal responses. Sample has been previously described; there were five families in each group. Results indicated that normals could solve the puzzle, while the others could not. The data on why they could not was felt to be consistent with the hypothesis that interpersonal problems in families significantly interfere with their collaborative problem-solving efforts.

REISS, D. Individual thinking and family interaction. IV: A study of information exchange in families of normals, those with character disorders, and schizophrenics. *Journal of Nervous and Mental Disease*, 1969, *149*, 473–490.
This is the third in a series of papers on interrelationships of family interaction and thinking and perception of family members. Methodology has been discussed in the earlier papers. This experiment was developed to test the family's efficiency in exchanging information *within* itself. Families of normals and schizophrenics were more sensitive than those with character disorders to cues from within the family. Families of schizophrenics appeared to represent a group of families who utilize cues from within but not from without the family.

REISS, D. Individual thinking and family interaction. V: Proposals for the contrasting character of experiemtnal sensitivity and expressive form in families. *Journal of Nervous and Mental Disease*, 1970, *151*, 187–202.
Based on three previous experiments 12 variables on family interactions and individual thinking were factor analyzed, and results were obtained from 14 of the families in the original sample (previously reported). Variables of shared experiential sensitivity in families were more closely asnd generally related, either as cause or effect to the thinking of its members rather than to variables in expressive form.

RISKIN, J. Family interaction scales: A preliminary report. *Archives of General Psychiatry*, 1964, *11*, 484–494.
A report on a research project where nine families were given a structured interview and the conversation categorized. Two minute segments of the conversation are categorized by the coder as clear, change of topic, commitment, and so on. At attempt is then made to describe the family from the coding sheets blindly. "Results suggest that it is possible to make clinically meaningful and accurate descriptions of the whole family and of its various members, based on the coded speeches and without focussing on the content."

RISKIN, J. Methodology for studying family interaction. *Archives of General Psychiatry*, 1963, *8*, 343–348.
A report of a pilot study with five families designed to develop a conceptual framework and methods for investigating the relationship between family interaction and personality formation. Family members are brought together in standardized structured interviews with the tape recorded conversation analyzed by a set of categories which include clarity, content, agreement, commitment, congruency, intensity, and attack or acceptance of the other person.

RISKIN, J. "Nonlabeled" family interaction: Preliminary report on a prospective study. *Family Process*, 1976, *15*, 433–439.
This paper outlines the procedures, sample selection, data collection and preliminary findings of an exploratory study which focuses on whole-family interaction. It is a preliminary report which discusses the first year of a two year study and the sample consists of two families who are interviewed at monthly intervals. Problem areas are identified and future plan are discussed.

RISKIN, J., & McCORKLLE, M. E. "Nontherapy" family research and change in families: A brief clinical research communication. *Family Process*, 1979, *18*, 161–162.
This is an interim report of an exploratory, prosepctive study of "well" family interaction. The study focuses on direct observation of the whole family over time.

ROSENTHAL, A., BEHRENS, M. I., & CHODOFF, P. Communication in lower-class families of schizophrenics. *Archives of General Psychiatry*, 1968, *18*, 464–470.
This is the first part, methodological, problems, of a two-part report on low socioeconomic families of schizophrenics. Groups compared were 17 black schizophrenics and their families, 11 black families in a control group, and 11 white schizophrenics and their families. The procedure included observation in the home with tasks requiring the family to maintain a focus of attention on a specific topic. (For Part II of this study see Behrens, M. I. Communication in lower-class families of schizophrenics. *Archives of General Psychiatry*, 1968, *18*, 689–696.)

RUBIN, J. A., & MAGNUSSEN, M. G. A family art evaluation. *Family Process*, 1974, *13*, 185–200.
See reference in Section 3.2.

RUSSELL, C. S. Circumplex model of marital and family systems. III: Empirical evaluation with families. *Family Process*, 1979, *18*, 29–45.
This paper describes a research study designed to test the hypotheses that family systems exhibiting moderate adaptability and moderate family cohesion are more functional than families exhibiting either extreme. The sample consisted of 31 families with one daughter ranging in age from 14–17 years who participated in a structured family interaction game (SIMFAM). They were then asked to answer questionnaires designed to measure the variables of cohesion and adaptability, support and creativity. Results from data analysis show that moderate family cohesion and adaptability as well as high family support and creativity are associated with high family functioning. Implications for practice and recommendation for practitioners are offered.

RYDER, R. G. Husband-wife dyads vs. married strangers. *Family Process*, 1968, *7*, 233–238.
A comparison of the behavior of spouses with each other and with strangers by use of the color matching test which induces a conflict situation. Sixty-four married dyads and 56 unmarried dyads were contrasted. Few differences were found, but persons "treat strangers more gently, and generally more nicely than they do their spouses."

RYDER, R. G. Two replications of color matching factors. *Family Process*, 1966, *5*, 43–48.
A replication of the color matching test of Goodrich and Boomer. The test was applied to 64 married couples and 56 split couples defined as a male and female pair not married. Comparisons with the original sample, and between the married and unmarried groups are made.

RYDER, R. G., & GOODRICH, D. W. Married couples responses to disagreement. *Family Process*, 1966, *5*, 30–42.
A report on the color matching test administered to 49 recently married couples. Husband and wife are exposed to colors and asked to match them when some of them do not match. Ways of handling the conflict are categorized and described.

SCHEFLEN, A. E. Stream and structure of communicational behavior. *Behavioral series Monograph No. 1*. Philadelphia: Eastern Pennsylvania Psychiatric Institute, 1965.
A context analysis of a family therapy session by Whitaker and Malone. The examination of the interview is in detail and includes kinesic, linguistic and contextual description.

SCHULMAN, R. E., SHOEMAKER, D. J., & MOELIS, I. Laboratory measurement of parental behavior. *Journal of Consulting Psychology*, 1962, *26*, 109–114.
Families were told to make up stories about a scene which included a variety of buildings and people with the hypothesis that in families with a conduct problem child, parents would exhibit more control over behavior of the child, and that in these families there would be significantly more aggression between parents. Parents and one son, age eight to 12, of 41 families were tested. In 20 families the child was considered a conduct problem while the other 21 had no reported conduct problems. Parents' behavior was rated by observers who found that parents of conduct problem children were more rejecting and hostile than parents of children without problems. It was concluded that there is a cause-effect relation between parental hostility and rejection and aggressive behavior in children.

SHAPIRO, I. N., & WILD, C. M. The product of the consensus Rorschach in families of male schizophrenics. *Family Process*, 1976, *15*, 211–224.
This study examined the use of families' conjoint Rorschach responses to identify families of schizophrenics. The sample consisted of 36 families with a schizophrenic member who had been hospitalized prior to the study and two control groups (38 families with no history of psychiatric hospitalization and 13 families of non-schizophrenics who were either past or present in-patients in a psychiatric hospital). Results showed highly significant ability of the test to distinguish the groups. The family Rorschach holds promise as an efficient and effective tool for distinguishing schizophrenic families from other families.

SHARAN, & SHLOMO. Family interaction with schizophrenics and their siblings. *Journal of Abnormal Psychology*. 1966, *71*, 345–353.
An experimental study contrasting the behavior of parents of schizophrenics with the patient and with a sibling. Twenty-four families were asked to solve collectively the questions from the comprehension and similarities subtests of the Wechsler-Bellevur intelligence scale. The conversations were compared for problem-solving efficiency, mutual support patterns, and parent-child sex role alignments. Parents and patient worked as efficiently as parents and siblings. parents supported both children equally and fathers and mothers were equally dominant. The patients were more supportive of their parents than were the sibilngs, and parental discord was more prominent when the patient was present than when the sibling was present.

SHERMAN, M. H., ACKERMAN, N. W., SHERMAN, S. N., & MITCHELL, C. Non-verbal cues in family therapy. *Family Process*, 1965, *4*, 133–162.

A discussion of non-verbal cues in family therapy with excerpts from an interview. Non-verbal expressions tend to occur in inverse proportion to verbal expressions which are ineffective, give clues to attitudes and traits, and act as hidden cues to shared emotional conflicts.

SIGAL, J. J., RAKOFF, V., & EPSTEIN, N. B. Indications of therapeutic outcome in conjoint family therapy. *Family Process*, 1967, *6*, 215–226.
A report on a study which attempted to predict the eventual success of family therapy by examining the degree of family interaction and emotional involvement as described by therapists in the initial stages of treatment. "The clinical observations in this study raise some doubts about the value of the interactional frame of reference in conjoint family therapy.

SINGER, M. Delinquency and family disciplinary configurations. *Archives of General Psychiatry*, 1974, *31*, 795–798.
This clinilcal study elaborates on the Johnson-Szurek hypothesis of superego lacunae as etiologic to "delinquency." Sample was 30 families treated in family therapy, and data were obtained from observations by the cotherapists and from a rating scale (not described). Results indicate that families with an antisocial identified patient operate with "very restrictive policy-making, loose policing, and very lenient punishing." No examples of "permissive" policy-making were observed.

SMITH. R. Discussion tasks as a measure of influence structure and reversal of role structure in normal families. Implications for the study of pathological families. *Journal of Psychiatric Research*, 1970, *8*, 51–61.
Influence of communication patterns in 12 American, white, middle-class families consisting of both parents and child were studied by recording and analyzing their interaction on decision-making tasks. Each task was oriented toward a different member of the family or the family as a whole. The response obtained depended on the type of task used to elicit structure.

SMITH, R. C. Verbal discussion versus note passing tasks in the study of family role structure. *Journal of Nervous and Mental Disease*, 1971, *152*, 173–183.
This study compares two methods of eliciting family interaction—verbal discussion (discussion tasks) and note passing in a communication network (communication network tasks). A sample of 12 white, middle-class families consisting of mother, father and adolescent child performed 8 tasks in which they had to reach a single final decision on family relevant problems; 4 discussion tasks and four similar communication network tasks were used. Analysis of data showed that the communication network medium yielded: (1) a significantlyl more equal influence and equal communication family role structure; (2) an influence structure which was more unusual or less expected than the role structure on discussion tasks; and (3) an influence structure which correlated significantly less well with the competence structure perceived by all family members.

SNELL, J., ROSENWALD, R., & ROBEY, A. The wifebeater's wife: A study of family interaction. *Archives of General Psychiatry*, 1964, *11*, 107–113.
A study of 37 families in which men were charged by their wives with assault and battery and who were referred to one of the psychiatric clinics which serve the courts of Massachusetts. Twleve of the families were studied in detail (both husband and wife were seen for three or more interviews). Four wives were in individual psychotherapy for more than 18 months. In addition some group therapy and couple therapy were attempted. A typical family structure is described: husband is passive, indecisive, and sexually inadequate; wife aggressive, masculine, frigid, and masochistic; relationship between the two characterized by alternation of passive and aggressive roles. An adolescent son may upset the equilibrium.

SOJIT, C. M. Dyadic interaction in a double blind situation. *Family Process*, 1969, *8*, 235–260.
Marital couples were exposed to a "double bind situation" to contrast parents of delinquents, ulcerative colitis patients, and normal controls. The couples were exposed to the proverb "a rolling stone gathers no moss" and were asked to reach agreement about its meaning. The responses were categorized and differences found.

SPECK, R. Family therapy in the home. *Journal of Marriage and the Family*, 1964, *26*, 72–76.
An essay based on the author's clinlical experience in doing family therapy in the home. Advantages of this technique are discussed and several new phenomena are described: the absent member, the most disturbed family member, the youngest member, the role of pets, the extended family, and family secrets.

SPECK, R. Family therapy in the home. In N. W. Ackerman (Ed.), *Expanding theory and practice in family therapy*. New York: Family Service Association of America, 1967.
A clinical paper from a research project in which family therapy was conducted at home. Advantages and disadvantages in techniques are discussed. It is thought to be advantageous over doing therapy in the office, but no definitive experiment "has yet been done." At least one home visit should be made to every family.

SPECTOR, R., GUTTMANN, H., SIGAL, J., RAKOFF, V., & EPSTEIN, N. Time sampling in family therapy sessions. *Psychotherapy*, 1970, *7*, 37–40.

This study is an attempt to obtain a representative picture of a family therapy session from a portion of it. Tape recordings of meetings with 6 one-child families were used. They were coded by assigning samples to one of three categories of affect—emergency, welfare, or neutral. The therapists' speeches were divided into drive (speeches aimed at stimulating interaction or conveying empathy) or interpretive. Interviews were divided into different segments to check uniformity. Results indicated that in terms of emergency affect there was good correlation with entire family participation and poor correlation with individual member participation. A sample of a session can give a global picture of the entire family's affect but is insufficient to assess the contribution of the individual family members to the over-all pattern.

STABENAU, J. R., TUPIN, J., WERNER, M., & POLLIN, W. A comparative study of families of schizophrenics, delinquents, and normals. *Psychiatry*, 1965, *28*, 45–59.
A report of a comparison of five families with a schizophrenic, five families with a delinquent, and five normal families tested with the revealed differences test, the object sorting test, and the thematic apperception test. "Data from the three different tests suggests that in the schizophrenic and delinquent families there were both individual disturbances in thought process and impaired communication at the family level . . . . There was relatively little evidence of communication impairment at the individual or family level in the normal families.

STACHOWIAK, J. Decision-making and conflict resolution in the family group. (In C. Larson, & F. Dancelzols.), *Perspectives on Communication*. Milwaukee:Speech Communication Center, University of Wisconsin, 1968, pp. 113–124.
The author discusses his previous research summarizing major findings on: (1) Family productivity—which is decreased in "maladaptive" families; (2) Influence of individual members —adaptive families showed distinct hierarchal ordering of members; (3) Conflict, in which maladaptive families showed more agression and hostility than adaptive, and (4) Communication, which was disturbed in maladaptive families. Implications for future research are discused.

STEINGLASS, P. The home observation assessment method (HOAM): Real-time naturalistic observation of families in their homes. *Family Process*, 1979, *18*, 337–354.
This paper describes a new method developed to obtain objective coding of family interaction over extended time periods in a home setting. This method has been applied to study 31 families for a total of over 250 sesions. Initial analysis of data indicates that coder reliability is high and the HOAM can measure dimensions of family behavior independent of home architecture. Preliminary findings indicate that although families differ significantly along the interacional dimensions, all families spent remarkably little time in decision making behavior suggesting that home behavior is mostly of a "maintenance type."

STEINGLASS, P., DAVIS, D. I., & BERENSON, D. Observations of conjointly hospitalized "Alcoholic couples" during sobriety and intoxication: Implications for theory and therapy. *Family Process*, 1977, *16*, 1–16.
A clinical description of a group of 10 couples of which one or both were alcoholic and were hospitalized at the same time. The inpatient experience was part of an intensive, 6-week, multiple couples, group therapy program. During hospitalization couples were encouraged to reproduce as closely as possible their usual drinking patterns and interactional behavior. Observations of interactional behavior during intoxication and sobriety led to the following conclusions: (1) intramarital interactional behavior associate dwith intoxication is even more highly patterned than behavior during sobriety; (2) interactional behavior becomes simplified to a few repetitive units, with the appearance of extreme ridigity; (3) alcohol operates as a problem-solver in system maintenance.

STRAKER, G., & JACOBSON, R. A study of the relationship between family interaction and individual symptomatology over time. *Family Process*, 1979, *18*, 443–450.
This study demonstrates that there is a positive correlation between family interaction and individual symptom-atology, and that changes in interaction have more influence on change in symptoms than vice-versa. Five families were taped in weekly sessions over 20 weeks, and five interactional dimensions were utilized. Each family had a mother-father-child triad with an encopretic child. The interaction dimension scores were abstracted weekly from these sessions by content analyses relying on various scales and compared to the frequency of encopresis. Results indicated that: 1) thwarted assertion and encopresis were significantly related; 2) the relationship between thwarted assertion and encopresis occurring in the week after the measurement of thwarted assertion was more significantly than in the week preceding the measurement.

STRODTBECK, F. The family as a three-person group. *American Sociological Review*, 1954, 23–29.
A research study attempting to replicate the findings of Mills in relation to three-person groups. The sample was 48 cases including father, mother, and adolescent son. They were asked to fill out alternatives to 47 items. The study was done in the family homes and tape recorded. Decision-making power was associated with high participation and when the two most active members who "solidarity" in their relation to one another, the stability of their rank participation is high. When the two most active members were in conflict, stability was as low for these families as for the other families.

STRODTBECK, F. Husband-wife interaction over revealed differences. *American Sociological Review*, 1951, *23*, 468–473.
A field study of ten Navajo, ten Texan, and ten Mormon couples, Balance of power can be shown using the revealed differeces. The technique depends both on power elements in a larger cultural organization and amount of participation in the small group situation.

STRODTBECK, F. The interaction of a henpecked husband with his wife. *Marriage and the Family Living*, 1952, *14*, 305–308.
A clinical case report on the psychodynamics of being "henpecked." Method was the revealed differences test. Compared to other couples, although the wife was more dominant, it was "not so painful in practice as the community gossip would lead one to believe." Interaction sequence is a more accurate way of assessing family dynamics than community observation.

TAYLOR, W. R. Research on family interaction, I: Static and dynamic models. *Family Process*, 1970, *9*, 221–232.
A comparison of static and dynamic models of family structure illustrated with a clinical example. The emphasis is upon the Markov process where a state is succeeded by other possible states.

TERRILL, H. M., & TERRILL, R. E. A method for studying family communication. *Family Process*, 1965, *4*, 259–290.
A description of the application of the Leary interpersonal system to family interaction. Rather than use a checklist, the system is applied to the actual interchange between family members in a standard interview.

THOMAS, E.J., WALTER, C. L., & O'FLAHERTY, K. A verbal problem checklist for use in assessing family verbal behavior. *Behavior Therapy*, 1974, *5*, 235–246.
An attempt was made to assess family verbal behavior by narrowing a large number of potential verbal responses to a small number, using the Verbal Problem Checklist (VPC) of 49 inductively derived categories of potentially problematic areas of verbal responding. Sample was 9 couples treated by marital therapies, with two raters making independent ratings of VPC categories for each husband and wife and four different discussion periods, each lasting approximately 20 minutes. Results indicated that the VPC narrowed the number of possible problem areas from a maximum of 49 to an average of 4 for husbands and 3 for wives. The VPC appears to be a useful assessment measure for family verbal behavior.

TITCHENER, J. L., D'ZMURA, T., GOLDEN, M., & EMERSON, R. Family transaction and deprivation of individuality. *Family Process*, 1963, *2*, 95–120.
A report of an experimental method in research on family interaction. Subjects were families of patients who applied because of neurotic symptoms. Task was for the family to "reconcile their differences in opinion previously revealed in a questionnaire administered to each family member." The observers used tapes, films and notes of direct observation to record the family transactions. The authors believe that a "young person elaborates an identity and develops his sense of it from the communicative interplay o the family." A case is presented in detail to illustrate.

TITCHENER, L., & GOLDEN, M. Predictions of therapeutic themes from observation of family interaction evoked by the revealed differences technique. *Journal of Nervous and Mental Disease*, 1963, *136*, 464–474.
A standard interview procedure with the family discussion observed and classification of formal content variables attempted. The results are said to be informative for prediction of the course of therapy.

TITCHENER, J., VANDER HEIDE, C., & WOODS, E. Profiles of family interaction systems. *Journal of Nervous and Mental Disease*, 1966, *143*, 473–480.
This is a report of a study designed to measure family interaction systems. Data were collected using Riskin's interaction scales, which were then modified. Advantages of this technique are discussed. Methods of sampling and data analysis are described, and several profiles of family interaction are exemplified. A discussion of variables in family interaction systems is made. Flow of information and quality of the flow are key variables in measuring how families function.

WADESON, H., & FITZGERALD, R. Marital relationship in manic-depressive illness. *Journal of Nervous and Mental Disease*, 1971, *153*, 180–196.
This is a study of nine patients with manic-depressive illness, and their spouses, using standardized conjoint art evaluation sessions in order to assess interpersonal dynamics. Blind raters were able to match pictures of patients and their spouses with 100 per cent accuracy but were unable to distinguish pictures made by the patients from those made by the spouses. The consistent dynamics that emerged was strong dependency needs in both patient *and spouse*, and the wish for the other to be strong.

WATZLAWICK, P. A structured family interview. *Family Process*, 1966, *5*, 256–271.
A report on the use of a standard interview developed in the Bateson project and applied at the mental research

institute on samples of families. The family is placed in a room and asked a series of standard questions, or given tasks to do together. It is said to be a simple and effective teaching and training aid and helpful to the therapist who is going to deal with the family. The procedure is given with examples.

WAXLER, N. E., & MISHLER, E. G. Scoring and reliability problems in interaction process analysis: A methodological note. *Sociometry*, 1966, *29*, 28–40.
A discussion of rater reliability when using Bales' interaction process analysis. Comparisons of tape recordings, typescripts, and combinations of both are given and comparisons are made of different ways of summarizing agreements between coders.

WELLS, C. F., RABINER, E. L. The conjoint family diagnostic interview and the family index of tension. *Family Process*, 1973, *12*, 127–144.
This paper describes a standardized assessment procedure for obtaining and recording comparable information across patient–family situations. A rating instrument, the Family Index of Tension, containing 15 dimensions, is utilized during a conjoint family diagnostic interview. Twenty-two measures of raw scores on the 15 FIT scales can be utilized for their correlations in follow-up studies. An attempt is made top select highly reliable factors having a manifest clinical relevance to patient outcome and for prediction of aftercare dropout and effectiveness.

WESTLEY, W., & EPSTEIN, N. Patterns of intra-familial communication. *Psychiatric research report No. 11.* Washington, D.C.: American Psychiatric Assocation, 1959.
A research report attempting to describe intrafamily communication patterns. Nine healthy families with an adolescent were studied using clinical interview, the Rorschach, and the TAT. Nine categories of family function are described and patterns of overt communication versus other types of communication are descibed.

WILD, C. Disturbed styles of thinking. *Archives of General Psychiatry*, 1966, *13*, 464–470.
Examiner's reactions to giving the object sorting test to parents of schizophrenics are described. Findings here are taken from the Wynne and Singer papers on "Thought Disorder and Family Relations of Schizophrenics." Examiners felt "frustrated and hopeless" in dealing with schizophrenic parents' inability to maintain a consistent task, inability to maintain role of subject being tested, and general negativism. Theoretical, tentative implications of the findings are discussed.

WILD, C. M., & SHAPIRO, L. N. Mechanisms of change from individual to family performance in male schizophrenics and their parents. *Journal of Nervous and Mental Disease*, 1977, *165*, 41–56.
This is a research study to provide data on the question of whether the disturbed behavior of parents with a schizophrenic child preexists or is a response to an identified patient's pathology. Method was to administer a conceptual task called the Twenty Questions Task individually to each family member and to the family as a unit with a sample of 36 schizophrenic families, 13 nonschizophrenic controls, and 38 normal controls, Results "indicated that far more schizophrenic sons than control sons were much more efficient individually than with their families." A number of schizophrenic sons performed competently as individuals, but the subsequent performance of parents and sons together on the same task was generally *inferior* to that of the son alone. Results suggest that the parental behavior plays a part in the etiology of schizophrenia.

WILD, C., SINGER, M., ROSMAN, G., RICCI, J., & LIDZ, T. Measuring disordered styles of thinking. *Archives of General Psychiatry*, 1966, *13*, 471–476.
Forty-four parents whose child was a schizophrenic in-patient were matched for age and education with 46 control parents (community volunteers) on the object sorting test. A scoring manual is described. Patient-parents scores differed significantly from controls. The object scoring test seems to discriminate between parents of schizophrenic patients and controls who do not have children with psychiatric pathology.

WILLI, J. Joint Rorschach testing of partner relationship. *Family Process*, 1969, *8*, 64–78.
A test of marital partners by the conjoint Rorschach procedure. A sample of 80 pairs was examined with each person administered the Rorschach individually and the again administered it conjointly with the partner. The goal was to measure the relative strength of the partners and how the personality of the subject changes in the discussion with the other.

WING, J. Ratings of behavior of patient and relative. *Journal of Psychosomatic Research*, 1964, *8*, 223–228.
A report of a test of the hypothesis that (1) high emotional involvement of patient and relative should lead to deterioration of the patient, and (2) that the amount of face-to-face contact between patient and relative would be related to outcome. Patients were evaluated by means of two raters' description and a checklist. Relatives were evaluated by means of scheduled ratings. Patients were hospitalized schizophrenics. Results indicated that if there was a high index of emotional involvement of relative with patient there was a high percentage of deterioration. In the case of patients who were moderately or severly ill at time of discharge, and who were living with relatives rated as showing a high degree of emotional involvement. relatively few hours of contact were associated with relatively better outcome.

WINTER, W. D., & FERREIRA, A. J. Interaction process analysis of family decision-making. *Family Process*, 1967, *6*, 155–172.
A sample of 90 triads of father, mother, and child were tested to contrast normals with abnormals. The families were exposed to a set of three TAT cards and asked to make up a story they all agreed upon which linked the three cards together. The protocols were scored with the Bales IPA system. It is concluded that "the Bales IPA system, in its present form, is not suited for work with families."

WINTER, W., & FERREIRA, A. Talking time as an index of intrafamilial similarity in normal and abnormal families. *Journal of Abnormal Psychology*, 1969, *74*, 574–575.
This study tested the hypothesis that normal families correlates more highly with each other than do abnormal families in terms of talking at length in extemporaneous speech. The sample consisted of 127 family triads—77 abnormals with identified patients being "emotionally disturbed maladjusted" (44), schizophrenic (16), and delinquents (17), and 50 normals. The families took the group Thematic Apperception Test, and the total number of seconds of speech of each of the family members was correlated with the other two family members. Results indicated that members of abnormal families resembled each other more than do members of normal families.

WINTER, W. D., FERREIRA, A. J., & OLSON, J. L. Hostility themes in the family TAT. *Journal of Projective Techniques*, 1966, *30*, 270–274.
Three TAT cards based on 3 cards were produced conjointly by 126 three-member families. These stories were scored for the relative amount of weighted hostility and the percentage of overt hostility themes, based on the Hafner-Kaplan system. There were 50 families with normal children, 44 with emotionally maladjusted children, 16 with schizophrenics, and 16 with delinquent children. Normal and schizophrenic groups produced sotries that were low both in weighted hostility and overt hostility, whereas stories by families with emotionally maladjusted children were high in both variables. The delinquent-child family scored high in weighted hostility and close to normals in overt hostility.

WINTER, W. D., FERREIRA, A. J., & OLSON, J. L. Story sequence analysis of family TATS. *Journal of Projective Techniques*, 1965, *29*, 392–397.
A group of 126 famlies, composed of parents and one child, were asked to produce TAT stories conjointly. The families were to make up a story based upon three TAT cards presented simultaneously to them. Three stories based on nine cards were composed by each family and scored by the Arnold system of story sequence analysis. In the sample there were 50 families with normal children. The abnormal group consisted of 44 emotionally maladjusted, 16 delinquent, and 16 schizophrenic children. The procedure successfully differentiated normal from abnormal families but the three abnormal group did not differ from each other. The stories of abnormal families are said to be characterized by negative attitudes toward achievement, morality, responsibility, human relationships, and reaction to adversity.

WYNNE, L. C. Consensus Rorschachs and related procedures for studying interpersonal patterns. *Journal of Projective Techniques and Persepctive Assessment*, 1968, *32*, 352–356.
This is a review of family research using the consensus Rorschach (a relatively standardized situation in which behavior of two or more persons interacting with one another can be observed, recorded, and studied using Rorschach cards). The entire family works on each card. The Family Rorschach and Spouse Rorschach have also been used. Advantages include simplicity and clinical freedom, but there is the hazard of a lack of standardization in administration and evaluation. In addition, the problem of degree of participation by the tester is still unsolved.

WYNNE, L. C. The study of intrafamilial alignments and splits in exploratory family therapy. In N. W. Ackerman, F. L. Beatman, & S. Sherman (Eds.), *Exploring the Base for family therapy*. New York: Family Service Association of America, 1961.
A discussion of families studied during family therapy with the emphasis upon alignments and splits as structural points of reference. Includes experiences with the family therapy of 30 families at NIMH with case examples and verbatim transcripts.

ZIERER, E., STERNBERG, D., FINN, R., & FARMER, M. Family creative analysis. I: Its role in treatment. *Bulletin of Art Therapy*, 1966, *5*, 47–65.
A report on the use of creative analysis (which is a technique by which paintings are used to understand the functioning of the ego) and its application to family treatment. The family agrees on a project to be done and then the sketch is made by one or many members of the family. It is the divided into as many sections as there are participants. From an understanding of the painting, the therapist then interprets the family and their conflicts. Observations are shared with the treatment team of the in-patient unit in which the identified patients are staying, and also with the members of the family. Short and long range goals of family treatment are formulated and worked out in at least 15 projects.

ZUCKERMAN, E., & JACOB, T. Task effects in family interaction. *Family Process*, 1979, *18*, 47–53.
This is an experimental study of the effects of different tasks on patterns of family activity. Conflict and influence were

assessed by means of multivariate procedures on a sample of 30 family triads. Findings indicate marked consistency in family interaction across the three experimental tasks: Thematic Apperception Test, Family Problem Question-naire, and Unrevealed Difference Technique. These findings of constancy in the family's internal organization are correlated with the process of homeostasis as described in general systems theory.

ZUK, G. H. A further study of laughter in family therapy. *Family Process*, 1964, *3*, 77–89.
A discussion of the function of laughter in the family illustrated excerpts from family therapy sessions. It is proposed that laughter is an important means of qualifying meaning for the purpose of disguise.

ZUK, G. On the pathology of silencing strategies. *Family Process*, 1965, *4*, 32–49.
A description and categorization of the ways people impose or enforce silence on one another. "There is a causal relation between silencing strategies and pathological silence and babbling which may themselves be used as powerful silencing strategies."

ZUK, G. On silence and babbling in family psychotherapy with schizophrenics. *Confinia Psychiatrica*, 1965, *8*, 49–56.
From the author's clinical work, two cases are presented in support of the idea that both silence and babbling can be understood as attempts to interrupt communication and silence others' interactions. They are often seen in schizophrenia, but patients learn these strategies from their parents. Techniques for dealing with this in treatment are discussed.

ZUK, G. On the theory and pathology of laughter in psychotherapy. *Psychotherapy*, 1966, *3*, 97–101.
See reference in Section 1.1.

ZUK, G. H., BOSZORMENYI-NAGY, I., & HEIMAN, E. Some dyanmics of laughter during family therapy. *Family Process*, 1963, *2*, 302–314.
An examination of the frequency of laughter in family therapy sessions with parents and a schizophrenic girl. Frequency of laughter was totalled for different intervals during the sessions. A correlation is suggested between tension or anxiety and laughter and it was found that the parents laughed most in the first interval of a session. Significantly more laughter of the daughter occurred in the third of four intervals, thus showing a reversal of patterns of laughter between parents and daughter over thirteen sessions.

3.4   FAMILY DATA FROM EXPERIMENTATION

ANANDAM, K., & HIGHBERGER, R. Child compliance and congruity between verbal and nonverbal maternal communication—A methodological note. *Family Process*, 1972, *11*, 219–226.
This paper describes a method to study congruity between verbal and non-verbal maternal communication with a group of 6 sons during 2, 30-minute sessions. These videotaped sessions were rated independently by three unbaised observers based on information from games played by mothers and sons. Data were categorized along verbal and nonverbal parameters into encouraging and restricting, positive and negative categories. Three classifications were utilized: (1) positive congruity; (2) negative congruity; and (3) incongruity. Mothers became less positively congruent when conditions for mother-son interactions were limited.

EPSTEIN, N. B., & SANTA-BARBARA, J. Conflict behavior in clinical couples: Interpersonal perceptions and stable outcomes. *Family Process*, 1975, *14*, 51–66.
This study examined the relation between a couple's perception of one another while engaged in a conflict situation and their managment of the conflict itself (N=180). The prisoner's dilemma (P.D.) and chicken (CK) were the standard conflict situations. Each couple's interactions were subjected to vector analysis and several differences were found. A cooperative couple perceived each other as cooperative and themselves expressed more appeasing intentions than any other group. Couples who waivered between cooperating and competing failed to attain any stable solution to the conflict.

FERREIRA, A. M. Decision-making in normal and pathologic families. *Archives of General Psychiatry*, 1963, *8*, 68–73.
An experiment to find differences between 25 normal and 25 abnormal families using a decision making test. The family members first make a choice of items on a questionnaire when alone and then are brought together and asked to reach agreement on the same items. Their choices separately and together are compared and the agreements are categorized as unanimous, majority, dictatorial, and chaotic. The two types of families are found to differ

FERREIRA, A. J. Interpersonal perceptivity among family members. *American Journal of Orthopsychiatry*, 1964, *34*, 64–71.
A report of a study investigating interpersonal perceptivity among members of families in terms of the individual's

ability to guess the rejecting behavior of the other two family members. The sample consisted of "25 normal and 30 pathologic families." The families were asked to color a number of flags on pieces of cardboard and asked to "throw away, i.e., to reject, the productions of the other family members: which they didn't like for any reason. They were also asked to guess how many of their own flags would be thrown away by other family members. Interpersonal perceptivity is greater in children than in adults.

FERREIRA, A. J. Rejection and expectancy of rejection in families. *Family Process*, 1963, *2*, 235–244.
A report of a study to investigate overt rejection and expectancy of rejection in normal and abnormal families. The sample was "25 normal and 30 pathologic families." The families were asked to color a number of flags on pieces of cardboard and asked to "throw away, i.e., to reject the productions of the other family members" which they didn't like for any reason. They were also asked to guess how many of their own flags would be thrown away by other family members. Differences were found between the two groups and there was a marked discrepancy between rejecting and expecting to be rejected in pathological families.

FERREIRA, A. J., & WINTER, W. D. Decision-making in normal and abnormal two-child families. *Family Process*, 1968, *7*, 17–36.
A report of a study of 85 families, 36 noraml and 49 abnormal (composed of parents and two children), were tested in a procedure similar to that previously used in a test of family triads. Differences were found between the two gorups on measures of "spontaneous agreement," "decision time," and "choice fulfillment."

FERREIRA, A. J., & WINTER, W. D. Family interaction and decision-making. *Archives of General Psychiatry*, 1965, *13*, 214–223.
A report of a study contrasting 50 normal families and 75 families with an abnormal child. The abnormal group included 15 schizophrenics, 16 delinquents, and 44 maladjusted children. The family members were asked to fill out a neutral questionnaire separately, and then they were brought together and asked to fill out the same questionnaire while reaching agreement on the items as a group. Generally this report is concerned with the extend of aggrement when family members make their choices separately, how much time is necessary to reach group decisions, and the appropriateness of the family decisions in fulfilling the wishes of the individual family members. Eighteen hypotheses are described and the results reported in terms of the differences found between the groups.

FERREIRA, A., WINTER, W. D., & POINDEXTER, E. J. Some interactional variables in normal and abnormal families. *Family Process*, 1966, *5*, 60–75.
See Reference in Section 3.3

GOODRICH, D. W., & BOOMER, D. S. Experimental assessment of modes of conflict resolution. *Family Process*, 1963, *2*, 15–24.
A report of an experiemental technique for studying the coping behavior of husband and wife when they attempt to resolve a martial conflict. Fifty paid volunteer couples between 18 and 27 years of age were asked to match colors—some unmatchable—to see how the couple coped with puzzling or ambiguous situations. A general discussion of results if given, with the authors relating the "ability to achieve perspective on the situation and maintenance of self-esteem" to adequacy of coping.

GORDON, B. N., & KOGAN, K. L. A mother-instruction program: Analysis of intervention procedures. *Family Process*, 1975, *14*, 205–221.
Instructions were given to mothers (N=30) via a "bug-in-the-ear" device while they were actively engaged in interaction with their children. Two variables were related to behavioral change: (1) the type of statements made to mothers; and (2) the kinds of behaviors which mothers were encouraged to exhibit. Results showed that the amount of interpersonal behavior change was not related to intervention statements but tended to be related to the number of problem behaviors originally indicated by mothers. There is some evidence that social class may affect the success of different techniques.

HALEY, J. Cross-cultural experimentation: An initial attempt. *Human Organism*, 1967, *3*, 110–117.
A comparison of Caucasian middle-class American families and Japanese-born families in an experimental setting where the measure is speech sequences. Differences are found.

HALEY, J. Experiment with abnormal families. *Archives of General Psychiatry*, 1967, *17*, 53–63.
A comparison of abnormal and normal families in an experimental setting where family members speak to each other from different rooms. Measures are who chooses to speak with whom and patterns of speech sequence.

HALEY, J. Family experiments: A new type of experimentation. *Family Process*, 1962, *1*, 265–293.
A report on a research project in which parents and schizophrenic children were contrasted with parents and normal children in an experimental game to test hypotheses about coalition patterns in normal and abnormal families. Differences were found between the 30 families in each group. There is a general discussion of the uniqueness of experimenting with families in theoretical, methodological, and sampling problems.

HALEY, J. Research on family patterns: An instrument measurement. *Family Process*, 1964, *3*, 41–65.
See Reference in Section 3.3

HALEY, J. Speech sequences of normal and abnormal families with two children present. *Family Process*, 1967, *1*, 81–97.
A comparison of families with an abnormal child and families with normal children in an experimental setting with parents and two children present. The measure is speech sequences.

HALEY, J. Testing parental instructions to schizophrenic and normal children: A pilot study. *Journal of Abnormal Psychology*, 1968, *73*, 559–566.
See Reference in Section 3.3

HARPER, J. M., SCORESBY, A. L., & BOYCE, W. D. The logical levels of complementary, symmetrical, and parallel interaction classes in family dyads. *Family Process*, 1977, *16*, 199–209.
This is a study of father–mother, father–child, and mother–child dyads of 48 families who were categorized into complementary, symmetrical, and parallel classes using the Relationship Styles Inventory. Each of the dyads in these 3 categories was then randomly assigned to 1 of 2 experimental conditions in which they jointly resolved a moral dilemma. In one condition, the dyads were asked to follow compelmentary rules, while in the second condition they were instructed to follow symmetrical rules. Results indicated that parallel dyads adjusted to both the complementary and symmetrical conditions, whereas symmetrical and complementary dyads did not successfully accommodate rules outside of their own class. Implications for therapy are discussed.

JACOB, T., & DAVIS, J. Family interaction as a function of experimental task. *Family Process*, 1973, *12*, 415–427.
This study evaluated family patterns of talking and interrupting, as elicited from discussions of a Plan Something Together Task, a set of TAT cards, and an Unrevealed Difference Questionnaire. With few exceptions data analyses indicated that such family patterns in 10 intact family triads were not altered significantly as a function of experimental tasks and, therefore, suggested considerable interactional stability across differing contexts.

LEVIN, G. Communicator–communicant approach to family interaction research. *Family Process*, 1966, *5*, 105–116.
A family experiment in which the experimenter asks the subject to make a tape recording which might be played subsequently to some specific other person in his family. The recordng includes specific instructions about a simple task. Individuals from families containing a schizophrenic (a sample of 33) were contrasted with normal individuals. The recordings were not actually played to family members, but the instructions were analyzed and classified with differences found between the two groups.

MOSHER, L., & KWIATKOWSKA, H. Family art evaluation: Use in families with schizophrenic twins. *Journal of Nervous and Mental Disease*, 1971, *153*, 165–179.
See reference in Section 1.1.

MOSHER, L., POLLIN, W., & STABENAU, J. Families with identical twins discordant for schizophrenia: Some relationships between identification, thinking styles, psychopathology and dominance-submissiveness. *British Journal of Psychiatry*, 1971, *118*, 22–28.
This is another in a series of studies attempting to assess the role of family variables in the development of schizophrenia. The variables were roles of identification, thinking styles, psychopathology, and dominance/submissiveness. The sample was eleven families with identical twins discordant for schizophrenia. They were tested on a variety of clinical and objective test variables, including the MMPI Ego Strength and MMPI Ms Scale. Results indicated the schizophrenic twin is more often identified with the less healthy parent, usually the mother, on the basis of clinical rather than objective tests. The schizophrenic patients were more "global" in their cognitive style and identified with the more "global" member of the parental pair. Schizophrenic members were most often submissive. The mothers were rated as less healthy but, paradoically, tended to be dominant.

RAKOFF, V., & ROSE, A. Patterns of response to out-of-focus slides of families with an emotionally disturbed member. *Family Process*, 1972, *11*, 339–346.
"Mutual facial recognition" was studies in 30 families; 15 with and 15 without a disturbed member (parent or child). Each family consisted of parents and two children. Parents completed a Quay-Peterson, Fels, and MacFarlane checklist for each child before each family member was shown slides of family and nonfamily members. Slides, initially out-of-focus, were brought into focus and the person was to signal the experimenter as they identified each slide either as a family member or a stranger. Families with a markedly disturbed child had longer recognition times, particularly for the mother. Also, there is a suggestion that the families with a disturbed parent have patterns of recognition entirely different from those of other families in the study.

RAVICH, R. Game-testing in conjoint marital psychotherapy. *American Journal of Psychotherapy*. 1969, *23*, 217–229.
See Reference in Section 1.3

RAVICH, R. A. The Ravich interpersonal game/test: Comments on Liebowitz and Black's paper. *Family Process*, 1975, *14*, 263–267.
This paper is a commentary by the test's author on a paper by Liebowitz and Black published in a previous volume of the same Journal. The author contends that the relative success or failure of male–female cotherapists can be predicted according to their interaction behavior in the Game/Test. A reply by Liebowitz is included in this article.

RAVICH, R., DEUTSCH, M., & BROWN, B. An experimental study of marital discord and decision making. In I. M. Cohen (Ed.), *Psychaitric research report No. 20*. Washington, D.C.: American Psychiatric Association, 1966.
A report on a study of 38 couples tested with a game in which the partners imagine that they are operating a truck and can effect each other's truck when they meet a one-lane road. Behavior is described in terms of sharing, dominating and submitting, being inconsistent, being competitive, and being dysjunctive.

REISS, D. Individual thinking and family interaction: Introduction to an experimental study of problem-solving in families of normals, character disorders, and schizophrenics. *Archives of General Psychiatry*, 1967, *16*, 80–93.
A report of an experimental study of the relationship between individual thinking and family interaction. Experimental procedures and methods of analysis are discussed. Subjects were families of five normals, five character disorders, and six schizophrenics. The test used was a puzzle that required active use of cognitive and conceptual capacities. The method of analysis was derived from the work of Riley which developed a systematic approach of computing scores from the raw data and rules concerning inferences.

REISS, D. Individual thinking and family interaction. II: A study of pattern recognition and hypothesis testing in families of normals, character disorders, and schizophrenics. *Journal of Psychiatric Research*, 1967, *5*, 193–211.
The second in a series of studies of the relationship of family process and individual thinking. Results indicate that following a period of family interaction, members of normal families showed improvement in pattern recognition; members of families of schizophrenics showed deterioration or no change; members of character disorder families showed results in between the other two.

REISS, D., & SALZMAN, C. Resilience of family process. *Archives of General Psychiatry*, 1973, *28*, 425–433.
To test the effects on family interaction of one of its members receiving psychotropic medication, secobarbital was administered to the offspring of family threesomes. Twenty-four families were seen, one-half given 175 mg of secobarbital and the other half receiving a placebo, on a double-blind basis. Outcome was measured by a card-sorting experimental procedure and computer analysis of automatically transcribed voice records. Results indicated that the drug produced no objective change in the problem-solving of the offspring or of the family, but produced marked changes in the family speech patterns.

RYDER, R. G. Husband-wife dyads vs. married strangers. *Family Process*, 1968, *7*, 233–238.
A comparison of the behavior of spouses with each other and with strangers by use of the color matching test which induces a conflict situation. Sixty-four married dyada and 56 unmarried dyads were contrasted. Few differences were found, but persons "treat strangers more gently, and generally more nicely than they do their spouses."

RYDER, R. G. Two replications of color matching factors *Family Process*, 1966, *5*, 43–48.
A replication of the color matching test of Goodrich and Boomer. The test was applied to 64 married couples and 56 split couples (defined as a male and female pair not married). Comparisons with the original sample, and between the married and unmarried groups are made.

RYDER, R. G., & GOODRICH, D. W. Married couples responses to disagreement. *Family Process*, 1966, *5*, 30–42.
A report on the color matching test administered to 49 recently married couples. Husband and wife are exposed to colors and asked to match them when some of them do not match. Ways of handling the conflict are categorized and described.

RYKOFF, V., SIGAL, J., & SANDERS, S. Patterns of report on the hearing of parental voices by emotionally disturbed children. *Journal of Psychiatric Research*, 1970, *8*, 43–50.
This is a first report of a series of experiments designed to examine factors that influence the ease or difficulty with which family members appear to hear one another. Thirty-two children with nonpsychotic mental illness were compared with a group of their siblings, plus two other control groups. The parents read statements carrying different affects that were then played on separate tracts on the same recording tape simultaneously into both ears of the children. The children were asked to report on what they heard. They also completed a Parent-Child Relationship Questionnaire and a Parental Dominance Questionnaire. Results indicated disturbed children have particularly patterns of perceiving verbal communication within the famliy, and these patterns are at least partially determined by a child's perception of the parent as rewarding or punishing.

RYLE, A., & LIPSHITZ, A. Recording change in marital therapy with the reconstruction grid. *British Journal of Medical Psychology*, 1975, *48*, 39–48.

This is a study of a method for measuring progress in family therapy. Prior to therapy, couples make a "grid" of 33 elements of their relationship, and then rate themselves on these elements serially before 11 of 16 sessions of conjoint therapy. Changes during the therapy which can be shown by the grid method are discussed. Results are said to show a considerable amount of change which correlated with clinical accounts.

RYLE, A., & LIPSHITZ, S. Repertory grid elucidation of a different conjoint therapy. *British Journal of Medical Psychology*, 1976, *49*, 281–285.

In an elaboration on the author's use of the "grid" method of measuring change in relationships, a couple rated their realtionship to each other as well as the therapists before each weekly session for one year. A second "background grid" rated the couples relationship to each other and their parents in the past. The ananlysis of the grids supported the clinical impression that this couple could not change in conjoint therapy.

SANTA-BARBARA, J., & EPSTEIN, N. B. Conflict behavior in clinical families: Preasymptotic interactions and stable outcomes. *Behavioral Science*, 1974, *19*, 100–110.

This research study explores interaction patterns in couples in an attempt to determine the types of stable outcomes occurring in conflict patterns between spouses. Sample was 180 married couples in family therapy. Conflict situations used were "extended prisoner dilemma" and "chicken games." Results indicated that there were predictable differences in outcomes of high cooperation, high conflict, and a dominant-submissive interaction. A later study will report on these interaction patterns and treatment outcome.

SEEMAN, L., WEITZ, L. J., & ABRAMOWITZ, S. I. Do family therapists' family ideologies affect their impressions of families. *Journal of Community Psychology*, 1976, *4*, 149–151.

The notion is tested that the values of family therapists influence their impressions of the families they treat. Method was to obtian data from 15 male and 35 female professionals and graduate students attending a one-day workshop in family therapy who were classified as either traditional or nontraditional in their beliefs about the family . They were give a transcript of a hypothetical family in which the parents' verbalizations were suggestive of either traditional or nontraditional values and asked to rate the families. Results indicate there was little diagnostic value bias thereby failing to confirm the notion that the therapists' values significantly influence their impressions of the family.

SHAPIRO, R. J., FISHER, L., GAYTON, W. F. Perception of cognitive ability in families of adolescents. *Family Process*, 1974, *13*, 239–52.

In order to explore the validity of the interpersonal/relational theory this experiment tested whether psychopathology lessens person's ability for perceiving people as they really are. Twenty families of hospitalized adolescents were compared with a control group of 20 normal families on the accuracy with which each family member could predict each other's performance on I.Q. tests. Accuracy of predition was measured by comparing actual scores and the scores other family members predicted. The results indicate that psychopathology is not the sole, or even the most crucial indicator determining how a person perceives another. Implication for future research is discussed as well as some issued involving family therapy evaluations.

SHARAN, & SHLOMO. Family interactions with schizophrenics and their siblings. *Journal of Abnormal Psychology*,1966, *71*, 345–353.

An experimental study contrasting the behavior of parents of schizophrenics with the patient and with a sibling. Twenty-four families were asked to solve collectively the questions from the comprehension and similarities subtests of the Wechsler-Bellevue intelligence scale. The conversations were compared for problem-solving efficiency, mutual support patterns, and parent-child sex role alignments. Parents and patient worked as efficiently as parents and siblings, parents supported both children equally, and fathers and mothers were equally dominant. The patients were more supportive of their parents than were the siblings, and parental discord was more prominent when the patient was present than when the sibling was present.

SHERMAN, H., & FARINA, A. Social adequacy of parents and children. *Journal of Abnormal Psychology*, 1974, *83*, 327–330.

This is an experimental study testing the general hypothesis that the family is specified in pathology in the offspring and the specific notion that inadequate skills in parents can be transmitted to their children. Method was to look at an index of "social adequacy" using a sample of male college students and their mothers. The subjects were rated as high- or low-socially adequate. Their mothers were then interviewed and also rated as to social adequacy, contingency and relevance of conversation, appropriateness of behavior and spontaneity. Results indicated that there was significant correlation between social adequacy in 17 of 23 families on social adequacy, contingency, and relevance. Although this is a correlational, not causal study, results suggested that "parents do seem to play a role in maladjustment of offspring."

SOLVBERG, H. A., & BLAKAR, R. M. Communication efficiency in couples with and without a schizophrenic offspring. *Family Process*, 1975, *14*, 515–534.

This is a description of an experimental method for studying language and communication in schizophrenics. Two subjects are given what they believe are identical maps. Comparison of five parent dyads of normals and five parent dyads of schizophrenics demonstrated that four of five of the latter group were unable to solve the problem. The experimental situation appears to demand flexibility in modifying communication patterns to solve the problem.

WAXLER, N. E. Parent–child effects on cognitive performance: An approach to the etiological and responsive theories of schizophrenia. *Family Process*, 1974, *13*, 1–22.
This experiment was designed to ask whether parents affect children (cause health or illness) or do children affect parents more in schizophrenic and normal families. Using the following four groupsings of: (1) parents of a schizophrenic child and another schizophrenic child; (2) parents of a schizophrenic child with a normal child; (3) parents of a normal child with a schizophrenic child; and (4) parents of a normal child with another normal child, these experiments constructed 45 "artificial" families. Each parent pair and each child participated twice, once each with schizphrenia type and normal type. They performed a game task of 20 questions. The major findings were that: (1) schizophrenic children do better with normal parents, improve more in completing the task; (2) schizophrenic children have a limited effect on normal parents, that they improve little, and (3) normal parents and normal children do well togther. General conclusions included reinforcement of the tenet that the schizophrenic child does not carry with him a fixed and irreparable cognitive deficit and that the social context around him does have an effect.

WIJESINGHE, O. B. A., & WOOD, R. R. A repertory grid study of interpersonal perception within a married couples psychotherapy group. *British Jouranl of Medical Psychology*, 1976, *49*, 287–293.
This is a pilot study of interpersonal perception by members of a multi-couples group. All members of a four couple group constructed a "repertory grid" of eight elements. Then each member ranked the spouse's grid as he/she thought the other had done. The therapist also ranked each member's grid as he thought the other had done. Principle component analysis of the grids showed that the constructs relating to (1) discussing problems, (2) showing feelings, and (3) dominance were important to the inter-group perception. It also showed that the recognition of the spouse's ability to show feelings was the main area of misperception between couples.

3.5   RESEARCH THEORY AND REVIEW

BEHRENS, M. L., BATESON, G., LEICHTER, H. J., LENNARD, H. L., & COTTRELL, L. S., JR. The challenge of research in family diagnosis and therapy—Sumary, Parts I–IV. In N. W. Ackerman, F. L. Beatman, & S. Sherman (Eds.), *Exploring the base for family therapy*. New York: Family Service Association of America, 1961.
Discussions about research by Bateson, Lennard, Cottrell and Leichter following an introductory summary by Behrens.

BELL, N. W. Terms of a comprehensive theory of family pychopathology relationships. In G. H. Zuk, & I. Boszormenyi-Nagy (Eds.), *Family therapy and disturbed families*. Palo Alto: Science & Behavior Books, 1967.
A discussion of the current status of family ideas and the work that needs to be done. There is a lack of shared language, of coordination with other sciences, of adequate scientific method in the research, and lack of consensus on the components of the systems investigated.

BODIN, A. Conjoint family assessment: An evolving field. In P. McReynolds (ed.), *Advances in psychological assessment*. Science and Behavior Books: Palo Alto, 1968.
This is a resume of testing methods designed for use with families in the fields of both family therapy and family research. Approaches have bene individual, conjoint, and combined. Subjective, technilques include family tasks, family strengths, inventory and family art. Objective techniques include analysis of communication, games, and how conflict is resolved. Critique of these methods is presented.

COLAPINTO, J. The relative value of empirical evidence *Family Process*, 1979, *18*, 427–441.
This paper reviews premises and assumptions utilized by different therapists that empirical evidence is a good guideline for the merits of their respective approaches. It has been suggested that epistomological premises behind individual and systems-oriented models are incompatible, and support opposing sociocultural values.

CORNELISON, A. R. Casework interviewing as a research technique in a study of families of schizophrenic patients. *Mental Hygiene*, 1960, *44*, 551–559.
A discussion of casework interviewing in family study as experienced by a caseworker with the Lidz project. The families of sixteen cases were studied by individual interviews with family members. Group interviews have been recently initiated. Caseworker-family contact begins upon hospital admission if not sooner and family patterns are frequently illuminated by the various and varying attitudes displayed toward the caseworker. A general discussion is offered of the special usefulness of combined casework service and research, practical aspects of the method, and problems involved.

DAVIS, A. J., & STEWART, N. J. Barriers to sample access. *JPN Mental Health Service*, 1976, *14*, 7–10.
This report from a reserach team describes problems in obtaining a sample to do family research. Institutional barriers, attitudinal barriers, procedural barriers, and guidelines for penetrating the barriers are discussed. Sample acquisition can be very time-consuming and nonrewarding unless researchers design techniques to deal with these problems in their projects.

DRECHSLER, R. J., & SHAPIRO, M. I. Two methods of analysis of family diagnostic data. *Family Process*, 1963, *2*, 367–379.
A description of the conjoint use of clinical and statistical analysis of the same data. Thirteen families were interviewed and also given a standard family task (discussing a questionnaire) to perform alone. Samples of the tape recordings were extracted and frequency count made of how often one person spoke to another. Clinical impressions were compared and similarities found.

FONTANA, A. F. Familial etiology of schizophrenia: Is a scientific methodology possible? *Psychology Bulletin*, 1966, *66*, 214–227.
A review of methodology in family research on schizophrenia, emphasizing clinical observation, retrospective recall, and direct observation of family interaction. The former two approaches are siad to be unsuitable "for a scientific body of eitological facts": the latter approach should be used with caution. Findings of various studies are reviewed. The author concludes the greatest value so far is in the guidelines provided for longitudinal research, but sufficient knowledge is not yet available to warrant the great expenditure involved in longitudinal research at the present time.

FRAMO, J. L. Systematic research on family dynamics. In I. Boszormenyi-Nagy, & J. L. Framo (Eds.), *Intensive family therapy.* New York: Harper & Row, 1965.
See Reference in Section 3.6

GELLES, R. J. Methods for studying sensitive family topics. *American Journal of Orthopsychiatry*, 1978, *48*, 408–424.
This is a discussion aimed at identifying some of the special problems in family research, focusing on the families' complexity and high incidence of "sensitive" areas. Problems with often-used methods of sampling, interviewing and handling of data are discussed with 64 references included.

GOLDBERG, E. Difficulties encountered in assessing family attitudes. *Journal of Psychosomatic Research*, 1964, *8*, 229–234.
A discussion of studies made which attempted to assess family organization and functioning in relation to disease (such as chronic ulcers, schizophrenia, etc.). Problems of methodology include interrelatedness of variables, objective assessment, comparisons, and measurement in relation to the family.

GREENWALD, S. Let us not confound the schizophrenic's family. *Comprehensive Psychiatry*, 1971, *12*, 423–429.
A paper reviewing previous research on the relation of family psychopathology to schizophrenia in the identified patient. At best, previous research makes a questionable cause and effect relationship; at worst, it had not identified any differences from normal families.

GUTTMAN, H., SPECTOR, R. M., SIGAL, J. J., EPSTEIN, N. B., & RAKOFF, V. Coding of affective expression in family therapy. *American Journal of Psychotherapy*, 1972, *26*, 185–194.
A research paper that describes the development of a coding system for family therapy "process," and reviews other coding systems. The Dollard and Auld system was used here and an example given. Preliminary results indicated an overall intercoder reliability of .74, but some categories fell as low as .50.

HADLEY, T. R., & JACOB, T. Relationship among measures of family power. *Journal of Social Psychology*, 1973, *27*, 6–12.
This is a research study assessing the relationship among various measure of family power. Sample was 20 three-membered families evaluated in terms of talking time, seccessful interruptions, and unrevealed difference technique, and a coalition game. Results indicated a positive relation between total talking time and successful interruptions, no relation between the coalition game and the unrevealed difference technique, and no relation between the process and outcome measures.

HILL, R. Marriage and family research: A critical evaluation. *Eugenic Quarterly*, 1954, *1*, 58–63.
See Reference in Section 3.6

HILL, R. Methodological issues in family development research. *Family Process*, 1964, *3*, 186–206.
A review of famil study oriented toward a family development frame of reference and the special requirements of the longitudinal method of data collection. Concepts of the family frame of reference are said to be developmental, structure–function, learning theory, personality development, and household–economic. Difficulties in and altern-atives to the longitudinal study are discussed.

HILL, R., & HANSEN, D. Identification of conceptual frameworks utilized in family study. *Marriages and Family Living*, 1960, *22*, 299–326.
See Reference in Section 3.6

HODGSON, J. W., & LEWIS, R. A. Pilgrim's progress. III: A trend analysis of family theory and methodology. *Family Process*, 1979, *18*, 163–173.
See reference in Section 6.0.

KAUFFMAN, J. Validity of the family relations test: A review of research. *Journal of Projective Techniques and Perspective Assessment*, 1970, *34*, 186–189.
This paper reviews research on the Family Relations Test (a clinical projective technique for assessing family interaction), and offers a critique of the design of the studies. Evidence of the test's validity is equivocal. Since few studies have thus far been reported, additional research is needed, and future directions for this are suggested.

LEVINGER, G. Supplementary methods in family research. *Family Process*, 1963, *2*, 357–366.
A review of methods in family research with a comparison of subjective report and objective observation with a discussion of their strengths and weaknesses. A study is reported of 31 families who were studied with both observationand self report. The results showed gross correspondence between the two methods, and it is suggested that both procedures should be used since they supplement each other.

LICKORISH, J. R. A behavioral interactional model for assessing family relationships. *Family Process*, 1975, *14*, 535–558.
This paper is a description of a model for conceptualizing family interaction. It incorporates theories of "dyadic" interactions and the data is obtained by having members of a family give responses to cards from the Family Relations Indicator, a projective test. A "constituent analysis" is used to code the responses, which were then subjected to an "Ingrid 72" statistical analysis program. Two parents' responses are supplied to illustrate the method.

LIEBOWITZ, B., & BLACK, M. The structure of the Ravich interpersonal game/test. *Family Process*, 1974, *13*, 169–183.
This study was designed to evaluate the use of simulation games to study the dyadic interactional process. Present testing technology and research instruments historically are entrenched in the assumption of individual pathology even when evaluating family process, e.g., family Rorschach and TATs. Using 75 married couples seeking marital therapy, these experimenters used the Ravich Interpersonal Game Test (RIG/T) to evaluate dyadic decision-making. The goal of the study was to investigate how well the RIG/T is representative of the process aspects of marital decision-making, i.e., to access content validity. It was concluded that this game's maximizing solution is too easily discovered—so the test may not be discriminating enough.

MALOUF, J. L., & ALEXANDER, J. F. Family therapy research in applied community settings. *Community Mental Health Journal*, 1976, *12*, 61–71.
This paper is concerned with the theory and practice of doing research in a community mental health center. Outcome from the CMHC should be compared to outcome from existing facilities. Four general methodological issues are discussed: design adequacy, issues related to dependent measures, situational factors, and issues of generalization and duration of treatments. Several clinical studies of family therapy outcome are presented in support of these ideas.

NYE, F. I., & MAYER, A. E. Some recent trends in family research. *Social Forces*, 1963, *41*, 290–301.
The research literature on the family in four leading sociological journals from 1947–61 (N=456) was analyzed. Changes in methodological aspects and substantive content are documented. Problems remain regarding the failure to use research competence fully, inadequate communication among researchers, and lack of attention to methodological research *per se*. Special attention is given problems, and potentials in the utilization of theory, in control of extraneous variables, in the validity of data, in using third variables as contingent conditions, and in longitudinal design.

POST, F., & WARDLE, J. *Family neurosis and family psychosis: A review of the problem. Journal of Mental Science.* 1962, *108*, 147–158.
A review of some of the work that has been done in social psychiatry—the psychiatry of relationships. After discussing early studies investigating families of various types of orientation the authors review the studies of the current families of child and adult patients. They conclude that even those studies of family events and interactions occurring shortly before the patient became ill, and not years previously, are prematurely concerned with proving some basic theoretical construct. It is essential to discover the proportion and type of psychiatric cases in which there is a clear link between emotional characteristics in relatives and friends and the patient's breakdown. A bibliography of 57 references is included.

RABKIN, L. The patient's family: Research methods. *Family Process*, 1965, *4*, 105–132.
A review of family research with speical emphasis upon the family of the schizophrenic. Critical examination is done of

case history studies, interviewing studies, psychodiagnostic testing, questionnaire studies, and observational research. A bibliography of 99 references is included.

RISKIN, J., & Faunce, E.E. An evaluative review of family interaction research. *Family Process*, 1972, *11*, 365–455. See reference in Section 6.0.

RISKIN, J., & FAUNCE E. Family interaction scales. I. Theoretical framework and methods. *Archives of General Psychiatry*, 1970, *22*, 504–512.
The authors present a theoretical framework and method used to evaluate the Family Interaction Scales (FIS), developed for measuring whole family interaction. Sample was 44 families, obtained through a local high school and from local therapists, including both normal and abnormal families. The families were administered a standard semi-structured interview, and a five-minute segment was scored using the FIS. The family was subsequently interviewed at home, and socioeconomic demographic data were obtained. They were then divided into five groups including multi-problem families, families with two or three labeled problems, families with child-labeled problems only, families with from the school sample with no labels but who seemed to have significant family problems,and families with no labels and no problems, considered normal. Data were analyzed using non-parametric statistical tests.

RISKIN J., & FAUNCE, E. Family interaction scales. II: Data analysis and findings. *Archives of General Psychiatry*, 1970, *22*, 513–526.
Results of the study of normal and abnormal families using the FIS demonstrated that the FIS taps meaningful areas of family interaction and that several of the scale categories have statistical significance. It was concluded that the scale will discriminate among different types of families.

RISKIN, J., & FAUNCE, E. Family interaction scales. III: Discussion of methodology and substantive findings. *Archives of General Psychiatry*, 1970, *22*, 527–537.
In a discussion of the Family Interaction Scales, methodological aspects of the study are critically reviewed, and profiles of different groups of families are presented. The significance of the study and possible future directions are indicated.

RITTERMAN, M. K. Paradigmatic classification of family therapy theories. *Family Process*, 1977, *16*, 29–48.
This article offers a method for classifying theories of family therapy. Communications theory and structural theory are examined and compared in terms of their "mechanistic" and "organismic" respective roots. Claims are presented that all therapies may be classified following this model.

ROBINS, L. N. Problems in follow-up studies. *American Journal of Psychiatry*, 1977, *134*, 904–907.
This essay reviews recent regulations concerning consent procedures and protection of privacy as they apply to children and their families. Rigorous sample selection, nearly complete follow-up, and objective assessment of outcome are virtually impossible at this point. It is concluded that compliance with current "subjects' rights" regulations sometimes seems potentially more harmful to the subjects than the research itself.

SCHULTZ, S. J. A scheme for specifying interaction units. *Family Process*, 1975, *14*, 559–578.
The specification of units of family interaction research is reviewed and a new Interaction Unitizing Scheme for preparing typescripts using "speech" is demonstrated with 25 families. Coding can be done directly from these unitized transcripts or they can be used to define units when coding from audio or videotape. Reliability methods are outlined and data is presented indicating that the unitizing scheme has high inter-coder reliability.

SINGER, M. & WYNNE, L. Principles for scoring communication defects and deviances in parents of schizophrenics: Rorschach and TAT scoring manuals. *Psychiatry*, 1966, *29*, 260–289.
A continuation of previous studies in which the authors have predictively related parental behavior on psychological tests with psychiatric diagnosis of their offspring. Two scoring manuals for use with the Rorschach and with the TAT are presented in an effort to pinpoint certain selective features of parental behavior which can be quickly scored (previous studies used inferences which required a great deal of time in analyzing a battery of tests). A discussion of the tests and their clinical correlates in the family of schizophrenics is also provided.

SLIPP, S. & KRESSEL, K. Difficulties in family therapy evaluation. I: A comparison of insight versus problem-solving approaches. II: Design critique and recommendations. *Family Process*, 1978, *17*, 409–422.
See reference in Section 2.0.

TAYLOR, W. R. Research on family interaction. I: Static and dynamic models. *Family Process*, 1970, *9*, 221–232.
Static and dynamic models of family structure are measured by a content-free assessment of the sequence of states of interactions in family sessions. Certain parallels between behavioral variables and the more abstract clinical concepts

of family structure are drawn. By subsuming the latter structural concepts unde a framework of "balance theory" considerable reduction in complexity may be achieved without sacrificing clinical relevance.

TITCHENER, J., VANDER HEIDE, C., & WOODS, E. Profiles in family interaction systems. *Journal of Nervous and Mental Diseases*, 1966, *143*, 473–483.
A report of a study designed to measure family interaction systems. Data were collected using Riskin's interaction scales which were then modified. Advantages of this technique are discussed. Methods of sampling and data analysis are described and several profiles of family interaction are exemplified with discussion of variables in family interaction systems. Flow of information and quality of the flow are key variables to measure how families function.

TURK, J. L. Power as the achievement of ends: A problematic approach and small group research. *Family Process*, 1974, *13*, 39–52.
Using theoretical models, this paper discusses the methodology in research studies of exploring group/family functions by examining an individual's power within a group to achieve an end result or activity. It is concluded that an individual's end is impossible to determine because families/groups are characterized by functionally diffused and ongoing relations. Substitute procedures for examining power without examining its resultant end are methodologically incorrect. The author concludes that an alternative to describing families/groups in terms of power is to describe them in terms of interactional patterns. This would preclude the reduction of group level phenomena to an individual's desires and actions, as well as to the need to speculate on intrapsychic states.

WAXLER, N. E. & MISHLER, E. G. Sequential patterning in family interaction: A methodological note. *Family Process*, 1970, *9*, 211–220.
A discussion of different ways of analyzing participation rates in family conversations when the measure is who speaks after whom.

WEAKLAND, J. The double-bind theory by self-reflexive hindsight. *Family Process*, 1974, *13* 269–277.
Reflecting upon his theory of the "double-bind," the author calls for more exploration in the field of communication. To make this theory more specific, and thereby prove or disprove it is nonfunctional, we need to examine communication by its effects.

WILD, C. M., SHAPIRO, L. N. & ABELIN, T. Sampling issues in family studies of schizophrenia. *Archives of General Psychiatry*, 1974, *30*, 211–215.
This research study examines problems of sampling in family interaction studies of schizophrenia. From a larger sample of 549 schizophrenic patients, only 21 ultimately cooperated in the study. The factors that account for the shrinkage were analyzed. Cooperating patients were found to be from a higher socioeconomic status, earlier birth order, younger when interviewed, younger when admitted to the hospital, and more likely to have been diagnosed acute rather than paranoid or chronic schizophrenic.

WYNNE, L. Methodologic and conceptual issues in the study of schizophrenics and their families. *Journal of Psychiatric Research*, 1968, *6*, 185–199.
This paper explores some of the conceptual and methodological issues in research studies on schizophrenic families. It also reviews the author's previous research and describes the samples used. Because of the early stages of work in this area, research methods have usually been worked out only *after* the base line data had been obtained and the plea is made to do it the opposite way.

YARROW, M. R.,CAMPBELL, J. D. & BURTON, R. V. Reliability of maternal retrospection: A preliminary report. *Family Process*, 1964, *3*, 207–218.
An examination of the retrospective method of family research where the data is self report of family members about the past. A study is reported where retrospection of mothers is obtained through interview methods and these data are compared with the reports of those mothers at the earlier period. The results "demonstrate a very large error in retrospective interview data on parent–child relations."

ZIEGLER-DRISCOLL, G. Family research study at Eagleville Hospital and Rehabilitation Center. *Family Process*, 1977, *16*, 175–189.
This article describes the Family Study Program at Eagleville Hospital and Rehabilitation Center. Some of the problem areas inherent in coordinating research with a new treatment program are presented. It discusses the sample of drug abusers, their families, and their course in family treatment. One observation regards the problem of disengagement, referring to separation of the adolescent or young adult from an overly dependent position in the family system toward a more differentiated and independent one. this was present in 10 of the 25 treated families. Family treatment facilitated the process.

3.6   FAMILY THEORY

ACKERMAN, N. A changing conception of personality: A personal viewpoint. *American Journal of Psychoanalysis,* 1957, *17*, 78–86.
This is a clinical essay focusing on some new ideas on personality development. A theory of personality development must take into account intrapsychic forces, social forces, family and hereditary factors. Personality integration is the sum total of all these factors.

ACKERMAN, N. W. Child and family psychiatry today: A new look at some old problems. *Mental Hygiene,* 1963, *47*, 540–545.
A paper evaluating some basic concepts of child psychiatry, which finds these concepts incomplete without amending them "so that child and family may be treated as a single entity, rather than piecing them apart." Some basic family dynamics are discussed in support of that idea.

ACKERMAN, N. W. Prejudice and scapegoating in the family. In G. H. Zuk & I. Boszormenyi-Nagy (Eds.) *Family therapy and disturbed families.* Palo Alto: Science & Behavior Books. 1967.
See Reference in Section 1.4.

ACKERMAN, N. W. Prejudicial scapegoating and neutralizing forces in the family group, with special reference to the role of family healer. *International Journal of Social Psychiatry,* 1964, (Special Edition No. 2) 90–96.
See Reference in Section 3.3.

ACKERMAN, N. W. Toward an integrative therapy of the family. *American Journal of Psychiatry,* 1958, *144*, 727–723.
Based on the author's clinical experience in family therapy, a method for understanding family pathology and a program of prevention is presented and illustrated by case examples. Illness is a function of the family as well as a manifestation of individual behavior.

ACKERMAN, N. W. & BEHRENS, M. L. A study of family diagnosis. *American Journal of Orthopsychiatry,* 1956, *26*, 66–78.
See Reference in Section 5.1.

ACKERMAN, N. W., PAPP, P., & PROSKY, P. Childhood disorders and interlocking pathology in family relationships. In E. J. Anthony, & C. Koupernik (Eds.), *The child in his family.* New York: Wiley, 1970.
A discussion of the concept of studying the child by moving from the dynamic study of the whole family back to the child. Case examples are given.

ACKERMAN, N. W., & SOBEL, R. Family diagnosis. *American Journal of Orthopsychiatry,* 1950, *20*, 744–753.
See Reference in Section 1.6.

ALANEN, Y. O. Round table conference of family studies and family therapy of schizophrenic patients. *Acta Psychiatrica Scandinavica,* (Supplement No. 169), 1963, *39*, 420–426.
See Reference in Section 5.2.

ANTHONY, E. J. The mutative impact of serious mental and physical illness in a parent on family life. In E. J. Anthony & C. Koupernik (Eds.), *The child in his family.* New York: Wiley, 1970.
A report of a study of families where a parent figure has succumbed to a serious mental or physical disorder necessitating hopitalization. Various views are offered of such illness as a disruption of family roles, as a crisis in accommodation, as a disconnection, and as a challenge. Family members were interviewed individually and in dyads and triads.

ANTHONY, E. J., & KOUPERNIK, C. (Eds.), *The child in his family.* New York: Wiley, 1970.
Volume I in the series of the International Yearbook for Child Psychiatry and Allied Disciplines. Included are papers from a variety of authors of different nations. The sections include family dynamics, family vulnerability and crisis, chronic fmaily pathology, and mental health and families in different cultures. 492 pp.

ARCHIBALD, H. The disturbed child-disturbed family. *Archives of Pediatrics,* 1950, *67*, 128–133.
An essay, based on the author's clinical practice, which describes presenting signs and symptoms of emotional nature seen in a pediatric practice. The emotional symptoms are seen as related to a disturbed family. The child is in a "vicious cycle." Suggestions for dealing with this problem are made.

ARNOLD, A. The implications of two-person and three-person relationships for family psychotherapy. *Journal of Health and Human Behavior,* 1962, *3*, 94–97.

An essay on the disinclinations of psychotherapists to work directly with families. A sociological formulation is offered in terms of the differences in the dynamics of dyadic and triadic relationships and how they impinge on the therapist.

AUERSWALD, E. H. Interdisciplinary vs. ecological approach. *Family Process*, 1968, *7*, 202–215.
A discussion of the difference between approaching a problem from the viewpoint of different disciplines or using an ecological systems approach. A case of a runaway girl is used for exploring this difference.

BATESON, G. The bisocial integration of behavior in the schizophrenic family. In N. W. Ackerman, F. L. Beatman & S. Sherman (Eds.), *Exploring the base for family therapy*. New York: Family Service Association of America, 1961.
A description of families and other systems in terms of feedback and calibration where calibration is at the "setting" level. Families of schizophrenics are described in terms of difficulties at the calibration level.

BATESON, G. Minimal requirements for a theory of schizophrenia. *Archives of General Psychiatry*, 1960, *2*, 477–491.
An essay on developing a theory of schizophrenia. The role of learning theory, genetics, and evolution is discussed. The double-bind model may be used in part to explain the symptoms of schizophrenia and perhaps other behavioral disorders.

BATESON, G., & JACKSON, D. D. Some varieties of pathogenic organization. *Disorders of communication No. 42*. Research Publications, Association for Research in Nervous and Mental Disease, 1964.
A discussion of symmetrical and complementary relationships, analogic, and digital communication models, and the relation of such ideas to pathological organization.

BATESON, G., JACKSON, D. D., HALEY, J., & WEAKLAND, J. Towards a theory of schizophrenia. *Behavior Science*, 1956, *1*, 251–264.
See Reference in Section 5.2.

BARNHILL, L. R., & LONGO, D. Fixation and regression in the family life cycle. *Family Process*, 1978, *17*, 469–478.
Using case examples to illustrate, this paper explores the use of a "developmental" view (progression of a family through a life cycle with regressions and fixations) in family therapy. By emphasizing a developmental view, therapists may understand variations in family functioning based on stages of family development. There is a need to increase the specificity with which assessments and interventions are tailored by incorporating this view.

BECKMAN-BRIDLEY, S. & TAVORMINA, J. B. Power relationships in families: A social-exchange perspective. *Family Process*, 1978, *17*, 423–436.
This paper presents an integrated approach to the issue of power in families from a social-exchange theory viewpoint. In a healthy family, one member should dominate permanently, since power involves a mutual relationship system that changes its content, though not its rules of operation, in specific decision-making situations.

BELL, N. W. Extended family relations of disturbed and well families. *Family Process*, 1962, *1*, 175–193.
The author's thesis is that "disturbed families have been unable to resolve conflicts with the extended kin outside the nuclear family" and that "well" families have achieved resolution of the problems of ties to extended kin. Most of the data were collected from observation and interviews in the home. Findings were that the "pathological" families used the extended family to (1) shore up group defenses, (2) act as stimuli of conflict, (3) act as screens for the projection of conflicts, and (4) act as competing objects of support.

BELL, N. W. Terms of a comprehensive theory of family psychopathology relationships. In G. H. Zuk & I. Boszormenyi-Nagy (Eds.), *Family therapy and disturbed families*. Palo Alto: Science & Behavior Books, 1967.
See Reference in Section 3.5.

BERNAL, G. & BAKER, J. Toward a metacommunicational framework of couple interactions. *Family Process*, 1979, *18*, 293–302.
This article describes a multi-level, "metacommunicational," framework for understanding couple interactions. Five interactonal levels are defined: (1) object (focused on object); (2) individual (focused on the person); (3) transactional (focused on the transactions); (4) relational (focused on the relationship); and (5) contextual (focused on the context). Case examples are provided and clinical implications are discussed.

BIRDWHISTELL, R. L. An approach to communication. *Family Process*, 1962, *1*, 194–201.
An essay on communication processes in general, emphasizing types and multi-functions of messages with particular applicability to the child receiving "messages" in growing up.

BIRDWHISTELL, R. The idealized model of the American family. *Social Casework*, 1970, *51*, 195–198.
This clinical essay focuses on the notion that the American family is organized around idealized goals (e.g., romanticized love) that are unobtainable, thus leading to a sense of hopelessness and failure in the parents. It is hypothesized that these feelings contribute to psychopathology in all members of the family. The author suggests that to improve health in the family, the impossible goals must be unmasked.

BOSZORMENYI-NAGY, I. The concept of schizophrenia from the perspective of family treatment. *Family Process*, 1962, *1*, 103–113.
A discussion of "the problems and mechanisms of family relationships." The author's hypothesis is that "schizophrenic personality development may in part be perpetrated by reciprocal interpersonal need complementaries between parent and offspring." Observations were collected from intensive psychotherapy of young female schizophrenics and concurrent conjoint therapy of their relatives at a psychiatric hospital.

BOSZORMENYI-NAGY, I. From family therapy to a psychology of relationships: Fictions of the individual and fictions of the family. *Comprehensive Psychiatry*, 1966, *7*, 408–423.
A theoretical paper examining some of the questions posed by having a "family orientation" to psychiatric problems. A comprehensive psychology of relationships would include both internal experience and observable behavior. Theories of family dynamics and other theories of psychology are discussed.

BOSZORMENYI-NAGY, I. Relational modes and meaning. In G. H. Zuk & I. Boszormenyi-Nagy (Eds.), *Family therapy and disturbed families*. Palo Alto: Science & Behavior Books, 1967.
An essay on the determinents and meaning of relationships. "Existential freedom is a dialectical process; it is not love through merger. It is a capacity for symmetrical self-other delineations and continuous new resolutions of opposing positions in relationships.

BOSZORMENYI-NAGY, I. A theory of relationships: Experience and transaction. In I. Boszormenyi-Nagy, & J. L. Framo (Eds.), *Intensive family therapy*. New York: Harper & Row, 1965.
A discussion of relationships from the point of view of a dialectical theory of personality and relatedness, alternate choices of self-delineation, and an object model of the formation of relational systems.

BOWEN, M. Family psychotherapy with schizophrenia in the hospital and in private practice. In I. Boszormenyi-Nagy, and J. L. Framo (Eds.) *Intensive family therapy*. New York: Harper & Row, 1965.
A discussion of a theory of the family and of family therapy with sections on differences between family and individual theory, a summary of the family theory of emotional illness with the emphasis upon schizophrenia, the parental transmission of problems to the child, the clinical approach to modify the family transmission process, and principles and techniques of this family therapy approach.

BOWEN, M., DYSINGER, R., & BASAMANIA, B. Role of the father in families with a schizophrenic patient. *American Journal of Psychiatry*, 1959, *115*, 1017–1020.
One of a series of papers on a study of families with schizophrenics in which the entire family was all hospitalized in the psychiatric research ward for periods of "up to two and a half years." Four families were hospitalized while an additional six famiies were seen in out-patient family therapy for periods of up to two years. The most frequent family dynamic observed was "emotional divorce" between mother and father and an intense relationship between mother and patient in which the father was excluded.

BRITTAIN, C. V. Adolescent choices and parent–peer cross-pressures. *American Sociological Review*, 1963, *28*, 385–391.
Adolescent choices when peers and parents indicate different courses were investigated as to variation by content area. Two hundred and eighty high school girls in two southern states responded to hypothetical dilemmas. On two occasions interviews were also held with 42 subjects. The data indicate that choice depended upon the area, and that a complex process of perception of and identification with peers and parents is involved.

BRODEY, W. M. A cybernetic approach to family therapy. In G. H. Zuk, & I. Boszormenyi-Nagy (Eds.), *Family therapy and disturbed families*. Palo Alto: Science & Behavior Books, 1967.
In this paper "the family is conceptualized as a self-perpetuating organism with a built-in regulatory system. Family therapy is directed to altering the family's self regulation . . . "

BRODEY, W. The family as the unit of study of treatment: Image, object, and narcissistic relationships. *American Journal of Orthopsychiatry*, 1961, *31*, 69–73.
An essay which attempts to outline the dynamics of family relationships starting from the intrapsychic point of view and moving to interactional models. Externalization, object relationships, image relationships and narcissism are all discussed in the family context in terms of building a conception of how a family operates.

BRODEY, W. M. The need for a systems approach. In N. W. Ackerman (Ed.), *Expanding theory and practice in family therapy*. New York: Family Service Association of America, 1967.
A clinical essay pointing out that there is still a great lack of standardized method to evaluate complex intervention into complex systems. Further study and methods are needed.

BRODSKY, C. M. The social recovery of mentally ill housewives. *Family Process*, 1968, 7, 170–183.
A report on a study of the relationship between social recovery and role among mentally ill housewives. A sample of 38

housewives admitted to an acute treatment research unit were examined and followed up. The housewife's role is said to be conductive to recovery.

BRODY, E. M. Aging and family personality: A developmental view. *Family Process*, 1974, *13*, 23–37.
This paper discusses the issues of aging, separation, loss and death in the developmental context of changing roles and responsibilities of family members. Societal trends in population aging are explored and the concept of family personality is elaborated.

BROFENBRENNER, U. The changing American child—A speculative analysis. *Journal of Social Issues*, 1961, *17*, 6–18.
A variety of studies show that American parents have changed their child-rearing techniques in the past 25 years. No solid comparative data exist, but one may infer existence of changes from known relationships between socialization techniques and outcome. Outcome varies by sex of child and authority-nurturance division between parents. Many signs point to the conclusion that a generation lacking intiative, inner direction, and responsibility has been produced. Recent changes suggest that parents may now be raising a more achievement-oriented generation, the motivation being inculcated by mothers in a family atmosphere of "cold democracy."

BRUCH, H. Changing approaches to the study of the family. In I. M. Cohen (Ed.), *Psychiatric research report No. 20*, Washington, D.C.: American Psychiatric Association, 1966.
A general discussion of family influence with the emphasis upon the salient aspects of family transactions centering on the continuous interactions of biological endorsement with environmental forces.

CHARNY, I. W. And Abraham went to slay Isaac: A parable of killer, victim, and bystander in the family of man. *Journal of Ecumenical Studies*, 1973, *10*, 304–317.
This is a reinterpretation of the parable of Abraham in which Abraham does kill Isaac. One of the family's main functions is to prevent individual destructiveness on the part of its members.

CHEEK, F. E. & ANTHONY, R. Personal pronoun usage in families of schizophrenics and social space utilization. *Family Process*, 1970, *9*, 431–447.
This is a study of the use of personal pronoun usage in interaction, as a measure of the social functioning of both individuals and groups. Male and female (N = 67) schizophrenic young adults and their parents were compared with normal young adults and their parents. Previous findings regarding disproportionate use of the first person singular by schizophrenics were confirmed; their parents were low in usage of these pronouns. Findings of other related studies seem to be supported by these findings.

CLARK, A. W., & VAN SOMMERS, P. Contradictory demands in family relations and adjustment to school and home. *Human Relations*, 1961, *14*, 97–111.
Intensive case studies of families of 20 maladjusted and 20 adjusted children, all families having one or more adults other than the parents living in the family. The concern was with "the process of explaining an unsatisfactory relationship between any two individuals in terms of the influence of a third individual." Data were obtained by detailed, focussed interviews, questionnaires to school staffs, group interviews with peers, and tests of ability. School difficulties were associated with unsatisfactory relationships in the home, one of which was dependence of one parent upon the other adult. Unsatisfactory relationships of adults contribute to withdrawal of father from family activities, difficulties between adults and children, maladjustment of children at home and school, and recurrence of symptoms in parents.

COHEN, C. I. & CORWIN, J. An application of balance theory to family treatment. *Family Process*, 1975, *14*, 469–479.
This paper reviews Heider's Balance Theory of family function. Applicability to family treatment is discussed in regard to the therapists ability to disrupt inflexible alliance patterns.

COLLVER, A. The family cycle in India and the United States. *American Sociological Review*, 1963, *26*, 86.
Systematic comparisons of age at marriage, interval before birth of the first child, total child-bearing period, and other stages of family cycle are made between the United States and a rural-Indian area. The stages are less clearly defined in India. The meaning in terms of kinship system and the ramifications for the society are explored.

DAVIS, D. Interventions into family affairs. *British Journal of Medical Psychology*, 1968, *41*, 73–79.
An essay using a case example from Ibsen's play, *The Lady From the Sea*. How the family problem was resolved in the play and how it might be resolved using present psychiatric treatment methods (ECT, behavior therapy, family therapy, and so forth) are discussed. Emphasis is placed on finding the "right" treatment course by an appraisal covering the entire family.

DELL, N., TRIESCHMAN, A., & VOGEL, E. A sociocultural analysis of resistances of working-class fathers treated in a child psychiatric clinic. *American Journal of Orthopsychiatry*, 1961, *31*, 388–405.

The author's hypothesis is that fathers have been excluded from the treatment process in the child guidance clinic setting. Ten "working-class" fathers were seen for periods ranging from one to four years. It was part of concurrent, simultaneous treatment of the identified patient (the child) and the mother. Familial dynamics are discussed. The child's treatment may be facilitated when the father is seen.

DUNHAM, R. M. Ex post facto reconstruction of conditioning schedules in family interaction. In I. M. Cohen (Ed.), *Psychiatric research report No. 20*. Washington, D. D.: American Psychiatric Association, 1966.
A discussion of family behavior from the point of view of learning theory. Given some of the descriptions of families of schizophrenics, "have the patients been exposed to a chronic pattern of aversive conditioning that has inhibited the develoment of ego strength and left them passive?"

ELDER, G. H. Structural variations in the child-rearing relationship. *Sociometry*, 1962, *25*, 241–262.
Seven types of parent–adolescent interdependence, ranging from parental autocracy to parental ignoring, were identified by focussed interviews. Questionnaires to 7,400 Ohio and North Carolina adolescents reveal that parental dominance is most common in lower-class, large, Catholic families. Parental autocracy is most likely to be associated with negative evaluations of parental policies by adolescents and with mutual rejection of each other.

ELDER, G. H., & BOWERMAN, C. E. Family structure and child-rearing patterns: The effect of family size, sex composition. *American Sociological Review,* 1963, *28*, 891–905.
The effects of family size, sex composition and social class on the involvement of the father in child rearing, on the type of parental control exerted, and on the disciplinary techniques used were studied. Data were from a 40% sample (N = 1261) of all seventh grade white Protestant students of unbroken homes in central Ohio and central North Carolina. Family size and sex composition were found to have effects on child-rearing methods, but the effects are highly contingent on the sex of the child and the social class of the family.

ENGLISH, O. S., SCHEFLEN, A. E., HAMPE, W. W., & AUERBACH, A. H. Strategy and structure in psychotherapy. *Behavioral Studies Monograph No. 2*. Philadelphia: Eastern Pennsylvania Psychiatric Institute, 1965.
A companion volume to *Stream and structure of communicational behavior* (by A. E. Scheflen) which includes three research studies of a family therapy interview by Whitaker and Malone.

EPSTEIN, N., & WESTLEY, W. Parental interaction as related to the emotional health of children. *Social Problems*, 1960, *8*, 87–92.
One of a series of papers concerned with the parents' relationship with, and emotional health of, their children. Methodology was previously described. Results indicated that there was no firm relationship between the level of the parental sexual relationship and the average level of emotional health among the children, but a clearcut degree of dependency needs in the father was directly related to unhealthiness in the children. The level of the father's unresolved dependency needs does not seem to affect the children's health as long as the father is stronger than the mother.

ERICSON, P. M., & ROGERS, L. E. New procedures for analyzing relational communication. *Family Process*, 1973, *12*, 245–267.
This paper presents a system for describing and indexing patterns of communication at the relational level, i.e., it refers to the control aspects of message exchanges that define an interactor's relationships with others. This coding system also focuses on the control defining aspects of communication, as well as the sequences of messages; it attempts to index the control dimensions of those messages according to their similarities or differences.

FAVAZZA, A. R. & OMAN, M. Overview: Foundations of cultural psychiatry. *American Journal of Psychiatry*, 1978, *135*, 293–303.
This is an essay discussing foundations of cultural psychiatry. There is a section discussion family and social networks that describe four types of family structure. The concept of "the family" may be too limited for effective therapeutic intervention,and if so, it suggests network therapy as the treatment of choice for family problems.

FELDMAN, M. J. Privacy and conjoint family therapy. *Family Process*, 1967, *6*, 1–9.
A discussion of whether greater or lesser degree of privacy effects the nature of therapeutic disclosures by contrasting individual and conjoint family therapy. There is no simple relationship between degree of privacy and kind and scope of disclosure. The private nature of individual therapy led to an ethical position which elevates an individual's welfare above others, which may even be to their detriment.

FERREIRA, A. J. Family Myths. In I. M. Cohen (Ed.), *Psychiatric Research Report No. 20*, Washington, D.C.: American Psychiatric Association, 1966.
See Reference in Section 1.1.

FERREIRA, A. Family myth and homeostasis. *Archives of General Psychiatry*, 1963, *9*, 457–463.
A discussion of a particular aspect of the family relationship, the family myth, which is defined as "a series of fairly

well integrated beliefs shared by all family members, concerning each other and their mutual position in the family life"—beliefs that go unchallenged despite reality distortions which they imply. Three family case reports are presented in support of the discussion; the author believes that the family myth is to the relationship what the defense is to the individual.

FERREIRA, A. J. Family myths: The covert rules of the relationship. *Confinia Psychiatrica*, 1965, *8*, 15–20.
A general discussion of the myths in families which express covert rules of family relationships. These well-systematized fabrications perform an important part as homeostatic mechanisms. "In fact, it seems that the family myth is to the family what the defense is to the individual." From family therapy observations, the author says that "pathologic families" can be overburdened with their own mythology and "seem to retain very little freedom for unrehearsed action, and to suffer in their ability to deal with new situations, and unexpected events."

FERREIRA, A. Psychosis and family myth: *American Journal of Psychotherapy*, 1967, *21*, 186–197.
In this essay, several case examples are given in support of the notion that psychotic behavior is a manifestation of not only the individual, but also as an elaboration of pre-existing family myths "upon which the preservation of the relationship may depend." Family myths prevent change and are concretizations of the family's interactional patterns. Family therapy is suggested as a method of changing psychotic behavior.

FLECK, S. An approach to family pathology. *Comprehensive Psychiatry*, 1966, *7*, 307–320.
Functions and tasks of normal families, as well as an approach to understanding family pathology based on deficiencies in performing their functions and tasks are outlined. Suggestions for research on the family are made.

FORD, F. R., & HERRICK, J. Family rules: Family life styles. *American Journal of Orthopsychiatry*, 1974, *44*, 61–69.
This clinical essay attempts to classify how families function. The family is a rule-governed system; thus understanding rules can predict behavior. Five family life styles are described. To change the behavior of the family, the therapist must restate the rules so that counter rules can be put into operation in order to renegotiate the original family rule.

FLECK, S. A general systems approach to severe family pathology. *American Journal of Psychiatry*, 1976, *133*, 669–673.
A general systems approach is proposed for examination and understanding of family functioning. Looking at the family as an open system, five areas are described: (1) evolutionary goals and tangible tasks, (2) a need for "semipermeable" boundaries, (3) cultural and subcultural communication models, (4) leadership effectiveness, and (5) the nature and age-appropriateness of the affective bonds. The advantage of such a framework of competencies and defects is that it can lead to a typology of family processes that can be evaluated regardless of symptoms or diagnosis of individual family members.

FRAMO, J. L. Symptoms from a family transaction viewpoint. In N. W. Ackerman (Ed.), *Family therapy in transition*. Boston, Brown, 1970.
A discussion of symptoms in terms of irrational role assignments, projective transference distortions, and internalized objects which become subidentities. Case examples, illustrate symptom choice, symptom maintenance, and pseudosymptoms.

FRANCES, V. & FRANCES, A. The incest taboo and family structure. *Family Process*, 1976, *15*, 235–244.
This paper draws from studies of animal sexual behavior, specifically patterns of mating, attachment and dominance. Parallels in the human family are hypothesized: that man brings with him an inheritance of symbolization thereby making the natural incest barrier, an incest taboo. These authors compare human separation–individuation and the oedipal conflict with detachment and cominance in animal "familial" structures. From this comparison these authors conclude that the operation of incest in the family is asymmetrical or that the mother–son incest taboo is strong than the father–daughter, brother–sister incest taboos.

FREEDMAN, D. S., FREEDMAN, R., & WHELPTON, P. K. Size of family and preference for children of each sex. *American Journal of Sociology*, 1960, *66*, 141–146.
An investigation of 889 white couples with two, three, or four children, to determine whether the question of American family size is influenced by a desire of parents to have at least one child of each sex.

FREEMAN, D. S. The family as a system: fact or fantasy? *Comprehensive Psychiatry*, 1976, *17*, 735–748.
Nine major myths involving family diagnosis and treatment are discussed clinically: myths about family structure, nature of family systems, resistance to change, disintegrating families, the most stable types of relationships, blaming, speaking for others, the role of the identified patient, and the problem patient.

GALDSTON, I. The need for an epidemiology of psychiatric disorders of the family. In N. W. Ackerman, F. L. Beatman, & S. Sherman (Eds.), *Exploring the base for family therapy*. New York: Family Service Association of America, 1961.

A clinical essay, which points out that although there are strong biases to the contrary, there is very little information about the epidemiology of either normal or pathologic families. Such information cannot be obtained during treatment. In addition to data about normal families, follow-up data of normal families must also be obtained.

GEHRKE, S., & KIRSCHENBAUM, M. Survival patterns in family conjoint therapy. *Family Process*, 1967, *6*, 67–80.
A discussion of 20 families studied in family therapy with the emphasis upon different patterns of emotional survival myths in the family. Three types of family are contrasted: the repressive family, the delinquent family, and the suicidal family. The survival myth has to do with the illusion of family members that they must continue their existing family ways of relating to survive psychologically.

GEISMAR, L. L. Family functioning as an index of need for welfare services. *Family Process*, 1964, *3*, 99–113.
A discussion of the need to have an objective means of assessing the need for welfare services. A standardized method of evaluating family functioning is offered with a report of a study of families.

GLASSER, P. H. Changes in family equilibrium during psychotherapy. *Family Process*, 1963, *2*, 245–264.
See Reference in Section 1.1.

GLASSER, P., & GLASSER, L. Adequate family functioning. In I. M. Cohen (Ed.), *Psychiatric research report No. 20* Washington, D.C.: American Psychiatric Association, 1966.
A report of a study of families in which at least one member was undergoing psychotherapy. The emphasis is upon five critera of adequate family functioning: internal role consistency, consistency of role and actual performance, compatibility of roles, meeting psychological needs, and the ability of the family to respond to change.

GRUNEBAUM, H. & CHASIN, R. Relabeling and reframing reconsidered: The beneficial effects of a pathological label. *Family Process*, 1978, *17*, 449–455.
This article examines the adaptive effect of pathological labeling of one family member through the presentation of five cases. There are many families in which a pathological label applied to one family member may have beneficial impact on the family system. The relabeling of one member, rather than the whole family, may relieve guilt and expectations, and thus free the family to engage in constructive action. The use of any label should be determined by its therapeutic impact.

HADER, M. The importance of grandparents in family life. *Family Process*, 1965, *4*, 228–240.
See Reference in Section 4.3.

HALEY, J. Family therapy: A radical change. In J. Haley (Ed.), *Changing Families: A Family Therapy Reader*. New York: Grune & Stratton, 1971.
See Reference in Section 1.1.

HALEY, J. Observation of the family of the schizophrenic. *American Journal of Orthopsychiatry*, 1960, *30*, 460–467.
See Reference in Section 3.3.

HALEY, J. The perverse triangle. In G. Zuk & I. Boszormenyi-Nagy (Eds.), *Family therapy and disturbed families*. Palo Alto: Science & Behavior Books, 1967.
A discussion of cross-generational coalitions as a cause of disturbance in family and other organizations.

HASSAN, S. A. Transactional and contextual invalidation between the parents of disturbed families: A comparative study. *Family Process*, 1974, *13*, 53–76.
This study was designed to examine the effect of parents' communication style on their offspring's psychopathology. Using 46 couples divided into six categories of varying degrees of pathology (schizophrenic, delinquent, psychosomatic, ulcerative colitis and a normal control group) seven scales were set up to measure parents verbal exchanges during the discussion task question, "How out of all the people in the world did you two get together?" Specifically, mutual "validation" was maximal in the control group couples and minimal in the groups having a delinquent or schizophrenic member. This study corresponds with other research which links parental communicational patterns with deviance of offspring.

HEARD, D. H. From object relations to attachment theory: A basis for family therapy. *British Journal of Medical Psychology*, 1978, *51*, 67–76.
This paper compares Winnicott's theory of object relations and Bowlby's theory of attachment. Reasons are given for preferring attachment theory as a basis for family therapy; e.g. its emphasis on homeostasis at different stages of development and shared goals.

HECKEL, R. V. A comparison of process data from family therapy and group therapy. *Journal of Community Psychology*, 1975, *3*, 254–257.
This is a clincial study of verbal response patterns occuring in family therapy. Method was to compare 6 families (with

27 members) in family therapy with 23 group therapy patients (in 3 different groups), all of whom were in mental health facilities and seen for eight sessions. Verbal behavior was scored in two of the eight sessions by a single rater utilizing the process analysis of Heckel and Salzber. Results indicated that family members, in contrast to therapy group members, responded less to the therapist, had more negative interactions, a higher readiness to deal with relevant issues, a lower need to elaborate on comments, and less need to build relationships.

HENRY, J. Family structure and the transmission of neurotic behavior. *American Journal of Orthopsychiatry*, 1951, *21*, 800–818.
Based on analysis of interaction patterns of one family attending a child guidance clinic, the author makes the following hypotheses: "(1) individuals learn relatively rigid patterns of interaction which they then tend to project upon the world in such a way as to expect reciprocal patterns from others, (2) from the standpoint of intrafamilial interaction, neurosis may be considered originating in rigid interaction pattersn of pathogenic, quality, (3) family interaction patterns may be described with relative precision that will enable therapists to state the general psychological characteristic of families, and (4) the transmission of a neurosis in a family line is a transmission of a rigid interactional pattern of pathogenic quality."

HENRY, J. The study of families by naturalistic observation. In I. M. Cohen (Ed.), *Psychiatric research report No. 20*. Washington, D.C.: American Psychiatric Association, 1966.
A discussion of the observation of psychotic children in the home with the emphasis upon the methodology and the experience of such observation. An illustration is given, and "when such observations are undertaken it quickly becomes apparent that the data is so rich as to compel reexamination of old theories and suggest hypotheses leading to new ones."

HOFFMAN, L. Deviation amplifying processes in natural groups. In J. Haley (Ed.), *Changing families*. New York: Grune & Stratton, 1971.
A theoretical paper on the limitations of a homeostatic theory to deal with change. The family view, systems theory, and sociological ideas about deviants are brought together in a discussion of the process of change in systems when a deviation is amplified.

HOFFMAN, L. "Enmeshment" and the too richly cross-joined system. *Family Process*, 1975, *14*, 457–468.
This paper proposes a connection between Minuchin's concept of an "enmeshed" family and Ashby's discussion of the problems inherent in a system in which all parts are tightly interlocked. Adaptive change in such a system is difficult and requires a loosening of these tight "joints" in the system. This is compared to interventions in family therapy which are aimed at restructuring boundaries and separating individuals from one another.

HOFFMAN, L., & LONG, L. A systems dilemma. *Family Process*, 1969, *8*, 211–234.
a description of a man's breakdown in terms of the social systems within which he moved, and the attempts to intervene to bring about change. The ecological field of a person is the area considered.

HOWELLS, J. G. The nuclear family as the functional unit in psychiatry. *Journal of Mental Science*, 1962, *108*, 675–684.
A discussion of the family, the nuclear family (defined as a sub-system of the social system and consisting of two adults of different sexes who undertake a parenting role to one or more children), and family psychiatry.

HUBBELL, R. D., BYRNE, M. C., & STACHOWIAK, J. Aspects of communication in families with young children. *Family Process*, 1974, *13*, 215–224.
This is a study about family interaction as studied through language usage. The contents of interaction were studied in 16 normal families with two children, ages 3 and 4 and 6 and 7. Results showed that the older children had more and more varied communication, and that female children got more positive feedback. This supports a conclusion of strong same-sex coalitions between parents and children.

JACKSON, D. D. Aspects of conjoint family therapy. In G. H. Zuk & I. Boszormenyi-Nagy (Eds.), *Family therapy and disturbed families*. Palo Alto: Science & Behavior Books, 1967.
See Reference in Section 1.1

JACKSON, D. D. Family rules: Marital, quid pro quo. *Archives of General Psychiatry*, 1965, *12*, 589–594.
See Reference in Section 4.1

JACKSON, D. D. The individual and the larger contexts. *Family Process*, 1967, *6*, 139–154.
An essay on the contexts in which individuals function. The emphasis is upon the system and includes a discussion of the individual in his family as well an any entity, such as a nation, in systematic relationship with other entities. The article is followed by discussions by George Vassiliou, Nathan B. Epstein, and Lyman C. Wynne.

JACKSON, D. D. The study of the family *Family Process*, 1965, *4*, 1–20.

An essay on the family emphasizing the family as a rule-governed, homeostatic system. It includes problems of family theory and research.

JACKSON, D. D., RISKIN, J., & SATIR, V. A method of analysis of a family interview. *Archives of General Psychiatry*, 1961, *5*, 321–339.
See Reference in Section 3.3

JACKSON, D. D., & SATIR, V. A review of psychiatric developments in family diagnosis and therapy. In N. W. Ackerman, F. L. Beatman, & S. Sherman (Eds.), *Exploring the base for family therapy*. New York: Family Service Association of America, 1961.
A clinical essay describing the development of family therapy. Clinical trends from psychiatry, social work, anthropology, and psychoanalysis as well as the literature are carefully reviewed in seeing a gradual development of a way of thinking about the individual patient as a reflection of a disturbed family. Family therapy offers an impressive laboratory for studying growth and change available to the researcher. Behavior that had formerly been thought of as "constitutional" could now be seen as interactional in etiologic terms.

JACKSON, D. D., & WEAKLAND, J. Schizophrenic symptoms in family interaction. *Archives of General Psychiatry* 1959, *1*, 618–621.
Based on psychological, sociological, and anthropological information about families, data collection from individual interviews of family members, and treatment of the family together, the authors hypothesize that schizophrenic behavior can be seen as (1) "resembling the behavior of other family members, though it may be exaggerated almost to a caricature," and (2) "appearing to subserve important functions within the family." Two case examples are given in support of this view.

KANTOR, R. E. Schizophrenia and symbolic interactionism. *Family Process*, 1964, *3*, 402–414.
A general discussion of the "basic assumptions of interactionism" presented in the form of seven issues: processes, contemporary causality, dynamic fields, self-concepts, emergents, and molarity and systems.

KLEBANOW, S. Parenting in the single parent family. *Journal of the American Academy of Psychoanalysis*, 1976, *4*, 37–48.
From the author's practice, this paper focuses on special responsibilities and burdens of the single parent family. The single parent's psychological problems (e.g., preoccupation with own loss and maintenance of feelings of self worth) are discussed from a psychoanalytic viewpoint and important reality problems (e.g., precarious finances and child care arrangements) are identified.

KLUGMAN, J. "Enmeshment" and "fusion." *Family Process*, 1976, *15*, 321–323.
This paper compares the concepts of fusion as described by Bowen and enmeshment as described by Minuchin. The author concludes that the concepts are similar and complementary. He further observes that enmeshment which describes the functioning of the family system, differs from fusion which describes the functioning of an individual within the system.

KLUGMAN, J. Owning and disowning: The structural dimension. *Family Process*, 1977, *16*, 353–356.
This paper reexamines Stierlin's concept of "owning and disowning" in the parent–child relationship from a structural dimension and discusses implicaitons for therapy. A commentary by Stierlin is included in the paper, pointing out weaknesses in the author's applications of the concept.

KOHL, R. N. Pathologic reactions of marital partners to improvement of patients. *American Journal of Psychiatry*, 1962, *118*, 1036–1041.
A discussion of the precipitation of a psychiatric illness in a marital partner when a patient shows clinical improvement based upon observation of 39 in-patients treated at the Payne Whitney psychiatric clinic over a period of ten years. In all cases it was necessary to include both spouses in the treatment plan to maintain the patient's improvement or recovery. Commonly there was denial of marital conflict as etiologically significant by both partners at the time of hospitalization and emphasis upon the "ideal" nature of the marriage and mutual denial of resentment or hostility. With improvement in the patient, the spouses displayed the first observable signs of psychopathology.

LABARRE, W. The biosocial unity of the family. In N. W. Ackerman, F. L. Beatman, and S. Sherman (Eds.), *Exploring the base for family therapy*. New York: Family Service Association of America, 1961.
A clinical essay by an anthropologist on the role of the family. The nuclear family is a "human universal," which is not culturally contingent, but rather biologically fundamental. All attempts at therapy, including individual psychotherapy, are essentially restructuring of the family.

L'ABATE, L., WEEKS, G., & WEEKS, K. Of scapegoats, strawmen, and scarecrows. *International Journal of Family Therapy*, 1979, *1*, 86–96.
This is a theoretical paper (with treatment implications) about how people externalize "hurt" feelings within the

family. Scapegoating is the process by which other members of a system select one to be "sick," but "strawmanning" is when that person accepts his sick role. "Scarecrowing" differs from the latter because then the person is also avoided and isolated by the system.

LAING, R. D. Mystification, confusion and conflict. In I. Boszormenyi-Nagy, & J. L. Framo (Eds.), *Intensive family therapy*. New York: Harper & Row, 1965.
The theoretical schema of Marx—where the exploiter mystifies with a plausible misrepresentation of what is going on with the exploited—is applied to the family of the schizophrenic. The act of mystifying and the state of being mystified are described with case examples. The therapist's task is to help such a person become demystified.

LAQUEUR, H. P. General systems theory and multiple family therapy. In W. Gray, F. Duhl, & N. Rizzo (Eds.), *General systems theory and psychiatry*. Boston: Little, Brown, 1969.
A discussion of multiple family therapy from the point of view of systems theory. The general theoretical base for multiple family therapy is offered within this framework.

LAQUEUR, H. P. Multiple family therapy and general systems theory. In N. W. Ackerman (Ed.), *Family therapy in transition*. Boston: Little, Brown, 1970.
The family from the point of view of general systems theory with the emphasis upon treating groups of families. Theory and technique are described with examples.

LAQUEUR, H. P. Multiple family therapy and general systems theory. *International Psychiatric Clinics*, 1970, 7, 99–124.
A discussion of multiple family therapy using the concepts of general systems theory. The family and its components are viewed as subsystems of a larger field of interrelations whose interface problems can be studied and dealt with.

LEBOVICI, S. The psychoanalytic theory of the family. In E. J. Anthony, & C. Koupernik (Eds.), *The child in his family*. New York: Wiley, 1970.
The psychoanalytic view of a child's development in his family and his fantasy life.

LEHRMAN, N. S. Anarchy, dictatorship, and democracy within the family: A biosocial hierarchy. *Psychiatric Quarterly*, 1962, *36*, 455–474.
An essay in which the author proposes "that the backbone of the family structure in most human societies, including our own, is basically a linear hierarchy of roles arranged along the ordinal of intrafamilial power." The hierarchy is headed by father followed by mother, followed by children in order of birth, A discussion of roles and of types of families is also presented.

LESLIE, G. R., & JOHNSON, K. P. Changed perceptions of the maternal role. *American Sociological Review*, 1963, *28*, 919–928.
See Reference in Section 3.2

LEWIS, R. A. A developmental framework for the analysis of premarital dyadic formation. *Family Process*, 1972, *11*, 17–48.
The pourpose of this study is a formulation of a pratial theory of premarital dyadic formation, given the complex dynamics of the mate selection process in open marriage systems. Research reviewed indicates six processes in a developmental sequence which seem to confront the heterosexual pair through the stages of courtship: processes that relate to the couple's perceiving similarities, achieving pair rapport, inducing self-disclosure, role-taking, achieving interpersonal role-fit, and attaining "dyadic crystalization."

LEVANDE, D. I. Family theory as a necessary component of family therapy. *Social Casework*, 1976, *58*, 291–295.
In order to do family therapy, the therapist has to have a theoretical model. Three models are discussed: (1) Structure-Functional Model, (2) Interactional Model, and (3) Developmental Model. Implications for curricula are discussed.

LEVETON, ALAN F. Elizabeth is frightened. *Voices*, 1972, *8*, 4–13.
This is a clinical paper giving one case example that synthesizes concepts of communication strategies and strategies derived from Gestalt therapy in a family setting. In Gestalt therapy, the only "real" time is the present; the issue of individual responsibility is delineated. Conflicts and symptoms are the here-and-now expressions of unfinished situations that can be completed in therapy and restore homeostasis.

LEVINGER, G. Marital cohesiveness and dissolution: An integrative review. In P. H. Glasser, & L. N. Glasser (Eds.), *Families in crisis*. New York: Harper & Row, 1970.
See Reference in Section 4.1

LEVINGER, G. Supplementary methods in family research *Family Process*, 1963, *2*, 357–366.
See Reference in Section 3.5

LEVINGER, G. Task and social behavior in marriage. *Sociometry*, 1964, *27*, 433–448.
See Reference in Section 3.3

LIDZ, T. The family as the developmental setting. In E. J. Anthony, & C. Koupernik (Eds.), *The child in his family*.
New York: Wiley, 1970.
A description of child development in terms of the family with the emphasis upon the parental nurturant function,
the dynamic organization of the family, the social roles learned in the family and the parental transmition of the
culture.

LIDZ, T. The psychoanalytic theory of development and maldevelopment: Recapitulation. *American Journal of
Psychoanalysis*, 1967, *27*, 115–127.
This lecture attempts to integrate both psychoanalytic and family concepts in developing a theory of normal family
functioning and malfunctioning. "When the family organization is disturbed, there can be a multiplicity of ways in
which things can go wrong." However when the parents can form a coalition, the child "can develop a reasonably firm
and satisfactory gender identity."

LIDZ, T., CORNELISON, A., FLECK, S., & TERRY, D. Intrafamilial environment of schizophrenic patients. II:
Marital schism and marital skew. *American Journal of Psychiatry*, 1957, *114*, 241–248.
See Reference in Section 5.2

LIDZ, T., CORNELISON, A., TERRY, D., & FLECK, S. Intrafamilial environment of the schizophrenic patient. VI:
The transmission of irrationality. *Archives of Neurological Psychiatry*, 1958, *79*, 305–316.
See Reference in Section 5.2.

LIDZ, T., & FLECK, S. Some explored and partially explored sources of psychopathology. In G. H. Zuk, & I.
Boszormenyi-Nagy (Eds.), *Family therapy and disturbed families*. Palo Alto: Science & Behavior Books, 1967.
An essay on the problem of how the infant develops as a person in relation to significant family members and the
family as a social system. Six sources of psychopathological development in offspring are presented.

LINDSAY, J. S. B. Balance theory: Possible consequences of number of family members. *Family Process*, 1976, *15*,
245–249.
This paper focuses on the number of family members and the multiple relationships that may exist and affect function
within the family structure. The relationships are categorized as hetero- or homosexual, and as one or two
generational, and significant differences characteristic of the relationship between parents, among siblings, and
between parents and siblings are discussed. Implications of this numerical perspective for family therapy are
examined.

LINDSAY, J. The structure within groups. *British Journal of Social and Clinical Psychology*, 1967, *6*, 195–203.
An analysis of a group therapy session with the emphasis upon the formal characteristics of the sequences in the
conversation. "Without any concern with the content of the conversation, it has been possible to demonstrate
significant dyadic, triadic, and other multiple person situations, and of the effect of the therapist's remarks and of
silences."

LINDSAY, J. Types of family and family types. *Family Process*, 1968, 7, 51–66.
A discussion of the application of the theory of logical types to family descriptions. Confusions between the monad,
the dyad, and the triad are described and a hypothesis for schizophrenia is presented.

LITWAK, E. Geographic mobility and family cohesion. *American Sociological Review*, 1960, *25*, 385–394.
A second paper reporting a study of the families of 920 married white women living in a middle-class urban area.
Several hypotheses about the relationship of identification with extended kin and occupational mobility are tested.
The data indicate that extended families do not hinder, but rather aid geographical, and hence, occupational mobility.

LUSTIG, N., DRESSEN, J., SPELLMAN, S., & MURRAY, T. Incest. *Archives of General Psychiatry*, 1966, *14*, 31–
41.
Family constellations in six cases of father–daughter incest are reported. Data were gathered from clinical interviews
with the families. From the cases and from reviewing the literature, intrapsychic and transactional dynamics are
hypothesized which contribute to choice of father–daughter incest as a family defense. Incest is seen as a "tension
reducing defence within a dysfunctional family serving to maintain the integrity of the family unit."

MABREY, J. H. Medicine and the family. In P. H. Glasser, & L. N. Glasser (Eds.), *Families in crisis*. New York:
Harper & Row, 1970.
See Reference in Section 7.1.

MacGREGOR, R. Each family member experiences a different environment. In I. H. Cohen (Ed.), *Psychiatric
research report No. 20*. Washington, D.C.: American Psychiatric Association, 1966.

A view of the family emphasizing the basic notion that much of psychiatric illness can be viewed as an arrest in development of a family unit. Four types of families have been diagnosed: those with infantile, childish, juvenile, and preadolescent functioning.

MacGREGOR, R. The family constellation from the standpoint of various siblings. In O. Pollak, & A. S. Friedman (Eds.), *Family dynamics and female sexual delinquency*. Palo Alto: Science & Behavior Books, 1969.
See Reference in Section 5.4.

MACHOTKA, P., PITTMAN, F. S., III, & FLOMENHALT, K. Incest as a family affair. *Family Process*, 1967, *6*, 98–116.
A discussion of incest from the point of view of the whole family. Two cases of father-daughter incest and one of sibling incest are discussed with the emphasis upon the crucial role of the nonparticipating member, the concerted denial of the incest, and where the focus of therapy should be.

MARCUS, L. M. Patterns of coping in families of psychotic children. *American Journal of Orthopsychiatry*, 1977, *47*, 388–399.
See Reference in Section 5.3.

MARTIN, F. E. Some implications from the theory and practice of family therapy for individual therapy (and vice versa). *British Journal of Medical Psychology*, 1977, *50*, 53–64.
Using the concept of "transactions" between theoretical systems, theories of individual and family therapy are compared. Methods of data collection, emphasis on "closed" or open systems, the importance of "insight," outcome studies, and choice of intervention are all discussed. It is important to be able to utilize both frameworks and shift between them during evaluation and treatment. Criteria for the choice of an individual or family intervention are outlined.

MAYER, J. E. People's imagery of other families. *Family Process*, 1967, *6*, 27–36.
A discussion of the ways people's ideas about other families significantly affect their familial relationships. The emphasis is upon the need for research in this area and a classification scheme.

McPEAK, W. R. Family interactions as etiological factors in mental disorders: An analysis of the American Journal of Insanity, 1844–1848. *American Journal of Psychiatry*, 1975, *132*, 1327–1329.
This historical view focuses on the etiolgy of psychiatric illness at a time that psychiatry did not recognize the importance of family dynamics.

MEAD, D. E., & CAMPBELL, S. S.: Decision-making and interaction by families with and without a drug-abusing child. *Family Process*, 1972, *11*, 487–498.
This is a study of 40 Caucasian family triads: father, mother and child between the ages of 14 and 19. Twenty families had a drug-abusing child. The test required that individual family members first alone, listed favorite and least favorite solutions to the following types of situations: choosing a color for a car, choosing a movie to attend, choosing a family chore. Family members were then brought together to choose group favorites and least favorites. The variables measured were spontaneous agreement, choice fulfillment, and chaotic responses. Eleven hoptheses are stated; results for each are reported and compared with the 1965 Ferreira and Winter study. Conclusions in general show that normal families tend to have more spontaneous agreement as families and between members of all dyads, but especially between mother and child.

MEISSNER, W. W. Family dynamics and psychosomatic processes. *Family Process*, 1966, *5*, 142–161.
A discussion of the impact of patterns of family interaction on patterns of physical health and illness, with a review of the literature.

MEISSNER, W. W. Thinking about the family: Psychiatric aspects. *Family Process*, 1964, *3*, 1–40.
A review of the ideas and the literature produced by the shift from individual orientation to a specifically family-centered orientation. The family studies are reviewed in terms of what has been said about mothers, fathers, parental interaction, and total family constellations. The ideas of the major research groups are presented and analyzed. A bibliography of 135 references is included.

MENDELL, D., & CLEVELAND, S. A three-generation view of a school phobia. *Voices*, 1967,*3*, 16–19.
A case report in support of the notion that psychopathology is "passed on from generation to generation with more or less specific way and expectation of handling it." Three generations of data from the identified patient (a 14-year-old boy), his mother, and maternal grandmother were obtained from clinical psychiatric interviews and the Rorschach and thematic apperception tests. School phobia of the identified patient is seen as an attempt to answer the obsessive concern of a boy's relationship to his mother and her relationship to her mother.

MENDELL, D., CLEVELAND, S., & FISHER, S. A five-generation family theme. *Family Process*, 1968, 7, 126–132.
A study examining projective test fantasies of family members. Five generations of one family, including examination

of 27 members, were conducted. It was found that a family selects one or two central themes which are perpetuated in the responses of family members across generations.

MILLER, D. R., & WESTMAN, J. C. Family teamwork and psychotherapy. *Family Process*, 1966, *5*, 49–59.
A discussion of primary questions about etiology and treatment developed in a study of functional retardation in reading. In one type of reading difficulty the problem can be explained by poor teaching or traumatic experiences, and in the other there is a function in the family. The roots of the symptom in family relationships is described with an emphasis upon family teamwork in maintaining the difficulty.

MINUCHIN, S. Family therapy: Technique or theory? In J. Masserman (Ed.), *Science and Psychoanalysis Vol. XIV: Childhood and Adolescence.* New York: Grune & Stratton, 1969.
A discussion of family therapy with the emphasis upon the need to take into account the total ecology of the family. "I think that family therapy . . . will be in danger of ossification if it fails to move towards an ecological theory of man."

MINUCHIN, S. The use of an ecological framework in the treatment of a child. In E. J. Anthony & C. Koupernik (Eds.), *The child in his family*, New York: Wiley, 1970.
A discussion of the three elements in the study of the child: as an individual, in his environment, and the linkage between the two. A case of an adolescent with *anorexia nervosa* is dealt within terms of his family and the family therapy approach to the problem.

MISHLER, E., & WAXLER, N. Family interaction processes and schizophrenia. *Internation Journal of Psychiatry*, 1966, *2*, 375–430.
A critical and extensive review of the theories of the relationship between family interaction and schizophrenia, with major space devoted to the work of the Bateson, Lidz, and Wynne groups. The purpose of the review was to see how the theories could be tested and used as guidelines for research. The major contributions of these groups are to the theory of the etiology of schizophrenia, by focussing on the family and its methods of interactions, rather than on the individual. Critical evaluations by Bateson, Lidz, Spiegel, and Wynne of the article and the various theories contained in it are included.

MISHLER, E. G. & WAXLER, N. E. The sequential patterning of interaction in normal and schizophrenic families. *Family Process*, 1975, *14*, 17–50.
This paper focuses n the sequential patterning of interaction through time. The primary statistical method used is a modification of multivariate informational analyses (MIA). The underlying rationale is provided by information theory. Families differed from each other more significantly in triact analyses. Normal families had frequent mother-father coalitions and included more triadic sequences. Differences tended to cluster in comparison where the patient-son dyad was present in the discussion.

MORRIS, G., & WYNNE, L. Schizophrenic offspring, parental styles of communication. *Psychiatry*, 1965, *28*, 19–44.
One of a series of papers reporting a study of parental styles of communication and schizophrenic children. Data were selected from excerpts of transcripts of conjoint family sessions with 12 families. Predictions about the most disturbed offspring were made by a judge blind to the clinical aspects of the case. Predictive criteria were then reformulated using the data from a parallel study utilizing psychological test material as predictors. These reformulated criteria were then utilized for blind predictions on eight new families. Results indicated that the style of the family communication can be related to the thought and affect disorder in schizophrenics.

MOSHER, L., WILD, C., VALCOV, A., et al. Cognitive style, schizophrenia, and the family: Methodological implications of contextual effects. *Family Process*, 1972, *11*, 125–146.
This study examines the nature of and the relationship between individual and family transactional cognitive styles. Measures included clinical examination of the family unit, dyads, triads, individual interviews, home visits and testing on the Object Sorting Test, Embedded Figures Test, TAT, Draw-a-Person Test, Wechsler Adult Intelligence Scale, and Rorschach of one family (parents and their one schizophrenic and one normal daughter). All members were independently rated for: global psychopathology, diagnosis of schizophrenia, type of thought disorder (qualitative), thought disorder (quantitative), cognitive style, and identification. Results showed that there were great individual and group variability across contexts. There are serious questions about generalizing from one-measure or one-context studies of cognitive functioning.

MUIR, R. The family and the problem of internalization. *British Journal of Medical Psychology*, 1975, *48*, 267–272.
An attempt is made to integrate concepts derived from family therapy with those from psychoanalytic therapy. Particular focus is on the concept of "internalization," and a case example is presented in support of the theory that family interactional forces may be more powerful than intrapsychic forces, i.e., family integrity may outweight all other considerations "including the subject's own libidinal interests, rights, and even survival."

MURRELL, S., & STACHOWIAK, J. The family group: Development structure and therapy. *Journal of Marriage and the Family*, 1965, *27*, 13–18.

From the literature, authors previous experience, and previous research, a theory of the family is presented. Assumptions in terms of therapy are discussed. Families are viewed as being unable to problem-solve and as resistant to change.

NIMKOFF, M. F. & MIDDLETON, R. Types of family and types of economy. *American Journal of Sociology*, 1961, *66*, 215–225.
The relationship between family types and subsistence patterns is explored with reference to 549 societies in the World Ethnographic Survey. Two family types—the independent (normally only one nuclear or polygamous family) and the extended (whether laterally, vertically, or both), and 11 subsistence types (e.g., hunting and gathering dominant, agriculture dominant) are distinguished. The independent family is found to be associated with hunting and the extended family with agriculture. The associations are accounted for in terms of food supply, demand for family labor, physical mobility and property.

O'CONNER, W. A. & STACHOWIAK, J. Patterns of interaction in families with low adjusted, high adjusted and mentally retarded members. *Family Process*, 1971, *10*, 229–241.
This experiment is designed to describe differences in patterns of family interaction in three groups of eight families: families with a low adjusted child prior to formal clinic contact, with a high (well) adjusted child, and families with a well adjusted mentally retarded child. Participants were selected by school personnel and all families had an eldest male child between 10 and 12 years of age and a younger school-age child. Interactions were measured with regard to adaptation, stability, productivity, specificity, overt power, conflict, cohesion and emotionality. Results indicate low cohesion in the low adjusted group, high cohesion and conflict in the high adjusted group and high cohesion in the group with mentally retarded children. The study also found that the retarded child is assigned the "youngest-sib" role in their families.

OPLER, M. K. Social and cultural influences on the psychopathology of family groups. In G. H. Zuk, & I. Boszormenyi-Nagy (Eds.), *Family therapy and disturbed families*. Palo Alto: Science & Behavior Books, 1967.
An essay considering the social context of the family as related to mental health. Examples from different cultures are given.

OTTO, H. A. Criteria for assessing family strength. *Family Process*, 1963, *2*, 329–339.
A discussion of family strengths and resources with the data collected by questionnaire. Twenty-seven families were queried. Married couples met for group discussions on family strengths. A set of criteria for assessing family strengths is offered.

PATTISON, E. M. et al. A psychosocial kinship model for family therapy. *American Journal of Psychiatry*, 1975, *132*, 1246–1251.
The focus here is on extending the family model beyond the intact, nuclear family to include different kinds of families (e.g., one-parent families). Based on the Pattison Psychosocial Kinship Inventory, the system and its role in creating disturbed behavior are described, as well as possible implications for treatment.

PENISTON, D. H. The importance of "death education" in family life. *Family Life Coordinator*, 1962, *11*, 15–18.
A discussion by a pastor of the need to educate families for preparation for a possible death in the family. Includes discussions of death as a taboo area like sex; disruption of family life caused by death; and the importance of preparing professional men to deal wisely with bereaved families.

POLLAK, O. Developmental difficulties and the family system. In O. Pollak, & A. S. Friedman (Eds.), *Family dynamics and female sexual delinquency*. Palo Alto: Science & Behavior Books, 1969.
A discussion of the development and growth of family members as a person moves from the family unit in which he is born, to the family he creates through marriage, to the family of his children to which he eventually relates as a dependent.

POLLAK, O. Family structure: Its implications for mental health. In O. Pollak, & A. S. Friedman (Eds.), *Family dynamics and female sexual delinquency*. Palo Alto: Science & Behavior Books, 1969.
A discussion of the implications for mental health of various types of family structure. Compared are middle-class families, fatherless families, and three-generation families.

PRINCE, A. J. A study of 194 cross-religion marriages. *Family Life Coordinator*, 1962, *11*, 3–7.
A report on a study of 142 interfaith marriages and 52 marriages between protestants of different demoninations. Data were obtained with questionnaires. Topics of interest are cross-religion marriages, major areas of conflict, changes in church attendance patterns, degree of satisfaction with marriage, and attitudes about cross-religion marriages for children.

PULVER, S. E., & BRUNT, M. Y. Deflection of hostility in folie à deux. *Archives of General Psychiatry*, 1961, *5*, 257–265.

Three cases are presented to illustrate a description of the psychodymnamics of the transfer of delusions. The partners are divided into the primary and secondary with the primary partner strongly dependent upon the secondary. As the primary partner begins to feel taken advantage of and increasingly angry, his anger against the secondary partner is projected onto an outsider as paranoid delusion. When the secondary partner does not support the delusion, the direct hositility toward the secondary partner becomes intolerable and the secondary partner deflects it by accepting the delusion and joining in the projection.

RABKIN, R. Uncoordinated communication between marriage partners. *Family Process*, 1967, *6*, 10–15.
A discussion of communication codes unique to particular family systems. Examples of couples' problems in developing mutual codes are given.

RANSOM, J. W. & SCHLESINGER, S. & DERDEYN, A. P. A stepfamily formation. *American Journal of Orthopsychiatry*, 1979, *49*, 36–43.
This paper discusses the evolution of families that include children from the parents' prior marriages. Borrowing from theories of the developmental stages of a biological family, three phases are described, ending with "reconstitution" of the family. Examples of problems, e.g., scapegoating, are discussed and one case report is included.

RAPORPORT, R. The family and psychiatric treatment. *Psychiatry*, 1960, *23*, 53–62.
A conceptual framework for analyzing family relationships and role performance of psychiatric patients applied to a case. Three areas are considered important in conceptualizing role difficulties: familial position, personal and social norms, and personality factors. This framework is applied to a case presented in detail.

RAUSH, H. L. Process and change—A Markov model for interaction. *Family Process*, 1972, *11*, 275–298.
This paper examines family, dyadic and group relationships, utilizing the finite Markov chain as a model. The Markov chain permits the analysis and evaluation of a complex mult-determined relation as it evolves through time. The model encompasses both stability and change, and it yields implications for personal, interpersonal, and environmental modifications. Illustrative examples demonstrate the applications of this model.

RAVICH, R. A. A system of dyadic interaction. *Family Process*, 1970, *9*, 297–300.
A description of a notation for two-person interaction based upon the *I Ching*, or *Book of changes*.

RAVICH, R. A. A system of notation of dyadic interaction. *Family Process*, 1970, *9*, 297–300.
The necessity of organizing the large quantity of data derived from the use of the Ravich Interpersonal Game-Test (RIG/T) has led to the development of a system of notation of two-person interaction. Only either-or decisions of each person in a dyad being tested is recorded. The source of the system of notation utilized is the I Ching, or Book of Changes.

RAYBIN, J. The curse: A study in family communication. *American Journal of Psychiatry*, 1970, *127*, 617–625.
The curse is a particular type of family communication usually expressing a wish that some harm befall another family member and often connoting that the one who curses has the magical power to cause the harm to occur. It usually spans several generations. Four case examples are presented in support of this concept—one patient thought she was a "bad seed," a second case involved homosexual incest, and the last two, suicidal behavior which ran through the family. Family therapy, as well as other therapies, are recommended to treat this disorder.

RAYMOND, M. E., SLABY, A. E., & LIEB, J. Familial responses to mental illness. *Social Casework*, 1975, *56*, 492–498.
This is a clinical essay describing the typical sequential pattern of response to the mental illness of one member of the family. Phases usually overlap and often vary in intensity and include: (1) beginning uneasiness; (2) need for reassurance; (3) denial and minimizing; (4) anger and blame; (5) guilt, shame and grief; (6) confusion in the changed family; and (7) acceptance of reality. Therapists often have similar responses to the family. Suggestions for dealing with these responses are made.

RENDON, M. The family and defense mechanisms. *American Journal of Psychoanalysis*, 1974, *34*, 347–350.
This is a paper presented at the Karen Horney Clinic which compares the psychoanalytic model of the individual to the family systems model. Several "defensive" family functions such as scapegoating, role reversal of parent and child, and family "secrets" are discussed and defined using psychoanalytic terms. Family therapy and psychoanalysis are not mutually exclusive, but complement each other. Antagonism between their proponents is explained as the result of "ideological" politics.

RICHARDSON, H. B. A family as seen in the hospital. In P. H. Glasser, & L. N. Glasser (Eds.), *Families in Crisis*. New York: Harper & Row, 1970.
Families who are involved with a medical hospital are studied from various points of view. The family is discussed as seen by staff, the records, the patient, and the conversation of individual family members.

RISKIN, J. Family interaction scales: A preliminary report. *Archives of General Psychiatry*, 1964, *11*, 484–494.
A report on a research project where nine families were given a structured interview and the conversation categorized. Two minute segments of the conversation are categorized by the coder as clear, change of topic, commitment, and so on. An attempt is then made to describe the family from the coding sheets blindly. "Results suggest that it is possible to make clinically meaningful and accurate descriptions of the whole family and of its various members based on the coded speeches and without focussing on the content."

RISKIN, J. Methodology for studying family interaction. *Archives of General Psychiatry*, 1963, *8*, 343–348.
A report of a pilot study with five families designed to develop a conceptual framework, including methods for investigating the relationship between family interaction and personality formation. Family members are brought together in standardized structured interviews with the tape recorded conversations analyzed by a set of categories which include clarity, content, agreement, commitment, congruency, intensity, and attack or acceptance of the other person.

ROSENBAUM, C. P. Patient–Family similarities in schizophrenia. *Archives of General Psychiatry*, 1961, *5*, 120–126.
See Reference in Section 5.2.

ROSENTHAL, M. J., NI, E., FINKELSTEIN, M., & BERKWITZ, G. K. Father–child relationships and children's problems *Archives of General Psychiatry*, 1962, *7*, 360–373.
A group of 405 new patients coming into the institute for Juvenile Research in Chicago were examined to determine whether the emotional problems of children were related to certain types of father-child relationships. the relationships was examined by interviews with parents and children. Certain of the children's problems were found to be correlated with types of father-child relationships being studied while others were not.

RUTTER, M. Sex differences in children's responses to family stress. In E. J. Anthony & C. Koupernik (Eds.), *The child in his family*. New York: Wiley, 1970.
A questionnaire study investigating the impact on the child of marital problems and parental psychiatric disorders. Antisocial behavior in boys is associated with disturbance in ramily relationships, but the marriage rating bore no relation to the rate of disorder in girls. Theoretical discussion is offered.

SANDER, F. M. Family therapy or religion: A rereading of T. S. Eliot's *The cocktail party*. *Family Process*, 1970, *9*, 279–296.
An analysis of the play, *The Cocktail Party*, from the view of analytic sociology, emphasizing family therapy as a response to changes in the structure of contemporary families.

SANDER, F. M. Marriage and the family in Freud's writings. *American Academy of Psychoanalysis*, 1978, *6*, 157–174.
See reference in Section 4.1.

SANUA, V. The sociocultural aspects of childhood schizophrenia. In G. H. Zuk, & I. Boszormenyi-Nagy (Eds.), *Family therapy and disturbed families*. Palo Alto: Science & Behavior Books, 1967.
A discussion of methodological issues, research strategies, and the problems inherent in studying parent-child relationships and interaction as an etiological factor in schizophrenia. Includes a review of the literature.

SAUNA, V. Sociocultural factors in families of schizophrenics: A review of the literature. *Psychiatry*, 1961, *24*, 246–265.
A review of the literature on the etiology of schizophrenia. Problems and methodology are looked at and the literature is discussed from the point of view of data from hospital records, from separate interviews with patients and families, from interviews of families together, from studies using personality tests, from questionnaires and rating scales, and from studies using the cross-cultural approach. All these studies boil down to looking at the problem one of four ways: (1) parental troubles transmitted to the children, (2) family structure, (3) disturbed interactional patterns, and (4) geneic and consitutional factors in the child.

SATIR, V. M. The family as a treatment unit. *Confinia Psychiatrica*, 1965, *8*, 37–42.
A discussion of family therapy with the emphasis on concepts of interaction. The family is discussed as a closed and open system and "appropriate outcomes" for the family are said to be "decisions and behavior which fit the age, ability, and role of the individuals, which fit the role contracts and the context involved, and which further the common goals of the family."

SATIR, V. Family systems and approaches to family therapy. *Journal of Fort Logan Mental Health Center*, 1967, *4*, 81–93.
An essay focussing on development of the concept of the famiy as a system. How it functions and what happens when the family system breaks down are discussed.

SCHEFLEN, A. E. Communicational arrangements which further specify meaning. *Family Process*, 1970, *9*, 457–472.
This paper is an excerpt presentation on the topic of "metabehavior and meaning." It relates to the communicational patterns utilized by an individual or by two persons in the course of presentations. Different combinations, patterns and sequences, are described; most of them are presented consciously and influenced by the cultural arrangements of the presenters and in the context of the audience.

SCHEFLEN, A. E. Regressive one-to-one relationships. *Psychiatric Quarterly*, 1960, *34*, 692–709.
A description of regressive attachments between two individuals. The characteristics of these "gruesome twosomes" are: limitations of relatedness to others, decreasing gratification within the relationships, and the maintenance of the attachment by mutual exploitation of the partner's anxieties by such means as threats of desertion and arousal of guilt. Several variations of this type of relationship are presented and illustrated with four case histories involving differing sex and age combinations. There is a discussion of differentiating between neurotic and non-neurotic one-to-one relationships.

SCHERZ, F. The crisis of adolescence in family life. *Social Casework*, 1967, *48*, 209–215.
Adolescence is seen as a time of crisis for the family, in addition to the patient. When behavioral symptoms come up, family treatment is indicated. The influence of grandparents in family communication is discussed.

SCHULMAN, G. L. The changing American family: For better or worse. *International Journal of Family Therapy*, 1979., *1*, 9–21.
This is a theoretical paper on the viability of the American family. It still exists because it is defined by its functions (e.g., childrearing), not its structure (i.e., member composition). Basic characteristics of all families, (e.g., conflicts of autonomy versus need to belong to a group) and current sources of pressure for change are discussed.

SCOTT, R. Perspectives on the American Family Studies in Schizophrenia. *Confinia Psychiatrica*, 1965, *8*, 43–48. See Reference in Section 5.2.

SHAPIRO, R. L. The origin of adolescent disturbances in the family: Some considerations in theory and implications for therapy. In G. H. Zuk, & I. Boszormenyi-Nagy (Eds.), *Family therapy and disturbed families*, Palo Alto: Science & Behavior Books, 1967.
The study of the current family relations of the adolescent helps to identify the nature of determinants in his developmental experience. Verbatim excerpts from interviews are presented and therapeutic design is discussed.

SHERMAN, S., BEATMAN, F. L., & ACKERMAN, N. W. Concepts of family striving and family distress: The contribution of M. Robert Gomberg. *Social Casework*, 1958, *39*, 383–391.
A review of the ideas of M. Robert Gomberg with emphasis upon his writings on family process, family stability and instability, and therapeutic intervention.

SHOHAN, S., & RAHAV, G. Social stigma and prostitution. *Ana. Int. de Criminolog.*, 1967, *6*, 479–513.
An attempt to relate the "stigma theory of crime and deviation to the etiology of prostitution in authoritarian oriental families." The population examined are the Jewish North-African immigrants to Israel and the conclusion is that "the processes of differential identification and association leading the girl to a full-fledged life of prostitution are the final stages of a dynamic process initiated by the girl's compliance with a stigmatizing role case on her within the family."

SLUZKI, C. Transactional disqualification: Research on the double bind. *Archives of General Psychiatry*, 1967, *16*, 494–504.
This is one of a series of papers stemming from a research project on communication in families with schizophrenic patients. Transactional disqualification is a form of communication in which the subject can verbally or non-verbally deny the previous communication. This persistant pattern of relating can lead to schizophrenic symptoms.

SLUZKI, C. & BEAVIN, J. "Simetria y Complementariada: Una Definición Operacional y Una Tipologia de Parejas," *Acta Psiquiatrica y Psicologica De America Latina*, 1965, *11*, 321–330.
A discussion of classifying relationships in terms of symmetry and complementarity, with a review of the literature on the subject. The variables are operationally defined and a speech score is derived based upon analysis of the transactional unit. A typology of couples and other dyads is proposed composed of seven possible configurations based upon these modalities of interaction.

SLUZKI, C. E. & VERON, E. The double bind as a universal pathogenic situation. *Family Process*, 1971, *10*, 397–410.
The authors examine the etiology of three types of neurosis: hysteric, phobic and obsessive-compulsive. They draw on specific learning contexts and experiences of several patients around the dependence versus independence conflict of development. They conclude that the paradoxes created by the double-bind lead to these pathological states and may well define a universal pathogenic situation, not limited to the genesis of schizophrenia.

SOJIT, C. M. The double bind hypothesis and the parents of schizophrenics. *Family Process*, 1971, *10*, 53–74.
See Reference in Section 5.2.

SOLOMON, M. A. A developmental, conceptual premise for family therapy. *Family Process*, 1973, *12*, 179–188.
This article subdivides the developmental stages of the family in five periods: the marriage, the birth of the first child
and subsequent child bearing, individuation of family members, the actual departure of children, and the integration
of loss. These various stages have implications for diagnostic and treatment purposes in family therapy.

SOLVBERG, H. A. & BLAKAR, R. M. Communication efficiency in couples with and without a schizophrenic
offspring. *Family Process*, 1975, *14*, 515–534.
See reference in Section 3.4.

SONNE, J. C. Entropic communication in families with adolescents. *International Journal of Family Therapy*, 1979, *1*,
276–289.
From the author's clinical work three case examples are used to define and illustrate the concepts of "entropy" and
"negentropy" as they relate to communication within a family. In a normal family with an adolescent, communication
will tend towards growth and more organization, i.e., "a negentropic shift." In a disordered family, communication will
tend to pull the family apart and isolate members, i.e., an "entropic shift."

SONNE, J. C. Entropy and family therapy: Speculations on psychic energy, thermodynamics, and family interpsychic
communication. In G. H. Zuk, & I. Boszormenyi-Nagy (Eds.), *Family therapy and disturbed families*. Palo Alto:
Science & Behavior Books, 1967.
An attempt to link together concepts from the physical sciences with observations of schizophrenic families in
treatment with special emphasis upon the concept of entropy.

SORRELLS, J., & FORD, F. Toward an integrated theory of families and family therapy. *Psychotherapy*, 1969, *6*,
150–160.
A theoretical paper describing a theory of family functioning and family treatment. All family members have self-
needs, self-want and self-concepts. The family operates in a system using certain communication devices which
maintain a homeostasis. Concepts of status quo, decision-making autonomy and distortion of feedback are discussed.
Techniques of treatment including making the contract, diagnosis, interventions, and goals are discussed.

SPARK, G. M., & BRODY, E. M. The aged are family members. *Family Process*, 1970, *9*, 195–210.
A discussion of the involvement of older family members and the important roles they play in family dynamics.
Including them in treatment can prevent cyclical repetition of pathological relationship patterns.

SPECK, R. Family therapy in the home. *Journal of Marriage and the Family*, 1964, *26*, 72–76.
An essay based on the author's clinical experience in doing family therapy in the home. Advantages of this technique
are dicussed and several new phenomena are described: the absent member, the most disturbed family member, the
youngest member, the role of pets, the extended family, and family secrets.

SPECK, R., & ATTNEAVE, C. Network therapy. In J. Haley (Ed.), *Changing families*. New York: Grune & Stratton,
1971.
A report on "network therapy" where all of the significant people of a natural group are brought together in relation to
a problem. The theory, practice, techniques, and effects of assembling the "tribe" are described.

SPEER, D. C. Family systems: Morphostasis and morphogenesis, or "Is Homeostasis Enough?" *Family Process*,
1970, *9*, 259–278.
It is argued that homeostasis is insufficient as a basic explanatory principle for family systems. The needs for
considering positive feedback processes and variety are emphasized.

SPIEGEL, J. Interpersonal influence within the family. In B. Schaffner (Ed.), *Group Processes: Transactions of the
third conference*. New York: Josiah Macy, Jr. Foundation, 1956.
A group discussion of the findings from the author's research project (which had been previously reported in a series
of papers) of an interdisciplinary study of the effects of conflicts between cultural-value orientations of the processes
of interaction within the family, and consequently the development of health or pathology of the individual members
of the family. There are discussions of normal and pathological equilibrium in the family and a classification of social
roles.

SPIEGEL, J. Mental health and the family. *New England Journal of Medicine*, 1954, *251*, 843–846.
"Complex psychological, social, and somatic forces are interwoven in the dynamics of family adjustment." Family
dynamics and a model of family relationships are discussed.

SPIEGEL, J. New perspectives in the study of the family. *Marriage and Family Living*, 1954, *16* 4–12.

A clinical essay attempting to formulate a dynamic model for understanding the whole family rather than individuals. There are marked value clashes and role conflicts within variant families that are in transition towards the dominant middle-class model. Family dynamics as well as individual dynamics must be taken into account to understand families. More information on values, and role and value conflicts encountered in various family systems are also needed.

SPIEGEL, J. The resolution of role conflict within the family. *Psychiatry*, 1957, *20*, 1–16.
An offshoot of a study between cultural value conflict and the emotional adjustment of the identified patient, this essay analyzes the concept of social role and its relation to the functional or dysfunctional behavior in the family. "Equilibrium—disequilibrium balance and its relationship to role" is examined, as well as how role modification is achieved. Disequilibrium can lead to symptoms in the patient.

SPIEGEL, J. Some cultural aspects of transference and counter transference. In J. Masserman (Ed.), *Science and psychoanalysis (Vol. II) Individual and family dynamics.* New York: Grune & Stratton, 1959.
See Reference in Section 5.4.

SPIEGEL, J., & BELL, N. The family of the psychiatric patient. In S. Arieti (Ed.), *American handbook of psychiatry.* New York: Basic Books, 1959.
A chapter in a textbook on psychiatry dealing with sections on the history of the role of the family in mental illness; etiologic studies of parent-child interactions and development of various mental illnesses including schizophrenia, psychoneurosis, and acting-out disorders; the impact of mental illness upon the family; the family and treatment procedures; and new approaches to the family and its pathology, including family therapy. There are 238 references.

STACHOWIAK, J. Decision-making and conflict resolution in the family group. In C. Larson & F. Dance (Eds.), *Perspectives on Communication*, Milwaukee: University of Wisconsin, Speech Communication Center, 1968.
The author discusses his previous research summarizing major findings on: (1) family productivity—which is decreased in "sick families," (2) influence of individual members—maladaptive families showed distinct hierarchal ordering of members, (3) conflict in which maladaptive families showed more aggression and hostility than adaptive families, and (4) communication, which was disturbed in maladaptive families. Implications for future research are discussed.

STENNETT, R. Family diagnosis: MMPI and CTP results. *Journal of Clinical Psychology*, 1966, *22*, 165–167.
MMPI and CTP (California Test of Personality) tests were done on 230 families over a five-year period in an out-patient clinic to answer several questions about family dynamics. Families were urban, Protestant, white with wide socioeconomic status. The CTP was given to children from age four up to 13. Findings were that a significant number of family members other than the identified patient had personality problems of their own, that there was a significant correlation in the level of psychopathology between the parents of troubled families, but no evidence was found of conflicting or complementary personality characteristics in the parents.

STIERLIN, H. Shame and guilt in family relations. *Archives of General Psychiatry*, 1974, *30*, 381–392.
This is a clinical essay about shame and guilt in terms of family theory and dynamics. These processes serve homeostatic functions in a family. The positive aspects are described and compared in two families in which the shame and guilt became restrictive and interfered with individuation and separation. Suggestions for therapy are made, and several case examples are presented in support of the theory.

STIERLIN, H., LEVI, D. L., & SAVARD, R. J. Parental perceptions of separating children. *Family Process*, 1971, *10*, 411–427.
The authors have drawn on some of the newer models of familial interactions which emphasize the importance of the parental perceptions of a child as a determinant of his/her own self-image and established relationships with others. They have examined this phenomenon in the context of the developmental phase of separation and individuation in adolescence in several family situations where treatment was sought. Some implications for therapy are discussed briefly.

STREAN, H. S. A family therapist looks at "Little Hans." *Family Process*, 1967, *6*, 227–234.
A reexamination of the case of Little Hans from the point of view of the family as the unit of diagnosis and treatment. The case is said to be "an excellent illustration of how a symptom of one member binds and protects a whole family constellation."

STRODTBECK, F. L. The family as a three-person group. *American Sociological Review*, 1954, 23–29.
A research study attempting to replicate findings of Mills in relation to three-person groups. The sample was 48 cases including father, mother, and adolescent son. They were asked to fill out alternatives to 47 items. The study was done in the family homes and tape recorded. Decision-making power was associated with high participation and when the two most active members show "solidarity" in their relation to one another, the stability of their rank participation is high. When the two most active members were in conflict, stability was as low for these families as for the other families.

STRODTBECK, F. L. The interaction of a "Henpecked" husband with his wife. *Marriage and Family Living*, 1952, *14*, 305–308.
A clinical case report on the psychodynamics of being "henpecked." Method was the revealed differences test. Compared to other couples, althought the wife was more dominant, it was "not so painful in practice as the community gossip would lead one to believe." Interaction sequence is a more accurate way of assessing family dynamics than community observation.

SUSSMAN, M. B. Adaptive, directive, and integrative behavior of today's family. *Family Process*, 1968, 7, 239–250. See Reference in Section 4.5.

TAYLOR, W. R. Research on family interaction. I: Static and dynamic models. *Family Process*, 1970, 9, 221–232.
A comparison of static and dynamic models of family structure illustrated with a clinical example. The emphasis is upon the Markov process where a state is succeeded by other possible states.

TAYLOR, W. R. Using sysems theory to organize confusion. *Family Process*, 1979, *18*, 479–488.
This paper is an attempt to apply the symbolic logic developed by Spencer Brown and elaborated by Francisco Varela to complex clinical situations. The author claims that this model is a useful transitional step toward the future use of quantitative models.

TESSMAN, L. H., & KAUFMAN, I. Variations on a theme of incest. In O. Pollak, & A. S. Friedman (Eds.), *Family dynamics and female sexual delinquency*. Palo Alto: Science & Behavior Books, 1969.
A discussion of incest occuring in families with young girls, either in fantasy or fact, with case examples.

THARP, R., & OTIS, G. Toward a theory for therapeutic intervention in families. *Journal of Consulting Psychology*, 1966, *30*, 426–434.
Family roles are characterized into five functional entities: solidarity, sexuality, internal instrumentality, external relations, and division of responsibility. Data were obtained from the authors' clinical work. A discrepancy between the expectations and the actual performance can lead to symptoms. Interventions to make the roles more consonant are described with three case illustrations presented in support of these concepts.

TITCHENER, J. L. Family systems as a model for ego system. In G. H. Zuk, & I. Boszormenyi-Nagy (Eds.), *Family therapy and disturbed families*. Palo Alto: Science & Behavior Books, 1967.
A discussion of the importance of an intrapsychic point of view in the comprehension of family process, the family system phase of ego development, and how family life influences the maturing ego.

TOWNE, R. D., MESSINGER, S. L., & SAMPSON, H. Schizophrenia and the marital family: Accommodations to symbiosis. *Family Process*, 1962, *1*, 304–318.
Another in a series of reports by this group of their study of 17 women who as young adults had experienced severe difficulties in their marital families, and were hospitalized with a diagnosis of schizophrenia. Here the focus was on the "symbiotic" nature of the family relationships which seem to serve to keep the families together, and when broken down led to hospitalization of the wife. Three patterns are described.

TYLER, E. A. The process of humanizing physiological man. *Family Process*, 1964, *3*, 280–301.
A general discussion of how "man, the physiological animal, becomes man, the social human" is presented as a social theory of human behavior. The individual is traced through various stages of socialization development from infancy to old age.

VERON, E., KORNBLIT, A., MALFE, R., & SLUZKI, C. E. Estructures de conducta y Sistemas de comunicacion social (Conduct structures and systems of social communication). *Acta Psiquiatrica Y Psicologica Argentina*, 1963, *9*, 297.
A conceptual model for the sociological study of psychoneurosis is described, which includes three strategic levels: individual; familial (group structure); and social stratification, including cultural structures. The recurrence of certain conduct structures in an individual, that is, of generalized ways of interaction, is the result of a meta-communicative process of learning, i.e., deutero-learning. The presence of recurrent ways of learning in a family group is a function of the family organization as communication system. The persistence of certain types of communication within the family group is a function of the socio-cultural context which influences the family.

VINCENT, C. E. Mental health and the family. In P. H. Glasser, & L. N. Glasser (Eds.), *Families in crisis*. New York: Harper & Row, 1970.
A selective review of broad developments and trends in the emerging role of the federal government in the mental health field. The relevance of the family to mental health and community mental health centers is discussed with a review. Present needs are discussed.

VISHER, F. B., & VISHER, J. S. Common problems of stepparents and their spouses. *American Journal of Orthopsychiatry*, 1978, *48*, 252–262.

Using case material from private practice, common problems experienced by stepparents and their spouses as well as common myths about stepfamilies are presented. Professionals should understand and support stepparents, whose difficult struggle to adjust to new families is a major modern family therapy problem.

VOGEL, E. F., & BELL, N. W. The emotionally disturbed child as the family scapegoat. In N. W. Bell, & E. F. Vogel (Eds.), *A modern introduction to the family*, Glencoe: Free Press, 1960.
A discussion of families with disturbed children in terms of the child's function as a scapegoat. Topics include selection of the child for scapegoating, the induction of him into this role, and the rationalizations.

WALKER, K. N., & MESSINGER, L. Remarriage after divorce: Dissolution and reconstruction of family boundaries. *Family Process*, 1979, *18*, 185–192.
This paper examines remarriage from the perspective of family boundaries and roles. Remarried persons have dual memberships in two families. "Successful" remarriage families would be those who acknowledge the prior allegiance and affection that may exist between parents and children, but also expect some sense of membership in the remarriage household. Members of these two families would have to learn to live with two sets of relatively permeable boundaries.

WALLACE, A. F., & FOGELSON, R. D. The identity struggle. In I. Boszormenyi-Nagy, & J. L. Framo (Eds.), *Intensive family therapy*. New York: Harper & Row, 1965.
Anthropological observers of a family therapy program discuss "representative instances of identity struggle" observed in the treatment of the family of the schizophrenic.

WARKENTIN, J. Marriage: The cornerstone of the family system. In O. Pollak, & A. S. Friedman (Eds.), *Family dynamics and female sexual delinquency*. Palo Alto: Science & Behavior Books, 1969.
A description of the inner assumptions and postulates about human nature and marriage of two experienced therapists. The emphasis is upon the importance of the therapist's views about life when dealing with a family.

WARKENTIN, J., & WHITAKER, C. Serial impasses in marriage. In I. M. Cohen (Ed.), *Psychiatric research report No. 20*. Washington, D.C.: American Psychiatric Association, 1966.
A discussion of marriage as both a legal and an emotional commitment with special emphasis upon the times "when we may expect difficulty and even impasse in the development of the emotional marriage." These times include the wedding night, pregnancy, the second baby, and the "ten year syndrome."

WATZLAWICK, P. A review of the double bind theory. *Family Process*, 1963, *2*, 132–153.
A presentation of the comments on the double bind theory occurring in the literature from 1957–1961. The comments are discussed and excerpts presented.

WAXLER, N. E., & MISHLER, E. G. Sequential patterning in family interaction: A methodological note. *Family Process*, 1970, *9*, 211–220.
Rate-of-participation scores have found widespread use to index certain features of family structure. Haley argued that a high level of predictability in who follows whom indicates a relatively rigid or organized family structure. A sample of schizophrenic families is compared with normal families; the results do not support Haley's hypothesis.

WEAKLAND, J. H. The double bind hypothesis of schizophrenia and three-party interaction. In D. D. Jackson (Ed.), *The etiology of schizophrenia*. New York: Basic Books, 1960.
A discussion of the double bind as it applies to three party situations. Described are mother, father, child relationships and such institutional relationships as administration–therapist–patient and doctor–nurse–patient.

WELLER, L. The relationship of birth order to anxiety: a replication of the Schacter findings. *Sociometry*, 1962, *25*, 415–417.
Schacter (*The psychology of affiliation*) showed that first-born and only children became more anxious in threatening situations than later-born children. Schacter's experimental procedures were repeated with 234 female under-graduates. Anxiety was assessed by an adjective check list and a questionnaire. No relationship of birth order and anxiety appear, contradicting Schacter's findings. The author suggests that birth order in itself may be too simple and needs to be considered in conjunction with other variables.

WERTHEIM, F. S. The science and typology of family systems. II: Further theoretical and practical considerations. *Family Process*, 1975, *14*, 285–309.
Typology of family systems is based on the assumption derived from general systems theory whereby under normal conditions human behavior is an adaptive, active organized process, subject to controls that regulate the ongoing exchanges between the given social system and its micro- and macro-environment. Morphostasis which insures systemic stability and morphogenesis which enables the system to change are discussed in terms of the system-

processing of pragmatic perceptual meaning. Implications of the present theoretical raitonale and general issues concerning psychological theory are explored.

WEST. S. S. Sibling configurations of scientists. *American Journal of Sociology*, 1960, *66*, 268–274.
Birth order and the number of siblings of 813 scientists were obtained as part of a study of six research organizations. The aim was to determine what type of family experience is associated with choice of research as a career. First, fifth, and sixth birth ranks are over-represented; second, third, and fourth are under-represented. Siblings are distributed randomly as regards sex. Comparison with data on the general population indicates that a sibship size increases, probability of a scientist coming from family decreased. Isolation in childhood is said to be important in developing the characteristics of a scientist. Data support either a hypothesis that relative isolation is necessary for research career, or the hypothesis that mothers of scientists have fewer children than normal.

WESTLEY, W., & EPSTEIN, N. Family structure and emotional health: A case study approach. *Marriage and Family Living*, 1960, *22*, 25–27.
One of a series of papers from a study of the emotional health of nine families, each of which contained at least one emotionally healthy adolescent. In studying the grandmothers of these emotionally healthy families, it was found that they were seen as "cold and manipulative," while the fathers were seen as "warm and supportive." The attitude of these mothers, as towards their husbands, was one of seeing husbands as they had seen their fathers. The marital relationship was "warm and well adjusted." The mental health of the subjects was influenced more by the organization of the nuclear families, than by the mental health of the grandparents.

WESTLEY, W., & EPSTEIN, N. Patterns of intra-familial communication. *Psychiatric research report No. 11.* Washington, D.C.: American Psychiatric Association, 1959.
A research report attempting to describe intrafamily communication patterns. Nine healthy families with an adolescent were studied using clinical interview, the Rorschach and the TAT. Nine categories of family function are described and patterns of overt communication versus other types of communication are described.

WESTMAN, J. C., MILLER, D. R., & ARTHUR, B. Psychiatric symptoms and family dynamics as illustrated by the retarded reader. In I. M. Cohen (Ed.), *Psychiatric research report No. 20.* Washington, D.C.: American Psychiatric Association, 1966.
See Reference in Section 5.3

WILD, C. M., SHAPIRO, L. N., & GOLDENBERG, L. Transactional communication disturbances in families of male schizophrenics. *Family Process*, 1975, *14*, 131–160.
This is a description of a method for comparing the interaction of male schizophrenics with their families to that of psychiatrically hospitalized nonschizophrenics and normals. Interactions were scored on attention, problem-solving, and dominance, by direct observation, by observation with videotapes and from transcripts. Tape scoring was the most efficient and effective in discriminating the three groups.

WINER, L. R. The qualified pronoun count as a measure of change in family psychotherapy. *Family Process*, 1971, *10*, 243–247.
See reference in Section 1.1.

WORLD HEALTH ORGANIZATION. Aspects of family mental health in europe. *Public Health Papers No. 28.*
Eight papers which were "working papers presented at a seminar on mental health and the family held by the WHO Regional Office for Europe at Athens in 1962" and specially commissioned chapters. These include "The Mother and the Family", "The Child in the Family", "Working Women and the Family", "Marriage Problems and their Implications for the Family", "Family Psychotherapy", "Mental Health and the Older Generation", "School for Parents", and "The Hampstead Child-Therap Clinic".

WYNNE, L., RYCKOFF, I., DAY, J., & HERSCH, S. Pseudo-mutuality in the family relations of schizophrenics. *Psychiatry*, 1958, *21*, 205–220.
See Reference in Section 5.2

WYNNE, L. C., RYCKOFF, I. M., DAY, J., & HERSCH, S. Pseudo-mutulaity in the family relations of schizophrenics. In N. W. Bell, & E. F. Vogel, *A modern introduction to the family.* Glencoe: Free Press, 1960.
See Reference in Section 5.2

ZIEGLER, R. G., & MULINER, P. J. Persistent themes: A naturalistic study of personality development in the family. *Family Process*, 1977, *16*, 293–305.
This is a pilot longitudinal study on the relationship between early childhood behavior and adolescent "concerns." The current family system of 30 families was studied in conjoint family sessions that included, when possible, the

grandparental generation. The Offer scale was administered to each adolescent, and a family Semantic Differential scale of interpersonal perception was given to mother, father and adolescent. A psychologist independently tested mother, father and subject with a WAIS, TAT and Rorschach. A case presentation illustrates the particular patterns of one of the family systems studied.

ZUK, G. On the pathology of silencing strategies. *Family Process*, 1965, *4*, 32–49.
A description and categorization of the ways people impose or enforce silence on one another. "There is a causal relation between silencing strategies and pathological silence and babbling which may themselves be used as powerful silencing strategies.

ZUK, G. H. Theories of family pathology: In what direction? *International Journal of Family Therapy*, 1979, *1*, 356–361.
This essay discussed three theories of family pathology. They are the: (1) intergenerational, (2) communicational, and (3) scapegoat theories. They are described and compared. They only point they have in common is their vision of a process of victimization in families that may lead to psychiatric symptoms in one member. The newer short term family therapy approaches are found to be inconsistent with intergenerational theory.

ZUK, G., & RUBINSTEIN, D. A review of concepts in the study and treatment of families of schizophrenics. In I. Boszormenyi-Nagy, & J. L. Framo (Eds.), *Intensive family therapy*. New York: Harper & Row, 1965.
A review of conceptual trends in family treatment of schizophrenics. Discusses the shift from parent pathology to nuclear family to three generational involvement.

ZUCKERMAN, M. Save the pieces! *Psychology Bulletin*, 1966, *66*, 78–80.
A brief comment correcting factual mistakes in Frank's review of the method and results of a study by Zuckerman, Oltean, and Moashkin. There is also an argument that the retrospective statistical approach to the study of the family's relation to psychopathology is valid and has contributed to the discovery of etiology in other disorders. Methodology involved in dealing with multiple factors and lack of reliability of instruments is discussed.

4. FAMILY DESCRIPTION

4.1 MARITAL DESCRIPTION

ACKERMAN, N. W. The diagnosis of neurotic marital interaction. *Social Casework*, 1954, *35*, 139–147.
A lecture based on the author's clinical work in which he lays out a theory of family pathology and marital disharmony. There is an extensive schema for evaluating the marital relationship, divided into 7 categories: (1) goals, (2) performance, (3) achievement, (4) dynamic interrelations, (5) neurotic interactions, (6) consequences of Neurotic interactions, and (7) patterns of compensation.

BAILEY, M. B. Alcoholism and marriage. *Quarterly Journal on the Studies of Alcoholism*, 1961, *22*, 81–97.
A review paper summarizing and discussing the major literature relating to alcoholism and marriage. Further research is said to be needed to attempt an integration of the two hypotheses that regard the course of an alcoholic marriage as a manifestation of a personality disorder or as a response to a particular kind of stress. "The past few years have witnessed a general growth of psychiatric interest in total family diagnosis and treatment, but this new emphasis has hardly begun to manifest itself in respect to alcoholism." A bibliography of 46 references is included.

BARNETT, J. Narcissism and dependency in the obsession-hysteric marriage. *Family Process*, 1971, *10*, 75–83.
Patterns of distortion, typical power struggles, as well as the communication and sexual difficulties in the obsessional–hysteric marriage are described. Underlying roots of conflict are the contrapunctual interplay of narcissism and dependency, both overt and covert, in the obsessional and hysteric partners.

BAUMANN, G., & ROMAN, M. Interaction testing in the study of marital dominance. *Family Process*, 1966, *5*, 230–242.
A sample of 50 couples was exposed individually and conjointly to the Wechsler Bellevue. In the conjoint testing, the couple was asked to reach agreement on the response. Comparisons of the individual test and the conjoint test were made as well as measures of dominance of the couple tested together.

BECK, D. F. Marital conflict: Its couse and treatment as seen by caseworkers. *Social Casework*, 1966, *47*, 211–221.
A clinical essay describing a theory of marital conflict. Data were obtained by sending an unstructured questionnaire to "400 caseworkers in 104 member agencies throughout the United States" and "stimulation of local study groups to prepare reports in depth on such topics." There is a "marital balance," which helps keep the family in equilibrium and which is derived from courtship and the early years of marriage,. The breakdown of the marital conflict and the conflicts resulting are described, including the point where couples apply for help. Good and bad prognostic factors in terms of casework intervention and treatment of marital conflict are described.

BECKER, B. J. Holistic, analytic approaches to marital therapy. *American Journal of Psychoanalysis*, 1978, *38*, 129–142.
This paper presents an overview of common problems that couples have for which they request or need marital therapy. Examples include problems of finance, communication, and expectations, as well as those concerning relationships with the extended family. Implications for treatment are discussed.

BECKER, J. V., & MILLER, P. M. Verbal and nonverbal marital interaction patterns of alcoholics and nonalcoholics. *Journal on the Studies of Alcoholism*, 1976, *37*, 1616–1624.
This is a research study testing the notion that wives help to maintain drinking behavior in their spouse. Sample compared 6 couples in which the husband was the hospitalized, alcoholic, identified patient to 6 couples in which the husband hospitalized for other psychiatric illness. Data was collected by videotape and rated independently and retrosepctively on verbal and nonverbal measures. Results indicated that husbands tended to speak during alcohol-related conversation, while wives spoke more when discussing other topics. Wives in both groups looked at their spouses more than their husbands did during alcohol-focused conversation.

BERGNER, R. M. The marital system of the hysterical individual. *Family Process*, 1977, *16*, 85–95.
This paper supplements previous descriptions of individual hysterical behavior with clinical observations on 16 couples. The husband of the hysterical female does not take a disagreeable stand on anything, enjoys playing his role as a "caretaker," seems always calm, unemotional, and detached. He does not hold up his end in the fulfillment of family duties and responsibilities. The female sees herself as weak and seeks a partner who can remain calm under stressful emotional situations. Development of long-standing resentment eventually characterizes their relationship. Hysterical behavior is one of the consequences of their deteriorating relationship.

BEUKENKAMP, C. Parental suicide as a source of resistance to marriage. *International Journal of Group Psychotherapy*, 1961, *11*, 204–208.
A review of 45 former patients seen in private practice who had remained unmarried despite their efforts to the contrary. Because 25 of them later married and 20 had not, the author renewed contact to explore the difference. He learned that of the 25 who had married, the fathers of 8 had committed suicide and the fathers of 17 had made attempts or implied they might do so. The author concludes that the 25 who married resolved in therapy an unhealthy identification with a suicidal father which was related to their reluctance to marry.

BOLTE, G. L. A communications approach to marital counseling. *Family Coordinator*, 1970, *19*, 32–40.
A clinical essay based on the hypothesis that communications difficulties provide an important avenue for understanding marital conflict. Therefore an interactional approach is advised for treating problems. Communication difficulties are outlined and interventions are suggested. Interactional techniques are seen as only one part of the marriage counselor's repertoire.

BRISCOE, C. W., & SMITH, J. B. Depression and marital turmoil. *Archives of General Psychiatry*, 1973, *29*, 811–817.
This is one of a series of research reports relating depressive illness to marital problems. The sample comprised 45 divorced females and 12 males with the diagnosis of unipolar, affective disease. Results indicate that (1) 43 of the 45 females had a depressive episode more than one month in duration at the time of the marital separation or divorce; and (2) 20 of the 22 who had had prior episodes of depression were again depressed at the time of marital disruption. The relation of the depression and the disruption is examined, and it is concluded that the depression was a cause, *rather than* a result, of the marital turmoil.

BUCK, C. W., & LADD, K. L. Psychoneurosis in marital partners. *British Journal of Pyschiatry*, 1965, *3*, 587–590.
See Reference in Section 3.1

BURCHINAL, L., & CHANCELLOR, L. E. Age at marriage, occupations of grooms, and interreligious marriage rates. *Social Forces*, 1962, *40*, 343–354.
The effects of age at marriage, status of the groom, and interaction effects, on the propensity for intra- or inter-religious marriage were tested in all Iowa first marriages, 1953 to 1957 (N = 17,636). Protestants are less likely to contract interreligious marriages than Catholics. Interreligious marriages are more frequent with higher age of marriage and higher status of the groom. There are also joint effects which vary by group. The data are interpreted as indicating that the saliance of religion varies in relation to the reference group experience specific to age and status levels.

BURCHINAL, L., & CHANCELLOR, L. E. Survival rates among religiously homogeneous and interreligious marriages. *Social Forces*, 1963, *41*, 353–0362.
All first marriages of white Iowa residents between 1953 and 1959 which lasted at least 12 months were recorded (N = 72,488). Divorces in such marriages during the period were also identified. Homogeneous marriages had a higher survival rate than interreligious marriages, but the age of the bride at marriage and the husband's occupational status are even stronger variables. Among Protestants, denominationally homogeneous marriages are less stable than denominationally-mixed marriages. Homogeneous Catholic marriages survive better than denominationally homogeneous Protestant marriages. In mixed marriages survival varies widely depending on the denomination of the Protestant spouse.

CHARNY, I. W. Marital love and mate. *Family Process*, 1969, *8*, 1–24.
A discussion of marriage with the emphasis upon how marital fighting is "inevitable, necessary, and desirable—not simply an unhappy byproduct of emotional immaturity or disturbance."

CHRISTODOULOU, G. Two cases of "Folie à deux" in husband and wife. *Acta Psychiatrica, Scandinavica*, 1970, *46*, 413–419.
This is a clinical report of two cases of "folie à deux." A review of the literature and of these two cases reveals there is usually a dominant and submissive partner in the marriage with complementary needs. Most often the dominant member communicates the delusion to the submissive one, but in the second case report, the reverse occurred.

COLE, C. L., SPANIER, G. B. Induction into mate-swapping: A review. *Family Process*, 1973, *12*, 279–290.
This paper summarizes some of the research findings that relate to mate-swapping activities. The mate-swapper searches for an alternative to compensate for an unhappy adjustment to his or her marriage. Poor relations with the family of orientation and low evaluation of the parents' marriage may have a profound influence. The male is generally the initiator in the mate-swapping activities; he convinces his wife to try to restore meaning and vitality to their marital relationship.

COLLINS, J., KREITMAN, N., NELSON, B., & TROUP, J. Neurosis and marital interaction. III: Family roles and functions. *British Journal of Psychiatry*, 1971, *119*, 233–242.
Another in a series of studies on neurosis and marital interaction, this one considers eight categories of family roles and functions. The investigators looked at not only what was being done, but who did it and how the decisions were made. Results indicated that the patient marriages were husband-dominated, had less joint decision-making, and more conflict over role function.

CONSTANTINE, L. L., & CONSTANTINE, J. M. Group and multilateral marriage: Definitional notes, glossary, and annotated bibliography. *Family Process*, 1971, *10*, 157–176.
The purpose of this paper is to define the phenomenon of *multilateral marriage* as a marriage of at least three

individuas, each of whom is married to at least two other members of the conjugal unit. Multilateral marriage differs from group marriage principally in including cetain three person marriages. Group marriage is defined as two or more men and two or more women.

DENIKER, P., DESAUGY, D., & ROPERT, M. The alcoholic and his wife. *Comprehensive Psychiatry*, 1964, *5*, 374–384.
A study focusing on the relationship between the alcoholic and his wife by studying three groups of patients: 50 alcoholics with psychiatric disorders called psychiatric alcoholics, 50 alcoholics with cirrhosis or gastritis called digestive alcoholics, and 67 in a control group where the husband was matched for age and sociomeconomic status. All couples were interviewed using a questionnaire designed for this study. Compared with the digestive alcoholics and the controls, the psychiatric alcoholics showed a relationship to birth order, had fathers who were also alcoholics, made lower salaries, had dominant wives, and drank relatively little at home. The wife of the psychiatric alcoholic "tends to unconsciously maintain her husband's alcoholism."

DOHERTY, J. P., & ELLIS, J. A new concept and finding in morbid jealousy. *American Journal of Psychiatry*, 1976, *133*, 679–683.
This is a clinical report of three marital couples in which the identified patient was the husband who was "pathologically jealous." In all three cases the men had witnessed the mother engage in "extramarital sexual activity." Implications for diagnosis and treatment are presented.

DUPONT, R., & GRUNEBAUM, H. Willing victims: The husbands of paranoid women. *American Journal of Psychiatry*, 1968, *125*, 151–159.
In an attempt to understand the dynamics of spouses of paranoid women, cases with paranoid delusions (both inpatient and outpatient) were evaluated over a 3-year period. Data were collected on 9 women with paranoid state, using clinical interviews with the husband alone, wife alone, and the couple together, plus the MMPI and interpersonal checklist. Results indicated that the wife expressed the anger and dissatisfaction in the marriage, while the husband manifested passivity and apparent resonableness and thus seemed to be a "willing victim."

DYER, W. G. Analyzing marital adjustment using role theory. *Marriage and Family Living*, 1962, *24*, 371–375.
Marriage partners enter marriage with certain ideas about their roles and how they should behave in this new position, and each also has certain expectations of how the other should behave in his role. Conflicts may come when one's self-perception does not agree with the perception of the partner, when the norms and personal preferences of the husband are in conflict with those of the wife, and when the role performance of one does not agree with role expectations of the other.

FALLDING, H. The family and the idea of a cardinal role. *Human Relations*, 1961, *14*, 329–350.
Thirty-eight Melbourne, Australia intact families were studied intensively by group and individual interviews. Three types of families were distinguished on the basis of the extent to which members' external involvements are made relevant or necessary to the group: (1) Adaptation type—husband and wife seek different satisfaction from life, but adapt to each other by giving independence to othei to follow personal interests without accountability to the family. (2) Identification type—husband's and wife's satisfactions largely derived from family life. Satisfactions independently derived from outside are incidental. (3) False identification type—Husband and wife have conflicting aims, individually and/or together. They strive to control conflicts by acting as if the family is of cardinal importance to both, resuting in dissatisfaction. Some of the external controls on family conduct and the nature of the unit provided by the cardinal role are explored.

FELDMAN, L. B. Depression and marital interaction. *Family Process*, 1976, *15*, 389–395.
See reference in Section 1.7.

FELDMAN, L. B. Marital conflict and marital intimacy: An integrative psychodynamic-behavioral-systematic model. *Family Process*, 1979, *18*, 69–78.
This paper presents a conceptual model to interpret some of the intrapsychic and interpersonal forces that stimulate and maintain repetitive, nonproductive marital conflict behavior. Intrapsychic anxiety stimulates interpersonal defensive behavior, and this in turn reinforces the persistence of the anxiety. Therapeutically it is necessary to integrate active, behaviorally oriented techniques (systematic desensitization, behavioral rehearsal, modeling, etc.). Hopefully, this would alter repetitive cycles of interpersonal conflict behavior, a major cause of the persistence of intimacy anxiety.

FERREIRA, A. J., & WINTER, W. D. On the nature of marital relationships: Measurable differences in spontaneous agreement. *Family Process*, 1974, *13*, 355–369.
In order to examine the "family pathology cycle," the authors pose two questions: (1) Is there more spontaneous agreement between man-wife at the time of marriage in normal or abnormal families?, or (2) Is initial spontaneous agreement between husband and wife the same in all families, differentiating over time between normal and abnormal relationships? This cross-sectional study evaluated the spontaneous agreement (SA) scores of 419 couples (242

normal couples and 177 abnormal couples) to a lengthened form of the Ferreira-Winter questionnaire. Results indicate that SA did not differ for the two groups for those couples married a short time. Overall SA was higher for normal couples and increased according to increased durations of marriage. There was no increase in SA with durations of marriage for the abnormal couples. Cautions as to validity of these results and their implications are discussed.

FISCHER, S., & FISCHER, R. L. The complexity of spouse similarity and difference. In G. H. Zuk, & I. Boszormenyi-Nagy (Eds.), *Family therapy and disturbed families*. Palo Alto: Science & Behavior Books, 1967.
A report on a study of similarities and differences among spouses based upon a sample of 119 families. The parents were exposed to a battery of test procedures intended to tap personality, value, and attitudinal dimensions. Measures of multiple levels of response would seem necessary, because "depending upon the variables one chooses to measure, spouses will appear to be similar, different, or both."

FOX, R. E. The effect of psychotherapy on the spouse. *Family Process*, 1968, 7, 7–16.
A discussion and review of the literature of the effect on a spouse when the partner is in individual psychotherapy. Problems of gathering data are presented and the ethical problem of adverse effects upon the spouse are discussed.

FRANK, E., ANDERSON, C., & KUPPER, D. J. Profiles of couples seeking sex therapy and marital therapy. *American Journal of Psychiatry*, 1976, *133*, 559–562.
This study attempts to delineate profiles of couples coming for either sex therapy (29 couples) or marital therapy (25 couples). Both clinics were at the same institution. Assessment instrument was the marital evaluation form. Results indicate that both groups were similar in the degree of sexual and marital difficulties and demographic characteristics. The relationships of the sex therapy couples generally were characterized by satisfaction and affection, whereas the marital therapy couples were often antagonisic. Implications for treatment are discussed.

FRY, W. F. The marital context of an anxiety syndrome. *Family Process*, 1962, *1*, 245–252.
A report from a project for the study of schizophrenic communication, whose hypothesis is that "the relationship with the marriage partner is intimately related to the psychopathology of the patient." The patients in the report had the syndrome of anxiety, phobias, and stereotyped avoidance behavior. Spouses are described, and it was found that the onset of symptoms correlated with an important change in the life of the spouse. The symptoms seemed to keep the couple united.

GEHRKE, S., & MOXOM, J. Diagnostic classifications and treatment techniques in marriage counseling. *Family Process*, 1962, *1*, 253–264.
A report by two case workers describing a marital counseling method with the diagnostic classifications and treatment techniques used. Indications for joint interviews with husband and wife are given.

GIOVACCHINI, T. Characterological aspects of marital interaction. *Psychoanalytic Forum*, 1967, 2, 7–29.
From a case example of a woman in her middle thirties who was being analyzed, this essay stresses the need for marital partners to use projection in maintaining a psychic balance in a marriage setting. The case is presented from the viewpoint of object relationships, character structure, and symbiosis. There is a discussion of the case by 7 other psychoanalysts with varying theoretical biases in terms of intrapsychic and interpersonal dynamics.

GOODE, W. J. Marital satisfaction and instability: A cross-cultural class analysis of divorce rates. In P. H. Glasser, & L. N. Glasser (Eds.), *Families in crisis*. New York: Harper & Row, 1970.
See Reference in Section 4.5

GOODRICH, D. W., & BOOMER, D. S. Experimental assessment of modes of conflict resolution. *Family Process*, 1963, 2, 15–24.
A report of an experimental technique for studying the coping behavior of husband and wife when they attempt to resolve a marital conflict. Fifty paid volunteer couples between 18 and 27 years of age were asked to match colors—some unmatchable—to see how the couple coped with puzzling or ambiguous situations. A general discussion of results is given, with the authors relating the "ability to achieve perspective on the situation and maintenance of self-esteem" to adequacy of coping.

GOODRICH, D. W., RYDER, R., & RAUSH, H. Patterns of newlywed marriage. *Journal of Marriage and the Family*, 1968, *30*, 383–391.
A report of an exploratory study of 50 average, middle-class marriages examined during the fourth month with interviews, problem solving situations, and questionnaires. Eight patterns of marriage are suggested.

GREEN, K. A. The echo of marital conflict. *Family Process*, 1963, 2, 315–328.
A study of the characteristics of couples coming to the Conciliation Court of the Superior Court of Los Angeles County. In 1960, 500 consecutive cases of couples applying to the conciliation service were examined. The sociocultural characteristics are presented.

HALEY, J. Marriage therapy. *Archives of General Psychiatry*, 1963, *8*, 213–234.
A discussion of the treatment of conflicts in marriage. Certain types of marital relationships, the kinds of conflicts which arise, and the ways a therapist intervenes to induce change are discussed. It is suggested that conflicts occur when husband and wife define their relationship in conflicting ways, thereby imposing paradoxical situations. The resolution of the conflict can occur when the couple faces paradoxical situations provided by marriage therapists.

HILL, R. Marriage and family research: A critical evaluation. *Eugenic Quarterly*, 1954, *1*, 58–63.
See Reference in Section 6

JACKSON, D. Family rules: Marital quid pro quo. *Archives of General Psychiatry*, 1965, *12*, 589–94.
This is a clinical paper in which a theory of marriage is proposed based on the characteristic relationship rather than the characteristics of the individuals. Similarities and differences between spouses comprise the "bargain" on which the marriage relationship is based. Advantages and disadvantages of this scheme of understanding the marital relationship are discussed.

JACKSON, T., & BODIN, A. Paradoxical communication and the marital paradox. In S. Rosenbaum, & I. Alger (Eds.), *The marriage relationship*. New York: Basic Books, 1968.
This is an attempt to provide a conceptual framework and techniques for dealing with a disturbed marital relationship. The marital situation is seen as a paradox in itself. As a result of that paradox, some examples of disturbed communication are discussed. In the treatment of such communication, labeling conflicting levels, encouraging the symptoms, and actually prescribing them are helpful.

JOHNSON, C. L., & JOHNSON, F. A. Attitudes toward parenting in dual-career families. *American Journal of Psychiatry*, 1977, *134*, 391–395.
This study from an upstate New York college community examines "role strain" and patterns of adaptation in families with dual careers and children under 12 years old. Twenty-eight randomly selected couples were studied with a semistructured interview scaled and scored by two raters. Results showed anxiety and guilt over parenting in the wives, suggesting that "role strain" was greatest there. Coping mechanisms included giving temporary priority to children, rationalization, and training children to be self-reliant. The authors conclude that individual psychotherapy directed to such role strain could alleviate some pressures on these women.

KAHN, M. Non-verbal communication and marital satisfaction. *Family Process*, 1970, *9*, 449–456.
The Marital Communication Scale (MCS) and the Primary Communication Inventory (PCI) were administered to 21 maritally satisfied and 21 maritally dissatisfied couples. The results indicate a relationship between marital satisfaction and accuracy of nonverbal communication as assessed by both measures. The two measures were also found to have little in common.

KARDENER, S. The family: Structure, pattern, and therapy. *Mental Hygiene*, 1968, *52*, 524–531.
See Reference in Section 1.1

KARPEL, M. Individuation: From fusion to dialogue. *Family Process*, 1976, *15*, 65–82.
This paper explores the processes of fusion and individuation as they relate to problems experienced by couples. Four modes of relating are described and ways in which dysfunctional dyadic relational patterns may represent the individual's attempt to move from fusion to dialogue are suggested. The author attempts to integrate concepts of individual theoretical perspective with practical usefullness.

KATZ, I., COHEN, M., & CASTIGLIONE, L. Effect of one type of need complementarity on marriage partners' conformity to one another's judgments. *Journal of Abnormal Social Psychology*, 1963, *67*, 8–14.
Fifty-five paid volunteer couples were examined using a forced-choice questionnaire to test the hypothesis that when the husband's need to receive affection is similar in strength to the wife's complementary need to give affection the tendency of spouses to be influenced by one another will be significant. Results indicated husbands could accept wives' judgments; the converse was not true.

KATZ, M. Agreement on connotative meaning in marriage. *Family Process*, 1966, *4*, 64–74.
A study of marriage based on the assumption that marital happiness is related to the degree of similarity between the spouses. Two groups of 20 couples, one seeking marriage counseling and one classed as happily married, were exposed to the Osgood semantic differential instrument and differences were found. Troubled couples were more discrepant in their semantic structures.

KERCKHOFF, A., & DAVIS, K. E. Value consensus and need complementarity in mate selection. *American Sociological Review*, 1962, *27*, 295–303.
Approximately 100 college couples seriously considering marriage were studied on 2 occasions, 7 months apart. Their need complementarity (measured by Schutz's FIRO scales) and value consensus (by Farber's index) were measured and related to length of association and progress toward a permanent union. The hypothesis that consensus related to

progress toward a permanent union holds only for short-term couples. The hypothesis that need complementarity is related to progress holds only for long-term couples. The findings are interpreted to mean that different factors are salient at different stages of mate selection.

KOHL, R. N. Pathologic reactions of marital partners to improvement of patients. *American Journal of Psychiatry*, 1962, *118*, 1036–1041.
A discussion of the precipitation of a psychiatric illness in a marital partner when a patient shows clinical improvement based upon observation of 39 inpatients treated at the Payne Whitney Psychiatric Clinic over a period of 10 years. In all cases it was necessary to include both spouses in the treatment plan to maintain the patient's improvement or recovery. Commonly there was denial of marital conflict as etiologically significant by both partners at the time of hospitalization and emphasis upon the "ideal" nature of the marriage with mutual denial of resentment or hostility. With improvement in the patient, the spouses displayed the first observable signs of psychopathology.

KREITMAN, N. Mental disorder in married couples. *Journal of Mental Science*, 1962, *108*, 438–446.
See Reference in Section 3.1

KRIETMAN, N. The patient's spouse. *British Journal of Psychiatry*, 1964, *110*, 159–174.
See Reference in Section 3.2

KUNSTADTER, P. A survey of the consanguine or matrifocal family. *American Anthropology*, 1963, *65*, 56–66.
A review and critique of historical, value-system, and functional explanations of the existence of the matrifocal family. It is concluded that "matrifocal families develop as a result of the division of labor separating adult males and adult females in a community" when other solutions to an unbalanced sex ratio of adults are unavailable.

LEVINGER, G. Marital cohesiveness and dissolution: An integrative review. In P. H. Glasser, & L. N. Glasser (Eds.), *Families in crisis*. New York: Harper & Row, 1970.
A discussion of cohesiveness in marriage as a special case of group cohesiveness in general. The framework is based upon two components: attractions toward or repulsions from a relationship, and barriers against its dissolution. Includes a review of factors associated with divorce.

LEVINGER, G. Sources of marital dissatisfaction among applicants for divorce. In P. H. Glasser, & L. N. Glasser (Eds.), *Families in crisis*. New York: Harper & Row, 1970.
See Reference in Section 3.1

LEVITT, H., & BAKER, R. Relative psychopathology of marital partners. *Family Process*, 1969, *8*, 33–42.
A study examining whether the member of a marriage who seeks treatment is the more disturbed of the spouses. A sample of 25 patients and their spouses were examined with questionnaire and psychological tests. Eleven psychologists served as judges to examine the test results and identify the "sicker" member. In 13 of the 25 cases the identified patient was judged to be the "sicker".

LEWIS, R. A. A developmental framework for the analysis of premarital dyadic formation. *Family Process*, 1972, *11*, 17–48.
See Reference in Section 3.6

LICHTENBERG, J. D., & PIN-NIE PAO The prognostic and therapeutic significance of the husband-wife relationship for hospitalized schizophrenic women. *Psychiatry*, 1960, *23*, 209–213.
A discussion of the types of husbands of hospitalized schizophrenic women and the importance of taking the spouse into account in psychotherpay. Observation of 43 patients indicated the husbands fell into certain groups, although no prototype personality was found. In terms of prognosis, the husbands are classified as constructively active, obstructively active, rejecting, maintaining the previous pathological relationship, and vacillating. Ways to include the husband in the therapeutic program were attempted and are recommended.

LUCKY, E. B. Marital satisfaction and congruent self-spouse concepts. *Social Forces*, 1960, *39*, 153–157.
Satisfactorily (S) and less satisfactorily (LS) married couples were identified by Locke's marital adjustment scale from a population of 594 married students. Couples in the two groups independently completed the Leary interpersonal checklist regarding the self and spouse. The congruence of the husband's perception of himself and his wife's percpetion of him was related to satisfaction, but the congruence of the wife's self concept and her husband's perception of her was not. Some implications and explanations of these results are offered.

LUCKEY, E. B. Perceptional congruence of self and family concepts as related to marital interaction. *Sociometry*, 1961, *24*, 234–250.
Forty-one satisfactorily married (S) and 40 less satisfactorily married (LS) couples completed Leary interpersonal check lists on self, spouse, mother, father, and ideal self. S and LS subjects were compared on agreement of self

concept and spouse's concept of subject, of self and ideal self, of self and parent, of spouse and parent, of ideal self and spouses. The many differences between S and LS subjects are used to refine the proposition that marital satisfaction is related to perceptual congruence, and to evaluate a theory of marital interaction.

MARKOWITZ, M., & KADIS, A. L. Parental interaction as a determining factor in social growth of the individual in the family. *International Journal of Social Psychiatry*, (special ed. 2), 1964, 81–89.
See Reference in Section 1.2

MARTIN, P. Dynamic considerations of an hysterical psychosis. *American Journal of Psychiatry*, 1971, *128*, 745–747.
This is a clinical study of the interpersonal dynamics in a hysterical psychosis. Wives were found to have a symbiotic attachment ot their husbands on whose ego functioning they depended. Husbands not only failed to support them, but became destructive forces that broke down neurotic, hysterical defensive structure. Psychosis was seen as a coping mechanism of last resort—a defense against separation. One case is presented in support of the above observations.

MEYEROWITZ, J. H., & FELDMAN, H. Transition to parenthood. In I. M. Cohen (Ed.), *Psychiatric research reports No. 20*. Washington, D.C.: American Psychiatric Association, 1966.
A report of a study of 400 couples based on interviews of individuals. Experiences during the first pregnancy are described as well as when the child is 1 month and 5 months old.

MITCHELL, H. E. Application of the Kaiser method to marital pairs. *Family Process*, 1963, *2*, 265–279.
See Reference in Section 3.2

MITCHELL, H. E., BULLARD, J. W., & MUDD, E. H. Areas of marital conflict in successfully and unsuccessfully functioning families. *Journal of Health and Human Behavior*, 1962, *3*, 88–93.
The nature and frequency of marital disagreements in 200 marriage counseling cases and in 100 self-selected, successful families. Data on both groups were obtained from the marriage adjustment schedule and from interviews. Both groups rank their problems in the same order: economic is highest, religious and educational are lowest. No differences in ranking of problems by husbands and wives were apparent, but conflicted families report a greater frequecy of problems. Some cultural implications of these findings are discussed.

MURPHY, D. C., & MENDELSON, L. A. Communication and adjustment in marriage: Investigating the relationship. *Family Process*, 1973, *12*, 317–326.
This is a study designed to find out the correlation between communication and adjustment levels in marriage. Thirty married couples in a university setting were asked to complete an adjustment inventory (the Locke Marital Adjustment Scale) and a communication measure (the Marital Communication Inventory). A positive correlation was established, supporting the hypothesis that marital communication and adjustment are highly interrelated.

NAPIER, A. V. The marriage of families: Cross generational complementarity. *Family Process*, 1971, *10*, 373–395.
Two couples without psychiatric illness and their parents were interviewed using a structured questionnaire in order to examine stasis and change in marital patterns across generations in normal families in an attempt to draw some conclusions as to their cross-generational complementarity. The author contends that in choosing a marital partner, an individual makes an unconscious effort "yet careful account" of his/her own family trends and in his/her prospective mate's family origin as well. The intention is to choose a partner that will make "the emergent family more satisfying than the one in which they were raised."

NAVRAN, L. Communication and adjustment in marriage. *Family Process*, 1967, *6*, 173–184.
A sample of married couples was exposed to the marital relationship inventory and the primary communication inventory, two questionnaires given to the couples individually. The 24 couples having a "happy" relationship were contrasted with 24 having an "unhappy" relationship. Differences were found and marital adjustment was shown "to be positively correlated with capacity to communicate."

NELSON, B., COLLINS, J., KREITMAN, N., & TROUP, J. Neurosis and marital interaction. II: Time sharing and social activity. *British Journal of Psychiatry*, 1970, *117*, 47–58.
See Reference in Section 3.3.

OLSON, D. H. The measurement of family power by self-report and behavioral methods. *Journal of Marriage and the Family*, 1969, *31*, 545–550.
A study comparing self report and observed behavior on the question of power in marriage. Thirty-five couples were given questionnaires and their responses compared with their behavior in the laboratory dealing with real problems. No relationship was found between what the couples said about the distribution of power in the marriage and what was observed when the dealt with one another. Explanatory factors are offered, and the conclusion is reached that this research reinforces "the idea that methodological research of this type should precede, rather than follow, substantive research in the field."

PERLMAN, C., & GIVELBER, F. Women's issues in couples treatment—The view of the female therapist. *Psychiatric Opinion*, 1976, *13*, 6–12.
Issues in the women's movement that focus on changing women's roles have caused conflict in marriages. Using clinical vignettes, transference, counter-transference, and management of such issues are discussed.

PERLOW, A., & MULLINS, S. Marital satisfaction as perceived by the medical student's spouse. *Journal of Medical Education*, 1976, *51*, 726–734.
A structured questionnaire was administered to 239 spouses of recent medical school graduates as a means of assessing the quality of marital relations during medical school. Although most respondents were satisfied with their marriages, 38 percent indicated they could have benefited from marital therapy. Reasons for marital dissatisfaction were discussed.

PITTMAN, F. S., & FLOMENHAFT, K. Treating the doll's house marriage. *Family Process*, 1970, *9*, 143–155.
Intervention procedures in the type of marriage where one spouse's incompetence is required or encouraged by the other. Therapy works best when the emphasis is upon respect for unique individual needs within the framework of the marriage.

PLONE, A. Marital and existential pain: Dialectic in Bergman's "Scenes from a Marriage." *Family Process*, 1975, *14*, 371–378.
Marital pain and existential pain are discussed in terms of the movie, "Scenes from a Marriage" by Bergman. The relationship between the lack of autonomy and inability to tolerate intimacy is discussed. The concept of the "third-party" in marriage is considered.

PRINCE, A. J. A study of 194 cross-religion marriages. *Family Life Coordinator*, 1962, *11*, 3–7.
A report on a study of 142 interfaith marriages and 52 marriages between protestants of different denominations. Data were obtained with questionnaires. Topics of interest are cross-religion marriages, major areas of conflict, changes in church attendance patterns, degree of satisfaction with marriage, and attitudes about cross-religion marriages for children.

QUINTON, D., RUTTER, M., & ROWLANDS, D. An evaluation of an interview assessment of marriage. *Psychological Medicine*, 1976, *6*, 577–586.
This is a research report on the development of an interview assessment scale for marital relationships, which was shown to have a good interrater reliability, high consistency across the accounts of both marriage partners, and resistance to methodologic bias. A 4-year follow-up study demonstrated high predictability for later marital breakdown. The assessment scale also shows strong association with behavioral deviancy in the children. A shortened version is described, and preliminary findings are given on its validity.

RABKIN, R. Uncoordinated communication between marriage partners. *Family Process*, 1967, *6*, 10–15.
A discussion of communication codes unique to particular family systems. Examples of couples' problems in developing mutual codes are given.

RAE, J., & DREWERY, J. Interpersonal patterns in alcoholic marriages. *British Journal of Psychiatry*, 1972, *120*, 615–621.
Marital patterns of 33 male alcoholics and their wives were compared with 51 controls, using the PD Scale of the MMPI. Results indicated that control men were more independent than dependent and control women were more dependent than independent. Furthermore, they were *perceived* as such by their spouses. The relation between marital patterns and outcome is discussed.

RAPOPORT, R. Normal crises, family structure and mental health. *Family Process*, 1963, *2*, 68–80.
An essay on some of the "ideas and methods" behind an exploratory study of how "the family handled "the newly married state." Six couples were thus studied via interviews both before and after marriage for variable periods of time.

RAPOPORT, R., & RAPOPORT, R. N. New light on the honeymoon. *Human Relations*, 1964, *17*, 33–56.
A general discussion of the honeymoon followed by a task description illustrated with a case example. The honeymoon ritual is described as part of the life-cycle transition point of marriage.

RAUSH, H. L., MARSHALL, K. A., & FEATHERMAN, J. M. Relations at three early stages of marriage reflected by the use of personal pronouns. *Family Process*, 1970, *9*, 69–82.
This study compares the use of pronouns "I-me-my-mine," to "We-us-our-ours," as these occurred in a series of interviews mainly with 21 couples. The three early stages of marriage-newlywed, late pregnancy, and early postnatal periods demonstrate how communications differ. Three general expectations in relative usage from "we" toward "I" as marriage progressed were confirmed by these data.

RAVICH, R. Game-testing in conjoint marital psychotherapy. *American Journal of Psychotherapy*, 1969, *23*, 217–229. See Reference in Section 1.3

RAVICH, R., DEUTSCH, M., & BROWN, B. An experimental study of marital discord and decision making. In I. M. Cohen (Ed.), *Psychiatric research report No. 20*. Washington, D.C.: American Psychiatric Association, 1966. See Reference in Section 3.4

ROMAN, M., BAUMAN, G., & BORELLO, J. et al: An effect of change in patient status on marital interaction. *Family Process*, 1976, *15*, 251–258.
This study explores the relational changes and implications of the role shift of one partner from "patient" to "non-patient." Using a technique called "interaction testing," alterations in marital relational patterns were identified particularly as they relate to decision making. In a sample of 16 couples, the authors were able to demonstrate significant improvement in couples' intellectual function; increased task efficiency, and appropriate decision making and positive changes in the pattern of decision making.

ROSSI, A. Family development in a changing world. *American Journal of Psychiatry*, 1972, *128*, 1057–1066.
This is an essay describing the changing role of women in the family in the last half century. It is believed that women now devote a smaller percentage of their adult life to rearing of children and have achieved higher levels of education, which has facilitated more egalitarian relationships between husbands and wives and has increased the proportion of married women who are capable of holding jobs. Marriage rates are not decreasing, but divorce rates are. The feminist movement may help in reshaping one's personal goals to keep pace with rapidly changing social changes.

RUBINSTEIN, D. Distortion and dilemma in marital choice. *Voices*, 1966, *2*, 60–64.
From an extensive case example, this essay hypothesizes that in a disturbed marital relationship there are distortions and dilemmas which can be summarized as follows: (1) the marital pair does not relate as real persons; (2) they relate through each other to the internal introjects; (3) they try to change each other into an internal introject to solve longstandig conflicts; (4) they become "bad objects;" and (5) as long as there is an externalized "bad object," the idealized "good" introject can be kept alive and hoped for. Family therapy attempts to uncover these distortions and help the marital pair to see each other realistically.

RYDER, R. G. Dimensions of early marriage. *Family Process*, 1970, *9*, 51–68.
This is an outline for a descriptive dimensional framework appropriate to the beginnings of marriage. Sample size was 48 couples. The procedure consisted of four evenings utilizing separate interviews and testing. Each of the final four factors were correlated with each of the original variables. Results showed that husband ambitiousness was a dissatisfaction variable.

RYDER, R. G. "Husband-Wife Dyads vs. Married Strangers. *Family Process*, 1968,1 *7*, 233–238.
A comparison of the behavior of spouses with each other and with strangers by use of the color matching test which induces a conflict situation. Sixty-four married dyads and 56 unmarried dyads were contrasted. Few differences were found, but persons "treat strangers more gently and generally more nicely than they do their spouses."

RYDER, R. G. A topography of early marriage. *Family Process*, 1970, *9*, 385–402.
This is a report of a study on patterns of early marriage. Two hundred "non-clinical" couples, ages 18–27 were interviewed. Twenty-one patterns of marriage, organized along fine axes (e.g., husband's effectiveness, wife's orientation toward the marriage) were derived from the interview material.

RYDER, R. G. Two replications of color matching factors. *Family Process*, 1966, 43–48.
A replication of the color matching test of Goodrich and Boomer. The test was applied to 64 married couples and 56 split couples (defined as a male and female pair not married). Comparisons with the original sample, and between the married and unmarried groups are made.

RYDER, R. G., & GOODRICH, D. W. Married couples' responses to disagreement. *Family Process*, 1966, *5*, 30–42.
A report on the color matching test administered to 49 recently married couples. Husband and wife are exposed to colors and asked to match them when some of them do not match. Ways of handling the conflict are categorized and described.

RYLE, A., & HAMILTON, M. Neurosis in fifty married couples. *Journal of Mental Science*, 1962, *108*, 265–273.
An investigation of 50 working-class marital couples to record the prevalence of neurosis as indicated by the Cornell medical index, the records of the general practitioner with whom the families were registered, and the home interviews of a psychiatric social worker. The information from these sources was compared and the presence of neurosis was correlated with some aspects of adverse childhood experience, marital adjustment, consumer status and social integration.

SAGER, C., GRUNDRACH, R., KRAMER, M., LANZ, R., & ROYCE, J. The married in treatment: Effects of psychoanalysis on the marital state. *Archives of General Psychiatry*, 1968, *19*, 205–217.
In order to asscertain the effects of psychoanalysis on the marital state, a study of 736 married patients (432 women and 304 men), age 21 to 68, in middle and upper socioeconomic class who were being treated in psychoanalysis. Seventy-ine psychoanalysts supplied data on "any ten consecutive patients." The data were obtained through a closed-ended questionnaire. Twelve percent of the patients had concurrent group therapy, 2 percent were in conjoint marital therapy, and about 20 percent of the patients had one or more conjoint consultations with their spouse and analyst. Results indicated that marriages rated poor initially improved and marriages rated better also improved. There was no evidence that as one marital partner got better another got worse. Overall individual patient improvement was rated at about 60 percent of the cases. Of the spouses who were in treatment, good effects were more frequently reported in cases in which both husband and wife were treated by the same psychoanalyst.

SAGER, C. J., KAPLAN, H. S., GUNDLACH, R. H. et al: The marriage contract. *Family Process*, 1971, *10*, 311–326.
This is an essay derived from material from private practice. The marriage contract concept is useful as a transactional and psychodynamic model to comprehend troubled marriages. The concept refers to the reciprocal relationships established between partners who have individual, expressed and unexpressed, conscious and unconscious, concepts of their obligations towards, and expectations, of each other. The degree to which a marriage can satisfy each partner's contractual expectations is an improtant determinant of the quality of that marriage. The aim of treatment is open communication between the spouses on conscious and unconscious levels, as each partner is encouraged to explore and verbalize the unspoken aspects of their contracts.

SAMOUILIDIS, L. Marital relationships: Frustration and fulfillment. *American Journal of Psychoanalysis*, 1975, *35*, 365–375.
General concepts that apply to marriage as well as meshing of personalities, premarital motivations that lead to marriage, and aspects of the marital process are discussed. Ways of identifying a growing, versus a nongrowing, marriage are discussed.

SANDER, F. M. Marriage and the family in Freud's writings. *Amerian Academy of Psychoanalysis*, 1978, *6*, 157–174.
This is an historical review of what Freud wrote about marriage and the family. The intent is to "build bridges between psychoanalytic and family theories." The author found 30 references to the family and 11 to marriage. The author feels that an integration between the two theories should "flow naturally."

SCHUERMAN, J. Marital interaction and posthospital adjustment. *Social Casework*, 1972, *53*, 163–172.
See Reference in Section 3.2.

SILVERMAN, J. The women's liberation movement: Its impact on marriage. *Hospital and Community Psychiatry*, 1975, *26*, 39–40.
Changing societal expectations of women's role in the family are hypothesized to disrupt the "dominant submissive marriage." Data were obtained from the author's clinical experience with marital therapy in a community mental health center. Marital therapy is thought to help to restore equilibrium in which both partners share the responsibilities of marriage.

SLUZKI, C. E., & BEAVIN, J. Simetria y complementariada: Una definicion operacional y una tipologia de parejas. *Acta Psiquiatrica Y Psicologica De America Latina*, 1965, *11*, 321–330.
See Reference in Section 3.6

SNELL, J., ROSENWALD, R., & ROBEY, A. The wifebeater's wife: A study of family interaction. *Archives of General Psychiatry*, 1964, *11*, 107–113.
A study of 37 families in which men were charged by their wives with assault and battery and who were referred to one of the psychiatric clinics which serve the courts of Massachusetts. Twelve of the families were studied in detail (both husband and wife being seen for three or more interviews). Four wives were in individual psychotherapy for "more than 18 months." In addition, some group therapy and "couple therapy" was attempted. A typical family structure is described: husband is passive, indecisive, and sexually inadequate; wife agressive, masculine, frigid, and masochistic; relationship between the two characterized by alternation of passive and aggressive roles. An adolescent son may upset the equilibrium.

STRODTBECK, F. Husband-wife interaction over revealed differences. *American Sociological Review*, 1951, *23*, 468–473.
A field study of ten Navajo, ten Texan, and ten Mormon couples. Balance of power can be revealed using this technique, and it depends both on power elements in a larger cultural organization and amount of participation in the small group situation.

THARP, R. Marriage roles, child development and family treatment. *American Journal of Orthopsychiatry*, 1965, *35*, 531–538.

Previous research on marriage has given "a small grain of knowledge" according to the author. He proposes a tentative structure of marriage roles: solidarity, sexuality, external relations, internal instrumentality, and division of reponsibility. Disturbed marriage roles may result in disturbed parent-child relations within the same role function. Advances of this theory as well as applications to treatment of the family are discussed.

VAN DEN BERGE, P. Hygergamy, hypergenation and miscegenation. *Human Relations*, 1960, *13*, 83–91.
The author suggests that marriage or mating of women upward in the status hierarchy is widespread, and that it occurs under, and leads to, certain specific conditions. The hypothesis of maximization of status is suggested to account for the marriage, mating, and also miscegenation patterns. Data from a variety of societies give support to the hypothesis.

VOGEL, E. F. The marital relationship of parents of emotionally disturbed children: Polarization and isolation. *Psychiatry*, 1960, *23*, 1–12.
In a study of 18 families seen by an interdisciplinary team, nine families with emotionally disturbed children were matched with 9 families with relatively healthy children. The marriage relationship in all families with an emotionally disturbed child was found to be more disturbed; the parents behaved as if they were polar opposites and each partner contended that his standards were right and the spouse's wrong. In the control families the parents had less physical separation, shared activities with each other more, and exhibited more flexibility in the handling of money.

WARKENTIN, J., & WHITAKER, C. Marriage—The cornerstone of the family system. In O. Pollak, & A. S. Friedman (Eds.), *Family dynamics and female sexual delinquency*. Palo Alto: Science & Behavior Books, 1969.
A description of the inner assumptions and postulates about human nature and marriage of two experienced therapists. The emphasis is upon the importance of the therapist's views about life when dealing with a family.

WARKENTIN, J., & WHITAKER, C. A. The secret agenda of the therapist doing couples therapy. In G. H. Zuk, & I. Boszormenyi-Nagy (Eds.), *Family therapy and disturbed families*. Palo Alto: Science & Behavior Books, 1967.
A discussion of the treatment of married couples with the emphasis upon the profound influence of the therapist's own pattern of personal living. Includes the authors' premises about marriage.

WARKENTIN, J., & WHITAKER, C. Serial impasses in marriage. In I. M. Cohen (Ed.), *Psychiatric research report No. 20*. Washington, D.C.: American Psychiatric Association, 1966.
A discussion of marriage as both a legal and an emotional commitment with special emphasis upon the times "when we may expect difficulty and even impasse in the development of the emotional marriage." These times include the wedding night, pregnancy, the second baby, and the "10-year syndrome."

WEISMAN, I. Exploring the effect of the marital relationship on child functioning and parental functioning. *Social Casework*, 1963, *44*, 330–334.
A report on a study investigating the relationship between child functioning and marital patterns. A sample was drawn of clients from the Community Service Society of New York and the data consisted of the judgments of the caseworkers who used a rating scale to indicte severity and persistence of conflict in several areas of child functioning and parental patterns.

WELLISCH, D. K., GAY, G. R., & McENTEE, R. The easy rider syndrome: A pattern of hetero- and homosexual relationships in a heroin addict population. *Family Process*, 1970, *9*, 425–430.
Based on case material from a free, medical clinic, a pattern of dyadic relationship in the addict subculture is described in terms of its familial antecedents, current dynamics, and treatment implications. The chief feature of this pattern is that the male member of the dyad is an "easy rider" supported and cared for by the female partner. (Includes seven references.)

WESTLEY, W. A., & EPSTEIN, N. B. Report on the psycho-social organization of the family and mental health. In D. Willner (Ed.), *Decisions, values, and groups*. New York: Pergamon Press, 1960.
A report of a study designed to investigate the relationship between family functioning and development of either mental health or pathology. The sample was 531 students of the first-year class at a university who were given a Rorschach, a Gordon-Personality test, and interviewed by a psychiatrist. Twenty were classified as being the most emotionally healthy, and of these, 17 were in the study. There is a schema for description, analysis, and evaluation of the family using a case example. Common features of these emotionally healthy families are described.

WILLI, J. Joint rorschach testing of partner relationships. *Family Process*, 1969, *8*, 64–78.
A test of marital partners by the conjoint Rorschach procedure. A sample of 80 pairs was examined with each person administered the Rorschach individually, and then again administered it conjointly with the partner. The goal was to measure the relative strength of the partners and how the personality of the subject changes in the discussion with the other.

WINTER, W. D., FERREIRA, A. J., & BOWERS, N. Decision-making in married and unrelated couples. *Family Process*, 1973, *12*, 83–94.

This is a study of family communications. Twenty married and 20 "synthetic" couples, all college students were given the Ferreira-Winter Questionnaire to study their decision-makling performance. Family communication variables measured in this study were: spontaneous agreement, decision time, choice fulfillment, silence, interruption, explicit information, and politeness. The purpose was to examine the effects of marriage and extensive closeness on the interaction of men and women.

WOLMAN, R. Women's issues in couples treatment—The view of the male therapist. *Psychiatric Opinion*, 1976, *13*, 13–19.
This is the second part of a two-part article on women's issues in Marital Therapy. Data is from the author's clinical practice. It is suggested that changes resulting from the "women's liberation movement" can increase motivation and potential for change in marital therapy or can increase resistance to therapy. Techniques of treatment are discussed.

4.2 SIBLING STUDIES

BANK, S., & KAHN, M. D. Sisterhood–Brotherhood is powerful: Sibling sub-systems and family therapy. *Family Process*, 1975, *14*, 311–337.
Different alliances and joint functions vis-à-vis their parents are explored, also the effects of death or departure of sibling and the functioning of "sick" or "well" sibling relationship operates throughout the life cycle.

DAY, J., & KWIATKOWSKA, H. The psychiatric patient and his "well" sibling: A comparison through their art productions. *Bulletin of Art Therapy*, 1962, *2*, 51–66.
See Reference in Section 3.3

FISCHER, A. The importance of sibling position in the choice of a career in pediatric nursing. *Journal of Health and Humn Behavior*, 1962, *3*, 283–288.
Questionnaires on sibling status and various other background characteristics and attitudes were administered to 109 student nurses in a children's hospital. The hypothesis that senior siblings are more likely to become pediatric nurses than junior siblings holds only for sibling groups of four or more. Further analysis shows that sex composition of the sibling group also affects this career choice. A theory to cover all sibling group sizes, based on opportunities for identification with feminine models is advanced. It is suggested that sibling position, handled more complexly, may be as significant as clinical studies suggest.

FOX, J. R. Sibling incest. *British Journal of Sociology*, 1962,*13*, 128–150.
A consideration of what motivates incestuous and non-incestuous behavior, i.e., the conditions under which incestuous behavior between siblings does and does not occur. Two types of pattern exist: when there is physical separaion before puberty, desire is strong after puberty and temptation must be controlled by strong sanctions; when there is pyhsical interaction before puberty, there will be aversion after puberty and little temptation, anxiety or strong sanctions. Ethnological evidence is introduced to support the hypothesis.

FRIEDMAN, A. S. The "well" sibling in the "sick" family: A contradiction. *International Journal of Social Psychiatry*, special edition *2*, 1964, 47–53.
A discussion of the function and importance of the sibling in treatment of families with a schizophrenic child. Emphasis is upon the sibling who is absent from the family therapy sessions, and it is said that typically this sibling is in "secret" alliance with one of the parents and the absence affects the outcome of the therapy. Clinical examples are given.

GREENBAUM, M. Joint sibling interview as a diagnostic procedure. *Journal of Psycholgy and Psychiatry*, 1965, *6*, 227–232.
See Reference in Section 1.6

JENSEN, S. Five psychotic siblings. *American Journal of Psychiatry*, 1962, *119*, 159–163.
Case report of a family in which 5 of 7 siblings and 10 of 17 members of the last two generations have had psychotic episodes. Genetic, environmental, and psychodynamic theories of etiology are discussed.

KEMPLER, W., IVERSON, R., & BEISSER, A. The adult schizophrenic and his sibling. *Family Process*, 1962, *1*, 224–235.
Sixty-five siblings in a group of 16 schizophrenic families were interviewed using a structured protocol to explore parent–child relationships as seen by the siblings. Findings included distortions in communications by both patients and siblings and appeared unrelated to the schizophrenic process. Four subjects, all of whom were "favorite" children in the family, showed no such distortions. A transcript from a single family is presented.

KRELL, R., & RABKIN, L. The effects of sibling death on the surviving child: A family perspective. *Family Process*, 1979, *18*, 471–477.
Based on material from an outpatient child clinic, family psychodynamics produced by the death of a child are described. Surviving siblings can become the focus of maneuvers unconsciously designed to alleviate guilt and control fate through silence and efforts to maintain silence, through substitution for the lost child, and through endowing the survivor child with qualities of the deceased.

LANE, E. A., & ALBEE, G. W. Early childhood differences between schizophrenic adults and their siblings. *Journal of Abnormal Sociology and Psychology*, 1964, *68*, 193–195.
The IQ tests which had been taken when they were in the second grade were obtained for 36 men and women who were later hospitalized for schizophrenia. These IQ results were compared with those of their siblings taken at the same time. The mean IQ of those who later became schizophrenic was lower than that of the siblings. A control group did not show such differences.

LIDZ, T., FLECK, S., ALANEN, Y. O., & CORNELISON, A. Schizophrenic patients and their siblings. *Psychiatry*, 1963, *26*, 1–18.
A study of the siblings of schizophrenics based upon individual interviews of family members, observation of family members with each other and hospital staff, and projective tests. Sixteen families were studied for periods ranging from 6 months to 6 years. As many siblings were psychotic as were reasonably well adjusted, and all except 5 of 6 of the 24 siblings suffered from severe personality disorders. Siblings of the same sex as the patient were more disturbed than those of the opposite sex.

LU, Y. C. Contradictory parental expectations in schizophrenia. *Archives of General Psychiatry*, 1962, *6*, 219–234.
A report of some preliminary findings of an investigation of the families of schizophrenics. The emphasis is upon comparison of the parents' relationship with patient and with nonschizophrenic siblings in an attempt to explain why one child in a family develops schizophrenia and not another. The parents expect a higher degree of dependence from the preschizophrenic than from the nonschizophrenic child, and they also expect a higher degree of achievement and responsibility. The author suggests that the relational pattern of contradictory parental expectations and the child's persistent effort to fulfill them could be called a "quadruple bind."

LU, Y. C. Mother–Child role relations in schizophrenia: A comparison of schizophrenic patients with non-schizophrenic siblings. *Psychiatry*, 1961, *24*, 133–142.
An investigation into why one child in a family develops schizophrenia and another does not, based upon interviews with 50 chronic schizophrenic patients, their siblings, and their parents. The patient is largely confined to his parents, especially his mother, while the siblings have several significant others.

MEISSNER, W. W. Sibling relations in the schizophrenic family. *Family Process*, 1970, *9*, 1–25.
The purpose of this paper is to review studies on sibling involvement in schizogenic families and to present clinical findings from a family in which the pattern of sibling involvement had striking impact on the development of schizophrenic illness within the family. The material supports the view that schizophrenia is a function of the interaction of parental pathologies. Collusion, paranoia, and anger are discussed.

NEWMAN, G. Younger brothers of schizophrenics. *Psychiatry*, 1966, *29*, 146–151.
As a contribution to intrafamilial dynamics in schizophrenic families, three cases are reported of siblings who had an older brother who was schizophrenic and who developed emotional disorder themselves. The cases were studied by the author in the course of psychotherapy. All three had great guilt from three sources—"letting the older brother bear the burden of the patient's demands, for not saving the older brother from mental illness, and for exercising his own perception, judgment, and initiative."

POLLACK, M., WOERNER, M., GOLDBERG, P., & KLEIN, D. Siblings of schizophrenic and nonschizophrenic psychiatric patients. *Archives of General Psychiatry*, 1969, *20*, 652–658.
This study attempts to test the relative power of genetic versus psychogenic etiology in schizophrenia. Sixty-four sibs of 46 schizophrenic patients 104 sibs of 68 personality disorder patients, and 16 sibs of 13 index cases with psychoneurotic and affective disorders were compared in terms of their psychiatric status. Method was clinical interview in most cases, but where siblings could not be personally contacted, descriptions from the family or from other records were used. Results indicated the sibs of the schizophrenic patients did not differ from those of nonschizophrenic patients in overall incidence of abnormality. None of the many specific family interaction patterns hypothesized to be pathogenic for schizophrenics have thus far been substantiated by methodologically sound studies.

SHARAN (SINGER), & SHLOMO. Family interaction with schizophrenics and their siblings. *Journal of Abnormal Psychology*, 1966, *71*, 345–353.
An experimental study contrasting the behavior of parents of schizophrenics with the patient and with a sibling. Twenty-four families were asked to solve collectively the questions from the comprehension and similarities subtests

of the Wechsler-Bellvue Intelligence Scale. The conversations were compared for problem-solving efficiency, mutual support patterns, and parent–child sex role alignments. Parents and patient worked as efficiently as parents and siblings, parents supported both children equally, and fathers and mothers were equally dominant. The patients were more supportive of their parents than were the siblings, and parental discord was more prominent when the patient was present than when the sibilng was present.

WEST, S. S. Sibling configurations of scientists. *American Journal of Sociology*, 1960, *66*, 268–274.
Birth order and the number of siblings of 813 scientists were obtained as part of a study of 6 research organizations. The aim was to determine what type of family experience is associated with choice of research as a career. First, fifth, and sixth birth ranks are over-represented; second, third, and fourth are under-represented. Siblings are distributed randomly as regards sex. Comparison with data on the general population indicates that as sibship size increases, probability of a scientist coming from family decreases. Isolation in childhood is said to be important in developing the characteristics of a scientist. Data support either a hypothesis that relative isolation is necessary for research career, the hypothesis that mothers of scientists have fewer children than normal.

WYNNE, L. C., & SINGER, M. T. Thought disorder and family relations of schizophrenics. I: A research strategy. II: A classification of forms of thinking. *Archives of General Psychiatry*, 1963, *9*, 191–206.
See Reference in Section 5.2.

ROSENTHAL, D. Confusion of identity and the frequency of schizophrenia in twins. *Archives of General Psychiatry*, 1960, *3*, 297–304.
The author sought to test the hypothesis that if the etiology of schizophrenia is on a familial basis, with gentic as well as psychodynamic factors playing equal roles, than schizophrenia should occur more frequently among twins than among nontwins and among monozygotic than amond dizygotic twins. Case material is from two previouslly reported studies in which the proportions of twins to nontwins with various psychotic illness could be calculated. Findings were that neither schizophrenic nor psychotic illness requiring hospitalization occurred more frequently in twins than in nontwins or in monozygotic than dizygotic twins. The finding suggests that "confusion of ego identity" said to occur more commonly among twins does not have etiological value with respect to schizophrenia.

4.3   FAMILY—MULTIPLE GENERATION

ATTNEAVE, C. L. Therapy in tribal settings and urban network intervention. *Family Process*, 1969, *8*, 192–210.
A comparison of network therapy and interventions in a network clan of a tribal minority culture. An example of treatment with an Indian tribe is contrasted with urban network treatment where the clanlike social structure must be reconstituted.

BEATMAN, F. L. Intergenerational aspects of family therapy. In N. W. Ackerman (Ed.), *Expanding theory and practice in family therapy.* New York: Family Service Association of America, 1967.
A clinical essay focusing on indications or contraindications for bringing in the third generation in family therapy. The third generation often incapacitates the nuclear family. Several case examples are presented in support of bringing in the third generation. The clinical rule of thumb is not on sociologic lines, but rather "lines of meaningful relationships and conflicts."

BELL, N. W. Extended family relations of disturbed and well families. *Family Process*, 1962, *1*, 175–193.
The author's thesis is that "disturbed families have been unable to resolve conflicts with the extended kin outside the nuclear family" and that "well" families have achieved resolution of the problems of ties to extended kin. Most of the data were collected from observations and interviews in the home. Findings were that the "pathological" families used the extended family to (1) shore up group defenses, (2) act as stimuli of conflict, (3) act as screens for the projection of conflicts, and (4) act as competing objects of support.

BOSZORMENYI-NAGY, I. Ethical and practical implications of intergenerational family therapy. *Psychotherapy and Psychosomatics*, 1974, *24*, 261–268.
Techniques of working with intergenerational families (two or three generations in the same family) are explored. It is stressed that "each member has to be both considered in his own rights and alerted to his responsibilities for improving his side of the family balance."

BRODY, E. H., & SPARK, G. Institutionalization of the aged: A family crisis. *Family Process*, 1966, *5*, 76–90.
A discussion of the importance of involving the family in the decision about institutionalizing an aged person. Case examples are given.

EHRENWALD, J. Neurosis in the family. *Archives of General Psychiatry*, 1960, *3*, 232–242.
Assuming that it is maladjusted attitudes rather than specific nosological entities which are subject to psychological contagion, this article discusses the potentially communicable nature of disturbed interpersonal attitudes. Examples are given of a family covering four generations and of three smaller family groups, presenting obsessive-compulsive, psychosomatic, and hysteric features. Epidemiologically, the emphasis is upon "elemenatry units of behavior as are included in our inventory of traits and attitude," rather than on the manifest symptoms.

ERICKSON, G. D. The concept of personal network in clinical practice. *Family Process*, 1975, *14*, 487–498.
This paper reviews the developing strands of network practice, examines some of the forms and characteristics of personal networks and considers several theoretical and practice issues. The importance of developing concepts that link and bridge the three network sectors: kinship, friendship, and care giving is discussed.

FISHER, S., & MENDELL, D. The communications of neurotic patterns over two and three generations. In N. W. Bell, & E. F. Vogel (Eds.), *A modern introduction to the family*. Glencoe: Free Press, 1960.
A report on a study of similarities in the patterning of fantasy and behavior in 2 or more generations of family groups. The data included projective tests and psychiatric interviews. Six families with 3 generations of kin, and 14 families with 2 generations of kin, were examined and impressions are given.

FRANKLIN, P. Famiy therapy of psychotics. *American Journal of Psychoanalysis*, 1969, *29*, 50–56.
A case report of a schizophrenic child and his parents and grandmother who were treated both individually and with famiy therapy over 7 years. The author's thesis is that schizophrenic symptoms are a manifestation of a process that "involves the entire family." The identified patient and the family improved after treatment.

HADER, M. The importance of grandparents in family life. *Family Process*, 1965, *4*, 228–240.
A discussion of the significance of grandparents in the life of young people and their significance to young people. The literature is reviewed on grandparents with a division between the positive and negative influences.

JENSEN, S. Five psychotic siblings. *American Journal of Psychiatry*, 1962, *119*, 159–163.
See Reference in Section 4.2.

LEADER, A. L. The place of in-laws in marital relationships. *Social casework*, 1975, *56*, 486–491.
The interpersonal relationships of in-laws with family of origin and current famiy are described. In-laws have various meanings to spouses, including working out past, positive, and negative relationships with their own parents (for example, adopted children or those children who have been raised extensively in foster homes). By the same token, inlaws have strong effects on sons- or daughters-in-law. For example, an inlaw may seek out a son-in-law to "give the nurturance they never gave before" or to punish, or infantilize etc. How this behavior contributes to symptoms of various family members is discussed.

LITWAK, E. Geographic mobility and family cohesion. *American Sociological Review*, 1960, *25*, 385–394.
A second paper reporting a study of the families of 920 married white women living in a middle class urban area. Several hypotheses about the relationship of identification with extended kin and occupational mobility are tested. The data indicate that extended families do not hinder but rather aid geographical, and hence, occupational mobility.

LITWAK, E. Occupational mobility and extended family cohesion. *American Sociological Review*, 1960, *25*, 9–21.
Parson's view that occupational mobility is antithetical to the extended family system is questioned. In this study of visiting and identification patterns in the families of 920 married white women living in a middle-class urban area, the findings support the modified view tht the extended family in a mature industrial society can provide aid across class lines without hindering mobility.

MENDELL, D., & CLEVELAND, S. A. Three-generation view of a school phobia. *Voices*, 1967, *3*, 16–19.
This is a case report in support of the notion that psychopathology is "passed on from generation to generation with a more or less specific way and expectation of handling it." Three generations of data from the identified patient, a 14-year-old boy, his mother, and maternal grandmother was obtained from clinical psychiatric interviews and the Rorschach and Thematic Apperception Tests. The School phobia of the identified patient is seen as an attempt to answer the "obsessive concern" of the boy's relationship to his mother and her relationship to her mother.

MENDELL, D., CLEVELAND, S., & FISHER, S. A five-generation family theme. *Family Process*, 1968, *7*, 126–132.
A study examining projective test fantasies of family members. Five generations of one family were examined, including examination of 27 members. It was found that a family selects one or two central themes, which are perpetuated in the responses of family members across generations.

MENDELL, D., & FISHER, S. An approach to neurotic behavior in terms of a three-generation family model. *Journal of Nervous and Mental Disorder*, 1956, *123*, 171–180.

This is one of a series of papers pointing out that psychopathology can be understood in terms of a three-generational family model. The data was obtained from the author's clinical experience, other studies in the literature, and projective data from the Rorschach and TAT. Data from one case is offered in support of these hypotheses.

NAPIER, A. Y. The marriage of families: Cross generational complementarity. *Family Process*, 1971, *10*, 373–395. See reference in Section 4.1.

PETURSSON, E. A study of parental deprivation and illness in 291 psychiatric patients. *International Journal of Social Psychiatry*, 1961, *7*, 97–105.
A group of 291 patients with functional psychiatric illness was observed by the author and information gathered about their parents from them, from spouses or relatives, or by direct observation in some instances. The parents suffered from functional psychiatric illness in 77.5 percent of the cases. The incidence of broken homes was 31.7 percent. There appeared to be a high incidence of patients developing the same type of psychiatric illness as the parents in various categories. Well integrated family units occurred in the background of patients in only 11.7 percent of the cases.

REISS, P. J. The extended kinship system: Correlates of and attitudes on frequency of interaction. *Marriage and Family Living*, 1962, *24*, 333–339.
A report of a study of urban middle-class kinship systems with emphasis upon frequency of contact and attitudes about it. A sample was selected from the metropolitan Boston area and interviewed. The conclusions are that frequency of interaction are not explained by the sex, ethnic background, or family cycle phase of the respondents. Degree of kin relationship and distance of residence of kin are the most important variables. Half of the respondents felt the frequency of contact with kin has been insufficient and there is a desire for kin to live close but not too close.

SCHERZ, F. The crisis of adolescence in family life. *Social Casework*, 1967, *48*, 209–215.
Adolescence is seen as a time of crisis for the family in addition to the patient. When behavioral symptoms come up, family treatment is indicated. The influence of grandparents in the chain of family communication is discussed.

SCOTT, R., & ASHWORTH, P. Closure at the first schizophrenic breakdown: A family study. *British Journal of Medical Psychology*, 1967, *40*, 109–146.
See Reference in Section 5.2.

SOBEL, D. E. Children of schizophrenic patients: Preliminary observations on early development. *American Journal of Psychiatry*, 1961, *118*, 512–517.
A report on observations of the early development of children whose parents are both schizophrenic. Four infants were raised by their schizophrenic parents and four raised by foster parents. Three of the four children raised by their original schizophrenic parents developed clear signs of depression and irritability in infancy. None of the four infants raised by foster parents developed any such clear signs of emotional disorder. The three schizophrenic mothers engaged in relatively little active play with their infants or showed pleasurable responsiveness. Case details are presented.

SPARK, G. M. Grandparents and intergenerational family therapy. *Family Process*, 1974, *13*, 225–237.
This article explores loyalty, justice and the balance of merit in the unsettled accounts between first and second generation family members. The author indicates that often second generation families live out unresolved conflicts/loyalties of first generation family members. Using a case example, the author demonstrates the technique of including parents and grandparents in therapy session. She shows a famiy changing fundamentally through the inclusion of their parents in treatment and through the therapist's ability to facilitate major intergenerational rebalancing.

SPARK, G. M. & BRODY, E. M. The aged are family members. *Family Process*, 1970, *9*, 195–210.
This paper suggests that inclusion of older family members when appropriate in the treatment of younger families can be beneficial in preventive repetition of the same pathological patterns. Family members in all generations may benefit from such treatment. Clinical evidence is presented.

STUCKERT, R. P. Occupational mobility and family relationships. *Social Forces*, 1963, *41*, 301–307.
Conflicting theories as to whether the extended family is compatibile with mobiity have been advanced. To resolve this issue and determine whether mobility affects other forms of interaction, 266 white married couples in Milwaukee were interviewed. Current status was assessed by occupation. Mobility was assessed relative to parental occupations. Mobility is shown to be conversely related to frequency of contacts, lesser identification with extended family, lesser tendency to use the extended family as a reference group, lesser tendency to use neighbors as a reference group, and higher participation of wives in voluntary associations. It is concluded that mobility is detrimental to extended family relations, and tends to produce social isolation of married women.

SUSSMAN, M. B. Adaptive, directive, and integrative behavior of today's family. *Family Process*, 1968, *7*, 239–250.
A discussion of the relationship between the nuclear family and its kinship structure, as well as between other social institutions. It is said that the kin network acquires commitments by rewards perceived as superior to those offered by other social structures and so establishes tradition-laden obligations among family members.

SWEETSER, D. A. Mother–daugther ties between generations in industrial societies. *Family Process*, 1964, *3*, 332–343.
A report of cross-generational family relations in Finland and Sweden. Although the nuclear family is relatively independent, strong kinship ties are maintained most frequently, with the married couples sharing a household with wives' parents rather than with those of the husbands.

TRIBBEY, J. A. Like father, like son: A projection-displacement pattern. *Bullentin of the Menninger Clinic*, 1964, *28*, 244–251.
A study concerned with the frequency with which a son begins to take up the behavior of an antisocial father. Case material was from 55 boys referred for treatment to the psychiatric diagnostic unit of a children's receiving home. Of the 55, 10 were judged by the author to have histories similar to that of the father. The overall family picture is "that of a boy whose parents are divorced, and whose father has a long-standing history of antisocial behavior. Before long, as the mother had always 'known,' the son begins to get into trouble." Dynamics are discussed. Poor treatment results with these cases are pointed out.

TOLSDORF, C. C. Social networks, support, and coping: An exploratory study. *Family Process*, 1976, *15*, 407–417.
This study examines the utility of the social network model by applying it to the areas of stress, support, and coping. Extensive interviews were conducted by the author with 20 subjects, 10 of whom were schizophrenic males and 10 of whom were recently hospitalized medical subjects. All subjects were veterans matched for age, education, socioeconomic status, and marital status. Quantitative data and qualitative data were gathered and analyzed. Psychiatric subjects reported fewer intimate network associations, more family members dominating the network and fewer but more powerful functional members. In contrast, medical subjects reported more intimate relationships, fewer family members and the power of functional members was more balanced with that of the subject. These differences suggest that the larger social systems within which persons interact may be explored through the network model, and that this approach may be a valuable tool in furthering research in the family.

YOUNG, T. L. Family neuropsychiatry. *Diseases of the Nervous System*, 1963, *24*, 243–246.
A report by a physician, trained in both neurology and psychiatry, of impressions gained from treating 114 cases from 43 families for neurologic, psychotic, and psychoneurotic states. Numerous cases are cited in support of the author's impressions that mental disturbances run in families, and that one family member's illness has significant effect on other family members.

WALSH, F. W. Concurrent grandparent death and birth of schizophrenic offspring: An intriguing finding. *Family Process*, 1978, *17*, 457–463.
See reference in Section 5.2.

4.4 FAMILY CRISIS STUDIES

BARD, M., & BERKOWITZ, B. A community psychology consultation program in police family crisis intervention: Preliminary impressions. *International Journal of Social Psychiatry*, 1969, *15*, 209–215.
This is the second in a series of reports describing training of police in family crisis intervention with patients of low socioeconomic class. Rationale for the program, methods of selection, and techniques of training (which included use of family crisis laboratory demonstrations and "human relations workshops") are presented. The unit operates by having a biracial pair on duty around the clock. There are three special groups, which meet weekly to discuss the ongoing program, and each policeman has an individual consultant for one hour a week. Although no data is presented, it is the author's impression that this technique provides more satisfactory crisis intervention than previous methods, has an indirect value for the community, and provides less danger to the policeman in fulfilling his role.

BARD, M., & BERKOWITZ, B. Training police as specialists in family crisis intervention: A community psychology action program. *Community Mental Health Journal*, 1967, *3*, 315–337.
A description of a project to train policemen in doing family crisis intervention based on the idea that family crises often precipitate criminal acts or that policemen are often called as a first line of defense during family crisis. During

the preparatory phase, volunteers were given lectures, field trips, and "learning by doing" demonstrations. An evaluation of the program is planned.

BOLMAN, W. Preventive psychiatry for the family: Theory, approaches, and programs. *American Journal of Psychiatry*, 1968, *125*, 458–472.
See Reference in Section 4.5.

BRODY, E. H., & SPARK, G. "Institutionalization of the Aged: A Family Crisis," *Family Process*, 1966, *5*, 76–90.
A discussion of the importance of involving the family in the decision about institutionalizing an aged person. Case examples are given.

CAPLAN, G. Patterns of parental response to the crisis of premature birth: A preliminary approach to modifying the mental health outcome. *Psychiatry*, 1960, *23*, 365–374.
Types of response to the crisis of a premature birth were derived from interview data of 10 cases where the baby weighed less than 4 pounds and the records were sufficiently detailed so a case could be assigned unambiguously to an extreme category of healthy or unhealthy outcome. Cases were classified as "healthy outcome" if all relationships in the family were as healthy or more healthy than before the birth and if parent-child relationships were healthy at the end of 12 weeks. "Unhealthy outcomes" were the reverse. It is hoped that further studies will help professional people recognize extreme patterns associated with poor outcome to a crisis so that they can intervene promptly.

COUNTS, R. Family crisis and the impulsive adolescent. *Archives of General Psychiatry*, 1967, *17*, 64–74.
A case example is presented in support of the hypothesis that the acting out of an adolescent can best be understood by seeing it as acting out of a family crisis. The adolescent is used as a scapegoat of the family who acts out somebody else's impulses, which helps to stabilize his or her own internal operations while it stabilizes the family.

EISLER, R. M. Crisis intervention in the family of a firesetter. *Psychotherapy: Theory, Research and Practice*, 1972, *9*, 76–79.
One case is presented in support of the thesis that family stresses are causal to the firesetting in the case. Family therapy was given. A 4-month follow-up revealed improvement, and one-year follow-up revealed no further firesetting.

EISLER, R. M. & HERSEN, M. Behavioral techniques in family-oriented crisis intervention. *Archives of General Psychiatry*, 1973, *28*, 111–116.
See Reference in Section 1.1.

EVERSTINE, D. S., BODIN, A. M., & EVERSTINE, L. Emergency psychology: A mobile service for police crisis calls. *Family Process*, 1977, *16*, 281–292.
This paper describes an emergency treatment center, which has been in operation since 1975. The 24-hour program for crisis intervention backs up police departments to provide help to people with family crises, suicide attempts, and severe emotional disturbances. The service provided to 340 families included initial and follow-up visits which were mostly conducted at the homes of the clients. Results of a pilot survey showed a significant reduction of costs compared to outpatient visits in the surrounding community mental health programs.

FLOMENHAFT, K., & LANGSLEY, D. After the crisis. *Mental Hygiene*, 1971, *55*, 473–477.
This is a follow-up report from a crisis intervention unit that stressed family therapy. It was previously found that "crisis intervention had little effect on long-term patterns of individual and family behavior." One reason for this was the impression that the referral to the crisis unit often came when the referring agency was unable to manage the patient or was frustrated with his refusal to follow its recommendation. The report describes methods of working with such agencies. Referrals should be 'live' (in contrast to a written letter or a name and address). Private physicians and community mental health clinics are the most difficult to work with in coordinating efforts with the patient and family, because once the family loses motivation, the case is dropped.

GARRISON, J. Network techniques: Case studies in the screening-linking-planning conference method. *Family Process*, 1974, *13*, 337–353.
This paper describes the Screening-Linking-Planning (SLP) conference method as a technique for social network intervention. The technique takes advantage of certain characteristics of people in crisis which makes them amenable to change. The technique includes involving a person's network in a supportive way, making known positive expectations, and relabeling negative behaviors into positive ones. Three case histories are used to describe this method and its success with acute and chronic hospital patients.

GLASSMAN, R., LIPTON, H., & DUNSTAN, P. Group discussions with a hospitalized schizophrenic and his family. *International Journal of Group Psychotherapy*, 1959, *9*, 204–212.
See Reference in Section 1.7.

GROUP FOR THE ADVANCEMENT OF PSYCHIATRY, Committee on the Family. *Integration and conflict in family behavior. Report No. 27.* Topeka, 1954.
A report by the committee on the family of GAP dealing with organizing data on the study of the family. It discusses the relation of the family to the social system, the system of values to which the family is oriented, and Spanish-American family patterns as well as American middle-class family patterns. 67 pp.

HADLEY, R. T., JACOB, T., MILLIONES, J. et al: The relationship between family developmental crisis and the appearance of symptoms in a family member. *Family Process*, 1974, *13*, 207–214.
This is a study of symptom formation in family member(s) following family crises. Ninety families were studied who had experienced the loss of a member or addition of a member. Results showed a significant correlation between time since the crisis and likelihood of symptoms in family members.

JENSEN, D., & WALACE, J. G. Family mourning process. *Family Process*, 1967, *6*, 56–66.
A discussion of mourning as a family crisis involving all members. Two case examples are given. Therapy is seen as intervening in maladaptive family interaction patterns resulting from the loss of a member.

KAPLAN, D. M., & MASON, E. A. Maternal reactions to premature birth viewed as an acute emotional disorder. *American Journal of Orthopsychiatry*, 1960, *30*, 539–552.
A study of the maternal reaction to premature birth being carried out in the Harvard School of Public Health Family Guidance Center. Examination of 60 families following the premature birth indicates a typical psychological experience for the mother. The maternal stress begins with the onset of labor and continues through delivery and after. Case examples are given of more and less successful resolution of the situation.

KRITZER, H., & PITTMAN, F. S. Overnight psychiatric care in a general emergency room. *Journal of Hospital and Community Psychiatry*, 1968, *19*, 303–306.
A clinical article reviewing the experience with 36 psychiatric patients who came to the emergency room because of a crisis. As alternatives to inpatient hospitalization, overnight hospitalization, and the emergency room were used. Rationale was that the patients' presenting problems were often a manifestation of underlying family problems, and, by temporarily relieving the crisis and working out the future management, inpatient hospitalization could be avoided. Results indicated that of 36 patients, 11 were essentially sent to a psychiatric hospital, 22 were discharged directly from the emergency room, and 3 signed out against medical advice.

LANGSLEY, D., PITTMAN, F., & SWANK, G. Family crisis in schizophrenics and other mental patients. *Journal of Nervous and Mental Disease*, 1969, *149*, 270–276.
A further report on a study using crisis therapy as an alternative to psychiatric hospitalization. In this study, 50 families which included a schizophrenic patient and 50 which included a nonschizophrenic mental patient were studied using an instrument which quanitified the events leading to a crisis in the family and the management of such crises. Nonschizophrenic mental patients were better able to handle crisis and were better able to interact with their families. Discussion of these findings is presented.

LANGSLEY, D. G., PITTMAN, F., MACHOTKA, P., & FLOMENHAFT, K. Family crisis therapy: Results and implications. *Family Process*, 1968, 7, 145–159.
A report on the crisis treatment unit established at Colorado Psychiatric Hospital in Denver. A total of 186 cases randomly selected were treated by brief family treatment and compared with control cases hospitalized in the usual way. Preliminary results are reported.

LANGSLEY, D., FLOMENHAFT, K., & MACHOTKA, P. Follow-up evaluation of family crisis therapy. *American Journal of Orthopsychiatry*, 1969, *39*, 753–759.
One of a series of papers on a research project in which families were assigned randomly either to tranditional hospital treatment or family crisis therapy with a focus on family therapy. Six-month follow-up evaluations of 150 family crisis therapy cases and 150 hospital treatment cases demonstrated that patients are less likely to be rehospitalized in the former group.

MORRISON, G., & COLLIER, J. Family treatment approaches to suicidal children and adolescents. *Journal of the American Academy of Child Psychiatry,* 1969, *8*, 140–154.
A study of 34 patients referred to a child psychiatry emergency service because of a suicide attempt. There were 28 girls and 6 boys in the sample, with 65 percent of the group between the ages of 15 and 17. They were seen with their families by a psychiatrist and social worker. Rationale was that the suicide attempt was an effort on the part of the child to reveal underlying family disruption. After the acute crisis was resolved using family therapy, 30 of the 34 patients were referred for further therapy. Of these 30, 28 accepted the recommendation, but only 8 made further interviews and only 2 were in treatment 1 year after the suicide attempt.

MOSS, S. School experience as family crisis. *Journal of the International Association of Pupil and Personnel Workers*, 1970, *15*, 115–121.
This clinical paper offers a critique of current methods for dealing with school "problem children." The school's focus has been on the child rather than on the family system. The event of the child going off to the school is a nodal point for the entire family. How the family deals with separation and the demands of the school has a direct effect on how the child is able to cope with the school. "A child's school problem must be seen in the light of the family's function."

NEALON, J. The adolescent's hospitalization as a family crisis. *Archives of General Psychiatry*, 1964, *11*, 302–312.
A study of the reactions of 25 sets of parents to the hospitalization of an adolscent member of the family. Data were collected from parents' initial interviews with caseworker. Interviews were held before admission or as soon as possible afterward. The hospitalization was defined as a family crisis because "of the impact of mental illness on the family, family disruption precipitating and following hospitalization, and the parent's expectation of the hospitalization." Family-oriented approach is stressed, and implications for treatment are discussed.

PARAD, H. J., & CAPLAN, G. A framework for studying families in crises. *Social Work*, 1960, 5, 3–15.
An approach to the observation and study of the family in crisis. Family members are seen individually and as a group in the home, while engaged in household activities. The concepts of family lifestyle, problem-solving mechanisms, and need–response patterns are illustrated with a case history. It is suggested that intervention is most effective at the moment the family is in crisis.

PATTISON, W. M. Treatment of alcoholic families with nurse home visits. *Family Process*, 1965, *4*, 75–94.
The use of public health nurses in making home visits is described in terms of preventive crisis intervention and family therapy. The results in a study of 7 families are offered with case examples and it is said the public health nurse can play a decisive role, particularly with lowerclass, multiproblem familes.

PITTMAN, F., DEYOUNG, C., FLOMENHAFT, K., KAPLAN, D., & LANGSLEY, D. Crisis family therapy. In J. Masserman (Ed.), *Current psychiatric therapies* (Vol. VI) New York: Grune & Stratton, 1966.
A report of the author's experiences in using a family approach in dealing with acute crisis situations, rather than using hospitalization or individual psychotherapy. Setting was an acute treatment facility which hospitalizes about 75 percent of patients referred. Of these, 25 percent were referred to the family treatment unit consisting of a psychiatrist, social worker, and nurse. Fifty cases were referred to this unit and in 42 cases hospitalization was "avoided completely." Techniques of treatment are discussed.

PITTMAN, F., LANGLSEY, D., FLOMENHAFT, K., DEYOUNG, D., & MACHOTKA, P. Therapy techniques of the family treatment unit. In J. Haley (Ed.), *Changing families*. New York: Grune & Stratton, 1971.
A report on the therapy techniques of the crisis treatment unit in Denver which did brief family therapy to keep people out of the hospital. Different approaches used are described.

PITTMAN, F., LANGSLEY, D., KAPLAN, D., FLOMENHAFT, K., & DEYOUNG, C. Family therapy as an alternative to psychiatric hospitalization. In I. M. Cohen (Ed.), *Psychiatric research report no. 20*. Washington, D.C.: American Psychiatric Association, 1966.
A report on the crisis treatment team at the Colorado Psychopathic Hospital which treated a random selection of patients and their families as an alternative to hospitalization. Case examples are given.

POLAK, P. R., EGAN, D., VANDENBERGH, R., & WILLIAMS, W. V. Prevention in mental health: a controlled study. *American Journal of Psychiatry*, 1975, *132*, 146–149.
This controlled study tests the notion that family therapy after a stressful event can prevent subsequent psychiatric illness in the family. Design included an experimental group of 39 families who received crisis intervention following a recent, sudden death; a control group of 66 families who received no crisis intervention following a recent, sudden death; and another control group of 56 families who experienced no death within 2 years prior to contact and who received no crisis intervention. Outcome measures, using a variety of self-report and family measurement devices, were obtained 6 months following the crisis. Data were analyzed using a principal-components factor analysis. Results indicate that there was no significant difference among groups in improving coping behavior, lowering instances of medical and psychiatric illness, or improving social functioning in bereaved families.

RUEVENI, U. Network intervention with a family in crisis. *Family Process*, 1975, *14*, 193–203.
The process of network intervention is described with a family triad ending with an assembly of 35 supportive individuals. Six distinct phases are described: (1) retribalization; (2) polarization; (3) mobilization; (4) depression; (5) break through; and (6) exhaustion and elation.

RUEVENI, V. The family therapist as a system inverventionist. *International Journal of Family therapy*, 1979, *1*, 63–75.

Crises are often resolved by families reconnecting with additional sources of support, frequently the extended family relatives. The therapist can function in the role of the "convenor" of such an extended network. Six phases of such intervention and the roles taken by the therapist in convening, mobilizing and directing such support are described. References to clinical work are used as examples.

SAMPSON, H., MESSINGER, S., & TOWNE, R. D. Family processes and becoming a mental patient. *American Journal of Sociology*, 1962, *68*, 88–96.
The accommodation of the family to the deviant behavior of the future patient, and the disruption of this accommodation which leads to hospitalization are described for a series of 17 married mothers. Patients were located at time of first admission and extensive data collected by interviews with family members, by professionals involved at any stage, and by direct observation in home and hospital. Types of accommodation found were: (1) spouses isolated, emotionally distant from each other, and (2) family not self-contained but revolved about a maternal figure who took over wife's duties. Each type has characteristic ways of disrupting, resulting in different implications in hospitalization.

SAMPSON, H., MESSINGER, S., & TOWNE, R. D. The mental hospital and family adaptations. *Psychiatric Quarterly*, 1962, *36*, 704–719.
The authors' purpose was to examine the effects of hospitalization on the family, not only during the hospitalization but also after discharge. Seventeen families in which the wife-mother was hospitalized for the first time and was diagnosed by the state hospital as schizophrenic were studied using interviews and records up to 2 years after release. Emphasis is placed on a more deliberate therapeutic intervention based on study of the crisis that precipitated hospitalization and ways in which these crises are coped with by the family.

SIMMONS, R., HICKEY, K., KJELLSTRAND, C., & SIMMONS, R. L. Family tension in the search for a kidney donor. *Journal of the American Medical Association*, 1971, *215*, 909–910.
This is a study of family relationships at the time that the donation of a kidney is needed from a family member. A series of 78 consecutive cases from a renal transplant center were reviewed. In 21, children were recipients; in the remainder, adults were the recipients. The focus, in contrast to previous studies, was on the family unit including the nondonor. Results indicated that children did not seem to generate the same kind of crisis in decision making as did adult recipients. In 13 of the 57 adult cases, significant family tensions involving potential sibling donors revealed marked mixed feelings of the donors in conflict with family members; e.g., the spouse of the potential donor refused to let the donor donate.

SIMMONS, R., & KLEIN, S. Family noncommunication: A search for kidney donors. *American Journal of Psychiatry*, 1972, *129*, 687–692.
Decision making in families during crisis was studied using a sample of 59 patients and their families on a kidney transplant service. Each family's members were interviewed intensely throughout the transplant period, and the family interaction was reconstructed to attempt to understand what transpired in making the decision about transplantation. Findings indicated that communication channels were "blocked." After the transplant, there was an improvement in family cohesion.

SLIVKIN, S. E. Death and living: A family approach. *American Journal of Psychoanalysis*, 1977, *37*, 317–323.
See Reference in Section 5.6.

WELLISCH, D. K. Adolescent acting out when a parent has cancer. *International Journal of Family Therapy*, 1979, *1*, 230–241.
Six case reports of adolescents with a parent with cancer are presented in order to document the adolescents' reactions to this stress and how these reactions in turn affect the family. "Acting out" is found to be a common problem, and if focal points for intervention are recognized (e.g., shifts in the adolescent's role) crisis intervention treatment can be effective.

WETHERILL, P. S. Predictability, failure and guilt in suicide: A personal account. *Family Process*, 1975, *14*, 339–370.
The lifetime medical, social, and psychiatric history of a young man, accumulated from the time he was 4 years old until he was 21 years old is presented. The observations are recorded by his mother. The predictability of the suicide is discussed, and questions are raised about personal and professional responsibility and guilt.

WHITIS, P. R. The legacy of a child's suicide. *Family Process*, 1968, *7*, 159–169.
A discussion of the effect on a family of a child's suicide illustrated with a case report. Prompt therapeutic intervention is recommended for the bereaved family.

4.5   THE FAMILY IN THE COMMUNITY

ACKERMAN, N. W. Adolescent problems: A symptom of family disorder. *Family Process*, 1962, *1*, 202–213.
An essay based on the thesis that adolescent problems represent in part not only a disorder of a particular stage of growth but also a symptom of a parallel disorder in the family, society, and culture. Clinical examples are given.

ACKERMAN, N. Family healing in a troubled world. *Social Casework*, 1971, *52*, 200–205.
This is a clinical essay stressing the point that disorders of society "invade and infect" daily family and community life. Family mechanisms to cope with these problems are listed. Attention must be paid not only to families, but the "families within the community" and the entire social community itself. It is suggested that family helpers *go to* the homes and offer direct "action" as well as talking therapies.

AHMED, F. Family and mental disorders in Pakistan. International Journal of Social Psychiatry, 1968, *14*, 290–295.
See Reference in Section 3. 1.

ANDERSON, L. M. & SHAFER, G. The character-disordered family: A community treatment model for family sexual abuse. *American Journal of Orthopsychiatry*, 1979, *49*, 436–445.
This study describes a model for treatment of "sexually abusive" families (defined as families in which a minor child is sexually mistreated by a parent or guardian). Demographic data collected on 62 families seen by an urban mental health agency is reported, and phases of treatment explained. Based on incidences of alcohol abuse (65 percent), criminality (37 percent), etc., the concept of the "character-disordered" family is developed. Interagency coordination of services and *involuntary* treatment is recommended.

ANDREWS, R. G. Adoption: Legal resolution or legal fraud? *Family Process*, 1978, *17*, 313–328.
This paper is part of a series in a symposium on "The Family and Child Placement Practices." It reviews the present status and effects of adoption procedures on the psychological development of the adoptee and on the biological and adoptive families. It suggests that the attitudes and practices of secrecy by the courts, agencies, and adoptive families have "intensified the adoptees' feelings of being different" and " cut off" from their roots. However, if adoption records are unsealed by new legal practices, the primary needs of the adoptive and biological parents can be undermined by the needs of the adopted adult. It recommends greater openness in adoption practices in order for less tension to develop.

APONTE, H. J. The family-school interview: An eco-structural approach. *Family Process*, 1976, *15*, 303–311.
The author describes a systems approach to students' problems that considers the interaction between and among the child, the school, and the family and attempts to define and integrate the resources of each system within this context of the school interview for the purpose of solving school-related problems.

ARONSON, J., & POLGAR, S. Pathogenic relationships in schizophrenia. *American Journal of Psychiatry*, 1962, *119*, 222–227.
See Reference in Section 5.2.

AUERSWALD, E. H. Families, change, and the ecological perspective. *Family Process*, 1971, *10*, 263–280.
This paper presents the state of families and of family therapy in the U.S. from an epistological viewpoint of ecology. Three groups are examined with this view: a segment of middle-class youth; a segment of the chronically poor who are mostly members of minority groups, largely black; and a group of ecologists within the older generation of scientists. Their family processes are reviewed, including the crises generated by influences coming from different sources within our society.

BELL, J. & BELL, E. Family participation in hospital care for children. *Chidren*, 1970, *17*, 154–157.
This is a report of the authors' experiences visiting hospitals in Africa and in Asia in order to determine the role of the family when a member is hospitalized. The more modern the facility, the less involved the family was with the patient. The more involved the family was, the more psychologically secure were both patient and family.

BERTRAND, A. L. School attendance and attainment: Function and dysfunction of school and family social systems. *Social Forces*, 1962, *40*, 228–233.
The hypothesis is advanced that the dropping out of school of capable youths is dysfunctional for the society but functional for family, school, and other primary social systems. Data were gathered in Louisiana from 369 students and 68 dropouts and from 125 and 68 of their parents, respectively. The families of dropouts are found to be farm-laborers rather than owners and managers, have less education, less involement in school affairs, place a low value on education, and were of lower status. Dropouts also are geographically distant from schools, have low grades, participate little in school activities, and do not find the school system compatible.

BOLMAN, W. Preventive psychiatry for the family: Theory, approaches and programs. *American Journal of Psychiatry*, 1968, *125*, 458–472.

A detailed paper attempting to integrate the ideas on preventive psychiatry for the family with systems theory. Goals, approaches, and specific programs are given for various types of populations, e.g., families in crisis due to loss of a member.

BRODEY, W., & HAYDEN, M. Intrateam reactions: Their relation to the conflicts of the family in treatment. *American Journal of Orthopsychiatry*, 1957, *27*, 349–356.
A clinical report emphasizing the notion that reactions of treating personnel to each other are in part a reenactment of conflicts of the family. Data were obtained from an outpatient child guidance clinic team of psychotherapist and caseworker. Five case examples were given to support this hypothesis. By focusing on the reactions of the workers, significant dynamics trends can be identified and therapy can be accelerated. The building of family conflicts that influence the intrateam reactions depends upon the power of the family conflict and the sensitivity of the team equilibrium to this particular stress.

BURSTEN, B. Family dynamics, the sick role, and medical hospital admissions. *Family Process*, 1965, *4*, 206–216.
A discussion of how the medical hospital may be used in the service of family patterns. There may be no organic difficulty, or an organic difficulty can be combined with psychosocial factors to resolve a family conflict. Case examples are given.

CAREK, D. J., & WATSON, A. S. Treatment of a family involved in fractricide. *Archives of General Psychiatry*, 1964, *11*, 533–543.
Case report of a family in which the eldest male sibling (age 10) shot and killed the youngest male sibling. The parents were treated with conjoint family therapy, and the oldest sibling was hospitalized. Data were collected from the conjoint family meetings and from observations of the hospitalized patient. Formulation and treatment is discussed. The data are related to "society's philosophical view of illegal behavior and treatment, and some speculations about therapeutic implementation."

CHATTERJEE, P. The deserving underclass: A focus for social work policy in the year 2001. *Family Process*, 1973, *12*, 189–196.
This paper poses the future changes in the roles and functions provided by social workers to individuals in our society that might result if the institution of marriage lost its traditional characteristics. By utilizing a hypothetical decision by the Supreme Court declaring the institution of matrimony as unconstitutional, the author speculates about the orientation given to social workers' professional activities. The decision would generate a new type of "sexual underclass," and the professional would need to develop policy guidelines to serve this new underclass.

CHOPE, H. D., & BLACKFORD, L. The chronic problem family: San Mateo County's Experience. *American Journal of Orthopsychiatry*, 1963, *33*, 462–469.
A report summarizing ideas developed by the San Mateo Department of Health and Welfare in dealing with the chronic, multiproblem famiy and their multiple agency services. They point out that the agencies helping the chronic, multiproblem family cannot function independently and suggest one worker to "represent the family."

CLARK, A. W., & VAN SOMMERS, P. Contradictory demands in family relations and adjustment to school and home. *Human Relations*, 1961, *14*, 97–111.
See Reference in Section 3.2.

COLLOMB, H., & VALANTIN, S. The black African family. In E. J. Anthony, & C. Koupernik (Eds.), *The child in his family*. New York: Wiley, 1970.
A description of the black African family with the emphasis upon demographic data, cultural and social frameworks, filiation and lineage, and intrafamilial relationships.

COLEMAN, S. B., & STANTON, M. D. An index for measuring agency involvement in family therapy. *Family Process*, 1978, *17*, 479–483.
This paper reports on the Progress Index for Family Therapy Programs, an instrument for measuring the relative level of involvement in family therapy by treatment programs. It was developed as part of a national survey on the use of family therapy for treating drug abuse. It includes data from 500 agencies, 76 of which were community mental health centers.

COLON, F. In search of one's past: An identity trip. *Family Process*, 1973, *12*, 429–438.
This paper is an autobiographical note in which the author shows that a person's identity is profoundly related to his sense of connection to his family of origin. As a foster child he tried to get himself reconnected to his natural family. It presents some questions about policies of foster-care agencies.

CONSTANTINE, L. L. 2001—Controversy continues. *Family Process*, 1974, *13*, 395–398.
On prostitution and intimacy, a review of Chatterjee's article "The deserving underclass . . . " (Family Process, 1973), with a reply by Chatterjee.

CULBERT, S. A. & RENSHAW, J. R. Coping with the stresses of travel as an opportunity for improving the quality of work and family life. *Family Process*, 1972, *11*, 321–337.
This paper describes a "workshop" that was set up in an industrial organization to help families cope with the problems created by business travel. Couples explored their individual and joint response to the stress and were aided in developing collaborative coping resources.

CURRY, A. E. The family therapy situation as a system. *Family Process*, 1966, *5*, 131–141.
A discussion of the processes that occur between a family unit and the family therapist which involve neutralizing the therapist, reestablishing the family's pretherapy equilibrium, and disrupting the overall family therapy situation. Processes of coalition, coalescence, and coagulation are presented with examples.

DIBELLA, G. A. W. Family psychotherapy with the homosexual family. *Community Mental Health Journal*, 1979, *15*, 41–46.
This is an essay on the need for (and lack of) family therapy in community psychiatry for homosexual families. The sample was 600 families treated over 5 years in a large community mental health clinic. The reasons for treatment included reactions to homosexuality, training difficulties, and pressure from the rest of the community. It is believed that family therapy is an effective way to treat homosexuals and should be available.

EPSTEIN, N., & CLEGHORN, J. The family transactional approach in general hospital psychiatry: Experiences, problems, and principles. *Comprehensive Psychiatry*, 1966, *7*, 389–396.
A paper dealing with the experiences and problems arising, and principles derived from, the introduction of concepts of famiy dynamics and family therapy in the psychiatry departments of two general hospitals. The concepts were used in the outpatient department, community department, inpatient service, and the day hospital. Ongoing supervision for family as well as for individual therapy is stressed.

ERICKSON, G. Combined family and service network intervention. *Service Worker*, 1973, *41*, 276–283.
This essay describes an approach to working with poverty families linked with a variety of health, social welfare, and educational agencies. The usual probelm is that such agencies often pull in separate directions, resulting in dissolution of the family rather than better functioning. The suggested goal is mutual agreement among the various helping professions of key tasks for problem-solving. "Working with networks" is thought to be a useful technique. One case example is presented in support of the techniques presented.

FINE, P. Family networks and child psychiatry in a community health project. *Journal of the American Academy of Child Psychiatry*, 1974, *12*, 675–689.
This is a clinical paper describing therapeutic approaches that involved the family network to treat problems of children in a community mental health center in an urban ghetto. Four cases are presented to illustrate the technique.

FLECK, S., CORNELISON, A., NORTON, N., & LIDZ, T. The intrafamilial environment of the schizophrenic patient. III: Interaction between hospital staff and families. *Psychiatry*, 1957, *20*, 343–350.
See Reference in Section 5.2

FRANCES, A., & GALE, L. Family structure and treatment in the military. *Family Process*, 1973, *12*, 171–178.
This paper examines the special situation of military families. Periodic separations, frequent moves, and rigid hierarchy test out the resourcefulness of military personnel and their families. As a result, several family constellations may appear, such as the compulsive male married to a dependent female, the symbiotic family with both partners estranged from external support, and the explosive family in which both parents are impulsive and violent. Treatment of these problems are most effective with the whole family involved rather than individual therapy.

GANSHEROFF, N. BOSZORMENYI-NAGY, I., MATRULLO, J. Clinical and legal issues in the family thearpy record. *Hospital and Community Psychiatry*, 1977, *28*, 911–913.
This paper suggests guidelines for writing family therapy charts. The writer of such a record must consider clnical needs and hospital accreditation standards as well as "rights to privacy" and other legal aspects. This may be more difficult when writing about a family, and the lack of an adequate privilege law has led some family therapists to keep no record at all.

GARDNER, R. A. A four day diagnostic-therapeutic home visit in Turkey. *Family Process*, 1970, *9*, 301–317.
A report of a 4-day visit in Istanbul to consult with a family of a 20-year-old Turkish patient. A Greek and a Turkish psychiatrist comment on the article.

GATTI, F., & COLMAN, C. Community network therapy: An approach to aiding families with troubled children. *American Journal of Orthopsychiatry*, 1976, *46*, 608–617.
A treatment program providing consultation to a public school system in a small, working-class community is based on involving the whole family network and its culture. Numerous case examples are presented to support the notion that this is a useful way to approach school problems.

GLASSER, P. H., & NAVARRE, E. L. The problems of families in the AFDC program. In P. H. Glasser & L. N. Glasser (Eds.), *Families in crisis*. New York: Harper & Row, 1970.
The effects of poverty on the family presented sociologically and psychologically, and from the point of view of the mother and the social worker.

GOODE, W. J. Marital satisfaction and instability: A cross-cultural class analysis of divorce rates. In P. H. Glasser, & L. N. Glasser (Eds.), *Families in crisis*. New York: Harper & Row, 1970.
A discussion of marital stability with the emphasis upon forms of instability and disorganization in families. Divorce is described in terms of class and across cultures, with divorce rates given for various countries.

GOULD, E., & GLICK, I. D. The effects of family presence and brief family intervention on global outcome for hospitalized schizophrenic patients. *Family Process*, 1977, *16*, 503–510.
Fifty-three families of long term hospitalized schizophrenics were studied to find out if the inclusion of family therapy and the presence of the family during hospitalization had any effect on the outcome. Results indicated that there were no significant differences in outcome either between individual family therapy, multiple family group therapy, or no family therapy at all. However, the data suggested that the *presence* of a family during hospitalization and after discharge, was clearly related to better posthospital functioning.

HALEY, J. Cross-cultural experimentation: An initial attempt. *Human Organism*, 1967, *3*, 110–117.
A comparison of Caucasion middle-class American families and Japanese-born families in an experimental setting where the measure is speech sequences. Differences are found.

HALLECK, S. L. Family therapy and social change. *Social Casework*, 1976, *57*, 483–493.
This clinical essay examines the effect of change in society on the family (i.e., problems in the family assumed to result, at least in part, from changes in society). The role of family therapy in dealing with the family is also discussed with the conclusion that resolution of internal and family conflicts does not ensure a good life. Many conflicts brought to therapy are engendered by social forces that cannot be dealt with in therapy with individuals and families.

HERZ, M. I., ENDICOTT, J., & SPITZER, R. Brief versus standard hospitalization: The Families. *American Journal of Psychiatry*, 1976, *133*, 795–801.
This is the second paper on a controlled study of three different type of inpatient treatment—standard inpatient care (discharged at the therapist's discretion), brief hospitalization (one week or less) with traditional day care available, and brief hospitalization without day care. Methodology and sample have been described in other papers. Results indicated that brief hospitalization had several positive effects on family functioning, primarily early resumption of occupational roles and less financial burden, with few deleterious effects. Overall there were few differences in any of the measures among the three treatment groups in terms of family burden.

HOFFMAN, L., & LONG, L. A systems dilemma. *Family Process*, 1969, *8*, 211–234.
A description of a man's breakdown in terms of the social systems within which he moved and the attempts to intervene to bring about change. The ecological field of a person is considered.

HOUSE, A. E., & STAMBAUGH, E. E. Transfer of therapeutic effects from institution to home: Faith, hope, and behavior modification. *Family Process*, 1979, *18*, 87–93.
This paper describes the case of a 10-year-old boy hospitalized for severe antisocial behavior. Therapeutic results obtained in the institutional setting were transferred effectively to the home setting. Three and 12-month follow-ups showed lasting improvement.

HUFFER, V. Australian aborigine: Transition in family grouping. *Family Process*, 1973, *12*, 303–315.
This paper describes marked transitions of family structure undergone in the last 50 years by a group of Australian aborigines; from polygymous to monogamous relationships. Presently there is a tendency for the youth not to marry but for the young women to incorporate their offspring into the household of their monogamous parents. A matrilocal pattern is developing that has the potential for matriarchal dominance. Parallels with transitions in American minority family groups are examined.

JEFFERS, C. Living Poor: Providing the basic necessities, priorities and problems. In P. H . Glasser, & L. N. Glasser (Eds.), *Families in crisis*. New York: Harper & Row, 1970.
A description of low-income families and the problems of a mother providing decent food, clothing, and shelter.

KAFFMAN, M. Family conflict in the psychopathology of the Kibbutz child. *Family Process*, 1972, *11*, 171–188.
An analysis of the incidence and nature of emotional disorders exhibited by the child population of about 100 Israeli Kibbutz settlements over a period of 20 years. In a group of 196 children, (ages 3 to 18) the most common etiologic factor (95%) was an obvious disharmony between parent and child. Overcontrol in the parent–child realtionship (54%), inconsistency (39%) and overprotection (28%) were characteristic of this disharmony. The existence of the culturally deprived child, who is brought up in a home characterized by few intellectual stimulations, was also present

as a pathogenic factor, although to a lesser degree and despite the rich resources for child stimulation in the Kibbutz society.

KAFFMAN, M. Family diagnosis and therapy in child emotional pathology. *Family Process*, 1965, *4*, 241–258.
A description of families treated in Israel based upon 194 kibbutz families and 126 families living in Haifa. Family treatment is said to be effective. Case examples are given.

KHATRI, A. A. Personality and mental health of indians (Hindus) in the context of their changing family organization. In E. J. Anthony, & C. Koupernik (Eds.), *The child in his family*. New York: Wiley, 1970.
A discussion of the Hindu patrilineal family and its impact on personality and mental health. The effects of social change are emphasized.

KINZIE, D., SUSHAMA, P. C., & LEE, M. Cross-cultural family therapy—A Malaysian experience. *Family Process*, 1972, *11*, 59–67.
This is a case report about family therapy in a non-Western culture. The case is a family with social, economic, cultural, and linguistic differences from the therapist. A meaningful, brief family therapy session was conducted in two languages. Follow-up visits indicated that a new pattern of relationship had developed. Family therapy can be done cross-culturally provided that the values of the patient and the therapist are recognized and that the goals are limited and consistent with those of the patient.

LANCASTER, L. Some conceptual problems in the study of family and kin ties in the british isles. *British Journal of Sociology*, 1961, *12*, 317–333.
A critique of studies of family and kinship in contemporary societies, with emphasis upon clarifying structural categories such as kinship systems, networks, sets, groups, and households.

LANGSDORF, R. Understanding the role of extrafamilial social forces in family treatment: A critique of family therapy. *Family Therapy*, 1978, *5*, 73–80.
This is an essay based on the premise that the family therapy field tends to isolate the family from its social, economic, and political environment. Therapists often do not see that families *cannot*, overcome the outside conditions that threaten their existence. Therefore, because the therapists do not understand these outside conditions, they do not include measures to deal with their treatment planning. Reasons for this failure are suggested.

LEAVITT, M. The discharge crisis: The experience of families of psychiatric patients. *Nursing Research*, 1975, *24*, 33–40.
This is a clinical study of families in which the identified patient was being discharged from psychiatric hospitalization. The sample was 16 families interviewed prior to discharge, using a semi-structured interview. Usually only one member of the family was interviewed (rather than the whole family). Results suggest that families were unprepared for the discharge of the patient and felt uninvolved in the identified patient's hospitalization.

LENNARD, S. H. C., & LENNARD, H. L. Architecture: Effect of territory, boundary, and orientation on family functioning. *Family Process*, 1977, *16*, 49–66.
This paper reviews the effect on the family's interaction of the home environment. Three concepts are utilized to examine the relation between the internal coherence of family and environment; "isomorphic fit," "complementarity fit," "non-fit." Three case illustrations are included.

MALOUF, J. L., & ALEXANDER, J. F. Family therapy research in applied community settings. *Community Mental Health Journal*, 1976, *12*, 61–71.
see Reference in Section 3.5.

MANNINO, F. V., & SHORE, M. F. Ecologically oriented family intervention. *Family Process*, 1972, *11*, 499–505.
In this article, the authors build on tenets proposed by Umbarger urging an ecological approach to family therapy for the poor. Family anxiety and dysfunction, regardless of social class, is often an ecological phenomenon, i.e., a consequence of discordant patterns of relation between family and nonfamily systems (school, health agencies, job situations, legal problems). Effective psychotherapy ought therefore to deal not only with psychological factors but also reality factors (employment, housing), with the emphasis on concrete action and the involvement of the therapist in these areas.

MANNINO, F. V., & SHORE, M. F. Family structure, aftercare, and post-hospital adjustments. *American Journal of Orthopsychiatry*, 1974, *44*, 76–85.
This research study explores the relation of family sturcture to posthospital outcome. Forty-one patients discharged from a state hospital and sent to an interrelated community aftercare program were compared with a control group discharged from the same state hospital but not in the interrelated program. The two groups were matched by sex, age, race, diagnosis, and date of discharge. Data were collected by a social work student at the patient' home and were completed on all subjects but one. Interview schedule consisted of a variety of functional, family adjustment scales.

Results indicated that (1) the only significant difference in outcome between experimental and control groups was that the group in the aftercare program had greater involvement in free-time activities; (2) posthospital adjustment of patients who lived in intact families of procreation and occupied central family positions was better than that of patients in reverse situations; and (3) the aftercare program worked best with high-risk patients.

MARCIANO, E. D. Middle class incomes, working class hearts. *Family Process*, 1974, *13*, 489–502.
In order to study the neglected area of blue collar marital patterns in middle class income and residential settings, this author examines the friendship nucleus of five couples residing in New Jersey. The study began in 1968 and concluded only after several months of observation and discussion. Sex-role segregation, sex in marriage, role-segregation, marital happiness, exposure to middle-class values, and husband and money power issues were discussed. This study indicates that blue-collar patterns are maintained after establishing middle-class income and residence due to the middle-class norms that have been established. The validity of socioeconomic status as a standard to study middle-class marriages is questioned.

MAZUR, V. Family therapy: An approach to the culturally different. *International Journal of Social Psychiatry*, 1973, *19*, 114–120.
This is a case report and analysis of an *unsuccessful* treatment of a family in which the identified patient was from Guam (which has a strong tradition of fatalism and strict matriarchal control). Observing the patient's family might help the therapist to understand the patient's culture and to afford more opportunities for techniques related to the patient's different lifestyle and values.

McADOO, H. Family therapy in the black community. *American Journal of Orthopsychiatry*, 1977, *47*, 75–79.
In addition to the usual family stresses, black families are subject to the additional strain of discrimination. Support is achieved mostly from the family and from the kinship network rather than the community. Treatment strategies for this situation are proposed.

McCORD, W., McCORD, J., & HOWARD, A. Early familial experiences and bigotry. *American Sociological Review*, 1960, *25*, 717–772.
The *Authoritarian Personality* concluded that bigots have experienced stern, moralistic, rejecting child rearing. The conclusion, much challenged, is evaluated in the light of data from the Cambridge-Somerville Youth Study. Ratable data on prejudices are available for 45 of 200 subjects reinterviewed in 1948 and 1956. No relation between degree of prejudice and family experiences as determined earlier could be established. The interpretation is suggested that prejudice in the lower class is a part of a generally stereotyped culture and does not relate to personality needs or family environment.

McKINLEY, C., RITCHIE, A., GRIFFIN, D., & BONDRANT, W. The upward mobile negro family in therapy. *Diseases of the Nervous System*, 1970, *31*, 710–718.
This is a report of treatment using multiple impact therapy on three "middle-class" black families. The identified patients were acting out *male children*, who were considered to be "severely disturbed." Although the families were intact, they were found to be grossly disorganized and chaotic with the primary dynamic being a power struggle between mother and father. Results of treatment indicated that the presenting symptoms of the identified patient could be alleviated and relationships among siblings improved. It was not possible, however, to change the "destructive relationship" between the parents. The "role reversal" technique of psychodrama was one of the more effective techniques utilized.

MINUCHIN, S. The use of an ecological framework in the treatment of a child. In E. J. Anthony, & C. Koupernik (Eds.), *The child in his family*. New York: Wiley, 1970.
A discussion of the three elements in the study of the child: as an individual, in his environment, and the linkage between the two. The ecological point of view is discussed. A case of an adolescent with *anorexia nervosa* is examined in terms of his family and the family therapy approach to the problem.

MOSS, S. Integration of the family into the child placement process. *Children*, 1968, *15*, 219–224.
This clinical paper criticizes current procedures for placing children in either a foster family or an institution. There has only been lip service paid to involving the family in a placement procedure. Family involvement helps in deciding whether or not to place, preplacement planning, and working through conflicts while the child is away. The ideal goal of placement is to enable the child to return to the family. For this reason, treatment for the family while the child is away is crucial.

NARAIN, D. Growing up in India. *Family Process*, 1964, *3*, 127–154.
A review of research on the socialization of the child in India with a detailed review of the studies on child rearing and parent–child relationships.

OPLER, M. K. Social and cultural influences on the psychopathology of family groups. In G. H. Zuk, & I. Boszormenyi-Nagy, (Eds.), *Family therapy and disturbed families*. Palo Alto: Science & Behavior Books, 1967.

An essay considering the social context of the family as related to mental health. Examples from different cultures are given.

OSTBY, C. H. Conjoint group therapy with prisoners and their families. *Family Process*, 1968, *7*, 184–201.
See Reference in Section 1.2

PAPAJOHN, J. Intergenerational value orientation and psychopathology in Greek-Amerian families. *International Journal of Family Therapy*, 1979, *1*, 107–132.
This is a report on the use of Kluckhohn's Value Orientation Theory and Spiegel's transactional theoretical framework to study the acculturation process and its effect on mental health in a minority group. Seventeen families of first and second generation Greek-Americans with a second generation schizophrenic member were compared to seventeen matched Greek-American controls. Data was obtained with the value orientation schedule—an individual questionnaire—and a detailed statistical analysis is included. Results showed a greater difference *between* generations in *both* groups than between groups.

POLLAK, O. Family structure: Its implications for mental health. In O. Pollak, & A. S. Friedman (Eds.), *Family dynamics and female sexual delinquency*. Palo Alto: Science & Behavior Books, 1969.
A discussion of the implications for mental health of various types of family structure. Compared are middle-class families, fatherless families, and three-generation families.

RANSOM, D. C., & VANDERVOORT, H. E. The development of family medicine. *Journal of the American Medical Association*, 1973, *225*, 1098–1102.
A clinical essay exploring the differences between family medicine and primary care. Based on their clinical experience in a family medicine program, the authors make the point that family medicine should be based on the "family approach" and suggest "putting the family into the center of medical care delivery." Problems in the implementation of such a procedure are discussed.

RENSHAW, J. R. An exploration of the dynamics of the overlapping worlds of work and family. *Family Process*, 1976, *15*, 143–165.
This study examines the relationship between the family life and working life of people in our society. The methodology used included grounded theory and systems theory approaches. The systems were found to be interdependent and stress was found to be a product of the interaction between the two systems. Successful coping was positively correlated with the perception of control over life events. The author suggests an open, nonblaming, joint problem solving approach with the organization accepting ultimate responsibility for considering family needs in the decision-making process.

RIEGER, W. A proposal for a trial of family treatment and conjugal visits in prison. *American Journal of Orthopsychiatry*, 1973, *43*, 117–122.
A proposal based on the author's personal impressions as a prison psychiatrist. No clinical material or data is given. Objections made in the past to conjugal visits in prison are examined. The author speculates that the objectives can be met if visits are part of a family treatment program and that such a program would improve the rehabilitative success of prisons.

SAMPSON, H., MESSINGER, S. L., & TOWNE, R. D. The mental hospital and marital family ties. *Social Problems*, 1961, *9*, 141–155.
The social processes affecting the marital family of 17 first admissions to a California state hospital and their families are described. Hospitalization for these cases did not interrupt ties to the community, but did provide a moratorium which allowed a reestablishment of outside ties.

SCHEFLEN, A. E. Living space in an urban ghetto. *Family Process*, 1971, *10*, 429–450.
This 2 year research study examines human territorial arrangements and behaviors through 1800 household interviews, 35 photographed space layouts, and 6 videos of Puerto Rican, Black and Italian-American families living in a Bronx ghetto. Several differences of interaction and uses of space have been highlighted to compare the different ethnic inhabitants. Implications as to the establishment of the therapeutic alliance are drawn.

SELIG, A. L. The myth of the multi-problem family. *American Journal of Orthopsychiatry*, 1976, *46*, 526–532.
The "multi-problem family" is a myth. Rather than the family being composed of a bunch of individuals, each with problems, the problem is that the health care delivery system isn't geared to meet the needs of families—that is, the health-care delivery system is fragmented. Therefore, the members of the families have to spread themselves out to get the services that a family needs.

SLUZKI, C. E. Migration and family conflict. *Family Process*, 1979, *18*, 379–390.
Following a model based on performance under stress, this paper describes the vicissitudes of the family system during the process of migration. The process is divided into five steps: prepartory stage, migration, period of over-compensation, period of crisis or decompensation, transgenerational phenomena. Each stage presents its own phenomenology, its own types of conflicts, and its own available coping modalities. The therapist may intervene preventatively at each one of these stages, requiring different techniques and strategies, according to the steps of the migratory process.

SONNE, J. C. Insurance and family therapy. *Family Process*, 1973, *12*, 399–414.
This paper examines the present difficulties involved in seeking reimbursement for family therapy through health and accident insurance. Payment is usually based on individual psychiatric diagnosis, and very few companies will insure a family for family therapy. This issue bears significance on the conflict between traditional concepts of individual psychopathology and recent concepts of socially shared family psychopathology.

SPECK, R. V. Psychotherapy of the social network of a schizophrenic family. *Family Process*, 1967, *6*, 208–214.
A description of the social network aproach to treatment. Procedure, goals, and future directions are described.

SPIEGEL, J. P. Some cultural aspects of transference and counter-transference. In J. Masserman (Ed.), *Science and psychoanalysis (Vol. II): Individual and family dynamics*. New York: Grune & Stratton, 1959.
A clinical essay based on work with working class Irish-American, Italian-American, and so-called "old American" families from two groups. The first were "well" families; the second were "sick" families. Data were gathered from clinic visits as well as home visits. Countertransference difficulties vary as to the cultural population. Having an entire family involved helps break the impasse that often develops. The family and the community are seen as important variables in the functioning of an individual.

SPITZER, S. P., SWANSON, R. M., & LEHR, R. K. Audience reactions and careers of psychiatric patients. *Family Process*, 1969, *8*, 159–181.
A study of the reaction of families and the ways these reactions influence the psychiatric patient career. The histories of 79 first admission patients were examined, and patient and a family member were interviewed. Two dimensions of famiy reaction to deviance are described leading to a typology of eight career patterns which allow for the classification of 95 percent of the cases reviewed.

STANTON, M. D. The military family: Its future in the all-volunteer context. In Goldman, N. L. & Segal, D. R. (Eds.), *Sage research progress series on war, revolution, and peacekeeping (vol. 6)*, Beverly Hills, CA: Sage Publications, 1976.
This is a chapter reviewing trends within the military family as part of a book on military research. The policies of the military (past, present, or proposed) toward family treatment, retirement, family disruptions, family mobility, etc. are discussed. Many of the changes in the military family reflect changes in families within the larger civilian society. It is important for the success of the all volunteer military program that these changes be recognized by the military.

STEIN, H. F. "All in the Family" as a mirror of contemporary American culture. *Family Process*, 1974, *13*, 279–315.
The specific relational positions of family members are examined in the television series, "All in the Family." Interpersonal and generational conflicts, identity structures, and value conflicts are explored in light of the Bunker family and the larger American population. This author concludes that there are parallels in the cultural patterning of the American people.

STEIN, H. F. Cultural specificity in patterns of mental illness and health: A Slovak-American case study. *Family Process*, 1973, *12*, 69–82.
This paper explores the way in which the perspective of "analytic relativism" is applied to the field data of mental health, as well as the implications of such an approach for family dynamics and the identity process. Mental illness and mental health have a cross-cultural validity as categories of a dichotomy existing within the dynamics of every culture. An illustrative case history of a Slovak-American family with a schizophrenic member is presented.

STEIN, H. F. The Slovak-Amerian "Swaddling Ethos": Homeostat for family dynamics and cultural continuity. *Family Process*, 1978, *17*, 31–45.
This paper describes the relationships among cultural ethos, family dynamics, personality configuration, and childrearing patterns among multi-generation Slovak-Americans. The "swaddling ethos" is assumed to serve as a homeostat whose regulatory function can be discerned through the analysis of family structure and process, especially through the family's values, affective patterns, roles, boundaries, and structural units. The core of the ethos is a dependency–security complex that attaches the individual to an extended family network of obligation, indebtedness, and reciprocity, towards the Slovak heritage.

STRODTBECK, F. Husband-wife interaction over revealed differences. *American Sociological Review*, 1951, *23*, 468–473.
A field study of 10 Navajo, 10 Texan and 10 Mormon couples. Balance of power can be revealed using this technique. The technique depends both on power elements in a larger cultural organization and amount of participation in the small group situation.

SUMER, E. A. Changing dynamic aspects of the Turkish culture and its significance for child training. In E. J. Anthony & C. Koupernik (Eds.) *The child in his family*. New York: Wiley, 1970.
A description of families in Turkey based upon "intensive psychiatric work with large numbers of families" who have applied at outpatient services. Childrearing, sexual education, and discipline are discussed.

SUSSMAN, M. B. Adaptive, directive, and integrative behavior of today's family. *Family Process*, 1968, *7*, 239–250.
A discussion of the relationship between the nuclear famiy and its kinship structure as well as other social institutions. It is said that the kin network acquires commitments by rewards perceived as superior to those offered by other social structures and so establishes tradition-laden obligations among family members.

TUCKER, B. Z., & DYSON, E. The family and the school: Utilizing human resources to promote learning. *Family Process*, 1976, *15*, 125–141.
This paper describes a project which seeks to promote understanding and communication between families and public school professionals with the consultation of a family therapist and the incorporation of family therapy processes. Outcomes of importance to the school and to the family are suggested and plans to continue and expand the pilot project are proposed.

VASSILIOU, G. Milieu specificity in family therapy. In N. W. Ackerman (Ed.), *Family therapy in transition*. Boston: Little, Brown. 1970.
A description of the Greek family, its historical development, and its problems as seen from a family therapy point of view.

VINCENT, C. E. Mental health and the family. In P. H. Glasser, & L. N. Glasser (Eds.), *Families in crisis*. New York: Harper & Row, 1970.
A selective review of broad develoments and trends in the emerging role of the federal government in the mental health field. The relevance of the family to mental health and community mental health centers is discussed with a review. Present needs are examined.

VINCENT, C. E. Mental health and the family. *Journal of Marriage and the Family*. 1967, *29*, 18–38.
A clinical essay by a sociologist focusing on creating a new speciality. The adaptation of the family to community and society, as well as to its own members, is crucial in the development of individual psychopathology.

WARKENTIN, J., & WHITAKER, C. A. The secret agenda of the therapist doing couples therapy. In G. H. Zuk, & I. Boszormenyi-Nagy (Eds.), *Family therapy and disturbed families*. Palo Alto: Science & Behavior Books, 1967.
See Reference in Section 1.3.

WYLAN, L., & MINTZ, N. L. Ethnic differences in family attitudes towards psychotic manifestations with implications for treatment programmes. *International Journal of Social Psychiatry*, 1976, *22*, 86–95.
Attitudes of Irish-American families are compared with Jewish-American families toward psychosocial dysfunction in a psychotic family member. The sample was 32 families (13 Jewish and 19 Irish) in which one member had either affective or schizophrenic disorder. A Family Attitude questionnaire was given by a psychiatric social worker to one member of the family designated as a "responsible relative." The psychiatric symptoms were collected from the psychiatrist in charge of the case. Results indicated that significantly more Irish families than Jewish families tolerated deviant thinking, while significantly more Jewish families than Irish families tolerated deviant verbal emotionality. Treatment implications are that intrapsychic and interpersonal problems must both be treated during hospitalization for a successful posthospital outcome.

WYNNE, L. C. The family as a strategic focus in cross cultural psychiatric studies. In W. Caudill, & T. Lin (Eds.), *Mental health research in Asia and the Pacific*. Honolulu: East-West Center Press, 1969.
The family lends itself particularly well to the four variables of primary conceptual systems: biology, personality, social structure, and culture. The changes in patterns between the nuclear family and the extended family are discussed as are family communication patterns. There is a review of the literature in this area.

5. TYPES OF FAMILIES

5.1 CONTRASTING FAMILY TYPES

AHMED, F. Family and Mental disorders in Pakistan. *International Journal of Social Psychiatry*, 1968, *14*, 290–295.
In order to study the effect of the structure of the family on mental illness, 967 cases from a privately owned psychiatric clinic in Pakistan were studied, using retrospective case records. Only psychotics and neurotics were used from the larger sample. Results revealed that there were more females psychotics, that psychotic patients were closer in age to their parents, that father was usually less than 25 years of age for the psychotics and more than 25 for the neurotics. That more psychotics were the oldest in the family and more neurotics were the youngest. There was more psychopathology in the family of psychotics than in that of neurotics. No relationship was found between mental disorders and marital status, sibling order, parental loss in childhood, and mother's age at birth.

BAXTER, J. C., & ARTHUR, S. Conflict in families of schizophrenics as a function of premorbid adjustment and social class. *Family Process*, 1964, *3*, 273–279.
A group of 16 hospitalized male schizophrenics was classified into 4 groups on the basis of the patient's premorbid adjustment and social class. Standard interviews with the parents were rated for conflict. "Results indicate that the amount of conflict expressed by the parents varies jointly with premorbid level of the patient and the social class of the family."

BAXTER, J. C., ARTHUR, S., FLOOD, C., & HEDGEPETH, B. Conflict patterns in the families of schizophrenics. *Journal of Nervous and Mental Disease*, 1962, *135*, 419–424.
Families of 12 male and 6 female schizophrenics were interviewed individually and as a group to explore conflict patterns in relation to the sex of the child. The amount of conflict is said to be comparable in the 2 groups while patterns of conflict differ. There is more interparental conflict in the group of families with a male patient and more involvement of the patient in conflict in the group with a female patient.

BAXTER, J. C., & BECKER, J. Anxiety and avoidance behavior in schizophrenics in response to parental figures. *Jouranl of Abnormal Social Psychology*, 1962, *64*, 432–437.
Good and poor premorbid schizophrenics were exposed to TAT cards of parent–child relationships. Poor premorbids produced more anxiety in response to a mother figure than a father figure. Good premorbids showed the reverse. Avoidance behavior in response to parental figures did not differ.

BAXTER, J. C., BECKER, J., & HOOKS, W. Defensive style in the families of schizophrenics and controls. *Journal of Abnormal Social Psychology*, 1963, *66*, 512–518.
Parents of good and poor premorbid schizophrenics were given Rorschach tests. Parents of poor premorbids showed a greater amount of immature behavior than parents of good premorbids or parents of neurotics.

BEAVERS, W. T., BLUMBERG, S., TIMKEN, D. R., & WEINER, M. F. Communication patterns of mothers of schizophrenics. *Family Process*, 1965, *4*, 95–104.
A study of the ways the mothers of schizophrenics communicate with an interviewer. Nine mothers of schizophrenics were contrasted with 9 mothers of hospitalized nonschizophrenic patients. The mothers of schizophrenics communicated their feelings in a quantitatively more ambiguous fashion.

BECK, S. F. Families of schizophrenic and of well children: Methods, concepts, and some results. *American Journal of Orthopsychiatry*, 1960, *30*, 247–275.
A report on a research study attempting to differentiate and compare families with schizophrenic children, families with neurotic children, and families with normal children. A list of trait items about individuals in 106 families were Q-sorted by a psychiatrist and 3 social workers. The clusterings are said to indicate similarities and differences.

BECK, S., & NUNNALLY, J. Parental attitudes in families. *Archives of General Psychiatry*, 1965, *13*, 208–213.
Differences in "attitudes" of parents of schizophrenic children were compared with those with well children. Eighteen attitudes were measured using the semantic differential test of Osgood (measures concepts like "my child, pregnancy," etc.). Schizophrenic families were obtained from 32 families of children resident in a therapeutic school; well children families came from the community. Concepts associated with greater mental health by the well families included "my mother, the kind of father I am, the kind of mother I am, myself when I was a father, clinic mothers, and clinic our family." There was no difference between samples in the other 9 concepts.

BECKER, J., TATSUOKA, M. & CARLSON, A. The communicative value of parental speech in families with disturbed children. *Journal of Nervous and Mental Diseases*, 1966, *14*, 359–364.
Hypothesis was the communicativeness of parents with emotionally disturbed children (11 sets of parents who had children coming to a clinic) would be lower than that of parents with normal children (12 parent sets who were paid volunteers). Communicativeness was assessed by Taylor's cloze procedure. The speech of nonclinic mothers was significantly more communicative than that of nonclinic fathers, clinic mothers, and clinic fathers. The latter 3 groups did not differ among themselves.

BEHRENS, M., & GOLDFARB, W. A study of patterns of interaction of families of schizophrenic children in residential treatment. *American Journal of Orthopsychiatry*, 1958, *28*, 300–312.
An attempt to differentiate families of schizophrenic children from those of nonschizophrenic children with a sample of 20 families who had a child diagnosed as schizophrenic and 5 with a behavior disorder, all of whom were inpatients. There were ten normals, all children living at home. Data were collected using family interaction scales; observations were recorded in the homes for both the normals and the patients when they were on a home visit. Results indicate that the schizophrenic families were more pathologic than the normal families and the families with behavior disorders.

BEHRENS, M., MEYERS, D. I., GOLDFARB, W., GOLDFARB, N. & FIELDSTEEL, N. D. The Henry Ittleson center family interaction scales. *Genetic Psychology Monograph*, 1969, *80*, 203–295.
A report on the manual used for the family interaction scales. The scales appraise the functioning of family groups, and derive from a clinical interest in the relationship between the identified patient and the family. Data are obtained through a 3-hour home visit at mealtime. Scales have been used to evaluate the functioning of the family with a schizophrenic child, to compare families which include children with various diagnoses with normal families, and to determine the nature of changes in family functioning over a specified length of time. A description of scales and scoring instructions, and 3 family illustrations are included.

BEHRENS, M., ROSENTHAL, A. J., & CHODOFF, P. Communication in lower-class families of schizophrenics. *Archives of General Psychiatry*, 1968, *18*, 689–696.
The second part of a study of low-socioeconomic families of schizophrenics. The study was doen in the home where the family was focused upon a task, particularly the Rorschach. Raters were asked to predict type of family from written transcripts. Results indicate that communication and interaction patterns of lower-class families with a schizophrenic differ from families whose class background is similar.

BEHRENS, M., & SHERMAN, A. Observations of family interaction in the home. *American Journal of Orthopsychiatry*, 1959, *29*, 243–248.
An essay on the author's previous studies using home visits in evaluating family interactional patterns to differentiate schizophrenic families from nonschizophrenic families. Difficulties in this type of research are discussed and suggestions for further data collection are made. It is felt that this is a useful technique for "diagnostic, treatment, and research purposes."

BENTINCK, C. Opinions about mental illness held by patients and relatives. *Family Process*, 1967, *6*, 193–207.
A study inquiring into the nature of the attitudes at home about mental illness in families of male schizophrenics. A control group of male medical patients was used. The data were gathered by a questionnaire administered in a home interview. The sample was 50 schizophrenics and 50 relatives, and 50 medical patients and 50 relatives. Opinions of relatives of schizophrenics had "more in common with blue collar employees than with mental health professionals."

BROWNING, C. J. Differential impact of family disorganization on male adolescents. *Social Problems*, 1960, *8*, 37–44.
Samples of 60 nondelinquent, 60 delinquent-truancy, and 60 delinquent-auto theft boys (age 15) were identified. Data were obtained from school, police, and probation records; from interviews with mothers; from family solidarity and marital adjustment scales filled out by parents; and California test of personality scales filled out by the boys. The incidence of broken homes is higher in the delinquent groups, but this variable is not a consistently good indicator of family disorganization and needs refinement.

CHEEK, F. Family interaction patterns and convalescent adjustment of the schizophrenic. *Archives of General Psychiatry*, 1965, *13*, 138–147.
An attempt to examine the relationship between family interaction patterns and outcome in schizophrenia. Data were obtained from 51 patients who had been hospitalized between the ages of 15 and 26, all of whom had living mothers and fathers. Each family member filled out a questionnaire relating to interaction patterns; all 3 family members together worked on 2 questionnaire problems; an interview with the mother on the adjustment of the patient was evaluated by means of a 40-item four point rating scale. One week later, in the home of the patient, 2 more 15-minute disucssions between family members were recorded. Fifty-six normal families were studied with identical procedures used as with the schizophrenics. Results indicated that it was the characteristics of the parents, rather than the degree of sickness of the patient "which was the decisive factor in producing a poor outcome."

CHEEK, F. Family socialization techniques and deviant behavior. *Family Process*, 1966, *5*, 199–217.
A study based upon Parson's theoretical framework in which deviant behavior is related to imbalance of systems inputs and outputs at various stages of development. A sample of 120 males adults from 4 different groups—schizophrenics, normals, alcoholics, and reformatory inmates—were exposed to a questionnaire on family problem situations. Differences were found and it is suggested that Parsons' theoretical scheme could be translated into reinforcement theory.

CHEEK, F. The father of the schizophrenic: The function of a peripheral role. *Archives of General Psychiatry*, 1965, *13*, 336–345.
In view of the absence of data on the role of the father in the intrafamilial environment of the schizophrenic, Bales' interaction process analysis technique and the social system theoretical framework of Parsons are used for studying the interaction of 67 families of young adult schizophrenics (40 male and 27 female). This sample was compared to 56 families with nonpsychotic young adults (31 male and 25 female). Outcome in schizophrenia was evaluated a year and a half following discharge from the inpatient setting. All discusion were tape recorded and coded, using the Bales interaction categories. Additionally, each member of the families was asked to fill in a questionnaire examining expectations and perceptions of how the others might behave in relation to one another in certain typical family problems. Schizophrenic fathers occupy a peripheral position in the family in which the mother and patient are closest by default. Profiles of mothers of schizophrenics however differed more widely from those of normals than fathers.

CHEEK, F. Parental role distortions in relation to schiozphrenic deviancy. In I. M. Cohen (Ed.), *Psychiatric research report No. 20.* Washington, D.C.: American Psychiatric Association, 1966.
A study investigating the nature of the schizophrenic interacting in the family and the relation of family interaction to the outcome of the schizophrenic. The study combined questionnaire and observational data. The sample included 67 schizophrenic contrasted with 56 nonpsychotic young adults.

CHEEK, F. A serendipitous finding. Sex roles in schizophrenia. *Journal of Abnormal Social Psychiatry*, 1964, *69*, 392–400.
One of a series of reports on an ongoing research project studying the family environment in schizophrenia. Interaction profiles of 67 young adults schizophrenics (40 male and 27 female) were compared with those of 56 normals (31 male and 25 female). Profiles were derived from 48 minutes of recorded interaction between father, mother, and patient with a variation of the Bales interaction categories. Male schizophrenics presented an interaction equivalent of withdrawal, with low total activity rates and low dominance behaviors. In contrast, female schizo-phrenics proved to be more active than female normals.

CLARK, A. W., & VAN SOMMERS, P. Contradictory demands in family relations and adjustment to school and home. *Human Relations*, 1961, *14*, 97–111.
In these intensive case studies of families of 20 maladjusted and 20 adjusted children, all of the families had one or more adults other than the parents living in the family. The concern was with "the process of explaining an unsatisfactory relationship between any 2 individuals in terms of the influence of a third individual." Data were obtained by detailed, focused interviews, questionnaires to school staffs, group interviews with peers, and tests of ability. School difficulties were associated with unsatisfactory relationships in the home, one of which was dependence of 1 parent upon the other adult. Unsatisfactory relationships of adults contribute to withdrawal of father from family activities, difficulties between adults and children, maladjustment of children at home and school, and recurrence of symptoms in parents.

COE, W. C., CURRY, A. E., & KESSLER, D. R., Family interaction of psychiatric patients. *Family Process*, 1969, *8*, 119–130.
A study using a questionnaire to examine family interaction patterns with emphasis upon everyday activities. Forty males and 40 females and their relatives who were psychiatric inpatients were contrasted with 54 husband and wife volunteers. Results include the finding that more family decision making is left to the child in the patient families. In these families the members tend not to recognize disagreement in their interactions.

CUMMING, J. H. The family and mental disorder: An incomplete essay. In *Causes of Mental Disorders: A review of epidemiological knowledge.* New York, Milbank Memorial Fund, 1961.
An essay called incomplete because it reviews only a portion of the very large number of studies which attempt to relate mental disorder with the family. After a review of ideas about the functions of the family unit, an attempt is made to provide a typology of family studies by survying studies in the field with emphasis upon the structure and function of socialization processes. Relating the various studies to each other , author concludes, "It is clear that organized study of the area of the family and mental illness is in a state of chaos."

CURRY, A. Toward the phenomenological study of the family. *Existential Psychiatry*, 1967, *6*, 35–44.
See reference in section 1.1.

DENIKER, P. dESAUGY, D., & ROPERT, M. The alcoholic and his wife. *Comprehensive psychiatry*, 1964, *5*, 374–384.
A study focusing on the relationship between the alcoholic and his wife by studying three groups of patients: 50 alcoholics with psychiatric disorders called psychiatric alcoholics, 50 alcoholics with cirrhosis or gastritis called digestive alcoholics, and 67 in a control group where the husband was matched for age and socioeconomic status. All couples were interviewed using a questionnaire designed for this study. Compared with the digestive alcoholics and the controls, the psychiatric alcoholics showed a relationship to birth order, had fathers who were also alcoholics,

made lower salaries, had dominant wives, and drank relatively little at home. The wife of the psychiatric alcoholic "tends to unconsciously maintain her husband's alcoholism."

DUHRESSEN, A. Preventive massnahmen in der familie. *Psychotherapy and Psychosomatics*, 1968, *16*, 319–322. See Reference in Section 3.6.

FARINA, A. Patterns of role dominance and conflict in parents of schizophrenic patients. *Journal of Abnormal Social Psychology*, 1960, *61*, 31–38.
Parents of 12 good premorbid schizophrenics, 12 poor premorbids, and 12 children hospitalized for tuberculosis were interviewed. They were exposed individually and as pairs to hypothetical incidents with children. The joint conversation was analyzed for dominance and conflict. Father dominance was associated with good premorbid adjustment of the son and mother dominance with porr premorbid adjustment. Parents of schizophrenics displayed more conflict than the control parents.

FARINA, A., & DUNHAM, R. M. Measurement of family relationships and their effects. *Archives of General Psychiatry*, 1963, *9*, 64–73.
A group of families of male hospitalized schizophrenic patients, divided into good premorbid and poor premorbid, was given a structural situation test. Each family member is exposed to some hypothetical problem situations with children, and the family is then brought together and exposed to the same situation. Indices of dominance, such as length of speeches, and indices of conflict were constructed. Immediately following this, a group of the patients was given a visual task individually and contrasted with a group given the same task a week after the situation test. The conclusions are that fathers are more dominant in good premorbid cases and mothers more dominant in bad premorbid cases. Conflict scores are higher for good premorbids.

FERBER, A., KLIGLER, D., ZWERLING, I., & MENDELSOHN, M. Current family structure. *Archives of General Psychiatry*, 1967, *16*, 659–667.
Hypothesis was that the family, in order to maintain equilibrium, will extrude to the hospital certain members (most usually those members functioning peripherally). Data were obtained from an emergency room psychiatric population of a large municipal hospital. Nine hundred and thirty-seven patients and/or their "closest companion" filled out a family information form. Families of psychiatric patients were compared with families from the general population. Reliability on the raw data was 90 percent. Findings were that being married (rather than single, widowed, etc.) coming from family of procreation, coming from an intact family, and being an emotionally important member of the household are associated with a lower risk of becoming a patient and of having a better outcome from treatment.

FERREIRA, A. J. Decision-making in normal and pathologic families. *Archives of General Psychiatry*, 1963, *8*, 68–73.
An experiment to find differences between 25 normal and 25 abnormal families using a decision-making test. The family members first make a choice of items on a questionnaire when alone and then are brought together and asked to reach agreement on the same items. Their choices separately and together are compared and the agreements are categorized as unanimous, majority, dictatorial, and chaotic. The two types of families are found to differ.

FERREIRA, A. J. Interpersonal perceptivity among family members. *American Journal of Orthopsychiatry*, 1964, *34*, 64–71.
A report of a study investigating interpersonal perceptivity among members of families in terms of the individual's ability to guess the rejecting behavior of the other two family members. The sample consisted of "25 normal and 30 pathologic families." The families were asked to color a number of flags on pieces of cardboard and asked to "throw away, i.e., to reject, the productions of the other family members" which they didn't like for any reason. They were also asked to guess how many of their own flags would be thrown away by other family members. Interpersonal perceptivity is greater in children than in adults.

FERREIRA, A. J. Rejection and expectancy of rejection in families. *Family Process*, 1963, *2*, 235–244.
A report of a study to investigate overt rejection and expectancy of rejection in normal and abnormal families. The sample was "25 normal and 30 pathologic families." The families were asked to color a number of flags on pieces of cardboard and asked to "throw away, i.e., to reject, the productions of the other families members" which they didn't like for any reason. They were also asked to guess how many of their own flags would be thrown away by other family members. Differences were found between the two groups and there was a marked discrepancy between rejecting and expecting to be rejected in pathological families.

FERREIRA, A. J., & WINTER, W. D. Decision-making in normal and abnormal two-child families. *Family Process*, 1968, *7*, 17–36.
A report of a study of 85 families, 36 normal and 49 abnormal, composed of parents and two children. The families were tested in a procedure similar to that previously used in a test of family triads. Differences were found between the two groups on measures of "spontaneous agreement," "decision time," and "choice fulfillment."

FERREIRA, A. J., & WINTER, W. D. Family interaction and decision-making. *Archives of General Psychiatry*, 1965, *13*, 214–223.

A report of a study contrasting 50 normal families and 75 families with an abnormal child. The abnormal group included 15 schizophrenic, 16 delinquent, and 44 maladjusted children. The family members were asked to fill out a neutral questionnaire separately, and then they were brought together and asked to fill out the same questionnaire while reaching agreement on the items as a group. Generally this report is concerned with the extent of agreement when family members make their choices separately, how much time to reach group decisions is necessary, and the appropriateness of the family decisions in fulfilling the wishes of the individual family members. Eighteen hypotheses are described and the results reported in terms of the differences found between the groups.

FERREIRA, A. J., & WINTER, W. D. Information exchange and silence in normal and abnormal families. *Family Process*, 1968, 7, 251–278.
A comparison of normal and abnormal families which measured exchange of information and amount of time spent in silence in doing a task. A sample of 30 normal and 45 abnormal families were contrasted by a rater judgement of tape recordings. Differences were found.

FERREIRA, A., & WINTER, W. D., Stability of interactional variables in family decision-making. *Archives of General Psychiatry*, 1966, *14*, 352–355.
In order to test the stability over time, and after family therapy, of three variables in family decision making, 23 randomly selected families (10 abnormal and 13 normal) were retested six months after the original research project. The abnormal families had received therapy. Results indicated that there was no significant difference between the means observed in tests and retests of the three variables for either normal or abnormal families. It is concluded that these three variables (spontaneous, agreement, decision-time, and choice-fulfillment) were consistent over time and were not changed by family therapy.

FISHER, L. On the classification of families—A progress report. *Archives of General Psychiatry*, 1977, *34*, 424–433.
A literature review from the last 20 years focuses on types of family classification. Family schemata have been organized into the following groups: (1) style of adaptation; (2) developmental family stage; (3) initial problem or diagnosis of the identified patient; (4) family theme or dimension; and (5) types of marital relationship. Six family types, based on multidimensional (rather than typological) framework, with prognostic statements about each type are presented.

FISHER, S., & MENDELL, D. The communication of neurotic patterns over two and three generations. In N. W. Bell, & E. F. Vogel (Eds.), *A modern introduction to the family*. Glencoe, Free Press, 1960.
A report on a study of similarities in the patterning of fantasy and behavior in two or more generations of family groups. The data included projective tests and psychiatric interviews. Six families with 3 generations of kin and 14 families with 2 generations of kin were examined and impressions are given.

FRIEDMAN, C. J., & FRIEDMAN, A. S. Characteristics of schizogenic families during a joint story-telling task. *Family Process*, 1970, *9*, 333–353.
A comparison of families with a schizophrenic and normal families in the task of telling a story. Observer ratings were used for the interaction and judges ratings for the final joint family story. Differences were found.

GARMEZY, N., CLARKE, A. R., & STOCKNER, C. Child rearing attitudes of mothers and fathers as reported by schizophrenic and normal patients. *Journal of Abnormal Social Psychiatry*, 1961, *63*, 176–182.
A group of 15 good premorbid and 15 poor premorbid schizophrenic patients were asked to think back when they were 13 or 14 years old and try to remember mother and father at that time. The experimenter then presented them with 75 statements describing various child-rearing attitudes and asked the patients if their parents would have agreed or disagreed with each item. A group of 15 patients hospitalized for medical problems was used as a control. The results indicate that the subject's level of social maturity and the extent of attitudinal deviance ascribed to parents are related. Poor premorbids reveal maternal dominance whereas good premorbids ascribe heightened paternal dominance in their responses.

GARMEZY, N., FARINA, A., & RODNICK, E. H. The structured situation test: A method for studying family interaction in schizophrenia. *American Journal of Orthopsychiatry*, 1960, *30*, 445–451.
A group of 36 sets of parents composed of parents of good and poor premorbids and of sons with tuberculosis ("normals") were exposed to 12 hypothetical misbehaviors of a son. Individually and then together they were asked to indicate how to handle the situation. From tape recordings of the interviews, measures of dominance behavior and conflict were made, such as who spoke first and last, acceptance of another's solution, amount of interruption, and so on. With good premorbids the fathers were dominant and in poor premorbids the mothers were. The "normals" share dominance. Poor premorbids show greater conflict than "normals."

GARTNER, R. B., FULMER, R. H., WEINSHEL, M. et al: The family life cycle: Developmental crises and their structural impact on families in a community mental health center. *Family Process*, 1978, *17*, 47–58.
A survey of the demographic and clinical characteristics of 110 families of patients treated in a day hospital leads to the development of a typology based on the configuration of family members and the position of the identified patient

within the family structure. Four constellations or types were categorized—families in which the identified patient is: (1) currently a spouse; (2) the grown child of a couple in an ongoing marriage; (3) a grown child of a single parent; (4) a single adult living with relatives other than parents. They seem to be distinct clinical entities in the population studied.

GEHRKE, S., & KIRSCHENBAUM, M. Survival patterns in family conjoint therapy. *Family Process*, 1967, *6*, 67–80.
A discussion of 20 families studied in family therapy with the emphasis upon different patterns of emotional survival myths in the family. Three types of family are contrasted: the repressive family, the delinquent family, and the suicidal family. The survival myth has to do with the illusion of family members that they must continue their existing family ways of relating to survive psychologically.

GERBER, G. L. Psychological distance in the family as schematized by families of normal, disturbed, and learning-problem children. *Journal of Consulting Clinical Psychology*, 1973, *40*, 139–147.
This is a comparative study of psychological distance within families (as measured by physical distance between dolls) made by matching families with a normal child, a disturbed child, and a child with a learning problem. Sample was 30 white, upper middle-class families (10 in each group) who had at least two children. Classification of "disturbed versus normal" was made by the principal of the school and her assistant. Each member of the family and the family group together did the "family doll placement technique" (previously described). Results indicated that in negative story themes both groups of disturbed boys put greater distances between the mother doll and the doll representing himself than normal boys did. Female siblings of disturbed boys placed greater distance between the father doll and the doll representing herself than female siblings of normal boys.

GETZELS, J. W., & JACKSON, P. W. Family environment and cognitive style: A study of the sources of highly intelligent and of highly creative adolescents. *American Sociological Review*, 1961, *26*, 351–359.
A study of adolescent boys and girls, 28 highly intelligent but not creative and 26 creative but not concomitantly intelligent, chosen from a school population on the basis of testing. These students proved equally superior in achievement to the remainder of the student body although they differed both functionally and in their goals. The central issue of this report deals with the role of the family environment in the differentiation of kinds of intellectual ability through interviews with the mothers. Significant group differences were found in parental type education, childhood memories, reading interests, values, degree of satisfaction with child and school, etc. The authors find less anxiety in the highly creative home and therefore more freedom for "individual divergence."

GREENBERG, I. M., & ROSENBERG, G. Familial correlates of the 14 and 6 CPS EEG positive spike pattern. In I. M. Cohen (Ed.), *Psychiatric research report No. 20*. Washington, D.C.: American Psychiatric Association, 1966.
A report on the results of a study of the families of young hospitalized psychiatric patients in which central nervous system function, individual psychodynamics, cognitive style, and social and familial factors are considered. A sample of nine patients were contrasted with ten with no EEG abnormality. Differences were found in the families.

HALEY, J. Cross-cultural experimentation: An initial attempt. *Human Organism*, 1967, *3*, 110–117.
A comparison of Caucasion middle-class American families and Japanese-born families in an experimental setting where the measure is speech sequences. Differences are found.

HALEY, J. Experiment with abnormal families. *Archives of General Psychiatry*, 1967, *17*, 53–63.
A comparison of abnormal and normal families in an experimental setting where family members speak to each other from different rooms. Measures are who chooses to speak with whom and patterns of speech sequence.

HALEY, J. Family experiments: A new type of experimentation. *Family Process*, 1962, *1*, 265–293.
A report on a research project in which parents and schizophrenic child were contrasted with parents and normal child in an experimental game to test hypotheses about coalition patterns in normal and abnormal families. Differences were found between the 30 families in each group. There is a general discussion of the uniqueness of experimenting with families in theoretical, methodological, and sampling problems.

HALEY, J. Research on family patterns: An instrument measurement. *Family Process*, 1964, *3*, 41–65.
A report of an investigation of patterns of interchange in families. The questions are whether families follow patterns, whether "normal" and "abnormal" families differ, and whether patterns change over time. A group of 40 normal and 40 abnormal families were given a standard stimulus for conversation and a frequency count was made of the order in which family members speak. Families were found to follow patterns and differences were found between the normal and abnormal groups.

HALEY, J. Speech sequences of normal and abnormal families with two children present. *Family Process*, 1967, *6*, 81–97.
A sample of 50 "abnormal" and 40 "normal" families were contrasted in an experimental setting where a measurement was made of the sequence in which family members speak. Differences had been found in a previous study were the families were tested in triads. In this study, where the sibling was included as well as the index child, differences were not found between the two groups.

HALEY, J. Testing parental instructions to schizophrenic and normal children: A pilot study. *Journal of Abnormal Social Psychology*, 1968, *73*, 559–566.
An experiment to test the hypothesis that parents communicate to their schizophrenic children in conflicting ways. Parental instructions were given from a separate room and tape recorded so that they could be played to matched children. On this small sample, the indications were the parents of schizophrenics do not communicate in more conflicting ways than parents of normal children when the measurement is the success of a child in following their instructions.

HASSAN, S. A. Transactional and contextual invalidation between the parents of disturbed families: A comparative study. *Family Process*, 1974, *13*, 53–76.
See Reference in Section 3.6.

HILGARD, J., & NEWMAN, M. F., Early parental deprivation as a function factor in the etiology of schizophrenia and alcoholism. *American Journal of Orthopsychiatry*, 1963, *33*, 409–420.
A study designed to consider the age at which loss by death was sustained during childhood by hospitalized schizophrenic and alcoholic patients. Comparison was made using hospital admission records of 1521 schizophrenic patients, 929 alcoholic patients, and a control group of 1096 cases selected using an area-sampling technique from an urban community. It was concluded that mother loss among women in both diagnostic categories was earlier than in the control group members who lost mothers. Schizophrenic women showed loss of both mother and father at a significantly earlier age than the control subjects.

HILGARD, J., & NEWMAN, M. F. Parental loss by death in childhood as an etiological factor among schizophrenic and alcoholic patients compared with a non-patient community samples. *Journal of Nervous and Mental Disease*, 1963, *137*, 14–28.
Hospital records were examined and a sample of 1,561 schizophrenic patients and 929 alcoholic patients were compared with a control sample of 1,096 cases. Schizophrenics had lost one or both parents more often than the control group members. Parent loss is said to one of the factors associated with an increase in vulnerability in coping with the stresses of adult life.

JENKINS, R. The varieties of children's behavioral problems and family dynamics. *American Journal of Psychiatry*, 1968, *124*, 1440–1445.
1500 children attending a psychiatric clinic were separated into three groups by computer clustering of their symptoms and correlated with family types. Overanxious children are likely to have an anxious, infantilizing mother. A critical, depreciative, punitive, inconsistent mother or stepmother is typical for the unsocialized, aggressive child. Socialized delinquents are likely to come from large families characterized by parental neglect and delegation of parental responsibilities.

KELLAM, S. G., ENSMINGER, M. E., & TURNER, R. J. Family structure and the mental health of children: Concurrent and longitudinal community-wide studies. *Archives of General Psychiatry*, 1977, *34*, 1012–1022.
See Reference in Section 3.2.

LANTZ, C. E. Strategies for counseling Protestant evangelical families. *International Journal of Family Therapy*, 1979, *1*, 169–183.
Because they have been historically ignored by psychotherapists, this paper discusses strategies for developing a therapeutic relationship with "evangelical" families. It is observed that family life is particularly important to "born-again" Christians. Different attitudes of therapists toward them and difficulties in translating what the family therapy field has to offer into terms they can use are examined.

LERNER, P. Resolution of intrafamilial role conflict in families of schizophrenic patients. *Journal of Nervous and Mental Disease*, 1966, *141*, 342–351.
Hypothesis was that there would be differences in the processes used to solve intrafamilial role conflict in parents with schizophrenic sons with marked thought disorder (12 families), less severe thought disorder (12 families), and control families (12 families). Thought disorder was measured by Rorschach protocol using the genetic level score of Becker. Intrafamilial role conflict solving was measured using a situational test with Strodtbeck's "revealed differences" technique. Results supported the hypothesis. Methodology of such research is discussed.

LEARNER, P. Resolution of intrafamilial role conflict in families of schizophrenic patients.II: Social Maturity *Journal of Nervous and Mental Disease*, 1967, *4*, 336–341.
A study attempting to evaluate the relationship between resolution of intrafamilial role conflict and premorbid level of social competence in schizophrenics. Sample and methods were the same as in a previous study except that here social competence was measured by a scale developed by Zigler and Phillips. Findings were that control families compromised and acknowledged disagreement, while schizophrenic families did not but let mother or father decide.

LEIK, R. K. Instrumentality and emotionality in family interaction. *Sociometry*, 1963, *26*, 131–145.
A comparison of discussion groups where nine families composed of father, mother, and daughter participated in

triadic sessions. One third of the discussion groups were made up of all fathers, all mothers, or all daughters. Another third were composed of a father, a mother, and a daughter not of the same family. The final third was of natural families. The three groups were exposed to standard questions and observed. Categories of acts were derived from theBales system with an emphasis upon instrumentality versus emotionality. It was found that sex role differentiation tends to disappear in family groups and the relevance of instrumentality and emotionality is quite different for family interaction than for interaction among strangers.

LENNARD, H. L., BEAULIEU, M. R., & EMBREY, N. G. Interaction in families with a schizophrenic child. *Archives of General Psychiatry*, 1965, *12*, 166–183.
A study contrasting ten families with a schizophrenic child and seven normal families. The families have a 15-minute discussion of three topics related to a child's life. The conversations are recorded, transcribed, and coded along 12 dimensions. Differences are found between the two groups. There is a discussion of the theoretical background and methodological problems.

LEVIN, G. Communicator–Communicant approach to family interaction research. *Family Process*, 1966, *5*, 105–116.
A family experiment in which the experimenter asks the subject to make a tape recording which might be played subsequently to some specific other person in his family. The recording includes specific instructions about a simple task. Individuals from families containing a schizophrenic (a sample of 33) were contrasted with normal individuals. The recordings were not actually played to family members, but the instructions were analyzed and classified with differences found between the two groups.

LIDZ, T., CORNELISON, A., FLECK, S., & TERRY, D. Intrafamilial environment of schizophrenic patients. II: Marital schism and marital skew. *American Journal of Psychiatry*, 1957, *114*, 241–248.
A study of the intrafamilial environment of the schizophrenic patient. In this study of 14 families, eight were split in two factions by "overt schism between the parents." Thus the identified patient cannot use one parent as a model for identification or as a love object without losing the support of the other parent. The other six families were "skewed" (defined as psychopathology in the dominant parent) which was accepted or shared by the other without trying to change it. Case examples are given.

MALMQUIST, C. School phobia: a problem in family neurosis. *Journal of the American Academy of Child Psychiatry*, 1965, *4*, 293–319.
In contrast to the traditional approach to school phobia, this essay puts forth the clinical notion that it can be seen as a reaction to family pathology. Four types for characterizing disordered families that have been reported in the literature are: (1) the perfectionistic family, (2) the inadequate family, (3) the egocentric family, and (4) the unsocial family. How these family types relate to the symptom are discussed. There is an extensive review of the literature.

McCORD, J., McCORD, W., & HOWARD, A. Family interaction as antecedent to the direction of male aggressiveness. *Journal of Abnormal Social Psychology*, 1963, *66*, 239–242.
See Reference in Section 5.4

McGHIE, A. A comparative study of the mother–child relationship in schizophrenia. I: The interview. II: Psychological testing. *British Journal of Medical Psychology*, 1961, *34*, 195–221.
In Part I of this two-part article there is a description of interviews with 20 mothers of schizophrenics, 20 mothers of neurotics, and 20 mothers of normals. Findings about families of schizophrenics reported in the literature were generally confirmed. There is more marital disharmony in the schizophrenic group and the fathers are said to be weak. However, mothers of schizophrenics do not appear as overprotective as mothers of neurotics. In Part II, the test findings for the three groups are reported. They were given a child rearing questionnaire, a sentence completion test, a word connection test, and the Rorschach.

MEYERS, D., & GOLDFARB, W. Studies of perplexity in mothers of schizophrenic children. *American Journal of Orthopsychiatry*, 1961, *31*, 551–564.
In order to document the association of parental complexity (defined as passivity, uncertainty, lack of spontaneity, absence of empathy; with diminished awareness of the child's needs, bewilderment, and blandness in the face of unacceptable behavior in the child, and an absence of parental control), 23 mothers of schizophrenic children and 23 mothers of normal children were studied. Techniques included a participant–observation technique (in which the observer spent three hours with the family at home), and a semistructured open-ended interview of the mothers. Results indicted that the mothers of the schizophrenic children without organic involvement have a greater difficulty in appropriately structing their child's environment, while the mothers of the organic group cannot be differentiated from mothers of the normals.

MISHLER, E. Families and schizophrenia: An experimental study. *Mental Hygiene*, 1966, *50*, 552–556.
A discussion of a way of testing families with a schizophrenic member and contrasting them with normal families. Findings are not given, but illustrations are offered of ways the families respond in the test situation.

MISHLER, E., & WAXLER, N. Family interaction in schizophrenica. *Archives of General Psychiatry*, 1966, *15*, 64–75.
A paper describing only methodology used in an experimental study of family interactions in schizophrenia. Subjects were 30 schizophrenic families (in which a schizophrenic child was hospitalized) and 16 normal families recruited from the community. Schizophrenic patients were newly admitted to the hospital, unmarried, white, living in the Boston area, living at home with both parents (who had to be alive and living together), and had one unmarried sibling of the same sex. Experimental procedure was Strodtbeck's revealed differences test. Coding and data analysis procedures are described.

MITCHELL, H. E., BULLARD, J. W., & MUDD, E. H. Areas of marital conflict in successfully and unsuccessfully functioning families. *Journal of Health and Human Behavior*, 1962, *3*, 88–93.
See Reference in Section 4.1

MOOS, R. H., & MOOS, B. S. A typology of family social environments. *Family Process*, 1976, *15*, 357–371.
This study attempts to derive an empirically tested taxonomy of the social environments of families so that the relationship betwen family environments and family outcomes may be better understood. A sample of 100 families was tested using the family environmental scale (FES) which assesses the family social environments as they are viewed by family members, interviewers or visitors. The results were subjected to a cluster analysis which yielded six categories of families: expression oriented, independence oriented, moral-religious oriented, structure oriented, and conflict oriented.

MORRIS, G., & WYNNE, L. Schizophrenic offspring, parental styles of communication. *Psychiatry*, 1965, *28*, 19–44.
One of series of papers reporting a study of parental styles of communication and schizophrenic children. Data were selected from excerpts of transcripts of conjoint family sessions with 12 families. Predictions about the most disturbed offspring were made by a judge blind to the clinical aspects of the case. Predictive criteria were then reformulated using the data from a parallel study, utilizing psychological test material as predictors. These reformulated criteria were then utilized for blind predictions on eight new families. Results indicated that the style of the family communication can be related to the thought and affect disorder in schizophrenics.

NURRELL, S., & STACHOWIAK, J. Consistency, rigidty, and power in the interaction patterns of clinic and non-clinic families. *Journal of Abnormal Psychology*, 1967, *72*, 265–272.
To study interaction patterns in families, 11 families (each having at least two children who were attending a child guidance clinic) were matched with 11 control families whose names were obtained from school (who were thought to be normal). Families were observed by two raters through a one-way mirror and were asked to (1) plan something together as a family, (2) answer a list of 11 questions about the families and agree on the answers, (3) list adjectives regarding their family, and (4) make up stories to seven TAT pictures. Results indicated that in all 22 families, the pattern of who talks to whom was consistent. Secondly, the control patients had more rigidity in speaking than the "sick" families. Thirdly, in the sick families the older child had more power within the family than in the controls. Fourthly, the sick families were not as productive as the well families.

NOVAK, A. L., & VAN der VEEN, F. Family concepts and emotional disturbance in the families of disturbed adolescents with normal siblings. *Family Process*, 1970, *9*, 157–171.
See Reference in Section 3.1

OLSON, D. H., SPRENKLE, D. H., & RUSSELL, C. S. Circumplex model of marital and family systems. I: Cohesion and adaptability dimensions, family types and clinical applications. *Family Process*, 1979, *18*, 3–28.
This paper describes the development of a model which can be used as a tool for diagnosing and establishing treatment goals with families and couples. Using the two dimensions of cohesion and adaptability which have been identified as central concepts in the analysis of family behavior, the authors develop a model which identified 16 types of marital and family systems. The focus is on maintaining a critical balance between degrees of cohesion and degrees of adaptability in relational systems.

PAUL, N., & GROSSER, G. Operational mourning and its role in conjoint family therapy. *Community Mental Health Journal*, 1965, *1*, 339–345.
Studies of records of 50 families with a schizophrenic member and 25 families with at least on psychoneurotic member revealed "patterns of inflexible interaction and maladaptive response to object loss." The way the sample was obtained is not stated. It is hypothesized from this data that incomplete mourning after object loss leads to an inability to deal with future object loss and this defect is transmitted to other family members. This is thought to lead to a "fixation of symbiotic relationships in the family." Therefore, "one possible way to dislodge this fixation would be to mobilize those affects which might aid in disrupting this particular kind of equilibrium." "Operational mourning" is the technique evolved by the authors to do this and is believed to "involve the family in a belated mourning experience with extensive grief reactions." A case report is included for illustration.

PEAL, E. "Normal" sex roles: An historical analysis. *Family Process*, 1975, *14*, 389–409.
Definitions of family normality are discussed in terms of parental sex-role performance. Sex roles assumed to be normative in the modern, urban, middle-class family were determined by economic and social changes occurring in the 19th century. These changes created serious psychological consequences. A behavior code formulated to facilitate adaptation is now defined b sociologists as normal. Social role performance, as an unsatisfactory criterion for identifying pathogenic families is discussed.

QUERY, J. M. N. Pre-morbid adjustment and family structure: A comparison of selected rural and urban schizophrenic men. *Journal of Nervous and Mental Disease*, 1961, *133*, 333–338.
A study which reviews schizophrenia in relation to cultural and familial settings. The hypothesis is that premorbid adjustment of rural schizophrenics will be better than that of urban subjects because the rural setting includes a more partriarchal family structure, more emphasis upon individualism, and better sex-role identification. Case history data were examined in terms of the Phillip's scale and supplemented by family interviews. Fifty-one families were interviewed and the hypothesis was supported by the evidence.

REISS, D. Individual thinking and family interaction: Introduction to an experimental study of problem-solving in families of normals, character disorders, and schizophrenics. *Archives of General Psychiatry*, 1967, *16*, 80–93.
A report of an experimental study of the relationship between individual thinking and family interaction. Experimental procedures and methods of analysis are discussed. Subjects were families of five normals, five character disorders, and six schizophrenics. The test used was a puzzle that required active use of cognitive and conceptual capacities. The method of analysis was derived from the work of Riley which developed a systematic approach of computing scores from the raw data and rules concerning inferences.

REISS, D. Individual thinking and family interaction. II: A study of pattern recognition and hypothesis testing in families of normals, character disorders, and schizophrenics. *Journal of Psychiatric Research*, 1967, *5*, 193–211.
The second in a series of studies of the relationship of family process and individual thinking. Results indicate that following a period of family interaction, members of normal families showed improvement in pattern recognition; members of families of schizophrenics showed deterioration or no change; and results of members of character disorder families were in between the two.

REISS, D. Individual thinking and family interaction. III: An experimental study of categorization performance in families of normals, character disorders, and schizophrenics. *Journal of Nervous and Mental Disease*, 1968, *146*, 384–404.
The second of a series of studies to measure the relationship between individual family interaction and individual thinking and to determine what differences in this relationship exist among families of normals, personality disorders, and schizophrenics. Method was to give the families a puzzle, tape their discussion, and to code verbal responses. Sample has been previously described; there were five families in each group. Results indicated that normals could solve the puzzle, while the others could not. The data on why they could not were felt to be consistent with the hypothesis that interpersonal problems in families significantly interfere with their collaborative problem-solving efforts.

REISS, D. Individual thinking and family interaction. IV: A study of information exchange in families of normals, those with character disorders, and schizophrenics. *Journal of Nervous and Mental Disease*, 1969, *149*, 473–490.
The third in a series of papers on interrelationships of family interaction and thinking and perception of family members. The experiment was developed to test the family's efficiency in exchanging information within itself. Families of normals and schizophrenics were more sensitive than those with character disorders to cues from within the family. Families of schizophrenics appeared to represent a group of families who utilize cues from within but not from without the family.

ROSENTHAL, A. J., BEHRENS, M. I., & CHODOFF, P. Communication in lower class families of schizophrenics. *Archives of General Psychiatry*, 1968, *18*, 464–470.
Part I, Methodological Problems, of a two-part report on low-socioeconomic families of schizophrenics. Groups compared were 17 black schizophrenics and their families, 11 in a black control group, and 11 white schizophrenics and their families. The procedure included observation in the home with tasks requiring the family to maintain a focus of attention on a specific topic. (For Part II of this study see Behrens, M. I. Communication in lower class families of schizophrenics. *Archives of General Psychiatry*, 1968, *18*, 689–696.

SCHULMAN, R. E., SHOEMAKER, D. J., & MOELIS, I. Laboratory measurement of parental behavior. *Journal of Consulting Psychology*, 1962, *26*, 109–114.
Families were told to make up stories about a scene which included a variety of buildings and people with the hypothesis that in families with a conduct problem child, parents would exhibit more control over behavior of the child, and that in these families there would be significantly more aggression between parents. Parents and one son (age 8–12) of 41 families were tested. In 20 families the child was considered a conduct problem while the other 21 had

no reported conduct problem. Parents' behavior was rated by observers who found that parents of conduct problem children were more rejecting and hostile than parents of children without problems. It was concluded that there is a cause–effect relation between parental hostility and rejection and aggressive behavior in children.

SHARP, V., GLASNER, S., LEDERMAN, I., & WOLFE, S. Sociopaths and schizophrenics—A comparison of family interactions. *Psychiatry*, 1964, *27*, 127–134.
To test the hypothesis that there would be differences in the family interaction of matched groups of sociopaths and schizophrenics, 20 subjects of each group were examined. These included every patient admitted to the authors' case load at the Philadelphia Naval Hospital. Sources of data were social service questionnaires, parental visits, and interviews with parents. Findings were that sociopaths joined the service "to escape from home," had shorter hospitalization, and their families were much more unconcerned and rejecting than the schizophrenic families who visited more.

SINGER, M. T., & WYNNE, L. C. Communication styles in parents of normals, neurotics, and schizophrenics: Some findings using a new rorschach scoring manual. In I. M. Cohen (Ed.), *Psychiatric research report No. 20*. Washington, D.C.:American Psychiatric Association, 1966.
A report of a study of 250 families in which the Rorschach was used as a stimulus for individual family members. Styles of parental communication are described and findings reported.

SINGER, M. T., & WYNNE, L. C. Differentiating characteristics of parents of childhood schizophrenics, childhood neurotics, and young adults schizophrenics. *American Journal of Psychiatry*, 1963, *120*, 234–243.
A study in which parents of 20 autistic children were blindly differentiated at a statistically significant level of accuracy from parents of 20 neurotic children. The data were TAT and Rorschach tests of the parents. Additionally, the parents of adolescent and young adult schizophrenics were compared with the parents of autistic children and differences were found.

SOJIT, C. M. Dyadic interaction in a double bind situation. *Family Process*, 1969, *8*, 235–260.
Marital couples were exposed to a "double bind situation" to contrast parents of delinquents, ulcerative colitis patients, and normal controls. The couples were exposed to the proverb "a rolling stone gathers no moss" and were asked to reach agreement about its meaning. The responses were categorized and differences found.

SPITZER, S. P., SWANSON, R. M., & LEHR, R. K. Audience reactions and careers of psychiatric patients. *Family Process*, 1969, *8*, 159–181.
A study of the reaction of families and the ways these reactions influence the psychiatric patient career. The histories of 79 first admission patients were examined, and patient and a family member were interviewed. Two dimensions of family reaction to deviance are described leading to a typology of eight career patterns which allow for the classification of 95 percent of the cases reviewed.

STABENAU, J. R., TUPIN, J., WERNER, M., & POLLIN, W. A comparative study of families of schizophrenics, delinquents, and normals. *Psychiatry*, 1965, *28*, 45–59.
A report of a comparison of five families with a schizophrenic, five families with a delinquent, and five normal families tested with the revealed differences test, the object sorting test, and the thematic apperception test. "Data from the three different tests suggest that in the schizophrenic and delinquent families there were both individual disturbances in thought process and impaired communication at the family level . . . . There was relatively little evidence of communication impairment at the individual or family level in the normal families."

STACHOWIAK, J. Decision-making and conflict resolution in the family group. In C. Larson, & F. Dance (Eds.), *Perspectives on Communication*. Milwaukee: University of Wisconsin, Speech Communication Center, 1968.
The author discusses his previous research summarizing major findings on (1) family productivity—which is decreased in "sick families," (2) influence of individual members—maladaptive families showed distinct hierarchal ordering of members, (3) conflict in which maladpative families showed more aggression and hostility than adaptive, and communication, which was disturbed in maladpative families. Implications for future research are discussed.

STEGER, C., & KOTLER, T. Contrasting resources in disturbed and nondisturbed family systems. *British Journal of Medical Psychology*, 1979, *52*, 243–251.
This is a review of studies on the effects of family functioning on child psychopathology using the concept of supportive or coping resources in a family systems framework. Areas reviewed included early parental experience, socioeconomic status, and marital/parental relationships. It is found that the notion of resources—especially nonfamily interactions which may offer compensating supports—enhances the family systems theory's ability to understand the quality of family life.

STURM, I. Attempt to dramatize the double-bind hypothesis of the schizophrenic family. *Journal of Psychology*, 1961, *77*, 55–66.

This is a report of a script written for a television program which portays a common family situation by two kinds of families—a normal family and a family which has a schizophrenic member. Its intent is to dramatize the "double bind" theory of the etiology of schizophrenia.

TSENG, W. S., et al: Family diagnosis and classification. *Journal of Child Psychiatry*, 1976, *15*, 15–35.
This is a report from a research team based on clinical material which attempts to define a family diagnostic and classificatory scheme. The scheme is based on developmental history, mental status examination, and outcome of diagnostic separation of the identified patient from the family. Families are described as: (1) child-reactive; (2) parent-reactive; (3) marital-reactive; (4) unresolved-triangular; (5) special-theme; and (6) pan-pathological families. A definition and case example is presented for each type. Therapeutic implications are suggested.

VAN DER VEEN, F., HUEBNER, B., JORGENS, B., & NEJA, P. Relationship between the parents' concept of the family and family adjustment. *American Journal of Orthopsychiatry*, 1964, *34*, 45–55.
To study the "significance of the family unit for the well-being of the individual" and "the perceptions of the family unit by each individual," two groups of ten families each were selected. One group was composed of families from the community which functioned well (called the higher adjustment group). The other group was composed of families which had applied to a guidance center for help with one of their children. They were matched as to sex and position of the child and size of family. Tests used were the family concept Q-sort, family semantic test, and a marital questionnaire. Results indicated that the adjustment of the families was a function of: (1) the amount of agreement between the "real" family concept of the parent and "ideal" family concept as determined by professionals, (2) the agreement between the "real" and "ideal" family concepts of the parent, and (3) the agreement between the "real" family concepts of the mother and the father.

VIDAL, G., PRECE, G., & SMULEVER, M. Convivencia y trastorno mental. *Acta Psiquiatrica Y Psicologica De America Latina*, 1969, *15*, 55–65.
A sample of 1,322 patients were studied for family size, birth order of the patient, and family integrity (number of years the offspring lived together with both parents). The hypothesis was that "the higher the amount of the family relationship the lower the severity of the mental disorder." Neurotics were expcted to show smaller families, first birth order positions, and intact families, while psychotics would show larger families, last birth order positions, and disrupted families. The hypothesis about neurotics was confirmed but that about psychotics was only partially confirmed.

VOGEL, E. F. The marital relationship of parents of emotionally disturbed children: Polarization and isolation. *Psychiatry*, 1960, *23*, 1–12.
In a study of 18 families seen by an interdisciplinary team, nine families with emotionally disturbed children were matched with nine families with relaivetly healthy children. The marriage relationship in all families with an emotionally disturbed child was found to be more disturbed; the parents behaved as if they were polar opposites and each partner contended that his standards were right and the spouse's wrong. In the control families the parents had less physical separation, shared activities with each other more, and exhibited more flexibility in the handling of money.

VOGEL, E. F., & BELL, N. W. The emotionally disturbed child as a family scapegoat. *Psychoanalytic Review*, 1960, *47*, 21–42.
Based upon intensive study of nine families with a disturbved child matched with a group of "well" families, this report emphasizes the use of the child as a scapegoat for conflicts between the parents. In all the disturbed families a particular child was involved in the tensions existing between parents, while in the "well" families the tensions were less severe or were handled in such a way that the child did not become pathologically involved.

WALDRON, S., SHRIER, D., STONE, B., *et al.*, School phobia and other childhood neuroses: A systematic study of the children and their families. *American Journal of Psychiatry*, 1975, *132*, 802–808.
This is a clinical study of the "family dynamics" of school phobia. The method was to compare 35 families having an identified patient with school phobia with 35 matched families having an identified patient with "neurosis" (using the classification of the Group for the Advancement of Psychiatry). Both groups were selected from larger groups attending an outpatient clinic and were the "healthiest" one-third of each group. A rating scale was developed to assess clinical aspects of child, parental, and family functioning as well as precipitating factors. Data were obtained from chart review. Results indicated that twice as many school phobic children (as children with other neuroses) showed excessive separation anxiety, dependency, and depression. Mutually hostile-dependent interaction was found in the school phobic children.

WALKER, K. N., & MESSINGER, L. Remarriage after divorce: Dissolution and reconstruction of family boundaries. *Family Process*, 1979, *18*, 185–192.
See Reference in Section 3.6.

WERNER, M., STABENAU, J., & POLLIN, W. TAT method for the differentiation of families of schizophrenics, delinquents, and normals. *Journal of Abnormal Psychology*, 1970, *74*, 139–145.

This is a research study attempting to differentiate patterns of parent-child interaction and their effects on subsequent development of pathology. Method was to assess the parent–child interaction using 240 TAT stories by parents of ten schizophrenics, ten delinquents, and ten normals. The interaction was defined as (1) personally involved, (2) impersonally involved, and (3) over-involved. Blind ratings of the stories into the three categories easily differentiated the three parents groups. Blind ratings of another separate series of stories from 20 mothers of schizophrenics and 20 mothers of normal children again differentiated the two parental groups.

WERTHEIM, E. S. Family unit therapy and the science and typology of family systems. *Family Process*, 1973, *12*, 361–376.
This paper descirbes a three-dimensional typology of family systems. Eight family types are isolated including; (1) two normal types; (2) two fairly integrated types, with relatively milder individual symptoms; (3) two pseudointegrated tupes, with more serious individual psychopathology, such as psychotic and psychosomatic behavior; (4) two nonintegrated types, whose members present a wide range of symptomatology, such as antisocial behavior.

WERTHEIM, E. S. The science and typology of family systems. II: Further theoretical and practical considerations. *Family Process*, 1975, *14*, 285–309.
See Reference in Section 3.6.

WESTLEY, W. A., & EPSTEIN, N. B. Report on the psychosocial organization of the family and mental health. In D. Willner (Ed.), *Decisions, values, and groups*, No. I. New York: Pergamon Press, 1960.
A report of a study designed to investigate the relationship between family functioning and development of either mental health or pathology. The sample was 531 students of the first-year class at a university who were given a Rorschach, a Gordon personality test, and interviewed by a psychiatrist. Out of these, 20 were classified as being the most emotionally healthy, and of these, 17 were in the study. There is a schema for description, analysis, and evaluation of the family. Common features of these emotionally healthy families are described.

WILD, C., SINGER, M., ROSMAN, G., RICCI, J., & LIDZ, T. Measuring disordered styles of thinking. *Archives of General Psychiatry*, 1966, *13*, 471–476.
Forty-four parents whose child was a schizophrenic in-patient were matched for age and education with 46 control parents (community volunteers) on the object sorting test. A scoring manual is described. Patient-parents scores differed significantly from controls. The object scoring test seems to discriminate between parents of schizophrenic patients and controls who do not have children with psychiatric pathology.

WINTER, W., & FERREIRA, A. A factor analysis in family interaction measures. *Journal of Protective Techniques and Personal Assessment*, 1970, *34*, 55–63.
This is a research study attempting to form a classification of families less dependent on the variable of psychiatric diagnosis of the identified patient. To do this 25 patients with normal children and 33 with abnormal children made up TAT stories and were tested by the technique of "unrevealed differences." Data were subjected to factor analysis, and seven factors were abstracted: (1) middle class adjustment, (2) fast performance, (3) sullen silence, (4) lack of task orientation, (5) insufficient communication, (6) hospital interaction, and (7) dependency. Advantages of giving a label to the whole family rather than to just one member of the family were discussed.

WINTER, W. D., & FERREIRA, A. J. Interaction process analysis of family decision making. *Family Process*, 1967, *6*, 155–172.
A sample of 90 triads of father, mother, and child were tested to contrast "normals" with "abnormals." The families were exposed to a set of three TAT cards and asked to make up a story they all agreed upon which linked the three cards together. The protocols were scored with the Bales IPA system. It is concluded that "the Bales IPA system, in its present form, is not suited for work with families."

WINTER, W. D., & FERREIRA, A. J. Talking time as an index of intrafamilial similarity in normal and abnormal families. *Journal of Abnormal Psychology*, 1969, *74*, 574–575.
A study testing the hypothesis that normal families correlate more highly with each other than do abnormal families in terms of talking at length in extemporaneous speech. 127 family triads were tested. Of these, 77 were abnormals with identified patients being "emotionally disturbed maladjusted;" 50 were normals. The families took the group thematic apperception test and the total number of seconds of speech of each of them indicated that members of abnormal families resembled each other more than do members of normal families.

WINTER, W. D., FERREIRA, A. J., & OLSON, J. Hostility themes in the family TAT. *Journal of Projective Techniques and Personal Assessment*, 1966, *30*, 270–275.
Second of a series describing a diagnostic test adapted for use with families. Results were obtained from use of three TAT stories based on three cards, each produced conjointly by 126 three-member families. Stories were scored for hostility in the story themes. Fifty familiesv had normal children, 44 had neurotic children, 16 had schizophrenic children, and 16 had delinquent children. Normal and schizophrenic groups produced stories low in hostility, neurotics produced stories high in hostility, and delinquents scored high on one hostility variable and low on another.

WINTER, W. D., FERREIRA, A. J., & OLSON, J. L. Story sequence analysis of family TATs. *Journal of Projective Techniques and Personal Assessment*, 1965, *29*, 392–397.
A group of 126 families, composed of parents and one child, were asked to produce TAT stories conjointly. The families were to make up a story based upon three TAT cards presented simultaneously to them. Three stories based on nine cards were composed by each family and scored by the Arnold system of story sequence analysis. In the sample there were 50 families with normal children. The abnormal group consisted of 44 emotionally maladjusted, 16 delinquent, and 16 schizophrenic children. The procedure successfully differentiated normal from abnormal families but the three abnormal groups did not differ from each other. The stories of abnormal families are said to be characterized by negative attitudes toward achievement, morality, responsibility, human relationships, and reaction to adversity.

WYNNE, L. C. The study of intrafamilial alignments and splits in exploratory family therapy. In N. W. Ackerman, F. L. Beatman, & S. Sherman (Eds.), *Exploring the base for family therapy*. New York: Family Service Association of America, 1961.
See Reference in Section 5.2

WYNNE, L. C., & SINGER, M. T. Thought disorder and family relations of schizophrenics. I: A research strategy. II: A classification of forms of thinking. *Archives of General Psychiatry*, 1963, *9*, 191–206.
See Reference in Section 5.2

YOUNG, M., & GEERTZ, H. Old age in London and San Francisco: Some families compared. *British Journal of Sociology*, 1961, *12*, 124–141.
A British and an American suburb are compared as to family attitudes of older people. No differences were found in the frequency of contact with adult children, the tendency to live close by, or in the greater importance of adult daughters in parents' lives. But the American respondents had more knowledge of and pride in their ancestors. Larger national samples confirmed the last finding.

5.2   FAMILY MEMBER WITH PSYCHOTIC DISORDER

ABLON, S. L., DAVENPORT, Y. B., GERSHON, E. S., & ADLAND, M. L. The married manic. *American Journal of Orthopsychiatry*, 1975, *45*, 854–866.
This paper describes the family dynamics of the identified patient with manic-depressive illness. Method included chart review of 53 families in which the identified patient had bipolar, manic-depressive illness; of these 57, 43 were married. Of these 43, 8 participated in 2, sequential, post-hospital, psychotherapy groups. Clinical observations noted were: (1) the threat of recurring mania, (2) hostility between spouses, (3) massive denial, (4) symbiosis and dependency, (5) weak or absent father. Therapy implications were discussed.

ACKERMAN, N. W. Family focused therapy of schizophrenia. In A. Scher, & H. Davis (Eds.), *The out-patient treatment of schizophrenia*. New York: Grune & Stratton, 1960.
Given at a conference on the out-patient treatment of schizophrenia, this clinical essay is on family therapy, schizophrenia, and the family. The family is relevant not only to the course and outcome but also to the origin of schizophrenia, and treatment should include the whole family together rather than only the identified patient. Techniques of treating the family are described.

ACKERMAN, N. W. The Schizophrenic patient and his family relationships. In M. Greenblatt, D. J. Levinson, & G. L. Klerman (Eds.), *Mental patients in transition. Steps in hospital-community rehabilitation*. Springfield: Thomas C. Charles, 1961.
A discussion of the influence of the family on the patient discharged from the hospital.

ACKERMAN, N. W., & FRANKLIN, P. F. Family dynamics and the reversibility of delusional formation: A case study in family therapy. In I. Boszormenyi-Nagy & J. L. Framo (Eds.), *Intensive family therapy*. New York: Harper & Row, 1965.
A report on a case of a 16-year-old schizophrenic and her family in which treatment "of the whole family seemed to move toward reversal of the patient's psychotic experience." Interview data and comment is provided.

ALANEN, Y. The families of schizophrenic patients. *Proceedings of the Royal Society of Medicine*, 1970, *63*, 227–231.
This is one of a series of research studies comparing parents and siblings of 30 schizophrenics with 30 neurotics. The parents of schizophrenics had a greater incidence of schizophrenia, personality disorders, and borderline disorders than did the normals. The siblings of the schizophrenics showed more varied disturbance than the parents. Of 30

schizophrenic families, 14 were "schizmatic" and 7 were "skewed"; 10 families were chaotic, 11 were rigid, 6 showed both patterns, and 3 were atypical. The families from which schizophrenics come are usually disturbed both genetically and evironmentally.

ALANEN, Y. Round table conference of family studies and family therapy of schizophrenic patients. *Acta Psychiatrica Scandinavica*,Supplement No. 169, 1963, *39*, 420–426.
A report of a panel discussion oriented toward family dynamics and therapy held at the Thirteenth Congress of Scandinavian Psychiatrists in 1962. Topics discussed included findings of the Yale studies on families, parental interaction and the resulting disturbed body images of schizophrenic patients, reactions of the family when the patient is in individual psychotherapy, and families of schizophrenics in relation to the "larger families" of our contemporary societies."

ALANEN, Y. Some thoughts on schizophrenia and ego development in the light of family investigations. *Archives of General Psychiatry*, 1960, *3*, 650–656.
Noting a divergence between the studies of family environment of the schizophrenic and classical psychoanalytical conceptions, the author reviews the problem and attempts to bring the ideas closer together with four main points in the pathological ego development of the schizophrenic.

ALANEN, Y. O., & KINNUNEN, P. Marriage and the development of schizophrenia. *Psychiatry*, 1975, *38*, 346–365.
Thirty schizophrenic patients whose marriage preceded the schizophrenia were interviewed clinically with their spouses and given a psychological examination using a modified WAIS and Consensus Rorschach. Eighteen of the 30 families were treated with marital therapy (at least ten sessions for 11 of the 18 families). Marriages were classified into three types using data on "interaction types" from the Consensus Rorschach. Therapeutic implications are discussed.

ALBERT, R. S. Stages of breakdown in the relationships and dynamics between the mental patient and his family. *Archives of General Psychiatry*, 1960, *3*, 682–690.
Since a family is a social system of many different interlocking roles, the absence or illness of a member produces a reaction throughout the family. Two guiding premises are (1) with disruption, the ongoing dynamics move patient and family into a poorer state with less possibility of a return to earlier, healthier stages of interaction, and (2) in the earlier stags other members of the family are equally ill and susceptible candidates for becoming the patient. Given a description of stages as a model, there could be better prediction and preparation for dealing with cases.

ANDERSON, C. M. Family intervention with severely disturbed inpatients. *Archives of General Psychiatry*, 1977, *34*, 697–702.
See Reference in Section 1.7.

ANTHONY, E. J. The mutative impact of serious mental and physical illness in a parent on family life. In E. J. Anthony & C. Koupernik (Eds.), *The child in his family*. New York: Wiley, 1970.
A report of a study of families in which a parent figure has succumbed to a serious mental or physical disorder necessitating hospitalization. Various views are offered of such illness as a disruption of family roles, as a crisis in accommodation, as a disconnection, and as a challenge. Family members were interviewed individually and in dyads and triads.

ARBOGAST, R. The effect of family involvement on the day care center treatment of schizophrenia. *Journal of Nervous and Mental Disease*, 1969, *149*, 277–280.
See Reference in Section 1.4.

ARIETI, S. Parents of the schizophrenic patient: A reconsideration. *Journal of the American Academy of Psychoanalysis*, 1977, *5*, 347–358.
Schizophrenia is due to a combination of genetic and environmental factors. The author asserts that there has previously been an error in conceiving the patient as being molded completely by external circumstances. In fact, it is the patient's behavior, which is a transformation of family irrationality, that constitutes schizophrenia. In 75 percent of cases of schizophrenia seen by the author in private practice, the mother did not fit the image of the so-called "schizophrenogenic mother."

ARONSON, J., & POLGAR, S. Pathogenic relationships in schizophrenia. *American Journal of Psychiatry*, 1962, *119*, 222–227.
Investigating 13 soldiers who developed overtly schizophrenic psychoses in the army, the authors interviewed 185 individuals on 11 army posts to gather data. Work performance and overt psychotic symptoms are said to depend upon the type of relationship established with significant others. Three types of relationship were distinguished: the quasitherapeutic, the pseudotherapeutic and the contratherapeutic. The authors suggest the data indicate the groups other than the family can be pathogenic.

AUERSWALD, E. H. Interdisciplinary vs. ecological approach. *Family Process*, 1968, 7, 202–215.
A discussion of the difference between approaching a problem from the viewpoint of different disciplines or using an ecological systems approach. A case of a runaway girl is used for exploring this difference.

BARTLETT, F. H. Illusion and reality in R. D. Laing. *Family Process*, 1976, *15*, 51–64.
This is a critical essay which describes the inconsistency between Laing's sensitivity for the experience of the schizophrenic and his censure of the schizogenic family. The author traces the development of this apparent contradiction beginning with Laing's earliest writings through his more recent efforts. The author concludes that Laing's emphasis on the exclusive value of the intrapsychic process is not congruent with contemporary society and therefore is counterproductive in terms of therapeutic goals and outcomes.

BASAMANIA, B. W. The emotional life of the family: Inferences for social casework. *American Journal of Orthopsychiatry*, 1961, *31*, 74–86.
A casework view of the Bowen research project where families with a schizophrenic member were hospitalized. Observations of 11 families are categorized into (1) interrelated personality problems among family members, and (2) interaction problems among family members. Case examples are given. A discussion of family therapy procedures is presented with the emphasis upon relating to more than one individual at a time. Inferences for social casework emphasize the dimension of the emotional life of the family rather than the integration of sociological concepts with casework practice.

BATESON, G. The bisocial integration of behavior in the schizophrenic family. In N. W. Ackerman, F. L. Beatman, & S. Sherman (Eds.), *Exploring the base for family therapy*. New York: Family Service Association of America, 1961.
A description of families and other systems in terms of feedback and calibration, where calibration is at the "setting" level. Families of schizophrenics are described in terms of difficulties at the calibration level.

BATESON, G. Minimal requirements for a theory of schizophrenia. *Archives of General Psychiatry*, 1960, *2*, 477–491.
See Reference in Section 3.6.

BATESON, G., JACKSON, D. D., HALEY, J., & WEAKLAND, J. H. A note on the double bind—1962. *Family Process*, 1963, *2*, 154–161.
A brief comment by the Bateson group on the context of their 1956 paper on the double bind and further developments after that time. Includes a bibliography of project members arranged by subject with 70 references.

BATESON, G., JACKSON, D. D., HALEY, J., & WEAKLAND, J. Toward a theory of schizophrenia. *Behavioral Science*, 1956, *1*, 251–264.
Based on the authors' previous clinical experience, experimental data, the theory of logical types (defined as a discontinuity between a class and its member), and communication theory, the authors hypothesize that schizophrenic symptoms may result from being caught in a double bind. This is defined as a situation in which no matter what a person does, he can't "win." Therapeutic implications are discussed—many therapeutic gambits are "borderline double binds."

BAXTER, J. C. Family relations and variables in schizophrenia. In I. M. Cohen (Ed.), *Psychiatric Research (Report no. 20)*. Washington, D.C.: American Psychiatric Association, 1966.
An article reviewing the variables used in the study of family relationships of schizophrenics. Whether child or family is "causal" is discussed, and the merits of one interpretation or the other is ambiguous at present.

BAXTER, J. C. Family relationship variables in schizophrenia. *Acta Psychiatiatrica Scandinavica*, 1966, *42*, 362–391.
See Reference in Section 3.6.

BAXTER, J. C., & ARTHUR, S. Conflict in families of schizophrenics as a function of premorbid adjustment and social class. *Family Process*, 1964, *3*, 273–279.
A group of 16 hospitalized male schizophrenics was classified into 4 groups on the basis of the patient's premorbid adjustment and social class. Standard interviews with the parents were rated for conflict. "Results indicate that the amount of conflict expressed by the parents varies jointly with the premorbid level of the patient and the social class of the family."

BAXTER, J. C., ARTHUR, S., FLOOD, C., & HEDGEPATH, B. Conflict patterns in the families of schizophrenics. *Journal of Nervous and Mental Disease*, 1962, *135*, 419–424.
Families of 12 male and 6 female schizophrenics were interviewed individually and as a group to explore conflict patterns in relation to the sex of the child. The amount of conflict is said to be comparable in the 2 groups while patterns of conflict differ. There is more interparental conflict in the group of families with a male patient and more involvement of the patient in conflict in the group with a female patient.

BAXTER, J. C., & BECKER, J. Anxiety and avoidance behavior in schizophrenics in response to parental figures. *Journal of Abnormal and Social Psychology*, 1962, *64*, 432–437.
Good and poor premorbid schizophrenics were exposed to TAT cards of parent–child relationships. Poor premorbids produced more anxiety in response to a mother figure than a father figure. Good premorbids showed the reverse. Avoidance behavior in response to parental figures did not differ.

BAXTER, J. C., BECKER, J., & HOOKS, W. Defensive style in the families of schizophrenics and controls. *Journal of Abnormal and Social Psychology*, 1963, *66*, 512–518.
Parents of good and poor premorbid schizophrenics were given Rorschach tests. Parents of poor premorbids showed a greater amount of immature behavior than parents of good premorbids or parents of neurotics.

BEAVERS, W. T., BLUMBERG, S., TIMKIN, D. R., & WEINER, M. F. Commmunication patterns of mothers of schizophrenics. *Family Process*, 1965, *4*, 95–104.
A study of the ways the mothers of schizophrenics communicate with an interviewer. Nine mothers of schizophrenics were contrasted with nine mothers of hospitalized nonschizophrenic patients. The mothers of schizophrenics communicated their feelings in a quantitatively more ambiguous fashion.

BECK, S. Families of schizophrenic and of well children: Methods, concepts, and some results. *American Journal of Orthopsychiatry*, 1960, *30*, 247–275.
A report on a research study attempting to differentiate and compare families with schizophrenic children, families with neurotic children, and families with normal children. A list of trait items about individuals in 106 families were O-sorted by a psychiatrist and three social workers. The clusterings are said to indicate similarities and differences.

BECK, S., & NUNNALLY, J. Parental attitudes in families. *Archives of General Psychiatry*, 1965, *13*, 208–213.
Differences in "attitudes" of parents of schizophrenic children were compared with those with well children. Eighteen attitudes were measured using the semantic differential test of Osgood (measures concepts like "my child, pregnancy," etc.). Schizophrenic families were obtained from 32 families of children resident in a therapeutic school; well children families came from the community. Concepts associated with greater mental health by the well families included "my mother, the kind of father I am, the kind of mother I am, myself when I was a father, clinic mothers, and clinic our family." There was no difference between samples in the other nine concepts.

BEHRENS, M., & GOLDFARB, W. A study of patterns of interaction of families of schizophrenic children in residential treatment. *American Journal of Orthopsychiatry*, 1958, *28*, 300–312.
An attempt to differentiate families of schizophrenic children from those of nonschizophrenic children with a sample of 20 families who had a child diagnosed as schizophrenic, and 5 who had a child with a behavior disorder, all of whom were inpatients. There were 10 normals, all children living at home. Data were collected using family interaction scales, and observations were recorded in the homes for both the normals and the patients when they were home on a visit. Results indicate that the schizophrenic families were more pathologic than the normal families and the families with behavior disorders.

BEHRENS, M., MEYERS, D. I, GOLDFARB, W., GOLDFARB, N. & FIELDSTEEL, N. D. The Henry Ittleson center family interaction scales. *Genetic Psychology Monograph*, 1969, *80*, 203–295.
A report of a manual used for the family interaction scales. The scales appraise the functioning of family groups, and derive from a clinical interest in the relationship between the identified patient and the family. Data are obtained through a three-hour home visit at mealtime. Scales have been used to evaluate the functioning of the family with a schizophrenic child, to compare families which include children with various diagnoses with normal families and to determine the nature of changes in family functioning over a specified length of time. A description of scales and scoring instructions, and three family illustrations are included.

BEHRENS, M., ROSENTHAL, A. J., & CHODOFF, P. Communication in lower class families of schizophrenics. *Archives of General Psychiatry*, 1968, *18*, 689–696.
The second part of a study of low socioeconomic families of schizophrenics. The study was done in the home where the family was focused upon a task, particularly the Rorschach. Raters were asked to predict type of family from written transcripts. Results indicate that communication and interaction patterns of lower-class families with a schizophrenic differ from families whose class background is similar.

BENTINCK, C. Opinions about mental illness held by patients and relatives. *Family Process*, 1967, *6*, 193–207.
A study inquiring into the nature of the attitudes at home about mental illness in families of male schizophrenics. A control group of male medical patients was used. The data were gathered by a questionnaire administered in a home interview. The sample was 50 schizophrenics and 50 relatives, and 50 medical patients and 50 relatives. Opinions of relatives of schizophrenics had "more in common with blue collar employees than with mental health professionals.

BERGER, A., A test of the double bind hypothesis of schizophrenia. *Family Process*, 1965, *4*, 198–205.
A sample of 20 schizophrenics, 18 maladjusted nonschizophrenics, 20 hospital employees, and 40 students were exposed to a questionnaire of items rated for their double bind nature. Differences were found.

BOSZORMENYI-NAGY, I. The concept of schizophrenia from the perspective of family treatment. *Family Process*, 1962, *1*, 103–113.
A discussion of "the problems and mechanisms of family relationships." The author's hypothesis is that "schizophrenic personality development may in part be perpetrated by reciprocal interpersonal need complementaries between parent and offspring. Observations were collected from intensive psychotherapy of young female schizophrenics and concurrent conjoint therapy of their relatives at a psychiatric hospital.

BOVERMAN, M., & ADAMS, J. R. Collaboration of psychiatrist and clergyman: A case report. *Family Process*, 1964, *3*, 251–272.
A description of a psychotic patient and family treated in collaboration. The different functions of psychiatrist and clergyman are discussed, each presenting his view of the case.

BOWEN, M. A family concept of schizophrenia. In D. D. Jackson (Ed.), *The etiology of schizophrenia*. New York: Basic Books, 1960.
Clinical observations based upon a research study of the families of schizophrenics. Includes a report on the project in which whole families of schizophrenics were hospitalized.

BOWEN, M. Family psychotherapy. *American Journal of Orthopsychiatry*, 1961, *31*, 40–60.
A discussion of the research program in which parents and their schizophrenic offspring lived together on a psychiatric ward. The paper includes a description of the history of the project, the sample of families, and the theoretical approach. The emphasis is upon the family as a unit of illness rather than upon individuals in the family group. Principles and techniques of family therapy emphasize utilizing the family leader, avoiding individual relationships with family members, and not accepting the position of omnipotence into which the family attempts to place the therapist. Results are discussed and examples given with case material.

BOWEN, M. Family psychotherapy with schizophrenia in the hospital and in private practice. In I. Boszormenyi-Nagy & J. L. Framo (Eds.), *Intensive family therapy*. New York, Harper & Row, 1965.
A discussion of a theory of the family and of family therapy with sections on: differences between family and individual theory; a summary of the family theory of emotional illness with the emphasis upon schizophrenia; the parental transmission of problems to the child; the clinical approach to modify the family transmission process; and principles and techniques of this family therapy approach.

BOWEN, M., DYSINGER, R., & BASAMANIA, B. Role of the father in families with a schizophrenic patient. *American Journal of Psychiatry*, 1959, *115*, 1017–1020.
One of a series of papers on a study of families with schizophrenics in which the entire family (mother, father, identified patient, and well sibling) were all hospitalized in the psychiatric research ward for periods of "up to two and a half years." Four families filled this criteria while an additional six famlies were seen in outpatient family therapy for periods of up to two years. The most frequent family dynamic observed was "emotional divorce" between mother and father and an intense relationship between mother and patient in which father was excluded.

BRODEY, W. Image, object and narcissistic relationships. *American Journal of Orthopsychiatry*, 1961, *31*, 69–73.
A discussion of the family unit with a conceptualization involving externalization, the narcissistic relationship, and the image relationship. It is suggested that the psychotic member has escaped from the bizarre pseudologicalness and stereotype of the family, but his astonishingly perceptive comments are dismissed by the family as entirely crazy.

BRODEY, W. Some family operations in schizophrenia. *Archives of General Psychiatry*, 1959, *1*, 379–402.
One of a series of papers from a research project in which entire families (all of which have a schizophrenic member) are hospitalized and observed for periods of 6 months to 2½ years. Data were collected from five families. Descriptions of the family and of staff–family relationships are reported. Based on the family histories an attempt is made to understand the pathology presented.

BRODSKY, C. M. The social recovery of mentally ill housewives. *Family Process*, 1968, *7*, 170–183.
A report on a study of the relationship between social recovery and role among mentally ill housewives. A sample of 38 housewives admitted to an acute treatment research unit were examined and followed-up. The housewife's role as said to be conducive to recovery.

CAPUTO, D. V. The parents of the schizophrenic. *Family Process*, 1963, *2*, 339–356.
A study to assess the role of the parents in the development of schizophrenia, with particular emphasis upon the concept of the passive father and dominating mother. Parents were given individual tests and after taking a parent attitude inventory they were asked to discuss the items on which they had disagreed. These discussions were assessed

with the Bales method. Reversal of role was not found to be a significant factor, and a hostile atmosphere is indicated in the home of the potential schizophrenic.

CHEEK, F. Family interaction patterns and convalescent adjustment of the schizophrenic. *Archives of General Psychiatry*, 1965, *13*, 138–147.
See Reference in Section 3.3.

CHEEK, F. Family socialization techniques and deviant behavior. *Family Process*, 1966, *5*, 199–217.
A study based upon Parsons' theoretical framework in which deviant behavior is related to imbalance of systems inputs and outputs at various stages of development. A sample of 120 male adults from 4 different groups— schizophrenics, normals, alcoholics, and reformatory inmates—were exposed to a questionnaire on family problem situations. Differences were found and it is suggested that Parsons' theoretical scheme could be translated into reinforcement theory.

CHEEK, F. The father of the schizophrenic: The function of a peripheral role. *Archives of General Psychiatry*, 1965, *13*, 336–345.
See Reference in Section 3.3.

CHEEK, F. Parental role distortions in relation to schizophrenic deviancy. In I. M. Cohen (Ed.), *Psychiatric research report no. 20*. Washington, D.C.: American Psychiatric Association, 1966.
A study investigating the nature of the schizophrenic interacting in the family, and the relation of family interaction to the outcome of the schizophrenic. The study combined questionnaire and observational data. The sample included 67 schizophrenic contrasted with 56 nonpsychotic young adults.

CHEEK, F. The "schizophrenic mother" in word and deed. *Family Process*, 1964, *3*, 155–177.
A study of the mothers of schizophrenics by direct observation of their behavior in a standard conversation with spouse and schizophrenic offspring. The data were analyzed with a revised version of the Bales process analysis. Sixty-seven families of schizophrenics were contrasted with 56 normal families. Differences in characteristics of the mothers were found.

CHEEK, F. A serendipitous finding: Sex roles in schizophrenia. *Journal of Abnormal Social Psychology*, 1964, *69*, 392–400.
One of a series of reports on an ongoing research project studying the family environment in schizophrenia. Interaction profiles of 67 young adult schizophrenics (40 male and 27 female) were compared with those of 56 normals (31 male and 25 female). Profiles were derived from 48 minutes recorded interaction between father, mother, and patient with a variation of the Bales interaction categories. Male schizophrenics presented an interaction equivalent of withdrawal, with low total activity rates, and low dominance behaviors. In contrast, female schizophrenics proved to be more active than female normals.

CHEEK, F. E., & ANTHONY, R. Personal pronoun usage in families of schizophrenics and social space utilization. *Family Process*, 1970, *9*, 431–447.
See Reference in Section 3.6.

COE, W. C., CURRY, A. E., & KESSLER, D. R. Family interaction of psychiatric patients. *Family Process*, 1969, *8*, 119–130.
A study using a questionnaire to examine family interaction patterns with emphasis upon everyday activities. Forty males and 40 females and their relatives who were psychiatric inpatients were contrasted with 54 husband and wife volunteers. Results include the finding that more family decision-making is left to the child in the patient families. In these families the members tend not to recognize disagreement in their interactions.

DAVIS, D. R. The family triangle in schizophrenia. *British Journal of Medical Psychology*, 1961, *34*, 53–63.
An attempt to answer the question, "What contribution to the etiology of schizophrenia in young males is made by conflicts arising out of the Oedipus complex?" with emphasis upon the patient's attitude toward parents. A review of the literature and a discussion of actual incest and patricide are presented. The author discusses 15 schizophrenic patients with emphasis upon the onset of illness. He concludes that the onset occurs during a crisis between the patient and his mother when anxiety becomes intense. Frustration of incestuous wishes contributes to this anxiety. Hatred for the father was clearly shown in a minority of the cases.

DAVIS, D. R. A re-appraisal of Ibsen's *Ghosts*. *Family Process*, 1963, *2*, 81–94.
A critical analysis of Ibsen's play, *Ghosts: A Domestic Drama*, in light of modern therapy of family psychopathology. Current ideas about the family of the schizophrenic are applied to this family drama.

DAY, J., & KWIATKOWSKA, H. The psychiatric patient and his "well" sibling: A comparison through their art productions. *Bulletin of Art Therapy*, 1962, *2*, 51–66.

A clinical paper comparing the "well" sibling to the "sick" sibling in a schizophrenic family. The setting was an in-patient ward, and observations were taken from the art work of the paired siblings, during art therapy. The data from three families reveal that the "sick" sibling art productions are quite disorganized, while the "well" sibling's productions are more normal.

DUNHAM, R. M. Ex post facto reconstruction of conditioning schedules in family interaction. In I. M. Cohen (Ed.), *Psychiatric research report no. 20*, Washington, D.C.: American Psychiatric Association, 1966.
See Reference in Section 3.6.

DUPONT, R., & GRUNEBAUM, H. Willing victims: The husbands of paranoid women. *American Journal of Psychiatry*, 1968, *125*, 151–159.
In an attempt to understand the dynamics of spouses of paranoid women, cases with paranoid delusions (both inpatient and outpatient) were evaluated over a three-year period. Data were collected on nine women with paranoid state, using clinical interviews, with the husband alone, wife alone, and the couple together, plus the MMPI and interpersonal checklist. Results indicated that the wife expressed the anger and dissatisfactions in the marriage, while the husband manifested passivity and apparent reasonableness and thus seemed to be a "willing victim."

DYSINGER, R. H. A family perspective on the diagnosis of individual members. *American Journal of Ortho-psychiatry*, 1961, *31*, 61–68.
A discussion of the characteristic view of health matters by members of families containing a hospitalized schizophrenic as part of the Bowen study. Typically mother, father, and identified patient are intensely involved emotionally over health issues. Siblings are not included in the same way. Confusion over feelings, physical symptoms and definite illness exists, and attempts to do something effective about a health matter are often stalemated. Intense emotional problems in the parental relationship are handled through a set of mechanisms that operate to support an inaccurate assumption that the problem is the health of one child. The development of psychosis in the child demonstrates the inefficiency of this displacement and also can become a focus for the perpetuation of the family mechanism.

EVANS, A. S., BULLARD, D. M., JR., & SOLOMON, M. H. The family as a potential resource in the rehabilitation of the chronic schizophrenic patient: A study of 60 patients and their families. *American Journal of Psychiatry*, 1961, *117*, 1075–1083.
A study of the relative value of drugs on social therapies in the treatment of chronic schizophrenia. The success or failure of plans for discharge was often found to be dependent upon the relationship between the patient and his family. This descriptive report summarizes some of the findings about these families, including the discovery that a surprising number of families maintained an active interest in the patient and regularly visited him after years of hospitalization. The need for psychiatric social workers and additional community resources is emphasized as imported for facilitating discharge.

FARINA, A. Patterns of role dominance and conflict in parents of schizophrenic patients. *Journal of Abnormal Social Psychology*, 1960, *61*, 31–38.
Parents of 12 good premorbid schizophrenics, 12 poor premorbids, and 12 children hospitalized for tuberculosis were interviewed. They were exposed individually and as pairs to hypothetical incidents with children. The joint conversation was analyzed for dominance and conflict. Father dominance was associated with good premorbid adjustment of the son and mother dominance with poor premorbid adjustment. Parents of schizophrenics displayed more conflict than the control parents.

FARINA, A., & DUNHAM, R. M. Measurement of family relationships and their effects. *Archives of General Psychiatry*, 1963, *9*, 64–73.
A group of families of male hospitalized schizophrenic patients, divided into good premorbid and poor premorbid, was given a structural situation test. Each family member is exposed to some hypothetical problem situations with children, and the family is then brought together and exposed to the same situation. Indices of dominance, such as length of speeches, and indices of conflict were constructed. Immediately following this, a group of the patients was given a visual task individually and contrasted with a group given the same task a week after the situation test. The conclusions are that fathers are more dominant in good premorbid cases and mothers more dominant in bad premorbid cases. Conflict scores are higher for good premorbid.

FEINSILVER, D. Communication in families with schizophrenic patients. *Archives of General Psychiatry*, 1970, *22*, 143–148.
In a study comparing communication in schizophrenic families and normal families there were 6 schizophrenic families (each consisting of mother, father, patient, and nonschizophrenic sibling) to compare with the control group of 6 normal families. The task was to communicate "essential attributes of common household objects from one person to another" and the verbal interaction was scored according to misidentification of the object, inappropriate conceptualization, and impaired focal attention. Results indicated that families of schizophrenic patients perform

significantly more poorly than the families of normals. In the schizophrenic families, there was no difference in communication from the parents to the schizophrenic sibling or to the nonschizophrenic sibling.

FERBER, A., KLIGLER, D., ZWERLING, I., & MENDELSOHN, M. Current family structure. *Archives of General Psychiatry*, 1967, *16*, 659–667.
Hypothesis was that the family , in order to maintain equilibrium, will extrude to the hospital certain members (most usually those members functioning peripherally). Data were obtained from an emergency room psychiatric population of a large municipal hospital. Nine hundred and thirty-seven patients and/or their "closest companion" filled out a family information form. Families of psychiatric patients were compared with families from the general population. Reliability on the raw data was 90 percent. Findings were that being married (rather than single, widowed, etc.) coming from family of procreation, coming from an intact famiy, and being an emotionally important member of the household are associated with a lower risk of becoming a patient and of having a better outcome from treatment.

FERREIRA, A. Psychosis and family myth. *American Journal of Psychotherapy*, 1967, *21*, 186–197.
See Reference in Section 3.6.

FERREIRA, A. J. & WINTER, W. D. Family interaction and decision-making. *Archives of General Psychiatry*, 1965, *13*, 214–223.
A report of a study contrasting 50 normal families and 75 families with an abnormal child. The abnormal group included 15 schizophrenic, 16 delinquent, and 44 maladjusted children. The family members were asked to fill out a neutral questionnaire separately and then they were brought together and asked to fill out the same questionnaire while reaching agreement on the items as a group. Generally this report is concerned with the extent of agreement when family members make their choices separately, how much time is necessary to reach group decisions, and the appropriateness of the family decisions in fulfilling the wishes of the individual family members. Eighteen hypotheses are described and the results reported in terms of the differences found between the groups.

FERREIRA, A. J., WINTER, W. D., & POINDEXTER, E. J. Some interactional variables in normal and abnormal families. *Family Process*, 1966, *5*, 60–75.
A study contrasting normal and abnormal families, with the abnormals including schizophrenics, delinquents, and maladjusted. The families were exposed to TAT cards three at a time and asked to make up a story tying them together. Differences that were found between the types of families were described.

FLECK, S. Family dynamics and origin of schizophrenia. *Psychosomatic Medicine*, 1960, *22*, 333–344.
A comprehensive review of the Lidz project with a discussion of the findings and of the general problem of investigating the family of the schizophrenic. All of the 16 families studied were severely disturbed. Typical characteristics include a failure to form a nuclear family; family schisms; family skews; blurring of generation lines; pervasion of the entire atmosphere with irrational, usually paranoid ideation; persistence of conscious incestuous preoccupation; and sociocultural isolation. Case examples are presented.

FLECK, S., CORNELISON, A., NORTON, N., & LIDZ, T. The intrafamilial environment of the schizophrenic patient. III: Interaction between hospital staff and families. *Psychiatry*, 1957, *20*, 343–350.
One of a series of papers on the effect of the family in the etiology and pathogenesis of schizophrenia. The role of the patient's family with the hospital staff was examined. Neglecting the relationship of the family to the staff can affect the patient's hospital course "deleteriously or even catastrophically."

FLECK, S., LIDZ, T., & CORNELISON, A. Comparison of parent–child relationships of male and female schizophrenic patients. *Archives of General Psychiatry*, 1963, *8*, 1–7.
A study of 17 families containing a schizophrenic child, emphasizing the differences between families containing schizophrenic sons and those with schizophrenic daughters. Schizophrenic males often come from skewed families with passive, ineffectual fathers and disturbed, engulfing mothers. Schizophrenic girls typically grow up in schismatic families with narcissistic fathers and emotionally distant mothers.

FLECK, S., LIDZ, T., CORNELISON, A., SCHAFER, S., & TERRY, D. The intrafamilial environment of the schizophrenic patient. In J. Masserman (Ed.) *Science & psychoanalysis (Vol. II): individual and familial dynamics*. New York: Grune & Stratton, 1959.
One of a series of papers on a study of schizophrenic families focusing on problems of incest in the understanding and treatment of schizophrenic patients. Essential requisites of normal family function and organization are described along with consistent disturbances in schizophrenic families.

FONTANA, A. F. Familial etiology of schizophrenia: Is a scientific methodology possible? *Psychology Bullentin*, 1966, *66*, 214–227.
A review of methodology in family research on schizophrenia emphasizing clinical observation, retrospective recall, and direct observation of family interaction. The former two approaches are said to be unsuitable "for a scientific

body of etiological facts", the latter approach should be used with caution. Findings of various studies are reviewed. The author concludes the greatest value so far is in the guidelines provided for longitudinal research, but sufficient knowledge is not yet available to warrant the great expenditure invovled in longitudinal research at the present time.

FOUDRAINE, J. Schizophrenia and the family: A survey of the literature 1956–1960 on the etiology of schizophrenia. *Acta Psychotherapy*, 1961, *9*, 82–110.
In a thorough review of the literature, the author describes the development of the family point of view of schizophrenia and summarizes the works of authors who have published on the subject during this period. He explores the problems of attempting to conceptualize the function of the family as a whole, and to connect pathological family structure with schizophrenia in the individual. A bibliography of 97 items is included.

FRANK, G. H. The role of the family in the development of psychopathology. *Psychology Bullentin*, 1965, *64*, 191–205.
See Reference in Section 6.

FRANKLIN, P. Family therapy of psychotics. *American Journal of Psychoanalysis*, 1969, *29*, 50–56.
See Reference in Section 1.1.

FREEMAN, H. E. Attitudes toward mental illness among relatives of former patients. *American Sociology Review*, 1961, *26*, 59–66.
The relatives of 649 newly discharged mental hospital patients (of a total population of 714) were successfully interviewed to investigate their attitudes about the etiology of mental illness, the mental hospital, the normalcy of patients after mental illness, and the responsibility of patients for their condition. As in other surveys, age and education were associated with attitudes. "Enlightened" attitudes were not associated with social class measured independently of education, but were associated with verbal skill. It is suggested that verbal skill may be more important than "style of life." However, attitudes were related to the patients' posthospital behavior and appear to be complexly determined and deeply rooted.

FREEMAN, H. E., & SIMMONS, O. G. Feelings of stigma among relatives of former mental patients. *Social Problems*, 1961, *8*, 312–321.
Feelings of stigma were elicited from the families of 649 members of a group of 714 functional psychotics released from hospitals in eastern Massachusetts. Data were gathered by means of standard items in a structured interview with a relative a month after the patient's release. One-quarter of the sample reported feelings of stigma, while two-thirds acknowledged management problems. These feelings are associated with the patient's posthospital behavior, the education, class status, and personality characteristics of the relatives. Wives are more likely than other kin to feel stigma.

FRIEDMAN, C. J., & FRIEDMAN, A. S. Characteristics of schizogenic families during a joint story-telling task. *Family Process*, 1970, *9*, 33–353.
See Reference in Section 3.3.

FRIEDMAN, C., & FRIEDMAN, A. Sex concordance in psychogenic disorders: Psychosomatic disorders in mothers and schizophrenia in daughters. *Archives of General Psychiatry*, 1972, *28*, 611–617.
To test the hypothesis that there is a higher incidence of psychosomatic illness in mothers of female schizophrenics than in mothers of male schizophrenics or mothers of nonschizophrenic control offspring, a sample of 128 families with a male child with schizophrenia, 67 with a female child, and 140 control cases was selected. Determination of each family members' presence or absence of schizophrenia, psychosomatic illness, and degree of illness was made using a questionnaire and blind judges. Results indicated that mothers of female schizophrenics had a significantly greater incidence of psychosomatic disorders, but no greater incidence of organic, nonpsychosomatic disorder than either of the other two groups of mothers.

GARMEZY, N., CLARKE, A. R., & STOCKNER, C. Child rearing attitudes of mothers and fathers as reported by schizophrenic and normal patients. *Journal of Abnormal Social Psychology*, 1961, *63*, 176–182.
A group of 15 good premorbid and 15 poor premorbid schizophrenic patients were asked to think back when they were 13 or 14 years old and try to remember mother and father at that time. The experimenter then presented them with 75 statements describing various child rearing attitudes and asked the patients if their parents would have agreed or disagreed with each item. A group of 15 patients hospitalized for medical problems was used as a control. The results indicate that the subject's level of social maturity and the extent of attitudinal deviance ascribed to parents are related. Poor premorbids reveal maternal dominance whereas good premorbids ascribe heightened paternal dominance in their responses.

GARMEZY, N., FARINA, A., & RODNICK, E. H. The structured situation test: A method for studying family interaction in schizophrenia. *American Journal of Orthopsychiatry*, 1960, *30*, 445–451.
A group of 36 sets of parents composed of parents of good and poor premorbids and of sons with tuberculosis

("normals") were exposed to 12 hypothetical misbehaviors of a son. Individually and then together they were asked to indicate how to handle the situation. From tape recordings of the interviews, measures of dominance behavior and conflict were made, such as who spoke first and last, acceptance of another's solution, amount of interruption, and so on. With good premorbids the fathers were dominant and in poor premorbids the mothers were. The "normals" share dominance. Poor premorbids show greater conflict than "normals."

GLICK, I. The "sick" family and schizophrenia—Cause and effect? *Diseases of the Nervous System*, 1968, *29*, 129–132.
A critique on the hypothesis is that there is a cause and effect relationship between disturbed family functioning and schizophrenia. A summary of a theory is presented, and questions raised by it are discussed. Data culled from other etiologic theories (biologic, genetic, and intrapsychic) pertinent to family theory are reviewed. Data obtained thus far are insufficient to form a unitary hypothesis for the etiology of schizophrenia.

GODUCO-AGULAR, C., & WINTROB, R. Folie à Famille in the Phillipines. *Psychiatric Quarterly*, 1964, *38*, 278–292.
A case report of folie à famille (defined as psychotic behavior in each of eight members of the family reported) in a Philippine family. A review of the literature and a sociocultural formulation of the case are presented.

GOLDFARB, W. The mutural impact of mother and child in childhood schizophrenia. *American Journal of Orthopsychiatry*, 1961, *31*, 738–747.
Childhood schizophrenia is a psychiatric classification which does not delineate a single and specific clinical entity but describes a broad diversity of serious ego impairments. Etiological diversity is hypothesized as well with a "continuum of causal factors ranging from primary somatic dificiencies within the child to a primary psychosocial disturbance within the family." In clinical practice it has been feasible to identify two general classes of disorder: children with abnormal organic status and the class of nonorganic children. The organic cluster contains children derived from families similar to those of normal children. A case of each type is presented and discussed with emphasis upon the complex mutual and reciprocating impact of the child on the family and the family on the child.

GREENWALD, S. Let us not confound the schizophrenic's family. *Comprehensive Psychiatry*, 1971, *12*, 423–429.
See Reference in Section 3.5.

GRUNEBAUM, H. U., & WEISS, J. L. Psychotic mothers and their children: Joint admission to an adult psychiatric hospital. American Journal of Psychiatry, 1963, *119*, 927–933.
See Reference in Section 1.4.

HALEY, J. The art of being schizophrenic. *Voices*, 1965, *1*, 133–142.
A description of the schizophrenic with special emphasis upon family and hospital context.

HALEY, J. Experiment with abnormal families. *Archives of General Psychiatry*, 1967, *17*, 53–63.
See Reference in Section 3.4

HALEY, J. Family experiments: A new type of experimentation. *Family Process*, 1962, *1*, 265–293.
See Reference in Section 3.4

HALEY, J. The family of the schizophrenic: A model system. *Journal of Nervous and Mental Disease*, 1959, *129*, 357–374.
A description of the family of the schizophrenic as a governed system with a verbatim excerpt from a family interview for illustration.

HALEY, J. Ideas that handicap therapy with young people. *International Journal of Family Therapy*, 1979, *1*, 29–45.
This is an essay proposing that treatment of young schizophrenics with biological, psychodynamic systems, and "double-bind" theories should be abandoned. Criteria for a successful theory are proposed and a "contemporary" theory for family therapy, which sees problems in relation to stages of life, is suggested.

HALEY, J.Observation of the family of the schizophrenic. *American Journal of Orthopsychiatry*, 1960, *30*, 460–467.
See Reference in Section 3.3

HALEY, J. Testing parental instructions to schizophrenic and normal children: A pilot study. *Journal of Abnormal Psychology*, 1968, *73*, 559–566.
See Reference in Section 3.4

HALEY, J. The perverse triangle. In J. Zuk, & I. Boszormenyi-Nagy (Eds.), *Family therapy and disturbed families*. Palo Alto: Science & Behavior Press, 1967.
See Reference in Section 3.6

HAYWARD, M. Schizophrenia in a double bind. *Psychiatric Quarterly*, 1960, *34*, 89–91.
A case example illustrating the use of the double bind in the development of schizophrenia. Understanding this concept is helpful in understanding schizophrenic behavior.

HERMAN, B. F., & JONES, J. E. Lack of acknowledgment in the family Rorschachs of families with a child at risk for schizophrenia. *Family Process*, 1976, *15*, 289–302.
The study focused on an analysis of acknowledgment patterns exhibited by 10 middle to upper class intact families with problem adolescents who presented for treatment. Parental communication deviance was assessed with the family Rorschach test and a judgment of potential risk for schizophrenia was made. Positive acknowledging responses were important characteristics of low-risk families and *vice-versa* in high-risk families, offering important implications for future research in family communication patterns.

HIGGINS, J. Sex of child reared by schizophrenic mothers. *Journal of Psychiatric Research*, 1966, *4*, 153–167.
In an attempt to assess the effect of child-rearing by schizophrenic mothers, two groups of 25 children of schizophrenic mothers were studied. One group was reared by the mothers and the other group was reared from an early age by agents without psychiatric illness. The sample was tested using a psychiatric interview of the child only, several psychological tests and a report from the school. Results failed to support the hypothesis that the mother-reared children would display greater maladjustment on the various measures than would the reared-apart child.

HILGARD, J., & NEWMAN, M. F. Early parental deprivation as a function factor in the etiology of schizophrenia and alcoholism. *American Journal of Orthopsychiatry*, 1963, *33*, 409–420.
A study designed to consider the age at which loss by death was sustained during childhood by hospitalized schizophrenic and alcoholic patients. Comparison was made using hospital admission records of 1521 schizophrenic patients, 929 alcoholic patients, and a control group of 1,096 cases selected using an area-sampling technique from an urban community. It was concluded that mother loss among women in both diagnostic categories was earlier than in the control group members who lost mothers. Schizophrenic women showed loss of both mother and father at a significantly earlier age than the control subjects.

HILGARD, H., & NEWMAN, M. F. Parental loss by death in childhood as an etiological factor among schizophrenic and alcoholic patients compared with a non-patient community sample. *Journal of Nervous and Mental Disease*, 1963, *137*, 14–28.
Hospital records were examined and a sample of 1,561 schizophrenic patients and 929 alcoholic patients were compared with a control sample of 1,096 cases. Schizophrenics had lost one or both parents more often than the control group members. Parent loss is said to be one of the factors associated with an increase in vulnerability in coping with the stresses of adult life.

HIRSCH, S., & LEFF, J. Parental abnormalities of verbal communication in transmission of schizophrenia. *Psychology Medicine*, 1971, *1*, 118–127.
See Reference in Section 3.2.

HOOVER, C. The embroiled family: A blueprint for schizophrenia. *Family Process*, 1965, *4*, 291–310.
An essay on the emotionally entangled family with an adolescent who becomes schizophrenic at adolescence. Schizophrenia is said to arise in the family when there is a combination of factors involving emotional "embroilment."

JACKSON, D. D. Conjoint family therapy. *Modern Medicine*, 1965, *33*, 172–198.
See Reference in Section 1.1

JACKSON, D. D., & WEAKLAND, J. H. Conjoint family therapy: Some considerations on theory, techniques, and results. *Psychiatry*, 1961, *24*, 30–45.
A report on conjoint family therapy of families with a schizophrenic member with a discussion of the theoretical point of view, the procedural arrangements, and typical problems. Case material is used to illustrate characteristic sequences in the therapy. The emphasis is upon the current interaction within these families and their resistance to change. Results are presented, and there is a discussion of countertransference problems and the shift in psychotherapeutic approach characteristic of therapists who attempt family psychotherapy.

JACKSON, D. D., & WEAKLAND, J. Schizophrenic symptoms in family interaction. *Archives of General Psychiatry*, 1959, *1*, 618–621.
See Reference in Section 3.6

JACKSON, D. D., BLOCK, J., & PATTERSON, V. Psychiatrists' conceptions of the schizophrenogenic parent. *Archives of Neurology and Psychiatry*, 1958, *79*, 448–459.
See Reference in Section 3.1

JOHNSTON, F., & PLANANSKY, K. Schizophrenia in men: The impact on their wives. *Psychiatric Quarterly*, 1968, *42*, 146–155.

A study on an in-patient unit rating 36 wives of chronic in-patients. Data were gathered from interviews with spouses obtained independently by four raters on the unit. As the patients regressed, about half the spouses rejected (divorced, separated, etc.), their husbands. Reasons for this are discussed.

KAUFMAN, I., FRANK, T., HEIMS, L., HERRICK, S., REISER, D., & WILLER, L. Treatment implications of a new classification of parents of schizophrenic children. *American Journal of Psychiatry*, 1960, *116*, 920–924.
A report of a study of the personalities of 80 schizophrenic children's parents. Material was gathered from psychotherapy, psychological testing, and direct observation of parent–child interaction. Parent personalities are classified as "psychoneurotic," "somatic," "pseudodelinquent," and "overtly psychotic." The first two types of personalities were found more frequently in an outpatient setting, while the last two were found more frequently in a state hospital setting. Treatment for these parents is discussed.

KEMPLER, W., IVERSON, R., & BEISSER, A. The adult schizophrenic and his siblings. *Family Process*, 1962, *1*, 224–235.
Sixty-five siblings in a group of 16 schizophrenic families were interviewed using a structured protocol to explore "parent–child relationships" as seen by the siblings. Findings included distortions in communications by both patients and siblings and appeared unrelated to the schizophrenic process. Four subjects, all of whom were "favorite' children in the family, showed no such distortions. A transcript from a single family is presented in illustration.

KIND, H. The psychogenesis of schizophrenia. *International Journal of Psychiatry*, 1967, *3*, 383–403.
A review article covering the data bearing on psychogenic factors in the etiology of schizophrenia. The literature is covered in five headings: (1) findings based on psychotherapy of schizophrenic patients, (2) investigations on interpersonal relationships in the earlier family life of schizophrenics (3) statistical investigations on the frequency of particular traumatic situations. (4) investigations by various methods on the attitudes of important figures to the children, and (5) social and cultural circumstances. The author concludes that a purely psychogenic theory of schizophrenia is just as untenable as a purely genetic one. Five critical evaluations by various authors are included.

KLEIN, H., & ERLICH, H. S. Some dynamic and transactional aspects of family therapy with psychotic patients. *Psychotherapy and Psychosomatics*, 1975, *26*, 148–155.
See Reference in Section 1.4.

LAING, R. D. Mystification, confusion, and conflict. In I. Boszormenyi-Nagy, & J. L. Framo (Eds.), *Intensive family therapy*. New York: Harper & Row, 1965.
See Reference in Section 3.6

LAING, R. D., & ESTERSON, A. Families and schizophrenia. *International Journal of Psychiatry*, 1967, *4*, 65–71.
A paper describing the authors' theoretical position for their work studying families with a schizophrenic member. Schizophrenia is seen as a social event—"a set of clinical attributions made by certain persons about the experience and behavior of others"—not as a disease. "Family" includes the extra-familial personal networks of family members. The authors' study is directed to observable interactions between these members and the family system itself and not to unconscious or inferred motives. Schizophrenia is seen as a reaction to family behavior.

LANGSLEY, D., PITTMAN, F., & SWANK, G. Family crisis in schizophrenics and other mental patients. *Journal of Nervous and Mental Disease*, 1969, *149*, 270–276.
A further report on a study using cirsis therapy as an alternative to psychiatric hospitalization. In this study 50 families that included a schizophrenic patient and 50 that included a nonschizophrenic mental patient were studied using an instrument that quantified the events leading to a crisis in the family and the managment of such crises. Nonschizophrenic mental patients were better able to handle crisis and interact with their families. A discussion of these findings is presented.

LASEQUE, C., & FALRET, J. La folie à deux ou folie communiquee. transl. R. Michaud, *American Journal of Psychiatry*, 1964, supplement no. 121. (Originally published in *Annales Medico-Psychologiques*, November, 1877, p. 18.
The first English translation of the classical paper written in 1877, it represents an attempt to delineate and understand the relationship between emotionally ill people and those who live in close contact with them. "Insanity" is not contagious (that is the passing of a delusion from a "sick" to a "healthy" person) except in the following circumstances: (1) the more sick individual is also more intelligent, the other more dependent, (2) both individuals must have lived together for a long time isolated from outside influences, (3) the delusion is within the realm of probability for both individuals. It is more common among women. Treatment is to separate the two patients; in the secondary patient the psychopathology is reversible. Case material is presented in support of the above ideas.

LEFF, J. P. Developments in family treatment of schizophrenia. *Psychiatric Quarterly*, 1979, *51*, 216–230.
See Reference in Section 6.0.

LENNARD, H., BEAULIEU, M. R., & EMBREY, N. G. Interaction in families with a schizophrenic child. *Archives of General Psychiatry*, 1965, *12*, 166–183.
A study contrasting 10 families with a schizophrenic child and 7 normal families. The families have a 15-minute discussion of 3 topics related to a child's life. The conversations are recorded, transcribed, and coded along 12 dimensions. Differences are found between the two groups. There is a discussion of the theoretical background and methodological problems.

LEVIN, G. Communicator-communicant approach to family interaction research. *Family Process*, 1966, 5, 105–116.
A family experiment in which the experimenter asks the subject to make a tape recording which might be played subsequently to some specific other person in his family. The recording includes specific instructions about a simple task. Individuals from families containing a schizophrenic (a sample of 33) were contrasted with normal individuals. The reocrdings were not actually played to family members, but the instructions were analyzed and classified with differences found between the two groups.

LEWIS, V. S., & ZEICHNER, A. N. Impact of admission to a mental hospital on the patient's family. *Mental Hygiene*, 1960, *44*, 503–509.
A report on a study of the effect on families when a member is hospitalized for mental illness. The study is based upon interviews with members of the families of 109 patients admitted to Connecticut's three state mental hospitals. Reported with tables are such categories as the recognition and acceptance of mental illness, the ways of coping with the patient's illness, assessment of help of resources tried, and treatment given prior to hospitalization.

LITCHTENBERG, J. D., & PIGN-NIE, PAO. The prognostic and therapeutic significance of the husband–wife relationship for hospitalized schizophrenic women. *Psychiatry*, 1960, *23*, 209–213.
A discussion of the types of husbands of hospitalized schizophrenic women and the importance of taking the spouse into account in psychotherapy. Observation of 43 patients indicated the husbands fell into certain groups, although no prototype personality was found. In terms of prognosis, the husbands are classified as constructively active, obstructively active, rejecting, maintaining the previuos pathological relationships, and vacillating. Ways to include the husband in the therapeutic program were attempted and are recommended.

LIDZ, R., & LIDZ, T. Homosexual tendencies in mothers of schizophrenic women. *Journal of Nervous and Mental Disease*, 1969, *149*, 229–235.
From 4 case studies of schizophrenic women whose mothers were also interviewed, the authors' thesis is that "incestuous homosexual tendencies of schizophrenic patients reflect similar proclivities in their parents." In therapy, the mothers attempt to focus on the therapist, rather than on the process of therapy.

LIDZ, T. The influence of family studies on the treatment of schizophrenia. *Psychiatry*, 1969, *32*, 237–251.
In this lecture, the author attempts to link up his work on schizophrenia as a family disorder with contributions of Freida-Fromm-Reichmann, as well as new advances with the tranquilizing drugs and milieu therapy. Dynamics of pathologic families as well as techniques of working with them are discussed in detail.

LIDZ, T. Schizophrenia and the family. *Psychiatry*, 1958, *21*, 21–27.
An essay dealing with the etiology of schizophrenia. The role of the family in the etiology is discussed with particular emphasis on how pathological family development can lead to different syndromes. The author's studies of schizophrenia are described briefly.

LIDZ, T., CORNELISON, A., TERRY, D., & FLECK, S. Intrafamilial environment of the schizophrenic patient. VI: The transmission of irrationality. *Archives of Neurology and Psychiatry*, 1958, *79*, 305–316.
A study of families of schizophrenics in which 9 of the 15 patients had at least one parent who could be called schizophrenic. Their "irrational" behavior was transmitted through disturbed communication to the children who were reared in intrafamilial systems of communication which distort or deny reality. The implications of these findings are discussed in terms of the etiology of schizophrenia.

LIDZ, T., & FLECK, S. Schizophrenia, human integration, and the role of the family. In D. D. Jackson (Ed.), *The etiology of schizophrenia*. New York: Basic Books, 1960.
A discussion of the deficiencies in families of schizophrenic patients as a way of clarifying the ego weakness of schizophrenic patients.

LIDZ, T., FLECK, S., ALANEN, Y. O., & CORNELISON, A. Schizophrenic patients and their siblings. *Psychiatry*, 1963, *26*, 1–18.
See Reference in Section 3.2

LIDZ, T., FLECK, S. CORNELISON, A., & TERRY, D. The intrafamilial environment of the schizophrenic patient. IV: Parental personalities in family interaction. *American Journal of Orthopsychiatry*, 1958, *28*, 764–776.
One of a series of papers dealing with observations from an intensive study of the intrafamilial environments of

schizophrenic patients. A long case report is presented in support of the hypothesis that the nature of the parental personalities will determine family interaction and will bear on the development of schizophrenia in siblings.

LIDZ, T, PARKER, B., & CORNELISON, A. The role of the father in the family environment of the schizophrenic patient. *American Journal of Psychiatry*, 1956, *113*, 126–132.
See Reference in Section 3.2

LINDSAY, J. S. B. Types of family and family types. *Family Process*, 1968, 7, 51–66.
A discussion of the application of the theory of logical types to family descriptions. Confusions between the monad, the dyad, and the triad are described and a hypothesis for schizophrenia is presented.

LOVELAND, N. T. The family Rorschach: A new method for studying family interaction. *Family Process*, 1963, *2*, 187–215.
A report of a study in which the Rorschach was used as a standardized stimulus for family conversations. The procedure is described, the advantages and disadvantages are discussed, and excerpts from a family Rorschach are presented.

LU, Y. C. Mother–Child role relations in schizophrenia: A comparison of schizophrenic patients with non-schizophrenic siblings. *Psychiatry*, 1961, *24*, 133–142.
An investigation into why one child in a family develops schizophrenia and another does not, based upon interviews with 50 chronic schizophrenic patients, their siblings, and their parents. The patient is largely confined to his parents, especially his mother, while the siblings have several significant others.

LU, Y. C., "Contradictory Parental Expectations in Schizophrenia," *Archives of General Psychiatry*, 1962, *6*, 219–234.
A report of some preliminary findings of an investigation of the families of schizophrenics. The emphasis is upon a comparison of the parents' relationship with patient and with nonschizophrenic siblings in an attempt to discover why one child in a family develops schizophrenia and not another. The parents expect a higher degree of dependence from the preschizophrenic than from the nonschizophrenic child, and they also expect a higher degree od achievement and resonsibility. The author suggests that the relational pattern of contradictory parental expectations and the child's persistent effort to fulfill them could be called a "quadruple bind."

MARCUS, E. M. Patterns of coping in families of psychotic children. *American Journal of Orthopsychiatry*, 1977, *47*, 388–399.
The nature and strength of family adaptation to severely disabled children is discussed theoretically, based on the author's experience in a clinic for "autistic and communications-disordered children." The effects on parents' self-concept, decision making, perception of the child, behavior and relations with others is examined and implications for intervention and research are suggested. The author compared this approach to that of ascribing an etiologic relation between the family and the child's illness and feels that this approach is less blaming and more practical for parents of psychotic children.

MARX, A., & LUDWIG, A. Resurrection of the family of the chronic schizophrenic. *American Journal of Psychotherapy*, 1969, *23*, 37–52.
A careful review of ths authors' experience treating psychiatric inpatients by systematically involving the family of the patient. Sample was 44 chronic schizophrenic patients and families studied over a 2 year period. Family resistances and methods to deal with these resistances are discussed. The treatment program included family therapist meetings, patient-family-therapist sessions, multiple family group meetings, and multiple, family-conjoint therapy sessions. Some of the effects of this treatment program, both positive (patient and family improvement) and negative (member of the family decompensating), as well as methods of dealing with these problems, practical theoretical implications, and ethics of this approach are discussed.

McCORD, W., PORTA, J., & McCORD, J. The familial genesis of psychoses. *Psychiatry*, 1962, *25*, 60–71.
A study of the influence of early environment on the development of psychosis based upon data gathered during the childhood of subjects who later became psychotic. In the middle 1930's in Massachusetts, a sample of boys was observed as part of a study on the prevention of delinquency. These past case histories were examined and twelve prepsychotics were matched with nonpsychotic controls. The familial environments of the prepsychotics differed from those of the nonpsychotics in a number of ways. Typically the prepsychotics were raised in an environment directed by an overprotective mother and an absent or passive father. This "silver cord syndrome" has also been noted by other investigators who used a retrospective approach.

McGHIE, A. A comparative study of the mother–child relationship in schizophrenia. I: The interview. II: Psychological testing. *British Journal of Medical Psychology*, 1961, *34*, 195–221.
In Part I of this two-part article there is a description of interviews with 20 mothers of schizophrenics, 20 mothers of neurotics, and 20 mothers of normals. Findings about families of schizophrenics reported in the literature were

generally confirmed. There is more marital disharmony in the schizophrenic group and the fathers are said to be weak. However, mothers of schizophrenics do not appear as overprotective as mothers of neurotics. In Part II, the test findings for the three groups are reported. They were given a childrearing questionnaire, a sentence completion test, a word connection test, and the Rorschach.

MEISSNER, W. W. Sibling relations in the schizophrenic family. *Family Process*, 1970, *9*, 1–25.
See Reference in Section 4.2.

MEYERS, D., & GOLDFARB, W. Studies of perplexity in mothers of schizophrenic children. *American Journal of Orthopsychiatry*, 1961, *31*, 551–564.
In order to document the association of parental complexity (defined as passivity, uncertainty, lack of spontaneity, absence of empathy, with diminished awareness of the child's needs, bewilderment, and blandness in the face of unacceptable behavior in the child, and an absence of parental control) 23 mothers of schizophrenic children and 23 mothers of normal children were studied. Techniques included a participant-observation technique (in which the observer spent 3 hours with the family at home), and a semistructured open-ended interview of the mothers. Results indicated that the mothers of the schizophrenic children without organic involvement have a greater difficulty in appropriately structuring their child's environment, while the mothers of the organic group cannot be differentiated from mothers of the normals.

MISHLER, E. G. Families and schizophrenia: An experimental study. *Mental Hygiene*, 1966, 552–556.
A discussion of a way of testing families with a schizophrenic member and contrasting them with normal families. Findings are not given, but illustrations are offered of ways the families respond in the test situation.

MISHLER, E. G., & WAXLER, N. E. Family interaction and schizophrenia: A review of current theories. *Merrill-Palmer Quarterly*, 1965, *11*, 269–315.
A review of the theories of schizophrenia and the family with special emphasis upon differences and similarities between the Bateson, Lidz and Wynne groups. A selected bibliography is included.

MISHLER, E. G., & WAXLER, N. E. Family interaction processes and schizophrenia. *International Journal of Psychiatry*, 1966, *2*, 375–430.
A critical and extensive review of the theories of the relationship between family interaction and schizophrenia, with major space devoted to the work of the Bateson, Lidz, and Wynne groups. The purpose of the review was to see how the theories could be tested and used as guidelines for research. The major contributions of these groups are to the theory of the etiology of schizophrenia by focusing on the family and its methods of interactions, rather than on the individual. Critical evaluations by Bateson, Lidz, Spiegel, and Wynne of the article and the various theories contained in it are included.

MORRIS, G., & WYNNE, L. Schizophrenic offspring parental styles of communication. *Psychiatry*, 1965, *28*, 19–44.
One of series of papers reporting a study of parental styles of communication and schizophrenic children. Data were selected from excerpts of transcripts of conjoint faily sessions with 12 families. Predictions about the most disturbed offspring were made by a judge blind to the clinical aspects of the case. Predictive criteria were then reformulated using the data from a parallel study, utilizing psychological test material as predictors. These reformulated criteria were then utilized for blind predictiitons on 8 new families. Results indicated that the style of the family communication can be related to the thought and affect disorder in schizophrenics.

MOSHER, L. R. Schizophrenogenic communication and family therapy. *Family Process*, 1969, *8*, 43–63.
A description of a technique of family therapy with a family of a schizophrenic. The emphasis is upon the structural and process aspects of the family's communication. Case material is used for illustration.

MOSHER, L. R., & FEINSILVER, D. Current studies on schizophrenia. *International Journal of Psychiatry*, 1973, *11*, 7–52.
See Reference in Section 6.0.

MOSHER, L., POLLIN, W., & STABENAU, J. Families with identical twins discordant for schizophrenia: Some relationships between identification, thinking styles, psychopathology and dominance-submissiveness. *British Journal of Psychiatry*, 1971, *118*, 22–28.
See Reference in Section 3.4.

MOSSIGE, S., PETTERSON, R. B., & BLAKAR, R. M. Egocentrism and ineffeiciency in the communication of families containing schizophrenic members. *Family Process*, 1979, *18*, 405–425.
This study is based on a methodology outlined by Blakar by which interaction is analyzed in terms of how and to what extent participants manage or fail to cope with the various prerequisites for successful communication under various circumstances. The interaction of 12 families—6 with a schizophrenic member and 6 normal controls—were analyzed

in Blakar's communication conflict situation with respect to the member's ability to take the perspective of each other. The pathologic families proved to be significantly more egocentric with resulting inefficient communication.

NEWMAN, G., Younger brothers of schizophrenics. *Psychiatry*, 1966, *29*, 146–151.
As a contribution to intrafamilial dynamics in schizophrenic families, three cases are reported of siblings who had an older brother who was schizophrenic and who developed emotional disorder themselves. The cases were studied by the author in the course of psychotherapy. All three had great guilt form three sources—"letting the older brother bear the burden of the parent's demands, for not saving the older brother from mental illness, and for exercising his own perception, judgment and initiative."

NIELSEN, N. P., & NAVA, V. Il ranking Rorschach Test Ed il PARI nello studio delle interazoni in un gruppo di famiglie di schizorenici. (The consensus Rorschach Test and the PARI in a study of interactions in a group of families of schizophrenics.) *Rivista di Psyichiatria* (Roma), 1975, *10*, 345–364.
See Reference in Section 3.3.

PALOMBO, S., MERRIFIELD, J., WEIGERT, W., MORRIS, G., & WYNNE, L. Recognition of parents of schizophrenics from excerpts of family therapy interviews. *Psychiatry*, 1967, *30*, 405–412.
This study attempts to explore the hypothesis that a judge, other than one trained by the authors, could distinguish parents of schizophrenics from nonschizophrenics, working only with excerpts of parental behavior taken from family therapy. Results indicated that other judges could, but only after being trained by the authors. When the procedure for sampling parental behavior was changed, the ability to make significant predictions was diminished.

PAUL, N. L. The role of a secret in schizophrenia. In N. W. Ackerman (Ed.), *Family therapy in transition*. Boston: Little, Brown, 1970.
A case of a family of a schizophrenic with a secret concerning the son's birth. Excerpts from family interviews are included to illustrate decoding of the transactions among the family members.

PAUL, N. L., & GROSSER, G. H. Family resistance to change in schizophrenic patients. *Family Process*, 1964, *3*, 377–401.
A description, with case excerpts, of the patterns of family response to schizophrenic patients that develop during the early phase of conjoint family therapy. It is said that families express desire for the patient to change while attempting to maintain the status quo in family relationships in ways that reinforce the patient's symptomatology.

PAUL, N. L., & GROSSER, G. H. Operational mourning and its role in conjoint family therapy. *Community Mental Health Journal*, 1965, *1*, 339–345.
Studies of records of 50 families with a schizophrenic member and 25 families with at least one psychoneurotic member revealed "patterns of inflexible interaction and maladaptive response to object loss." The way the sample was obtained is not stated. It is hypothesized from this data that incomplete mourning after object loss leads to an inability to deal with future object loss, and this defect is transmitted to other family members. This is thought to lead to "fixation of symbiotic relationships in the family."

PARSONS, A. Family dynamics in south italian schizophrenics. *Archives of General Psychiatry*, 1960, *3*, 507–518.
If family factors play an etiological role in schizophrenia, comparative studies of the family background of schizophrenics in different cultures is important. After observation of south Italian patients in the United States, a sample of 25 patients hospitalized in public hospitals in Naples and vicinity was investigated. Patterns in the families are described in terms of exclusive dyads, imbedded dyads, competitive and unstable situations, and isolates. Comparing pathological family constellations in different cultures, the taboo areas are important, and the problem of differentiating the normal from the pathological must be resolved. "We would doubt that these probelms can ever be resolved in a framework in which any particular set of social values or conditions is considered as inherently schizogenic."

PETURSON, E. A study of parental deprivation and illness in 291 psychiatric patients. *International Journal of Social Psychiatry*, 1961, *7*, 97–105.
A group of 291 patients with functional psychiatric illness was observed by the author and information gathered about their parents from them, from spouses or relatives, or by direct observation in some instances. The parents suffered from functional psychiatric illness in 77.5 percent of the cases. The incidence of broken homes was 31.7 percent. There appeared to be a high incidence of patients developing the same type of psychiatric illness as the parents in various categories. Well-integrated family units occurred in the background of patients in only 11.7 percent of the cases.

PITTMAN, F. S., III, & FLOMENHAFT, K. Treating the doll's house marriage. *Family Process*, 1970, *9*, 143–155.
See Reference in Section 4.1.

POLLACK, M., WOERNER, M., GOLDBERG, P., & KLEIN, D. Siblings of schizophrenic and nonschizophrenic psychiatric patients. *Archives of General Psychiatry*, 1969, *20*, 652–658.
A study attempting to test the relative power of genetic versus psychogenic etiology in schizophrenia. Sixty-four siblings of 46 schizophrenic patients, 104 siblings of 68 personality disorder patients, and 16 siblings of 13 index cases with psychoneurotic and affective disorders were compared in terms of their psychiatric status. Method was clinical interview in most cases, but where siblings could not personally be contacted, descriptions from the family or from other records were used. Results indicated the siblings of the schizophrenic patients did not differ from those of nonschizophrenic patients in overall incidence of abnormality. None of the many specific family interaction patterns hypothesized to be pathogenic for schizophrenia have thus far been substantiated by methodologically sound studies.

PULVER, S. E., & BRUNT, M. Y. Deflection of hostility in folie à Deux. *Archives of General Psychiatry*, 1961, *5*, 257–265.
Three cases are presented to illustrate a description of the psychodynamics of the transfer of delusions. The partners are divided into the primary and secondary, with the primary partner strongly dependent upon the secondary. As the primary partner begins to feel taken advantage of and increasingly angry, his anger against the secondary partner does not support the delusion, the direct hostility toward the secondary partner becomes intolerable and the secondary partner deflects it by accepting the delusion and joining in the projection.

QUERY, J. M. N. Pre-morbid adjustment and family structure: A comparison of selected rural and urban schizophrenic men. *Journal of Nervous and Mental Disease*, 1961, *133*, 333–338.
A study which reviews schizophrenia in relation to cultural and familial settings. The hypothesis is that premorbid adjustment of rural schizophrenics will be better than that of urban subjects because the rural setting includes a more patriarchal family structure, more emphasis upon individualism, and better sex-role identification. Case history data were examined in terms of the Phillip's scale and supplemented by family interviews. Fifty-one families were interviewed and the hypothesis was supported by the evidence.

RABKIN, L. Y. The patient's family: Research methods. *Family Process*, 1965, *4*, 105–132.
A review of family research with special emphasis upon the family of the schizophrenic. Critical examination is done of case history studies, interviewing studies, psychodiagnostic testing, questionnaire studies, and observational research. A bibliography of 99 references is included.

RAVICH, R. A. A system of dyadic interaction. *Family Process*, 1970, *9*, 297–300.
A description of a notation for two-person interaction based upon the I Ching, or *Book of Changes*.

REISS, D. The family and schizophrenia. *American Journal of Psychiatry*, 1976, *133*, 181–185.
It is suggested that family interaction abnormalities are often associated with schizophrenia and may play a causal, rather than epiphenomenal, role in its pathogenesis. Such communication processes affect development of attentional and conceptual capacities that also have strong biological roots. Such a model would be a meeting ground for researchers in the areas of biological and familial theories of schizophrenia.

REISS, D. Individual thinking and family interaction: Introduction to an experimental study of problem-solving in families of normals. character disorders, and schizophrenics. *Archives of General Psychiatry*, 1967, *16*, 80–93.
A report of an experimental study of the relationship between individual thinking and family interaction. Experimental procedures and methods of analysis are discussed. Subjects were families of 5 normals, 5 character disorders, and 6 schizophrenics. The test used was a puzzle that required active use of cognitive and conceptual capacities. The method of analysis was derived from the work of Roley, which developed a systematic approach of computing scores from the raw data and rules concerning inferences.

REISS, D. Individual thinking and family interaction. II: A study of pattern recognition and hypothesis testing in families of normals, character disorders, and schizophrenics. *Journal of Psychiatric Research*, 1967, *5*, 193–211.
The second in a series of studies of the relationship of family process and indivdiual thinking. Results indicate that following a period of family interaction, members of normal families showed improvement in pattern recognition; members of families of schizophrenics showed deterioration or no change; and results of members of character disorder families were in between the two.

REISS, D. Individual thinking and family interaction. III: An experimental study of categorization performance in families of normals, those with character disorders, and schizophrenics. *Journal of Nervous and Mental Disease*, 1968, *146*, 384–404.
The third of a series of studies to measure the relationship between individual family interaction and individual thinking, and to determine what differences in this relationship exist among families of normals, personality disorders, and schizophrenics. Method was to give the families a puzzle, tape their discusion, and to code verbal responses. Sample has been previously described; there were 5 families in each group. Results indicated that normals could solve the puzzle, while the others could not. The data on why they could not were felt to be consistent with the hypothesis that interpersonal problems in families significantly interfere with their collaborative problem-solving efforts.

REISS, D. Individual thinking and family interaction. IV: A study of information exchange in families of normals, those with character disorders, and schizophrenics. *Journal of Nervous and Mental Disease*, 1969, *149*, 473–490.
The fourth in a series of four papers on interrelationships of family interaction and thinking and perception of family members. Methodology has been discussed in the earlier papers. This experiment was developed to test the family's efficiency in exchanging information within itself. Families or normals and schizophrenics were more sensitive than those with character disorders to cues from within the family. Families of schizophrenics appeared to represent a group of families who utilize cues from within but not from without the family.

RETTERSTOL, N. Paranoid psychosis associated with impending or newly established fatherhood. *Acta Psychiatrica Scandinavica*, 1968, *44*, 51–61.
A study of 169 consecutive male psychiatric patients with a diagnosis of paranoid psychosis, admitted over a 20-year period to an inpatient service. Follow-ups averaged 5 years, but went up to 20 years in some cases. There were 4 cases in which the precipitant appeared to be impending fatherhood. A shift of the homeostasis between the father and the mother of the baby appeared to have been caused.

RICHMOND, A. H., & LANGA, A. Some observations concerning the role of children in the disruption of family homeostasis. *American Journal of Orthopsychiatry*, 1963, *33*, 757–759.
A report from a day-hospital of observations on families and patients whose psychiatric illness had led the families to request removal of the patient from the community. The authors noted 3 patterns of family dynamics in which the child, by its (1) birth, (2) maturation, and (3) efforts to achieve independence, served to disrupt family homeostasis.

ROSENBAUM, C. P. Patient-family similarities in schizophrenia. *Archives of General Psychiatry*, 1961, *5*, 120–126.
A discussion of the family of the schizophrenic based upon conjoint interviews with such families during several research projects. It is suggested that the disordered thinking and interpersonal relations of the schizophrenic have recognized counterparts in his family. Such primary symptoms of schizophrenia as disorders of association, selective inattention, and ambivalence, as described by Bleuler, are compared with similar thought patterns in the family, illustrated with case material. A review and synthesis is made of research in the field of the schizophrenic family with the emphasis upon the appropriateness of schizophrenic symptoms in this context.

ROSENTHAL, D. Confusion of identity and the frequency of schizophrenia in twins. *Archives of General Psychiatry*, *Archives of General Psychiatry*, 1968, *18*, 464–470.
See Reference in Section 4.2

ROSENTHAL, A. J., BEHRENS, M. I., & CHODOFF, P. Communication in lower-class families of schizophrenics. *Archives of General Psychiatry*, 1968, *18*, 689–696.
The first part of a two-part report on low-socioeconomic families of schizophrenics. Groups compared were 17 black schizophrenics and their families, 11 in a black control group, and 11 white schizophrenics and their families. The procedure included observation in the home with tasks requiring the family to maintain a focus of attention on a specific topic. (For Part II of this study *see* Behrens, M. I. Communication in lower class families of schizophrenics. *Archives of General Psychiatry*, 1968, *18*, 689–696.

ROSMAN, B., WILD, C., RICCI, J., FLECK, S., & LIDZ, T. Thought disorders in the parents of schizophrenic patients: A further study utilizing the object sorting test. *Journal of Psychiatric Research*, 1964, *2*, 211–221.
A second replication of a study by McConughy who found that parents of schizophrenic patients received scores in the object sorting test that were indicative of pathology in conceptual thinking. Sixty-eight parents of schizophrenic patients and 115 control parents were used. The hypothesis of greater frequency of pathological scores in the patient–parent group was supported only with subjects from higher levels of intelligence, education, and occupation.

RYCKOFF, I., DAY, J., & WYNNE, L. Family role structure and schizophrenia. *Proceedings of the Twentieth Annual Meeting of St. Elizabeth's Hospital*. Washington, D.C.: 1957, pp. 22–26.
Two cases are presented in support of the concept that in families of schizophrenics, individuals attempt to fit themselves into rigid roles without trying to rework them. It is postulated that the family system has hindered ego differentiation from which critical faculties might develop.

RYCKOFF, I., DAY, J., & WYNNE, L. Maintenance of stereotyped roles in the families of schizophrenics. *Archives of General Psychiatry*, 1959, *1*, 93–99.
One of a series of papers on a study of family relationships and schizophrenia. Data were collected from a study of the identified patient who was a hospitalized schizophrenic. Parents were seen twice weekly on an outpatient basis. Schizophrenic family dynamics are described in terms of "role patterns" in an attempt to understand identity development. Unconscious determinants of these roles are discussed through the use of clinical examples.

SAFILIOS-ROTHSCHILD, C. Deviance and mental illness in the Greek family. *Family Process*, 1968, 7, 100–117.
See Reference in Section 3.2.

SANDER, F. M. T. S. Eliot's *The family reunion*—"Schizophrenia" reconsidered. *Family Process*, 1971, *10*, 213–228.
This paper discussed T. S. Eliot's play *The Family Reunion* as a representation of a "schizophrenic" and his family. It illustrates some of the clinical insights of both individual and family psychiatry. It concludes with a reconsideration of the concept of schizophrenia.

SANUA, V. D. The sociocultural aspects of childhood schizophrenia. In G. H. Zuk, & I. Boszormenyi-Nagy (Eds.), *Family therapy and disturbed families*. Palo Alto: Science & Behavior Books, 1967.
A discussion of methodological issues, research strategies, and the problems inherent in studying parent–child relationships and interaction as an etiological factor in schizophrenia. Includes a review of the literature.

SANUA, V. D. Sociocultural factors in families of schizophrenics: A review of the literature. *Psychiatry*, 1961, *24*, 246–265.
A review of family studies which includes problems of methodology, studies using hospital records, interviews with relatives, data from psychotherapy, studies using tests, cross-cultural comparisoins of the schizophrenic environment and that of other pathologies. The author concludes that etiological factors fall into 4 general categories: (1) undesirable traits in the parents, (2) family sturcture—early parental or sibling deaths or broken families, (3) undesirable interpersonal patterns, and (4) genetic or constitutional factors. He points out the inconsistency and wide variation in methodology and sampling and the neglect of social variables, and suggests an international research organization to coordinate research in mental illness.

SCHAFFER, L., WYNNE, L. C., DAY, J., RYCKOFF, I. M., & HALPERIN, A. On the nature and sources of the psychiatrist's experience with the family of the schizophrenic. *Psychiatry*, 1962, *25*, 32–45.
A detailed discussion of the experience of the therapist as he performs family therapy with the family of the schizophrenic where "nothing has a meaningful relation to anything else." It is said to be different from work with other families, and case illustrations are given.

SCHATZMAN, M. Paranoia or persecution: The case of Schreber. *Family Process*, 1971, *10*, 177–212.
Through exploring Schreber's paranoid schizophrenia in the context of the family, particularly Schreber's father's beliefs and actual child-rearing techniques, this author raises several interesting areas of further exploration: (1) paranoid ideation is a representation of the patient's own experiences and can be explained through the exploration of the patient's primary experiences in his family of origin; (2) treatment includes matching the intra-psychic account of behavior with other sources within one's family or by observing family interaction; (3) the social network to which a child is born has impact on that child's development and continued mental health, and (4) historical events (or societal behaviors) are representations of the larger societal culture; its beliefs and mores.

SCOTT, R. Perspectives on the American family studies in schizophrenia. *Confina Psychiatrica*, 1965, *8*, 43–48.
A review of the American literature on family studies of schizophrenia with questions and criticisms. There is a selective bias in leaving out family history of schizophrenics and focusing on interactional aspects. The concept of the double bind is questioned and explained in a different way.

SCOTT, R., & ASHWORTH, P. The "axis value" and the transfer of psychosis. *British Journal of Medical Psychologty*, 1965, *38*, 97–116.
A report of a study of seven families with a schizophrenic member using a self-report test in which parents and child mark a check list of 42 items. The family members check off what applies to themselves and to each of the others, then what each thinks the other will check off about him. Contrasts are made between "shadow parents" (the parent who is most involved with the patient and also had a significant involvement with a mad ancestor), and non-shadow parents. Differences are said to be found, and descriptions of the families are offered.

SCOTT, R., & ASHWORTH, P. Closure at the first schizophrenic breakdown: A family study. *British Journal of Medical Psychology*, 1967, *40*, 109–146.
One of a series of papers on the preillness familial relationships of schizophrenics with their families at the time of the first decompensation. Sample included 23 families (19 female patients and 4 male patients), average age 26, who were seen over 2½ years, with an average number of interviews totalling 27 and lasting 3 hours apeice. Using a three-generational hypothesis, one or both parents has had a significant traumatic event (such as death or insanity of a parent). Their feelings about this event are studied pertinent to the development of a schizophrenic reaction in their children. "Signs of disturbance in the child are regraded by the parent as if a catastrophic event is occurring again," and their reaction often then seems inappropriate.

SHARAN (SINGER), S. Family interaction with schizophrenics and their siblings. *Journal of Abnormal Psychology*, 1966, *71*, 345–353.
An experimental study contrasting the behavior of parents of schizophrenics with the patient and with a sibling. Twenty-four families were asked to solve collectively the questions from the comprehension and similarities subtests of the Wechsler-Bellvue intelligence scale. The conversations were compared for problem-solving efficiency, mutual support patterns, and parent–child sex role alignments. Parents and patient worked as efficiently as parents and

siblings, parents supported both children equally, and fathers and mothers were equally dominant. The patients were more supportive of their parents than were the siblings, and parental discord was more prominent when the patient was present than when the sibling was present.

SHARAN (SINGER), S. Family interaction with schizophrenics and their siblings. In E. G. Mischler, N. E. Waxler (Eds.), *Family interaction processes and schizophrenia*. New York: Science House, 1968.
A report of a research investigation discussing 3 aspects of family theory: (1) problem-solving within the family (2) the formation of rival intrafamilial dyads, and (3) parental role reversals and the crossing of sex-generation boundaries. The sample was 24 schizophrenic patients, including both parents and a normal child in addition to the identified patient. The interaction testing technique was used as a research instrument. Results indicated that parents were equally supportive of the identified patient as well as the well sibling. The patient was associated with greater interparental conflict than was the normal child. Implications of these findings in comparison with other research are discussed.

SHARP, V., GLASNER, S., LEDERMAN, I., & WOLFE, S. Sociopaths and schizophrenics—A comparison of family *interactions. Psychiatry*, 1964, *27*, 127–134.
To test the hypothesis that there would be differences in the family interaction of matched groups of sociopaths and schizophrenics, 20 subjects of each group were examined. These included every patient admitted to the authors' case load at the Philadelphia Naval Hospital. Sources of data were social service questionnaires, parental visits, and interviews with parents. Findings were that sociopaths joined the service "to escape from home," had shorter hospitalizations, their families were much more unconcerned and rejecting than the families of the schizophrenics, who visited more.

SINGER, M. T., & WYNNE, L. C. Communication styles in parents of normals, neurotics, and schizophrenics: Some findings using a new Rorschach scoring manual. In I. M. Cohen (ed.), *Psychiatric research report no. 20*. Washington, D.C.: American Psychiatric Association, 1966.
See Reference in Section 3.2

SINGER, M. T., & WYNNE, L. C. Differentiating characteristic of parents of childhood schizophrenic, childhood neurotics, and young adults schizophrenics. *American Journal of Psychiatry*, 1963, *120*, 234–243.
See Reference in Section 3.2

SINGER, M. T., & WYNNE, L. C. Thought disorder and family relations of schizophrenics. III: Methodology using projective techniques: Results and implications. *Archives of General Psychiatry*, 1965, *12*,187–212.
See Reference in Section 3.2

SLIPP, S. The symbiotic survival pattern: A relational theory of schizophrenia. *Family Process*, 1973, *12*, 377–398.
This paper presents a theoretical, formulation regarding schizophrenia and family functioning. The symbiotic survival pattern found in these families is a mutually controlling system of interaction in which each individual feels responsible for the self–esteem and survival of the other. The genesis of this pattern appears to be that the parents have not integrated their own ambivalent attitudes toward their parents and achieved, self and object differentiation. Two cases are presented to demonstrate how the various transactions within the symbiotic survival pattern are useful in understanding individual and system dynamics.

SLUZKI, C. Transactional disqualification: Research on the double bind. *Archives of General Psychiatry*, 1967, *16*, 494–504.
See Reference in Section 3.6

SOBEL, D. E. Children of Schizophrenic Patients: Preliminary observations on early development. *American Journal of Psychiatry*, 1967, *118*, 512–517.
See Reference in Section 4.3

SOJIT, C. M. The double bind hypothesis and the parents of schizophrenics. *Family Process,* 1971, *10*, 53–74.
A description and analysis of the interaction of parents of schizophrenics and parents of nonschizophrenics in both double bind and non-double bind situations is presented. The test asks parents to determine together, then transmit to their child, *the* meaning of two proverbs: one proverb having two mutually exclusive meanings, the other, only one meaning. The interaction of eight couples who are parents of adolescent or young adult schizophrenic is compared with the interaction of parents of nonschizophrenics (normal or other disorder). Results indicated a general distorted system of communication between the parents of schizophrenics. This is felt to be a key factor undermining the family structure, causing the schizophrenic to produce incongruent messages of his own and to respond to all communication as incongruent and binding.

SONNE, J. C., & LINCOLN, G. The importance of a heterosexual co-therapy relationship in the construction of a

family image. In I. M. Cohen (Ed.), *Psychiatric research report no. 20.* Washington, D.C.: American Psychiatric Association, 1966.
A discussion of the use of co-therapy to provide a heterosexual image in the treatment of the family of the schizophrenic.

SONNE, J. C., SPECK, R. V., & JUNGREIS, J. E. The absent-member maneuver as a resistance in family therapy of schizophrenia. *Family Process,* 1962, *1,* 44–62.
A report of a specific type of resistance encountered while using family treatment in 10 families containing a schizophrenic offspring. The absent-member maneuver, defined as the absence of a family member from the family sessions, was seen in one form or another in all 10 families. Some of the dynamics of this manuever are discussed, the authors believing that the absent member (often seen as "healthy" by the rest of the family) tends to pathologically maintain unresolved Oedipal problems in the family.

SPECK, R. V., & RUEVENI, U. Network therapy: A developing concept. *Family Process,* 1969, *8,* 182–191.
A description of network therapy where all members of the kinship system, all friends of the family, and other significant people are brought together. A description of the method and a case illustration are offered.

SPIEGEL, J., & BELL, N. The family of the psychiatric patient. In S. Arieti (Ed.), *American handbook of psychiatry* (Vol. I): New York: Basic Books, 1959.
A chapter in a textbook on psychiatry dealing with sections on the history of the role of the family in mental illness; etiologic studies of parent-child interactions and development of various mental illnesses including schizophrenia, psychoneurosis, and acting-out disorders; the impact of mental illness upon the family; the family and treatment procedures; and new approaches to the family and its pathology, including family therapy. There are 238 references.

SPITZER, S. P., SWANSON, R. M., & LEHR, R. K. Audience reactions and careers of psychiatric patients. *Family Process,* 1969, *8,* 159–181.
A study of the reaction of families and the ways these reactions influence the psychiatric patient's career. The histories of 79 first admission patients were examined and patient and a family member were interviewed. Two dimensions of family reaction to deviance are described leading to a typology of eight career patterns which allow for the classification of 95 percent of the cases reviewed.

STABEANU, J. Schizophrenia: A family's projective identification. *American Journal of Psychiatry,* 1973, *130,* 19–23.
One case history of a family with a set of monozygotic male twins discordant for schizophrenia is used to present a theory that by means of projective identification the parents may contribute to the differential life course leading to schizophrenia in a family member. This defense is utilized to a greater degree in schizophrenia than in other psychiatric illnesses.

STABENAU, J. R., TUPIN, J., WERNER, M., & POLLIN, W. A comparative study of families of schizophrenics, delinquents, and normals. *Psychiatry,* 1965, *28,* 45–59.
A report of a comparison of five families with a schizophrenic, five families with a delinquent, and five normal families tested with the revealed differences test, the object sorting test, and the thematic apperception test. "Data from the three different tests suggest that in the schizophrenic and delinquent families there were both individual disturbances in thought process and impaired communication at the family level ... There was relatively little evidence of communication impairment at the individual or family level in the normal families."

STEINFELD, G. Parallels between the pathological family and the mental hospital: A search for process. *Psychiatry,* 1970, *33,* 36–55.
This is an essay based on the thesis that there are parallels between the pathological environment existing in families that produce schizophrenics and the environments found in mental hospitals. The author points out that there are no research findings supporting the notion that the family is a necessary and sufficient condition in producing schizophrenia. Hospitals, although potentially therapeutic, are often pathological and tend to duplicate the family life of schizophrenics. The author suggests changes in the inpatient treatment of schizophrenics, particularly focussing on a "setting which provides a place were a person's dignity and self-respect can be regained" rather than the opposite.

STIERLIN, H. The dynamics of owning and disowning: Psychoanalytic and family perspectives. *Family Process,* 1976, *15,* 277–288.
This paper discusses the intrapsychic and interpersonal dynamics of "inner" and "other-ownership" and presents a case of parental over-owning in a family with schizophrenic members. The advantages and disadvantages of being over-owned are identified and therapeutic implications are explored. The concept of being under-owned is elaborated and societal implications are drawn.

STIERLIN, H. Psychoanalytic approaches to schizophrenia in the light of a family model. *International Review of Psychoanalysis,* 1974, *1,* 169–178.
This is an essay comparing the family approach and the psychoanalytic approach to schizophrenia. These two

approaches are seen as complementary, emphasizing different etiologic and therapeutic possibilities. Ways in which both intrapsychic and interpersonal conflicts are interrelated are described and treatment implications made.

TAICHERT, L. C. Two adolescents at risk for schizophrenia: A family case study. *International Journal of Family Therapy*, 1979, *1*, 152–162.
One case of two step-brothers, ages 12 and 15, is presented in support of the thesis that neurological and psychological factors may be implicated in etiology of adolescent psychoses. The emphasis is on the need for family and individual therapists to consider the importance of these developmental problems, i.e. "soft" neurological signs, learning disabilities, and parents' fears and conflicts over these in their work.

TOWNE, R. D., MESSINGER, S. L., & SAMPSON, H. Schizophrenia and the marital family: Accommodations to symbiosis. *Family Process*, 1962, *1*, 304–318.
Another in a series of reports by this group of their study of 17 women who as young adults had experienced severe difficulties in their marital families and were hospitalized with a diagnosis of schizophrenia. Here the focus was on the "symbiotic" nature of the family relationships, which seem to serve to keep the families together when broken down led to hospitalization of the wife. Three patterns are described.

WAHL, C. W. The psychodynamics of consummated maternal incest. *Archives of General Psychiatry*, 1960, *3*, 186–193.
A report of two cases of hospitalized schizophrenic men who had sexual relations with their mothers. The author discusses dynamics of maternal incest and states that his case material supports the view that incestuous problems in schizophrenic patients play a role in the development of schizophrenia.

WAINWRIGHT, W. H. The reaction of mothers to improvement in their schizophrenic daughters. *Comprehensive Psychiatry*, 1960, *1*, 236–243.
At the Payne Whitney Psychiatric Clinic 8 mother–schizophrenic daughter combinations were interviewed and observed for a period ranging from 4 to 48 months, including up to 30 months after the patient's hospital discharge. Of these 8 mothers, 2 responded favorably to their daughter's improvement, 2 showed fluctuation in response which seemed dependent upon the severity of the daughter's symptoms, and 4 mothers showed signs of illness as their daughters improved. The author sees a common need with these 4 mothers to keep the daughter partially ill. Where hostility emerges during the recovery phase, he suggests evaluation for treatment of the mother.

WALSH, F. W. Breaching of family generation boundaries by schizophrenics, disturbed, and normals. *Interactional Journal of Family therapy*, 1979, *1*, 254–275.
This study tested the hypothesis that fantasies of role reversals in families of schizophrenics occur less often than nonschizophrenics. The method was to give the TAT, and Make a Picture Study tests to parents and index children (ages 18–28) alone and then conjointly. Groups compared were (1) schizophrenic child (N = 23), (2) disturbed nonschizophrenic child (N = 19), and (3) normal child (N = 20). Results showed no differences in "parentification" fantasies on child or parent's part, but strong differentiation of the schizophrenic group in child-as-mate fantasies. Methodological issues and theoretical implications are discussed. Thirty-one references are included.

WALSH, F. W. Concurrent grandparent death and birth of schizophrenic offspring: An intriguing finding. *Family Process*, 1978, *17*, 457–463.
This study calls attention to a family stress factor that may contribute to the development of schizophrenia: the concurrent stresses of the death and birth in the same family. The study compared 140 families in 3 groups of young adults; schizophrenic (N = 70), disturbed nonschizophrenic (N = 45), and normal (N = 25). Results showed a grandparent death within 2 years of birth of 41 percent of schizophrenics, 20 percent disturbed nonschizophrenics, and in 8 percent of normals. Two conclusions are suggested: (1) that a bereaved parent may be emotionally unavailable to spouse and infant, and (2) that attention to a child may block mourning and absorb painful feelings, with the child assuming a special replacement role.

WARING, M., & RICKS, D. Family patterns of children who become adult schizophrenics. *Journal of Nervous and Mental Disease*, 1965, *140*, 351–364.
A study comparing family variables of three groups of adult patients, who were seen as adolescents at a child guidance center. The 3 groups were (1) 30 patients, who as adults developed schizophrenia and remitted (defined as leaving the hospital): (2) 20 patients, who as adults developed schizophrenia and did not remit; and (3) a control group of 50 patients, selected from the clinic population who did not develop schizophrenia and were never hospitalized. Data were obtained retrospectively from work-ups at the time the patients were adolescents, and also from subsequent follow-ups with schools, hospitals, and other agencies, and finally in some cases with interviews with patient and family. There were significant familial differences between the remitting and unremitting groups, and less significant differences between the total schizophrenia group and the controls.

WATSON, D., BROWN, E., & BEURET, L. A family of five schizophrenic children. *Diseases of the Nervous System*, 1969, *30*, 189–193.

This is a case report of a family of seven children in which five were clearly schizophrenic. Neither parent had schizophrenia. Genetic and family dynamic explanations were presented. The etiology remained unclear.

WATZLAWICK, P. A review of the double bind theory. *Family Process*, 1963, *2*, 132–153.
A presentation of the comments on the double bind theory occurring in the literature from 1957–1961. The comments are discussed and excerpts presented.

WAXLER, N., & MISHLER, E. Parental interaction with schizophrenic children and well siblings. *Archives of General Psychiatry*, 1971, *24*, 223–231.
This study tests the assumption that there are systematic differences in how parents interact with their patient–child and nonpatient children. The samples were drawn from families from an inpatient unit for schizophrenics versus normals from the community matched for income, education, religion, and other variables. A revealed difference questionnaire was used in two situations—one, in which parents were with the patient–child and another in which they were with another child of the same sex and close to the patient's age. Results indicated there were no consistent predictable changes from a situation in which the patient was present to one in which the sibling was present, and thus the data did not support the assumption.

WEAKLAND, J. H. The double-bind hypothesis of schizophrenia and three-party interaction. In D. D. Jackson (Ed.), *The etiology of schizophrenia*. New York: Basic Books, 1960.
A discussion of the double bind as it applies to three party situations. Described are mother, father, child relationships, and such institutional relationships as administration–therapist–patient and doctor–nurse–patient.

WEAKLAND, J. H., & FRY, W. F. Letters of mothers of schizophrenics. *American Journal of Orthopsychiatry*, 1962, *32*, 604–623.
Several selected letters to schizophrenic patients from their mothers are presented with a microscopic and macroscopic examination of their characteristic and significant patterns. The letters exhibit similar influential patterns consisting of concealed incongruence between closely related messages. Almost no statement is ever allowed to stand clearly and unambiguously but is disqualified in a variety of ways. Patients' statements support the hypothesis that the letters induce paralysis or frantic activity in the recipients, which would be reasonable in response to "such a pervasive and general pattern of concealed strong but incompatible influence."

WEBLIN, J. Communication and schizophrenic behavior. *Family Process*, 1962, *1*, 5–14.
An essay in which the author's hypothesis is that "schizophrenic communication is a highly goal-directed activity towards avoiding almost any clearly defined relationships." This mode of relating is learned from the family—particularly from the parents. Several segments of tapes from two schizophrenic families are given.

WELLDON, R. M. C. "The shadow-of-death" and its implication in four families, each with a hospitalized schizophrenic member. *Family Process*, 1971, *10*, 281–302.
Through the description and careful examination of four families, each with a diagnosed schizophrenic member and each with an unresolved death in the immediate family, the author concludes that there are three areas which impede the family's and parent's eventual health. The "shadow of death" is enacted by the patient through a psychotic or "living death" and the patient will remain in this condition because of: (1) the parents unresolved feelings toward dead family member; (2) the child/patient will act as a repository for the parent's unresolved feelings; and (3) the family forms a "schizophrenic rigidity" or maintenance of status quo because of lack of knowledge of how to change or willingness to do so. The therapist often allows the family the "smokescreen" of mental illness by framing it as the primary problem.

WIEDORN, W. S. Intra-family adaptive significance of disordered communication and reality misperception in families of schizophrenic persons. In I. M. Cohen (Ed.), *Psychiatric research report no. 20*. Washington, D.C.: American Psychiatric Association.
A discussion of why families of schizophrenics show disordered communications and reality misperceptions, based upon psychoanalytical therapy with psychotic schizophrenic inpatients. It is said to represent an adaptive attempt in the family to maintain a symbiotic pairing. Case illustrations are offered.

WILD, C. M. Communication patterns and role structure in families of male schizophrenics. *Archives of General Psychiatry*, 1977, *34*, 58–70.
This research study explores the relationship between communication patterns and role structure in families of male schizophrenics. Automated "Who-to-Whom" data were collected from 69 families consisting of both parents and a son between the ages of 15 and 36. The family included 30 families of schizophrenics, 13 families of psychiatrically hospitalized nonschizophrenic controls, and 26 families of normal controls. Each family was seen for one two-hour session and given the following tests: (1) Patterns of interaction in the Dinner-Coffee break, (2) Twenty Questions test; (3) Family Group Rorschach; and (4) Best and Worst Experiences. There were automatic data collections with an observer blind to the group identity of the family. Results indicated that there are clear patterns of dominance in the families of schizophrenics with fathers most and sons least active, while activity was more evenly distributed among

family members in both control groups. The mother-son channel of communication was used more in both control groups than in families of schizophrenics. Results indicate that there are distinctive patterns of family interaction associated with having the identified patient as a son with a diagnosis of schizophrenia.

WILD, C. Disturbed styles of thinking. *Archives of General Psychiatry*, 1966, *13*, 464–470.
See Reference in Section 3.3.

WILD, C. M., SHAPIRO, L. N., & GOLDENBERG, L. Transactional communication disturbances in families of male schizophrenics. *Family Process*, 1975, *14*, 131–160.
See Reference in Section 3.6.

WILD, C., SINGER, M., ROSMAN, G., RICCI, J., & LIDZ, T. Measuring disordered styles of thinking. *Archives of General Psychiatry*, 1966, *13*, 471–476.
See Reference in Section 3.3.

WING, J. Ratings of behavior of patient and relative. *Journal of Psychosomatic Research*, 1964, *8*, 223–228.
A report of a test of hypothesis that (1) high emotional involvement of patient and relative should lead to deterioration of the patient, and (2) that the amount of face-to-face contact between patient and relative would be related to outcome. Patients were evaluated by means of two rater's description, and a checklist. Relatives were evaluated by means of scheduled ratings. Patients were hospitalized schizophrenics. Results indicated that if there was a high index of "emotional involvement" of relatives with patient, there was a high percentage of deterioration. In the case of patients who were moderately or severely ill at time of discharge and who were living with relatives rated as showing a high degree of emotional involvement, relatively few hours of contact were associated with relatively better outcome.

WINTER, W., FERREIRA, A., & OLSON, J. Hostility themes in the Family TAT. *Journal of Projective Technique and Personality Assessment*, 1966, *30*, 270–275.
Second of a series describing a diagnostic test adapted for use with families. Results were obtained from use of three TAT stories based on three cards, each produced conjointly by 126 three-member families. Stories were scored for hostility in the story themes. Fifty families had normal children, 44 had neurotic children, 16 had schizophrenic children and 16 had delinquent children. Normal and schizophrenic groups produced stories low in hostility, neurotics produced stories high in hostility, and delinquents scored high on one hostility variable and low on another.

WOLMAN, B. B. The fathers of schizophrenic patients. *Acta Psychotherapy and Psychosomatics*, 1961, *9*, 193–210.
See Reference in Section 3.2.

WYNNE, L. Communication disorders and the quest for relatedness in families of schizophrenics. *American Journal of Psychoanalysis*, 1970, *50*, 100–114.
Based on previous research, this is a clinical essay on communication disorders and the quest for relatedness in schizophrenic families. Schizophrenic families tend to relate at the expense of individuality and goal-directedness. A case example as well as previous work of Singer and Reiss are presented in support of this concept.

WYNNE, L. C. The study of intrafamilial alignments and splits in exploratory family therapy. In N. W. Ackerman, F. L. Beatman, & S. Sherman (Eds.), *Exploring the base for family therapy*. New York: New York Family Service Association of America, 1961.
From a clinical research project of 20 schizophrenic families and 10 families of nonschizophrenic psychiatric patients, it has been observed that schizophrenic families use as one of their main mechanisms of coping "pseudo-mutuality and pseudo-hostile mechanisms that disguise but help perpetuate the underlying problems." Conjoint family therapy based on understanding the family organization, and maneuvers in terms of alignments and splits, can benefit the disturbed family.

WYNNE, L, RYCKOFF, I. M., DAY, J., & HERSCH, S. I. Pseudo-mutuality in the family relations of schizophrenics. *Psychiatry*, 1958, *21*, 205–220.
An essay which postulates that the disturbance in the family is an important causal factor in schizophrenia. Data were obtained as part of a long-term research project on schizophrenia in which patients were hospitalized and parents were seen on an out-patient basis. Most of the data are drawn from clinical work with families. Patients with schizophrenia have families in which the relations can best be described as "pseudo-mutual." The acute schizophrenic experience is derived from internalization of the pathogenic family organization.

WYNNE, L. C., RYCKOFF, I. M., DAY, J., & HERSCH, S. I. Pseudo-mutuality in the family relations of schizophrenics. In N. W. Bell, & E. F. Vogel (Eds.), *A modern introduction to the family*. Glencoe, Free Press, 1960.
A description of families of schizophrenics studied with family therapy. Characteristic was pseudo-mutuality in the family; the family supports an illusion of a well-integrated state even when this is not supported by the emotional structure of the members. The strains contribute to the development of schizophrenia.

WYNNE, L. C., & SINGER, M. T. Thought disorder and family relations of schizophrenics. I: A research strategy. II: A classification of forms of thinking. *Archives of General Psychiatry*, 1963, *9*, 191–206.
A general discussion of the approach of the Wynne project. Families with schizophrenic members are contrasted with families of nonschizophrenic psychiatric patients, and siblings are contrasted with patients. The emphasis is upon the links between family patterns and schizophrenic thought disorder, defined broadly to include experience. The first part outlines the clinical and conceptual basis, the setting, and the kinds of research data. The second part presents a classification of schizophrenic thought disorders, including discrimination among varieties of schizophrenic and paranoid thinking.

ZUK, G. On silence and babbling in family psychotherapy with schizophrenics. *Confinia Psychiatrica*, 1965, *8*, 49–56.
From the author's clinical work, two cases are presented in support of the idea that both silence and babbling can be understood as attempts to interrupt communication and silence others' interactions. They are often seen in schizophrenia, but patients learn these strategies from their parents. Techniques for dealing with this in treatment are discussed.

ZUK, G. The victim and his silencers: Some pathogenic strategies against being silenced. In G. H. Zuk & I. Boszormenyi-Nagy (Eds.), *Family therapy and disturbed families*. Palo Alto: Science & Behavior Books, 1967.
A discussion of the strategies family members use to silence a member and the reciprocal relationship between the silencer and the victim. "Silencing strategies contribute to the development of paranoid, delusional, or hallucinatory states."

ZUK,. G., BOSZORMENYI-NAGY, I., & HEIMAN, E. Some dynamics of laughter during family therapy. *Family Process*, 1963, *2*, 302–314.
An examination of the frequency of laughter in family therapy sessions with parents and a schizophrenic girl. Frequency of laughter was totalled for different intervals during the sessions. A correlation is suggested between tension or anxiety and laughter and it was found that the parents laughed most in the first interval of a session. Significantly more laughter of the daughter occurred in the third of four intervals, thus showing a reversal of patterns of laughter between parents and daughter over 13 sessions.

ZUK, G., & RUBINSTEIN, D. A review of concepts in the study and treatment of families of schizophrenics. In I. Boszormenyi-Nagy & J. L. Framo (Eds.), *Intensive family therapy*. New York: Harper & Row, 1965.
A review of conceptual trends in family treatment of schizophrenics. Discusses the shift from parent pathology to nuclear family to three generational involvement.

ZWERLING, I., & MENDELSOHN, M. Initial family reactions to day hospitalization. *Family Process*, 1965, *4*, 50–63.
A report of a study on the relationship between the course of hospital treatment and certain family responses at the time of admission of a psychotic member. The sample consists of 100 patients consecutively admitted to a day hospital. It includes responses to admission, to family treatment and to improvement.

5.3 FAMILY MEMBER WITH DISORDER USUALLY FIRST EVIDENT IN CHILDHOOD

BAIRD, M. Characteristic interaction patterns in families of encopretic children. *Bullentin of the Menninger Clinic*, 1974, *38*, 144–153.
This is a clinical essay based on "impressions from 25 years experience as a social worker dealing with families of encopretic children." Family patterns include withholding (either between members or by a member), infantilization, mishandled anger, and miscommunication. Indicated treatment is family therapy. Several cases are presented in support of the impressions.

BENTOVIN, A. & KINSTON, W. Brief focal family therapy when the child is the referred patient. *Journal of Child Psychology and Psychiatry*, 1978, *19*, 1–12, 119–144.
See Reference in Section 1.1.

BYASSEE, J. & MURRELL, S. Interaction patterns in families of autistic, disturbed, and normal children. *American Journal of Orthopsychiatry*, 1975, *45*, 473–478.
In order to test the hypothesis that childhood autism results from "psychogenic factors," six "normal families" were compared with six families with an identified patient who had autism and six families with an identified patient who had other "nonpsychotic psychiatric illness." The test used was the Ferreira and Winter Unrevealed Differences Test

administered to all families in thier homes. Results indicated that there were no differences between families with autistic children and those with normal children. Families with disturbed children were found to have less agreements between father and mother than did autistic or normal families. The data did not support the psychogenic theory of the etiology of autism.

CRABTREE, L. H., BRECHT, J. A., & SONNE, J. C. Monadic orientation: A contribution to the structure of families with autistic children. *Family Process*, 1972, *11*, 255–274.
This paper describes the treatment of a family with an autistic child and presents the view that such families tend to maintain self-isolation and disaffiliation. This is considered an essential feature of the autistogenic process; it is labeled as the monadic orientation in the system, different than the process observed in schizophrenogenic families, where many interactions appear to function to maintain pathologic dyadic alliances.

DAVIS, D. Family processes in mental retardation. *American Journal of Psychiatry*, 1967, *124*, 340–350.
A lecture pointing out that in addition to genetic factors, mental retardation may result from failure of the family to give the child protection from stress during critical periods of learning in early childhood. Data were obtained from 50 cases (36 boys and 14 girls) with I.Q. below 75 (median 55)—all cases seen by the author prior to age seven. Retrospective historical data was obtained from parents—mothers were found to be depressed through much of the child's life including the period prior to recognition of the child's retardation. These mothers were found to have lost their fathers during adolescence and to have gotten "ineffective lifelong support" from the maternal grandmother. Prevention and treatment are discussed.

DURELL, V. Adolescents in multiple family group therapy in a school setting. *International Journal of Group Psychotherapy*, 1969, *19*, 44–52.
A clinical report of four families in multifamily therapy studied in over 11 sessions in a junior high school setting where the identified patients are having difficulty in school. The course of a group is discussed, and it was felt that a group was helpful in terms of the patient's school performance. Problems with school administration were discussed.

FARBER, G. Perceptions of crisis and related variables in the impact of a retarded child on the mother. *Journal of Health and Human Behavior*, 1960, *1*, 108–118.
An extension of earlier findings that a retarded child produces a tragic crisis (shock of diagnosis) or a role organization crisis (inability to develop roles to cope wth the child). A sample of 268 mothers and fathers of retarded children were interviewed and administered questionnaires. The hypotheses concern the reaction of mothers to the crises, relating type of crisis, role definitions of mother, and her self-perceived health. The general conclusion is that health-symptom status of mother is related to the type of crisis experienced.

FOSTER, R. M. A basic strategy for family therapy with children. *American Journal of Psychotherapy*, 1973, *27*, 437–445.
This paper recommends an appraoch for use with all families in which the identified patient is a child. The goal is to get the parents to see that they can get the child to do what they want, if *they* believe he can do it *if* the child believes he can do it. To do this, the therapist first elicits the desired behavior, then explores what they have tried to do to change the behavior, and then confronts the parents with their failure to direct the behavior they desire.

FOWLE, C. The effect of the severely mentally retarded child on his family. *American Journal of Mental Deficiency*, 1968, *73*, 468–473.
In order to test the effect of a severely mentally retarded child on the family a group of 35 families who had institutionalized their child were compared with 35 families who had kept their child in the home. There were 20 males and 15 females in each group. They were predominantly white middle- and lower-class families. Marital and sibling tension was measured using the Forbes sibling role tension index. Results indicated that there was no significant difference in "marital integration," but that there was a significant increase in "role tension" of the siblings if the child was not placed.

FRENCH, A., & STEWARD, M. Family dynamics, childhood depression, and attempted suicide in a 7-year-old boy: A case study. *Suicide*, 1975, *5*, 21–37.
Based on treatment of one family (the identified patient was a 7-year-old boy who made a suicide attempt), family dynamics for other such cases are hypothesized. Data were obtained from treatment of the identified patient over five months in play therapy while the parents were seen in marital therapy. The identified patient was found to be the family scapegoat.

GRUNEBAUM, M. G., HURWITZ, I., PRENTICE, N. M., & SPERRY, B. M. Fathers of sons with primary neurotic learning inhibitions. *American Journal of Orthopsychiatry*, 1962, *32*, 462–472.
An investigation which includes the treatment of 18 elementary school boys with severe learning difficulties. The resistance to therapeutic modification "persuaded us that this symptom was deeply embedded in the total family organization." The fathers are described in terms of their self image of inadequacy and resignation, their passive or explosively demanding orientation to their wives, their views of their sons as competitors for mother's support and

admiration, and their unconscious subversion of the child's achievement in the face of their conscious wish that the child succeed. The mothers maintain an image of masculinity that was dangerous or devalued and limit the son's attempt to form an achieving masculine identification. The parents' neurotic attitudes are internalized by the child and the conflict is displaced to the school situation.

GUERNEY, B., & GUERNEY, L. Analysis of interpersonal relationships as an aid to understanding family dynamics, a case report. *Journal of Clinical Psychology, 1961, 17,* 225–228.
A case of a 9 year-old girl who refused to go to school and had fears of death is presented in terms of the traditional evaluation and in terms of interpersonal famiy dynamics. The interpersonal analysis is based upon "a few of the non-quantitative conceptualizations of Leary's system," particularly "interpersonal reflexes" and the principle of "reciprocal interpersonal relations."

HALL, J., & TAYLOR, K. The emergence of Eric: Co-therapy in the treatment of a family with a disabled child. *Family Process*, 1971, *10,* 85–96.
This paper focuses on the socialization of the disabled child within the family. The family must each the child *how to be human* and *how to be disabled* in the larger society. Family therapy helps them to achieve these goals. A case illustration is included to demonstrate the use of family interviewing with a congenitally blind adolescent boy. It is concluded that the child's family is the most powerful resource for the successful habilitation of the disabled child into larger society.

HECKEL, R. V. The effects of fatherlessness on the preadolescent female. *Mental Hygiene,* 1963, *47,* 69–73.
A discussion of five fatherless preadolescent girls referred for treatment because of school problems, excessive sexual interest, daydreaming, and acting-out behavior. The girls responded more seductively to male staff members and more indifferently to females. Interviews were conducted with both mother and child. Developmental similarities, treatment, and follow-up information are discussed.

KAPLAN, S. L., & POZNANSKI, E. Child psychiatric patients who share a bed with a parent. *Journal of American Academy of Child Psychiatry,* 1974, *13,* 344–356.
Based on the screening of 700 records of children seen in a child psychiatric clinic, about 60 were coded as sharing a bed with a parent and of that 60, 27 had a consistent pattern of this behavior. They were compared with a control group of 26 children who did not share a bed with a parent. Dynamics of such behavior in families is described.

MALMQUIST, C. School phobia: A problem in family neurosis. *Journal of the American Academy of Child Psychiatry,* 1965, *4,* 293–319.
See Reference in Section 5.1.

MARCUS, L. M. Patterns of coping in families of psychotic children. *American Journal of Orthopsychiatry,* 1977, *47,* 388–399.
This paper, based on clinical experience with the population of a clinic for the treatment of autistic and communication-disordered children and their families, examines the strength and nature of the families adaptation to their child's illness. The parents' self-concept, decision making, perception of their child, behavior and relations with others outside the family are discussed as a practical approach to treatment and research.

MARTIN, B. Famiy interaction associated with child disturbance: Assessment and modification. *Psychotherapy: Theory, Research, & Practice,* 1967, *4,* 30–35.
This is a report testing the author's notion that disturbances in the interaction between parents and child can lead to disturbed behavior in the child. An experimental procedure was developed in order to limit communication to just one member of the family at a time. Sessions were recorded on audiotape and rated according to degree of blaming. In a pilot study the four families, two received modification procedures designed to decondition blaming, and two did not. The experimental families showed a greater proportion of decrease in blaming scores.

MENDELL, D., & CLEVELAND, S. A three-generation view of a school phobia. *Voices,* 1967, *3,* 16–19.
See Reference in Section 4.3.

MESSER, A. Family treatment of a school phobic child. *Archives of General Psychiatry,* 1964, *11,* 548–555.
Case report of family treatment over two years of a phobic child and his family. Hypothesis was that the phobia expressed publicly a disruption in the family equilibrium.

MILLAR, T. P. The child who refuses to attend school. *American Journal of Psychiatry,* 1961, *118,* 398–404.
The child who doesn't attend school with the knowledge of the parent, but beyond the parent's control, appears to be less fearful of school than concerned over separation from the mother. The child is protective of the mother and also able to manipulate and control his parents through mobilizing and exploiting guilt feelings. Treatment must be instituted promptly and must include early return to regular school attendance.

MILLER, D. R., & WESTMAN, J. C. Family teamwork and psychotherapy. *Family Process*, 1966, *5*, 49–59.
A discussion of primary questions about etiology and treatment developed in a study of functional retardation in reading. In one type of reading difficulty the problem can be explained by poor teaching or traumatic experiences, and in the other there is a function in the family. The roots of the symptom in famiy relationships are described with an emphasis upon family teamwork in maintaining the difficulty.

MILLER, D. R., & WESTMAN, J. C., Reading disability as a condition of family stability. *Family Process*, 1964, *3*, 66–76. See Reference in Section 3.2

MORRISON, J. R. Parental divorce as a factor in childhood psychiatric illness. *Comprehensive Psychiatry*, 1974, *15*, 95–102.
See Reference in Section 3.2.

MORRISON, J. R. & STEWART, M. A. A family study of the hyperactive child syndrome, *Biological Psychiatry*, 1971, *3*, 189–195.
See Reference in Section 3.2.

NOVAK, A. L., & VAN DER VEEN, F. Family concepts and emotional disturbance in the families of disturbed adolescents with normal siblings. *Family Process*, 1970, *9*, 157–171.
The present study is a preliminary investigation of the hypothesis that a child's degree of disturbance is a function of his/her perception of the family. Thirteen families with 9th graders were selected from clinic and nonclinic groups. Clinic families with at least two children, one who was professionally diagnosed as emotionally disturbed, were chosen. The lowest level of family functioning in the family concept measures was demonstrated by the identified patient. The factor analyses of the parents' family concepts suggests that the family concepts of parents in nondisturbed families are complementary.

PATTERSON, G. R., SHAW, D. A., & EBNER, M. J. Teachers, peers, and parents as agents of change in the classroom. In S. A. N. Benson (Ed.), *Modifying deviant social behaviors in various classroom settings*. Eugene: University of Oregon Press, 1969.
An approach to correcting deviant behavior in the classroom by using a combined systems and reinforcement theory approach.

PITTMAN, F., LANGSLEY, D., & DEYOUNG, C. Work and school phobias: A family approach to treatment. *American Journal of Psychiatry*, 1968, *124*, 1535–1541.
Eleven cases of work phobia (the patient experiencing overt anxiety associated with having to go to work or staying at work) are thought of as being "the adult form of school phobia." Treatment goal is to allow the wife or mother to allow the man to separate. One-year follow-up shows that five cases treated with conjoint family therapy were able to return to work; the six in long-term individual therapy had not.

PLIONIS, E. M. Family functioning and childhood accident occurence. *American Journal of Orthopsychiatry*, 1977, *47*, 250–263.
See Reference in Section 3.3.

ROSENBERG, J. B. & LINDBLAD, M. B. Behavior therapy in a family context: Treating elective mutism. *Family Process*, 1978, *17*, 77–82.
This paper discusses the use of behavioral and family approaches in the treatment of electively mute children. A case history illustrates the use of behavioral methods, reinforcement, counter-conditioning and successive approximations, in combination with family therapy, to maintain the changes that have occurred. The conclusion is that either approach by itself will not be effective in helping electively mute children, i.e., the treatment of choice is a combination of therapeutic techniques.

SCHEINFELD, D., BOWLES, D., TUCK, S., & GOLD, R. Parents' values, family networks, and family development: Working with disadvantaged families. *American Journal of Orthopsychiatry*, 1970, *40*, 413–425.
See Reference in Section 5.7.

SETLEIS, L. A philosophy of the family as a practical necessity. *Social Casework*, 1974, *55*, 562–567.
Based on the author's clinical experience as a consultant to a school that treats children with "learning disabilities," it is stated that the family is the primary resource for the child with learning disabilities. There is a discussion of family functions and the family's role with such children.

SHELLOW, R. S., BROWN, B. S., & OSBERG, J. W. Family group therapy in retrospect: Four years and sixty families. *Family Process*, 1963, *2*, 52–67.
A review of experience with family group therapy (authors' term for conjoint family therapy) with 60 families in a child

guidance clinic over a four-year period. Referral sources were mainly from physicians and school. Several "hidden" factors influenced choice of this form of therapy by staff members: (1) the identified patient was often the oldest child, and (2) there was a large proportion of school achievement problems represented.

SKYNNER, A. School phobia: A reappraisal. *British Journal of Medical Psychology*, 1974, *47*, 1–16.
See Reference in Section 1.1.

SMITH, I. W., & LOEB, D. The stable extended family as a model in treatment of atypical children. *Social Work*, 1965, *10*, 75–81.
A report of a multiple-impact therapeutic program in the treatment of six severely disturbed children and their families. Three boys and three girls, aged four-seven, were referred as mentally retarded, were intolerable in school, and appeared psychotic in the first interview. Two female therapists, assuming grandmotherly roles, treated the families conjointly in three overlapping phases: (1) individual treatment for the patient and parents, (2) family group therapy, and (3) peer experiences for all family members. Patients showed rapid symptomatic recovery, enabling them to return to school and participate in social situations. Parents and siblings, relieved of anxiety, functioned more efficiently and experienced improved interpersonal relationships.

TOOLEY, K. M. "Irreconcilable differences" between parent and child: A case report of interactional pathology. *American Journal of Orthopsychiatry*, 1978, *48*, 703–716.
See Reference in Section 1.6.

WALDRON, S., SHRIER, D., STONE, B. et al. School phobia and other childhood neuroses: A systematic study of the children and their families. *American Journal of Psychiatry*, 1975, *132*, 802–808.
See Reference in Section 5.1.

WESTMAND, J. C., MILLER, D. R., & ARTHUR, B. Psychiatric symptoms and family dynamics as illustrated by the retarded reader. In I. M. Cohen (Ed.), *Psychiatric research report no. 20*. Washington, D.C.: American Psychiatric Association, 1966.
A disucssion of the family of the retarded reader to illustrate how indivdual psychopathology can be linked with interpersonal relationships through symptoms and signs.

5.4   FAMILY MEMBER WITH DISORDER USUALLY FIRST EVIDENT IN ADOLESCENCE

ACKERMAN, N. W. Adolescent problems: A symptom of famiy disorder. *Family Process*, 1962, *1*, 202–213.
An essay based on the thesis that adolescent problems represent in part not only a disorder of a particular stage of growth, but also a symptom of a parallel disorder in the family, society, and culture. Clinical examples are given.

APONTE, H., & HOFFMAN, L. The open door: A structural approach to a family with an anorectic child. *Family Process*, 1973, *12*, 1–44.
This article is a step-by-step discussion about a videotape of an initial family interview with a family of an anorectic girl. It demonstrates a set of therapeutic techniques based on a structural view of family organization and dysfunction. A connection is made between the child's anorexia and the family's structural organization. At the end, the child's eating habits seem incidental compared to the changes in family relationships.

BARCAI, A. Family therapy and treatment of anorexia nervosa. *American Journal of Psychiatry*, 1971, *128*, 286–290.
Two cases are reported in support of the thesis that family therapy enables the family to change patterns that prevent the identified patient from regaining lost weight.Weight gain that subsequently occurs allows therapy to focus on family conflicts and process rather than on the weight gain itself.

BARDILL, D. Family therapy in an army mental hospital hygiene clinic. *Social Casework*, 1963, *44*, 452–457.
From an out-patient Army mental hygiene clinic, the author presents his experience in using family therapy with adolescents. Manifest problems represent a breakdown in the family system. Aims and techniques are discussed and illustrated by clinical examples.

BERKOWITZ, D. A., SHAPIRO, R. L., ZINNER, J., & SHAPIRO, E. R. Family contributions to narcissistic disturbances in adolescents. *International Review of Psycho-Analysis*, 1974, *1*, 353–362.
This paper attempts to formulate dynamics based on clinical material from family sessions rather than based on individual reconstruction. It is believed that the identified adolescent patient regresses with narcissistic symptoms

because, in the struggle for independence, he upsets the family equilibrium. The parents emerge from their adolescence with low self-esteem and the need for the support of external objects. The adolescent's separateness from the family recreates the problem for the parents and prevents his individual growth as well as his separation from the family.

BRANDZEL, E. Working through the oedipal struggle in family unit sessions. *Social Casework*, 1965, *46*, 414–422.
A discussion of the use of family-unit sessions to help a famiy work through its problems with a young adolescent. Case examples are given.

BRITTAIN, C. V. Adolescent choices and parent–peer cross–pressures. *American Sociological Review*, 1963, *28*, 385–391.
Adolescent choices when peers and parents indicate different courses were investigated as to variation by content area. Two hundred and eighty high school girls in two southern states responded to hypothetical dilemmas. On two occasions interviews were also held with 42 subjects. The data indicate that choice depended upon the area and that a complex process of perception of and identification with peers and parents is involved.

BROWNING, C. J. Differential impact of family disorganization on male adolescents. *Social Problems*, 1960, *8*, 37–44.
Samples of 60 nondelinquent-auto theft boys (aged 15) were identified. Data were obtained from school, police, and probation records; from interviews with mothers; from family solidarity and marital adjustment scales filled out by parents; and California test of personality scales filled out by the boys. The incidence of broken homes is higher in the deinquent groups, but this variable is not a consistently good indicator of family disorganization and needs refinement.

BRUCH, H. Family transaction and eating disorders. *Comprehensive Psychiatry*, 1971, *12*, 238–248.
Three cases are presented in support of the thesis that transactional patterns in families of anorexic children are causal to the symptomatology. Patterns developed during the early years of the identified patient's life determine the accuracy of perception and conceptualization of hunger as a distinct and identifiable sensation. The more distorted the development of these patterns, the more severe the psychopathology. Biologic and psychologic forces are on a continuous feedback circuit, and both contribute to the development of the psychopathology.

BYNG-HALL, J., & BRUGGEN, P. Family admission decisions as a therapeutic tool. *Family Process*, 1974, *13*, 443–459.
See Reference in Section 1.7.

CAILLE, P., ABRAHAMSEN, P., GIROLAMI, C., et al: A systems theory approach to a case of anorexia nervosa. *Family Process*, 1977, *16*, 455–465.
A case illustration describes treatment utilizing a systems theory approach to anorexia. The symptoms are viewed as natural consequences of a dysfunctional human interactional group. A dysfunctional family becomes dependent on mental or behavioral deviations in one of its members as a means of preventing disintegration.

CAREK, D. J., HENDRICKSON, W. J., & HOLMES, D. J. Delinquency addiction in parents. *Archives of General Psychiatry*, 1961, *4*, 357–362.
A discussion of parental participation in the cause and cure of delinquency traits. These parentally sanctioned traits "have been observed with regular frequency in some 400 cases" of hospitalized adolescents who had not been admitted primarily for delinquency in the legal sense. It is suggested that a rough analogy for parental participation is to be found in the drug addict. Clinical examples are used to illustrate seven mechanisms parents use to communicate unconscious approval. Complete separation is advised with anticipation of the parental anxiety which occurs if the child abandons delinquency.

CAREK, D. J., & WATSON, A. S. Treatment of a family involved in fratricide. *Archives of General Psyciatry*, 1964, *11*, 533–543.
See Reference in Section 4.5

CHEEK, F. Family socialization techniques and deviant behavior. *Family Process*, 1966, *5*, 199–217.
A study based upon Parson's theoretical framework in which deviant behavior is related to imbalance of systems inputs and outputs at various stages of development. A sample of 120 male adults from four different groups— schizophrenics, normals, alcoholics, and reformatory inmates—were exposed to a questionnaire on family problem situations.Differences were found and it is suggested that Parsons' theoretical scheme could be translated into reinforcement theory.

CONRAD, D. E. A starving family: An interactional view of anorexia nervosa. *Bulletin of the Menninger Clinic*, 1977, *41*, 487–495.

This is a case report of a patient with primary anorexia nervosa. The subject is reviewed theoretically and the family treatment described.

COUNTS, R. Family crisis and the impulsive adolescent. *Archives of General Psychiatry*, 1967, *17*, 64–74.
A case example is presented in support of the hypothesis that the acting out of an adolescent can best be understood by seeing it as acting out of a family crisis. The adolescent is used as a scapegoat of the family and he acts out somebody else's impulses, which helps to stabilize his own internal operations while it stabilizes the family.

DIETZ, C. R. Implications for the therapeutic process of a clinical team focus on family interaction. *American Journal of Orthopsychiatry*, 1962, *32*, 395–398.
A discussion of the treatment of children and adolescents with an emphasis upon the contrast with adult patients. Psychotherapy with adolescent patients is not a simple contractual relationship between therapist and patient but in the family oriented approach the goal is to strengthen the family equilibrium. Parents carry leadership in family affairs, and decisions about therapy with the child should be oriented within that framework. Initiating therapy, the content of the interviews, and termination should be done with the rights and responsibilities of the parents in mind.

EASSON, W. M., STEINHILBER, R. M. Murderous aggression by children and adolescents. *Archives of General Psychiatry*, 1961, *4*, 27–35.
A review of murderous aggression in families, with a detailed discussion of seven boys who had made murderous assaults and one boy who had committed murder. The background family psychopathology varied in character and malignancy but showed definite psychodynamic patterns. All cases demonstrated that one or both parents had fostered and condoned murderous assault. Typically the boys were emotionally tied to mother in a hostile way, the fathers were not available for healthy identification, and the boys were allowed to retain weapons even after episodes of violent and menacing behavior. In each case the child was informed of parental expectations that he would be violent even to the point of murder.

EHRLICH, S. S. The family structure of hospitalized adolescents. *Journal of Health and Human Behavior*, 1962, *3*, 121–124.
A descriptive study of the family structure of 55 hospitalized adolescents. Characteristics studies were socioeconomic status (religion, ethnicity, father's occupation, and employment of mother), family composition (family intactness and separations, ordinal postion), and family roles (mental conflict, role of grandparents).

EVANS, H. A., CHAGOYA, L., RAKOFF, V. Decision making as to the choice of family therapy in an adolescent inpatient setting. *Family Process*, 1971, *10*, 97–110.
See Reference in Section 3.1.

FERREIRA, A. J. The "Double bind" and delinquent behavior. *Archives of General Psychiatry*, 1960, *3*, 359–367.
A discussion of the double-bind theory as it related to delinquency. Double-binds are not confined to schizophrenic relationships but appear in the genesis of delinquent behavior. In delinquency, the source of messages is split; messages of distinct logical type, conflicting in themselves, emanate from two equally important parental figures. The child is a "victim" in that he is caught, for example, between a message emanating from father which requires certain behavior from him and a message from mother which is a destructive comment about that message. A case history is presented, and formal sequences of this delinquent pattern are diagrammed in symbolic logic style.

FERREIRA, A. J., & WINTER, W. D. Family interaction and decision-making. *Archives of General Psychiatry*, 1965, *13*, 214–223.
See Reference in Section 3.4

FERREIRA, A. J., WINTER, W. D., & POINDEXTER, E. J. Some interactional variables in normal and abnormal families. *Family Process*, 1966, *5*, 60–75.
See Reference in Section 3.3

FRIEDMAN, A. S. Delinquency and the family system. In O. Pollak, & A. S. Friedman (Eds.), *Family dynamics and female sexual delinquency*. Palo Alto: Science & Behavior Books, 1969.
A review article of what has been written about delinquency in relation to the family.

FRIEDMAN, A. S. The family and the female delinquent: An overview. In O. Pollak, & A. S. Friedman (Eds.), *Family dynamics and female sexual delinquency*. Palo Alto: Science & Behvaior Books, 1969.
A discussion of young female delinquents and what has been written about the cause, with illustrations from treatment of families of such girls.

FRIEDMAN, P. H. Family system and ecological approach to youthful drug abuse. *Family Therapy*, 1974, *1*, 63–78.
One case example is presented from the author's experience in working in a "street clinic" in an urban area with approximately 30 families with young middle-class drug abusers. No data were available on the amount or type of drug

abuse. A comparison of the "individual approach" with the "family approach" to such problems in terms of dynamics and therapy is discussed. Etiological hypotheses using both models are offered.

GETZELS, J. W., & JACKSON, P. W. Family environment and cognitive style: A study of the sources of highly intelligent and of highly creative adolescents. *American Sociological Review*, 1961, *26*, 351–359.
A study of adolescent boys and girls, 28 highly intelligent but not creative and 26 creative but not concomitantly intelligent, chosen from a school population on the basis of testing. These students proved equally superior in achievement to the remainder of the student body although they differed both functionally and in their goals. The central issue of this report deals with the role of the family environment in the differentiation of kinds of intellectual ability through interviews with the mothers. Significant group differences were found in parental type education, childhood memories, reading interests, values, degree of satisfaction with child and school, etc. The authors find less anxiety in the highly creative home and therefore more freedom for "individual divergence."

GOLDSTEIN, M., JUDD, L., RODNICK, E., ALKIRE, A., & GOULD, E. A method of studying social influence and coping patterns within families of disturbed adolescents. *Journal of Nervous and Mental Disease*, 1968, *127*, 233–252.
The first report of a project dealing with family interaction patterns between parents and adolescents. Twenty families with the identified patient aged 13 to 19 were seen for five sessions at the UCLA psychology clinic. Data collected included psychological testing (TAT and a partial WAIS), psycho-physiological recordings, and videotape recordings of both actual and simulated verbal interaction. The results of simulated interactions indicated that social power usage among family members was related to type of psychopathology manifested by the adolescents.

GORDON, J. S. Working with runaways and their families: How the SAJA community does it. *Family Process*, 1975, *14*, 235–262.
Development, philosophy and service delinvery to runaways (ages 10–18) and their families is described. An exploration is undertaken to show some of the relationships between the work of effective counseling, the set of counselors and the setting in which counseling takes place. Running away was not seen as evidence of psycho-pathology and potential criminality but as a symptom of a family's decay and a society in turmoil. The family seminar was established and an outline of a "way-of-looking-at-family" sessions evolved.

GROSSMAN, B. M. Identification and intervention for scapegoating in families with hospitalized adolescents. *Journal of Psychiatric Treatment & Evaluation*, 1979, *1*, 19–24.
This is a case report of the inpatient treatment of a 17-year-old adolescent and his family. The concept of scapegoating in adolescence is reviewed and the treatment interventions described. Treatment was by conjoint family therapy over several months as an inpatient and 18 months as an outpatient. Five year follow-up shows some improvement, but scapegoating is still evident.

HALLOWTIZ, D. Family unit treatment of character-disordered youngsters. *Social Work Practice*, Columbia University Press, 1963.
A report on the family treatment of 38 children with a diangosis of character disorder. Procedures and descriptions of the family are offered along with tabular reports of outcome. Sixty-one percent had a favorable outcome, with the treatment averaging 17 hours per case.

HARBIN, H. T. Episodic dyscontrol and family dynamics. *American Journal of Psychiatry*, 1977, *134*, 1113–1116.
Based on the author's practice on an inpatient unit that specialized in the study of aggressive behavior, he describes family dynamics and treatment when the identified patient suffers from "episodic violent behavior." The sample focuses on adolescents, most of whom had episodes of suicidal behavior and who had some evidence of "organic involvement." Typical family patterns include overly close alliances by the adolescent with one or both parents and transmission by parents of inconsistent values regarding aggression. Family therapy is seen as the preferred treatment approach and emphasizes family ways of handling dyscontrol episodes and the responsibility of the patient for his or her actions. No results are reported.

HARBIN, H. T., & MADDEN, D. J. Battered parents: A new syndrome. *American Journal of Psychiatry*, 1979, *136*, 1288–1291.
Clinical observations are presented from a pilot study of 28 families in which a parent has been assaulted or abused by a child member (usually adolescent). Disturbances in the family's authority structure, family denial, and relevant intrapsychic and cultural factors are discussed, and are used to support the conclusion that this is a distinct subtype of family violence requiring identification and special treatment.

HARMS, E. Defective parents, delinquent children. *Corrective Psychiatry*, 1962, *8*, 34–42.
A discussion of the relationship between delinquency and defective parents. In 300 cases of children stealing and lying, it was found that in 264 of them "at least on parent was, in one respect or another, deficient." Where the father is the defective factor, the boys will be found to be lying and the girls stealing. Where the mother is the defective factor, the girls will be found lying and the boys stealing.

KAZAMIAS, N. Intervening briefly in the family system. *International Journal of Social Psychiatry*, 1979, *25*, 104–109.
See Reference in Section 1.1.

KIERMAN, I. R., & PORTER, M. E. A study of behavior-disorder correlations between parents and children. *American Journal of Orthopsychiatry*, 1963, *33*, 539–541.
A report of three cases of youthful offenders who had been institutionalized, seemingly reformed, later married and reared children who eventually were referred to a child guidance clinic. In all cases, an almost perfect correlation was found between the behavior of the preadolescent child and that of his parent at the time he or she was a youthful offender.

KING, C. Family therapy with the deprived family. *Social Casework*, 1967, *48*, 203–208.
From the author's clinical work with delinquent boys at the Wiltwyck School, techniques with working with low-socioeconomic class patients and their families are described. Selection, rationale, and scope of family therapy is discussed. Basic techniques consisted of educational and therapeutic maneuvers focussed on clarity of communication, and the teaching of parent and sibling roles.

MANDELBAUM, A. A family centered approach to residential treatment. *Bulletin of the Menninger Clinic*, 1977, *41*, 27–39.
See Reference in Section 1.1.

McCORD, J., McCORD, W., & HOWARD, A. Family interaction as antecedent to the direction of male aggressiveness. *Journal of Abnormal and Social Psychology*, 1963, *66*, 239–242.
A continuation of earlier studies on delinquency, exploring the question, "What family environments tend to produce antisocial as opposed to socialized aggressiveness?" Results suggest that extreme neglect and punitiveness, coupled with a deviant-aggressive parental model, produce the former, while moderate neglect and punitiveness and ineffectual controls produce the latter.

MacGREGOR, R. The family constellation from the standpoint of various siblings. In O. Pollak, & A. S. Friedman (Eds.), *Family dynamics and female sexual delinquency*. Palo Alto: Science & Behavior Books, 1969.
A typology of families in relation to delinquency with case illustrations.

McPHERSON, S. R., BRACKELMANNS, W. E., NEWMAN, L. E. Stages in the family therapy of adolescents. *Family Process*, 1974, *13*, 77–94.
This paper describes eight consecutive stages in the family therapy process with an adolescent member. Through the "induction of crisis" or disequilibrium in the family system, therapeutic interventions are outlined through actual case representations which correspond to the eight stages. In the first stage, the crisis induced is the recognition that the individual's problem is a family problem. The induction of cirsis is then used by the therapist to produce growth in the family. It is concluded that the therapist must believe in the marital relationship and its future possibilities for health.

MEAD, D. E., & CAMPBELL, S. S. Decision-making and interaction by families with and without a drug-abusing child. *Family Process*, 1972, *11*, 487–498.
See Reference in Section 3.6.

MINUCHIN, S., AUERSWALD, E., KING, C., & RABINOWITZ, C. The study and treatment of families that produce multiple acting-out boys. *American Journal of Orthopsychiatry*, 1964, *34*, 125–134.
An early report of experience with families of delinquent boys at the Wiltwyck School for Boys in New York. The report focuses on some aspects of familial functioning, in particular "the socializing function of parental control, guidance and nurturance." The group's technique of family diagnosis and therapy with delinquent families is also presented.

MORRISON, G., & COLLIER, J. Family treatment approaches to suicidal children and adolescents. *Journal of the American Academy of Child Psychiatry*, 1969, *8*, 140–154.
See Reference in Section 4.4

ORVIN, G. H. Intensive treatment of the adolescent and his family. *Archives of General Psychiatry*, 1974, *31*, 801–806.
See Reference in Section 1.1.

RABINOWITZ, C. Therapy for underprivileged delinquent families. In O. Pollak, & A. S. Friedman (Eds.), *Family dynamics and female sexual delinquency*. Palo Alto: Science & Behavior Books, 1969.
See Reference in Section 5.7

RASHKIS, H. Depression as a manifestation of the family as an open system. *Archives of General Psychiatry*, 1968, *19*, 57–63.

Seven cases are presented in support of the idea that depression in the middle-aged is regarded as a part of a reciprocal relationship involving the adolescent and his parent. It is treated by "family psychiatry" (simultaneous treatment of one or more family members).

RAVENSCROFT, K. Normal family regression at adolescence. *American Journal of Psychiatry*, 1974, *131*, 31–35. Based on a sample of 20 families with hospitalized adolescents ranging from 14 to 19, with a wide variety of diagnostic disorders, this study examines "family regression," defined as a return to early modes of personal experience and interpersonal behavior. Data came from individual, family, and marital therapy sessions. It is believed that such regression results in mutual growth for both family and adolescents.

RINSLEY, D. B., & HALL, D. D. Psychiatric hospital treatment of adolescents. *Archives of General Psychiatry*, 1962, 7, 286–294.
A report on a study of the metaphorical communications among patients, parents, and staff members of an inpatient unit for the treatment of psychiatrically ill adolescents. Parental resistances to their children's treatment are described as they are expressed in metaphors to the staff. The child's problem of conflicting loyalties is also discussed. Optimum psychiatric treatment is accomplished only if the parents are meaningfully involved in the treatment process.

ROBEY, A., ROSENWALD, R., SNELL, J., & LEE, R. The runaway girl: A reaction to family stress. *American Journal of Orthopsychiatry*, 1964, *34*, 762–768.
A study of 42 adolescent girls who were brought before the Framingham Court Clinic. These 42 girls were referred by the court for further study and treatment. Their ages ranged from 13 to 17½. Data were obtained from "at least three interviews with parents and the girl . . . in some cases from data from treatment for as long as two years . . . and where the father was uncooperative, information was gathered from the probation officer." Typical family constellations are described. The authors state that the family dynamics revolve around "a threatened unconscious incestuous relationship with the father incited by the mother. Subsequent acting out of the unresolved Oedipal conflict through running away represents an attempted solution."

ROSMAN, B. L., MINUCHIN, S., LIEBMAN, R. Family lunch sessions: An introduction to family therapy in anorexia nervosa. *American Journal of Orthopsychiatry*, 1975, *45*, 846–853.
See Reference in Section 1.1.

RUTTER, M. Sex differences in children's responses to family stress. In E. J. Anthony, & C. Koupernik (Eds.), *The child in his family*. New York: Wiley, 1970.
A questionnaire study investigating the impact on the child of marital problems and parental psychiatric disorders. Antisocial behavior in boys is associated with disturbance in family relationships but the marriage rating bore no relation to the rate of disorder in girls. Theoretical discussion is offered.

SCHERZ, F. The crisis of adolescence in family life. *Social Casework*, 1967, *48*, 209–215.
Adolescence is seen as a time of crisis for the family as well as the patient. When behavioral symptoms come up, family treatment is indicated. The influence of grandparents in the chain of family communication that result from the sum total of all these factor's is discussed.

SERRANO, A. C., McDANALD, E. C., GOOLISHIAN, H. A. MacGREGOR, R., & RITCHIE, A. M. Adolescent maladjustment and family dynamics. *American Journal of Psychiatry*, 1962, *118*, 897–901.
A summary of the dynamics of 63 disturbed adolescents and their families. The patients are said to fall into four diagnostic categories each associated with a type of family interaction. These categories of maladjustment reaction in adolescence are: the infantile, the childish, the juvenile, and the preadolescent. The adolescent functions as a stabilizing factor in the family and when his behavior becomes unendurable to himself, the family, or society this precipitates a crisis which mobilizes the family to seek help.

SHAPIRO, R. L. The origin of adolescent disturbances in the family: Some considerations in theory and implications for therapy. In G. H. Zuk, & I. Boszormenyi-Nagy (Eds.), *Family therapy and disturbed families*. Palo Alto: Science & Behavior Books, 1967.
See Reference in Section 3.6

SOJIT, C. M. Dyadic interaction in a double bind situation. *Family Process*, 1969, *8*, 235–260.
Marital couples were exposed to a double-bind situation to contrast parents of delinquents, ulcerative colitis patients, and normal controls. The couples were exposed to the proverb "a rolling stone gathers no moss" and were asked to reach agreement about its meaning. The responses were categorized and differences found.

STABENAU, J. R., TUPIN, J., WERNER, M., & POLLIN, W. A comparative study of families of schizophrenics, delinquents, and normals. *Psychiatry*, 1965, *28*, 45–59.
A report of a comparison of five families with a schizophrenic, five families with a delinquent, and five normal families tested with the revealed differences test, the object sorting test, and the thematic apperception test. "Data from the

three different tests suggest that in the schizophrenic and delinquent families there were both individual disturbances in thought process and impaired communication at the family level . . . . There was relatively little evidence of communicaton impairment at the individual or family level in the normal families."

STIERLIN, H., A family perspective on adolescent runaways. *Archives of General Psychiatry*, 1973, *29*, 56–62.
This is a paper that discussed the family patterns of adolescent runaways, who are the identified patients. Four patterns of runaways are described: abortive runaways, schizoid runaways, casual runaways, and crisis runaways. Some runaways were expelled from the family, some kept bound to the family, and some were expected to fulfill different "missions" in the family (for example, to provide vicarious experiences for the parents). Suggestions for therapy are made.

TAICHERT, L. C. Two adolescents at risk for schizophrenia: A family case study. *International Journal of Family Therapy*, 1979, *1*, 152–162.
See Reference in Section 5.2.

TESSMAN, L. H., & KAUFMAN, I. Variations on a theme of incest. In O. Pollak, & A. S. Friedman (Eds.), *Family dynamics and female sexual delinquency*. Palo Alto: Science & Behavior Books, 1969.
A discussion of incest occuring in families with young girls, either in fantasy or fact, with case examples.

TRIBBEY, J. A. Like father, like son: A projection-displacement pattern. *Bulletin of the Menninger Clinic*, 1964, *28*, 244–251.
A study concerned with the frequency with which a son begins to take up the behavior pattern of an antisocial father. Case material was from 55 boys referred for treatment to the psychiatric diagnostic unit of a children's receiving home. Of the 55, 10 were judged by the author to have histories similar to that of their fathers. The overall family picture is "that of a boy whose parents are divorced, and whose father had a longstanding history of antisocial behavior. Before long, as the mother had always 'known,' the son begins to get into trouble." Dynamics are discussed. Poor treatment results with these cases are pointed out.

VAN DER VEEN, E., NOVAK, L. Perceived parental attitudes and family concepts of disturbed adolescents, normal siblings and normal controls. *Family Process*, 1971, *10*, 327–343.
This study tested the hypothesis that distrubed adolescents perceive poorer parental attitudes toward them (e.g., positive regard, empathic understanding, genuineness and unconditional regard) compared to normal siblings and normal controls. Two groups of 13 families (a clinic group and a nonclinic group, each with one child as an identified patient) were tested on the Barrett-Lennard's Relationship Inventory and the Family Concept Q Sort. Results showed that family disturbance is inversely related to the perception of parental positive regard, empathic understanding and genuineness; that there is less coherence among the parental and family perceptions of distrubed than nondisturbed children; and that the family satisfaction and adjustment of the children are strongly related to perceived parental attitudes, especially those of their fathers.

VOGEL, E., & BELL, N. W. The emotionally disturbed child as the family scapegoat. In N. W. Bell, & E. F. Vogel (Eds.), *A modern introduction to the family*. Glencoe: Free Press, 1960.
A discussion of families with distrubed children, in terms of the child's function as a scapegoat. Included is the selection of the child for scapegoating, the induction of him into this role, and the rationalizations.

WHITIS, P. R. The legacy of a child's suicide. *Family Process*, 1968, *7*, 159–169.
A discussion of the effect on a family of a child's suicide, illustrated by a case report. Prompt therapeutic intervention is recommended for the bereaved family.

WINTER, W. D., FERREIRA, A. J., & OLSON, J. L. Hostility themes in the family TAT. *Journal of Projective Technique and Personality Assessment*, 1966, *30*, 270–275.
Second of a series describing a diagnostic test adapted for use with families. Results were obtained from use of three TAT stories basedon three cards each, produced conjointly by 126 three-member families. Stories were scored for hostility in the story themes. Fifty families had normal children, 44 had neurotic children, 16 had schizophrenic children, and 16 had delinquent child. Normal and schizophrenic groups produced stories low in hostility, neurotics produced stories high in hostility, and delinquents scored high on one hostility variable and low on another.

WINTER, W. D., FERREIRA, A. J., & OLSON, J. L. Story sequence analysis of family TATs. *Journal of Projective Technique and Personality Assessment*, 1965, *29*, 392–397.
A group of 126 families, composed of parents and one child, were asked to produce TAT stories conjointly. The families were to make up a story based upon three TAT cards presented simultaneously to them. Three stories based on nine cards were composed by each family and scored by the Arnold system of story sequence analysis. In the sample there were 50 families with normal children. The abnormal group consisted of 44 emotionally maladjusted, 16 delinquent, and 16 schizophrenic children. The procedure successfully differentiated normal from abnormal families but the three abnormal groups did not differ from each other. The stories of abnormal families are said to be

characterized by negative attitudes toward achievement, morality, responsibility, human relationships, and reaction to adversity.

WOLD, P. Family structure in three cases of anorexia nervosa: The role of the father. *American Journal of Psychiatry*, 1973, *130*, 1394–1397.
See Reference in Section 1.1.

5.5   FAMILY MEMBER WITH NONPSYCHOTIC ADULT DISORDER

ALEXANDER, B. K., & DIBB, G. S. Opiate addicts and their parents. *Family Process*, 1975, *14*, 499–514.
The characteristics of 18 addict families are described. The relation between process and persistence of addiction is analyzed. Speculation on how addiction begins will be addressed.

ANASTASIADIS, Y. S. A study on psychopathological influence of parental environment in neurotic and schizoid patients. *Acta Psychotherapy*, 1963, *11*, 370–391.
A report from Istanbul "aiming to prove to what extent the neurotic and schizoid forms of personality defects are due to familial conflicts." Sample was 50 normals contrasted with 30 neurotics and 30 schizoid mental patients. The research method was psychotherapy and/or narcosis. Parents of mental patients are reported to be "a problem" and certain factors relating to the parent–child intervention are discussed.

ARLEN, M. S. Conjoint therapy and the corrective emotional experience. *Family Process*, 1966, *5*, 91–104.
The use of family therapy with families containing a person with severe character disorder described within a framework of providing a corrective emotional experience.

BAILEY, M. B. Alcoholism and marriage. *Quarterly Journal of Studies on Alcoholism*, 1961, *22*, 81–97.
See Reference in Section 4.1

BROWN, D. G. Homosexuality and family dynamics. *Bulletin of Menninger Clinic*, 1963, *27*, 227–232.
This review of the literature and of the author's experiences in treating male homosexuality points to a consistent pattern of family dynamics, that is, a combination of a dominating, overly intimate mother and a detached, hostile, or weak father.

BUCK, C. W., & LADD, K. L. Psychoneurosis in marital partners. *British Journal of Psychiatry*, 1965, *3*, 587–590.
A study of records of physician's diagnoses from a health insurance plan in a Canadian city. There was a definite association between the occurrence of psychoneurotic illness in husbands and wives who had been married for many years, little association for partners recently married, and no association during the premartial period. The authors interpret these findings as evidence that a process of contagion rather than mate selection determines the concordance between marital partners in psychoneurotic illness.

CHEEK, F. Family socialization techniques and deviant behavior. *Family Process*, 1966, *5*, 199–217.
A study based upon Parson's theoretical framework in which deviant behavior is related to imbalance of systems inputs and outputs at various stages of development. A sample of 120 male adults from four different groups—schizophrenics, normals, alcoholics, and reformatory inmates—were exposed to a questionnaire on family problem situations. Differences were found, and it is suggested that Parson's theoretical scheme could be translated into reinforcement theory.

DOWNING, R., COMER, N., & EBERT, J. Family dynamics in a case of Gilles de la Tourette's Syndrome. *Journal of Nervous and Mental Disease*, 1964, *138*, 548–557.
A case report of a patient with Gilles de la Tourette's syndrome in which all the members of the family were interviewed and tested with a WAIS, Rorschach, TAT, and word association test. A Leary interpersonal checklist was done in the home. From this data a dynamic, genetic, and familial formulation of the case was made.

EWING, J. A., LONG, V., & WENZEL, G. G. Concurrent group psychotherapy of alcoholic patients and their wives. *International Journal of Group Psychotherapy*, 1961, *11*, 329–338.
A description of concurrent but separate group psychotherapy meetings of alcoholic outpatients and their wives. The authors find that more husbands continue to attend group meetings if the wife is involved, and there is greater improvement in alcoholic patients whose wives also attend group meetings. The participation of the wife in the husband's drinking is examined. An example is the wife who accidentally put a shot of whiskey into her husband's iced tea after he had stopped drinking. The authors highly recommended involving the wives of alcoholics in group therapy.

FERREIRA, A. J. Family myth and homeostasis. *Archives of General Psychiatry*, 1963, *9*, 457–463.

A discussion of a particular aspect of the family relationship: the family myth, which is defined as "a series of fairly well integrated beliefs shared by all family members, concerning each other and their mutual position in the family life"—beliefs that go unchallenged despite reality distortions which they imply. Three family case reports are presented in support of the discussions; the author believes that the family myth is to the relationship what the defense is to the individual.

FERREIRA, A. J. Family myths: The convert rules of the relationship. *Confinia Psychiatrica*, 1965, *8*, 15–20.
A general discussion of the myths in families which express covert rules of family relationships. These well-systematized fabrications perform an important part as homeostatic mechanisms. "In fact, it seems that the family myth is to the family what the defense is to the individual." From family therapy observations, the author says that "pathologic families" can be overburdened with their own mythology and "seem to retain very little freedom for unrehearsed action, and to suffer in their ability to deal with new situations, and unexpected events."

GANGER, R., & SHUGART, G. The heroin addict's pseudoassertive behavior and family dynamics. *Social Casework*, 1966, *57*, 643–649.
A discussion of heroin addiction based upon interviews with addicts and family members. Addiction is said to have a function within the family. The authors conclude, "Our clinical observations and our experience with casework treatment provided to the total family unit, including the addicted person, lead us to the conviction that addiction is specifically a 'familiogenic' disease; consequently, any attempt to cure it must be undertaken within the context of the family unit."

GEHRKE, S., & KIRSCHENBAUM, M. Survival patterns in family conjoint therapy. *Family Process*, 1967, *6*, 67–80.
A discussion of 20 families studies in family therapy with the emphasis upon different patterns of emotional survival myths in the family. Three types of family are contrasted: the repressive family, the delinquent family, and the suicidal family. The survival myth had to do with the illusion of family members that they must continue their existing family ways or relating to survive psychologically.

GORAD, S. L. Communication styles and interaction of alcoholics and their wives. *Family Process*, 1971, *10*, 475–489.
Based on an interpersonal interactional theory of alcoholism, 20 normal couples were compared with 20 couples with an alcoholic husband as demonstrated in a game-playing situation. Couples were matched as to age, length of marriage, number of children, ethnic background, and religion. Statistical control measures were employed for differences in social class and education. The 3 hypotheses tested were: (1) the alcoholic uses a responsibility-avoidance style of communication with his wife; (2) the wife of the alcoholic has a responsibility-accepting style of communication with her husband; (3) the communication between the alcoholic husband and his wife does not result in the mutual benefit of the couple but rather results in rigidity or escalation. Results indicate that all 3 hypotheses were confirmed. Some additional ramifications of this experiment and its results are discussed briefly.

KLAGSBRUN, M., & DAVIS, D. I. Substance abuse and family interaction. *Family Process*, 1977, *16*, 149–173.
See Reference in Section 6.

MACHOTKA, P., PITTMAN, F. S., & FLOMENHAFT, K. Incest as a family affair. *Family Process*, 1967, *6*, 98–116.
A discussion of incest from the point of view of the whole family. Two cases of father–daughter incest and one of sibling incest are discussed with the emphasis upon the crucial role of the nonparticipating member. the concerted denial of the incest, and where the focus of therapy should be.

PITTMAN, F., LANGSLEY, D., & DeYOUNG, C. Work and school phobia: A family approach to treatment. *American Journal of Psychiatry*, 1968, *124*, 1535–1541.
Eleven cases of work phobia (tha patient experiencing overt anxiety associated with having to go to work or staying at work) are thought of as being "the adult form of school phobia," Treatment goal is to allow the wife or mother to allow the man to separate. One-year follow-up shows that 5 cases treated with conjoint family therapy were able to return to work; the 6 cases in long-term individual therapy had not.

RAPOPORT, R. The family and psychiatric treatment. *Psychiatry*, 1960, *23*, 53–62.
A conceptual framework for analyzing family relationships and role performance of psychiatric patients applied to a case. Three areas are considered important in conceptualizing role difficulties: familial position, personal and social norms, and personality factors. This framework is applied to a case presented in detail.

RYLE, A., & HAMILTON, M. Neurosis in fifty married couples. *Journal of Mental Science*, 1962, *108*, 265–273.
An investigation of 50 working class marital couples to record the prevalence of neurosis as indicated by the Cornell medical index, the reocrds of the general practitioner with whom the families were registered, and the home interviews of a psychiatric social worker. The information from these sources was compared and the presence of neurosis was correlated with some aspects of adverse childhood experience, marital adjustment, consumer status, and social integration.

SCHEFLEN, A. E. Regressive one-to-one relationships *Psychiatric Quarterly*, 1960, *34*, 692–709.
A description of regressive attachments between two individuals. The characteristics of these "guresom twosomes" are: limitations of relatedness to others, decreasing gratification within the relationship, and the maintenance of the attachment by mutual exploitation of the partner's anxieties by such means as threats of desertion and arousal of guilt. Several variations of this type of relationship are presented and illustrated with four case histories involving differing sex and age combinations. There is a discussion of differentiating between neurotic and non-neurotic one-to-one relationships.

SCHWARTZMAN, J. The addict, abstinence, and the family. *American Journal of Psychiatry*, 1975, *132*, 154–157.
An uncontrolled clinical study attempted to define the family dynamics involved in drug abuse and subsequent abstinence. Sample was 21 white, working-class families with the identified patient having either heroin or barbiturate addiciton. Data obtained from the entire family during family theray indicate that those families who were functioning better were able to tolerate abstinence of the identified patient, while families with other conflicts or inadequate functioning tended to reinforce the addiction.

SCHWARTZMAN, J., & BOKOS, P. Methadone maintenance: The addict's family recreated. *International Journal of Family Therapy*, 1979, *1*, 338–355.
Based on observations of 100 heroin addicts and their families in four state-run methadone maintenance clinics, it is speculated that families gave a covert message to "be out of control" and that the methadone maintenance treatment system continues this message. Failures of abstinence are seen as validating the "flaw" in the addict, rather than paradoxes in the system.

SNELL, J., ROSENWALD, R., & ROBEY, A. The wifebeater's wife, a study of family interaction. *Archives of General Psychiatry*, 1964, *11*, 107–113.
A study of 37 families in which men were charged by their wives with assault and battery and who were referred to one of the psychiatric clinics which serve the courts of Massachusetts. Twelve of the families were studied in detail (both husband and wife being seen for three or more interviews). Four wives were in individual psychotherapy for more than 18 months. In addition, some group therapy and "couple therapy" was attempted. A typical family structure is described: husband is passive, indecisive, and sexually inadequate: wife aggressive, masculine, frigid, and masochistic; relationship between the two characterized by alternation of passive and aggressive roles; an adolescent son may upset the equilibrium.

STANTON, M. D. The addict as savior: Heroin, death and the family. *Family Process*, 1977, *16*, 191–197.
This paper interprets the high mortality rate among drug addicts as a suicidal phenomenon with a family basis. The addict's death is seen as a noble, self-sacrificing gesture that secures him into a permanent bonding position within the family system. Two case examples illustrate the author's thesis.

STEINGLASS, P. Experimenting with family treatment approaches to alcoholism 1950–1975: A review. *Family Process*, 1976, *15*, 97–123.
After reviewing and assessing the clinical and experimental literature of the last 25 years, Dr. Steinglass suggests two issues for consideration: (1) the reluctance of family therapists to treat alcoholic families, and (2) the evidence of positive results from family therapy with alcoholic families. He concludes by suggesting a family systems approach for middle to upper class, intact families and a traditional medical model approach for individual alcoholics.

TABACHNICK, N. Interpersonal relations in suicidal attempts. *Archives of General Psychiatry*, 1961, *4*, 42–47.
A description of the interpersonal context, largely familial, of the attempted suicide: "a product of reflection of over 100 cases of suicidal attempts studied by a team of social scientists at the Suicide Prevention Center at Los Angeles." One could deduce from the fact that attempted suicides are dependent and masochistic that the significant individuals in their environment would also be dependent and masochistic. Observation supports such an expectation, and in numerous situaions both members of the unit are suicidal. Three cases are presented. Treatment suggestions are separation by hospitalization, and intervention to decrease the mutual dependence.

TITCHENER, J. L., D'ZMURA, T., GOLDEN, M., & EMERSON, R. Family transaction and derivation of individuality. *Family Process*, 1963, *2*, 95–120.
A report of an experimental method in research on family interaction. Subjects were families of patients who applied because of neurotic symptoms. Task was for the family to "reconcile their differences in opinion previously revealed in a questionnaire administered to each family member." The observers used tapes, films, and notes of direct observation to record the family transactions. The authors believe that "a young person elaborates an identity and develops his sense of it from the communicative interplay of the family." A case is presented in detail to illustrate.

VERNON, E., KORNBLIT, A., MALFE, R., & SLUZKI, C. E. Estructures de conducta y sistermas de comunicacion social. (Conduct structures and systems of social communication). *Acta Psiquiatrica Y Psicologica Argentian*, 1963, *9*, 297.
A conceptual model for the sociological study of psychoneurosis is described, including three strategic levels:

individual, familial (group structure), and social stratification, including cultural structures. The recurrence of certain conduct structures in an individual, that is, of generalized ways of interaction, is the result of a meta-communicative process of learning, i.e., deutero-learning. The presence of recurrent ways of learning in a family group is a function of the family organization as communication system. The persistence of certain types of communication within the family group is a function of the sociocultural context which influences the family.

VIDAL, G. PRECE, G., & SMULEVER, M. Convivencia y trastorno mental. *Acta Psiquiatrica Y Psicologica de America Latina*, 1969, *15*, 55–65.
A sample of 1,322 patients were studied for family size, birth order of the patient, and family integrity (number of years the offspring lived together with both parents).The hypothesis was that "the higher the amount of the family relationship the lower the severity of the mentla disorder." Neurotice were expected to show smaller families, first birth order positions, and intact families, while psychotics would show larger families, last birth order, positions, and disrupted families. The hypothesis about neurotics was confirmed but that about psychotics was only partially confirmed.

WEITZMAN, E. L., SHAMOIAN, C. A., & GOLOSOW, N. Family dynamics in males transsexualism. *Psychosomatic Medicine*, 1971, *33*, 289–299.
This is a case report describing the family dynamics in male transsexualism. Data were derived from both individual and family interviews over a 30-month period. Mother was characterized as depressed and masochistic, father as bisexual and emotionally labile. Childrearing patterns were those of overcloseness and overstimulation by the parents. The identified patient wanted to become a female as an adolescent; simultaneously, he showed a number of psychotic symptoms such as loosening of associations and delusional and paranoid thinking. Hypotheses as to the family dynamics are discussed.

WHITAKER, C. Family treatment of a psychopathic personality. *Comprehensive Psychiatry*, 1966, *7*, 397–402.
From part of a summary of treatment of a woman—identified as having "eight years of treatment, three psychotherpists, two near successes of suicide, and two successful divorces,"—and her family, the author has evolved a theory of the development of the psychopathic personality. The child divides a weak parental relationship and then adopts this approach to all situations in later life. A team approach is suggested.

WYATT, G. L., & HERZAN, H. M. Therapy with stuttering children and their mothers. *American Journal of Orthopsychiatry*, 1962, *32*, 645–659.
A study of the therapy of stuttering children, indicating that therapy should start from a sound theory of the interpersonal aspects of language learning in children. The techniques should be adapted to the age of the child, and the mother should be included in the treatment program. Twenty-six children were included in the sample with some children seen in the presence of their mothers and some seen separately. Stuttering was considered to be the result of a disruption of the complementary patterns of verbal interaction between mother and child.

5.6   FAMILY AND PHYSICAL ILLNESS

ANTHONY, E. The impact of mental and physical illness on family life. *American Journal of Psychiatry*, 1970, *127*, 138–146.
In a sample of schizophrenics, manic-depressive and patients with tuberculosis, the author attempted to assess the impact of their illness on the family. Method was to live with the family for a week; number of families is unspecified. Following emotional illness, there is a disruption in family members and the family as a whole, followed by re-integration or disintegration, depending on the family's premorbid adjustment, the previous socioeconomic and cultural level, as well as the severity of the illness. Medical illness creates a fear of "contamination" and this causes subsequent disturbances in the interpersonal relationships.

ANTHONY, E. J. The mutative impact of serious mental and physical illness in a parent on family life. In E. J. Anthony, & C. Koupernik (Eds.), *The child in his family*. New York: Wiley, 1970.
A report of a study of families where a parent figure has succumbed to a serious mental or physical disorder necessitating hospitalization. Various views are offered of such illness: as a disruption of family roles, as a crisis in accommodation, as a disconnection, and as a challenge. Family members were interviewed individually and in dyads and triads.

BOSWELL, J., LEWIS, C., FREEMAN, D., & CLARK, K. Hyperthyroid children: Individual and family dynamics. *Journal of the American Academy of Child Psychiatry*, 1967, *6*, 64–85.
A retrosepctive study describing twelve children(ten girls, two boys; six black, six white; four lower-, eight middle-class) who developed hyperthyroidism between the ages of four and 14. Data were gathered from individual psychiatric interviews, psychologic tests, parents, and from social agencies—but not from family interviews. Parents

were found to have given minimal care and expected maximum self-sufficiency from the child. Children were found to be fixated at a pregenital stage.

BRANDAN, W., TALMADGE, J., & VAN SICKLE, G. Familial communicational patterns of a patient with Gilles de la Tourette Syndrome. *Journal of Nervous and Mental Disease*, 1972, *154*, 60–68.
This is an experimental study attempting to document the hypothesis that verbal behavior could be correlated with diffeences in posture of participants in a family therapy session. Method was to film a family including mother, father, and identified patient, who had Gilles de la Tourette Syndrome. Verbal and nonverbal coding systems were set up and results analyzed, using the Chi Square Test. Results indicated that measurements of adequacy and responsibility in verbalizations were correlated with congruent time periods (those in which at least two participants in conversation were an identical or mirror image position for the given postural modality of the study). There were no significant results obtained for interpersonal word references, positive-negative verb forms, content phrases, or affect-laden phrases.

BURSTEN, B. Family dynamics, The sick role, and medical hospital admissions. *Family Process*, 1965, *4*, 206–216.
A discussion of how the medical hospital may be used in the service of family patterns. There may be no organic difficulty or an organic difficulty can be combined with psychosocial factors to resolve a family conflict. Case examples are given.

CRISP, A., & TOMS, D. Primary anorexia nervosa or a weight phobia in the male: Report of 13 cases. *British Journal of Medicine*, 1972, *1*, 334–337.
Thirteen male patients with anorexia nervosa are described and have the same characteristics as with previously described female patients. The syndrome was found to be associated with a high degree of family psychopathology and marital difficulty.

DAVIES, N. H., & HANSEN, E. Family focus: A transitional cottage in an acute-care hospital. *Family Process*, 1974, *13*, 481–488.
This paper illustrates with three case examples, the "Family Focus" program developed in 1971 and active at Stanford Hospital. The program consisted of patients in need of physical therapy and who were willing to participate in this live-in program. The patient and his family reside in a specially constructed "cottage" for up to a three day period. Family members are taught to assist the patient in caring for his/her disability. This mode of intervention could serve as a model for professionals other than physical therapists, in either the medical and/or psychiatric hospital settings.

DYSINGER, R. H. A family perspective on the diagnosis of individual members. *American Journal of Orthopsychiatry*, 1961, *31*, 61–68.
A discussion of the characteristic view of health matters by members of families containing a schizophrenic hospitalized as part of the Bowen study. Typically, mother, father and identified patient are intensely involved emotionally over health issues. Siblings are not included in the same way. Confusion over feelings, physical symptoms, and definite illness exists, and attempts to do something effective about a health matter are often stalemated. Intense emotional problem in the parental relationship is handled through a set of mechanisms that operate to support an inaccurate assumption that the problem is the health of one child. The development of psychosis in the child demonstrates the inefficiency of this displacement and also can become a focus for the perpetuation of the family mechanisms.

GREENBLUM, J. The control of sick care functions in the hospitalization of a child: Family vs. hospital. *Journal of Health and Human Behavior*, 1961, *2*, 32–38.
The author hypothesizes that parents are more willing to give up control of instrumental functions involved in the sickness situation (medical tasks associated with care and treatment of illness) than of the associated functions (merging socio-emotional needs and socializing into desirable behavior). Interviews were conducted with 18 children suffering from paralytic polio and their parents. Fourteen families participated in two repeat interviews. The degree of dissatisfaction with various aspects of hospital care was taken as an index of resistance to transfer of parental control. In the acute phase of illness dissatisfaction is greatest regarding primary functions, but decreases in the convalescent phase. Dissatisfaction regarding instrumental functions is low in the acute phase, and increases in the convalescent phase, especially in regard to providing of medical information. Some problems arising in the posthospital period from the "trained incapacities" the child acquires through hospital experience are discussed.

GOLDBERG, E. Difficulties encountered in assessing family attitudes. *Journal of Psychosomatic Research*, 1964, *8*, 229–234.
See Reference in Section 3.5

GROLNICK, L. A family perspective of psychosomatic factors in illness: A review of the literature. *Family Process*, 1972, *11*, 457–486.
See Reference in Section 6.

GROTJAHN, M. The aim and technique of psychiatric family consultations. In W. Mendell, & P. Solomon (Eds.), *The psychiatric consultation*. New York: Grune & Stratton, 1968.
Two case reports are presented in support of a technique of consultation in which the entire family is seen along with a referring physician in cases where the identified patient has a medical problem. The consultation takes place in the internist's office. Further management is left to the family and referring physician. Family psychopathology is usually the cause of the identified patient's problems.

HUBERTY, D. J. Adapting to illness through family groups. *International Journal of Psychiatric Medicine*, 1974, *5*, 231–242.
Based on the author's experience in a medical setting working with "healthy" families in which the identified patient has a chronic physical illness such as diabetes, cancer, or a "cardiac" problem, it is felt that involving the families in "counseling groups" is useful in dealing with the chronic illness. Anxiety of patients and families is reduced and "all members can function better within the limitations of the physical illness."

HOROWITZ, L. Treatment of the family with a dying member. *Family Process*, 1975, *14*, 95–106.
The focus of this report is on the treatment of two families with dying members. The therapist utilized her own life threatening experience as transferential and countertransferential elements in the therapeutic process.

HOEBEL, F. C. Brief family interactional therapy in management of cardiac-related high-risk behaviors. *Journal of Family Practice*, 1976, *3*, 613–618.
This is a study of the use of couple therapy to help patients who must modify their lifestyle to prevent worsening of a cardiac condition. Nine patients and their wives were seen after identifying the specific behaviors that required change. Results showed that the necessary changes were achieved in seven cases.

JACKSON, D. D. Family practice: A comprehensive medical approach. *Comprehensive Psychiatry*, 1966, *7*, 338–344.
The relationship of nonfunctional illness and the family is examined. Patterns of seeking medical care by families are listed; familial factors in relation to specific illness, e. g., ulcerative colitis and the "restrictive family" are discussed; and the family physician is encouraged to think of the patient's illness with the knowledge of the family as a whole.

JACKSON, D., & YALOM, I. Family research on the problem of ulcerative colitis. *Archives of General Psychiatry*, 1966, *15*, 410–418.
This study attempts to correlate parental behavior and the onset of ulcerative colitis. Eight patients were intensively studied using 4 to 20 conjoint family therapy 90-minute sessions, which were tape-recorded. Identified patients were all children ranging in ages from 7–17. Sociality of the family was limited, and they related in a "psuedo-mutual" fashion. Suggestions for further study were made.

JAFFE, D. T. The role of family therapy in treating physical illness. *Hospital & Community Psychiatry*, 1978, *29*, 169–174.
This is an essay based on clinical experience with medical patients of family stress as a causal factor in physicl illness. Several case examples are given to illustrate the effect of short term family therapy on such problems as scapegoating and a "learning for health" program is described.

LANGSLEY, D. G. psychology of a doomed family. *American Journal of Psychotherapy*, 1961, *15*, (4) 531–538.
A report on a family suffering from an inherited renal disorder, all of whom face premature death. Of ten siblings, nine have been observed (six by a psychiatrist). Their psychological defenses are discussed, with emphasis upon why one of them was more mature in facing death than were the others.

LANTZ, J. E. Extreme itching treated by a family systems approach. *International Journal of Family Therapy*, 1979, *1*, 244–253.
A case study is presented in which the identified patient was a sixteen year old with severe pruritis and scratching. It was thought to be triggered by parental conflict, so the treatment focused on this issue in sixteen weekly sessions. Outcome was assessed by monitoring the rate of scratching which declined steadily to zero by the fourteenth session, and was still absent at 6 month follow-up.

LIEBMAN, R., MINUCHIN, S., & BAKER, L. The role of the family in the treatment of anorexia nervosa. *Journal of Child Psychiatry*, 1974, *13*, 264–274.
This is one of a series of papers describing the "family" approach to treatment of anorexia nervosa. The treatment involves operant reinforcement techniques plus "structural family therapy." This particular report goes into detail about the process of a case and the application of the treatment. An 18-month follow-up indicated the identified patient continued to be symptom-free.

LIEBMAN, R., MINUCHIN, S., & BAKER, L. The use of structural family therapy in the treatment of intractable asthma. *American Journal of Psychiatry*, 1974, *131*, 535–540.
This is an uncontrolled clinical report of the use of family therapy in the treatment of selected families with an identified patient with intractable asthma. The family characteristics and dynamics are evaluated, and a family

treatment program in terms of goals, process, and techniques are described. Results indicated that all patients-families and individuals-improved over pretreatment intervention over a period of time ranging from 10 to 22 months.

LINTON, H. BERLE, B. B., GROSS, M., & JACKSON, E. Reaction of children within family groups as measured by the Bene-Anthony Tests. *Journal of Mental Science*, 1962, *107*, 308–325.
A study of 69 children in 28 families who were given the Bene-Anthony family relations test in which they were asked to match statements with representatives of family members. The test scores were rated high or low on six qualitative variables in family life. The child rated as sick by pediatrician and nurse was more involved with parent of the opposite sex, and in families with episodes of illness the children express a marked preference for mother. Significant patterns were found in boys and girls of different age groups and in the group as a whole.

LISS, J., & SHARMA, C. Multi-generational dynamics in a case of ulcerative colitis. *The Psychiatric Quarterly*, 1970, *44*, 461–475.
One case is presented in support of the notion that ulcerative colitis is an illness due to family pathology. In this case, the symptoms reflected "threatened loss of the symbiotic relationship with the mother." There is a review of the literature of ulcerative colitis.

MABREY, J. H. Medicine and the family. In P. H. Glasser, & L. N. Glasser (Eds.), *Families in crisis*. New York: Harper & Row, 1970.
A consideration of family relationships in the promotion of health and the treatment of illness. Included are medicine and family functioning, the family as a unit in medical care, and the family's nursing function.

MacNAMARA, M. Family stress before and after renal homotransplantation. *Social Work*, 1969, *14*, 89–98.
A renal transplantation unit found that involving the families of both donors and recipients prior to the transplant will avert complicated crises in the families and the patients.

MAURIN, J., & SCHENKEL, J. A study of the family unit's response to hemodialysis. *Journal of Psychosomatic Research*, 1976, *20*, 163–168.
This is a descriptive study of family response to hemodialysis. Twenty families were studied using the Conjoint Family Diagnostic Interview and the Family Index of Tension. Results showed that the identified patient had great control in the family, and little regard for the needs of others. There was little open communication and a general withdrawal from social life.

McNICHOL, K. N., WILLIAMS, H. E., ALLAN, J., & McANDREW, I. Spectrum of asthma in children. III: Psychological and social components. *British Medical Journal*, 1973, *4*, 16–20.
This is one of a series of papers whose purpose is to define the range, natural history, and clinical and physiologic manifestations of asthma in children up to 14 years of age. This report compares the physiological characteristics of 350 families of asthmatic children, whose degree of illness was of varying severity, with 82 controls. The data were gathered by a standardized questionnaire interviewing mother and child separately and by a school questionnaire given to teachers. Interviews were done at 7, 10, and 14 years. Results indicate that behavioral disturbances, maternal overconcern, and family stress were present only in the most severe cases. There were no differences in socioeconomic conditions between the asthmatic children and the controls.

MARSHALL, J. R., & NEILL, J. The removal of a psychosomatic symptom: Effects on the marriage. *Family Process*, 1977, *16*, 273–280.
The study examines the effects on the marriages of 12 patients who underwent intestinal surgery for extreme obesity. Marked conflict and disruption were observed. Most striking were changes in the areas of sexuality and dependence/independence parameters. The presence of marked obesity in one partner appeared to serve as a stabilizing function for the marital system, often protecting the spouse by denying a marital problem and thereby avoiding resolution. The symptom removal promoted marked affective changes in one partner that led to disruption and disorganization of the relationship.

McCORD, W., McCORD, J., & VERDEN, P. Familial correlates of psychosomatic symptoms in male children. *Journal of Health and Human Behaviors*, 1960, *1*, 192–199.
Further study of data from the Cambridge-Somerville Youth Study (1935–1945). Data were available on the physical condition of youths, their family backgrounds, and delinquent activities. Hypotheses that children with psychosomatic disorders would have been raised in families with a high degree of interpersonal stress and with anxious, hypochondriacal, symptom-ridden parents were not confirmed. But when boys were cross-classified as extropunitive or intropunitive, some regularities are observed. It is concluded that degree of extropunitiveness and nature of parental "sick-role" models are variables which affect childhood diseases.

MEISSNER, W. W. Family dynamics and psychosomatic processes. *Family Process*, 1966, *5*, 142–161.
A discussion of the impact of patterns of family interaction on patterns of physical health and illness, with a review of the literature.

MEISSNER, W. W. Family process and psychosomatic disease. *International Journal of Psychiatry in Medicine*, 1974, 5, 411–431.
Based on an extensive review of the literature (164 references), a theory of psychophysiologic disorders based on family pathology is elaborated. It is hypothesized that when a family system goes into strong disequilibrium, the individual members also go into disequilibrium. In ways that are not understood but are in some way related to "family affect," psychosomatic symptoms may be precipitated in individual members.

MILLER, J. Cognitive dissonance in modifying families' perceptions. *American Journal of Nursing*, 1974, 74, 1468–1470.
Thus is a clinical essay from the author's experience as a researcher interviewing spouses of surgical patients. Based on such experience, the author suggests that nurses who encounter unrealistic views of the identified patient's illness should work with the rest of the family by introducing a dissonant notion (i.e., a notion that is different from the family's experience). This will result in family change.

MINUCHIN, S. The use of an ecological framework in the treatment of a child. In E. J. Anthony & C. Koupernik (Eds.), *The child in his family*. New York: Wiley, 1970.
A discussion of the three elements in the study of the child: the child as an individual, in his environment, and the linkage between. The ecological point is discussed. A case of an adolescent with *anorexia nervosa* is examined in terms of his family and the family therapy approach to the problem.

MINUCHIN, S., & BARCAI, A. Therapeutically induced family crisis. In J. Masserman, *Childhood and adolescence, science and psychoanalysis* (Vol. XIV). New York: Grune & Stratton, 1969.
A report on a family treatment approach where a crisis is induced and resolved. A family with a child regularly hospitalized for diabetic acidosis was treated by assigning tasks which induced a crisis situation to which the family members had to respond by changing.

PALAZZOLI, M. S., BOSCOLO, L., CECCHIN, G. F., et al: The treatment of children through brief therapy of their parents. *Family Process*, 1974, 13, 429–442.
This paper reports on the successful resolution of encopresis and anorexia respectively, in two small children through brief therapy with their parents. The therapeutic techniques utilized are based on systems theory and the cybernetic model. The pros and cons of the treatment process and resulting rapid behavior changes are discussed.

PECK, B. B. Physical medicine and family dynamics: The dialectics of rehabilitation. *Family Process*, 1974, 13, 469–479.
In this paper, the relationship between illness, the rehabilitation process and the impact the family has on this process is examined. Through a clinical-casework study conducted in three medical settings over a 2-year period, four familial patterns of interaction were identified. Four case examples illustrating each one is discussed in terms of specific dynamics, key persons and the resultant rehabilitation process. The major finding of the study is that if patient rehabilitation failed, usually another or other family members were uncooperative. More effective ways to engage the family in the treatment of the disabled are suggested.

PURCELL, K., & METZ, S. R. Distinctions between subgroups of asthmatic children: Some parent attitude variables related to age of onset of asthma. *Journal of Psychosomatic Research*, 1962, 6, 251–258.
A continuation of the authors' previous work with asthmatic children at the Children's Asthma Research Institute and Hospital in Denver. Previous work had tentatively classified these 86 children as "steroid dependent" and "rapidly remitting" in terms of their clinical course once at the hospital and separated from home. Parents' attitudes were measured using the parent attitude research instrument. Positive findings of this study were that within the group of rapidly remitting children relatively late age of onset (after 12–18 months) was associated with autocratic and restrictive attitudes on the part of their mothers. These findings were not found in other group.

ROSENSTOCK, H. A. & CAMBOR, C. G. Family therapy approach to incapacitating migraine. *International Journal of Family Therapy*, 1979, 1, 46–55.
This is a case report on a nine year old boy with migraine headaches treated with family therapy for six months and then the parents treated with family therapy for an additional ten months (after all available medical treatment had failed). Goals were to (1) identify the triggers for the headaches and eliminate them, (2) improve school functioning, and (3) improve family functioning in relation to communication, strictness, and scapegoating. These were achieved and the patient remained asymptomatic at 5-year follow-up. A review of the literature on psychotherapy of migraines is included.

SERRANO, A. C., & WILSON, N. S. Family therapy in the treatment of the brain-damaged child. *Diseases of the Nervous System*, 1963, 24, 732–735.
The authors review their experiences with 34 children diagnosed as having organic brain syndromes with behavior disorders. They emphasize including the evaluation of the total family constellation (here using their multiple impact

therapy method previously reported on), in addition to the more traditional physical and psychological studies of the child.

SHAPIRO, R. J., & HARRIS, R. I. Family therapy in treatment of the deaf: A case report. *Family Process*, 1976, *15*, 83–96.
This is a case presentation of a family with a deaf member. The deaf member had been unsuccessfully treated individually for problems with impulsive behavior, lack of insight, communication deficits and poor motivation. Family counseling was initiated and problems of guilt, denial, and parental conflicts quickly emerged suggesting that the whole family system was in need of and receptive to intervention. The authors conclude after working for two years with families with deaf member that family therapy has advantages over other forms of therapy.

SHEPARD, K. F., BARSOTTI, L. M. Family focus–transitional health care. *Nursing Outlook*, 1975, *23*, 574–577.
The identified patients are those with problems related to physical therapy. The clinical notion behind this study is that the family should get involved with the treatment of the patient *before* the patient is discharged from the hospital. Families move on the hospital grounds into a special cottage designed for this purpose for a two-day, two-night span. Problems and advantages are discussed using case reports to illustrate.

SIMMONS, R., HICKEY, K., KJELLSTRAND, C. & SIMMONS, R. L. Family tension in the search for a kidney donor. *Journal of the American Medical Association*, 1971, *215*, 909–910.
See Reference in Section 4.4.

SIMMONS, R., & KLEIN, S. Family noncommunications: A search for kidney donors. *American Journal of Psychiatry*, 1972, *129*, 687–692.
See Reference in Section 4.4.

SKELTON, M., & DOMINIAN, J. Psychological stress in wives of patients with myocardial infarction. *British Journal of Medicine*, 1973, *2*, 101–103.
This is a clinical study of the reactions of wives to the myocardial infarction of their husbands. Sample was 65 wives of patiens admitted to a general hospital who were interviewed without their spouses. Results indicated that during the immediate postcoronary period, the wives felt depressed and guilty and felt their marriages were more problematic. At 1-year follow-up, most of these problems had disappeared.

SLIVKIN, S. E. Death and living: A family approach. *American Journal of Psychoanalysis*, 1977, *37*, 317–323.
This is a clinical paper on the treatment of families with a terminally ill member. Three case reports from a veteran's hospital are presented to illustrate the effects of this stres on the family system. The role of the psychiatrist in fostering communication between the patient, family and medical team is found to be particularly important.

SOJIT, C. M. Dyadic interaction in a double bind situation. *Family Process*, 1969, *8*, 235–260.
Marital couples were exposed to a double-bind situation to contrast parents of delinquents, ulcerative colitis patients, and normal controls. The couples were exposed to the proverb "a rolling stone gathers no moss" and were asked to reach agreement about its meaning. The responses were categorized and differences found.

STEELE, T. E., FINKELSTEIN, S. H. & FINKELSTEIN, F. O. Hemodialysis patients and spouses, marital discord, sexual problems, and depression. *Journal of Nervous and Mental Disease*, 1976, *162*, 225–237.
This is a clinical description of marital dynamics and problems when the identified patient is on demodialysis. Method was to use a sample of 17 chronic hemodialysis patients (10 men, 7 women) and their spouses currently in treatment at two hospitals using individual, self-rating instruments. Results indicated that while couples rated their degree of marital discord as low, the investigators rated it as high—with a high prevalence of sexual problems. Patient's depression scores were comparable to those of psychiatric patients, while spouses' depression scores resembled those of normals.

STRELTZER, J. et al. The spouse's role in home hemodialysis. *Archives of General Psychiatry*, 1976, *33*, 55–58.
This is a clinical report of 16 married couples in which a spouse was receiving home dialysis. Advantages and disadvantages of home dialysis (versus hospital dialysis) are discussed, and the case reports suggest that success or failure depend upon the role of the spouse. For example, there is an increased risk of failure if the spouse is dependent upon the home dialysis patient. Treatment implications are discussed.

SUMMERS, F. Severe hypertension treated successfully by marital psychotherapy. *American Journal of Psychiatry*, 1978, *135*, 989–990.
One case example was presented in support of the thesis that marital therapy is useful in treating medication-refractory hypertension.

TILLER, J. W. G. Brief family therapy for childhood tic syndrome. *Family Process*, 1978, *17*, 217–223.

This paper reports on the use of brief analytically oriented family therapy in the treatment of multiple tics. The identified patient was an eight year old girl with tics of the facial, thoracic, and upper limb musculature. The patient remained asymptomatic for a nine month followup period. Success is related to the rapidity of intervention, before rigid symptom and relationship patterns are instituted. Other favorable factors in the prognosis include: responsiveness of tics to family change, vulnerability factors in the child, intrafamilial emotional problems, changing dynamic responses in both child and family.

TITCHENER, J. L., RISKIN, J, & EMERSON, R. The family in psychosomatic process: A case report illustrating a method of psychosomatic research. *Psychosomatic Medicine*, 1960, *22*, 127–142.
A report of a study of a family in which one son developed ulcerative colitis. The mother-child symbiosis is looked at in terms of the total family milieu. A detailed case history is presented, and it is suggested that the object relations aspect of psychosomatic hypotheses can be more comprehensively investigated by inquiry into the patterns of interlocking relationships in the family.

TREUSCH, J., & GROTJAHN, M Psychiatric family consultations, the practical approach in family practice for the personal physician. *Annals of Internal Medicine*, 1967, *66*, 295–300.
In psychiatric consultations for patients with psychosomatic problems, the focus once was on the presence of the psychiatrist in the internist's office with the internist in charge. However, over the years it was recognized that the family seemed to be etiologic "in almost all psychiatric conditions likely to occur" in the internist's office. Techniques of the family consultation are described.

WEAKLAND, J. H. "Family somatics"—A neglected edge. *Family Process*, 1977, *16*, 263–272.
This paper is a plea for the relevance of interactional approaches to somatic illness, both in reference to its causation as well as its prognosis and outcome.

WELLISCH, D. K. Adolescent acting out when a parent has cancer. *International Journal of Family Therapy*, 1979, *1*, 230–241.
See Reference in Section 4.4.

WHITE, M. Structural and strategic approaches to psychosomatic families. *Family Process*, 1979, *18*, 303–314.
This paper presents a practical guide to working with psychosomatic families. Psychosomatic manifestations are viewed as a result of triangulation in a couple with difficulties with fusion and distance. Effective interventions must recognize the child's role in maintaining the cohesion of the family group. The program described was effective with ten families in the sample; symptom control was established withing one to two weeks and symptom-free status between one to five weeks. In a followup of 15 to 24 months, there was minimal recurrence in three of the sample, and two of these families viewed the recurrence as an opportunity to practice their new skills.

WIKRAN, R., FALEIDE, A., & BLAKAR, R. M. Communication in the family of the asthmatic child: An experimental approach. *Acta Psychiatrica Scandinavica*, 1978, *57*, 11–26.
This is an experimental study of the communication patterns and effectiveness of parents of asthmatic children (N = 17) versus controls (N = 5). The couples were given Blakar's conflict-road map test and the consensual solutions analyzed qualitatively. One-third of the asthmatice group showed significantly less effective communication (marked by egocentricity, vagueness, pretense and pseudoagreement) compared to the other two-thirds or to the control group. Seventy-nine references are included.

5.7 LOW SOCIOECONOMIC CLASS FAMILIES

ADAMS, P. Functions of the lower-class partial family. *American Journal of Psychiatry*, 1973, *130*, 200–203.
This is a study describing characteristics of the partial (defined as fatherless) family. This type of family functions as a viable form fulfilling many of the same functions as a complete family, but the sexual conjugal relationship is missing, there is a continual lack of security, children learn little of "power" relationships and constantly feel derogated and ill at ease.

ATTNEAVE, C. L. Therapy in tribal settings and urban network intervention. *Family Process*, 1969, *8*, 192–210.
A comparison of network therapy and interventions in a network-clan of a tribal minority culture. An example of treatment with an Indian tribe is contrasted with urban network treatment where the clanlike social structure must be reconstituted.

BARD, M., & BERKOWITZ, B. A community psychology consultation program in police family crisis intervention: Preliminary impressions. *International Journal of Social Psychiatry*, 1969, *15*, 209–215.

The second in a series of reports describing training of police in family crisis intervention with low socioeconomic class patients. Rationale for the program, methods of selection, and techniques of training (which include use of family crisis laboratory demonstrations and "human relations workshops") are presented.

BEHRENS, M. Brief home visits by the clinic therapist in the treatment of lower-class patients. *American Journal of Psychiatry*, 1967, *124*, 371–375.
A paper reviewing the author's experience with home visits. The sample was 80 patients attending an outpatient clinic. These were chronic schizophrenics, the majority black and female of low socioeconomic class with certain exceptions. Home visits were made on the average of one home visit per year per patient. At first the visits were done only at times of crisis situations, later routinely. The visits have been found useful in obtaining data about the patient and family, improving the relationship between patient and therapist, and in decreasing rehospitalizations.

BEHRENS, M., ROSENTHAL, A. J., & CHODOFF, P. Communication in lower-class families of schizophrenics. *Archives of General Psychiatry*, 1968, *18*, 689–696.
The second part of a study of low-socioeconomic families of schizophrenics. The study was done in the home where the family was focussed upon a task, particularly the Rorschach. Raters were asked to predict type of family from written transcripts. Results indicate that communication and interaction patterns of lower-class families with a schizophrenic differ from families whose class background is similar.

CORNWELL, G. Scapegoating: A study in family dynamics. *American Journal of Nursing*, 1967, *67*, 1862–1867.
See Reference in Section 1.1.

ELBERT, S., ROSMAN, B., MINUCHIN, S., & GUERNEY, F. A method for the clinical study of family interaction. *American Journal of Orthopsychiatry*, 1964, *34*, 885–894.
Two methods are described to obtain data on family interactions which were developed by the family research unit at the Wiltwick School for Boys. Families were from low-socioeconomic status with more than one delinquent child. The family interaction apperception test is a TAT-style test consisting of ten pictures showing family members in different activities. The family task is designed to permit observations of the family relations and their interactions. The family is seated in a room and by operating a tape recorder they hear six different tasks, which they must all discuss and answer together. During the time they are discussing the tasks, a continuous report on nonverbal behavior is being dictated by an observer (looking through a one-way mirror). Verbal behavior is recorded by a tape.

GEISMAR, L. L. Family functioning as an index of need for welfare services. *Family Process*, 1964, *3*, 99–113.
A discussion of the need to have an objective means of assessing the need for welfare services. A standardized method of evaluating family functioning is offered with a report of a study of families.

GREEN, A., GAINES, R., & SANDGRUND, A. Child abuse: Pathological syndrome of family interaction. *American Journal of Psychiatry*, 1974, *13*, 882–886.
See Reference in Section 3.2.

HOFFMAN, L, & LONG, L. A systems dilemma. *Family Process*, 1969, *8*, 211–234.
A description of a man's breakdown in terms of the social systems within which he moved and the attempts to intervene to bring about change. The ecological field of a person is the area considered.

KING, C. Family therapy with the deprived family. *Social Casework*, 1967, *48*, 203–208.
From the author's clinical work with delinquent boys at the Wiltwyck School, techniques with working with low-socioeconomic class patients and their families are described. Selection, rationale, and scope of family therapy is discussed. Basic techniques consisted of educational and therapeutic maneuvers focussed on clarity of communication, and the teaching of parent and sibling roles.

KOSSORIS, P. Family therapy: An adjunct to hemodialysis and transplantation. *American Journal of Nursing*, 1970, *70*, 1730–1733.
See Reference in Section 1.4.

LEVINE, R. Treatment in the home. *Social Work*, 1964, *9*, 19–28.
A clinical report of treatment of seven low-income, multiproblem families who came to a mental hygiene clinic for help with the identified patient, usually a child. Treatment of the family rather than the individual was begun because it seems more economical, more family members could be helped, and the therapist could be more accurate in understanding problems. Treatment was done in the home. Techniques included talking, demonstration, and family activity. The seven families were rated in terms of improvement.

McKINNEY, J. Adapting family therapy to multi-deficit families. *Social Casework*, 1970, *51*, 237–333.
This is a clinical paper on adopting family therapy for low socioeconomic class families. Techniques, rationale, and a clinical case are presented. It is pointed out that work with a family can be more effective than work with the individual

members alone. Agencies interested in this approach must be willing to restructure caseloads, take on a position of advocacy, and institute more flexible hours because of the necessity for home visit and community work. Paraprofessionals should also be involved in treatment.

MINUCHIN, S. Conflict-resolution family therapy. *Psychiatry*, 1965, *28*, 278–286.
A description of a method of family therapy developed at Wiltwyck School for Boys in which the therapist brings members of the family behind the one-way mirror with him to observe the conversation of the remainder of the family. The procedure is said to be particularly effective with multiproblem families. The family members are usually asked in family therapy to be a participant observer and in this method these two functions are separated. "The one-way mirror maintains the emotional impact of interpersonal experiences, while it does not provide an opportunity for impulsory discharge." The family members impulse to react with action, which is generally characteristic of the families treated, is delayed and channeled into verbal forms.

MINUCHIN, S. Family structure, family language and the puzzled therapist. In O. Pollak (Ed.), *Family theory and family therapy of female sexual delinquency*. Palo Alto: Science & Behavior Books, 1967.
An approach to family therapy derived from treating low socioeconomic families at the Wiltwyck School for Boys. "We began to look anew at the meaning and effectiveness of therapist interventions and to focus on two aspects of the family: family language and family structure." Ways of challenging the family structure and other procedures are described with illustrations.

MINUCHIN, S. Psychoanalytic therapies and the low-socioeconomic population. In J. Marmor (Ed.), *Modern Psychoanalysis*. New York: Basic Books, 1968.
The failure of psychoanalytic therapies and psychotherapy to reach the low-socioeconomic population is discussed in terms of the implicit requirements of those approaches and the characteristics of the population. Alternate approaches such as living group therapy, remedial learning therapy, and family therapy are discussed.

MINUCHIN, S., AUERSWALD, E., KING, C., & RABINOWITZ, C. The study and treatment of families that produce multiple acting-out boys. *American Journal of Orthopsychiatry*, 1964, *34*, 125–134.
An early report of experience with families of delinquent boys at the Wiltwyck School for Boys in New York. The report focuses on some aspects of familial functioning, in particular "the socializing function of parental control, guidance, and nurturance." The group's technique of family diagnosis and therapy with delinquent families is also presented.

MINUCHIN, S., & MONTALVO, B. An approach for diagnosis of the low socioeconomic family. In I. M. Cohen (Ed.), *Psychiatric research report no. 20*. Washington, D.C.: American Psychiatric Association, 1966.
A report on the diagnostic techniques used in appraisal of the individual and the family at the Wiltwyck School for Boys. The emphasis is upon communication style and affect. Clinical illustrations are provided.

MINUCHIN, S., & MONTALAVO, B. Techniques for working with disorganized low socioeconomic families. *American Journal of Orthopsychiatry*, 1967, *37*, 880–887.
A paper describing some modifications of family therapy techniques useful for dealing with some families of low-socioeconomic class. The techniques include changing the family composition so that some members observe the family sessions through a one-way mirror, treating various subgroups within the natural family separately (e.g., all adolescents), actively manipulating these subgroups in relation to the whole family group, and finally helping the family to discuss what they want to act on.

POWELL, M., & MONOGHAN, J. Reaching the rejects through multifamily group therapy. *International Journal of Group Psychotherapy*, 1969, *19*, 35–43.
A clinical report based on use of multifamily therapy (two or more families meeting together). The setting was a child guidance clinic. Data were obtained from five groups, each consisting of three families. Each family included mother, father, and the identified patient, with siblings introduced when it was considered "appropriate." They were mostly of low-socioeconomic class. One group was reported on, and the results indicated that communication improved with all family members. Premature termination was not a problem.

RABINOWITZ, C. Therapy for underpriviledged delinquent families. In O. Pollak, & A. S. Friedman (Eds.), *Family dynamics and female sexual delinquency*. Palo Alto: Science & Behavior Books, 1969.
A report on a family therapy approach to low-socioeconomic families. Includes a detailed description of the process of therapy with such a family based on work at the Wiltwyck School.

ROSENTHAL, A. J., BEHRENS, M. I., & CHODOFF, P. Communication in lower-class families of schizophrenics. *Archives of General Psychiatry*, 1968, *18*, 464–470.
This is the first part of a two-part report on low-socioeconomic families of schizophrenics. Groups compared were 17 black schizophrenics and their families, 11 in a black control group, and 11 white schizophrenics and their families. The procedure included observation in the home with tasks requiring the family to maintain a focus of attention on a

specific topic. (For Part II of this study see Behrens, M.I., "Communication in lower class families of schizophrenics. (*Archives of General Psychiatry*, 1968, *18*, 689–696.)

ROSENTHAL, P. A., MOSTELLER, S., WELLS, J. L, & ROLLAND, R. S. Family therapy with multiproblem multichildren families in a court clinic setting. *Journal of Child Psychiatry*, 1974, *13*, 126–143.
This is a clinical paper describing the family approach in treating five families with a delinquent child, all in a lower socioeconomic-class area. All families had failed in other treatment modalities. Specific issues were that the therapists should not (1) convey the feeling that they shared the family's negative image of themselves; (2) get caught up in famiy crises; (3) be discouraged by periods of no improvement or getting worse; and (4) take the role of "parents" to families. One case is presented in detail.

SCHEINFELD, D., BOWELES, D., TUCK, S., & GOLD, R. Parents' values, family networks, and family development: Working with disadvantaged families. *American Journal of Orthopsychiatry*, 1970, *40*, 413–425.
This is a clinical paper reporting a strategy for workng with disadvantaged families with preschool children who are showing signs of "slow development." There are seven operating principles: (1) Go to the parent rather than vice versa; (2) Discover the parents' own ideas concerning child rearing and work within that framework; (3) Introduce concrete activities; (4) Work with parent and child together; (5) Work with as many family members as possible; (6) Give positive reinforcement to family members; (7) Work with a network of social relationships that already exists among the family and other families in the community. Four phases of the project are described and an evaluation is made of six "key mothers." It is felt that "significant changes had been made in all the families." Results comparing the six experimental mothers to a control group, as well as to a group whose children were not having learning troubles, are inconclusive.

SZALITA, A. Deprived families. *Bulletin of Family Mental Health Clinic of The Jewish Family Service*, 1969, *1*, 5–7.
This is a clinical essay on the effect of poverty on families. Deprived families have a deficiency in leadership, in self-reliance, and self-esteem, as well as an inability to meet their needs successfully. If the family has been poor in earlier generations, later generations, although successful financially, often feel "insecure and unsuccessful." The therapist has to differentiate "his own sense of deprivation from that of the family he is treating."

6. SURVEYS OF THE LITERATURE

ACKERMAN, N. W. The growing edge of family therapy. *Family Process*, 1971, *10*, 143–156.
This paper is a survey of the expansion of the field of family therapy on the occasion of the 10th anniversary of the Family Institute of New York. Also it presents Ackerman's position in the field, at the end of 35 years of contributions.

BAILEY, M. B. Alcoholism and marriage. *Quarterly Journal of Studies on Alcohol*, 1961, *22*, 81–97.
A review paper summarizing and discussing the major literature relating to alcoholism and marriage. Further research is said to be needed to attempt an integration of the two hypotheses that regard the course of an alcoholic marriage as a manifestation of a personality disorder or as a response to a particular kind of stress. "The past few years have witnessed a general growth of psychiatric interest in total family diagnosis and treatment, but this new emphasis has hardly begun to manifest itself in respect to alcoholism." A bibliography of 46 references is included.

BATESON, G., JACKSON, D. D., HALEY, J., & WEAKLAND, J. H. A note on the double bind—1962. *Family Process*, 1963, *2*, 154–161.
See Reference in Section 5.2.

BAXTER, J C. Family relations and variables in schizophrenia. In I. M. Cohen (Ed.), *Psychiatric research report no. 20*. Washington, D.C.: American Psychiatric Association, 1966.
An article reviewing the variables used in the study of family relationships of schizophrenics. Whether child or family is "causal" is discussed and the merits of one interpretation or the other is ambiguous at present.

BAXTER, J. Family relationship variables in schizophrenia. *Acta Psychiatrica Scandinavica*, 1966, *42*, 362–391.
A very complete review of the literature starting from as far back as 1892 to the present with the focus on variables related to the family and child development. Topics covered are (1) sibling position of the patient; (2) loss of one or both parens; (3) presence of a distressed childhood in the patient's background; (4) atypical mother-child relationship; (5) atypical father-child relationship; (6) emotional immaturity in the parents; (7) dominance and disturbances between the parents; (8) interpersonal conflict in the family; (9) family-centered pathological behavior; and (10) special position of sib set for the patient.

BERMAN, E. M. & LIEF, H. I. Marital treatment from a psychiatric perspective: An overview. *American Journal of Psychiatry*, 1975, *132*, 583–592.
An overview of current theories of marital therapy. Different systems of marital classification, diagnosis and methods of treatment are examined. The marital life cycle and emerging trends in marital treatment are also discussed. More training in these areas for psychiatric residents is recommended. Seventy-nine references are included.

BODIN, A. Family therapy training literature: A brief guide. *Family Process*, 1969, *8*, 727–279.
The literature on training in family therapy is described and a bibliography of 32 articles listed.

BODIN, A. M. A review of family therapy, training and study in the San Francisco Bay area. *Family Process*, 1971, *10*, 111–121.
This is a detailed review of training and study facilities available in the San Francisco Bay area. It includes a listing of organizations and institutions, clinical services, training programs, and specialized activities in family therapy.

BOWEN, M. Use of family therapy in clinical practice. *Comprehensive Psychiatry*, 1966, *7*, 345–374.
An extensive review of the history of the family therapy movement, dynamics of family functioning, techniques of family therapy, and some of the clinical uses of family therapy. Current status and possible future of the "family movement" are discussed. The family field is in a state of "healthy, unstructured chaos," and the future will see much more research and further development of theory.

BRUGGEN, P. & DAVIES, G. Family therapy in adolescent psychiatry. *British Journal of Psychiatry*, 1977, *131*, 433–447.
This is a review article about family therapy with disturbed adolescents. The indications for family therapy are discussed. The potential contributions to the treatment of such patients from family and psychodynamic theories are contrasted. Different techniques and therapeutic pitfalls of family therapy are described. Seventy-five references are included.

CRAGO, M. Psychopathology of married couples. *Psychology Bullentin*, 1972, *77*, 114–128.
This is an article reviewing the literature on psychopathology in married couples. The incidence of psychopathology is lower in married couples compared with any other marital status group. When one partner has psychiatric illness, there is an association of psychiatric illness in the spouse. The spouse is affected not only by the partner's disorder, but also by the spouse's hospitalization and treatment. No cause and effect relationship of marital stress with a specific type of psychopathology has been clearly demonstrated. Suggestions for research design are made, and an extensive bibiliography is included.

CROMWELL, R. E., OLSON, D. H. L., & FOURNIER, D. G. Tools and techniques for diagnosis and evaluation in marital and family therapy. *Family Process*, 1976, *15*, 1–49.

This paper is an initial attempt at a text of tools and techniques for diagnosis and evaluation in marital and family therapy. The pertinent literature is reviewed and a model that interfaces a diagnostic procedure with the counseling process is presented. The assumption is made that effective methods provide additional data to assist in diagnosis, as well as in evaluating the effectiveness of treatment and comparing different treatments.

CUMMING, J. H. The family and mental disorder: An incomplete essay. In *Causes of mental disorders: A review of epidemiological knowledge, 1959*. New York: Milbank Memorial Fund, 1961.
See Reference in Section 5.1.

DOANE, J. A. Family interaction and communication deviance in disturbed and normal families: A review of research. *Family Process*, 1978, *17*, 357–376.
This paper is a review of recent family interaction studies with an emphasis on differences among disturbed and normal families. Several dimensions along which disturbed families differ from normal ones include: disturbed families are marked by a preponderance of parent–child coalitions and a corresponding weak parental coalition, as well as conflicted marital relationships; normal families have more flexible patterns of interacting, exhibit a greater level of general harmony or closeness, and are able to function more effectively on a variety of tasks. Rorschach and TAT communication deviance measure can discriminate accurately among parental pairs of autistic, withdrawn, acting-out, and young adult schizophrenic offspring. Implications for clinical practice and further research are discussed.

DOANE, J. A. Questions of strategy: Rejoinder to Jacob and Grounds. *Family Process*, 1978, *17*, 389–394.
This paper is a response to the critique by Jacob and Grounds of her review of family interaction research appearing in the same issue. She reviews systematically some of the issues raised by those authors.

FOUDRAINE, J. Schizophrenia and the family, a survey of the literature 1956–1960: On the etiology of schizophrenia. *Acta Psychotherapy*, 1961, *9*, 82–110.
In a thorough review of the literature, the author describes the development of the family point of view of schizophrenia and summarizes the works of authors who have published on this subject during this period. He explores the problem of attempting to conceptualize the function of the family as a whole and to connect pathological family structure with schizophrenia in the individual. A bibliography of 97 items is included.

FRAMO, J. L. Systematic research on family dynamics. In I. Boszormenyi-Nagy, & J. L. Framo (Eds.), *Intensive Family Therapy*. New York: Harper & Row, 1965.
A review of family research relevant to family dynamics. Includes a discussion of small group research, family interaction studies, and methodological problems.

FRANK, G. H. The role of the family in the development of psychopathology. *Psychology Bulletin*, 1965, *64*, 191–205.
A review of some of the literature on family influence as it relates to personality development and psychopathology. Studies of schizophrenia and neurotic problems are examined in terms of method of collecting data on family influence, including case history, psychiatric interview, psychological evaluation, and observation. The review concludes "we have not been able to find any unique factors in the family of the schizophrenic which distinguishes it from the family of the neurotic or from the family of controls, who are ostensibly free from evidence of patterns of gross psychopathology."

FREEMAN, V. J. Differentiation of "unity" family therapy approaches prominent in the United States. *International Journal of Social Psychiatry*, (Special Edition No. 2), 1964, 35–46.
A review and classification of family therapy with six "unit" or "conjoint" methods described, as well as eight closely related approaches. Similarities between methods are discussed in terms of frame of reference, family composition and activity of the therapist. A bibiography of 53 items on family therapy is included.

GREENBERG, F. S. The family interactional perspective: A study and examination of the work of Don D. Jackson. *Family Process*, 1977, *16*, 385–412.
This is a review article of the contributions of Don D. Jackson. It analyzes and attempts to unify the central concepts of what he referred to as conjoint family therapy. Emphasis is upon the theoretical components leading to the development of a behaviorally oriented, nontransference, focuses-treatment format, labeled as "family interactional psychotherapy."

GROLNICK, L. A family perspective of psychosomatic factors in illness: A review of the literature. *Family Process*, 1972, *11*, 457–486.
There is a trend away from the conception of the psychosomatic patient as a self-contained unit to that of the patient in a nexus of relationships. The author reviews literature in intrapsychic, dyadic, and especially familial categories. Some conclusions noted are: family relationships influence the onset and course of many organic illnesses; some family factors are changes in role, membership, and biological status (puberty, marriage, pregnancy, illness,

menopause, senium, and death).The family functions as a system in relation to the physically ill member. Within the family system, mothers play a central role in labeling illness, and other members, especially fathers, collude in this process. An extensive bibliography of 129 references concludes the review.

GURMAN, A. S. Marital therapy: Emerging trends in research and practice. *Family Process*, 1973, *12*, 45–54. See Reference in Section 1.3.

GURMAN, A. S., & KNISKERN, D. P. Behavioral marriage therapy. II: Empirical perspective. *Family Process*, 1978, *17*, 139–148.
This article reviews additional literature on behavioral marital therapy from an empirical point of view. A summary of the results of 23 studies using this approach led to the conclusion that the data on controlled and comparative studies do little to prove efficacy of behavioral marraige therapy. A flexible and open mind is probably the best avenue to advance the field.

GURMAN, A. S. & KNISKERN, D. P. Deterioration in marital and family therapy: Empirical, clinical and coneptual issues. *Family Process*, 1978, *17*, 3–20.
This paper reviews the literature for empirical evidence of deterioration during both behavioral and nonbehavioral marital and family therapy. Some conceptual issues relevant to a definition of worsening in marital and family therapy are discussed. A bibliography of 89 references is included.

GURMAN, A. S. & KNUDSON, R. M. Behavioral marriage therapy. I: A psychodynamic-systems analysis and critique. *Family Process*, 1978, *17*, 121–138.
This is the first of a series of articles published sequentially. The authors summarize the major theoretical premises and treatment strategies of Behavioral Marital Therapy, and review critically its major assumptions. The conceptual and clinical limitations of Behavioral Marital Therapy are described and refocused with regard to object relations theory and communication theory perspectives on marital dysfunction. One hundred and one references are included.

GURMAN, A. S., KNUDSON, R. M., & KNISKERN, D. P. Behavioral marriage therapy. IV: Take two aspirins and call us in the morning. *Family Process*, 1978, *17*, 165–180.
This is the fourth article of a series reviewing the validity of behavioral marriage therapy, in comparison to other approaches. It contains a reanalysis of the literature with a conclusion that the strenght of the empirical foundation of this approach has been greatly exaggerated.

HADER, M. The importance of grandparents in family life. *Family Process*, 1965, *4*, 228–240.
A discussion of the significance of grandparents in the life of young people and their significance to young people. The literature is reviewed on grandparents with a division between attitudes of positive and negative influences.

HANDEL, G. Psychological study of whole families. *Psychology Bullentin*, 1965, *63*, 19–41.
A review of family research and theory with an emphasis upon its development from a psychological point of view. Includes the emergence of this area, family structure descriptions, the interactional and interpersonal emphases, and research methods. A bibliography of 100 references is included.

HARBIN, H.T., & MAZIAR, H. M. The families of drug abusers: A literature review. *Family Process*, 1975, *14*, 411–431.
Relevant literature concerning the family background of compulsive drug abusers is reviewed. The main content of completed research is summarized and methodological criticisms are made. Future considerations for research on families of drug abusers are suggested.

HILL, R. Marriage and family research: A critical evaluation. *Eugenic Quarterly*, 1954, *1*, 58–63.
An essay undertaking a critical review of the literature on marriage and the family, covering trends in research, contemporary emphasis, and prospects for the future research. The essay covers primarily the sociologic literature.

HILL, R., & HANSEN, D. Identification of conceptual frameworks utilized in family study. *Marriage and Family Living*, 1960, *22*, 299–326.
An article which reports on a ten-year study attempting to inventory research on the family in terms of: (1) findings, (2) research procedures, and (3) theoretical propositions derived from the research. Five different research approaches (interactional, structure-function, situational, institutional, and developmental) and the disciplines they are developed in are presented and discussed.

HODGSON, J. W., & LEWIS, R. A. Pilgrim's progress III: A trend analysis of family theory and methodology. *Family Process*, 1979, *18*, 163–173.
This is a review of the current state of development of family theory, based on 614 family articles published from 1969 through 1976. The findings are as follows: (1) there is a continued scarcity of family theory articles; (2) developmental, institutional and systems frameworks have increased in writings; (3) samples were relatively large, but still

nonrandomly selected, with more sophisticated, statistical techniques; and (4) the interactionist approach seems to encourage more sophisticated experimental designs.

HOLLANDER, L, & KARP, E. Youth psychopathology and family process research. *American Journal of Psychiatry*, 1973, *130*, 814–817.
This is a review of the literature comparing (1) "normal" and "abnormal" families and (2) one or more diagnostic categories with normal controls or multiple comparisons. The focus was on hard data, controlled studies. Methodological problems in these studies are discussed, and an extensive bibliography is included.

JACOB, T., & GROUNDS, L. Confusions and conclusions: A response to Doane. *Family Process*, 1978, *17*, 377–387.
This paper is a critical review of Doane's article in the same issue.

JACOBSON, N., & WEISS, R. L. Behavioral marriage therapy. III: The contents of Gurman, et al. may be hazardous to our health. *Family Process*, 1978, *17*, 149–163.
This paper is a reply to the critique of behavioral marital therapy by Gurman, Kniskern, and Knudson. This reply includes a review of the conceptual model utilized in this approach, a review of techniques, and an analysis of the literature investigating the therapeutic efficacy of Behavioral Marriage Therapy, utilizing the same literature sources reviewed by Gurman, et al. The conclusion is reached that this approach is demonstrably effective, and that it is a viable framework for conceptualizing and treating relationship problems.

KASLOW, F., COOPER, B., & LENSENBERG, M. Family therapist authenticity as a key factor in outcome. *International Journal of Family Therapy*, 1979, *1*, 184– 199.
This article reviews the literature on the controversy about therapist self-disclosure to patients regarding the therapist's theoretical school, personality, etc. It also explores arguments for and against it, using several case examples. If disclosure is done authentically and appropriately it can be very helpful.

KLAGSBRUN, M., & DAVIS, D. I. Substance abuse and family interaction. *Family Process*, 1977, *16*, 149–173.
This paper reviews current literature on the belief that family processes contribute to the maintenance of individual substance abuse and may be of crucial importance in the understanding of the substance abuser. Drug use is of central importance in maintaining interactional equilibrium, at least once a chronic pattern of abuse has evolved. The individual's substance abuse is intimately involved with the level of functioning of the family system. Prior to the drug-taking event, there is an increased disorganization of the family system; during the drug-taking episode one finds repetitive and stereotyped behavior; following the drug-taking, there is a decrease in disorganization, with resolution of conflict in the family system as the drug-taker becomes the focus for previously unsolved feelings of frustration, danger, blame and contempt.

L'ABATE, L., & WEEKS, G. A bibliography of paradoxical methods in psychotherapy of family systems. *Family Process*, 1978 *17*, 95–98.
This is a list of 90 references dealing with the theory, research, and applications of paradoxical psychotherapy.

LEFF, J. P. Developments in family treatment of schizophrenia. *Psychiatric Quarterly*, 1979, *51*, 216–230.
This is a literature review of the application of family therapy to the treatment of schizophrenia since the 1950's. The original notion that families *caused* schizophrenia is re-examined, and the author questions whether family systems theory has anything to contribute to understanding schizophrenia. The literature (seven studies) suggests that family therapy can produce desired changes in some disorders, but there is no conclusive evidence that it is effective for families with schizophrenic identified patients.

LIDZ, T. The relevance of family studies to psychoanalytic theory. *Journal of Nervous and Mental Disease*, 1960, *135*, 105–112.
A lecture attempting to assimilate the theory of family dynamics into the theory of psychoanalytic psychology. There is a review of both the family therapy literature and the psychoanalytic literature which discusses the family. Integrating family theory into psychoanalytic theory can lead to "a more dynamic and complete understanding of human behavior."

MALMQUIST, C. School phobia: A problem in family neurosis: *Journal of the American Academy of Child Psychiatry*, 1965, *4*, 293–319.
In contrast to the traditional approach to school phobia, this essay puts forth the clinical notion that phobia can be seen as a reaction to family pathology. Four types for characterizing disordered families that have been reported in the literature are (1) the perfectionistic family, (2) the inadequate family, (3) the egocentric family, and (4) the unsocial family. How these family types relate to the symptom are discussed. There is an extensive review of the literature.

MEISSNER, W. W. Family dynamics and psychosomatic processes. *Family Process*, 1966, *5*, 142–161.
A discussion of the impact of patterns of family interaction on patterns of physical health and illness, with a review of the literature.

MEISSNER, W. W. Thinking about the family—Psychiatric aspects. *Family Process*, 1964, *3*, 1–40.
A review of the ideas and the literature produced by the shift from individual orientation to a specifically family-centered orientation. The family studies are reviewed in terms of what has been said about mother, fathers, parental interaction, and total family constellations. The ideas of the major research groups are presented and analyzed. Includes a bibliography of 135 references.

MISHLER, E., & WAXLER, W. Family interaction processes and schizophrenia. *International Journal of Psychiatry*, 1966, *2*, 375–430.
A critical and extensive review of the theories of the relationship between family interaction and schizophrenia with major space devoted to the work of the Bateson, Lidz, and Wynne groups. Purpose of the review was to see how the theories could be tested and used as guidelines for research. The major contributions of these groups are to the theory of the etiology of schizophrenia by focussing on the family and its methods of interactions, rather than on the individual. Critical evaluations by Bateson, Lidz, Spiegel, and Wynne of the article and the various theories contained in it are included.

MISHLER, E., & WAXLER, N. Family interaction processes and schizophrenia: A review of current theories. *Merrill-Palmer Quarterly*, 1965, *11*, 269–315.
a review of the theories of schizophrenia and the family with special emphasis upon differences, and similarities between the Bateson, Lidz, and Wynne groups. A selected bibliography is included.

MOSHER, L. R., & FEINSILVER, D. Current studies on schizophrenia. *International Journal of Psychiatry*, 1973, *11*, 7–52.
This is an extensive review of current knowledge on schizophrenia drafted by the National Institute of Mental Health. Included is a selection on family dynamics and treatment. Recent investigations have shown the presence of pathological interaction in the families of schizophrenic patients. However, the nature of their relationship to schizophrenia is still unresolved. What is clear is that the kinds of "peculiar" communication that are found in the identified patient have also been found in the family of the schizophrenic.

MOTTOLA, W. Family therapy: A review. *Psychotherapy*, 1967, *4*, 116–124.
A review of the literature of family therapy to this time. it is organized along problems of definition, history, examinations, issues, and research.

MURNEY, R., & SCHNEIDER, R. Family therapy: Understanding and changing behavior. In F. McKinney (Ed.), *Psychology in Action*. New York: Macmillian, 1957.
A review of articles in a book of collected articles for psychologists. It describes rationale, indications, methods, and theory of family therapy for the beginner.

NYE, F. I., & MAYER, A. E. Some recent trends in family research. *Social Forces*, 1963, *41*, 290–301.
The research literature on the family in four leading sociological journals from 1947–61 (N = 456) was analyzed. Changes in methodological aspects and substantive content are documented. Problems remain regarding the failure to use research competence fully, inadequate communication among researchers, and lack of attention to methodological research *per se*. Special attention is given problems and potentials in the utilization of theory, in control of extraneous variables, in the validity of data, in using third variables as contingent conditions, and in longitudinal design.

OLSON, D. H. Empirically unbinding the double bind: Review of research and conceptual reformulations. *Family Process*, 1972, *11*, 69–94.
This is a review of empirical research on the double-bind concept, focusing on conceptual and methodological limitations. Most studies have not adequately tested substantive issues related to the double bind and the final measure had little resemblance to the actual double-bind phenonmenon. So while the results are generally negative, the double-bind still has not been rigorously tested.

POOL, M. L., & FRAZIER, J. R. Family therapy: A review of the literature pertinent to children and adolescents. *Psychotherapy*, 1973, *10*, 256–260.
This paper reviews the literature on family therapy with children and adolescents from 1969 through 1972. Included are synopses on conjoint family therapy, multifamily therapy, family therapy in relation to crisis therapy, and new experimental techniques. It is concluded that there have been no outcome studies of family therapy using objective criteria.

POST, F., & WARDLE, J. Family neurosis and family psychosis: A review of the problem. *Journal of Mental Science*, 1962, *108*, 147–158.
A review of some of the work that has been done in social psychiatry—the psychiatry of relationships. After discussing early studies investigating families of orientation of various types of adult patients, the authors review the studies of the current families of child and adult patients. They conclude that even those studies of family events and

interactions occurring shortly before the patient became ill, and not years previously, are prematurely concerned with proving some basic theoretical construct. It is essential to discover the proportion and type of psychiatric cases in which there is a clear link between emotional characteristics in relatives and friends and the patient's breakdown. A bibliography of 57 references is included.

RABKIN, L. Y. The patient's family: Research methods. *Family Process*, 1965, *4*, 105–132.
A review of family research with special emphasis upon the family of the schizophrenic. Critical examination is done of case history studies, interviewing studies, psychodianostic testing, questionnaire studies, and observational research. A bibliography of 99 references is included.

REISINGER, J. P., & FRANGIA, G. W. Parents as change agents for their children: A review. *Journal of Community Psychology*, 1976, *4*, 103–123.
This is a review of the literature of behavioral, psychoanalytic, and client-centered therapy studies in which parents are involved in the clinical treatment of their own preschool and preadolescent children. Evidence, attitudes, and opinions suggest that it is feasible to utilize parents as change agents and that parents can be trained to function as effective change agents for their children.

RISKIN, J., & FAUNCE, E. E. An evaluative review of family interaction research. *Family Process*, 1972, *11*, 365–455.
This article critically reviews the status and direction of family interaction research. Problems with the studies reviewed include: (1) the lack of replication studies; (2) the vast amount of premises, assumptions and purposes of studies; (3) the incomparability of sample populations; (4) misuse of terms/words; (5) experimental setting problems; (6) the use of individual (as opposed to family) nosology, and (7) the continued use of labeled, unhealthy families. Specific examples are given. The authors include several recommendations for future study, a glossary of terms/experiments/techniques and an 18 page bibliography.

RUBINSTEIN, D. Family therapy. In E. A. Spiegel (Ed.), *Progress in Neurology and Psychiatry* (Vol. XVIII). New York: Grune & Stratton, 1963.
A review article of the literature on family dynamics and therapy for 1961 and 1962. Articles are grouped in the following categories: (1) theory and research, (2) dynamics, (3) technique, and (4) miscellaneous.

RUBINSTEIN, D. Family therapy. In E. A. Spiegel (Ed.), *Progress of neurology and psychiatry* (Vols XIX, XX) New York: Grune & Stratton, 1965, 1966.
In these two annual reviews of family therapy, the 1965 review emphasizes a shift to a concern with the creation of a conceptual framework to understand the dynamics of the family system. There were 54 references. In the 1966 annual review, there is a similar emphasis with articles summarized under the following headings: theory and research, dynamics, technique, and miscellaneous. Included are 54 references.

RUBINSTEIN, D. Family therapy. In J. Spiegel (Ed.), *Progress in Neurology and Psychiatry* (Vol. XXIII). New York: Grune & Stratton, 1968.
In this annual review of family therapy, a trend was noted toward some critical articles on methodology. It was noted that family studies might have *predictive* validity in various forms of psychopathology. There are 63 articles summarized.

RUBINSTEIN, D. Family therapy of schizophrenia—Where to?—What next? *Psychotherapy and Psychosomatics*, 1975, *25*, 154–162.
This is a theoretical paper that presents an overview of the field of family therapy focusing on therapeutic problems, process resistances, as well as a brief review of the literature on outcome studies. The author makes the point that most such studies are uncontrolled and effectiveness is unknown.

SACER, C. The development of marriage therapy: An historical review. *American Journal of Orthopsychiatry*, 1966, *36*, 458–468.
An historical review of the literature on marital therapy and an attempt to integrate current theoretical and therapeutic techniques. Transference from both a transactional and psychoanalytic frame of reference is discussed and felt to be a valuable tool in marital therapy.

SANUA, V. D. The sociocultural aspects of childhood schizophrenia. In G. H. Zuk, & I. Boszormenyi-Nagy (Eds.), *Family therapy and disturbed families*. Palo Alto: Science & Behavior Books, 1967.
A discussion of methodological issues, research strategies, and the problems inherent in studying parent–child relationships and interaction as an etiological factor in schizophrenia. Includes a review of the literature.

SAUNA, V. D. Sociocultural factors in families of schizophrenics: A review of the literature. *Psychiatry*, 1961, *24*, 246–265.
A review of family studies which includes problems of methodology, studies using hospital records, interviews with

relatives, data from psychotherapy, studies using tests, cross-cultural comparisons, European studies, and comparisons of the schizophrenic environment and that of other pathologies. The author concludes that etiological factors fall into four general categories: (1) undesirable traits in the parents, (2) family structure—early parental or sibling deaths or broken families, (3) undesirable interpersonal patterns, and (4) genetic or constitutional factors. He points out the inconsistency and wide variation in methodology and sampling, and the neglect of social variables, and suggests an international research organization to coordinate research in mental illness.

SCOTT, R. Perspectives on the American family studies in schizophrenia. *Confina Psychiatrica*, 1965, *8*, 43–48.
A review of the American literature on family studies of schizophrenia with questions and criticisms. There is a selective bias in leaving out family history of schizophrenics and focusing on interactional aspects. The concept of the double bind is questioned and explained in a new way.

SPECK, R. V. & SPECK, J. L. On networks: Network therapy, network intervention, and networking. *International Journal of Family Therapy*, 1979, *1*, 333–337.
This is a review of the literature on the concept of networks from primitive tribal societies to present day systems. Treatment applications relevant to the family model such as half-way houses, "therapeutic family reunions," and issues of privacy and confidentiality are discussed.

SPIEGEL, J., & BELL, N. The family of the psychiatric patients. In S. Arieti (Ed.), *American handbook of psychiatry*, (Vol. 1) New York: Basic Books, 1959.
A chapter in a textbook on psychiatry dealing with sections on the history of the role of the family in mental illness; etiologic studies of parent-child interactions and development of various mental illnesses including schizophrenia, psychoneurosis, and acting-out disorders; the impact of mental illness upon the family; the family and treatment procedures, and new approaches to the family and its pathology, including family therapy. There are 238 references.

STANTON, M. D. Family treatment approaches to drug abuse problems: A review. *Family Process*, 1979, *18*, 251–280.
This is a review of literature dealing with family therapy of drug abuse problems. Sixty-eight different studies or programs are compared as to their techniques and results. These are classified within different modalities; marital treatment, group treatment for parents, concurrent treatment for parent and identified patient, treatment with individual families, sibling-oriented treatment, multiple family therapy, and social network therapy. It is concluded that family treatment has been gaining acceptance as a therapeutic approach for problems of this type.

STRELNICK, A. H. Multiple family group therapy: A review of the literature. *Family Process*, 1977, *16*, 307–325.
See Reference in Section 1.2.

WALKER, L., BROWN, H., CROHN, H., et al. An annotated bibliography of the remarried, the living together, and their children. *Family Process*, 1979, 18, 193–212.
This is an annotated bibliography on the remarried and those living together in a committed relationship. The bibliography is divided into six sections: (1) demography; (2) remarried couples; (3) step-parents and step-children; (4) divorce as a precursor to remarriage; (6) remarriage—prophylactic and therapeutic aspects. Articles include cover publication dates through 1978.

WEISSMAN, M. M. & KLERMAN, G. L. Sex difference and the epidemiology of depression. *Archives of General Psychiatry*, 1977, *34*, 98–112.
This is a review of different rates of depression between the sexes in the U.S. and elsewhere during the past 40 years with critical analysis of the literature. There is a differential rate of depression between males and females with a higher rate for females. Marriage has a protective effect for males, but a detrimental effect for women. There appears to be a circular relationship between depression and marital problems.

WELLS, R. A., DILKES, T. C., & TRIVELLI, N. The results of family therapy. A critical review of the literature. *Family Process*, 1972, *11*, 189–207.
This is a review of studies evaluating outcome of family therapy. A total of 18 studies met minimal standards for inclusion; however, only two of these studies were considered adequate in their research design. Some of the difficulties included: (1) no consensus on a definition of family therapy; (2) lack of control group or utilization of poor controls; (3) methodological flaws, such as similar reliability upon therapist's evaluation and patient's self-reports and neglect of any pretherapy or follow-up measurements.

WINTER, W. Family therapy: Research and theory. *Current Topics in Clinical and Community Psychology*, 1971, *3*, 95–121.
This is a review article on theory and research in family therapy. Research in family therapy has been nonsystematic and poorly designed. Therapist characteristics, therapeutic techniques, family characteristics, and therapy setting and stage in therapy are relevant research variables to study. Family therapy outcomes studies have been inconclusive, and there has as yet been no controlled study to indicate that it works.

ZUK, G. H. The three crises in family therapy. *International Journal of Family Therapy*, 1979, *1*, 3–8.
This is an editor's introduction to a new journal in family therapy. The author traces the development of family therapy from its original focus on schizophrenia in the fifties to contribution to the proliferation of short term, community oriented techniques in the sixties, to its "professionalization" in the seventies. The need now is for adequate empirical testing of leading theories of family therapy.

ZUK, G. H., & RUBINSTEIN, D. A review of concepts in the study and treatment of families of schizophrenics. In I. Boszormenyi-Nagy, & J. L. Framo (Eds.), *Intensive family therapy*. New York: Harper & Row, 1965.
A review of conceptual trends in family treatment of schizophrenics. Discusses the shift from parent pathology to nuclear family to three generational involvement.

7. BOOKS

7.1 EDITED BOOKS

ACKERMAN, N. (Ed.). *Family Process*. New York: Basic Books, 1970.
Taken from the first 17 issues of the journal, *Family Process*, this collection of 24 papers is divided into a section on theory and practice and a section on focused research studies. 416 pp.

ACKERMAN, N. W. (Ed.). *Family therapy in transition*. Boston: Little, Brown, 1970.
A two-part book: the first part is a series of papers by different authors on the theory and practice of family therapy; the second part includes critical incidents with discussions by different family therapists.

ACKERMAN, N. W., BEATMAN, F. L., & SHERMAN, S. N. (Eds.). *Expanding theory and practice in family therapy*. New York: Family Service Association of America, 1967.
A collection of material on: the need for a systems approach; family therapy as a unifying force in social work; intergenerational aspects; family therapy in the home; and multiple impact therapy. There are two panel discussions, one on the classification of family types and the other on communication within the family. There are also papers on problems and principles, training family therapists through "live" supervision, and an actual family therapy session with comments by the therapists on why certain interventions were made. 182 pp.

ACKERMAN, N. W., BEATMAN, F. L., & SHERMAN, S. (Eds.). *Exploring the base for family therapy*. New York: Family Service Association of America, 1961.
A collection of material on family therapy including papers on the biosocial unity of the family, concept of the family in casework, family diagnosis and therapy, dynamics, prevention, epidemiology, and research. 159 pp.

ANTHONY, E. J., & KOUPERNIK, C. (Eds.). *The child in his family*. New York: Wiley, 1970.
Volume 1 in the series of *The International Yearbook for Child Psychiatry and Allied Disciplines*. Included are papers from a variety of authors of different nations. The sections include family dynamics, family vulnerability and crisis, chronic family pathology, and mental health and families in different cultures. 492 pp.

ARD, B. N., & ARD, C. C. (Eds.). *Handbook of marriage counseling*. Palo Alto: Science & Behavior Books, 1969.
A collection of previously published material on marriage counseling. There are sections on the place of philosophy on values; theoretical issues; conjoint marriage counseling; group marriage counseling; premarital counseling; special techniques; counseling regarding sexual problems; professional issues and ethics in marriage counseling; counseling divorce; and technical assistance for the marriage counselor. Includes an annotated bibliography. 474 pp.

AUERBACK, A. (Ed.). *Schizophrenia: An integrated approach*. new York: Ronald Press, 1959.
A collection of papers oriented toward research in schizophrenia. Included is a paper by Bateson on cultural problems posed by studying the schizophrenic process and a paper by Bowen on family relationships in schizophrenia. 224 pp.

BELL, N. W., & VOGEL, E. S. (Eds.). *A modern introduction to the family*. Glencoe: Free Press, 1961.
A collection of original material and previously published articles by multiple authors that attempts to provide a "sociology of the family." It includes: a framework for a functional analysis of family behavior: a study of different family systems; and papers on the family and economy, the family and policy, the family and community, and the family and value systems. It also includes a section on how normal families function and how family function relates to personality development and maldevelopment. 691 pp.

BENNIS, W., SCHEINE, E., BERLEW, D., & STEELE, F., (Eds.) *Interpersonal dynamics*. Homewood: Dorsey Press, 1964.
A collection of previously published material that includes discussions of the family scapegoat, the family theory of schizophrenia, interpersonal relationships within the family, and role conflict.

BLOCH, D. (Ed.). *Techniques of family psychotherapy: A primer*. New York: Grune & Stratton, 1973.
This is a collection of articles by 14 prominent contributors covering topics such as evaluation, home visits, multiple family therapy, marital therapy and crisis. The emphasis is on practical instruction. Editorial comments and suggested readings are included in many sections. 124 pp.

BOSZORMENYI-NAGY, I., & FRAMO, J. L. (Eds.). *Intensive family therapy: Theoretical and practical aspects*. New York: Harper & Row, 1965.
A collection of articles that includes: a review of the literature; rationale, dynamics, techniques, and indications and contraindications of family therapy; theory of relationships; countertransference; family therapy with schizophrenics in inpatient and outpatient settings; and research on family dynamics.

BRADT, J., & MOYNIHAM, C. (Eds.), *Systems/Therapy*. Washington, D.C.: J. Bradt and C. Moynihan 1972.

This is a collection of 26 papers by Bowen's students presented at the Georgetown Symposium on Family Psychotherapy, published privately in paperback. Topics included are on theory, techniques, and research.

BUCKLEY, T., MCCARTHY, J., NORMAN, E., et al. (Eds.). *New Directions in family therapy*. Oceanside, New York: Dahor, 1977.
This is a collection of previously presented works. It is divided into new theoretical discussions, specific treatment considerations not previously focused on by family therapists (e.g., crisis intervention with families of chronic psychotics, and controversial issues such as use of cotherapists. 148 pp.

CHRISTENSEN, H. T. (Ed.). *Handbook of marriage and the family*. Chicago: Rand McNally, 1964.
A collection of new material on marriage and the family, including sections on theoretical orientation; methodological developments; the family in its social setting; member roles and internal processes; applied and normative interests including family life, education, and the field of marriage counseling. 1028 pp.

COHEN, I. M. (Ed.). *Family structure, dynamics and therapy. Psychiatric research report no. 20*. Washington, D.C.: American Psychiatric Association, 1966.
A collection of material that includes discussions of research methods, family functioning, communication styles, dynamics, family myths, family relations where there is a retarded reader, family relations where the patient has 14 + 6 cps EEG positive spike patterns, family resistances, methods for family work-ups, techniques for dealing with the low socioeconomic class family, effects of videotape playback on family members, family therapy as an alternative for psychiatric hospitalization, use of heterosexual cotherapists, and multiple impact therapy as a teaching device. 234 pp.

CORFMAN, E. (Ed.). Families today: A research sampler on families and children. Rockville, Maryland: NIMH, 1979.
This is a collection in two volumes of works by NIMH investigators on many topics related to the family. Most are research oriented and the focus is on the modern family's problems such as divorce, poverty, unemployment, child abuse, mental illness. Abstracts of each article are included. 1013 pp.

CROMWELL, R., & OLDON, D. (Eds.). *Power in families*. New York: Halstead Press, 1975.
This book (available in paperback.) is a collection of works on theories of power, concepts of how power works in families, and ideas for research. Researchers have paid too little attention to the concept of power in families rather than in individuals. 264 pp.

EISENSTEIN, V. (Ed.). *Neurotic interaction in marriage*. New York: Basic Books, 1956.
A collection of material that includes discussions (mostly from the psychoanalytic point of view) on a cultural perspective on marriage, the effects of marital conflicts on child development, neurotic choices of mate, analysis of interaction patterns, psychological assessment in marital maladjustment, changes as a result of treatment of one member, casework with a disturbed family, approaches to treatment of marital problems, and problems of prediction of marital adjustment. 352 pp.

ERICKSON, G., & HOGAN, T., (Eds.). *Family therapy: An introduction to theory and technique*. New York: Aronson, 1976.
This book is a collection of previously published papers on family therapy—both theory and technique. It was originally published as a college textbook. Sections include works of history of family therapy, theoretical modes, specific techniques and new directions for family therapy. 408 pp.

FARBER, S. M., MUSTACCHI, P., & WILSON, R. H. L. (Eds.). *Man and civilization: The family's search for survival*. New York: McGraw-Hill, 1965.
A collection of material given at a conference concerned with the changes in the family secondary to changes in society. It includes articles on the "necessity of the family"; sacrifice of family structure; the family role; and new paths. 210 pp.

FERBER, A., MENDELSOHN, M., & NAPIER, A. (Eds.). *The book of family therapy*. New York: Aronson, 1972.
A collection of previously published works and many new contributions, with comments of patients (including some from panels and workshops). This book is a paperback textbook on family therapy. It is intended for beginners, as well as for supervisors, and includes chapters on basic theory, becoming a family therapist, techniques of treatment, and teaching techniques. 725 pp.

FRAMO, J. (Ed.). *Family interaction: A dialogue between family researchers and family therapists*. New York: Springer, 1972.
This is the report on a conference of 29 distinguished researchers and clinicians who met in 1967 to discuss methodological and clinical problems in family research. Seven position papers, not published elsewhere, and one anonymous autobiographical work are presented with excerpts from the discussions and comments by the editor. 248 pp.

GLADSTON, I. (Ed.). *The family: A focal point in health education.* New York: International University Press, 1961.
A collection of material from a conference with sections on: a discussion of the family in general; a profile of the American family; psychological dynamics of the "familial organism;" an approach to the study of family mental health; education for personal and familial living; education for parenthood; family and physician; social worker and family; family health maintenance; the anthropology of the American family; ethnic differences in behavior and health practices; and social differences in health practices. 216 pp.

GALDSTON, I. (Ed.). *The family in Contemporary Society.* New York: International Universities Press, 1958.
A collection of material from a conference on the family with discussions of the previous conference on the family given in 1956; the history of the family as a social and cultural institution; changing dynamics of the contemporary family; social and economic basis; behavioral trends and disturbances of the contemporary family; homeostatic mechanisms within the family; and emotionally disturbed and healthy adolescents and their family backgrounds. 147 pp.

GLASSER, P. H., & GLASSER, L. N. (Eds.). *Families in crisis.* New York: Harper & Row, 1970.
A collection of original material and previously published articles which includes discussions of families in poverty, disorganization of marriages and families, and families in terms of physical and mental health. 405 pp.

GREENE, B. L. (Ed.). *The psychotherapies of marital disharmony.* New York: Free Press, 1965.
A collection of previously presented material on treatment of marital problems using different approaches. There are papers on a multi-operational approach, sociologic and psychoanalytic concepts in family diagnosis, marital counseling, the classical psychoanalytic approach, treatment of marital partners separately where the therapists collaborate, concurrent psychoanalytic treatment for the marital partners, conjoint marital therapy, a combination of approaches, and the family approach to diagnosis. 191 pp.

GUERIN, P. *Family therapy: Theory and practice.* New York: Gardner Press, 1976.
This is a collection of articles and essays by prominent writers in the field. Topics include "historical overview, different theoretical concepts, clinical and format issues (such as who to include in a therapy session) and treatment techniques." Different theoretical concepts ranging from psychoanalytic to communication theory paradigms are detailed. 553 pp.

GURMAN, A., & RICE, E., (Eds.). *Couples in conflict.* New York: Aronson, 1975.
This is a collection of previously published articles and essays and some new material with an emphasis on new directions in marital therapy. Beginning with a section on the then current status of the field, it goes on to sections on treatment issues, specific approaches and a section on outcome research.

HALEY, J. (Ed.). *Changing families: A family therapy reader.* New York: Grune & Stratton, 1971.
A textbook bringing together 21 articles that describes different approaches to family therapy. Both previously published and new articles are included, and there is an extensive bibliography.

HANDEL, G. (Ed.). *The psychosocial interior of the family: A sourcebook for the study of whole families.* Chicago: Aldine, 1967.
An anthology of previously published articles on the social psychology of the family. It includes sections on the family as a psychosocial organization, research methods, the family as mediator of the culture, the meanings of family boundaries, the family as a universe of cognition and communication, patterning separateness and connectedness, and a reviw of family theories. 560 pp.

HOWELLS, J. G. (Ed.). *Advances in family psychiatry* (Volume I). New York: International University Press, 1979.
This is a collection of previously published articles intended to bring the reader up to date on the family therapy literature on the topics of theory, family psychopathology, family diagnosis, and family symptomatology. Editorial comments are included prior to each of the 36 selections. 559 pp.

HOWELLS, J. (Ed.). *Theory and practice of family psychiatry.* Edinburgh and London: Oliver & Boyd, 1968.
A collection of new material and previously published articles that include discussions of the theory and practice of family psychiatry; illustrations of the dimensions of the family; individual, relationship, group properties, material circumstances, and community interaction; and illustrations of clinical practice, including organization, the presenting patient, clinical syndromes, and therapy. There is an extensive bibliography. 953 pp.

JACKSON, D. D. (Ed.). *Communication, family and marriage.* Palo Alto: Science & Behavior Books, 1968.
A collection of previously published papers covering early generalizations on family dynamics from clinical observations, papers on the double-bind theory, communication, systems and pathology, and research approaches and methods. 289 pp.

JACKSON, D. D. (Ed.). *The etiology of schiozphrenia.* New York: Basic Books, 1960.
A collection of original material dealing with the etiology of schizophrenia. It includes a section on an overview of the

problems, genetic aspects, biochemical aspects, physiologic aspects, psychological studies, and family theories of schizophrenia. 456 pp.

JACKSON, D. D. (Ed.). *Therapy, communication and change*. Palo Alto: Science & Behavior Books, 1968.
A collection of previously published papers covering psychotic behavior and its interactional context, the interactional context of other kinds of behavior, interactional views of psychotherapy, and conjoint family therapy. 76 pp.

LOMAS, P. (Ed.). *The predicament of the family*. New York: International Universities Press, 1967.
A collection of original material oriented toward the theme of psychoanalytic concepts of the family. There are articles on family relationships in contemporary society; mirror roles of mother and family in child development; family interaction and adolescent therapy; the family pattern of distress; simultaneous analysis of mother and child; the family and individual structure; and a study of marriage as a critical transition for personality and family development.

MASSERMAN, J. (Ed.). *Science and Psychoanalysis (Vol. II): Individual and family dynamics*. New York: Grune & Stratton, 1959.
In this book there are sections on familial and social dynamics. Included are papers on survey of trends and research in the practice of family therapy, psychoanalytic approaches to the family, family homeostasis, family dynamics in schizophrenia, cultural aspects of transference and countertransference, techniques of family therapy, and a panel discussion and review on the family. 218 pp.

MISHLER, E. G., & WAXLER, N. W. (Eds.). *Family process and schizophrenia*. New York: Science house, 1968.
A collection of previously published articles that includes discussions of current theories; experimental studies; parents of the schizophrenic, dyadic interactions; parents with a schizophrenic child; pathogenic triad; parent and sibling; the family tetrad; and commentaries, which is a discussion of the articles by four family therapy theoreticians. 323 pp.

NASHE, E. M., JESSNER, L., & ABSE, D. W. (Eds.). *Marriage counseling in medical practice*. Chapel Hill: University of North Carolina Press, 1964.
A collection of original material and previously published articles that includes discussions of marriage counseling by the physician; premarital medical counseling; concepts of marital diagnosis and therapy; and marital counseling instruction in the medical school curriculum. There is an annotated bibliography. 368 pp.

PAPP, P. (Ed.). *Family therapy: Full-length case studies*. New York: Gardiner, 1977.
This collection of articles by well-known clinicians who have different approaches to selected cases, includes 12 case studies and extensive bibliographies. 210 pp.

POLLAK, O., & FRIEDMAN, A. S. (Eds.). *Family dynamics and female sexual delinquency*. Palo Alto: Science & Behavior Books, 1969.
A volume containing 18 previously unpublished papers that were based on a seminar on the family system as it influences the personality and behavior of sexually acting-out adolescent daughters. Sections include: family system theory, socioeconomic and cultural factors in sexual delinquency, psychodynamic factors in sexual delinquency, family interactional factors, and family therapy applications. 210 pp.

REISS, D., & HOFFMAN, H. (Eds.). *The American family*. New York: Plenun Press, 1979.
This is a collection of papers originally presented at a conference in Washington, D.C., in 1978 on dilemmas of the American family. Each of the seven chapters deal with topics, such as those of urban black families, single-parent families, and public policy, and are followed by discussions of "practical considerations." These examine implications for treatment, services planning, research, etc. 246 pp.

RIESS, F. B. (Ed.). *New directions in mental health* (Vol. I). New York: Grune & Stratton, 1968.
A collection of articles on various psychiatric topics including papers on practice of family treatment in kibbutz and urban child guidance clinics; short term analytic treatment of married couples in a group by a therapist couple; the therapeutic field in the treatment of families in conflict; recurrent themes in literature and clinical practice; and patterns of interaction in families of borderline patients. 304 pp.

ROSENBAUM, S., & ALGER, I. (Eds.). *The marriage relationship: Psychoanalytic perspectives*. New York: Basic Books, 1967.
A collection of some original and some previously presented papers focussing on the marital relationship from a family and psychoanalytic point of view. It includes discussions of communication; monogamy; femininity; resistance to marriage; mate choice; expectations in marriage; changing attitudes of marital partners towards each other; marital problems of older persons; the effects of chilren; effects of pathology of parents on the children; effects of sexual disturbances; effects of marital conflicts on psychoanalysis; different treatment approaches to marital problems

including individual psychoanalysis, with different analysts, family therapy, group psychotherapy with couples, growth and maturation in marriage, and marital dissolution. 366 pp.

SILVERMAN, H. L. (Ed.). *Marital counseling.* Springfied: Charles C. Thomas, 1967.
A collection of original material on marital counseling which includes discussions of psychological factors, ideological factors, scientific factors, and a summary of marital counseling concepts. 530 pp.

SLUZKI, C., & RANSOM, D. *The double bind: The foundation of the communicational approach to the family.* New York: Grune & Stratton, 1976.
This collection includes six previously published papers as well as new work on the applications of the "double bind" theory of interpersonal interaction to family therapy as well as to other social or psychopathological situations. Sections are divided into descriptions of the core theory, historical accounts of the development of the theory, a research review and explorations of the range of applications of the theory. An extensive bibliography is included. 359 pp.

STEIN, E. (Ed.). *Fathering: Fact or fable?* Nashville: Abingdon, 1977.
This is a collection of essays on the functions of fathering, the effects of absent fathering, and the need for "refathering." Suggestions are made for changing the role of many present-day fathers. 181 pp.

STEIN, M. I., (Ed.). *Contemporary psychotherapies.* Glencoe: Free Press, 1961.
A book containing a series of lectures on psychotherapy given in a seminar series. In it are two papers by Ackerman on family therapy and two papers by Jackson, one a general paper and the other on family therapy where the identified patient is schizophrenic. 386 pp.

STIERLIN, H. *Psychoanalysis and family therapy.* New York: Aronson, 1977.
Putting together his previously published writings on the subject, the author attempts to provide an orientation that will integrate psychoanalytic and family systems theory. Focusing on unconscious, intra-psychic mechanisms, which also show up in family theory, the author includes essays on family myths, "invisible loyalties" delegated roles, etc. A section on the practice of "psychoanalytic family therapy" is included.

VINCENT, C. D. (Ed.). *Readings in marriage counseling.* New York: Thomas Y. Crowell, 1957.
A collection of 52 articles on marriage counseling. The book includes sections on marriage counseling in an emerging and interdisciplinary profession; premarital counseling; definitions, methods, and principles in marriage counseling; marriage counseling of individuals, couples, and groups; theories of personality formation and change applicable to marriage counseling; research in marriage counseling; and questions related to marriage counseling as an emerging profession.

WATZLAWICK, P., & WEAKLAND, J. *The interactional view: Studies at the mental research institute 1965–1974.* New York: Norton, 1977.
As in the two previous collections from MRI, edited by Don Jackson in 1968, this collection of previously published articles and excerpts from books supports the interactional view of family function, pathology, and therapy. Chapters include theory, research, and training applications. 405 pp.

WHITAKER, C. (Ed.) *Psychotherapy of chronic schizophrenic patients.* Boston: Little, Brown, 1958.
A transcript of a conference on schizophrenia in which there were eight sessions, each oriented toward a particular topic in which no formal presentation is made, but rather a general discussion with a moderator for each section was held. The book includes sections on diagnosis and prognosis, schizophrenic distortion of communication, orality, anality, family and sexuality, countertransference, mangement of the patient, and family management. 219 pp.

ZUK, G. H., & BOSZORMENYI-NAGY, I. (Eds.). *Family therapy and disturbed families.* Palo Alto: Science & Behavior Books, 1967.
A collection of original material and previously published articles that includes discussions of family theory and psychopathology, relationships between family and sociocultural systems, and specific techniques of family and marriage therapy. 243 pp.

7.2   AUTHORED BOOKS

ABLES, B., & BRANDSMA, J. *Therapy for couples: A Clinicians guide for effective treatment.* San Francisco: Jossey-Bass, 1977.

This is a textbook of marital therapy that utilizes many verbatim transcripts. Its theoretical stance is described as "eclectic," and the emphasis is on teaching therapy techniques. 364 pp.

ACKERMAN, N. W. *Psychodynamics of family life, diagnosis and treatment in family relationships*. New York: Basic Books, 1958.
A collection of original material and previously published articles that includes a discussion of the psychodynamics of the family, the relation of family theory to psychoanalytic theory, social role and personality, family dynamics, techniques in diagnosis, techniques of treatment and research. There are special sections dealing with disturbances of marital pairs, parental pairs, childhood, adolescence, sociopathy, and psychosomatic illness. 379 pp.

ACKERMAN, N. W. *Treating the troubled family*. New York: Basic Books, 1966.
A book concerned with techniques of family therapy, including discussions of family crises, goals, the process of illness developing in the family, functions of the therapist, treatment of husband and wife, treatment when the family includes children, and some special techniques in dealing with the "scapegoat." 306 pp.

ALDOUS, J., & REUBEN, H. *International bibliography of research in marriage and the family 1900–1964*. Minneapolis: Univeristy of Minneapolis Press, 1967.
An extensive bibliography of the literature on the family. There are sections on transactions within groups, family as a small group, mate selection, and many other subject classes. 507 pp.

ANDREWS, E. *The emotionally disturbed family*. New York: Aronson, 1974.
This is a beginner's text from the Family Institute in Cincinnati, Ohio. It views families as transactional systems and includes individual chapters on specific transactions such as manipulation, bonding, etc. Other sections discuss family functions and training issues. 257 pp.

BANDLER, R., GRINDER, J., & SATIR, V. *Changing with families*. Palo Alto: Science and Behavior Books, 1976.
This book is intended to educate family therapists. It examines the process of therapy to clarify what is actually being communicated by therapists (which may not be what is intended). By way of illustration, it presents excerpts from transcripts of sessions and seeks to identify the patterns they contain. 194 pp.

BEAVERS, W. R. *Psychotherapy and growth: A family systems perspective*. New York: Brunner/Mazel, 1977.
General systems theory and ideas of normal and disturbed family functioning are used to examine the nature of psychotherapy and compare several schools of therapy. The final section contains the author's model for "growth-promoting" psychotherapy. 388 pp.

BELL, J. E., *Family group therapy*. Public Health Monograph No. 64. Washington, D.C.: Department of Health, Education and Welfare, 1961.
A manual of one approach to family therapy that discusses rationale and techniques phase by phase from the first conference through the terminal period. 52 pp.

BELL, J. E. *Family therapy*. New York: Aronson, 1975.
This book is a personal account of the author's work with families and his contribution to family therapy since the early 1950's. Included are accounts of families that first interested the author in seeing the family as "the unit to be treated," early work with "phases of therapy," and sections on newer applications and future possible applications of his work. 421 pp.

BERGLER, E. *Parents not guilty! Of their children's neuroses*. New York: Liveright, 1964.
A clinical report based on the notion that "there is no direct connection between acts, words, or attitudes of parents on the child's behavior and later development." 283 pp.

BOSZORMENYI-NAGY, I., & SPARK, G. *Invisible loyalties: Reciprocity in intergenerational family therapy*. New York: Harper and Row, 1973.
This book utilizes the experience of two well known family therapists and some previously published work to develop the theoretical concept of "loyalty" as it applies to social and individual behavior. This is discussed as it applies to normal and abnormal relationships and to transference in therapy. A detailed treatment account is included. 408 pp.

BRODEY, W. M. *Changing the family*. New York: Potter, 1968.
A personal view of families with many styles of family life described. "The stories . . . are little descriptions of families mixed with just enough comment and contrast to tell their own story and insist that you listen and feel . . . "

BRODY, E. *Long-term care of older people: A practical guide*. New York: Human Sciences Press, 1977.
Based on the notion that family therapists will be dealing more and more with problems of aging and the aged, this

book gives the therapists information on how to help families help their older members and provides them with a knowledge of geriatrics. 402 pp.

CHANCE, E. *Families in treatment*. New York: Basic Books, 1959.
A report on a research study of families in treatment in which the identified patient was the child. Father, mother, and patient were in individual treatment and there were no conjoint sessions. One section of the book is on the differences in looking at the data from the points of view of researcher, patient, and therapist respectively, and the other section is on research design, descriptions of the families at the beginning of treatment, the treatment relation, process of change, and interpretations of the data. 234 pp.

CONSTANTINE, L., & CONSTANTINE, J. *Group marriage: A study of contemporary multilateral marriage*. New York: MacMillan, 1973.
This is a preliminary report on research into alternative lifestyles. Nine group marriages were studies for three years and the book presents the author's views on the mobility and desirability of their lifestyle. 299 pp.

COUCH, E. H. *Joint and family interviews in the treatment of marital problems*. New York: Family Service Association of America, 1969.
A report of a project designed to collect data on rationale and techniques of caseworkers dealing with "troubled marriages." There are sections on special values of joint and family interviews for diagnosis and for treatment: conditions considered favorable and unfavorable to the use of joint interviews and family interviews; expansion of the circle of treatment participants and related experimental approaches; and summary and implications. 330 pp.

DICKS, H. V. *Marital tensions: Clinical studies toward a psychological theory of interaction*. New York: Basic Books, 1967.
A clinical research report investigating marital problems. Concepts of the study, rationale, social setting, individual setting, development of the study, evolution of concepts, symptomatology, diagnosis, treatment, and treatment results are reported. 354 pp.

DUVALL, E. *Family development*. Philadelphia: Lippincott, 1967.
A book on the family for "preprofessionals" who work with the family. It focuses on family lifestyles, tasks, how families reflect social changes, how families change with the introduction of children, and how families change after the children leave the family. 532 pp.

EHRENWALD, J. *Neurosis in the family and patterns of psychosocial defense*. New York: Harper & Row, 1963.
A collection of some original and some previously published material including chapters on family traits and attitudes; patterns of family interaction and of sharing and parent–child symbiosis, a description of a family with obsessive–compulsive personality; dynamics from both an interpersonal and intrapersonal point of view; patterns of contagion; the Mozart and Picasso families, psychiatric epidemiology, pattern changeability, and interpersonal dynamics in family therapy. 203 pp.

FERBER, J. & SCHOONBECK, J. *Crisis: A handbook for systemic intervention*. New York: Gardiner, Insitute for Human Studies, 1977.
This is a short work that describes how to set up and run a crisis team that approaches problems from a systems theory point of view. It also discusses some training issues involved in this approach, such as "discarding" individual psychiatric nomenclature. 64 pp.

FISHER, E. O. *Help for today's troubled marriages*. New York: Hawthorn Books, 1968.
A book on marriage counseling that covers the problems of marriage, aspects and procedures of marriage counseling, the problems of divorce and widowhood, and comments on remarriage. 288 pp.

FITZGERALD, R. *Conjoint marital therapy*. New York: Aronson, 1973.
This book presents the authors ideas on marital therapy. The first part contains an explanation of his methods, using analytic tools and stressing process more than content. The second part contains a case history with verbatim interviews. 248 pp.

FOLEY, V. *An introduction to family therapy*. New York: Grune & Stratton, 1974.
Published in paperback, this book is intended to introduce the field of family therapy to university students. Essential concepts of systems theory and seminal ideas such as the double bind are explored. Therapists such as Ackerman, Bowen, Haley and Jackson are compared and contrasted. Different models of clinical practice are described. 207 pp.

FRENCH, A. *Disturbed children and their families: Innovations in evaluation and treatment*. New York: Human Science Press, 1977.

By conceptualizing psychotherapy as an attempt to restore adaptiveness and homeostasis to an "open" system, rather than using a "disease" model, the author attempts to integrate general systems theory and accept developmental concepts. Exploratory of normal family functioning as well as pathology (e.g., symptoms are maladaptive compensation for imbalance) are presented. 333 pp.

FRIEDMAN, A. S., BOSZORMENYI-NAGY, I., JUNGREIS, J. E., LINCOLN, G., et al. *Psychotherapy for the whole family: Case histories, techniques, and concepts of family therapy of schizophrenia in the home and clinic.* New York: Springer, 1965.
A research project on treatment of schizophrenia using family therapy done in the home. The papers cover rationale, of treatment, experience with families, problems and concepts in treatment, and results of treatment. There is a section on a search for a conceptual model of family psychopathology.

FRIEDMAN, R. *Family roots of school learning and behavior disorders.* Springfield, Ill: Charles C. Thomas, 1973.
This textbook is based on the premise that family factors are the decisive element in many school difficulties. It provides a framework for evaluating and treating such disorders and for family intervention. 346 pp.

GLICK, I. D., & HALEY, J. *Family therapy and research: An annotated bibliography.* New York: Grune & Stratton, 1971.
An annotated bibliography of papers and books published from 1961–1970 that updates an earlier 1965 work. Sections include theory, research, therapy techniques, family descriptions (and classification), and literature surveys. Relevant films and videotapes are also included. 280 pp.

GLICK, I.D., & KESSLER, D. R. *Marital and family therapy.* New York: Grune & Stratton, 1981 (first edition, 1974).
This is the second edition of an introductory textbook on family therapy covering: development and definition of the field; past, present, and future of the family; understanding the functional and dysfunctional family; evaluation and setting goals; family treatment; the family model and other fields; results, guidelines, research and training. Numerous case examples and a transcript are included in this pluralistic orientation to the text.

GOODE, W. *The Family.* Englewood Cliffs: Prentice Hall, 1964.
The author discusses sociological theory as applied to family realtionships. He points up the complex relationships between family systems and the larger social structure, the biological basis of the family, legitimacy and illegitimacy, mate selection and marriage, forms of household, organized descent groupings, role relations, stratification, dissolution of family role systems, and changes in the family patterns. 120 pp.

GROTJOHN, M. *Psychoanalysis and the famiy neurosis.* New York: Norton, 1960.
A book based on clinical experience that combines psychoanalytic as well as interactional factors in the etiology of mental illness. Topics covered are: the history and etiology of the development of family therapy, psychodynamics of health and complementary neurosis of a family, and treatment techniques, including the diagnostic interview, training analysis, family treatment, and the dynamics of the therapeutic process. 320 pp.

Group for the Advancement of Psychiatry, Committee on the Family. *The case history method in the study of family process.* (Report No. 76). New York: 1970.
The purpose of this report is to demonstrate a systematic approach to modifying the traditional psychiatric "case history" for use in family diagnosis, treatment, and research. There are sections on principles for compiling a family case history, a typical case is presented and contrast made between a Puerto-Rican working-class and American middle-class family. Contrast in values within the nuclear family as well as in the extended family network are described. There is an appendix with a family case history outline. 380 pp.

Group for the Advancement of Psychiatry, Committee on the Family. *The field of family therapy.* New York: 1970.
A report on the field of family therapy which is meant to be a "snapshot" taken during the winter of 1966–67. Data are based upon a questionnaire answered by 312 persons who considered themselves family therapists as well as the opinions of the members of the family committee. The work deals with who are the practitioners of family therapy, how do the families typically enter treatment, what are the goals an conceptual approaches, what techniques are used, and what ethical problems arise.

Group for the Advancement of Psychiatry, Committee on the Family. *Integration and conflict in family behavior* (Report No. 27). Topeka: 1954.
A report by the committee on the family of GAP dealing with organizing data on the study of the family. It discusses the relation of the family to the social system, the system of values to which the family is oriented, and Spanish-American family patterns as well as American middleclass family patterns. 67 pp.

HALEY, J. *Problem-solving therapy.* San Francisco: Jossey-Bass, 1976.
Based on new and old material, the author outlines his current views on strategy and tactics of therapy and training issues. A major focus is on the reason for therapy. Included is the view that almost all problems stem from a marital

conflict that the family will not acknowledge, which makes their particular symptom(s) necessary for them. 275 pp.

HALEY, J. *Strategies of psychotherapy*. New York:Grune & Stratton, 1963.
A description of a variety of forms of psychotherapy from an interactional point of view. Includes chapters on marriage therapy and family therapy.

HALEY, J., & GLICK, I. *Psychiatry and the family: An annotated bibliography of articles published 1960–64*. Palo Alto: Family Process, 1965.
An annotated bibliography of papers published from 1960–1964. Content includes articles on family therapy as well as family research studies that are relevant to psychiatry and psychology. Papers from the fields of sociology and anthropology were excluded unless they pertained directly to the psychiatric field.

HALEY, J., & HOFFMAN, L. *Techniques of family therapy*. New York: Basic Books, 1967.
A presentation of the work of five family therapists. Interviews were done with Virginia Satir, Don D. Jackson, Charles Fulweiler, Carl Whitaker, and a therapy team doing crisis therapy. There is intensive examination of a first interview with a family to illustrate their approaches.

HEADLEY, L. *Return to the source: Adults and their parents in family therapy*. New York, Plenum Press, 1977.
In a book which attempts to combine the individual psychodynamic and family systems models, the author suggests that the identified patient's family members be brought into their therapy at certain points. This will aid in changing old patterns of behavior. Suggestions for overcoming resistance to this idea are included.

HINCHLIFFE, M., HOOPER, D., & ROBERTS, J. *The melancholy marriage*. New Jersey: Wiley, 1978.
This is a book about the relationship between marital problems and depression. The literature on this subject is reviewed and a model for depression that will account for the coincidence is proposed. 150 pp.

HORIGAN, F. D. *Family therapy: A survey of the literature*. Psychiatric Abstracts No. 11, Bethesda: Department of Health, Education and Welfare, 1964.
A selected, annotated bibliography of the literature of family therapy from 1949 to 1964.

HOWELLS, J. *Family psychiatry*. Springfield: Charles C. Thomas, 1963.
A collection of some original and some previously published material intended to be a textbook of family psychiatry. There are sections on theory and practice of family psychiatry; illustrations of the dimensions of the family; individual, relationships, group, maternal circumstances, and community interaction; and finally, illustrations from clinical practice, divided into organization, the presenting patient, clinical syndromes, and therapy itself. There is an extensive bibliography. 953 pp.

JACKSON, D. D. *Myths of madness*. New York: Macmillan, 1964.
A discussion of madness emphasizing its different mythologies and expressing a more social view.

JACKSON, D. D., & LEDERER, W. J. *Mirages of marriage*. New York: Norton, 1969.
A book focusing on the nature of marriage, marital problems, and procedures for bringing about change. Illustrations of different problems are given. Exercises for improving marital relations are provided for couples.

JACOBSON, N., & MARGOLIN, G. *Marital Therapy: Strategies based on social learning and behavior exchange principles*. New York: Brunner/Mazel, 1979.
This book presents a model fo marital treatment that is based on behavioral learning theory. There are sections on specific techniques (such as communication training, problem solving training, paradoxical directives, sex therapy), as well as on outcome research, two case studies, and a discussion of the similarities and differences between behavioral and nonbehavioral approaches to marital therapy. 415 pp.

KELLNER, R. *Family ill health: An investigation in general practice*. Springfield: Charles C. Thomas, 1963.
A report by a general practitioner concerning the incidence of physical and emotional illness and its relationships to family dynamics. It includes a plan of the investigation, description of the cases, method of analyzing the data, results, and a summary. 112 pp.

KEMPLER, W. *Principles of gestalt family therapy*. Oslo: A. S. IOH. Nordahls Trykkeri, 1973.
This short paperback is an introduction to a model for family therapy that utilizes the principles of Gestalt therapy. 127 pp.

KIESLER, D., BERNSTEIN, A., & ANCHIN, J. *Interpersonal communication: relationship and the behavior therapies*. New York: Psychological Dimensions, 1977.

This book is an attempt to combine communications theory (e.g., that which is derived from the work of Watzlawick, Jackson, etc.) with the techniques of behavioral therapy. The communications model is used to define the range and type of behavior to be observed. Implications for therapy and research are explored. 300 pp.

KLEMER, R. H. *Counseling in marital and sexual problems.* Baltimore: Williams & Wilkins, 1965.
A collection of original material and previously published articles that includes discussions of counseling in marital problems; counseling in sexual problems; other marriage problems; premarital counseling; and marriage counseling instruction in the medical curriculum. There is an extensive reading list. 309 pp.

KNOX, D., Marriage happiness: *A behavioral approach to counseling.* Champagne, Ill.: Research Press, 1971.
This is a short, paperback that is an instructional guide to behavioral treatment of marital problems. Case abstracts are included to illustrate techniques such as desensitization and assertiveness training. 171 pp.

KWIATKOWSKA, H. *Family therapy and evaluation through art.* Springfield: Thomas, 1978.
Written by a well-known art therapist, this book gives ideas about the usefulness of art therapies for the evaluation and treatment of families, as well as for research. The development of this technique is reviewed and case histories from the NIMH with illustrations are included. 280 pp.

L'ABATE, L. *Understanding and helping the individual in the family.* New York: Grune & Stratton, 1976.
This is a mostly theoretical book about how people develop in a normal family and how pathology develops in a dysfunctional family. The theory is based on notions of the functions of individual "boundaries," "personal space" and diffrentiation.

LAING, R. D. *The divided self.* London: Tavistock, 1960.
A clinical book focusing on a theory of schizophrenia in existential terms. There are sections on the existential foundation for understanding this phenomenon, the prepsychotic role of the schizophrenic, and the psychotic role of the schizophrenic—all related to the social context of this symptomatology.

LAING, R. D., & ESTERSON, A. *Sanity, madness and the family (Vol. I): Families of schizophrenics.* London, Tavistock, 1964.
A book describing a research project investigating 11 families in which the identified patient was a female with schizophrenia. The data were obtained from clinical interviews with family members both individually and together. "The behavior of schizophrenics is much more socially intelligible than has come to be supposed by most psychiatrists." Rather than having an illness, the symptoms are seen as a "strategy" invented by the person to live in an "unlivable" situation. 272 pp.

LAING, R. D., PHILLIPSON, H., & LEE, A. *Interpersonal perception—A theory and a method of research.* London: Tavistock, 1966.
A research project oriented toward understanding interaction of two persons. It includes sections on self and other; interaction and interexperience in dyads; the spiral of reciprocal perspective; historical view of the method; the interpersonal perception methods (IPM); disturbed and nondisturbed marriages; study of a dyad; developments; and the IPM questions. 179 pp.

LANGSLEY, D., & KAPLAN, D. *The treatment of families in crisis.* New York: Grune & Stratton, 1968.
A report of a research project where family crisis therapy was offered as an alternative to psychiatric hospitalization. Rationale, techniques of therapy, data on the patients, and results and implications are presented. 208 pp.

LENNARD, H., & BERNSTEIN, A. *Patterns in human interaction.* San Francisco: Jossey-Bass, 1969.
A textbook on "clinical sociology" which discusses interaction processes, methodological problems in describing interaction processes, interaction patterns in the family, psychotherapeutic interaction, and functions of human interaction. Patterns of schizophrenic and control families are described. 224 pp.

LEWIS, J., BEAVERS, W., GOSSETT, J., et al: *No single thread.* New York: Brunner/Mazel, 1976.
This book describes an ongoing research project that utilizes videotape recordings of families to identify quantifiable interactional variables necessary to healthy family functioning. The 44 families reported on in this work were actually volunteer controls for research on dysfunctional families. 260 pp.

LIDZ, T. *The family and human adaption.* New York: International Universities Press, 1963.
A collection of three lectures dealing with the role of the family in normal development, the role of the family in a changing society, and specific requisites for successful family functioning; the parents' ability to form a coalition, maintain boundaries between generations, and adhere to their appropriate sex-linked role. Finally, the book covers the family's capacity to transmit the basic adaptive techniques of the culture by means of communication. Failures in these functions are explored in terms of an etiologic theory for schizophrenia. 120 pp.

LIDZ, T., FLECK, S., & CORNELISON, A. R. *Schizophrenia and the family*. New York: International Universities Press, 1965.
A collection of original material and previously published articles by the Yale research group concerning their investigations of the intrafamilial environment in which schiophrenic patients grow up. The book includes the rationale for the study, some articles of the family environment of schizophrenic patients, a number of articles on the 17 study families (including aspects of casework techniques, family interaction, the hospital staff, familial dynamics, and psychological testing) and the implications of this data for a new theory of schizophrenia based on a disturbed intrafamilial environment. There is also a section documenting the type of thought disorder found in families with schizophrenic patients as seen on the object sorting test. There is an extensive bibliography. 477 pp.

LUTHMAN, S., & KIRSCHENBAUM, M. *The dynamic family*. Palo Alto: Science and Behavior Books, 1974.
This textbook from the Family Therapy Institute in Marin, California combines elements from the work of Satir and of communications theories of interaction (e.g., "positive intent"), treatment techniques, cotherapy, and training. The overall emphasis is a family growth model.

MacGREGOR, R., RITCHIE, A. M., SERRANO, A. C., SCHUSTER, F. , et al. *Multiple impact therapy with families*. New York: McGraw-Hill, 1964.
A report of a clinical project using a new technique for families who consult a child guidance clinic and who live a great distance away. The book includes a section on the development of family therapy, illustrations of the method; discussion of the method; and discussions of the family, family dynamics, therapeutic movement, the team, and results. 320 pp.

MARTIN, P. A marital therapy manual. New York: Brunner/Mazel, 1976.
This book aims at teaching techniques of marital psychotherapy to beginning therapists. It is based on the author's experience as a clinician and teacher and the emphasis is on practical "how to do it" instruction. The theoretical framework is psychodynamic and a section is included on "normal" values in marriage. 206 pp.

MESSER, A. *The individual in his family: An adaptational study*. New York: Thomas, 1970.
This book is based on a view of the family as having certain basic adaptive functions (e.g., coping with a change in its membership) and views pathology in terms of maladaptive behavior. Implications for treatment for several specific probems (childhood phobia, marital dysfunction, etc.) are discussed and an extensive bibliography of basic family psychology works is included.

MIDELFORT, C. F., *The family in psychotherapy*. New York: McGraw-Hill, 1957.
A report of a clinical project involving family therapy and the use of relatives in the care of psychiatric patients on both an inpatient and outpatient basis. It discusses the purpose of the project, and the use of family treatment in schizophrenia, depression, paranoid illness, psychopathic personality, and psychoneurosis. 202 pp.

MILLER, J. G. Living systems. New York: McGraw Hill, 1978.
This is a reference work and textbook describing the "general living system theory." The author describes universal characteristics of all living systems and, using many examples, describes some 19 necessary functions of a viable system. Some injunctions for treatment of dysfunction are discussed. 1102 pp.

MINUCHIN, S., *Families and family therapy*. Cambridge: Harvard University Press, 1974.
Derived from a series of lectures by a reknowned clinician and theorist, this book presents the author's ideas about "structural" family therapy. In this model, change is brought about by altering patterns of interaction and effect so as to change family structure, rather than by cognitive or affective experiences. The theory and techniques of this model are presented around six chapter-length transcripts of family sessions by the author and other clinicians. 268 pp.

MINUCHIN, S., MONTALVO, B., GUERNEY, B. G., et al. *Families of the slums: An exploration of their structure and treatment*. New York: Basic Books, 1967.
A book on a research project dealing with family treatment of low socioeconomic class families where the identified patient was delinquent. Research strategy, rationale, dynamics, techniques, and assessment of results are presented. 460 pp.

MINUCHIN, S., ROSMAN, B., & BAKER, L. *Psychosomatic's families: Anorexia Nervosa in context*. Cambridge: Harvard University Press, 1978.
This book is based on the idea that the family systems perspective is the best way to treat anorexia nervosa. This is compared to other models (for example, the medical model), and the authors' research in other psychosomatic syndromes is presented. Chapters detailing treatment sessions and outcome are included. 351 pp.

MISHLER, E. G., & WAXLER, N. W. *Interaction in families*. New York: Wiley, 1968.
A report on a research project with the aim of systematically identifying distinctive patterns of interaction in families

of schizophrenic patients. It includes background and aims of the study; research design; measurement techniques; strategy for data analysis; research findings focused around expressiveness, power, disruptions in communication, and responsiveness; case examples of findings; and a review and implications of the study. 436 pp.

MUDD, E. H. *The practice of marriage counseling*. New York: Association Press, 1951.
A study of the development of marriage and family counseling in the United States, and a description of its practice with case examples. It includes types of organizations and professions involved. 336 pp.

NAPIER, A., & WHITAKER, C. *The family crucible*. New York: Harper & Row, 1978.
In this detailed case study by two cotherapists, the author describes his relationship to Carl Whitaker and their approach to family therapy. The family included a VIP father, mother and three children. The oldest teenage daughter was the original identified patient. 301 pp.

NATIONAL CLEARINGHOUSE FOR MENTAL HEALTH INFORMATION. *Family therapy: A selected annotated bibliography*. Bethesda: Department of Health, Education and Welfare, 1965.
An annotated bibliography on the literature of family therapy up to 1964, which includes general theoretical articles, therapy with adolescents, child-oriented family therapy, therapy in the home, therapy with families of psychiatric inpatients, marital counseling applications, therapy with schizophrenics, and training family therapist. 27 pp.

PALAZZOLI, M. Self-starvation: *From the intrapsychic to the transpersonal approach to anorexia nervosa*. London: Chaucer, 1974.
Translated from the original 1963 Italian version (and revised), this book is a study of the family systems aspects of treating anorexia nervos (compared to other approaches). Bibliography of over 700 references is included. 289 pp.

PAOLINO, T., & McCRADY, B. *The alcoholic marriage: Alternative perspectives*. New York: Grune & Stratton, 1977.
By presenting five theoretical ways of understanding the "alcoholic marriage," and then proposing a choice among them, this book explores many theoretical principles of human behavior generally (e.g., psychoanalytic, learning theory, systems theory). Another major emphasis is placed on criteria for research into each of these theoretical perspectives. 211 pp.

PAPAJOHN, J., & SPIEGEL, J. *Transactions in the family*. San Francisco: Jossey-Bass, 1975.
Using case histories of three immigrant families in the United States (Puerto Rican, Greek, Italian), this book examines the acculturation process. The theoretical point of view is the "ecological systems" framework which sees cultural, social, psychological, and biological events as part of a "transactional field." 316 pp.

PARSONS, T., & BALES, R. F. *Family, socialization and interaction process*. Glencoe: Free Press, 1955.
A collection of papers oriented toward the family and its relation to personality development, social structure, child socialization, role differentiation in a nuclear family and small groups, and the role of the famiy in the general culture.

PATTERSON, G. *Families: Application of social learning to family life*. Champagne, Ill.: Research Press, 1975.
A paperback intended for parents and professionals, this book attempts to apply the concepts of social learning theory to behavior changes in families as an aid to effective childrearing. Procedures for eliminating unwanted behavior in children are given. 180 pp.

PATTERSON, G. R., RAY, R., & SHAW, D. *Direct intervention in families of deviant children*. Eugene: Oregon Research Institute, 1969.
A description of a conditioning approach in family therapy in which the ways parents deal with children is systematically modified and examined before and after. 70 pp.

PAUL, N., & PAUL, B. *A marital puzzle: Transgenerational analysis in marriage counseling*. New York: Norton, 1975.
This book is primarily a verbatim transcript of seven therapy sessions with a young couple, with commentary by the authors/therapists. The authors techniques included video and audio playback and sexual counseling. 302 pp.

PINCUS, L., & DARE, C. *Secrets in the family*. New York: Pantheon, 1978.
Using case material from their clinical experience, the authors describe the family life cycle from the psychodynamic viewpoint with emphasis on "secrets." These are unconscious wishes, myths, fears, etc., which are shared by family members and influence their interactions. 144 pp.

PRATT, L. *Family structure and effective health behavior: The engaged family*. Boston: Houghton Mifflin, 1976.
Using interviews with different families as well as theoretical discussion, this book discusses the relationship of the health care system to family structure. Ineffective health care can be due to defects in either family functioning or the health care system or both. Suggestions for change are made. 230 pp.

RABKIN, R. *Inner and outer space*. New York: Norton, 1970.
A book about social psychiatry with the emphasis on the shift from the inner space of the individual to social organisms. 215 pp.

RAPOPORT, R. & RAPOPORT, R. Dual-career families. Baltimore: Penquin, 1971.
This is a paperback about a study of five dual-career families by a husband and wife team in Great Britain. Interviews and comments are presented to analyze the families' motivations and functioning. Success seems to depend on mutual commitment and efficient planning.

RAVICH, R., & WYDEN, B. Predictable pairing: The structure of human atoms. New York: Wyden, 1974.
In this book, the authors describe Ravich's Interpersonal Game/Test that uses electric trains hooked up to a computer. Couples are asked to guide their train to a point, and analyses of their attempts—including collisions, blocking each other, or avoiding each other—are used to infer the nature and future of their relationship. Results are categorized into types of relationship, for example, dominant–submissive or cooperative. Therapeutic implications are discussed.

ROGERS, C. *Becoming partners: Marriage and its attenuation*. new York: Delacorte Press, 1972.
Using interview material from married people, this book discusses the state of marriage now and possible better ways on interacting. It is intended for both popular and professional reading.

ROSENTHAL, D. *The genian quadruplets: A case study and theoretical analysis of heredity and environment in schizophrenia*. New York: Basic Books, 1963.
A case study in schizophrenia of a family in which quadruplets were schizophrenic. The book is divided into sections dealing with the case history, tests and studies dealing with basic characteristics in response processes, projective tests and their analysis, systematic analysis of observations of the family by the research staff and the community, conceptualization of the family members in their interrelationships, and a theoretical analysis of the heredity-environment problem in schizophrenia. 609 pp.

RUBIN, L. *Worlds of pain: Life in the working class family*. New York: Basic Books, 1976.
This is a book about working class marriage and family life. It is based on an interview survey of 50 white, working class families in and around San Francisco. It is organized chronologically according to phases of a marriage (e.g., courtship, early marriage) and includes many quotations from the interviews. The author argues against the myth of an upwardly mobile American society. 268 pp.

RYLE, A. *Neurosis in the ordinary family: A psychiatric survey*. London: Tavistock, 1967.
A report of the author's study of the psychiatric health and personal relationships of 112 working-class families with children of primary school age. The study was done while the author was a general practitioner. It covers the methods of collecting data, social circumstances and characteristics of the population, parents' childhood, parents' psycho-dynamics, their parents' marriages, child-rearing practices and their relation to other parental attributes, psycho-logical disturbances in the children, parental factors associated with the disturbance in the children, family diagnosis, consultation and treatment, and evaluation and conclusions. 153 pp.

SAGER, C. *Marriage contracts and couples therapy*. New York: Brunner/Mazel, 1976.
Using the concept that each partner brings to a marriage an unwritten contract (i.e., "a set of expectations . . . conscious to unconscious"), this book offers an approach to therapy that is based on understanding these contracts. Marital therapy in this context is also seen as valuable for individual problems. Chapters on techniques and case examples are included. 335 pp.

SAMPSON, H., MESSINGER, L., & TOWNE, R. *Schizophrenic women: studies in marital crises*. New York: Atherton Press, 1963.
A book on a research project studying family relations of 17 schizophrenic women who had to be hospitalized. The book discusses the crisis that led up to hospitalization and its context, the process of separation, becoming a mental patient in terms of family processes, and the crisis resolution in the hospital and posthospital period. A summary is presented, and implications of this study are discussed. 174 pp.

SANDER, F. *Individual and family therapy: Toward and integration*. New York: Aronson, 1979.
Using several famous dramas as illustrations, this book discusses the shift in emphasis in psychiatry from the individual to the family and its sociocultural context. Hamlet, for example, is singled out as an "identified patient" in a dysfunctional family, and T. S. Eliot's, *The Family Reunion*" is discussed with regard to symbiosis and separation. 242 pp.

SATIR, V. M. *Conjoint family therapy: A guide to theory and technique*. Palo Alto: Science & Behavior Books, 1964.

A textbook on family therapy covering a theory of normal family functions, communication theory, and techniques of family diagnosis and treatment. There is an extensive bibliography. 196 pp.

SATIR, V., STACHOWICK, J., & TASHCHMAN, H. *Helping families to change*. New York: Aronson, 1975.
This is a book directed at "improving the effectiveness of family therapy." Sections on theoretical basis for family therapy and clinical skills are followed by "personal awareness exercises" to be done by the reader. Topics include intervention techniques, pitfalls in working with families and developments in family therapy. 296 pp.

SCHEFLEN, A. E. *Stream and structure of communicational behavior*. Behavioral series monograph no. 1. Philadelphia: Eastern Pennsylvania Psychiatric Institute, 1965.
A context analysis of a family therapy session by Whitaker and Malone. The examination of the interview is in detail and includes kinesic, linquistic and contextual description.

SELVINI PALAZZOLI, M., CECCHIN, G., PRATA, G., et al: *Paradox and counterparadox. A new model in the therapy of the family schizophrenic transaction*. New York: Aronson, 1978.
Using clinical examples from Milan, Italy, this book presents the use of paradoxical injunction in family therapy of families of schizophrenics. This technique is used to "break up" the pathological equilibrium in the family. 186 pp.

SKYNNER, A. *Systems of family and marital psychotherapy*. New York: Brunner/Mazel, 1976.
This book is an introductory textbook for the beginner. It offers a theoretical overview and practical guidelines, based primarily on the authors own work. The theoretical sections begin with the individual (for example, object relations theory and the unconscious) and builds up to the marital relationship and the wider social network. Application sections make use of extensive clinical examples. 425 pp.

Social Work Practice, 1963, Selected Papers. 90th Annual Forum, National Conference on Social Welfare, Cleveland, Ohio, May 19–24, 1963. New York: Columbia University Press, 1963.
A collection of papers given at a social work conference which includes a paper on family diagnosis and treatment, family unit treatment of character-disordered youngsters, and schizophrenia and family therapy. 255 pp.

THOMAS, E. *Marital communication and decision making: Analysis of assessment and change*. New York: The Free Press, 1977.
This book is an in-depth analysis of marital communications. It attempts to define functional as well as dysfunctional communication and provides rules for effective decision making between marital partners. Implications for strategies for change in therapy are stressed.

THORMAN, G. *Family therapy: Help for troubled families*, Public Affairs Pamphlet No. 356. New York: 1964.
Rationale, indications, family dynamics, techniques, and future trends are described in this report.

TOMAN, W. *The family constellation: Its effects on personality and social behavior*. New York: Springer, 1969.
A book describing a theory of the effects of the family constellation on personality and social behavior. The theory is described, as well as the major types of sibling positions and the major types of relations of the parents. Prediction of behavior is based on 6 case examples. 280 pp.

VICTOR, B., & SANDER, J. *The family: The evolution of our oldest human institution*. Indianapolis/New York: Bobbs-Merrill, 1978.
Using specific examples from many different societies, past and present, this book describes the social, economic, political, geographical, etc. context that reflects and is reflected by each of the family structures examined. Examples range from ancient Egypt to Kibbutz Israel. 151 pp.

VISHER, E., & VISHER, J. *Stepfamilies: A guide to working with stepparents and stepchildren*. New York: Brunner/Mazel, 1979.
The incidence of stepfamilies is increasing and such families have significant differences from nuclear families. The authors suggest that the same therapeutic approaches that help nuclear families and their members will help stepfamilies—if their different complexities are understood.

WALROND-SKINNER, S. *Family therapy: The treatment of natural systems*. London, Henley, and Boston: Rautlege and Kegan Paul, 1976.
This book is intended as an introductory text for beginning family therapists. It explains the systems theory outlook on families and includes sections on basic techniques, guidelines, indications and contraindications for family therapy. Some specific techniques such as family sculpture are also included. 164 pp.

WATZLAWICK, P. J. *An anthology of human communication*. Palo Alto: Science & Behavior Books, 1964.
A textbook and tape recording dealing with family dynamics, interaction, and communication patterns. Com-

munication theory is outlined, and there are sections on agreement and disagreement, types of relationships, disqualifications, schizophrenic communication, double binds, coalitions, and a suggested reading list. 63 pp., plus an audiotape.

WATZLAWICK, P. J., BEAVIN, H., & JACKSON, D. D. *Pragmatics of human communication, A study of interactional patterns, pathologies, and paradoxes.* New York: Norton, 1967.
A book dealing with "behavioral effects of human communication with special attention to behavior disorders." There are discussions of the frame of reference of the book, some axioms of communication, pathological communication, the organization of family interaction, analysis of the play, *Who's Afraid of Virginia Woolf?*, paradoxical communication, paradoxes in psychotherapy, and existentialism and the theory of human communication. 296 pp.

WATZLAWICK, P., WEAKLAND, J., & FISCH, R. *Change: Principles of problem formation and problem resolution.* New York: Norton, 1974.
This is a book about what is supposed to happen in any kind of therapy. "Second-order" change is a shift that affects a whole system, as opposed to shifts within an unchanged system ("first-order" change). There are discussions of how to decide which is indicated and how to implement it, for example, these concepts are related to various paradoxical techniques in therapy. 172 pp.

WEISS, R. *Marital separation.* New York: Basic Books, 1975.
Based on the idea that therapists must understand the problems of the newly separated to help them in individual therapy, the author reports on his program of "seminars for the separated," which consists of 8 weekly lectures with discussion groups. Topics included are establishing a new identity, impacts on friends and family, and forming new attachements. 352 pp.

WINTER, W. D., & FERREIRA, A. J. *Research in family interaction.* Palo Alto: Science & Behavior Books, 1969.
A collection of some original and some previously published material dealing with studies and research on family interaction. There are sections on methodological issues in family interaction research; studies of individual family members; studies of family interaction; and studies of intrafamily communication. There is a lengthy bibliography.

ZUK, G. *Family therapy: A triadic based approach.* New York: Behavioral Publications, 1971.
This book contains previously published articles and new interviews with families and discussions of the interviews. The author's approaches and techniques to family therapy (such as the "go-between" method) are detailed. 239 pp.

ZUK, G. *Progress and practice in family therapy.* Haverford, Pa.: Psychiatry and Behavioral Science Associates, 1974.
This book details new family therapy concepts (e.g., the role of the therapist as "celebrant"). Transcripts of both teaching and therapy sessions are used to teach guidelines for family interventions, goals, duration, etc. 120 pp.

8. AUDIOVISUAL CONTRIBUTIONS

ACKERMAN INSTITUTE. *Divorce-legal consultations*. New York: Ackerman Institute (149 East 78th Street, New York, N.Y. 10021).
This film presents a "simulated couple" contemplating divorce. Husband and wife are interviewed separately by two practicing attorneys who specialize in matrimonial law. In the final segment, the couple consults a family therapist. Therapists are often unfamiliar with their clients' experience with lawyers. These interviews capture the flavor of this kind of experience with our legal system.

ACKERMAN, N. *The enemy in myself*. New York: Ackerman Institute (149 East 78 Street, New York, N.Y. 10021).
This is a composite of four interviews spanning a period of 1½ years and conducted by Dr. Nathan Ackerman. The family groups consist of mother, father, and twin sons, 9 years old. Treatment commences following the suicide threat of one son, who is perceived by the family as disruptive and rebellious. Written material is included, covering family history and diagnosis.

ACKERMAN, N. *In and out of psychosis*. New York: Ackerman institute (149 East 78 Street, New York, N.Y. 10021).
This is a composite of interviews (including an individual session) conducted by Dr. Nathan Ackerman in the ongoing treatment of a severely disturbed adolescent girl and her family. The daughter is considered unmanageable and withdrawn and retreats into "mental voyages" to another planet, "Queendom." Family members are mother, father, daughter, and the maternal grandmother. Written material is included, covering family history and diagnosis.

ACKERMAN, N., BOWEN, M., JACKSON, D., & WHITAKER, C. *Hillcrest family series*. Pennsylvania: Psychological Cinema Register (Pennsylvania State University, University Park, Pennsylvania, 16802).
This is a series of eight films consisting of four separate family interviews with the same family by each of the authors, followed by the author discussing what he did.

ALGER, I. *Marital Crisis*. New York: IEA Productions (520 East 77 Street, New York, N.Y. 10021).
This tape follows the course of a couple in a brief (nine session) therapy in which there is a resolution of the acute crisis that threatened their marriage and a commitment to continue in a longer growth-oriented series of sessions. Voice over explains techniques.

ALGER, I. *Time mirror*. New York: IEA Productions (520 East 77 Street, New York, N.Y. 10021).
The author presents an overview on the use of videotape for therapy followed by three simulated family therapy sessions.

ALGER, I. & McMAHON, A. *Videotape in couples group therapy*. New York: IEA Productions (520 East 77 Street, New York, N.Y. 10021).
The authors present a segment of couples' group therapy with a focus on an illustration of video-playback technique to show one couple's interactions with them. The therapists utilize a role-play technique to act out the unspoken thoughts and feelings of the couple.

APONTE, H. *Too many bossess: Actions speak louder than words*. New Jersey: Monica McGoldnick (Department of Psychiatry, Rutgers Medical School, Piscataway, New Jersey).
Author deals with a family in which incest is an issue.

BATESON, G. *Cancer epistemology and the family*. New York: IEA Productions (520 East 77 Street, NewYork, N.Y. 10021).
The author discusses issues of his own experiences with cancer. He suggests a need for a new epistemology for cancer in order for its treatment and understanding to progress.

BATESON, G. *Double bind and epistemology*. New York: South Beach Psychiatric Center, Education Department (777 Seaview Avenue, Staten Island, N.Y. 10305).
Bateson talks about communication theory and double binds. Contains comments also made by author of the "Beyond the Double Bind" conference in New York City in 1977.

BATESON, G. *A workshop with Gregory Bateson*. New York: South Beach Psychiatric Center, Education Department (777 Seaview Avenue, Staten Island, N.Y. 10305).
The Author elaborates on "knowing," patterns of relationship, patterns of learning, levels of perception in context, genetic and context binds in relationships, the evolution of theories, and many more "Batesonian" topics.

BEAL, E. *Divorcing family systems*. Washington, D.C.: Georgetown University Family Center (4380 MacArthur Blvd., N.W., Washington, D.C. 20007).
Dr. Beal focuses on the impact of divorce on nuclear and extended families, as well as social and legal impact on families. Segments of clinical sessions show the marital dyad and the extended family.

BLAKE, P. *Childhood aggression: A social learning approach to family therapy*. Pennsylvania: Audio-Visual Services (Special Services Building, University Park, Pennsylvania 16802).

The social learning approach is applied to a family with a socially aggressive child. It demonstrates behavior modification techniques as used in a family setting.

BLOCH, D. & KORELITZ, A. *The initial interview.* New York: Ackerman Institute (149 East 78 Street, New York, N.Y. 10021).
Excerpts of a first session conducted by Dr. Bloch and Ms. Korelitz with a family of five—mother, father, adolescent son, who is identified as the problem in the family, middle son, and young daughter. Clinical material is interspersed with commentary by Phoebe Prosky, who discusses elements of particular importance in beginning work with a family.

BOSZORMENYI-NAGY, I. *Consultation with a family.* New York: South Beach Psychiatric Center, Education Department (777 Seaview Avenue, Staten Island, N.Y. 10305).
The author, using the vehicle of a consultation-evaluation with a family, focuses on his concepts of: (1) development of trustworthiness of relationships; (2) connectedness, and (3) multidimensional partiality. Later, drawing on material from the interview, he directly explains his thinking and approaches.

BOWEN, M. *Anxiety and emotional reactivity in therapy.* Washington, D.C.: Georgetown University Family Center (4380 MacArthur Blvd., N.W., Washington, D.C. 20007).
Dr. Bowen focuses on the way anxiety is manifested in a family and how the level of differentiations affects family's ability to respond to stress. He addresses the importance of the theapist becoming more "self-contained" within the emotional arena of his own family in order to be more effective clinically.

BOWEN, M. *Defining a self in one's family of origin* (Parts I and II). Washington, D.C.: Georgetown University Family Center (4380 MacArthur Blvd., N.W., Washington, D.C. 20007).
In these two tapes Dr. Bowen deals with common misconceptions about his theories including the notion of triangles, differentiation of one's self, emotional cutoff, and multigenerational history taking. He deals with some common mistakes that family therapists make.

BOWEN, M. *Interview with a schizophrenic family.* New York: South Beach Psychiatric Center, Education Department (777 Seaview Avenue, Staten Island, N.Y. 10305).
Bowen demonstrates his interviewing techniques, e.g., defusing emotionalism, increasing intellectual awareness and objectivity, decreasing triangulation, and promoting individuation.

BOWEN, M. *Schizophrenia as a multigenerational phenomenon.* New York: South Beach Psychiatric Center, Education Department (777 Seaview Avenue, Staten Island, N.Y. 10305).
Bowen explains his major concepts of differentiation, fusion, and the multigenerational development of schizophrenia. He reviews other theoretical models and compares them with those of this own.

DELL, P. *I don't want to be a fool.* Texas: University of Texas Medical Branch (Galveston, Texas 77030).
Brief strategic family sesion that shows the management of a family with an unstable diabetic member.

EPSTEIN, N., & BISHOP, D. *Two teaching tapes which describe the McMaster model. I: Problem centered systems therapy of the family. II: McMaster model of family functioning.* Rhode Island: Butler Hoop (345 Blackstone Blvd., Providence, R.I., 02906).
The tapes are representative of the authors models of family functioning and family therapy.

FAMILY ASSESSMENT SERIES. Pennsylvania: Psychological Cinema Register (Pennsylvania State University, University Park, Pennsylvania, 16802). 240 min.
A family is interviewed by four different family therapists. It is not a therapy interview but a consultation, or assessment, which lasts 30 minutes. The interviewer then spends 30 minutes immediately afterward discussing the interview and its implications with the family's regular therapist. The interviewers are Nathan Ackerman, M.D., New York, Murry Bowen, M.D., Maryland, Don D. Jackson, M.D., California, and Carl Whitaker, M.D., Wisconsin.

FAMILY ASSESSMENT SERIES. Pennsylvania: Psychological Cinema Register (Pennsylvania State University, University Park, Pennsylvania, 16802).

FERBER, A. *Two couples: two sessions each.* New York: Family Studies Section (Bronx State Hospital, 1500 Waters Plaza, Bronx, N.Y. 10461).
These are complete 1 hour, color films of the third and fourth sessions with two couples who continue in therapy. The tape demonstrates many of the skills of a marital therapist.

FOGARTY, T. F. *Lucille: A family consult interview with an individual.* New York: The Center for Family Learning (10 Hanford Avenue, New Rochelle, N.Y. 10805).
This is a demonstration of how to track the focus of "movement" through the individual and the family system.

GARFIELD, R., & SCHWOERI, L. *When an impasse arises in therapy.* New York: IEA Productions (520 East 77 Street, New York, N.Y. 10021).
The authors demonstrate a format for the family consultation interview. Special attention is given to the "entry" and "exit" processes of consultation, illustrating the return of therapeutic authority to the therapist.

GLICK, I.D., & MARSHALL, G. J. *Family therapy: An introduction* New York: Payne Whitney Clinic (525 East 68 Street, New York, N.Y. 10021).
This film, designed for family therapists as an introduction to family therapy, is based on treatment of a family over a 16-month period. The film demonstrates techniques (including videotape playbacks) and problems, but its primary purpose is to give an overview of the course of family treatment from beginning to end.

GUERIN, P. J. *Single parent family interview.* Rental $75. New York: The Center for Family Learning (10 Hanford Avenue, New Rochelle, N.Y. 10805).
This is an edited consult exploring the common structural problems and "toxic" issues typical of divorced, single-parent families.

HALEY, J. *Ideas which handicap a therapist.* New York: South Beach Psychiatric Center, Education Department (777 Seaview Avenue, Staten Island, N.Y. 10305).
This tape presents Haley's theory of change, why a particular therapist is successful, a guide to therapist action rather than reflection, recognizing failure when it has occurred, and ideas that he believes have impeded a theory of schizophrenia.

HALEY, J. *A modern "Little Hans."* Philadelphia: Philadelphia Child Guidance Clinic (34 Street & Civic Center Blvd., Philadelphia, Pa. 19104).
This tape shows Haley supervising a trainee on a specific family case. It is written and narrated by Haley and accompanied by a written text.

KEMPLER, W. *Family therapy.* California: Kempler Institute (6233 Wilshire Boulevard, Los Angeles, California, 90048).
This film shows a family trying to work out their problems together in family therapy.

KERR, K. *Focus on the extended family in family therapy.* Washington, D.C.: Georgetown University Family Center (4380 MacArthur Blvd., N.W., Washington, D.C. 20007).
Using Bowen's concepts, the therapist shows segments of family sessions that extend over 5 years dealing especially with the extended family.

KESSLER, D. R. *Family in crisis.* New Jersey: Sandoz Pharmaceuticals (Hanover, New Jersey 07936, or local Sandoz representatives).
The film is intended as an introduction to the understanding of family functioning and family treatment. Material presented includes sequences of a family at home and in therapy sessions, as well as of a professional seminar discussion group. The aim is to highlight specifically a number of fundamental family concepts of general usefulness to professionals rather than to present a chronological sequence of one family in therapy.

LORIO, J. *The family evaluation interview.* Washington, D.C.: Georgetown University Family Center (4380 MacArthur Blvd., N.W., Washington, D.C. 20007).
Segments of an initial clinical session are used to illustrate family data collecting (especially history of relationships), surveying the extended family, and bridging to the next session.

McCULLUOUGH, G. *Family cutoffs and psychosomatic response.* Pittsburgh: Western Psychiatric Institute and Clinic (3811 O'Hara Street, Pittsburgh, Pa. 15261).
This tape shows an anorectic woman with allergies, who regains physical and psychological functioning by reestablishing connections with members of her extended family.

MEYER, P. *A review of four techniques.* Washington, D.C.: Georgetown University Family Center (4380 MacArthur Blvd., N.W., Washington, D.C. 20007).
A demonstration of how theory determines which technique will be most productive. Reviewed here are the "I position," de-triangling, leader-reversal, and not bailing others out.

MINUCHIN, S. *A family interview with an 18-year-old schizophrenic, his parents and three siblings.* New York: South Beach Psychiatric Center, Education Department (777 Seaview Avenue, Staten Island, N.Y. 10305).
The tape presents Minuchin's approach as an active therapist. He physically moves members of the family in his efforts to reformulate and restructure the family.

MINUCHIN, S. *Interview with a divorced mother, her son (age 10) and daughter (age 7).* New York: South Beach

Psychiatric Center, Education Department (777 Seaview Avenue, Staten Island, N.Y. 10305).
A confused, divorced mother is "joined" by the therapist while data, diagnosis, goals, and tasks for transformation of dysfunctional patterns are shown. The therapist shows how he facilitates restructuring of the family.

MINUCHIN, S. *Interview with a teenage anorectic patient and her family*. New York: South Beach Psychiatric Center, Education Department (777 Seaview Avenue, Staten Island, N.Y. 10305).
The tape includes a family interview by Minuchin, techniques of taking a case history, and Dr. Minuchin having lunch with the family. Presentation clearly reveals the anorexia as a symptom of the family power struggle.

PAPP, P. Making the invisible visible. New York: Ackerman Institute (149 East 78 Street, New York, N.Y. 10021).
The use of sculpting as a therapeutic technique is demonstrated. Papp conducts an initial interview with a family of four—mother, father, and their adult son and daughter. She describes the basic dysfunctional triangle, which is visually traced and readjusted through the family sculpting. The therapist then comments on the process during a replay.

SAGER, C. *Marital or sex theapy*. New York: South Beach Psychiatric Center, Education Department (777 Seaview Avenue, Staten Island, N.Y. 10305).
The tape demonstrates the elucidation of the marriage contract as a therapeutic device with a couple who initially presented both sexual and marital problems. In a simulated session the author demonstrates what his techniques do to deal with these problems.

SATIR, V. *The nurturing triad*. Massachussetts: Boston Family Institute (251 Harvard Street, Brookline, MA. 02146).
The author demonstrates the use of a growth model in the treatment of a family.

SCHEFLEN, A. *Cancer and the family*. New York: IEA Productions (520 East 77 Street, New York, N.Y. 10021).
Shortly before his death, the author relates his own experiences with cancer and his family.

SCHEFLEN, A. *On communications*. New York: South Beach Psychiatric Center, Education Department (777 Seaview Avenue, Staten Island, N.Y. 10305).
Communications serve not only to transmit information but, more importantly, to establish, maintain, and regulate human interpersonal relationships. The film brings together the ideas of Bateson, Birdwhistle, Scheflen, and others.

SELVINI-PALAZZOLI, M., et al. *Three edited family interviews*. New York: Family Institute of Westchester (346 Mamaroneck Avenue, White Plains, N.Y. 10605).
This tape consists of edited segments illustrating the interviewing and intervention techniques of the Milan associates, in particular, circular interviewing, systemic hypothesizing, the role of the family consultant, and the use of paradox and rituals.

STEWART, S., & JOHANSEN, R. *Sybil's plight: A family's adjustment to chronic illness*. Pittsburg: Western Psychiatric Institute and Clinic (3811 O'Hara Street, Pittsburgh, Pa. 15261).
This tape demonstrates problems experienced by a family in its adjustment to a chronic catastrophic illness, in this case, renal failure and home dialysis. Topics dealing with forced dependency and intimacy, denial, genetic implications, and life and death are discussed.

WEAKLAND, J. *Pursuing the evident into schizophrenia and beyond*. New York: South Beach Psychiatric Center, Education Department (777 Seaview Avenue, Staten Island, N.Y. 10305).
The author focuses on the interactional views of schizophrenia and leans heavily on the context of communication for understanding and interventions to bring about change. He applies this interaction view also to the managing of violent behavior, psychosomatic disorders, and organizational problems.

WHITAKER, C. *Consultant for a multi-family group*. New York: South Beach Psychiatric Center, Education Department (777 Seaview Avenue, Staten Island, N.Y. 10305).
Dr. Whitaker's model as a consultant is demonstrated here. His active role in influencing families to change their patterns and his unorthodox use of humor and the absurd are shown in dealing with a "locked-in" relationship system within the group.

WHITAKER, C. *Consultant for a schizophrenic young man and his family*. New York: South Beach Psychiatric Center, Education Department (777 Seaview Avenue, Staten Island, N.Y. 10305).
Dr. Whitaker presents a consultation to the therapist–family unit and to the supra-system established over a period of years. In a "non-rational" approach, he is convinced they should go beyond the limits of absurdity that the family presents so that they (the family) can move toward the chaos and disorganization necessitated for any change to occur.

WHITAKER, C. *Consultation with a fragmented family at impasse*. New York: South Beach Psychiatric Center, Education Department (777 Seaview Avenue, Staten Island, N.Y. 10305).

This interview with divorced parents and their adolescent, "schizophrenic" children is followed by a discussion in which Dr. Whitaker comments that "family therapy is almost always a crisis intervention." He brings multiple generations together and turns over the responsibility of the family problem to the family. He stimulates a union of hostility against himself and double binds the family by apparently not "doing something" to help.

WHITAKER, C. *Consultation with a teenage adolescent and his family.* New York: South Beach Psychiatric Center, Education Department (777 Seaview Avenue, Staten Island, N.Y. 10305).
Dr. Whitaker interviews a family and focuses on the role of the identified patient as a symptom of the family's illness. Cotherapists are included in the interview.

WHITAKER, C. *Co-therapy of chronic schizophrenia.* New York: South Beach Psychiatric Center, Education Department (777 Seaview Avenue, Staten Island, N.Y. 10305).
In his interview Dr. Whitaker offers a statement on the development of a schizophrenic family with a schizophrenic child. He metaphorically conceptualizes the problems of interpersonal distance, control dependency, power triangulation symbiosis, and multigenerational confusion. He discusses the issue of using a co-therapist.

WHITAKER, C. *Family therapy consultation.* New York: IEA Productions (520 East 77 Street, New York, N.Y. 10021).
In the first part of this two-part tape, Dr. Whitaker joins the therapist and the family for a consultation interview. Part I shows the flexibility of a consultant compared to that of the usual therapist. Part II is a debriefing session with Dr. Whitaker and therapist with a discussion of the strategic interventions.

WYNNE, L. *Interview with a family of double binders.* New York: South Beach Psychiatric Center, Education Department (777 Seaview Avenue, Staten Island, N.Y. 10305).
A consultation interview with a family in which three of its members have eruptions of suicidal behaviors that bind the family members to their therapists so that separation and individuation are unlikely. The author comments on this common bind to therapists and institutions.

WYNNE, L. *Knotted relationships and communication deviance.* New York: South Beach Psychiatric Center, Education Department (777 Seaview Avenue, Staten Island, N.Y. 10305).
Dr. Wynne presents his views on double binds and his own concepts of pseudomutuality, pseudohostility, and communication deviance. Research data on schizophrenics and preschizophrenics are presented.

ZUK, G. *A family therapy with follow-up.* Philadelphia: Eastern Pennsylvania Psychiatric Institute (Henry Avenue, Philadelphia, Pennsylvania 19129).
An interview and follow-up session with a family, both of which demonstrates the author's techniques of understanding and working with sick families.

AUTHOR INDEX